THE LAW RELATING TO DOMESTIC BANKING

BANKING LAW
VOLUME 1

by

G. A. PENN, LL.B., LL.M.
Assistant Director, The Centre for Commercial Law Studies,
Queen Mary College, University of London;
Editor, Journal of International Banking Law;
Chief Examiner in the Practice and Law of International Banking,
Chartered Institute of Bankers

A. M. SHEA, B.A., LL.B., D.Phil., *Barrister and Solicitor (N.Z.)*
Head of Centre for Legal Studies, City University, London;
Deputy Editor, Journal of International Banking Law;
Chief Examiner in the Law Relating to Banking,
Chartered Institute of Bankers;
Cameron Markby Senior Research Fellow in Banking Law,
The Centre for Commercial Law Studies, Queen Mary College, University of London

A. ARORA, LL.B., Ph.D., *Barrister*
Lecturer in Law, University of Liverpool

LONDON
SWEET & MAXWELL
1987

Published in 1987 by
Sweet & Maxwell Ltd. of
11 New Fetter Lane, London.
Computerset by Promenade
Graphics Ltd., Cheltenham.
Printed in Scotland.

British Library Cataloguing in Publication Data

Penn, G. A.
    Banking law
    Vol. 1; The law relating to domestic banking.
    1. Banking law —— Great Britain
    I. Title II. Shea, A.M. III. Arora, A.
    IV. The law relating to domestic banking.
    344.106'82   KB1715

    ISBN 0–421–39000–X
    ISBN 0–421–36060–7 Pbk

THE LAW RELATING TO DOMESTIC BANKING

BANKING LAW

VOLUME 1

AUSTRALIA AND NEW ZEALAND
The Law Book Company Ltd.
Sydney : Melbourne : Perth

CANADA AND U.S.A.
The Carswell Company Ltd.
Agincourt, Ontario

INDIA
N. M. Tripathi Private Ltd.
Bombay
and
Eastern Law House Private Ltd.
Calcutta and Delhi
M.P.P. House
Bangalore

ISRAEL
Steimatzky's Agency Ltd.
Jerusalem : Tel Aviv : Haifa

MALAYSIA : SINGAPORE : BRUNEI
Malayan Law Journal (Pte.) Ltd.
Singapore and Kuala Lumpur

Preface

The idea for a two volume work in banking law, the first of which deals with domestic banking law and the second dealing with international banking law, arose out of a series of meetings between Graham Penn and Don Fiddes, a former Director of Studies at the Chartered Institute of Bankers, who were both concerned about the absence of an up-to-date text which covered the entire spectrum of banking law. It soon became clear that such a project would require the specialist knowledge of more than one individual, hence Tony Shea and Anu Arora were invited to "join the team" of authors.

This new work was originally conceived as being intended for degree and post-graduate students and for practitioners who regularly find themselves engaged in this complex area of law. The emphasis in both volumes is directed firmly towards the law in practice, and it is hoped that those who concern themselves with banking law, in its broadest sense, will find some of the answers to the often difficult questions which arise. Where the material fails to provide an answer we hope it will at least lead to other sources, and thus assist in solving practical banking law problems, hence the heavy referencing which is to be found throughout both volumes.

The original conception became slightly altered during production in order that the two volumes would cover the Chartered Institute of Bankers' examinations in both Law Relating to Banking and Practice and Law of International Banking. This slight change in emphasis has led to the omission of some material but the addition of other new chapters, namely, the sizeable chapters on Securities and Insolvency, and the expansion of the original material dealing with Agency, Partnerships and Corporate Customers.

Anybody who writes a book of this sort could not possibly start without the benefit of the learning of others. We have relied heavily upon a number or articles (many of which are acknowledged in the footnotes), and upon the publications listed in the Table of Abbreviations. Special mention must be made, however, of Philip Wood's excellent book, *Law and Practice of International Finance* and of the *Encyclopaedia of Banking Law* which provides the most comprehensive coverage of English Banking Law presently available.

In addition to published material we have placed considerable reliance on the knowledge and practical expertise of many lawyers and bankers, who have made helpful suggestions during the preparation of this work. Unfortuantely, the individuals themselves are too numerous to mention. The authors would, however, wish to acknowledge the very considerable assistance given by the following people:

David Lewis of the Reserve bank of Australia (Volume 1, Chapter 1 on the Regulation of Banks); Maurice Allen of Clifford Chance (Volume 2, Chapter 8 on Transferability of Loans and Loan Participations); Stephen Edlmann of Linklaters and Paines (Volume 2, Chapter 10 on Notes and Commercial Paper); Armel Cates, Robert Palache and Phillip Palmer of Clifford Chance (Volume 2, Chapter 11 on Swaps and Related Instruments); Andrew McKnight of Cameron Markby (Volume 2, Chapter 16 on

Legal Opinions). These experts are not, of course, responsible for any errors or omissions, which remain those of the authors alone.

The authors would also like to express their indebtedness to National Westminster Bank PLC for permission to reproduce their standard form documentation in Volume 2, Chapter 12 and for supplying copies.

The law is stated as at May 31, 1987.

London
May 31, 1987

G. A. Penn
A. M. Shea
A. Arora

To the late Don Fiddes
who is greatly missed

Table of Abbreviations

Books

Byles   *Byles on Bills of Exchange*, ed. Megrah & Ryder, (Sweet & Maxwell, 25th ed., 1983)

Chorley   Chorley, *Law of Banking*, (Sweet & Maxwell, 6th ed. 1974)

Encyclopaedia   *Encyclopaedia of Banking Law*, ed. Cresswell, Blaire, Hill, Wood (Butterworths, 1982)

Goode LPCS   Goode, *Legal Problems of Credit and Security*, (Sweet & Maxwell/CCLS, 1982)

Goode CL   Goode, *Commercial Law*, (Penguin, rev. 1985)

Gower   *Gower's Principles of Modern Company Law*, (Stevens, 4th ed., 1979 with 1987 supplement)

Holden   Holden, *The Law and Practice of Banking*, Vol. 1 and 2 (Pitman 3rd ed., 1982)

Paget   *Paget's Law of Banking*, ed. Megrah & Ryder (Butterworths, 9th ed., 1982)

Pennington   *Pennington's Company Law*, (Butterworths, 5th ed., 1985)

Journal

J.I.B.L.   *Journal of International Banking Law* (ESC Publishers Ltd.)

Reports

F.T.   *Financial Times* (Law Report)
L.D.A.B.   *Legal Decisions Affecting Bankers*

Statutes

B.O.E. Act	Bills of Exchange Act 1882
C.A.	Companies Act (year stated)
C.D.D.A.	Company Directors Disqualification Act 1986
I.R.	Insolvency Rules 1986
I.A.	Insolvency Act 1986
I.P.O.	Insolvent Partnerships Order 1986
L.P.A.	Law of Property Act (year stated)
L.C.A.	Land Charges Act 1972
L.R.A.	Land Registration Act (year stated)
L.R.R.	Land Registration Rules 1925
M.H.A.	Matrimonial Homes Act 1983

Contents

Section Four
Guarantees and Securities

Section Five
Insolvency

Table of Cases

Table of Statutes

Table of Statutory Instruments

Rules of the Supreme Court

Section One
Bank Regulation

1. Supervision of Banking

'In wild periods of alarm, one failure makes many and the best way to prevent the derivative failures is to arrest the primary failure which causes them'—Walter Bagehot (1873).[1]

Introduction

The continuing validity of Bagehot's aphorism has long provided the rationale for prudential supervision of financial intermediaries. However, only comparatively recently have attempts been made to place prudential supervision in the United Kingdom upon a formal footing. The law pertaining to the supervision of banks and other financial intermediaries is now fast growing into a discipline worthy of study in its own right. Not only does banking supervision encompass numerous facets of the law of banker and customer, but it transgresses regularly into the fields of public law, securities regulation and, more generally, financial economics. **1.01**

It is now generally accepted that a mechanism for ensuring adherence to appropriate prudential standards is a necessary component of a developed banking sector. Not only do banks play a key role in distributing financial resources to the rest of the economy, but in doing so they act as repositories for the public's savings. Their stability is a matter of considerable political concern; yet banks are peculiarly susceptible to instability and collapse. The nature of their business necessitates relatively high financial gearing and involves extensive maturity transformation. There is always an element of risk.[2] This rather fragile scheme depends on the continuing confidence of investors. When confidence deserts a financial intermediary, diaster is almost inevitable and the effect can be highly contagious throughout a financial system. The vulnerability of banks to sudden demand for withdrawal of deposits increases the likelihood that such withdrawals will take place. In the event of a disturbance in confidence, depositors will be alert to the need to withdraw their funds ahead of a "run" on deposits. The danger is that pessimistic prophecies can be self-fulfilling; they need not be well-founded. This loaded situation is exacerbated by an inadequate supply of information to depositors and market analysts which might enable them to make a reliable assessment of a bank's investment portfolio.

The imposition of a régime of prudential supervision aims to foster an environment of bank safety and soundness, and thus to dispel those errant fears that may overcome depositors. This is done by establishing procedures to ensure that risk is properly recognised and measured and that the institutions concerned have adequate capital in place to support the level of business and risks which they run. It is also necessary to ensure that financial institutions maintain adequate liquidity to meet prospective net cash requirements. Further, many prudential régimes put in place a safety net by way of deposit insurance or a lender of last resort facility in order to bolster depositor confidence. **1.02**

---

[1] *Lombard Street*, (1873), p. 51.
[2] For a useful economic account of banking risk, see J. W. Dean & I. H. Giddy, *Averting International Banking Crises*, (Solomon Brothers Center 1981), for the Study of Financial Institutions.

Nevertheless, the task of bank supervision is becoming increasingly complex. The last two decades have seen a dramatic boom in competitive banking activity. Financial institutions have expanded and diversified. At the same time, traditional banking markets have been invaded by other financial intermediaries. There has been a rapid expansion in international lending and extensive interpenetration of markets. The global debt crisis has focused attention on the growing interdependence of national banking systems, while at the same time highlighting the inadequacies of international supervision. Novel financial instruments are frequently being deployed. The Study Group established by the Group of Ten to examine recent innovations in the conduct of international banking introduced its brief as follows:

> "A sharp acceleration in the pace of innovation, deregulation and structural change in recent years has transformed the international financial system in important ways. Major new financial instruments—mostly taking the form of off-balance-sheet commitments—have either been created or have dramatically increased their role in the financial structure; international credit flows have shifted away from loans through large international banks into direct credit markets; the volume of daily transactions has multiplied; financial markets have become far more closely integrated worldwide; capital has become much more mobile."[3]

1.03 The stimulus for financial innovation is strong. It derives from a rapid growth in international trade and capital flows, expanding technology, a changing regulatory climate, and the emergence of a volatile and competitive financial marketplace. The developments have vastly improved the efficiency and profitability of financial markets, but have been accompanied by an increasing incidence of instability and risk, exposing the inherent vulnerability of banking institutions.

Innovation is forcing changes to the supervisory techniques customarily employed by central banks. Traditionally conservative, players in financial markets are now less averse to risk-taking. The information in which they deal is highly complex and increasingly difficult to assess against general pre-determined standards. Moreover, it can move rapidly through the market. Prudential supervision is itself becoming as risky as the business it seeks to oversee. The suddenness of the demise of Johnson Matthey Bankers testifies to that risk. Again, to cite the Group of Ten Study Group:

> "The policy responses required under present circumstances may need to be more rapid than in the past and may call for closer co-operation between banking authorities and those responsible for capital-market regulation at national and international level. Because of the market's ability to innovate rapidly and flexibly, it can be more difficult than in the past to design policy changes and be confident that those changes will for long achieve desired results, without unwanted side effects."[4]

Herein lies the paradox faced by central banks. In promoting the need for prudential safeguards, a supervisor cannot be oblivious to the need to foster

---

[3] Study Group established by the Central Banks of the Group of Ten Countries, *Recent Innovations in International Banking*, Bank for International Settlements (April, 1986), p. 1. A number of these new off-balance sheet instruments are considered in Vol. II of this work.
[4] *Ibid.* pp. 1–2.

a competitive banking environment. Indeed, in recent years considerable efforts have been made to promote deregulation and to bring about a reduction in structural rigidities in the financial marketplace. However, the result has been a more volatile marketplace and in such an environment it is difficult for supervisors to adopt a long-term perspective. Further, deregulation is a domestic matter and consequently will not be consistent across national boundaries. The uneven regulatory background throughout international financial markets has promoted lending based more on regulatory anomalies than on principles of comparative advantage. The phenomenon known as regulatory arbitrage was, for example, a major force behind the emergence of the Euromarkets. As Gardener observes: "Supervisors and bankers do not live in the economist's perfectly competitive world of longer-term equilibrium. All too often recently, shorter-term disequilibria have dominated both supervisory practices and philosophy."[5]

Background to the Banking Act 1979 and Banking Bill (1986–7)[6]

The development of the supervisory régime in the United Kingdom has **1.04** been punctuated by crises. Until 1979, banking supervision in this country was implemented on a relatively informal basis with no comprehensive legislative backing. The Banking Act 1979 was precipitated, at least in part, by the secondary banking crisis. The collapse at Johnson Matthey Bankers has pointed to the need for the Act's revision. The law relating to banking supervision in the United Kingdom remains in a state of transition.

Unlike many countries, legislative intervention in banking has been rare in the United Kingdom. The developing supervisory régime has sought to retain many of the attributes that have marked its informal traditions. Prudential supervision in the United Kingdom places considerable emphasis on flexibility and co-operation. Its elemental characteristics have been depicted as flexible, personal, progressive and participative.[7] It exists in sharp contrast to the approach taken in the United States and many European countries where rule-based systems are applied. In the United States, numerous supervisory authorities exist—both at Federal and State level—with jurisdictions that commonly overlap. They supervise some 14,000–15,000 banks. Supervisory responsibility is not divided on functional grounds, but depends on the type of charter obtained by each bank. Not only do the various authorities directly examine the institutions they supervise, but they also ensure compliance with an extensive range of banking regulations. Much of the legislation has been shaped by a strong populist tradition, present since the days of independence and wary of large banking conglomerates. This has produced a banking system that is both geographically, and functionally fragmented. Significantly, commercial and investment banking are separated; there are limitations on interstate branching (and in some

[5] E. P. M. Gardener, *U.K. Banking Supervision—Evolution, Practice and Issues*, (Allen and Unwin, 1986) p. 46.
[6] At the time of writing (March 1987) there was a new Banking Bill before Parliament. This Bill received the Royal Assent in May 1987 when it became the Banking Act 1987. It is understood that the commencement date for the Act in general will be in October 1987.
[7] G. Blunden, currently Deputy Governor of the Bank of England, "The Supervision of the U.K. Banking System," *Bank of England Quarterly Bulletin*, (1975) p. 188 and pp. 189–190.

states, *intra* state branching); and companies within banking groups are confined to activities closely related to banking.[8]

1.05   The United Kingdom has no comparable provisions. Superficially, at least, the United Kingdom's approach to banking supervision has always appeared distinctly *laissez-faire* when viewed against the extensive network of controls applied in the United States. And indeed, such a perception of banking supervision in the United Kingdom is commonplace. It is, however, misguided to consider supervision purely in terms of legislative parameters. Informal methods of regulation need not imply that regulation is non-existent or that it is lax. Over recent years, the Bank of England has enhanced the mechanics of its approach by issuing numerous discussion papers and guidance notes on contemporary supervisory issues—which, by and large, represent a consensus of views held by the supervisors and the supervised. And, prior to the Banking Act 1979, supervision of recognised banks and of some (but not all) deposit-taking institutions was conducted reasonably effectively by the Bank of England on a non-statutory basis.

Nevertheless, the Bank of England's informal approach to supervision had its limitations, and these were show-cased by the secondary banking crisis. The crisis was precipitated by so-called fringe banks who had been borrowing short and lending long without sufficient regard for their liquidity over time. In addition, many had become over-committed in a property market which had turned against them and, for these institutions, insolvency also threatened. The inevitable result was a liquidity crisis which threatened to escalate to other parts of the banking system as depositors realised the precarious nature of their exposures to these institutions. The crisis was only averted by the launch of a "Lifeboat" by the Bank of England and the major clearing banks which bridged the credit gap.[9] In many respects the problem was one of definition. The question "what is a bank?" has long proved to be an elusive one.[9a] The absence of a formal system of banking supervision has led to the growth of a large number of deposit-taking institutions operating on the fringes of banking and outside the surveillance of the Bank of England. The crisis also demonstrated that many of the Bank's supervisory techniques were in need of improvement and required a much greater commitment of resources. The growing scale and complexity of the banking system demanded a greater degree of technical rationality.

1.06   At the same time, compliance with the first EEC Banking Directive, which sought harmonisation of the law relating to credit institutions necessitated the passage of legislation by the end of 1979. Nevertheless, most of the key features of the Banking Act 1979 were not demanded by the EEC Directive. The eventual shape of the Act remained attributable to the lessons learned during the secondary banking crisis. The Act sought to reconcile the Bank of England's flexible and participatory style with a desire to place the scheme of supervision within a more formal legal framework. It should be apparent, however, that these objectives tend to pull in different directions and that much of the rationale that went into the Act is internally

---

[8] I cannot hope to unravel the complexities of the U.S. banking system here. See K. Spong, *Banking Regulation—Its purpose, Implementation and Effects* (2nd ed., 1985) Federal Reserve Bank of Kansas; C. H. Golembe and D. S. Holland, *Federal Regulation of Banking*, (1983) Gollembe Associates Inc.

[9] For a full account of the secondary banking crisis, see M. Reid, *The Secondary Banking Crisis, 1973–75—Its Causes and Course* (Macmillan, 1982).

[9a] The question "what is a bank"? is considered in greater detail in Chap. 2 below.

inconsistent and confused. Moreover, the complexities of contemporary banking supervision have proved to be more deep-seated than at first imagined and are not to be solved by encasing existing practices within a statutory framework. The collapse of Johnson Matthey Bankers demonstrated that the Banking Act 1979 was not the final solution but merely the first move.

In the late evening of Sunday, September 30, 1984 the Bank of England felt compelled to take over JMB. This move was consequent upon the Bank's discovery of substantial misreporting by JMB of certain large single exposures in its loan book. Investigations revealed that JMB's assets required significantly larger provisions—on a scale that would have effectively exhausted the capital of all companies within the JMB group. JMB's role as one of the five main participants in the London bullion market meant that its failure would have had a severe knock-on effect on the stability of the banking system and this was a consequence which the Bank of England was not prepared to countenance.

Any supervisory régime will be shocked by failures. Nevertheless, there **1.07** are aspects of JMB's collapse that raise special cause for concern. For one, unlike the failures that precipitated the secondary banking crisis, JMB fell squarely within the supervisory net; it simply slipped through. Its problems went unnoticed until much too late. The informal approach enabled JMB to divert the supervisors from the dangers building up in its loan book. For another, JMB's failure was not in the least attributable to the pace of change in the financial system—a factor present in recent failures overseas. JMB was brought down by elementary errors of banking prudence: excessive exposures to individual customers of doubtful credit–worthiness, inadequate or no security supporting those exposures and the absence of any coherent system of internal controls. The significance of JMB's collapse was not that it occurred. Quite the opposite; it was that its impending demise could go undetected for so long by the system of supervision.

In the event, the collapse spawned a Review Committee chaired by the Governor of the Bank of England. Its report[10] identified a number of weaknesses in the system of supervision. The Committee's recommendations were, in the main, adopted in a subsequent White Paper.[11] The new Banking Bill implements the proposals contained in the White Paper. But those who anticipated a more formal system of supervision—one based on codification and inspection—to arise from the ashes of JMB will find their expectations unfulfilled. In many respects, the events at JMB were merely illustrative of inadequacies in the Banking Act 1979 that were already apparent. Many of the compromises embodied in the Act had begun to unravel and a number of legislative omissions had come to light. The collapse at JMB provided a catalyst to facilitate a wide-ranging review of the whole system of banking supervision.

Scheme of the Banking Act

The Act's title is something of a misnomer. Its ambit is essentially that of **1.08** prudential supervision. It does not extend to other matters of banking and monetary policy—often covered within banking legislation overseas. It

[10] Cmnd. 9550 *Report of the Committee set up to consider the system of Banking Supervision*, (1985)—(the Leigh-Pemberton Committee).
[11] Cmnd. 9695 *Banking Supervision*, (1985).

does not deal with the contract of banker and customer, which is the conventional focus of banking law and currently in need of revision.[12]

There are two main limbs to the Banking Act 1979: the regulation of deposit-taking business and the establishment of a deposit protection scheme. In addition, the Act provides for regulation of the issue, form and content of advertisements for deposits and it controls the use of banking names and descriptions. It also requires overseas banks establishing representative offices to give notice to the Bank of England. The central provisions of the Act provide for a scheme requiring the vetting and prior authorisation of deposit-taking institutions. Conjunctively, there is provision for revocation in the case of a failure to fulfil any of the minimum criteria set out for authorisation. Between authorisation and revocation, the formal powers afforded the Bank are sparse.

The Bill closely follows the scheme of supervision set down in the Banking Act 1979. However, its provisions are set out with much greater precision and many of the Bank's powers are strengthened. The number of clauses employed by the Bill is more than double that of its predecessor. Yet, despite this additional legislative prescription, the Bill does not make radical changes to the scheme of supervision. The characteristic feature of supervision in the United Kingdom has always been its flexibility. The Bill adheres to this philosophy. Like the 1979 Act, the Bill does not purport to regulate every aspect of prudential supervision. There are no prescribed ratios for liquidity, capital adequacy or foreign currency exposure. The mechanics of continuing supervision are deliberately left for the Bank of England to implement without recourse to detailed statutory provisions. In this sense, the Bill's reforms are evolutionary rather than revolutionary.

The restriction on deposit-taking

1.09 The generic questions of what is a bank and what constitutes the business of banking have persistently vexed banking lawyers. Notwithstanding frequent use of these terms in statutes, they have eluded prescriptive definition. Prior to the Banking Act 1979, statutory definitions were either circuitous[13] or left the question to be resolved by administrative *fiat*.[14] Different institutions were recognised as banks for different purposes under various statutes. There were no formal and consistent criteria for recognition. Even the apparent objectivity of the three point test outlined in the frequently cited case of *United Dominion Trust* v. *Kirkwood*[15] proved indecisive. In that case, the Court of Appeal identified three characteristics consistent with the conduct of banking business: keeping customers' running accounts; honouring cheques drawn on the business; and collecting cheques on behalf of customers. However, the usefulness of these factors was undermined by the Court's unwillingness to rest its decision upon them. In reality, the decisive considerations in the case were putative standing and

---

[12] It is noted, however, that with the publication of the Bill came a Treasury announcement of a comprehensive review of banking law. This is a welcome move.

[13] See, for example, the Building Societies Act 1962 and the Income and Corporation Taxes Act 1970.

[14] See, for example, the Bank of England Act 1946, and the Companies Act 1967.

[15] [1966] 2 Q.B. 431.

community acceptance.[16] Historically, it seems we have been content to assume that we can always tell a bank when we see one.

The enigmatic character of the concept of banking encouraged the draftsman of the 1979 Act to steer clear of it. Instead, the central prohibition in the Act fixes on one aspect of banking business—that of deposit-taking. The object of the Act is the protection of depositors and the integrity of the deposit-taking system. There is little scope for the Bank of England to have regard to wider considerations when exercising its powers. Nevertheless, it is obvious that the effective supervision of deposit-taking institutions must necessarily involve the Bank in supervision of the uses to which deposits are put. Section 1(1) is the linchpin of the Act. It prohibits the acceptance of a deposit in the United Kingdom in the course of carrying on a deposit-taking business without the authorisation of the Bank or exemption under section 2. The system of banking supervision rests upon the need for deposit-taking institutions to obtain authorisation from the Bank. Clause 3 of the new Bill substantially reiterates the section 1(1) prohibition. It has however, been reworded to clarify the point that the territorial scope of the prohibition is confined to the acceptance of deposits in the United Kingdom—a point left ambiguous by the 1979 Act. Furthermore, the geographical scope has been widened under the new Bill to cover carrying on a deposit taking business anywhere in the world providing, of course, the deposit is accepted in the United Kingdom.

1.10 The prohibition on deposit-taking is wide in scope. It extends some way beyond those institutions which might commonly be regarded as banks to capture institutions which finance their own business materially from deposits or from the interest earned on them.

Numerous exemptions were necessary under the 1979 Act and these are in the main, repeated under the Bill. Clause 4(1) of the Bill exempts the Bank of England and those persons specified in schedule 2. The schedule includes numerous intergovernmental financial agencies, local authorities, the National Savings Bank, penny savings banks and school banks. It also exempts building societies, credit unions, friendly societies and certain insurance companies, these being regulated under other legislation. The schedule no longer contains the trustee savings banks or the National Giro-bank. In addition, clause 4(5) will again enable regulations to be made by the Treasury exempting the Bill's application to certain transactions. The policy here has been to grant exemptions where appropriate safeguards to the depositors are in place. Currently, the Banking Act 1979 (Exempt Transactions) Regulations (SI 1986/1712) exempt a diverse range of transactions. In particular, these include deposits taken in connection with the purchase of certain sterling debt securities and commercial paper,[16a] certain charitable deposits, deposits accepted by solicitors in the course of their profession and pre-contract deposits accepted in the course of estate agency work.

1.11 The Bill also continues to follow the 1979 Act in providing for a number of more general exemptions. These are given effect by extensive definition

---

[16] One author has commented that the decision appears to have been reached largely on grounds of expediency and "does not provide any better definition than previously existed of the term 'banker' or 'banking business' "—8 *Legal Decisions Affecting Bankers*, 523–4.

[16a] For a fuller discussion of how the exemption operates in relation to commercial paper, see Vol. II, Chap. 10 of this work. See also, G. Penn, "Sterling Commercial Paper" [1986] B.F.L. Rev., pp. 195–209.

of the meaning of "deposit" and of "deposit-taking business" in clauses 5 and 6 respectively.[17] In broad terms, a deposit will encompass any loan or other repayable funds. However, excluded from the definition is money paid which is referable to the provision of property or services or to the giving of security (but only when paid in compliance with the further requirements laid down in clause 5(2)). Loans from authorised institutions and others whose business consists mainly of lending money are also excluded, as are certain categories of connected lending within companies or between associated persons. However, the taking of a deposit alone is not sufficient to activate the prohibition laid down in clause 3. The deposit must be taken in the course of a deposit-taking business in which monies deposited are on-lent or used to finance the business to any material extent. The concept of "deposit-taking" business excludes incidental deposit-taking, taken on "particular occasions" by a person "not holding himself out as accepting deposits on a day-to-day basis."

1.12   The equivalent provisions in the 1979 Act have recently been considered by the Court of Appeal in *SCF Finance Company Limited* v. *Masri*.[18] The Court's decision gives considerable width to exclusions available both from the definition of "deposit" and of "deposit-taking business." The facts of *Masri* are complex. However, their essence can be summarised as follows; SCF carried on business as licensed brokers in commodity and financial futures. They held themselves out as willing to deal in the market on a client's behalf and for this purpose required clients to place funds with them to cover the transactions made as well as "margins" to cover the risk of loss on the transactions. Nevertheless, these proved inadequate in Masri's case and SCF incurred substantial losses in the course of trading on his behalf. When Masri failed to settle his account, SCF brought an action against him for the amount due. In rebuttal, Masri contended that his agreement with SCF contravened section 1 of the Banking Act 1979 in that the payments made constituted the acceptance of "deposits" in the course of an unauthorised "deposit-taking business." Accordingly, he contended that SCF were not entitled to recover sums due under the agreement and counterclaimed to recover sums already paid. At first instance, Legatt J. rejected Masri's contentions and gave judgement for SCF.[19] His decision was affirmed by the Court of Appeal. The Court considered the statutory parameters of "deposit" and of "deposit-taking business." In relation to "deposit," the Court found that the amounts paid by Masri to SCF had been paid by way of security for payment for the provision of property or services to be provided by SCF and thus were not "deposits" for the purposes of the 1979 Act. The Court reasoned that if a futures contract resulted in actual delivery of the commodity then SCF had provided "property" and if, as was usual, it did not then SCF had provided "services" by incurring risk and consequent lossess and through the extension of incidental credit on the course of their dealings. In either case, the payments made by Masri were to be regarded as security to protect SCF against the risk that Masri might default in reimbursing them for expenses incurred on his behalf.

This conclusion contradicted the existing interpretation. Prior to the decision it had been thought that for a payment to be exempt from the definition of a deposit, being referable to the provision of property or services,

---

[17] Sub-sections 1(4), (5), (6) and sub-sections 1(2), (3) of the 1979 Act.
[18] [1987] 1 All E.R. 175.
[19] [1986] 1 All E.R. 40. Analysed by Jane Welch in (1986) 1 J.I.B.L. 54.

it must be referable to a *specific* item of property or service. The Bank of England's *Guide for Intending Applicants for Authority to Take Deposits* states that the Bank regards this exemption:

" . . . as referring to advance or part payments for a *specific* item of property (*e.g.* the suit ordered from a tailor) or service and not, say, to monies placed in a budget account (for unspecified goods) run by a shop where part of the arrangements is that monies paid in are withdrawable. Similarly, monies placed with an investment manager for an investment at his discretion or the proceeds of the sale of securities held pending instructions for the client for disbursement do not in the Bank's view fall within the terms of section 1(b)(*a*)."[20]

This interpretation does not appear to have attached itself to the Court of Appeal and it is not one that fits easily within the wording of the 1979 Act. The relevant exclusion from the definition of deposit under the 1979 Act[21] makes no reference to *specific* property or services and there is no suggestion that such property or services be identified in advance. Indeed, under the 1979 Act the exclusion is expressed to include the provision of property or services "of any kind." (The new Bill now deletes these words.) While the Court's decision could be confined solely to cases where money is paid *by way of security* for payment of the provision of property or services, it is difficult to see why the same reasoning would not be applied more generally to advance or part payments for the provision of property or services. As a consequence, the *Masri* decision must raise doubts over the status of budget accounts—whether these be bill-paying facilities or store accounts. If forward payments of the type made in *Masri* are capable of being described by the Court as money "paid by way of security for payment for the provision of property or services," then it seems open for a court to conclude that forward payments to a bill-paying institution are an "advance payment" for the provision of a service. Equally, a court might now regard payments into a store account as an "advance payment" against the provision of property or services. By merely deleting the words "of any kind" the new Bill appears to leave these issues unresolved. **1.13**

The second limb of the *Masri* decision relates to the definition of a "deposit-taking business." Here, the Court found that **1.14**

"a person 'holds himself out to accept deposits on a day to day basis' only if (by way of express or implicit invitation) he holds himself out as being generally willing on any normal working day to accept such deposits from those persons to whom the invitation is addressed and who may wish to place moneys with him by way of deposits."[22]

The Court held that a *request* by SCF for specific payments to be made by a client does not come within this concept. However, such a distinction appears particularly artificial and compliance with this aspect of the decision could well require supervisors to make some particularly "hair-splitting" distinctions. Further, the Court considered that such requests would come within the meaning of "particular occasions." The mere fact that these occasions may be numerous did not render them any less particular. This

---

[20] Bank of England, *Guide for Intending Applicants for Authority to Take Deposits*, p. 2.
[21] s.1(6).
[22] [1987] 1 All E.R. 175, p. 190.

again conflicts with the previously accepted view. The Bank of England's Guide for Intending Applicants interprets the term:

> "as referring both to the frequency of deposit-taking and to the circumstances prevailing when the deposits were accepted. The more distinctive the circumstancs prevailing when deposits are accepted, the more frequent deposit-taking can be; and, *vice versa*, the more frequently deposits are accepted, the more peculiar the prevailing circumstances need to be for the occasions to be 'particular'."[23]

Clause 6(4) of the Bill will address this issue by requiring that regard shall be had to the frequency of "occasional deposits" and to any characteristics that distinguish them from each other. It is doubtful however that this position alone will be sufficient to override the effect of the decision in *Masri*.

The definitions of "deposit" and "deposit-taking business" are complicated. This can only lead to anomalies—the potential for which *Masri* clearly demonstrates. Given the speed at which change is taking place in the banking sector, the Bill contains an important addition. Clause 7 will empower the Treasury, in consultation with the Bank, to amend the definition of "deposit" and "deposit-taking business" by secondary legislation. The diversification of banking activities, particularly in the international finance markets, may well necessitate further reappraisal of the deposit-taking concept.

Unauthorised deposit-taking

1.15   The new Banking Bill also removes a procedural anomaly in relation to deposit-taking. While the Bank is a prosecuting authority under the 1979 Act, it is given no powers to investigate institutions which have not been authorised. The Bill confers new wide-ranging powers on the Bank to enable it to investigate unauthorised deposit-taking. Where a breach is suspected, the Bank will be empowered to require the person concerned to furnish information, produce documents or answer questions. The Bank will also be given a power of entry when it suspects that documents provided to it are incomplete or that documents covered by this clause may be suppressed or destroyed.

There are powers concerning the unauthorised acceptance of deposits to parallel those given by the Secretary of State under the Financial Services Act 1986 in relation to investments. The Bank will be entitled to apply to the court for an order directing the repayment of unauthorised deposits. In addition, the court may order a person who has profited from unauthorised deposit-taking to pay into court such sums as it considers just and direct their disbursement to those who made the deposits and to other just recipients. A further clause entitles the Bank and other prosecuting authorities to apply to the court for an injunction to prevent contravention of the Bill by unauthorised persons. And in Part VI of the Bill there is provision to enable the Bank to petition for the winding-up of an illegal deposit-taker.

Abolition of the two-tier system

1.16   The most significant change brought about by the Bill is the abolition of the two-tier system (*i.e.* the differentiation between recognised banks and licensed deposit-takers). The two-tier system was one of the key features of

[23] Bank of England, *op. cit.*, p. 4.

the 1979 Act. The system has shown itself to be an anachronism. It was designed to allow the Bank to continue its close relationship with the major banks while at the same time giving it greater powers of scrutiny and control over licensed deposit-takers whose readiness to comply with the bank's views could not be assumed. However, the different styles of supervision that developed can no longer be justified on prudential grounds. Indeed, the Review Committee notes that JMB's status as a recognised bank hindered the supervisor's ability to detect its growing problems.[24]

Under the 1979 Act, both recognised banks and licensed institutions are required to meet criteria covering legal form, prudent conduct and management. Recognised banks must in addition demonstrate high reputation and standing in the financial community and provide a wide range of banking services. Recognised banks are also generally required to have minimum net assets at the time of authorisation of £5 million while licensed institutions need only have £250,000.

The Bill amalgamates the two tiers and provides for a unitary system for authorisation. Schedule 5 provides for the continuing authorisation of existing recognised banks and licensed institutions under the 1979 Act. Nevertheless, the criteria for authorisation remain significant to them as their continued fulfilment is required by the Bill. The criteria for authorisation are laid down by clauses 8 and 9 and in Schedule 3. These are drawn from the criteria used in the 1979 Act, but the Bill spells out their elements more fully. The Bill envisages that the Bank will continue to apply the criteria flexibly. As a corollary, clause 16 will require the Bank to publish a statement of the principles that it from time to time applies in interpreting the criteria.

Clause 8 lays down the procedure by which an institution can apply to the Bank for authorisation. The Bill's interpretation clause defines an institution to be a body corporate or a partnership. It does not include sole traders. At present, there is only one partnership licensed under the Act. However, continuing availability of authorisation to partnerships is a requirement under the EEC Banking Directive. The Bill will no longer permit access to partnerships formed outside the EEC. **1.17**

Schedule 3 sets out the Bill's prudential requirements. Every director, controller and manager must be fit and proper persons to hold their respective positions. The Bill clarifies this requirement by referring both to probity and competence and by specifying a range of improper conduct to which the Bank may have regard in considering a person's suitability to hold these positions. The board of an authorised institution must include as many non-executive directors as the Bank considers appropriate. At least two individuals must effectively direct the business of the institution (termed the "four eyes" criterion). The schedule elaborates what is envisaged by the concept of "prudent conduct." An institution must maintain adequate capital, adequate liquidity and make adequate provisions for bad and doubtful debts. Capital must be (a) commensurate with the nature and scale of an institution's operations, and (b) sufficient to safeguard the interests of its depositors having regard to the nature, scale and risk of the institution's operations (although it is difficult to see how the former can add anything to the latter). Prudent conduct now also encompasses the need to maintain adequate accounting and other records and adequate systems of internal

---

[24] Leigh-Pemberton Committee, *op. cit.*, p. 4.

control. All institutions (not just recognised banks) must behave with integrity and professional skill. A single net asset requirement of £1 million will apply to all new institutions.

One vestige of the two-tier system will remain. Part III prohibits the use of banking names by any United Kingdom incorporated institution without paid up capital or undistributable reserves of not less than £5 million. However, this prohibition does not apply to existing recognised banks or to overseas institutions. Notwithstanding the restriction on banking names, banking descriptions will be open to all authorised institutions. The Bank will also have powers to object to names which it considers to be misleading or undesirable.

Revocation and restriction

1.18   The ultimate sanction which the Bank can invoke is revocation of an institution's authorisation and the Bill expands the grounds on which the Bank can do this. Primarily, these centre upon a failure to comply with the criteria specified in Schedule 3. However, the "catch-all" in clause 11(1) has been extended to enable the Bank to take account of matters external to the institution which threaten the interests of depositors. This provision now also encompasses the proposed future conduct of an institution and is not merely retroactive as under the 1979 Act.

The existence of grounds for revocation does not oblige the Bank to act on them. Indeed, the Bank must be prepared to justify its action and to conform generally with the reqirements of administrative law. It may also be quite possible for grounds for revocation to exist against an institution in circumstances where the best interests of depositors would be served by attempting its rehabilitation. Where the Bank considers a lesser sanction to be more appropriate, clause 12 enables the Bank to place restrictions upon an authorisation as an alternative to revocation. Clause 12 provides a more flexible mechanism to supersede the issue of conditional licences under the 1979 Act. The Bank also has power under clause 19 to issue directions to an institution once it has given notice of its intention to revoke the institution's authorisation or after the time limit upon a restricted authorisation has expired. These directions can cover any matter which the Bank considers to be desirable in the interest of depositors.

Changes in control

1.19   Section 14 of the 1979 Act imposes a duty on licensed institutions (but not recognised banks) to notify the Bank within 21 days of it becoming aware of a change in control. The duty does not extend to the controllers themselves; nor do the sanctions that can be imposed. Clearly, this has left the Bank with too little room to manoeuvre and so the Bill provides the Bank with much wider powers to control major changes in the ownership of authorised institutions.

The Bill will empower the Bank to prohibit, on prudential grounds, acquisitions of (or increases in) controlling shareholdings in authorised institutions incorporated in the United Kingdom. All those intend to acquire 15 *per cent.* or more of the voting power of an authorised institution will be required to obtain the Bank's prior consent before acquiring their stake. Similarly, no minority shareholder controller may become a majority (over 50 *per cent.*) shareholder, nor majority shareholder a principal (over 75 per cent.) shareholder without seeking the Bank's prior consent. The provisions also apply to those who exercise control by indirect means. Once the Bank is notified of a prospective change in control, it has three months in which it can serve notice of any objection it may have to the change. There is also provision for the Bank to serve a notice of objection on any shareholder controller (*viz.* 15 *per cent.* or more) that it considers is no longer fit and proper to be in such a position of control. In addition, any person who acquires a significant shareholding in a bank (defined as 5 *per cent.* or more) must give notice to the Bank of such a holding.

The Bank is empowered to delare an offending transaction void or to remove voting rights from the shares concerned. The Bank may also apply to the court for an order requiring the sale of specified shares. However, such an order cannot be made until any avenues of appeal have first been exhausted. A further clause enables the Treasury to direct the Bank to object (on grounds of international reciprocity) to the acquisition of controlling shareholdings in banks before they take place. This may in turn lead to the blocking of voting rights on the shares or to their divestment.

Information and large exposures

Effective supervision by the Bank depends heavily on the voluntary provision of financial information by institutions. This will always be so in a system which lays emphasis on co-operation and participation rather than on codification and inspection. Under the 1979 Act, the Bank's powers to compel the production of information are limited. Section 16 empowers the Bank, by notice in writing, to require a licensed institution (but not a recognised bank) to provide information and produce specified documents. Under the new Bill, this power will extend to all authorised institutions. This change is consequent upon the abolition of the two-tier system. The Bank can also require an institution to provide it with a report on the information by an accountant or other relevant professional. Where the institution concerned is part of a group of companies, the Bill extends the Bank's powers to other companies within the group. Also, directors, controllers and managers can be compelled to provide the Bank with the information that may reasonably assist it in determining whether they are fit and proper persons. **1.20**

Should these powers prove insufficient, the Bank is afforded a general right to enter the premises of a person upon whom notice to provide information or documents has been served. Entry is permitted without notice where the Bank reasonably believes that the relevant documents would be removed, tampered with or destroyed. Section 17 of the 1979 Act gives the Bank a power to appoint investigators and to examine the business of an authorised institution if the interests of depositors appear to be threatened. This provision is repeated in the Bill. New offences will cover those who provide the Bank with information that is false or misleading. These will extend to authorised institutions that suppress information knowing, or having reasonable cause to believe, it to be of relevance to the Bank in the performance of its supervisory functions.

The 1979 Act makes no reference to large exposures. (Indirectly, however, excessive exposures might well reflect upon the prudence of an institution's management.) Nevertheless, loan concentrations give rise to particular concern because of the risk that excessive exposure to an individ- **1.21**

15

ual customer, group of customers, country or economic sector, can threaten the solvency of an authorised institution should the exposure prove to be irrevocable. The dangers of such a scenario were amply demonstrated by the events at JMB. It is, therefore, essential for effective supervision that large exposures can be contained to an appropriate level and that they be reported promptly and accurately.

The Bill does not impose any ceiling on large exposures. Rather, it imposes a duty of notification upon authorised institutions. Notification is required following the assumption of any exposure to an individual customer (or group of connected customers) over 10 per cent. of its capital base and prior notification where a similar exposure in excess of 25 per cent. is proposed. The Bank can, by notice in writing, include exposures undertaken by subsidiaries of an authorised institution, when the subsidiary concerned is not itself an authorised institution. In such a case, the subsidiary's capital is also taken into account. The frequency, form and content of reports made is left to the discretion of the Bank. Failure to report as required will be an offence. However, it will be a defence to demonstrate that the relevant facts were not known at the time when the report was required provided that a report was made within 7 days of the institution becoming aware of those facts.

Of course, even a reporting régime is not without its difficulties. The task of defining the concepts of "exposure," "capital" and "connected borrowers" for prudential purposes is not easily accommodated within legislation. It is not attempted in the Bill. These concepts must be capable of reflecting evolving market practices. Further, they must be capable of accurately weighing the effect of contingent liabilities, off-balance sheet items and other risk bearing factors. The Bill makes it clear that any question regarding exposures to individuals, shall be determined in accordance with principles published by the Bank. In this regard, the Bank has published two consultative papers on the treatment of large exposures.[25] The papers emphasise that, notwithstanding the two reporting thresholds, the Bank's approach will be to take into account, particular characteristics pertaining to individual institutions. Indeed, it notes that in many circumstances exposures within the reporting thresholds may nevertheless be regarded as excessive. Exposures over 25 per cent. would only be countenanced by the Bank in exceptional circumstances. Compliance with the Bill will necessitate an understanding of these consultative papers.

Accounts and auditors

1.22   The most innovative change brought about by the new Bill is to clear the way for auditors to play a greater part in the supervisory process. Hadden has noted that, over the course of this century, auditors have progressively strengthened the independence and professional standing of their role.[26] The influence of professional standards on accounting and auditing techniques has been instrumental in substantially improving the accuracy and consistency of financial statements. Without this growth in accounting professionalism, laws designed to foster prudence and honesty in banking risk are ineffectively constructed and imperfectly applied. The Leigh-Pemberton

[25] "Large Exposures undertaken by Institutions authorised under the Banking Act 1979: Consultative Paper by the Bank of England," (July 1986) and (February 1987).
[26] T. Hadden, *Company Law and Capitalism* (Weidenfeld and Nicholson, 2nd ed., 1977), pp. 137–40.

Committee noted that if the Bank is not to carry out detailed inspections of its own, it must be able to rely on the assistance and co-operation of auditors whose duties necessitate first-hand knowledge of an institution's accounts.[27] The Bank intends to draw on this knowledge and require auditors to prepare reports on particular aspects of their client's business. Aside from strengthening the supervisory régime, this move is a cost effective one, sparing banks the alternative of facing two largely overlapping enquiries.

Of course, the complementary roles of auditor and supervisor have long been recognised but co-operation between them has hitherto been largely precluded by confidentiality constraints. An auditor's primary duty is to the institution and its shareholders and this duty restricts the information he can make available to third parties—including (at present) the Bank of England. The Bank's ability to communicate with auditors directly is also restricted by the tightly drafted confidentiality provisions contained in section 19 of the 1979 Act. The Bill will override an auditor's duty of confidentiality to enable him to pass on information to the Bank concerning the business affairs of his client. Such information must be acquired by him in his capacity as auditor and be communicated to the Bank in good faith. Note that the Bill does not impose a *duty* upon auditors to disclose information to the Bank. Nevertheless, they remain open to suit in negligence should they fail to communicate with the Bank when circumstances indicate that they ought reasonably to have done so. At the time of writing, the Bank of England is in consultation with the accountants' professional bodies with a view to developing a code of practice which will govern the circumstances in which accountants will be required to communicate to the Bank matters coming to their attention, and also matters which should be contained in their regular reports. For the Bank's part, it will again be required, as a general proposition, to observe confidentiality in the information supplied to it in accordance with the Bill's provisions. However, this general duty will be relaxed to permit disclosure by the Bank when necessary to facilitate the discharge of its functions under the Bill. In this context, specific reference is made to auditors.

Although not stated in the Bill, the White Paper makes it clear that in the majority of cases the Government expects that communications between auditors and supervisors should take place on a trilateral basis, involving an authorised institutions management.[28] The Bill is framed to accommodate the more rare circumstance where direct communication between auditors and supervisors may be warranted (*e.g.* in cases of suspected fraud). More commonly, it is envisaged that reporting accountants should advise supervisors on the adequacy of an authorised institution's books and records and internal controls. These must be sufficient to enable the directors and management of an institution to conduct its business in a prudent manner. This requirement will be supported by a guidance note to be issued by the Bank. Auditors will be required to notify the Bank if they decide to resign or not to seek re-appointment or if they propose to include a qualification to their report on an authorised institution's accounts. Equally, an institution must notify the Bank if it proposes not to re-appoint or to terminate the appoint-

[27] Leigh-Pemberton Committee, *op. cit.*, p. 3.
[28] The White Paper, (Cmnd. 9695) contains a guidance note on dialogue between auditors and supervisors (see Annex 4).

ment of its auditor. Failure to comply with these provisions will be an offence under the Bill.

Deposit protection scheme

1.23   Part II of the Banking Act 1979 established a mandatory deposit insurance scheme. The scheme is backed by a revolving Deposit Protection Fund of £5–6 million which is administered by a Deposit Protection Board. It provides partial protection to relatively small depositors. Under the scheme, 75 per cent. of the first £10,000 of a deposit placed with a recognised bank or licensed institution qualifies for protection in the event of insolvency. There is little protection for large depositors and, significantly, for other banks lending on the interbank market. Larger depositors are expected to make their own credit judgments. Also, interbank, foreign currency and secured deposits as well as deposits of more than five years to maturity do not come within the scheme. However, even small depositors must take some responsibility for assessing the credit-worthiness of the institution in which they place their deposits—hence the 75 per cent. limit on payments from the Fund. The Fund is financed by contributions levied on recognised banks and licensed institutions as a percentage of their deposit base, subject to a minimum initial contribution of £2,500 and a maximum of £300,000.

The Bill perpetuates the Deposit Protection Fund and the Deposit Protection Board. The level of deposit protection under the scheme has been raised from £10,000 to £20,000. In future, the parameters governing payment from the Fund (*i.e.* 75 per cent. of the first £20,000 deposited) can be altered by statutory instrument. The minimum initial contribution payable by newly-authorised institutions will be increased from £2,500 to £10,000. The maximum will remain at £300,000. The Bill will remove the Treasury's power under the 1979 Act to exempt overseas banks from the obligation to contribute. The application of the scheme has been extended to administration orders made under section 8 of the Insolvency Act 1986.

Co-operation between supervisors

1.24   The growing internationalisation and diversification of banking activities has generated a need for greater co-ordination and liaison between supervisors—both nationally and internationally. The Bill identifies a range of domestic authorities to which the Bank may release information to assist in the discharge of certain specified functions performed by those authorities. These include regulatory bodies established under the Financial Services Act 1986, the Building Societies Act 1986, the Insurance Companies Act 1982 and the Consumer Credit Act 1974. The Bill will also allow certain disclosures to be made to Government departments when in the interests of depositors or in the public interest and will enable the Bank to exchange information internationally with supervisors exercising comparable functions.

The Bank of England and the Board of Banking Supervision

1.25   Although clearly implicit in the 1979 Act, clause 1 of the Bill explicitly imposes a duty on the Bank to supervise the institutions that it authorises and to keep the operation of the Act and other relevant banking developments under review. It also contains the Bank's obligation to publish an annual report of its activities under the Bill. Clause 1(4) follows the Financial Services Act 1986 in conferring on the Bank and its staff an immunity from suit arising from anything done in purported discharge of the Bank's functions under the Bill.

Clause 2 (and schedule 1) establish the Board of Banking Supervision. In fact, the Board is already functioning on a non-statutory basis. Its role is to advise the Bank on the exercise of its functions under the Bill. The Board consists of the Governor, the Deputy Governor and the Executive Director responsible for supervision as *ex-officio* members and six independent members appointed by the Governor and the Chancellor of the Exchequer. The Board's constitution is unusual. Clause 2(3) imposes a duty on the independent members to advise the *ex-officio* members and clause 2(5) requires the *ex-officio* members to give written notice to the Chancellor of the Exchequer in any case where it is decided not to follow the advice of the independent members. But independent members are also entitled to approach the Chancellor directly. It is not clear how these provisions are intended to function. Is the duty to report to the Chancellor activated by the disagreement of one, some or all of the independent members? Presumably, it is not envisaged that the Board will meet as sub-groups. While not clear, it is unlikely that the duty imposed on independent members by sub-clause 2(3) is a several one. It follows that the existence of one independent dissentient would be sufficient to activate the *ex-officio* members' obligation to notify the Chancellor. Nevertheless, given that the Board has been attacked in the House of Commons as a "cosmetic exercise,"[29] the ambiguous nature of clause 2 is to be regretted.

Judicial review

Under the 1979 Act there is a right of appeal to the Chancellor of the Exchequer against a decision by the Bank to refuse or revoke a licence or recognition or to issue a direction in connection with a revocation. (Appeals under the Bill extend also to the imposition of restrictions upon an authorisation and to notices of objection issued to prospective controllers.) In the case of a revocation, the Bank's decision does not take effect until the appeal has been determined or the time limits have expired. Appeals under the 1979 Act are heard *de novo* by a tribunal of persons appointed by the Chancellor who reaches his decision after receiving the benefit of the tribunal's recommendations. There is also provision for further appeal to the High Court on points of law and this avenue is continued under the Bill. **1.26**

The Bill will enhance the standing of the tribunal. The membership of a tribunal is made more specific under the Bill. It must consist of a legally qualified chairman appointed by the Lord Chancellor and of two other persons with experience in accountancy and banking respectively. Under the Bill, the decision on appeal will be taken by the tribunal itself. The tribunal will have power to suspend the effect of a restriction or direction pending the oucome of a hearing. However, its mandate will be to conduct a judicial review rather than a rehearing. This move is likely to reduce the incidence of appeals but it will also reduce the Bank's influence upon their outcome by confining the issues in dispute to procedural aspects and removing them from the policy arena.

[29] Parliamentary Debates (Commons) November 28, 1986, Cols. 553–55 and 567.

There is also scope for the Bank's decisions to be reviewed more generally upon an application for judicial review under Order 53 of the Rules of the Supreme Court. Administrative action can be attacked by judicial review on grounds which are now conveniently grouped under the categories of "illegality," "irrationality" and "procedural impropriety."[30] With the rapid growth in administrative law that has taken place over the past two decades,[31] the Bank's decisions have become steadily more susceptible to judicial review. Clearly the passage of the Banking Act in 1979, which had the effect of placing banking supervision within a statutory framework, has accelerated the readjustments necessary to accommodate these developments. Administrative law has had a marked impact on decision-making processes at the Bank. The quasi-judicial character of many of the Bank's functions under the Act bring them directly within the purview of administrative law. In carrying out its functions the Bank must inevitably exercise discretions and make judgments about institutions and individuals. Further, it is apparent that administrative law is reaching into a wider range of the Bank's regulatory and supervisory activities. Persuasion is no longer an extra-legal activity.

1.27   Indeed, it is now clear that self-regulatory bodies established under private law can be brought within the sphere of judicial review. This was made clear in the *McCorquodale* case[32] when the Court of Appeal had cause to consider the role performed by the City Panel on Take-overs and Mergers. The Panel had argued that the Court's jurisdiction in public law extended only to bodies whose power is derived from legislation or the exercise of the prerogative. Moreover, it argued that the nature of the determinations made by the Panel required speed and finality and thus that it would be inappropriate to subject them to judicial review. Both arguments were rejected by the Court. The Court found that public law jurisdiction was not to be determined solely from the source of a body's power but also by whether it operates as an integral part of a system which has a public law character; is supported by public law in that public law sanctions are applied if its edicts are ignored, and performs what might be described as public law functions. After examining the structure and methods of the Panel, the Court found that its source of power is only partly based on moral persuasion and the assent of institutions and their members. Where extra-legal sanctions failed, the Panel drew support from a backdrop of statutory powers exercised by the Department of Trade and Industry and the Bank of England. However, in reaching this conclusion the Court went some considerable way to accommodate the need to give certainty to the Panel's determinations. First, the need to obtain leave to apply for judicial review will filter trivial and vexatious claims. Secondly, the Court stressed that it would normally allow contemporary decisions by the Panel to stand and merely make declaratory orders to guide the Panel on the future exercise of its powers. Only in cases of a breach of the rules of natural justice in disciplinary proceedings would the Court be prepared to upset a Panel ruling in retrospect.

Recent cases have also revealed a greater propensity on the part of the courts to review recommendations made by bodies constituted to advise

[30] *Council of Civil Service Unions* v. *Minister for Civil Service*, [1984] 3 W.L.R. 1174 (esp., *per* Lord Diplock).
[31] More particularly, since *Ridge* v. *Baldwin*, [1964] A.C. 40.
[32] *R.* v. *Panel on Take-overs and Mergers; ex p. Datafin and Prudential-Bache Securities Inc.*, (Judgment 5/12/86); *The Times* Law Report, December 8, 1986.

rather than to make final determinations.[33] It now seems that where a final decision-maker is obliged by statute to take full account of the advice tendered by an expert advisory body, that body must also act in accordance with the requirements of administrative law. Decisions of the Board of Banking Supervision are thus unlikely to be beyond scrutiny by the courts.

POSTCRIPT

The Banking Bill received the Royal Assent in May 1987, when it became the Banking Act 1987. It is understood that the commencement date for the Act, in general, will be sometime in October 1987.

---

[33] R. v. *Agricultural Dwelling-House Advisory Committee for Bedfordshire, Cambridgeshire and Northamptonshire*, (1986) Q.B.D.: Hodgson J. (*The Independent*, November 11, 1986). See also, S. A. de Smith, *The Judicial Review of Administrative Action*, (Sweet and Maxwell, 4th ed., by J. M. Evans) pp. 233–7.

Section Two

Banker and Customer

2. Definition of Bank and Customer

A. What is a bank?

There are, essentially, two reasons for wishing to know the answer to the question, "what is a bank." First, the nature of the relationship between bank and customer has certain characteristics which may, to some degree, distinguish it from other relationships. Even if not always so distinguishable, many of the incidents or characteristics of the relationship are well known, and may be presumed to attach to whatever body one has identified as a bank.[1] Secondly, a variety of statutes refer to banks, or to bankers, or to the business of banking. Well known examples are the Bills of Exchange Act 1882 (especially ss.60, 73, 79, 80) and the Cheques Act 1957 (ss.1–4). Section 2 of the 1882 Act defines the term "banker" as including "a body of persons, whether incorporated or not, who carry on the business of banking."[2] In a number of statutes the word has a complete definition, but that will apply only for the particular purpose of the statute. It is more common to find only partial definitions or no definition at all. One statutory device has been to enable a government department concerned with particular legislation to draw up a list of the institutions which count as "banks" for the purpose in question. Generally, the advice of the Bank of England would be sought. The existence of a number of lists led to a hierarchy or ladder of banking recognitions, and the more lists an institution appeared on, the more it resembled the idea of an all round bank. Whether or not there is some list of this kind, the problem in any statute must be resolved by reference in part to the purposes of the statute in question, and a general definition, therefore, must always be suspect. Leaving that aside, however, one may say certain things about the whole matter.

2.01

First, the relationship of banker and customer is characterised by the special relationship of confidence and secrecy. If that were to be excluded, (by, say, contract) one would tend to think that the institution to that extent did not resemble a bank. On the other hand, not all persons who have such a relationship are banks.[3]

2.02

Secondly, the relationship is one where the bank is ordinarily debtor and the customer is creditor, with a right, unless otherwise agreed, to payment on demand.[4] If a relationship is otherwise, then to that extent it does not resemble a banker-customer relationship. Obviously, however, not every borrower is a banker, even if he is to repay on demand.

Thirdly, the banker generally offers to maintain a current account for his

---

[1] If it is a bank, the incidents generally attach: if the incidents are obvious, it may be regarded as a bank.
[2] See also, *e.g.* The Post Office Act 1953, s.21, as amended, or the Banker's Books Evidence Act 1879, the Moneylenders Acts 1900 and 1927 (see s.6(d) of the Act of 1900 which exempts bankers from the requirements under the Act), the Stamp Act 1891, Agricultural Credits Act 1928, the Insolvency Act 1986, s.284(5) (though this refers to "a banker or other person") and so on. For a list of statutes see *U.D.T.* v. *Kirkwood* [1966] 2 Q.B. 431, 442, or schedule 6 to the Banking Act 1987. For an excellent discussion of the whole problem, see Morrison, Tillet and Welch, *Banking Act 1979*.
[3] Doctors, solicitors, accountants, trustees, for example.
[4] Below, Chap. 3.

customer, but it appears unnecessary that there be a deposit account. Further, it may be that a deposit account alone may suffice.[5]

Fourthly, it would appear to be an essential feature of banking that the repayment is made against a written order or mandate, generally in the form of a cheque. It does not follow that everyone who operates a repayment system which is by a similar means is a banker.[6]

2.03 Fifthly, it is part of a banking business that money be lent at a profitable rate of interest.[7] The same, however, may be said of any moneylender.[8]

Sixthly, it is part of a modern banking business that the banker issues his customer with cheque forms and arranges to collect payment due under cheques or bills paid into the customer's account, and drawn on other bankers or persons.

Seventhly, a banker will ordinarily "keep open shop for the receipt of money from all who choose to deposit it with him" so that he will accept any customer.[9] But some undoubted banks will only accept customers with a certain degree of wealth, or (merchant banks) with certain kinds of business, and in theory at least, any bank reserves the right to decline the business of a customer with bad references.

Finally, it may be that no one can be a banker who has not a reputation amongst the banking community as a banker.[10] It is uncertain what this means, but it perhaps refers to the prudential reputation of the alleged banker, and possibly to his professional skills and range of activities.

2.04 Ordinarily, therefore, and perhaps necessarily, one expects to see a current account, the issue of cheques, and the payment in and collection of cheques. Apart from that, the most that can be said is that the further the relationship diverges from one involving the features mentioned here, the less likely it is to be one of banker and customer. It may be the case that in a financial conglomerate, where the business is not divided into subsidiary companies, the element of the banking business must be a substantial part of the business, and perhaps the substantial part, before the business is that of a "banker."[11]

2.05 In *U.D.T.* v. *Kirkwood*[12] a garage company borrowed from the plaintiffs in order to obtain stock for their business. They gave bills of exchange as security, and the defendant endorsed these. The bills were dishonoured and the garage company was wound up. The plaintiffs sued the endorser, who pleaded that the Moneylenders Act 1900 applied to the plaintiffs (they had not been licensed under the Act, and if they were not bankers, who require no licences, the money loaned would be irrecoverable and no action lay on the bills). By a majority, the Court of Appeal held that the plaintiffs were bankers. The majority identified as essential features of a banking business:

[5] *Commercial Banking Co. Ltd.* v. *Hartigan* (1952) 86 I.L.T. 109. There was no true current account in *U.D.T.* v. *Kirkwood*, below, n. 12.
[6] By s.73 of the Bills of Exchange Act 1882, a cheque must, by definition, be drawn on a banker, and it cannot be a cheque if the drawee is not a banker.
[7] *Re Shield's Estate* [1901] I.R. 172, 198.
[8] See *Hafton Properties Ltd.* v. *McHugh (Inspector of Taxes)* November 28, 1986, where lending alone was said to be insufficient, in a case where the alleged bank took no deposits from the U.K. and did not, therefore, "carry on a banking business" in the U.K. for the purposes of s.54, Income and Corporation Taxes Act 1970.
[9] *Re Shield's Estate* [1901] I.R. 198, and *Hafton Properties Ltd.* v. *McHugh (Inspector of Taxes)* November 28, 1986, above, n. 8.
[10] See *U.D.T.* v. *Kirkwood*, below, n. 12.
[11] In *U.D.T.* v. *Kirkwood*, below, n. 12.
[12] [1966] 2 Q.B. 431.

(i) the maintenance of current accounts, (ii) the payment in to those accounts of cheques and their collection by the banker, and (iii) a reputation in the banking community as bankers. U.D.T. showed that they got money on deposit and that they operated a kind of current account but this was not the sort characteristic of a banking business. They had, however, a reputation in the banking community as bankers, and that community ought to be able to recognise a banker.[13] This decision appears to be exceptionally merciful to the plaintiffs (whose whole enormous moneylending business would have been brought down otherwise), and the majority warned that other cases might not be decided similarly in future.[14]

Building Societies or co-operative societies may be banks, if they operate current accounts, take deposits and offer banking facilities such as cheques payable on demand.[15] When trustee savings banks could not issue cheques, they were held not to carry on the business of banking,[16] but the position has probably been otherwise since they were permitted in 1964 to issue cheques.[17]

THE BANKING ACTS 1979 AND 1987

The 1979 Banking Act has been repealed and replaced by the 1987 Act. Both Acts are concerned only with the taking of deposits, which is, of course, only one of the functions of a banking business. The 1979 Act differentiated between "recognised banks" and "licensed institutions" and the main purpose of the distinction was to indicate those banks (the recognised variety) which were thought to need less supervision. Under the 1979 Act, a recognised bank was subject to prudential obligations or requirements like those applicable to all institutions under the 1987 Act. In addition, it had to provide either a wide range of banking services, or a highly specialised banking service. Further, it had to enjoy (and must have enjoyed for a reasonable period of time) a "high reputation and standing in the financial community." The 1979 Act specifically said that it did not affect banking status for any other purposes, so that many of the licensed institutions were banks for the purposes of other statutes. **2.06**

The failure of a recognised bank led in 1987 to the abolition of the distinction between recognised banks and licensed deposit takers. Like the 1979 Act, the 1987 Act also deals primarily with deposit taking businesses,[18] and requires authorisation for the purpose, unless an institution is exempted. Under the 1979 Act, the use of words such as "bank" or "banker" was restricted to recognised banks and a few others. After 1987, no person may use in his name the words "Bank, Banker" or indicate in his name that he is carrying on a banking business, unless he is an authorised institution with paid-up equity capital of not less than £5 million, or falls within certain other exceptions. The use as descriptions (other than in the name) of words such as these is also prohibited. There are exceptions as to names and des- **2.07**

---

[13] But the court did not regard itself as bound by banking opinion.
[14] Following this decision, s.123 of the Companies Act 1967 was enacted, enabling such institutions to be listed as bankers for the purpose of exemption from the Moneylenders Act. This was repealed by the Consumer Credit Act 1974.
[15] *Re Bottomgate Industrial Co-operative Society* (1891) 65 L.T. 712: *Re Birkbeck Permanent Building Society* [1912] 2 Ch. 183.
[16] *R.* v. *Industrial Disputes Tribunal ex p. East Anglian Trustee Savings Bank* [1954] 2 All E.R. 730.
[17] By the Trustee Savings Bank Act 1964. Clearly, the new T.S.B. is a bank.
[18] Considered above, Chap. 1.

criptions for such organisations as the National Savings Bank, penny savings banks, municipal banks, school banks, and foreign banks. It is expressly provided that the prohibitions do not prevent a person from describing himself as banker where this is necessary in order to comply with or take advantage of any enactment or rule of law or commercial usage or practice (clause 65(4)). Generally, therefore, the Act does not advance the definition of "banker," being concerned only with the regulation of deposit-taking businesses and with investor protection, and the stability of the financial system. But since at common law the "reputation" of a banker is not unimportant, the minimum criteria for authorisation (set out in schedule 3) may be of some significance. These refer to the fitness of individuals who manage the institution, to direction by two individuals, to the prudent conduct of the business, to the integrity and professional skills with which the business will be carried on, and to minimum net assets. The "prudent conduct" of the business contains references to a certain level of net assets, to adequate liquidity, to provision for depreciation, bad debts, and contingent liabilities, and to adequate record keeping.

B. What is a customer?

2.08 It is necessary to examine the word "customer" where it is used in some statutes: for example, section 75 of the Bills of Exchange Act 1882,[19] or in subsections 1 and 4 of the Cheques Act 1957.[20]

In addition to discerning the meaning of the word when used in these statutes (which do not define it), a variety of cases have held that between banker and customer there is a special relationship (primarily of a contractual nature) which has certain "incidents," (arising by express contract, or by implication of contractual terms) which is to say, that the bank owes the customer certain duties (these are the more important) and the customer owes the bank other duties. It is to some extent necessary, therefore, to examine for this purpose the legal definition of "customer," though there is a danger (so far as the common law is concerned) that this exercise will result in the drawing of a distinction between one who is and one who is not a customer which is more hard and fast than is justified. When statutory construction is not a question, the boundaries between customers and others are blurred, and a bank may owe duties to non-customers which are very much like, or in some cases identical to, those owed to customers. The point is, that if it can be said of an individual that he is certainly a customer, then certain duties towards him will be held to exist, unless excluded by contract. If he is not a customer, similar duties towards him may exist, but it will depend on the precise circumstances of every case. Even so, a bank may owe different duties to different customers, depending on their different circumstances, and what the bank undertakes to do. In any case, the question (at common law) is partly circular: a customer is a person to whom certain obligations are owed, and a person to whom those obligations are owed may be a customer (but is not necessarily so).

---

[19] Dealing with a banker's duty to pay on a cheque which is countermanded, or where the customer is dead.

[20] s.1 deals with the paying banker's liability regarding indorsements on cheques; s.4 with the collecting banker's liability where he receives payment for a customer not entitled to be paid.

The problem of definition also involves a consideration of the nature of **2.09**
"bank" and "banker."[21] A bank cannot be completely defined without
reference to its customers, and vice versa. Thus, for example, it was said in
U.D.T. v. *Kirkwood*[22] that the essential elements of a banker's business
were the maintenance for customers of current accounts, the payment of
cheques, and the collection of cheques for the customer. It would seem,
however, that if a person has only a deposit account,[23] or a credit card
account, he should be considered a customer, even though not the most
usual type of customer. It has also been said that an essential incident of the
relationship between bank and customer (whose account is in credit) is that
in relation to monies deposited the bank stands in the position of debtor to
the customer-creditor.[24] But a person remains a customer, if he is indebted
to the bank[25] or if the bank performs for him functions other than the holding of monies, (*e.g.* holding goods or documents for safekeeping, selling
securities, giving investment advice, advising on company take-overs and
mergers, selling insurance services, and all the other things which, in an era
of financial conglomerates, banks will do for their customers). Moreover, a
bank may hold funds as express or "constructive trustee," or subject to a
Quistclose trust[26] being obliged to use the funds for a purpose specified on
paying in, and not, say, for the purpose of appropriation to a particular
account of the bank's choice, or for subsequent combination of accounts.
The relationship is still one of banker and customer, though the relationship
is not merely one of debtor-creditor.

The following matters are also established: **2.10**

(i) A person may be a customer[27] even though his only connection with
the bank at the time in question was payment in to an account opened for
the purpose of a single cheque for collection. Duration not being of the
essence of the relationship, the first payment in constituted the person a customer.[28] This remains true even if the cheque has not been collected, and
even if the "customer" may not draw on the uncleared effects.[29] Indeed, it
has been said that a person who offers to open an account with a bank is a
customer as soon as his contractual offer is accepted.[30] Though an initial
credit is the normal practice, such a person might have a cheque book before
the account is credited.

(ii) A person is not a customer if the bank "performs a casual service"
for him, such as, for instance, cashing a cheque for a person who has no
account at the bank, introduced by a customer.[31] Banks often cash cheques
nowadays for strangers who have a cheque card from another bank, and
clearly the payee is not a customer of the bank which does so (nor is the
bank collecting for the payee, for it has bought the cheque and collects on its

[21] Examined above, para. 2.01.
[22] [1966] 2 Q.B. 431, above, para. 2.05.
[23] *Great Western Railway Co. Ltd.* v. *London and County Banking Co. Ltd.* [1901] A.C. 414.
[24] *Foley* v. *Hill*, below, para. 3.05.
[25] *Clarke* v. *London and County Banking Co.* [1897] 1 Q.B. 552.
[26] *Barclays Bank Ltd.* v. *Quistclose Investments Ltd.* [1970] A.C. 567.
[27] For the purpose of s.82 of the Bills of Exchange Act 1882 (this section was a predecessor of
the Cheques Act 1957, and is now abolished.
[28] *Commissioners of Taxation* v. *English, Scottish and Australian Bank Ltd.* [1920] A.C. 683.
[29] *Ladbroke & Co.* v. *Todd* (1914) 19 Com.Cas. 256, referred to with approval in *Barclays Bank
Ltd.* v. *Okenarhe* [1966] 2 Lloyds Rep. 87.
[30] *Barclays Bank Ltd.* v. *Okenarhe*, previous note.
[31] *Ibid.*

own behalf). It would seem, therefore, that the mere existence of a contract to purchase a bill of exchange is insufficient to constitute the seller a customer of the purchaser bank.[32] The crediting of cheques thus cashed to "Sundry Customers' Account" does not make those concerned customers.[33]

2.11   (iii) If a contract exists, a person may be a customer from the time a bank accepts instructions to collect monies from a third party, to pay part to a fourth party, and to retain the balance to the customer's order, although no account is formally opened: *Woods v. Martins Bank Ltd.*[34] The court in that case was concerned to find that the plaintiff was a customer, because it held that between customer and banker there was a fiduciary relationship, sufficient to maintain an action by the customer for negligent misrepresentation when he suffered loss after seeking investment advice. The existence of a fiduciary relationship is difficult to support, nowadays.[35] Moreover, it is now clear that liability for negligent misrepresentation may be owed by banks even to non-customers,[36] (though the existence of a contract may make a difference to disclaimers) so that the finding that the misrepresentee was a "customer" would not considered essential. However, the functions accepted by Martins Bank were "banking" functions, so that one might say that if a bank performs banking functions for a person with whom the bank has a contractual relationship, that person is a customer.

2.12   (iv) A bank may be a customer of another bank either if it has a drawing account with the other bank, or if it is a non-clearing bank which regularly uses a clearing bank to clear its cheques.[37] In a sales transaction involving the use of documentary credits, the issuing bank may be the customer of another bank which settles with the beneficiary, so as to give the settling bank the right to a special banker's lien (with right of sale) over the documents involved.[38]

(v) A person may (generally) be a customer of a bank, but for the particular purposes of a statute, may perhaps not be considered a customer. In *E.B. Savory & Co. v. Lloyds Bank Ltd.*[39] persons with accounts at one branch of a bank took stolen cheques to other branches of the same bank, which collected the cheques for them. The bank was not entitled to the protection of section 82 of the Bills of Exchange Act 1882, on the ground that it had been negligent in not ensuring a proper liaison between the branches. Further, in the Court of Appeal Lawrence L.J. held that the account holders were not customers of the collecting offices, which is to say, that the statutory protection was not intended for those collecting offices. The account holders "might just as well have been customers of some other bank."[40]

---

[32] See also, *Great Western Railway Co. Ltd.* v. *London and County Banking Co. Ltd.* [1901] A.C. 414, where a bank over a period of time cashed cheques for a person who had no account with them, and who was held not to be a customer. The bank collected for themselves, not for him. See also, *Tate* v. *Wilts and Dorset Bank* (1899) 1 L.D.A.B. 286.

[33] *Matthews* v. *Brown & Co.* (1894) 10 T.L.R. 386.

[34] [1959] 1 Q.B. 55; approved in *Warren Metals Ltd.* v. *Colonial Catering Co. Ltd.* [1975] N.Z.L.R. 273.

[35] After *National Westminster Bank P.L.C.* v. *Morgan*: see para. 19.03 below.

[36] See below, Chap. 3.

[37] *Importers Company Ltd.* v. *Westminster Bank Ltd.* [1927] 2 K.B. 297.

[38] *Aschkenasy* v. *Midland Bank Ltd.* (1934) 51 T.L.R. 34. For the lien, see below, Chap. 13.

[39] [1932] 2 K.B. 122, aff'd by H.L [1933] A.C. 201.

[40] No other judge considered this point.

(vi) The mere deposit of a sum of money with a bank with instructions to **2.13** transfer it to another bank does not of itself make the person requesting the transfer a customer of the bank, certainly where the depositor is a bank.[41]

(vii) The opening of an account by a person purporting to act with the authority of another, but who has no such authority, will not create a contractual relation of banker and customer between either the actual applicant or the purported customer, and the bank. The person opening the account, will, however, be liable on a warranty of authority.[42] In the case of forgery, it seems that the alleged customer cannot ratify what the unauthorised person has done so as to make the former retrospectively a customer.[43] Since accounts may be opened for fraudulent purposes, a request by a person to open an account for another must be met with particular caution, and the authority carefully established. An obvious risk is that the account is opened so that cheques payable to the named customer and fraudulently obtained by the person opening the account may be paid in, in which case the collecting bank would be liable in conversion to the true owner of the cheque. It would not be protected by section 4 of the Cheques Act 1957, precisely because it has not received payment for a "customer."[44] But the bank would not be liable to a purported customer for funds passing through the account and not otherwise belonging to him.[45] If there is authority to open the account, it matters not whether it is actual or ostensible, oral, written, by power of attorney, or howsoever.

(viii) A person may be a customer though he opens an account in an **2.14** assumed name. There is not, in England and Wales, any objection to a person using whatever name he wishes, though if he fraudulently deceives the bank the contract may be voidable at the bank's option. It may be fraud to say, "I am Smith" if the object is to make the bank think that the customer is not Jones, a bank-robber. Jones does not attempt to pass himself off as another existing person, but attempts to deceive the bank into thinking that he is not the bank robber, Jones.[46]

(ix) A person may be a customer though he opens an account in an **2.15** assumed name, purporting to be another existing person. This is clearly fraud, and the contract is voidable.[47] Again, the purpose may be fraudulently to pay cheques payable to the named person into the account, and then to withdraw the money. If this happens, prima facie the bank is liable in conversion, but as the person concerned is a customer, the bank has the protection of section 4 of the Cheques Act 1957, provided that it receives payment in good faith and without negligence (proper references being taken on opening the account, etc.).

At the heart of the notion of "customer," then, is (a) that there is a person with whom at the material time the bank has a contractual relationship, and

---

[41] *Aschkenasy* v. *Midland Bank Ltd.* (1934) 50 T.L.R. 209 (the depositor was a foreign bank, and transfer was to another foreign bank); *Kahler* v. *Midland Bank Ltd.* [1948] 1 All E.R. 811; aff'd [1950] A.C. 24.

[42] For which, see below, Chap. 15.

[43] *Stony Stanton Supplies (Coventry) Ltd.* v. *Midland Bank Ltd.* [1966] 2 Lloyds Rep. 373.

[44] *Ibid.*

[45] *e.g. Robinson* v. *Midland Bank Ltd.* (1925) 41 T.L.R. 170, 402.

[46] As to whether such a contract would be void for mistake, see Treitel, *Law of Contract*, (7th ed., 1987) Chap. 8. It is submitted that unless the bank very clearly (objectively) makes "not being Jones" a condition, the contract is merely voidable, and not void for mistake.

[47] Though not generally void for mistake, as submitted already.

(b) that the relationship includes the maintenance (or an agreement to maintain) by the bank of an account of some kind for that person.

OPENING THE BANK ACCOUNT

2.16 In order to avoid liability in certain cases described below, a bank must take reasonable care in opening an account (as by taking references, etc.).[48]

The customer is asked to sign a "mandate" which is the general authority given to the bank to operate the account (as opposed to specific mandates, like cheques, which are orders and authority to pay the payee of the cheque.) This may authorise another to sign cheques, but if so, then if authority is to be given to overdraw, this must be expressly stated, for no such power is implied.[49] In England and Wales, it is not the practice for the mandate to contain large numbers of terms and conditions,[50] or clauses protective of the bank. This seems to be more common abroad, but it may increasingly become the practice here.

---

[48] Below, Chap. 5.
[49] Cf. *Jacobs* v. *Morris* [1902] 1 Ch. 816.
[50] Discussed further below, para. 3.10.

3. Incidents of the Banker–Customer Relationship

A. Relationship based on contract

In *Joachimson* v. *Swiss Bank Corpn.*[1] the Court of Appeal, in a judgment often cited, held that the relationship between customer and banker was essentially a matter of contract, and that there was a single and indivisible contract[2] governing all general relations between the parties, even if separate contracts might be entered into for specific purposes (such as a contract where the customer borrows money, or the bank sells securities, etc.). The terms of the contract might be expressed, but (the court noted) were usually unwritten and undefined, and a matter for implication. The contract arose in the ordinary way, by offer (usually to open an account) and by acceptance, and it continues until ended by consent or other means. The incidents of the banker–customer relationship consist, therefore, largely of these implied terms.

3.01

B. "Special" tortious relationship

Since 1963, when the House of Lords decided *Hedley Byrne & Co. Ltd.* v. *Heller & Partners Ltd.*[3] it has been clear that as between a banker and his customer, or, for that matter any person who comes to the bank and seeks advice of a sort which it is reasonable to expect a banker to be able to give, there is a "special" relationship sufficient to give rise to a duty in tort (for customers or non-customers) or in contract (for customers or those who pay for the advice) if the bank assumes a duty to give the advice, and does not exclude its liability successfully. The bank may be liable even though the recipient of the advice has not paid for it.[4] Although the relationship is "special" enough to give rise to tortious liability, it is submitted that after *National Westminster Bank P.L.C.* v. *Morgan*, the decision in *Woods* v. *Martins Bank Ltd.*[5] that there is a fiduciary relationship between banker and customer seeking advice is insupportable and, in any case, it is unnecessary, following *Hedley Byrne & Co. Ltd.* v. *Heller & Partners Ltd.* (which does not require a fiduciary relationship).

3.02

Although there is a special relationship for tortious purposes between banker and customer, it does not follow that liability in tort is more extensive than in contract or that anything is to be gained by framing an action in tort rather than in contract. This possibility was expressly denied by the Privy Council, in *Tai Hing Cotton Ltd.* v. *Liu Chong Bank Ltd. and Others*[6] where the question concerned the customer's duties to the bank, rather than the converse.

---

[1] [1921] 3 K.B. 110.
[2] *Per* Atkin L.J. whose dictum has been recently approved in *Tai Hing Cotton Ltd.* v. *Liu Chong Bank Ltd. and Others* [1985] 2 All E.R. 947, 956. Bankes L.J. thought that there might be a primary contract, with separate added collateral obligations.
[3] [1964] A.C. 465.
[4] These matters are discussed below, Chap. 5.
[5] [1959] 1 Q.B. 55, above, para. 2.11. For the Morgan case, see below, para. 19.03.
[6] [1985] 2 All E.R. 947. above, para. 2.12.

C. Liability for breach of trust

3.03   The bank may have the "fiduciary" duties of a trustee over trust funds. Some funds may be the subject of an express trust, some of a constructive trust, and some of a type of trust called "Quistclose" which arises where A pays money to the bank for a specific purpose. These matters are discussed in Chapter 10.

D. Dominating influence by bank

3.04   It will be extremely rare that the bank obtains an influence over the customer such that any transaction is affected by the doctrine of "undue influence." This matter is considered elsewhere.[7]

E. Debtor–creditor relationship in respect of deposits

3.05   In *Foley* v. *Hill*[8] the House of Lords ruled that where a bank held funds belonging to its customer, the relationship between the parties was that of debtor (bank) and creditor (customer), rather than that the bank was trustee or agent. If the bank had fiduciary duties in respect of the funds, it would have had to account for their use, and profits made from employment of the funds might have been claimed by the customer. But the decision was that the bank might use the funds as it saw fit, being merely a debtor in the meantime. The House of Lords added that if the customer drew a cheque on the bank, the bank's obligation as debtor was to honour the demand if there were sufficient funds.[9]

The question still existed, whether the banker was liable only on demand. If not, then the Statute of Limitations,[10] which imposes a six-year period of limitations for actions based on a simple debt, would cause time to run from the time the banker received the money (unless he later acknowledged the debt, causing time to start running again). If the banker was liable on demand, time ran only from the making of a demand. Earlier cases suggested the former[11] but in *Joachimson* v. *Swiss Bank Corpn.*[12] the Court of Appeal held that demand was necessary as a condition precedent to the banker's liability constituting a present enforceable debt. Otherwise, the practice of banking would be detrimentally affected, and odd and uncontemplated results would follow. For example, the banker would be entitled to tender the amount of the credit balance at any time to the customer, and then refuse to honour outstanding cheques, because an ordinary debtor has a right to repay his debt at any time. Similarly, the customer would be able to demand repayment at any branch of the bank at any time. But these conclusions contradicted well-established authorities, and were insupportable. A demand, therefore, was required, and time did not run until then.[13] A demand could be made by presentation of cheque, or by the issue of a writ by the customer without previous demand. (If the customer did this, he

---

[7] Below, Chap. 19.
[8] (1848) 2 H.L.Cas. 28; see also *Midland Bank Ltd.* v. *Conway Corpn.* [1965] 2 All E.R. 972.
[9] This duty is further considered, below, Chap. 6.
[10] The Limitation Act 1980.
[11] *Pott* v. *Clegg* (1847) 16 M.&W. 321; *Re Tidd, Tidd* v. *Overell* [1893] 3 Ch. 154; *Bradford Old Bank Ltd.* v. *Sutcliffe* [1918] 2 K.B. 833. It was recognised that it all depended on the intention of the parties: *Walton* v. *Mascall* (1844) 13 M.&W. 452, 455.
[12] [1921] 3 K.B. 110.
[13] See also *Re Footman, Bower & Co. Ltd.* [1961] Ch. 443.

would probably be made to pay costs, or the bank could at once pay into court.)

If, on the other hand, the customer is indebted to the bank, the position is **3.06** different. In a term loan, time runs from the date at which the loan is repayable. But in an overdraft, the rule where nothing to the contrary is agreed is that time runs from the date of each advance.[14] Firstly, however, the rule in *Clayton's case*[15] would assist the bank, by discharging the earlier debts, and secondly, obligations under overdrafts, guarantees, and so on are usually expressly stated to arise on demand, in which case the rule in *Joachimson* v. *Swiss Bank Corpn.* applies.[16]

Further incidents of the debtor–creditor relationship, (*e.g.* duty to pay on cheques, and effect of garnishee orders and trust funds) are considered below.

A further question is whether the principle of *Foley* v. *Hill* applies where **3.07** the bank is given funds so that it may act as trustee. Funds held "as trustee" are not available to the debtor's creditors on the former's insolvency, and if the bank holds "as trustee" the monies would not be available on the insolvency of the bank, for the bank's creditors. In *Space Investments Ltd.* v. *Canadian Imperial Bank of Commerce Trust Co. (Bahamas) Ltd.*[17] the Privy Council decided that *Foley* v. *Hill* applied even to trust funds held by the bank. Having pointed out the general rule (from *Foley* v. *Hill*) applying to ordinary depositors, Lord Templeman discussed the special rules applicable to bank trustees. First, one might consider the case of funds wrongly misappropriated by the bank. In that case, the equitable remedy of tracing had the effect of creating an equitable charge for the beneficiaries, over all the assets of the bank, and this charge took priority over the unsecured creditors. But this required wrongdoing, and equity gave no similar protection where the bank exercised powers conferred by the trust instrument, in good faith. Some of the settlements here of which the bank was trustee empowered the bank (as trustee) to deposit with itself (as banker) monies which it had received in trust. The effect of that was that just as with ordinary deposits, the monies received as banker were held beneficially by the bank, on a debtor–creditor relationship with the beneficiaries. The beneficiaries had no rights to any asset (or in all the assets) of the bank. The bank continued to have obligations as trustee, but in respect of the proper management of the account, not in a proprietary respect of the money transferred to its general banking business.

This reasoning seems to be of general application, wherever monies are **3.08** deposited in trust with a bank not for a specific purpose, but for general investment. But it may not apply to the Quistclose trust, which arises where monies are deposited with the bank for the specific purpose of being paid to other persons.[18] On the other hand, in none of the modern "Quistclose cases" was a bank the insolvent party, and it would seem that unless the "purpose" is to be effected immediately the funds are received, the bank has the right to apply those funds generally in the meantime. If it has the

---

[14] *Parr's Banking Co. Ltd.* v. *Yates* [1898] 2 Q.B. 460.
[15] Discussed below, Chap. 13.
[16] See *Bradford Old Bank Ltd.* v. *Sutcliffe* [1918] 2 K.B. 833, for a case concerning guarantees. See also, the Limitation (Enemies and War Prisoners) Act 1945 which suspends the running of time while a person is an enemy or a prisoner of war.
[17] *The Times*, July 8, 1986 (J.C.).
[18] See *Barclays Bank Ltd.* v. *Quistclose Investments Ltd.* [1970] A.C. 567.

right to do so then, there being no breach of trust to cause an equitable charge to affix to the bank's assets, the reasoning of the *Space Investments* case may be applicable. It that is correct, then unless the bank is in some way prohibited from dealing with the funds as banker, the beneficiary has no right over the assets of the bank, although the bank retains obligations as trustee properly to manage the account, and not to misappropriate the money in breach of trust. Whether or not one can say that in relation to the deposit the relation is one of debtor-creditor, the result is the same. This casts a new light on *Foley* v. *Hill*.

F. Other implied terms mentioned in *Joachimson* v. *Swiss Bank Corpn.*

3.09   Atkin L.J. mentioned the following implied terms:

(i) the bank undertakes to receive money and to collect bills for its customer's account, and it borrows the proceeds and promises to repay them,

(ii) the bank promises to repay at the branch of the bank where the account is kept (and not at any other branch) and during banking hours,

(iii) it promises to repay any part of the amount due against the customer's written order at the branch (though whether a written order is necessary was not decided)

(iv) it promises not to cease to do business with the customer except on reasonable notice (because cheques, etc., may be outstanding for two or three days)

(v) the customer promises to exercise reasonable care in executing his written orders so as not to mislead the bank or to facilitate forgery.

G. Effect of express terms

3.10   It is a universal practice in the United Kingdom for intending customers to be asked to sign a bank's mandate form on opening an account, and this form will contain some terms of the contract. Mandate forms do not, however, attempt to spell out all the features of the relationship. If the customer is given special facilities, such as a cheque guarantee card, or a bank credit card[19] the customer then makes a separate agreement on the special terms notified to him at the time, and at every renewal. If a term loan is made, generally this is upon express terms notified at the time. On the general contractual principle of *L'Estrange* v. *Graucob*[20] a customer has notice of the terms of a contract which he signs, whether he reads the contract or not. Ambiguities will, however, be construed against the bank, and the weaker the negotiating position of the other party, the more likely are the courts to seek to hold that an exclusion of liability is ambiguous. Under the Unfair Contract Terms Act 1977, s.3, if there are written standard terms, or if a customer contracts as a consumer (if he does not make the contract in the course of a business)[21] then any contractual terms which the court considers unreasonable may be unenforceable if they attempt to exclude the bank's liability for loss caused to the customer by breach of contract, or attempt to entitle the bank to render a contractual performance substantially different from that reasonably expected of it, or to render none at all in respect of the whole or part of its obligations. Furthermore, if the bank is "negligent"

---

[19] Many of which are issued by separate subsidiary companies of the bank.
[20] [1934] 2 K.B. 394.
[21] s.12.

(which means, in breach of a contractual or tortious duty of reasonable care) then under section 2, any term excusing the bank from liability is enforceable only if reasonable. This requirement of reasonableness applies to terms purporting to define the bank's duty, as well as to terms excluding liability for breach.[22] The onus of proving reasonableness is on the bank[23] and it would seem that in judging reasonableness the court will have regard to the bank's (considerable) resources and ability to underwrite its losses by insurance[24] and probably also to such matters as the degree of notice given, or whether the customer ought to have known of the term in question, the strength of the bargaining positions of the parties, whether the customer received any inducement to agree to it, whether he could go elsewhere and bank with others who would not impose such terms on him, and whether compliance with any condition imposed on him as a prerequisite to complaining, etc., was reasonably expected to be practicable.[25]

An instructive case is *Burnett* v. *Westminster Bank Ltd.*[26] where a bank printed on the covers of cheque books (containing magnetic ink characters) a warning that cheques and credit slips in the books must be applied only to the account for which they had been prepared. The customer had accounts at two branches of the bank. One branch used the magnetic-ink system and the other did not. The customer used one of the cheques which he paid into the former branch, but he altered the numbers in ordinary ink so to draw on the "prohibited" account at the latter branch. He then ordered the latter branch to stop payment, but the cheque was routed to the former branch, because of the magnetic ink coding, and it was paid, no one there noticing the alterations. The court held that as the banker-customer relationship predated the introduction of the new cheque books, that relationship could not be altered unless the bank could show that the customer had read the words, or had otherwise agreed in writing to what was demanded. Had there been similar wording on a cheque, signing the cheque would presumably have prevented the customer from denying that he had notice. The position might have been different if the cheque book had been the first issued to a new customer. **3.11**

A more recent and important case is the decision of the Privy Council in *Tai Hing Cotton Ltd.* v. *Liu Chong Bank Ltd. and Others*[27] The Tai Hing company had current accounts with three Hong Kong banks, which were authorised to honour cheques bearing certain signatures. A dishonest employee of the company forged some 300 cheques over six years, his employers having left him unsupervised and having no proper financial control. The banks all had terms of business by which monthly statements were deemed to be correct unless the customer notified the bank of any error within a specified period. Under the general law[28] the customer's account could not be debited on a forgery. One question, however, was as to the effect of the express terms. These differed in phrasing, but one read **3.12**

"A statement of the customer's account will be rendered once a month.

---

[22] s.13.
[23] s.11(5).
[24] s.11(4).
[25] All these matters are mentioned in schedule 2, though strictly that does not apply to ss.2 and 3.
[26] [1966] 1 Q.B. 742.
[27] [1985] 2 All E.R. 947, [1986] A.C. 80.
[28] Below, Chap. 7.

Customers are desired: (i) to examine all entries in the statement of account and to report at once to the bank any error found therein. (ii) to return the confirmation slip duly signed. In the absence of any objection to the statement within seven days after its receipt by the customer, the account shall be deemed to have been confirmed."

These rules were made known to the company when it opened the accounts. On one account, the company was sent and returned confirmation slips, on another account no slips were issued (the bank did not say it would) and the customer did not otherwise confirm, and on the third the bank said it would send slips, but did not, and the customer did not confirm.

3.13   The Privy Council held that these terms of business did not protect the banks. They were contractual in effect, but "in no case do they constitute what has come to be called "conclusive evidence clauses.""[29] Their terms were not such as to bring home to the customer the importance of the inspection he had to make, or the conclusive effect of the statements. If the banks wished to impose an obligation on the customer to inspect his account, etc., and to make the statements unchallengeable for failure to do so, "the burden of the obligation and of the sanction imposed must be brought home to the customer." This test is "undoubtedly rigorous" because the banks are seeking to exclude rights which the customers would otherwise enjoy. Thus "clear and unambiguous provision is needed" to bind the customer. (For the same reasons, no estoppel could arise from the failure to reply, since there was no duty to reply.)[30] This is an example of the common-law "*contra proferentem*" rule whereby clauses which attempt to exclude a liability which would otherwise arise are construed against the person who seeks to reply upon them. At common law it is possible to exclude liability, but only if the clause is abundantly clear. Greater leeway is allowed between persons who contract "at arm's length." The decision does not appear (as in the *Burnett* case) to be based on lack of notice of the existence of the terms, for the customers signed the bank's conditions. Rather, it is a question of construction of the terms. Had the terms said simply "In the absence of such confirmation within . . . days the statement of account shall be conclusive evidence for all purposes of the state of accounts between bank and customer" it appears that this would have been sufficient. All this, however, concerns the common law. In the light of their Lordships' obvious disapproval of the terms in question, it is hard to resist the conclusion that such a modified term as suggested would, if the Unfair Contract Terms Act 1977 applied to the contract in question, have been held by the Privy Council to be unreasonable.

With an eye to the effect of the Act, a more reasonable term might seek to apportion the loss in case of the customer's negligence. The contract might provide a duty on the customer to check his statements, and for the apportionment of liability (perhaps on an arbitrator's[31] determination) if the customer is guilty of contributory negligence. It is difficult to see why that should be considered unreasonable.

---

[29] *Ibid.*, n. 27, at 959 (All E.R.).
[30] Below,, Chap. 7.
[31] Such as the Banking Ombudsman.

In summary therefore, **3.14**

(i) subject to the Unfair Contract Terms Act 1977 the terms of the contract are a matter for agreement,

(ii) in the absence of express terms, certain terms will arise by implication,

(iii) if those terms arising by implication confer advantages on the customer, then the exclusion of those rights requires (a) notice to the customer of the existence of the terms, (generally, by his signing a document referring to or preferably containing the terms), (b) unambiguous terms, and (c) (under the Act) that the terms be reasonable.

H. Duty to avoid conflicts of interest

This is a "fiduciary" duty applicable to "fiduciary" relationships. On **3.15** occasion, and especially with the diversification of banking businesses, the bank may act as agent, in which case the question of conflicts of interest and other duties of agents (avoiding secret profits, and so on) will arise. This is considered below in Chapter 15.

I. Duty correctly to inform customer of state of accounts

A "settled account" (an agreed one) or an "account stated" (an admitted **3.16** one) are both prima facie evidence of a debt for the amount stated, though error or fraud may be shown to rebut the creditor's claim.[32] In some cases, however, it might be agreed that the statement shall be conclusive, and if proper notice is given, this may be effective to bind both parties.[33] The question is, therefore, whether the bank, or customer, is bound (on the basis of conclusive evidence) if the statement is incorrect, being either an over-credit, or an over-debit. It seems clear that neither a passbook nor loose-leaf statements are regarded as conclusive evidence. Some older cases (relating to passbooks) suggest that while the entry in the book itself is not conclusive, it may become conclusive if, after having had the chance to inspect it and rectify it, the customer fails to do so. His silence is regarded as an admission that the entries are correct.[34] The great weight of authority, however, is otherwise, and, while treating a passbook (which the customer on receipt does not immediately challenge) as prima facie evidence, allows either the bank or the customer to show that the entry in the passbook or other statement is in error.[35]

It follows from this, that the customer is under no duty to check his state- **3.17** ments, and that an estoppel cannot arise against him from his failure to do so, even if, say debits have occurred through the customer's negligence

---

[32] There is some ambiguity in the phrases: some use them as if they meant "conclusive account."

[33] See *Bishund Chand Firm* v. *Seth Girdhari Lal* (1930) 50 T.L.R. 465, 468–469; *Tai Hing Cotton Mill Ltd.* v. *Liu Chong Hing Bank Ltd. and Others* [1985] 2 All E.R. 947 (J.C.) [1986] A.C. 80. This latter case, discussed above, illustrates the difficulty in an established relationship of making the statement conclusive evidence, even by express terms.

[34] *Devaynes* v. *Noble, Clayton's Case* (1816) 1 Mer.529, 572; *Blackburn Building Society* v. *Cunliffe, Brooks & Co.* (1882) 22 Ch.D. 61, 72.

[35] *Commercial Bank of Scotland* v. *Rhind* (1860) 3 Macq.643, 648; *Holland* v. *Manchester and Liverpool District Banking Co. Ltd.* (1909) 25 T.L.R. 386; *Vagliano Bros.* v. *Bank of England* (1889) 23 Q.B.D. 263 (C.A.) *cf.* [1891] A.C. 107, 114, 116; *Kepitigalla Rubber Estates Ltd.* v. *National Bank of India Ltd.* [1909] 2 K.B. 1010; *Chatterton* v. *London County Bank* (1890) *The Miller*, November 3, 1890, 394; *Walker* v. *Manchester and Liverpool District Banking Co. Ltd.* (1913) 108 L.T. 728; *Brewer* v. *Westminster Bank Ltd.* [1952] 2 All E.R. 650.

which has facilitated forgery. The most recent decision to this effect is *Tai Hing Cotton Mill Ltd.* v. *Liu Chong Hing Bank Ltd. and Others*[36] to which reference has already been made.[37] In that case the Privy Council held that a customer had no duty to the bank so to supervise his employees or agents so as to prevent forgeries, and no duty to check his statements. Nor, for reasons already given, did written terms purporting to make the statements conclusive have any effect.[38] In *Tai Hing* the Privy Council held that there was binding authority, in the form of *London Joint Stock Bank Ltd.* v. *Macmillan and Arthur*[39] in which the House of Lords appeared to eliminate such an implied contractual duty on the customer's part. In any case, the test for the implication of a term was necessity, and there was no necessity for such a term as here suggested. If the matter had become burdensome for banks, they could protect themselves in their express contractual terms of business, or they could seek to have the law changed, by Parliament. Further, the Privy Council held that developments in the law of tort since the *Macmillan* case in 1918 had not affected the position, and that the parties' obligations in tort could be no greater than those to be found expressly or by necessary implication in their contracts.[40] One doubt concerning the decision is that the arguments were based entirely on the existence of a duty to check the statements of account. In *London Intercontinental Trust Ltd.* v. *Barclays Bank Ltd.*[41] an account was wrongly debited (on one signature, instead of two) but the corporate customer had examined their statements and observed the debits in question. They did not inform the bank of the breach of mandate and this was held to amount to a representation that the cheques were validly drawn. Yet the bank relied only on their silence, and that was no more than it would have done had they not read the statements. It is difficult to see how, unless the bank knows that the customer has read the statement, there could be a representation. Either one postulates a duty to inform of known errors, or, after the *Tai Hing* case, the decision has been deprived of authority in this respect. Another ground for the decision (given by Slynn J.) is that of ratification (which would seem to require no reliance by the bank), and the decision may be explicable on this ground, and not on the ground of estoppel.

3.18   Subject to the last mentioned point, the *Tai Hing* decision settles that the customer has no duty to check his bank statements. It is thought that there may be two practical reasons for the decision. First, the bank is able to "spread the risk" of forgery to all customers, through its system of charges. Secondly, if the bank had succeeded in establishing a duty on the customer's part, the doctrine of estoppel would have operated in an "all or nothing" fashion, completely defeating the plaintiff's claim.[42]

A better solution would be the application of the principles of contributory negligence, which would allow the apportionment of the loss. That principle, however, seems at present not to apply to actions for debt, in

[36] [1985] 2 All E.R. 947 (J.C.), [1986] A.C. 80.
[37] Above, para. 3.12.
[38] Contrast Canadian cases referred to in Paget, 113.
[39] [1918] A.C. 777.
[40] In the U.S.A. the Uniform Commercial Code places an obligation on the customer to check his statements: ss.4–406. In *Wealden Woodlands (Kent) Ltd.* v. *National Westminster Bank Ltd. The Times*, March 12, 1983, McNeill J. rejected a suggestion that he bring the law in this country into line with that in the U.S.A.
[41] [1980] 1 Lloyds Rep. 241.
[42] That it cannot work partially is shown by *Avon C.C.* v. *Howlett* [1983] 1 All E.R. 1073.

which the customer frames his action. It is, however, possible for a bank to give proper notice (say, in its original mandate form) so as to provide contractually for the apportionment of loss, and it is thought that such a term should not be regarded as "unreasonable" within the meaning of the Unfair Contract Terms Act 1977.

Although the customer owes no duties to the banker in respect of the **3.19** statement, the converse is not true. There is probably an implied term that a customer is entitled either to a passbook or, in modern times, to regular (loose-leaf) statements of account. In addition, it is clear that the general principles of estoppel apply to the statement. Estoppel operates if there is (a) a statement of fact (or an omission to speak, where there is a duty), (b) reliance upon the statement (or its omission) and (c) the person relying suffers detriment from his reliance, or the circumstances are such that it is inequitable to allow the other party to go back on what he has said (or omitted to say)[43] In *Skyring* v. *Greenwood*[43a] bankers overcredited a customer for five years, and informed him of the credits. On discovering the error they sought to retain other funds of his, but were held not to be entitled to do so, for the credit entries were statements upon which the customer had relied and he had altered his position by spending more than he would otherwise have done.[44] In *Holland* v. *Manchester and Liverpool District Banking Co. Ltd.*[45] the bank's right to correct an entry was recognised, but the bank had no right to dishonour cheques drawn on the faith of the statements of account while uncorrected, and it was liable in damages for doing so. It is essential that the customer relies on the incorrect entry, and if he is unaware of it, estoppel cannot operate.[46] Naturally, if the customer knows that there has been a mistake, he cannot rely upon estoppel, and indeed, if he draws on the account with that knowledge, he may be guilty of a criminal offence.[47] "Reliance" and the requirement that it be inequitable for the bank to demand repayment also generally entails that the customer change his position in some way (or not changing, when otherwise he would have done so). In *United Overseas Bank* v. *Jiwani*[48] the defendant was wrongly advised of a credit, in circumstances in which he must have known (and the judge held he did know) that he was not entitled to it. He used the money towards a purchase which he had already embarked upon and had part paid towards, and the court held that he would have gone ahead with the purchase in any case, finding the money elsewhere. He was able to repay the bank. In these circumstances, it was not inequitable for the bank to demand repayment.

In summary, the position is that bank statements are prima facie evidence, but that they may be proved to be erroneous by either party. The customer has no duty to check his statements, and cannot be estopped by his negligence, though perhaps some behaviour by him may amount to a

---

[43] For a clear statement to this effect, see *United Overseas Bank* v. *Jiwani* [1976] 1 W.L.R. 964.
[43a] (1825) 4 B. & C. 281, approved in *Deutsche Bank (London Agency)* v. *Beriro Co.* (1895) 73 L.T. 669; *R.* v. *Blenkinsop* [1892] 1 Q.B. 43; *Holt* v. *Markham* [1923] 1 K.B. 504.
[44] For a very similar case to the same effect, see *Lloyds Bank Ltd.* v. *Brooks* (1950) 72 J.I.B. 114.
[45] (1909) 25 T.L.R. 386.
[46] *British and North European Bank Ltd.* v. *Zalstein* [1927] 2 K.B. 92.
[47] Theft, under s.1 of the Theft Act 1968. He may not commit theft simply by giving the cheque to another payee *R.* v. *Navvabi Times*, July 9, 1986, (as the giving of the cheque is not itself an appropriation of the bank's money) but it may still be an offence of obtaining by deception, if he deceives the payee in some way.
[48] [1976] 1 W.L.R. 964.

representation sufficient for an estoppel. The bank's statement may give rise to an estoppel, in a particular case.

J. Other duties of a bank to its customer

3.20   The following are dealt with elsewhere.

(i) The duty of confidence or secrecy concerning the customer's account.[49]

(ii) The duty to tell the customer of known forgeries of his account.[50]

(iii) The duty of a paying bank to honour a customer's cheques.[51]

(iv) The duty of a paying bank to obey its customer's countermands and to act upon notice of his death.[52]

(v) The duty of a paying bank not to pay without a valid authority (and the effect of forgeries.)[53]

(vi) The duties of a collecting bank in collecting cheques.[54]

Duties of banks to non-customers

3.21   Duties of this sort may arise in (a) equity, concerning trusts, (b) in tort. The latter particularly concern liability for negligent advice[55] or in conversion (where for example, the bank handles a cheque belonging to a third party).[56]

[49] Below, Chap. 4.
[50] Below, Chap. 7.
[51] Below, Chap. 6.
[52] Below, Chap. 6.
[53] Below, Chap. 7.
[54] Below, Chap. 9.
[55] Below, Chap. 3.
[56] Below, Chaps. 8, 9.

4. The Banker's Duty of Secrecy or Confidence towards his Customer

A. Introduction: *Tournier*'s case

Many countries have a statutory law relating to banker's duties of secrecy. **4.01** In England, the law is generally judge-made,[1] and is explained as the result of terms implied into the contract between banker and customer.

In *Tournier* v. *National Provincial and Union Bank of England*[2] the Court of Appeal held that the banker owed to his customer a legal, and not merely a moral, duty of confidentiality, or secrecy, so that the banker could not lawfully disclose to third parties information concerning the customer's affairs. Tournier was about £10 overdrawn on his bank account, and he agreed to repay this at the rate of £1 per week. As he then had no fixed address he gave to the bank the name and address of employers for whom he was about to work. He broke his agreement to repay, and the branch manager, in an attempt to find out the private address, telephoned the employers and spoke to a director. In the course of the conversation, the manager disclosed the overdraft and the default in repayment and expressed the opinion that the customer was betting heavily. Because of that, the employers refused, after the probationary period, to renew Tournier's employment. In this action, the court held that there was an implied duty of secrecy or non-disclosure. Despite *Foley* v. *Hill*,[3] therefore, there is a "fiduciary" element to the banker-customer relationship.

NATURE OF THE DUTY

A majority in *Tournier's* case held that the duty came into existence along **4.02** with the banker-customer relationship, and that thereafter the bank must release no information about the customer, or his account, whether the information was acquired before or after the account was opened, or after it ceased, and whether obtained directly from the customer or from other sources, and whether the account is in credit, or overdrawn. Moreover, information could not be released even after he ceased to be a customer (even, probably, after his death).[4]

A matter which is not finally resolved is whether the bank's duty is absolute, or a duty of reasonable care. It would seem that like other fiduciary duties, it is merely a duty of reasonable care. If, say, an unauthorised person managed to tap into electronic systems notwithstanding sophisticated electronic "defences" the bank should not be liable, if it had taken due care.[5] Similarly, if a written request was made by a clever forgery, then the bank may not be liable, though it has a duty to know its customer's signature,

---

[1] One statutory requirement is contained in The Banking Act 1987, which provides for the confidentiality of information obtained by the Bank of England. See also, the Data Protection Act 1984, for information held on computers.
[2] [1924] 1 K.B. 461.
[3] Above, para. 3.05.
[4] Scrutton L.J. thought that the duty did not extend to knowledge acquired while the banker-customer relation was not in existence, or from other sources.
[5] No more than if a thief stole bank mail from a Post Office van.

and should be liable for a poor forgery, and perhaps also if the address given differs from the bank's records.

B. Qualifications to the duty of secrecy

4.03   The duty, however, was qualified: Bankes L.J. said "On principle, I think the qualifications can be classed under four heads: (a) where disclosure is under compulsion by law; (b) where there is a duty to the public to disclose; (c) where the interests of the bank require disclosure; (d) where the disclosure is made by the express or implied consent of the customer." As examples of cases where disclosure was justified, Bankes L.J. referred to the duty to obey an order made by a court under the Bankers' Books Evidence Act 1879, or cases where danger to the state, or a public duty may supersede the duty of an agent to his principal,[6] or cases where a bank sues a customer for the amount of his overdraft (when they must mention the amount of the overdraft), or the "familiar" case where a customer authorises his banker to give a reference.

COMPULSION BY LAW, JUSTIFYING DISCLOSURE

4.04   The duty of confidence is a contractual duty, and any contractual term is illegal and unenforceable where there is a general legal duty of a contradictory nature.[7] Thus, if the banker is in the witness box for any reason then, like any other witness, he must answer relevant questions put to him if so directed by the court.[8]

Bankers Books Evidence Act 1879

4.05   The Bankers Books Evidence Act 1879, and R.S.C. Ord. 38, r. 13/2 aims to prevent bankers from being obliged (compellable) to produce their books in legal proceedings to which they are not party.[9] Without specific authority to the contrary, the rules of evidence normally require the "best evidence" to be called, and this would be considered to be the verbal testimony of the person who had compiled the books. That person might refer to written records not as evidence in themselves, but on the assumption that he was "refreshing his memory." The evidential weight of the books themselves, however, was considerable, and counsel sought to have the books produced.[10]

The Act therefore provides that not only the books themselves, but also duly authenticated copies of any entry in a banker's books shall be substantive evidence in all legal proceedings.[11] A banker's books[12] include ledgers, day books, cash books, account books and other records used in the ordinary business of the bank, whether the records are in written form, or kept on microfilm, magnetic tape, or any other form of mechanical or electronic data retrieval mechanism. This definition has been held to include micro-

---

[6] This refers to what Lord Finlay said, in *Weld-Blundell* v. *Stephens* [1920] A.C. 956, 965.

[7] This was said by Diplock L.J. (with reference, *inter alia*, to the banker's duty) in *Parry-Jones* v. *Law Society* [1969] 1 Ch. 1, 9.

[8] *Ibid.*

[9] So said in *Parnell* v. *Wood* [1892] P. 137.

[10] According to Bowen L.J. in *Arnott* v. *Hayes* (1887) 36 Ch.D. 731, 738, the books were in fact treated as the substantive evidence.

[11] s.3. This includes arbitrations, and proceedings of solicitors' disciplinary tribunals: s.10 (as extended by s.86 of the Solicitors Act 1974).

[12] s.9, as amended by the Banking Act 1979, Sched. 6.

film of the bank's other records, and was said to include any form of permanent record by means made available by modern technology. Thus, where
paper records are replaced by microfilm (a common practice, for space-
saving reasons), the microfilm records are the "books."[13] Where records are
in electronic form, those records are the books, and a computer print-out,
duly verified, would be sufficient evidence. Correspondence is not part of
the "books".[14] Books need not be in use every day, to be part of the "ordinary business": records kept for occasional reference are included.[15] "Bank"
means recognised bank, licensed deposit taker, municipal bank, trustee savings bank, National Savings Bank, and the Post Office (in relation to its
banking services.) The evidence contained in the books is not, of course,
conclusive, but merely prima facia evidence of what it states,[16] even against
the plaintiff.[17] Verification of the records is done by a partner or officer of
the bank, either orally, or by affidavit, saying that the "book" from which
the document produced was copied was (i) an ordinary book of the bank, as
defined, (ii) the entry was made in the ordinary course of the business of the
bank, (iii) the book is in the custody and control of the bank (or its successors), (iv) that the copy has been examined with the original, and is correct.

Whether the bank is party or not, the lack of records of an alleged debt is   **4.06**
itself capable of acting as proof that there is no debt.[18]

Even though a bank is not a party, it may still be compelled to produce
the books if a judge so orders for special cause[18a] and a party to any proceedings (civil or criminal) may, under section 7 of the Act, obtain from a judge
(including a magistrate in criminal proceedings)[19] an order entitling the
party to inspect the banker's books. It is probable that compliance with the
order (which must be served on the bank three clear days before it is to be
obeyed) may be achieved by producing authenticated copies (which are
prima facia evidence in all proceedings).[20] The bank does not have the protection against (compellable) production in court until it complies with the
order.[21] The court has a discretion as to whether to make the order[22] and it
will weigh the need to respect confidentiality against the public interest.[23] It
has been said that the power will be exercised with great caution, and only if
the grounds for it are clearly established and "sufficient."[24] Since accounts
may be in various names, the court must be satisfied either that the account
in question is that of a party to the litigation, or that he is so concerned with
the account that items in it would be evidence against him.[25] Thus, inspection of a husband's account may be ordered on the ground that his wife (the

---

[13] *Barker* v. *Wilson* [1980] 2 All E.R. 81.
[14] *R.* v. *Dadman, The Times*, March 11, 1983.
[15] *Idiot's Asylum* v. *Handysides* (1906) 22 T.L.R. 573.
[16] s.3.
[17] *Harding* v. *Williams* (1880) 14 Ch.D. 197.
[18] *Douglass* v. *Lloyds Bank Ltd.* (1929) 34 Com.Cas. 263 (The debt was not shown after 1873,
and there were no earlier records. The debt alleged to have been incurred in 1866 was held to
have been proved to have been repaid).
[18a] s.6.
[19] *R.* v. *Kinghorn* [1908] 2 K.B. 949.
[20] See Paget, 152.
[21] *Emmot* v. *Star Newspaper Co.* (1892) 62 L.J.Q.B. 77
[22] Below, this para.
[23] *R.* v. *Grossman* (1981) 73 Cr.App.R. 302, 307.
[24] *Arnott* v. *Hayes* (1887) 36 Ch.D. 731.
[25] *Ibid.* See also *South Staffs. Tramways Co.* v. *Ebbsmith* [1895] 2 Q.B. 669, 674; *Re Marshfield,
Marshfield* v. *Hutchings* (1886) 32 Ch.D. 499; *Pollock* v. *Garle* [1899] 1 Ch. 1.

party to the litigation) may have been using his account as a cloak for her transactions in securities (the subject of the litigation)[26] or has stolen the money and put it in his account.[27] In such a case notice of the application to the court must be given not merely to the bank, but to the third party concerned.[28] The process of obtaining evidence (by compulsion) before the trial is called "discovery," and that process is regulated by established principles.[29] For example, the courts object to making orders for "fishing expeditions" where there is no real ground for believing that there is a cause of action, but where it is hoped that documents revealed will show one. This principle has been held to apply to orders under section 7.[30] Hence, the order should not extend beyond the true purposes of the (criminal) charge which a court is considering, and the time period of the account over which it should be disclosed should be relevant to the charge, and it should be considered whether the prosecution has any real evidence.[31] In a legal action, irrelevant evidence is excluded. It must be shown, therefore, that the order relates to entries which are relevant, so that if produced at the trial, they could be used.[32] But where a defendant tells the police that he will plead guilty, this does not debar the prosecution from seeking an order, for the accused may not plead guilty at the trial.[33] In *Emmott* v. *Star Newspaper Co.*[34] Smith L.J. implied that an order would not be given to the defendant in a libel case, to enable him to justify the libel. But this dictum (which illustrates the court's discretion) has not been followed abroad.[35] It may well depend on the degree to which the applicant can convince the court that he is not merely "fishing" for a defence.

Foreign Complications

4.07 The court will not ordinarily make an order affecting documents held by a foreign branch of a U.K. bank and relating to that branch's non-U.K. resident customer, especially where the customer is not party to proceedings, and the disclosure abroad would be unlawful (as, *e.g.* a breach of confidence).[36] Further, it has been said that unless in exceptional circumstances, the court should not make an order under section 7 directed to the London branch of a foreign (New York) bank, requiring the bank to produce documents held at the overseas head office, relating to transactions which took place there on an account maintained by a non-U.K. resident, even if he is a party to the proceedings, and even if disclosure abroad is not unlawful there. The fact that the foreign bank had submitted itself to jurisdiction in

---

[26] *Ironmonger & Co.* v. *Dyne* (1928) 44 T.L.R. 579.

[27] *R.* v. *Andover Justices, ex p. Rhodes* [1980] Crim.L.R. 644 (D.C.) (she admitted it).

[28] Otherwise, s.7 does not require the bank or any other party to be summonsed, though generally the courts will insist that the application not be *ex parte, i.e.* that notice to the parties affected should be given: see *R.* v. *Marlborough Street Magistrates' Court Metropolitan Stipendiary Magistrate, ex p. Simpson* (1980) 70 Cr.App.R. 291.

[29] Regulated ordinarily by R.S.C. Ord. 24.

[30] *Williams* v. *Summerfield* [1972] 2 Q.B. 512.

[31] *Ibid.*, and see *R.* v. *Marlborough Street Magistrates' Court Metropolitan Stipendiary Magistrate, ex p. Simpson* (1980) 70 Cr.App.R. 291; *R.* v. *Nottingham Justices, ex p. Lynn* (1984) 79 Cr.App.R. 238.

[32] *R.* v. *Bono* (1913) 29 T.L.R. 635, 636; *Arnott* v. *Hayes* (1887) 36 Ch.D. 731; *Howard* v. *Beall* (1889) 23 Q.B.D. 1; *Perry* v. *Phosphor Bronze Co. Ltd.* (1894) 71 L.T. 854.

[33] *Owen* v. *Sambrook* [1981] Crim.L.R. 329.

[34] (1892) 62 L.J.Q.B. 77.

[35] *Sommers* v. *Sturdy (No. 2)* (1957) 10 D.L.R. (2d.) 269 (C.A. of British Columbia).

[36] *R.* v. *Grossman* (1981) 73 Cr.App.R. 302.

the sense of applying to the Bank of England under the Banking Act 1979 for recognition here made no difference. Since the bank was foreign and the business took place outside the U.K. the order might be seen an infringement of the sovereignty of the U.S.A. (since a subpoena was a procedural matter involving not the enforcement of a private right, but an exercise of sovereign authority).[37] There was no urgent necessity justifying a different approach, since the money allegedly taken by the customer had long since been spirited away. The court also decided that even though the foreign bank might be joined as defendant (in which ordinary discovery would be available) the principles applicable to the order under section 7 were not directly comparable to what might be done by discovery.[38]

Other Foreign Proceedings

If the banker–customer relationship is centred in the U.K. and the plaintiff **4.08** to an action brought in the U.S.A. (or elsewhere, abroad) serves in the U.S.A. a *subpoena* on a bank requiring it to disclose documents, including documents held in the London branch of the bank (an American bank) an English court may, if justified on the balance of convenience, grant and continue an injunction here to prevent disclosure by the London branch of confidential information. In considering the balance of convenience, it is relevant that the foreign court would accept the English court's injunction as a defence to its subpoena.[39] In one case, where a party to an action brought in the U.K. sought to use overseas wider processes of discovery which may be available overseas (*e.g.* against a branch of or in relation to business activities of the other party in the U.S.A. where "fishing expeditions" seem not to be discouraged) the court by injunction restrained the party concerned from using overseas the foreign procedural remedies.[40] The ground for this was that all procedural matters are a matter for the *lex fori* (law of the forum, or place where litigation takes place) and if litigation is begun here, the parties submit to English procedure. Procedural "forum shopping" ought to be discouraged. But the House of Lords disagreed: an injunction should not be given unless the plaintiff invaded a right of the defendant, or if his behaviour was unconscionable, in the sense of interfering with the due process of the court's jurisdiction.

Letters Rogatory

There is a procedure by which an application may be made to an English **4.09** court, by which it may request a foreign court (by "letters rogatory" or "letters of request")[41] to assist in collecting information for the purposes of

---

[37] *McKinnon* v. *Donaldson, Lufkin and Jenrette Securities Corpn. The Times* November 12, 1985. Mr. Justice Hoffman noted that a New York court had followed the same approach in relation to English banks with New York offices, in *Laker Airways Ltd.* v. *Pan American World Airways* (unrep. March 22, 1985).

[38] The non-U.K. resident customer was a Bahamian company, which had been dissolved, so that no order for discovery could be obtained against it. For the same reason, civil actions by that customer against the bank were unlikely.

[39] *X A.G.* v. *A bank* [1983] 2 Lloyds Rep. 535.

[40] *South Carolina Insurance Co.* v. *Assurantie Maatschappij de Zeven Provincien' NV* [1985] 2 All E.R. 1046; rev'd [1986] A.C. 24. See also, *Bank of Tokyo Ltd.* v. *Karoon* [1986] 1 A.C. 45.

[41] R.S.C. Ord. 70. See also s.5 of the Extradition Act 1873, which allows a magistrate here, if required by a Secretary of State, to take evidence from witnesses (who may be compelled as if in an ordinary criminal case) to assist in any non-political criminal matter taking place abroad. In conjunction with this, the Secretary of State may seek a s.7 order. There is no appeal from this order when made in these circumstances: *Bonalumi* v. *Secretary of State for the Home Department* [1985] 1 All E.R. 797.

an English action. In the *Settebello* case[42] the court refused to make a request to an overseas court to assist the English court to gather information which would tend to show that the laws of the overseas country were punitive (so that they need not be observed in England). It may be thought that it would have been impertinent for the English court to have made any such request, and the decision is hardly surprising. Similarly, by an Act of 1975, the foreign court may request the help of an English court, for the examination (by the court or someone else) of witnesses, and for the production of documents, inspection, etc., of property, and other assistance.[43] Under the Protection of Trading Interests Act 1980, where foreign legislation is thought to infringe English sovereignty there may be exceptions to the provision of information for foreign legal proceedings. (The Secretary of State may, by regulation, prohibit compliance with foreign rules).[44] In *Rio Tinto Zinc Corpn.* v. *Westinghouse Electric Corporation*[45] the House of Lords refused to allow this procedure to be used for a "fishing expedition." The request was phrased in vague terms ("such other director or other person who has knowledge of the facts" and "any memoranda, correspondence or other documents relating thereto"). The House was prepared to edit the request to allow examination of witnesses shown to have relevant evidence, and for the production of specifically identified documents, but it stressed that only direct evidence for use at trial was obtainable, and not information which might lead to the discovery of such evidence. It has been said elsewhere that not only must particular documents be specified,[46] but that the court must be satisfied that actual documents (to be contrasted with "conjectural documents which may or may not exist) do exist.[47] The 1975 Act[48] provides for claims of privilege to be raised (under either English or foreign law), and where this is raised the examiner himself (not being a court) may not decide this.[49] The witness should refuse to answer, and the court should determine the question before the answer is given (so as to avoid the other side seeing the answer). Where foreign privilege is raised, a "sealed envelope" procedure may be used by the examiner (by agreement of the parties, or perhaps, the English court will permit this) before the question of privilege is ruled upon by the foreign court.

Orders for Discovery

4.10   The Bankers Books Evidence Act 1879 does not change the law relating to proceedings in which the banker is party. "Discovery" is the pre-trial process by which each party is entitled to discover the nature of the other's case, and to obtain documents, etc. Naturally, bankers must comply with these discovery orders. The jurisdiction is particularly extensive in fraud cases and an order may be made at a very early stage of proceedings, and even if the bank is not personally liable for the fraud (it may be a party because a

---

[42] *Settebello* v. *Banco Totta and Acores* [1985] 1 W.L.R. 1050
[43] Evidence (Proceedings in Other Jurisdictions) Act 1975, governed by R.S.C. Ords. 70 and 39.
[44] For an example, see *British Airways Board* v. *Laker Airways Ltd.* [1985] A.C. 58.
[45] [1978] A.C. 547.
[46] Not "all A's bank statements for 1984," (which refers to a class of documents) but "A's monthly bank statements for his current account for 1984" (which is sufficiently particular).
[47] *Re Asbestos Insurance Coverage Cases* [1985] 1 W.L.R. 331: thus, in the second example in the previous note, it must be shown that monthly statements were made.
[48] See n. 43 above.
[49] *R.* v. *Rathbone ex p. Dikko* [1985] 2 W.L.R. 375.

tracing order can be made against it).[50] In *Bankers Trust Company* v. *Shapira and others*[51] an order of discovery was made against a bank. The plaintiff wished to trace the proceeds of two forged cheques, which were alleged to have been paid into the defendant's account with the Discount Bank (Overseas). The writ had not been served on two defendants (one untraceable, one in a Swiss prison) but the bank was made co-defendant to a tracing action. As a party to the action, the bank might be ordered to produce documents (other than by a section 7 order), and the court ordered discovery of the state of its customer's account and the documents and correspondence relating to it.[52] The court ruled that in a fraud case, the customer, who has been guilty of fraud, cannot rely on the confidential relationship between him and the bank.[53] However, such an order was a "strong thing" and needed good evidence for thinking that the money in the account was the plaintiff's money. In addition to that, the plaintiff must give an undertaking to pay damages to the bank if it becomes liable to anyone as a result of the disclosure, and the documents, once seen, must be used solely for the purpose of following and tracing the money, and not for any other purposes.

Subpoenas

In civil proceedings, a party may be made to produce documents by writ of **4.11** *subpoena*[54] and there is no defence of confidence, or that the authority of depositors is required.[55] The *subpoena* may be set aside if the witness cannot give relevant evidence, or the request was not issued bona fide for that purpose, or if it is oppressive or an abuse of the process of the court.[56]

In criminal proceedings *subpoenas* are not used, and the procedure to compel attendance of a witness (and documents) is to use a witness summons.[57] The court may direct that the summons shall be of no effect if satisfied that the witness cannot give material evidence or produce any material document, etc.[58]

Unlike discovery, or the section 7 orders, neither the *subpoena* nor the witness summons requires the production of documents, etc., before the hearing or trial.

Writs of Sequestration

Sequestration[59] is a process invoked by a court when a person (a contem- **4.12** nor) has been found in contempt of court, and has been fined, but has not paid, or when the contempt seems likely to continue. The court may issue a writ of sequestration, appointing a sequestrator to take possession of the contemnor's assets, so as to satisfy the fine, or to be retained until the con-

---

[50] *Norwich Pharmacal Co.* v. *Customs and Excise Comrs.* [1974] A.C. 133.

[51] [1980] 1 W.L.R. 1274.

[52] Not all of which would be banker's books, for the purpose of a s.7 order.

[53] *Initial Services Ltd.* v. *Putterill* [1968] 1 Q.B. 396, 405 was cited by Lord Denning M.R., along with *Mediterranea Reffineria Siciliana Petroli SpA* v. *Mabanaft GmbH* [1978] C.A. Transcript 816, and *London and Counties Securities Ltd.* v. *Caplan* (1978) (unrep.).

[54] Governed by R.S.C. Ord. 38, rr. 14–19. The *subpoenas* are *subpoena duces tecum*—"under penalty bring with you", or *subpoena ad testificandum*—"under penalty you must come to bear witness." Under R.S.C. Ord. 32, r. 7 a witness may be made to attend to give evidence in chambers.

[55] *R.* v. *Daye* [1908] 2 K.B. 333.

[56] *Senior Holdsworth, ex p. Independent Television News Ltd.* [1976] Q.B. 23.

[57] Under the Criminal Procedure (Attendance of Witnesses) Act 1965.

[58] s.2(2) of the Act, and R.S.C. Ord. 79, r. 10. See *R.* v. *Cheltenham Justices ex p. Secretary of State for Trade* [1977] 1 All E.R. 460.

[59] Governed by R.S.C. Ord. 45, r. 1; Ord. 46, r. 5.

tempt is "purged" (*e.g.* by an apology). If the writ is issued against the bank's customer, the bank is unaffected until it knows of the issue of the writ. When the bank knows of the issue of the writ it must refrain from any action (*e.g.* transferring funds out of the country) which may frustrate the object of the writ, unless the transactions are of an ordinary kind (*e.g.* honouring cheques for general business purposes).[60] If in doubt, the bank should inform the sequestrators, so as to protect themselves. Thus, without demand by the sequestrators, a bank may (in its own interest) be permitted to break its duty of confidence.[61] Once the sequestrators demand information about the contemnor's property, this must be answered "promptly, fully and accurately," and must reveal whether property is held, or when it was disposed of. The sequestrators are "as much entitled to the information as is the contemnor."[62] If the sequestrators demand the transfer of the property, or that it be held to their order, the bank must comply unless someone else may have an interest (*e.g.* the bank under a charge, or a joint account holder, or the beneficiary of a trust) or there is doubt that the property is liable to sequestration. In those cases the bank must explain its failure to comply, so that the sequestrators may decide whether to seek a specific order from the court.[63] It is contempt of court for any person knowingly to take any action which prevents the sequestrators from carrying out their duty.[64]

Garnishee Orders

4.13 A garnishee (or attachment) order may on the application of a judgment creditor be made by a court against a person who owes money to a debtor.[65] The order "attaches" the debt. If a creditor seeks to attach the debt which the bank owes its customer, then as part of the process of attaching the funds in question, the bank may be ordered to give details of the account. The order is usually made "nisi" at first (freezing the debt) and on full hearing will be made "absolute," ordering the bank immediately to pay the creditor. The order nisi acts as a "demand"[66] (the banker being liable only on demand).

Taxation

4.14 Under the Taxes Management Act 1970 (T.M.A.) and the Income and Corporation Taxes Act 1970 (I.C.T.A.) the Inland Revenue has powers to require banks to give information concerning securities held on behalf of customers,[67] bank interest payable to one customer exceeding £15 p.a.,[68] information about the customer and his associates or anyone connected with him (*e.g.* customers, suppliers, banks),[69] income from securities for persons resident in the U.K.[70] and in connection with the transfer of assets abroad (if the bank acts for the customer in connection with the formation

---

[60] *Eckman* v. *Midland Bank Ltd.* [1973] 1 Q.B. 519.
[61] *Ibid.*
[62] *Ibid.*
[63] *Ibid.*
[64] *Messenger Newspapers Group Ltd.* v. *N.G.A.* [1984] 1 All E.R. 293.
[65] R.S.C. Ord. 49.
[66] *Joachimson* v. *Swiss Bank Corpn.* [1921] 3 K.B. 110.
[67] s.13, T.M.A.
[68] s.17, T.M.A.
[69] s.20, T.M.A.
[70] s.24, T.M.A.; see, *ibid.*, s.518 if residence is in a place where there is a double taxation relief.

or management of close companies outside the U.K. or in connection with the creation or execution of trusts involving payments of income to persons outside the U.K., or does not act in the ordinary course of business).[71] The Finance Act 1985 gave[72] powers to the Commissioners of Customs and Excise, to obtain access to computer records when investigating VAT payments. The Act also[73] amended the Finance Act 1984,[74] Sched. 8, of which concerns information to be provided by banks as to interest paid, etc., on deposits. The amendment allows the Board of Inland Revenue to make regulations as to the certificates given by banks about these deposits "containing such information as may reasonably be required by the Board."

The Companies Act 1985, and the Financial Services Act 1986

Banks may be required to disclose information under various provisions of the Act, relating for example to the investigation of companies and their affairs,[75] the prosecution of "delinquent" officers and members,[76] the inspection of books where offences in connection with the management of the company by officers are suspected,[77] the provision of information concerning interests in the company's voting shares, and for the investigation of insider dealing.[78]

4.15

The Insolvency Act 1986

Under this Act an administrator (under an administration order) of a company has the general powers of the company as its agent, and the bank would not be in breach of a duty of confidence in giving information to him.[79] The same would apply to the liquidator, in a voluntary winding up of a company. Section 234 of the Act applies to an administrator, liquidator, provisional liquidator, or administrative receiver (the "office holder"), and entitles the court to order any persons with property, books, papers or records to which the company appears to be entitled, to pay, deliver, convey, surrender or transfer these to the office holder.[80] Under sections 236–237 any person whom the court thinks capable of giving information about the company may be summonsed, and may be required to submit an affidavit concerning his dealings, or to produce any books, papers or

4.16

---

[71] s.481, I.C.T.A. (the predecesor of this was s.414 of I.C.T.A. 1952): on the court's power to intervene see *Clinch* v. *I.R.C.* [1974] Q.B. 76; *Royal Bank of Canada* v. *I.R.C.* [1972] Ch. 665 (bond washing transactions not in the ordinary course of business); *Wilover Nominees Ltd.* v. *I.R.C.* [1974] 3 All E.R. 496; *Cutner* v. *I.R.C.* [1974] STC 259; *Essex* v. *I.R.C.* (1979) L (TC) 2776.

[72] s.10.

[73] s.38.

[74] Sched. 8, para. 3A.

[75] ss.431–453, C.A. 1985. Nothing in ss.431–446 of the Act requires disclosure by banks of information about any other person but the company in question—s.452(1)(b)—and note s.452(3) relating to s.447. The Financial Services Act 1986, however, allows a court to order any person to disclose information (unless there is a reasonable excuse) for the investigation of offences such as insider dealing. These powers are very wide.

[76] s.632, C.A. 1985, now in s.218, I.A.1986.

[77] s.721, C.A. 1985.

[78] s.212, C.A. 1985.

[79] s.14, I.A. 1986.

[80] Officers of the company, promoters, employees, etc., may be required to give information, under s.235. See also ss.22, 47, 131, 133–134.

records in his possession or control relating to the company.[81] They do not have to be the company's books, etc. In relation to an individual bankrupt, the Act imposes duties on the bankrupt to deliver up property, books, records, etc., to the trustees, and for a banker or agent to deliver up property[82] but does not otherwise directly authorise the trustee to demand the bank's records. The trustee may, however, apply to the court for various authorities and orders[83] and under sections 366–368 the official receiver or trustee may (after a bankruptcy order) apply to the court to summons before it any person appearing to be able to give information about the bankrupt's dealings, affairs or property, and to require them to submit an affidavit and produce any documents, etc.[84] It may be that since the estate of the bankrupt vests in the trustee or official receiver that those persons may require from a bank information about the bankrupt's affairs without a court order, on the assumption that they are, for the purpose, the bankrupt's authorised agents, or, where the bankrupt has funds with the bank, on the ground that the new owner of that property is entitled to demand it and is entitled to a statement of account for the purpose of verifying what is his property.[85] It is clearly the case that except as already said, no one has the right to demand from the bank information about a customer who is not the bankrupt, merely because he may have had dealings with the bankrupt.

Drug Trafficking Offences Act 1986

4.17 Section 8 of this Act enables the police or Customs and Excise to obtain an order prohibiting any person (including a bank) from dealing with the defendant's property, (as by paying him a debt)[86] where proceedings have been brought against the defendant and are still continuing and the court has reasonable grounds to think that the defendant has profited from drug trafficking.[87] A circuit judge may, under section 27, make an order requiring disclosure of information which will assist in an investigation into drug trafficking, if the information is likely to be of "substantial" value and should be disclosed in the public interest. It is by section 24 made an offence if any person knowing or suspecting that A does or has trafficked in drugs or benefited from this, retains or controls the proceeds of drug trafficking or places funds so obtained at A's disposal. But no offence is committed if the belief or suspicion is disclosed to the police as soon as possible, and the disclosure is not to be treated as a breach "of any restriction upon the disclosure of information imposed by contract." It follows that a bank which fails to disclose suspicions is guilty of an offence, and effectively is under an obligation to disclose.

It may be that the provisions of the Act will be extended to other crimes.

---

[81] Under the old requirement, s.561, C.A. 1985, see *Re Castle New Homes Ltd.* [1979] 2 All E.R. 755.

[82] See s.312.

[83] See ss.303, 311, 363.

[84] Similar to s.100, for companies.

[85] See *Questions on Banking Practice* (11th ed.), 694, which says that this is "of course" the case; but it is doubtful. It is nowhere directly stated in the 1986 Act, though it is stated in relation to companies in a compulsory winding up.

[86] s.8(7).

[87] It was previously possible to seize the profits of crime but only if not held in a mixed fund with other untained assets. *Chief Constable of Kent* v. *V* [1982] 3 All E.R. 36, *Chief Constable of Hampshire* v. *A* [1984] 2 All E.R. 385.

DUTY TO THE PUBLIC, JUSTIFYING DISCLOSURE

The easiest example to comprehend is that of a customer who in time of war **4.18** trades with the enemy.[88] Clearly, the bank's public duty requires it to disclose these facts to the authorities. If the bank has information which leads it positively and definitely to believe[89] that its customer is using the account for the purpose of committing a crime it is certain that it must decline to allow him to do so (for this may amount to aiding and abetting him, and if funds are received, the bank may be liable as constructive trustee). It is likely that in such a case the bank is justified in informing the police. On the other hand, juries, and not banks, try the question of guilt, and where the bank merely suspects that the customer is using the account for criminal purposes, it is likely that there is no justification for disclosure.[90] The problem may be most acute if the customer has already been convicted of (say) theft, and the police then discover the account, which may contain stolen money, at a time when it may be too late to obtain an order for disclosure.[91] Nevertheless, there seems to be no duty to disclose, nor protection based upon public interest if they do disclose. It must be recalled, however, that the bank is liable only in damages, and in the circumstances, these may be nominal.

The position may be further affected by proposals to confiscate the proceeds of crime.

WHERE DISCLOSURE IS JUSTIFIED, IN THE BANK'S INTEREST

The obvious case here is where the bank is sued in debt by the customer. It **4.19** must be able to refer to the accounts in order to defend itself, provided that it refers to no more than is necessary. Similarly, if the account is guaranteed, the bank must be able to disclose the extent of the debt to the guarantor when suing him, or demanding payment, and it seems that the guarantor has a right to know at any time the extent of his liability. Whether this is justified on the ground of the bank's interest, or implied consent by the customer, is uncertain, and unnecessary to decide. It may be that "defence" may go beyond defence in legal proceedings, if there is an attack, even a private attack, on the bank's reputation or behaviour. In *Sunderland* v. *Barclays Bank Ltd*.[92] the bank dishonoured the plaintiff's cheques, ostensibly on the ground of insufficient funds, but really because the bank knew she was gambling. She complained to her husband (who was then unaware of the gambling) and he told her to take it up with the bank. She telephoned the bank in his presence, and after while he took up the phone to add his protests, upon which the bank disclosed the facts of his wife's gambling to him. The court held that this disclosure was in the bank's interests, and that, in any case, the customer had impliedly consented. This was a private attack on the bank's reputation. It is essential for a bank to maintain its public reputation, and if a customer made a public attack, then clearly public rebuttal would be permitted.

[88] *Weld-Blundell* v. *Stephens* [1920] A.C. 956, 965.
[89] One can hardly say "knows", for it may be wrong.
[90] Paget, 154, has no doubts. He refers to Bankes L.J. in *Tournier* v. *National Provincial and Union Bank of England* [1924] 1 K.B. 461, 474.
[91] s.7 orders, or discovery, etc., apply only when proceedings are continuing. If the police hope to recover money, or to find evidence to implicate another against whom proceedings have not yet been brought, no court order is available.
[92] (1938) 5 L.D.A.B. 163.

DISCLOSURE JUSTIFIED BY THE CUSTOMER'S CONSENT

4.20 The customer may, of course, consent to disclosure, expressly or impliedly. A case of implied consent may be where the bank gives a reference to a person to whom a customer has given his bank's name[93] Implied consent may also explain the revelation to a guarantor of the extent of his liability (though he is told no more than is necessary).[94]

If the customer expressly prohibits disclosure, the bank must comply with that instruction, even as to references. The consequences as to references (a refusal to give a reference may be seen as condemnation of the customer by the bank) should be pointed out, and the bank should consider whether to open or to continue an account under these circumstances.[95]

A matter which has caused difficulties is telephone disclosure. It is clear that some banks did (and perhaps, still do) give information over the telephone to those they believed to be their customers.[96] While the giving of information over the telephone is justified if in fact it is given to the customer, the risk is that it may be anyone at all.

---

[93] Below, Chap. 5.
[94] Below, Chap. 20.
[95] *Questions on Banking Practice*, (11th. ed.), 693.
[96] The Committee of London Clearing Bankers, in their evidence to the Younger Committee on Privacy, found this difficult to believe, which may display considerable ignorance of and optimism about what went on at branch level. However, branch practice may now have been tightened up.

5. Bank's Liability for Status Opinions and Investment Advice

A. Bank's liability for incorrect references

One of the financial services which banks provide is the giving of references **5.01** (also called "status opinions") in respect of their customers. These references are given without fee to persons who may or may not be customers of the bank in question. They may be given to other banks, when a customer opens an account elsewhere (and are considered necessary, to protect the new bank from allegations of negligence in handling the account), or from finance companies, or from prospective trading partners, employers, landlords and others (we shall refer to these as the "recipient" of the reference).

Some banks may be prepared to give references directly to the (non-bank) recipient, while others may give them only to another bank, through whom the recipient makes the request. Some requests may be made by the recipient directly to the bank, with a request for a reply through the recipient's bank.

For reasons given later, most references are not signed by the bank, and they contain a "disclaimer" to the effect that "This reference/opinion is given without responsibility on the part of the bank and its officers and employees, and is intended for and made available to the named recipient only on a confidential basis, and is not to be passed on to third parties."

Although the bank does not charge the recipient of the reference, the costs are, of course, passed on to the bank's customers, through the general system of charges. It has been said that "The service that a bank performs in giving a reference is not done simply out of a desire to assist in commerce. It could discourage the customers of the bank if their deals fell through because the bank had refused to testify to their credit when it was good."[1] It is important to remember that banks are commercial institutions, receiving commercial rewards for providing bank references. They charge a fee for it (indirectly) and they gain, and keep, customers. This must be said, for it is very frequently said by bankers that the service is unprofitable, and that they would be happy to give it up. This should be treated with scepticism.

1. BANK'S LIABILITY TO ITS CUSTOMER

An initial question which arises is the justification for the bank departing **5.02** from its duty of confidence to its customer, for that duty normally prevents the revelation to others of any information which comes to the banker concerning a customer. One of the exceptions to that duty is, however, that the customer has consented to the revelation of the information, and it is generally thought that the practice of giving references is justified on the ground of an "implied consent" given by customers. The practice of giving references is widely known, and (although the value of references in assessing credit risk is often doubted) is (at least by banks, and many recipients) considered to be essential. In *Tournier* v. *National Provincial and Union Bank of England*[2] Bankes L.J. gave as an example of the case where disclosure is

---

[1] *Per* Lord Devlin, in *Hedley Byrne & Co. Ltd.* v. *Heller & Partners Ltd.* [1964] A.C. 465, 529.
[2] [1924] 1 K.B. 461.

made by express or implied consent "the familiar case where the customer authorises a reference to his banker."[3] Often, of course, the customer gives his banker's name to the person who seeks the information, and there can then be no doubt as to the justification for it. It is unclear if there is any difference between cases where the reference is given directly to the recipient, or indirectly, through another bank. It is difficult to see why the result should be different, for the bank giving the advice must know that it will often be passed on. However, it may be that the judges will distinguish between the cases.[4]

If there is implied consent, then it must surely be to the release of the minimum of information. Often, references may be expressed in what seems to the lay observer to be an uninformative fashion, such as "He is reliable and trustworthy." If the recipient has a particular credit figure in mind and so informs the bank, the reference may add "and good for your figures." Where the bank has nothing good to say about its customer, it will generally answer in a non-committal fashion, which may be as vague as "We confirm that he has an account with us" (which may be taken as an indication of considerable difficulties with the account) or "He is reliable and trustworthy, but we cannot answer for your figures" (which may mean that there have been no severe problems, but merely that the bank has no evidence from the account that the customer is good for the credit figure in mind.) There is sometimes pressure on banks for the provision of more information, but that pressure ought to be resisted, for it is not for the customer's benefit, nor for the banks' (it exposes them to greater potential liability, and would increase public unease about the system).

The Younger Committee[5] felt that banks overestimated the extent to which customers knew or accepted the practice of giving references, and thought that it was desirable that customers know what inquiries had been made about them, and what replies had been given. It recommended that banks make the existence and manner of operation of the system clear, and give the customer either an opportunity to grant a standing authority for the giving of references, or to require the bank to seek their consent on any occasion. These suggestions have not been implemented. The Data Protection Act 1984 will enable customers to request, for a modest charge, personal information about them held on computer records. Since most banks hold details of financial transactions on computer, those would be available, but of course, they are already made available to customers in regular statements. More personal comments and observations about customers are usually kept by branches on memorandum cards, rather than on computer, and the customer has no rights under the Act to see those records.

If the reference is incorrect, and harmful to the customer, then the customer would be entitled to sue the bank, either in contractual negligence, or more simply, in Defamation, for libel. Negligence requires proof of lack of reasonable care. Defamation requires the plaintiff to show that the report would lower his reputation in the estimation of right-thinking people, and the bank must then justify itself by showing that what it said was true, fail-

---

[3] See also Atkin L.J., who, however, expressed "no final opinion" as to whether the banker is justified in giving references.

[4] See, *e.g.*, *Parsons* v. *Barclay & Co. Ltd.* (1910) 103 L.T. 196, where the "wholesome and useful habit" to which Cozens-Hardy M.R. referred involved references given to another banker.

[5] Report of the Committee on Privacy, 1972, Cmnd. 5012.

ing which it is liable, even if it had some grounds for thinking that what it said was true. However, given the non-committal nature of references, this may not be difficult. The plaintiff would be driven to argue that the bland statements used contained an "innuendo," or suggestion that he was not creditworthy. Since defamation actions are still decided by juries, the question is one of fact. Damages would be reduced if, on discovering an error, the bank promptly apologised to the customer and (more importantly) to the recipient, thus mitigating the effect on the plaintiff's reputation. In the case of a business customer, the damages may be substantial,[6] though in the case of a non-business customer they may well be nominal, unless the customer shows a specific loss, such as refusal of a credit card facility.[7] It may be added that it is possible that banker's references enjoy, for the purposes of defamation, "privilege." That means that they cannot be used for the purposes of a defamation action. One case in which privilege exists is where the recipient of the statement has a common "interest" with the subject of it, provided that the maker of the statement (in defamation terms, its "publisher") bona fide believes in what he says, and believes in the interest of the recipient, and acts without malice or motives of private gain. It has been held that privilege is available to one who provides information about the credit of another, where the recipient has an interest which justifies it, and where the publisher bona fide believes this.[8] It is essential that the bank which gives the information believes bona fide in the "interest" of the recipient. Where banks provide information through another bank, and restrict information to that bank (as references usually do) while knowing or suspecting that the information is for another, it may be difficult for banks to claim that they bona fide believe that the bank-recipient has an interest.

2. BANKS' LIABILITY TO RECIPIENT

One question which may arise[9] is whether the bank, if a corporation, has **5.03** authority to give references, (*i.e.* whether it is not liable, because it is acting *ultra vires*).[10] The question was left open by the House of Lords in *Banbury* v. *Bank of Montreal*[11] though other cases have considered the giving of references to be part of the business of a banker[12] and the question can hardly be in doubt. Most banks will have specific rules allowing branch managers to provide references, and to delegate authority, etc., but in *Banbury* v. *Bank of Montreal* two of the three majority judges reasoned that if the bank had authority, a branch manager had authority[13] to bind his principals.

An interesting, but unresolved, problem is whether there is a difference in the content of the duty which the bank has when it gives a reference, depending on whether the action is in contract or in tort. Clearly, in either

---

[6] No "special damage" need be proved: *Fleming* v. *Bank of New Zealand* [1900] A.C. 577.

[7] *i.e.* the customer must prove special damages: see, *e.g.*, *Gibbons* v. *Westminster Bank Ltd.* [1939] 2 K.B. 882, where the plaintiff was awarded £2.

[8] See *Waller* v. *Loch* (1881) 7 Q.B.D. 619; *Robshaw* v. *Smith* (1878) 38 L.T. 423; *London Association for Protection of Trade* v. *Greenlands Ltd.* [1916] 2 A.C. 15.

[9] It may cease to matter soon, if the *ultra vires* rule affecting corporations is abolished.

[10] s. 35, C.A. 1985 would, in any case, possibly protect the recipient.

[11] [1918] A.C. 626.

[12] See *Swift* v. *Jewsbury and Goddard* (1874) L.R. 9 Q.B. 301; *Parsons* v. *Barclay & Co. Ltd.* (1910) 103 L.T. 196.

[13] Presumably, implied authority, but at least apparent authority.

case it has a duty not to be fraudulent[14] but it may be that there is a higher duty in contract. In *Robinson* v. *National Bank of Scotland*[15] the House of Lords said (in a fraud case) that the bank had no duty to take reasonable care (to be careful), but only to be honest. This, however, applied only if the recipient stood "in no special relation" to the banker.[16] In *Parsons* v. *Barclay & Co. Ltd.*[17] Cozens-Hardy M.R. said "emphatically" that a banker's duty was not "to do anything more than answer the questions put to him honestly from what he knew from the books and accounts before him." These cases may be explicable on the basis that at the time they were decided there was (apart from contract) no general principle of liability for negligent misrepresentation. However, when in *Hedley Byrne & Co. Ltd.* v. *Heller & Partners Ltd.*[18] the House of Lords accepted that if a banker assumed any tortious duty, it was a duty of reasonable care, in defining the content of that duty, (*i.e.* what was reasonable) Lord Hodson said that it would be unreasonable to impose on a banker a duty to spend much time and trouble on ascertaining the facts "if that obligation really adds anything to the duty of giving an honest answer." The banker is "permitted to give an impromptu answer in the words that immediately come to his mind on the basis of the facts which he happens to remember or is able to ascertain from the files . . . "[19] These approaches, and especially the last, are extremely benevolent to bankers. Sometimes it is thought that this is justified because the bank is unpaid for what it does. If the courts take this view, then where the bank has a direct contractual relationship with the recipient, more may perhaps be expected. We have remarked, however, that banks are not charitable institutions,[20] and that indeed they are always "paid," albeit indirectly, both in cash and in goodwill. In addition, it must never be forgotten that (at common law) it is possible for a bank to limit its liability by a disclaimer, and that if the advice is not to be relied upon, the disclaimer might say so. In our view, the attitude to banker's references shown in the older cases is explicable by the absence of any general duty of care, and the attitude expressed by Lord Hodson in *Hedley Byrne* is too benevolent.

a. Liability in Contract

5.04 This presupposes either a contract to give specific information, or that the recipient is a customer of the bank, so that in failing to give him reliable information the bank breaks an implied term of the contract (to take reasonable care in the management of the customer's affairs). The bank would be liable for the acts of its authorised agents, and (subject to a resolution of the content of its duty) it might be itself in breach of contract if it employed incompetent staff. A successful action by a customer-recipient occurred in *Cornish* v. *Midland Bank P.L.C.*[21] where a bank clerk negligently advised a customer that a bank mortgage was "just like a building society mortgage" (whereas a building society mortgage is for a limited amount, and the bank mortgage is of an "all moneys" type). Actions not for breach but for "mis-

---

[14] Subject to what is said below as to the effect of Lord Tenterden's Act.
[15] (1916) 53 Sc.L.R. 390, H.L.
[16] *Per* Lord Haldane, p. 392.
[17] (1910) 103 L.T. 196.
[18] [1964] A.C. 465.
[19] This was approving what Pearson L.J. had said in the Court of Appeal.
[20] And see also *National Westminster Bank P.L.C.* v. *Morgan* [1983] 3 All E.R. 85, 91 per Dunn L.J. who makes this exact point.
[21] [1985] 3 All E.R. 513.

representation" lie, of course, only if the misrepresentation is in the forma-tion of a contract, which is unlikely in the present type of case. If it occurred, then an action for damages under section 2(2) of the Misrepresen-tation Act 1967 would not succeed unless an action for fraud would succeed, which requires that the representation be signed by the maker (and bank references are unsigned).[22] Otherwise, Lord Tenterden's Act, which imposes the requirement for a signed representation, does not apply to con-tractual actions.[23]

As to disclaimers, it may be that they are ineffective even at common law, being given after the formation of the contract. If the contract contains an implied term to manage the customer's affairs with due care, then a non-contractual term added subsequently may be of no effect.[24] It seems that the disclaimer is non-contractual, being unsupported by fresh consideration, and being given in circumstances where the transaction is part of the orig-inal contract, rather than a fresh contract. In any case, it is clear that if the bank has been "negligent" the provisions of section 2(2) of the Unfair Con-tract Terms Act 1977 apply, and that the disclaimer must be reasonable. (Section 3 of the Act, which applies to contractual terms, would appear not to apply, because the disclaimer is probably not a contractual term.) The onus of proving reasonableness is on the bank, and it may be doubted that in the "blanket" form in which they are expressed, the disclaimer is reason-able. Much, however, depends on the content of the bank's duty. If it has little more than a duty of honesty, then if it is honest, it is not liable, and the disclaimer would make little difference, except to recognise the underlying legal position.

b. Liability in Tort

Liability may arise in Deceit, if a statement is made which is not honestly **5.05** believed by its maker to be true and if another relies on this and suffers loss.[25] However, Lord Tenterden's Act[26] provides that the bank is not liable for a fraudulent representation concerning the credit, etc., of another, unless the representation is written and signed by the maker or by the maker's authorised agent. For this purpose, the signature of a corporation may be made by an authorised agent.[27] *Banbury* v. *Bank of Montreal*[28] held that the Act applied only to actions for fraud, in the tort of Deceit. Contractual actions, or actions for Negligence, are unaffected by the Act, except actions for negligent misrepresentation under section 2(1) of the Misrepresentation Act 1967 (which can only be brought in circumstances—other than as to the defendant's state of mind—where Deceit would lie). It is, of course, for this reason that bank references are not usually signed, and this protects against actions in Deceit.

Liability may also arise in Negligence, following the decision in *Hedley*

---

[22] *U.B.A.F. Ltd.* v. *European American Banking Corpn.* [1984] 2 All E.R. 226; [1984] Q.B. 713.
[23] *Banbury* v. *Bank of Montreal* [1918] A.C. 626.
[24] See, *e.g.*, *Olley* v. *Marlborough Court Ltd.* [1949] 1 K.B. 532; *Chapelton* v. *Barry U.D.C.* [1940] 1 K.B. 532.
[25] *Derry* v. *Peek* (1889) 14 App.Cas. 337.
[26] The Statute of Frauds Amendment Act 1828, s.6.
[27] *U.B.A.F. Ltd.* v. *European American Banking Corpn.* above, n. 22, C.A. disagreeing with *Hirst* v. *West Riding Banking Co. Ltd.* [1901] 2 K.B. 560 which said that the principal himself had to sign, and that a company's seal had to be affixed.
[28] [1918] A.C. 626.

Byrne & Co. Ltd. v. *Heller & Partners Ltd.*[29] Before this decision, liability for negligent misrepresentation existed only if there was (a) a contractual relation between plaintiff and defendant,[30] or (b) a fiduciary relation.[30a] (This may explain dicta in the older cases—where fraud was in issue—that the bank's only duty is a duty of honesty.) Under the ordinary law of Negligence (which is generally taken to be based upon the principles enunciated in *Donoghue* v. *Stephenson*)[31] liability for negligence is imposed by the general law. But in *Hedley Byrne* the House of Lords were concerned that the "floodgates of litigation" should not be opened so wide as to catch (for example) people who casually gave information, or who did so without being paid for it. They held, therefore, that a duty of reasonable care existed only where such a duty was voluntarily undertaken. No such duty was imposed by law. Lord Devlin said "I do not understand any of your Lordships to hold that it is a responsibility imposed by law . . . It is a responsibility that is voluntarily accepted or undertaken . . . "[32] The significance of this was that the bank in question had used a disclaimer, saying that it accepted no responsibility. Given that, the bank could not be said to be accepting a duty, when in the same breath it said it was not doing so. For this reason, banks' references always contain disclaimers.[33] The English position may be contrasted with one taken in Australia, where the High Court held that liability was imposed by law, and that if a disclaimer worked at all, it was because it made it unforeseeable by the representor that the representee would rely on the advice.[34]

5.06   The common-law position in respect of disclaimers may have been affected by the Unfair Contract Terms Act 1977. Section 2(2) of that Act applies to the exclusion or restriction of liability for financial losses caused by "negligence." "Negligence" according to section 1 means, in addition to breach of contractual duties and occupiers' duties "the breach . . . of any common law duty to take reasonable care or exercise reasonable skill. . . . " The difficulty is that *Hedley Byrne* held that there was no duty unless one was assumed, and if there is no duty, there cannot be a "breach" within section 1, and, therefore, no "negligence" which, under section 2(2) is excluded or restricted. Section 13 of the Act provides that, to the extent that the Act prevents excluding or restricting any liability, it also prevents doing so by reference to terms and notices which exclude or restrict the relevant obligation or duty. This may solve the difficulty, but it is not clear. Can one "exclude or restrict" a duty which does not even exist if one does not undertake it? Is "not undertaking" something an "exclusion" or "restriction"? It may be that it is, for if advice is given without a disclaimer, liability does

---

[29] [1964] A.C. 465.

[30] See, *e.g.*, *Midland Bank Ltd.* v. *Seymour* [1955] 2 Lloyds Rep. 147, 157. in relation to *Batts Combe Quarry Co.* v. *Barclays Bank Ltd.* (1913) 48 T.L.R. 4.

[30a] *Nocton* v. *Lord Ashburton* [1914] A.C. 932. See *Woods* v. *Martins Bank Ltd.* [1959] 1 Q.B. 55 where, a few years before *Hedley Byrne*, a court imposed liability on a bank for negligent advice on what must now be regarded as the entirely spurious grounds that there was a fiduciary relationship.

[31] [1932] A.C. 562.

[32] [1964] A.C. 465, 529. See also *ibid.*, 492, 504, 511, 533, 540.

[33] In some cases involving negligent advice where a disclaimer has been omitted, a bank has been held liable: see *W. B. Anderson & Sons Ltd.* v. *Rhodes (Liverpool Ltd.* [1967] 2 All E.R. 850; *Box* v. *Midland Bank Ltd.* [1979] 2 Lloyds Rep. 391.

[34] *Mutual Life & Citizens Assurance Co. Ltd.* v. *Evatt* [1968] 122 C.L.R. 566, especially, *per* Barwick C.J. (The court's actual decision was reversed by the Privy Council in [1971] A.C. 793.)

arise, from the "situation" as it were, without needing an express undertaking of liability, and if that is so, then putting in a term which prevents it from arising may be said to "exclude " it. The matter requires judicial resolution.

A further question is whether the disclaimer binds third parties. As with the example given earlier[34a] banks may attempt to stipulate that the information is given only for the use of a named recipient, and is confidential to them. In *Junior Books Ltd.* v. *Veitchi Co. Ltd.*[35] (a case involving for financial loss arising from physical damage to property) there was some discussion in the House of Lords of the effect of an exemption clause in a contract between A (a property owner) and B (say, a builder for whose benefit the clause existed) when A sold to C, the plaintiff. Lord Fraser thought that if C knew of the exemption clause, it would bind him, but that possibly even if C did not know he would be in no better position than A, his vendor. Lord Roskill did not decide the matter, but thought that in principle, depending on its wording, the clause might limit the duty of care. Lord Keith of Kinkel would see no principle by which B could limit his duty to C (a comprehensible view, there being no contractual relationship, and liability being imposed here by law, unlike the case for negligent misstatements). Whichever of these views is correct, the same may not apply to negligent misstatements, where the duty is undertaken, not imposed.

In *Yianni* v. *Edwin Evans & Sons*[36] the plaintiff relied upon a surveyor's inspection and valuation done for a building society. He sued the valuers, arguing that their valuation meant that the house was worth the sum in question, and that it was foreseeable that the statement would be passed on to him. The court held that the valuer was liable, but said that only the purchaser named in the valuer's report could sue, and further, that the valuers were not liable for that part of the report described as confidential, since they had not authorised it to be passed on. However, the judgment is erroneously given in terms of a duty imposed by law, without consideration of the fact that the duty in relation to negligent misstatements is not imposed, but voluntarily undertaken, and that liability cannot depend merely on foreseeability of loss.

It is submitted that the question reduces itself to a question of A's authority to pass the reference on to C. That authority may be either actual, or apparent. Apparent authority cannot come from A's own representation that he has authority, but if C knows that A (which may be his own bank) has asked for information in C's name, or where B knows it is not for A alone, then when A receives the information B has apparently undertaken a duty (and B is bound, unless A communicates an effective disclaimer to C), and A has apparent authority from B to reveal the information to C. In these circumstances, where A asks B in C's name, or when B knows the information will be passed on, it is unlikely that a statement restricting the information to A, in confidence, could sensibly mean anything, and would probably be ineffective even at common law, let alone under the Unfair Contract Terms Act 1977. If the statement was effective, it would deprive A of actual authority to reveal the information to C, and A would be in breach of confidence in doing so, even though he asked for it for that very purpose. It may be, however, that if A asks for information in his own name, and

5.07

5.08

[34a] Above, para. 5.01.
[35] [1982] 3 All E.R. 201, [1983] 1 A.C. 520.
[36] [1982] Q.B. 438.

without specifying a purpose which makes it clear that he is asking for someone else, that B cannot be liable to C if the reference is given for A only, in confidence. B does not undertake a duty to C, and A has no apparent or actual authority to say so.[37] These conclusions follow from the restriction in the reference as to the parties to whom it may be given, rather than from the disclaimer, though certainly if C knows of the disclaimer, he cannot (subject to the Unfair Contract Terms Act 1977) say that any duty towards him has been undertaken.

5.09   The last question which we will consider here is whether the disclaimer (if subject to the Act) is reasonable. Again, one must first consider the content of the duty, and whether it much exceeds a duty of honesty (which disclaimers would not seem to attempt to exclude, and which, if they did, would be ineffective even at common law).[38] This in turn involves a consideration of whether one takes the view that banks are unrewarded for the service, so that no onerous obligations should be imposed, or whether (as we have suggested) such a view is too benevolent. In our view, the "blanket-exemptions" represented by the standard phrasing on references are unreasonable. A disclaimer in the form of a warning, (*e.g.* "This information may not be accurate and should not be relied on" or "This information was compiled after a brief reference to the customer's accounts, and should not be relied on as a full and accurate financial report, and no responsibility . . . etc.") may be effective. Again, the matter calls for judicial resolution.

B. Liability for investment advice

5.10   Much of what has been said above is relevant here. When a bank gives investment advice it has a contractual duty to customers and a tortious duty to those with whom it has a special relationship, under the principle of *Hedley Byrne & Co. Ltd.* v. *Heller & Partners Ltd.*[39] and it must take reasonable care in the provision of the advice. In *Banbury* v. *Bank of Montreal*[40] a manager gave fraudulent advice to invest in a company (whose account was causing the bank difficulty). The House of Lords held (by a majority of three to two) that the bank was not liable because there was insufficient evidence to show that the giving of advice on investments was within the scope of the bank's business, (*i.e.* the bank was acting *ultra vires*). But two of the majority held that if the bank had had authority, the manager who gave the advice would have had authority. In *Woods* v. *Martins Bank Ltd.*[41] the bank had held itself out as willing to advise, and that its managers could give "the very best advice" and could be consulted freely. The bank contemplated that the managers would obtain advice from brokers, and forbade managers to give direct advice to customers. The plaintiff, who had no business experience, sought the bank's advice, and acting upon what he was told by a manager (without actual authority to give advice), invested £5000 in a company. Later he opened an account with the bank, and subsequently (after further advice) invested more sums in the company, and guaranteed the account of an associated company. During the whole period the company's account with the bank was overdrawn, and the bank's district office

---

[37] See, *e.g. Overbrooke Estates Ltd.* v. *Glencombe Properties Ltd.* [1974] 1 W.L.R. 1335.
[38] *S. Pearson & Son Ltd.* v. *Dublin Corpn.* [1907] A.C. 351, 353, 362.
[39] [1964] A.C. 465.
[40] [1918] A.C. 626.
[41] [1959] 1 Q.B. 55.

had been pressing it for reductions. The plaintiff sued, alleging fraud, or negligence. Fraud was not found, but Salmon J. held that the bank was grossly negligent. He found that even though at the time of the original advice the plaintiff had no account with the bank, the plaintiff was a "customer," which is to say, that there was a contractual relationship because the bank accepted the plaintiff's instructions. There was, additionally, a "fiduciary" relationship between the parties, which caused the plaintiff to rely upon the bank. He held that the advertisements clothed the manager with apparent authority. As to whether giving advice was part of the bank's business, this must in each case be a question of fact, and what may have been true of the Bank of Montreal in 1918 was not necessarily true of Martins Bank in 1958. While it cannot now[42] be asserted that there is a "fiduciary" relationship between bank and customer, it is clear, following the *Hedley Byrne* case, that if the customer reasonably relies on the bank[43] there is a "special" relationship sufficient to give rise to a duty of reasonable care. This would seem to be the case whether the customer sues in contract, or in tort. As to the bank's business, it is submitted that (as Salmon J. suggests) the nature of a bank's business has changed since 1918, and that in today's "deregulated" circumstances, it cannot be doubted that the giving of advice is part of a bank's business. In any case, even if it is not, not being provided for by the Memorandum of Association of the Bank, section 35 of the Companies Act 1985 would protect a customer who in good faith relied on a transaction decided upon by the directors. If the directors authorise the giving of advice by branch managers, etc., the giving of advice by the managers may well be a "transaction" which has been "decided upon by the directors."[44]

As with banker's references, a disclaimer will at common law protect the **5.11** bank, but may be subject to the Unfair Contract Terms Act 1977 (certainly, if there is a contractual relationship between bank and recipient of the advice).

The principles mentioned apply not only to "investment" advice, but to any sort of negligent misstatement made by the bank, upon which the customer (or non-customer) reasonably relies.[45] In *Box* v. *Midland Bank Ltd.*[46] the plaintiff was advised that the bank would make an advance to finance a contract, but that head office sanction was needed. This, said the branch manager, was a mere formality provided that an E.C.G.D.[47] policy was obtained, and he added that such policies were obtainable. The manager did not explain the difference between an E.C.G.D. policy (which could be obtained) and an E.C.G.D. Bankers Guarantee (Bills and Notes) policy (which could not be obtained, but which alone head office would accept). The plaintiff made the necessary applications, and received a quotation for a policy, which head office rejected. Being unable to obtain an acceptable policy, the plaintiff then got into financial difficulties, and became bankrupt. He sued the bank for negligence. The court held that the bank had

---

[42] After *National Westminster Bank P.L.C.* v. *Morgan* [1985] 1 All E.R. 821, [1985] A.C. 686.
[43] See *Esso Petroleum Co. Ltd.* v. *Mardon* [1976] Q.B. 801.
[44] See Sealy, *Cases and Materials in Company Law*, (3rd. ed.), p. 121.
[45] *W. B. Anderson & Sons Ltd.* v. *Rhodes (Liverpool) Ltd.* [1967] 2 All E.R. 850; *Box* v. *Midland Bank Ltd.* [1979] 2 Lloyds Rep. 391.
[46] Previous note.
[47] Export Credits Guarantee Department: a government department established to promote foreign trade.

failed to take reasonable care "that is to say the care to be expected of an ordinary competent bank manager." The manager gave the customer the impression that the head office's sanction would be a mere formality, whereas he ought to have known that there was never the slightest prospect of the facility being made available. The bank was liable.

5.12   It seems then, that as long as the advice given or statement made is within the actual or apparent authority of the bank official who gives it, and is part of the bank's business (or the plaintiff is protected by section 35 of the Companies Act 1985) and the misrepresentation is made in circumstances in which it is reasonable for the plaintiff to rely upon it, and contains no disclaimer (or the disclaimer is unreasonable under the Unfair Contract Terms Act 1977, if that applies) then the bank may be liable if it fails to take reasonable care in making the misrepresentation. This is the case whether it is a reference, or investment advice, or some other sort of statement, as in *Box* v. *Midland Bank Ltd*. The major difference between references and other cases may be (though we have suggested that it should not be) that with bank references the "content" of the duty of reasonable care differs little from the duty of honesty (if Lord Hodson, in *Hedley Byrne*, is correct in following the older cases).

6. Paying Bank and Customer: Duty to Pay and Obey Countermands

A. Duty to pay (to honour cheques)

It is not the case that a banker has the duty to honour all his customer's **6.01** instructions.[1] Rather, there is a duty to honour all instructions which the banker has, at the time of the original contract, or subsequently, undertaken to honour, and this depends on any specific undertakings in a particular case, and on the general "holding out" of those things which the banker will do, which arises from the nature of a banker's business. One general holding out involves the use of cheques.

1. CHEQUE, AS MANDATE

The cheque is not merely a negotiable instrument, but also a mandate[2] to the bank from its customer, and it is an implied term of the contract that the bank, as debtor, will repay its customer-creditor on receipt of his order at the branch where he keeps his account.[3] If the bank pays within the mandate it fulfils the terms of the contract, and becomes entitled to debit the customer's account. Moreover, if a third party is paid, this has the effect of discharging the customer's liability to that party, for the bank pays as agent of the customer. If, however, the bank acts outside the mandate, it has no authority to debit the account, but the customer may ratify what the bank has done, or the customer may be estopped, in certain cases, from denying the bank's right to debit the account.

2. CHEQUES, AND THIRD PARTIES

Since the banker-drawee does not accept (by signing) cheques, he cannot be **6.02** liable in contract for non-payment to a holder as such[4] (though he may be liable in conversion to the true owner in some cases). It would be otherwise if the giving of the cheque by the customer to a third party amounted to an assignment of the funds in the account, for then, by section 136 of the Law of Property Act 1925, the presentation of the cheque to the bank would amount to written notice of the assignment, and the third party could sue the bank (and he alone could give a good discharge for the money).[5] However, while in Scotland a cheque may have the effect of assigning a debt, in England the mere drawing and delivery of a cheque (or any bill of exchange) does not do so.[6] It follows that the third party may not demand payment, for he is not legal or equitable owner of the debt. It is, however, possible for a customer to indicate other than by means of the cheque itself, that he intends to assign the debt, and if it is an assignment of the whole

---

[1] *London Joint Stock Bank Ltd.* v. *Macmillan and Arthur* [1918] A.C. 777.
[2] One must distinguish the original mandate taken at the time of opening the account, and particular mandates, such as cheques, relating to the operation of the account.
[3] So said in *Joachimson* v. *Swiss Bank Corpn.* [1921] 3 K.B. 110. In *London Joint Stock Bank Ltd.* v. *Macmillan and Arthur* [1918] A.C. 777 the obligation is said to arise simply out of the debtor-creditor relationship. This seems to mean the same thing as said in *Joachimson.*
[4] See *Dublin Port and Docks Board* v. *Bank of Ireland* [1976] I.R. 118.
[5] *Hughes* v. *Pump House Hotel Co.* [1902] 2 K.B. 190.
[6] s.53, B.O.E. Act 1882.

debt, the bank must pay the payee-assignee.[7] On the other hand, if the customer clearly assigns part of the debt, that can only operate as an equitable assignment, and only the customer can give a good discharge.[8] It seems to follow from this that the bank has no obligation to the third party payee. However, the customer's signature on the cheque is both an authority to pay and an order, and if there are sufficient funds, the bank has an obligation to the customer to pay. It is also established that the bank has no obligation to the customer to pay a reduced sum, where there are insufficient funds to pay the whole amount of a cheque, and it follows, therefore, that since the equitable assignee cannot sue the bank in his own name, no obligation is owed to him in this case, either. As already said, however, in the normal case the payee is not legal or equitable assignee, and *a fortiori* there is no obligation to pay him the reduced amount to the extent of the sufficiency of funds.

Generally, therefore, except for the possibility of liability in conversion, the cheque may be viewed by the banker, as against his customer, solely as a mandate to pay. Thus considered, the mandate has two aspects: first, it is authority to pay justifying a debit to the account (for example, it has only this characteristic if there are insufficient funds), and secondly, it may in addition impose a requirement to pay (if it is properly drawn, and there are sufficient funds, etc.)

3. NATURE OF THE DUTY

6.03 The duty is to obey the mandate, and in obeying it to do so with reasonable care so as not to cause loss to the customer.[9] Negligence is not only a direct and actionable breach of duty, but may also deprive the banker of statutory protection against his customer (in debt or damages) or a third party (in conversion) where he pays the wrong person.[10]

4. GENERAL CONDITIONS FOR PAYMENT

a. Branch, and Time

6.04 Although a bank is a corporate personality, the customer may not make demand of his debtor wherever he finds him, but only at the branch where he keeps the account.[11] The customer has no right to require the demand to be honoured at one branch on the ground that there are funds at another branch. The right thus to "combine" accounts is ordinarily that of the banker alone.[12] Demand may be made only during banking hours, or within a reasonable time thereafter.[13]

---

[7] *Walker* v. *Bradford Old Bank Ltd.* (1884) 12 Q.B.D. 511: contrast *Schroeder* v. *Central Bank of London Ltd.* (1876) 34 L.T. 735, where Brett J. said that there was no debt, capable of assignment, until demand on the banker was made. This seems to confuse the existence of the debt with the conditions for its repayment.

[8] *Re Steel Wing Co. Ltd.* [1921] 1 Ch. 349; *Bank of Liverpool and Martins Ltd.* v. *Holland* (1926) 43 T.L.R. 29; *Williams* v. *Atlantic Assurance Co. Ltd.* [1933] 1 K.B. 81; *Walter and Sullivan Ltd.* v. *J. Murphy & Sons Ltd.* [1955] 1 Q.B. 584; *Re Kent and Sussex Sawmills Ltd.* [1947] Ch. 177.

[9] *Bellamy* v. *Marjoribanks* (1852) 7 Exch. 389; *Carlon* v. *Ireland* (1856) 5 E. & B. 765.

[10] Under The Cheques Act 1957, and under ss.79–80 of the B.O.E. Act 1882 (and possibly, under s.60), discussed below, Chaps. 8, 19.

[11] *Joachimson* v. *Swiss Bank Corpn.* [1921] 3 K.B. 110.

[12] *Woodland* v. *Fear* (1857) 7 E. & B. 519; *Garnett* v. *McKewan* (1872) L.R. 8 Ex. 10; *McNaughten* v. *Cox & Co.* (1921) *The Times*, May 11, See below Chap. 13 for combination.

[13] Below para. 6.29.

b. Written Demand

We have observed[14] that the banker-debtor is not ordinarily liable to repay **6.05** the customer-creditor unless demand is made of him. Unless the original mandate (written statement of terms) says otherwise, it would seem that if the customer demands repayment of all his monies, he need not do so by written order, but this way of expressing it is perhaps misleading, for ordinarily the bank would be entitled to his signature as verification of his identity[15] and in any case the bank would be entitled to demand from him a written receipt. It would seem likely, however, that if the customer requests payment of less than the full sum, or requests payment to a third person, that the bank may require a written demand.

c. Unambiguous Form

The customer's demand mut be "in a form which is clear and free from **6.06** ambiguity" and which leaves the banker with no "room for misgiving as to what he is called upon to do."[16] Even if a "cheque" is not in fact a cheque it may be a good mandate. Thus, it may not be a cheque because it is not payable on demand (if postdated, for example)[17] or because it is not a bill of exchange (*e.g.* if expressed in terms which make it an authority, but not an order, to pay). It does not necessarily follow that because this is authority to pay, the bank is required to pay. In *Brooks & Co.* v. *Blackburn Benefit Society*[18] Lord Blackburn says the bank need only pay "cheques properly drawn." In *Griffiths* v. *Dalton*[19] Macnaghten J. said that a bank was not bound to honour an undated cheque, apparently on the ground that such a bill might be overdue.[20] This may be correct, (even though the instrument is still a valid "bill")[21] though the bank would presumably still be entitled to pay, as it is a valid mandate from the customer. But it is submitted that if the mandate (even if not a cheque, in law) is unambiguous and exposes the bank to no unusual risks,[22] then it must pay, unless its terms of contract otherwise stipulate. An example of an unusual risk is, for instance "where a cheque or draft is negotiated abroad and on which appears a special indorsement in Arabic or other Oriental characters, conveying absolutely nothing to the drawee bank."[23] In such a situation, the customer must give the bank authority to act reasonably for its own protection. It is clear that the bank may not defer payment until it is satisfied that indorsements are genuine, if the bill is "regular and complete" on its face.[24]

Other examples of improperly drawn cheques which entitle a bank to **6.07** refuse to pay are postdated cheques[25] (the bank must pay on the date, but

---

[14] Above, para. 3.05.

[15] Unless the cashier or branch manager knew him.

[16] *London Joint Stock Bank Ltd.* v. *Macmillan and Arthur* [1918] A.C. 777, *per* Lord Haldane.

[17] *Orbit Mining and Trading Co. Ltd.* v. *Westminster Bank Ltd.* [1963] 1 Q.B. 794.

[18] (1884) 9 A.C. 857, 864.

[19] [1940] 2 K.B. 264.

[20] Within s.36 B.O.E. Act 1882. This affects the ability of the transferor to give perfect title to the transferee.

[21] s.3(4) B.O.E. Act 1882.

[22] *London Joint Stock Bank Ltd.* v. *Macmillan and Arthur* [1918] A.C. 777.

[23] Paget, 231, citing *Carlisle and Cumberland Banking Co.* v. *Bragg* [1911] 1 K.B. 489; *Arab Bank Ltd.* v. *Ross* [1952] 2 Q.B. 216.

[24] *Vagliano Bros.* v. *Bank of England* [1891] A.C. 107, disagreeing with *Robarts* v. *Tucker* (1851) 16 Q.B. 560. The bank has the protection of the Cheques Act 1957, and of s.60 of the Bills of Exchange Act 1882, discussed below, Chaps. 8, 19.

[25] *Orbit Mining* case, above, n.17.

has no mandate to pay before); cheques on which words and figures disagree (the bank has a mandate to pay according to the words[26] but is not obliged to do so); or cheques crossed specially to more than one banker (the bank has a mandate to pay if it is the customer's order and not a forgery, but has no protection if it pays the wrong person, and may refuse to pay).[27]

d. Indorsements

6.08 So far as the paying banker is concerned, there are by virtue of statutory provisions[28] now few cases in which the lack of indorsement, or an irregular or forged indorsement need concern the bank. Apart from the statutory provisions, the lack of an indorsement to the person paid would be (a) a conversion as against the true owner, and (b) a breach of the mandate from the bank's customer, who has not authorised payment to this person.

e. Express Contractual Modifications

6.09 The implied terms relating to the form of cheques may be altered by contract, but if an attempt is made to do so in an established relationship, we have observed that the courts may be reluctant to give effect to the purported change.[29] Thus, in *Burnett* v. *Westminster Bank Ltd.*[30] an attempt was made on a cheque book to stipulate that cheques and credit slips would be applied to the account for which they had been prepared, and that customers must not permit their use on any other account. When a customer altered a cheque drawn on one account making it payable on the other account, but the bank debited the original account, it was held that this term did not bind the customer. First, it had not become part of the contract: (i) the plaintiff was bound only if he had notice of it, and it was not shown that he had read it, or that the bank had otherwise done enough to bring it to his attention, and (ii) there was no consideration to support such a variation of the contract.[31] and (iii) it was not clear that there was any contractual intention—*i.e.* that the term was intended to affect the contractual relationship. (Had the term been contained in the original signed mandate, this first ground for the decision would have been otherwise.) Secondly, even if the term was contractually binding, it was irrelevant as a defence,[32] for at most the customer's disobedience to the terms meant that he was in breach of contract, and the altered cheque was still no mandate to debit the account at the issuing branch. (The original mandate would need to give the bank a right to debit an account at the issuing branch regardless of alterations.)

f. Sufficient Funds

6.10 The banker has no obligation to extend an overdraft to his customer, and unless he has done so, he need honour a cheque only if there are "sufficient funds to meet it."[33] Since the customer has no right of combination of accounts for funds held at other branches, this refers to sufficiency of funds in the branch on which the cheque is drawn. The bank may, however, pay the cheque if it chooses, and debit an account elsewhere, exercising its right

---

[26] s.9 B.O.E. Act 1882.

[27] ss.79–80 B.O.E. Act 1882.

[28] Discussed in Chapters 7, 19.

[29] See above, para. 3.10.

[30] [1966] 1 Q.B. 742, [1965] 2 Lloyd's Rep. 218 (the facts are given above, para. 3.11).

[31] This second point, it is submitted, is very debateable.

[32] Though not to a counterclaim for damages.

[33] *Joachimson* v. *Swiss Bank Corpn.* [1921] 3 K.B. 110. See also *Whitaker* v. *Bank of England* (1835) 1 Cr.M. & R. 744.

of combination without notice.[34] Where there is a debt elsewhere, the bank may exercise its right of combination so as to refuse to pay on an account which appears to have a sufficient credit. The ground for that is simply that the total indebtedness of bank to customer is less than the amount of the cheque. Ordinarily, no notice need be given to the customer of the bank's intention. This right of combination (or "consolidation") is fully discussed elsewhere.[35]

If the customer pays in funds so as to meet a particular cheque, the banker may decline to honour another cheque on the ground that he must retain funds sufficient to meet the cheque earmarked by the customer. This is an example of the customer's right of "appropriation."[36] Funds paid in to an account for a specific purpose may also be subject to a Quistclose trust[37] and are not available for the banker's use by way of combination (nor, on the customer's insolvency, are they assets for his liquidator or trustee) so that the banker must honour the cheque in question. The cheque earmarked by reference to funds previously paid in must be honoured even if, by the bank having honoured another cheque, there are no longer sufficient funds.

Even where cash has been paid in, the bank may delay or refuse to honour **6.11** cheques until it has time to carry out the necessary book-keeping obligations.[38] Cash becomes "available" as soon as it is credited to the account.[39] But cash differs from uncleared effects (*i.e.* other cheques paid in, but not yet cleared) and the bank may decline to meet a cheque where there are uncleared effects, even if those funds have been credited to the account. The contrary is suggested by *Gordon* v. *Capital and Counties Bank Ltd.*[40] where it was said that if the bank credited the account with uncleared effects the customer was entitled to draw upon it. But there the bank had "credited as cash" the effects in question, which is to say, they had allowed the customer to draw against the funds, and he had done so. It is made clear by *A. L. Underwood Ltd.* v. *Bank of Liverpool*[41] that unless the bank intends to "credit as cash" and to allow the customer to draw against uncleared effects the mere crediting of the account does not prevent the dishonouring of cheques on the ground of insufficient funds. (Apart from the question of honouring cheques, the question may arise whether the bank is holder in due course, or otherwise receives for value, and it will be a holder for value if the customer's account is overdrawn on receipt, or if the bank credits for cash and allows the customer to draw on the uncleared effects.) A note on paying in slips to the effect that the bank may refuse to pay against uncleared effects may serve to clarify that the general rule (from the *Underwood* case) applies, even if, in a particular case, there is evidence of an agreement to the contrary.[42] But if the crediting is communicated to the

---

[34] Not all accounts may be so debited, (*e.g.* not trust accounts) nor is combination possible for all debts (*e.g.* contingent ones). In addition to combination, there may be a right of contractual set-off, and in insolvency cases, s.323 of the Insolvency Act 1986 may be relevant. These are considered below, Chaps 13. 27.

[35] Below, Chap. 13.

[36] Discussed below, Chap. 13.

[37] See below, Chap. 10.

[38] *Marzetti* v. *Williams* (1830) 1 B. & Ad. 415; *Griffiths* v. *London County and Westminster Bank* (1912) (unrep.).

[39] *Capital and Counties Bank Ltd.* v. *Gordon* [1903] A.C. 240, 249; *Re Mills, Bawtree & Co. ex p. Stannard* (1893) 10 Morr. 193.

[40] [1902] 1 K.B. 142, aff'd [1903] A.C. 240.

[41] [1924] 1 K.B. 775.

[42] See *Westminster Bank Ltd.* v. *Zang* [1966] A.C. 182.

customer, this is such a representation as may give rise to an estoppel, if the customer acts in reliance on the representation so as to incur expenditure, or to draw on the account.[43] Unless an estoppel arises, the bank would not be bound, for there is no new consideration to bind it.

It is no reason to refuse to pay that the bank knows that other (non-earmarked) cheques will shortly be presented, and that there is insufficient for all.[44]

6.12   There is no obligation to meet a cheque drawn for a certain amount where there are funds of a lesser amount, even to the extent of the lesser amount. Not only is the bank not required to make part payment, but probably it would be in breach of mandate if it did so. However, if the payee is aware of the shortfall, and tenders for the credit of the account a sum sufficient to make it up, the bank may be justified in receiving that sum and (after a delay for the purpose of clearing any cheque thus paid in) paying on the customer's cheque.[45]

If more than one cheque is presented, and there may be insufficient funds for all, they should be paid in the order of presentment, but if there is insufficient for the first according to this rule, then the first for which there is sufficient funds should be paid.[46] The general rule as to payment in order of presentment must, however, be observed with due regard to the customer's interests, and might be displaced, for example, where delays occurred as a result of a strike of bank-staff, and a consequent backlog in processing.[47] If two or more cheques are presented simultaneously, the one(s) for which there are sufficient funds should be paid, or, if either (but not both) could be paid, the smaller ones should be paid first (because the dishonour of a smaller sum might have a greater effect on the customer's reputation).[48]

6.13   If the bank decides to pay where there are insufficient funds, it acts within its mandate, and the customer is rightly debited, and his debt to any other payee discharged, etc.

g. Stale Cheques

It is the custom of banks not to pay cheques which are stale, and cheques are generally so treated if presented more than six months after their ostensible dates of issue. However, this period may vary from bank to bank. It is not clear whether the custom is so well known that it has become an implied term, justifying it, and there is no other justification for the banks' disobeying their mandates. If there is an implied term, perhaps it amounts to this, that the bank may refuse to honour a cheque if not presented until an unreasonable time after its date. It may be observed that any bill may become "overdue," and that a demand bill may become overdue after being in circulation for an unreasonable time[49] with the consequences stated in section 36 of the Bills of Exchange Act 1882: namely, that if the bill is thereafter negotiated, subsequent holders take it subject to defects of title affect-

---

[43] *Holland v. Manchester and Liverpool District Banking Co. Ltd.* (1909) 25 T.L.R. 386; *Akrokerri (Atlantic) Mines Ltd. v. Economic Bank* [1940] 2 K.B. 456; *Bevan v. National Bank Ltd.* (1906) 23 T.L.R. 65.

[44] *Sednaoni Zariffa Nakes & Co. v. Anglo-Austrian Bank* (1909) 2 L.D.A.B. 208.

[45] *Questions on Banking Practice* (10th ed.) No. 417.

[46] *Sednaoni Zariffa Nakes & Co. v. Anglo-Austrian Bank* (1909) 2 L.D.A.B. 208.

[47] *Dublin Port and Docks Board v. Bank of Ireland* [1976] I.R. 118.

[48] *Sednaoni Zariffa Nakes & Co. v. Anglo-Austrian Bank* (1909) 2 L.D.A.B. 208.

[49] s.36(3), B.O.E. Act 1882.

ing their transferors. This does not justify the banks' practice, but may explain it.[50]

The answer "Out of date" or "Stale" on the cheque, would not be defamatory.

h. Postdated Cheques

A postdated cheque would not be relevant in this context if the postdating is **6.14** noticed, and the cheque (or instrument, since it is not a cheque) is not paid (as is proper) until its date. But if it is wrongly paid early, the bank has not observed its mandate, and must not consider this debit in deciding whether to decline to honour other cheques on the ground of insufficient funds. It is for this reason that banks may seek to persuade customers not to postdate cheques. One of the checks a bank should make before dishonouring a cheque is to see whether any postdated instruments have wrongly been paid.

i. Garnishee Orders

A garnishee *order nisi* (or "freezing" order) is a court order, which requires **6.15** the bank to retain the funds of a customer until the court otherwise orders. If the order becomes absolute, the bank will be ordered to pay another person. The effect of such an order may be that the bank need not pay, on the ground of insufficiency of funds. This will depend on the nature of the order, which may be limited to a certain amount, leaving sufficient for other cheques, etc. Even if there would be insufficient funds, if the bank chooses, it may obey the mandate, but if the order becomes absolute and the bank is ordered to pay the funds to another, it must pay the funds without debit, and at that time it runs the risk that the customer will be unable to meet the debit. Sequestration orders[51] have a similar effect, inasmuch as the bank is obliged to follow the orders of the sequestrator, not the customer.

j. Countermands, etc.

The bank must not pay if it knows of a countermand, or of the customer's **6.16** death or incapacity. Countermands are further discussed below.[52]

k. Insolvency

If the customer becomes insolvent, and goes into liquidation, or bank- **6.17** ruptcy, the bank's right to pay is affected. This is considered elsewhere.[53]

l. Third Party Rights

Generally, the bank need not investigate its customer's title to the money, **6.18** and should not refuse to pay on the ground that the funds might belong to others. It would be otherwise if the bank knew that the drawer had no title to the funds, whether he stole them or received them by mistake.[54] Where there is a known trust or agency the bank may pay on the trustee's or agent's order unless the bank knows of a breach of trust or duty. In some circumstances the bank may be liable if it pays when it knows or ought to know of facts which would reveal to a reasonable banker that a customer is exceeding his authority or acting in breach of trust (*i.e.* for constructive

---

[50] See *Griffiths* v. *Dalton* [1940] 2 K.B. 264.
[51] Discussed above, Chap. 3.
[52] At para. 6.23.
[53] Below, Chap. 28.
[54] For recovery of money received by mistake, see below, Chap. 11.

knowledge). These principles (of "constructive trust") are discussed in Chapter 11.

SUMMARY

6.19   The position is, therefore, that a bank must honour a customer's cheques, provided that the cheque is presented to the correct branch, during opening times, by written demand in unambiguous, complete and regular form, not being a stale or postdated cheque, with sufficient funds, and there being no contrary legal order, no countermand or notice of death or incapacity, no insolvency complications, and no known contravention of third party rights.

5. CUSTOMER'S REMEDIES FOR BANKER'S BREACH OF DUTY

6.20   If the banker fails to comply with his duty the customer may sue him either in contract, for damages, or in the tort of defamation, for damages.

Defamation[55] (libel, where the defamation is written) requires that an untrue statement which would lower the plaintiff in the estimation of right thinking persons has been "published" to a third party, as by returning a cheque unpaid to that party. The banker is always justified if there are insufficient funds (true statements are not defamatory) but mistakes happen, and naturally, in returning a cheque, the banker attempts to avoid defamatory phrases. But that is difficult. In considering the cases, it must be recalled that the judge rules on whether words are capable of being defamatory, but the jury[56] decides whether they were defamatory in the particular case, and awards damages. "Not sufficient" or "insufficient funds" are probably defamatory (if untrue). "Present again" or "Refer to drawer" are probably defamatory since these words may be understood by most people to mean "insufficient funds."[57]

6.21   The following steps may be taken[58] if a cheque is to be dishonoured: (a) to ensure that all cheques were signed by the customer, and not by someone with a similar name, and by error debited to the customer's account, (b) to ensure that no postdated cheques were paid early, by error, (c) to ensure that regular credits have, in error, not been credited, (d) to ensure that the cheque was not drawn with a cheque card, (e) if the cheque is to be dishonoured, the least defamatory words possible should be used: if possible, "Words and figures disagree," or "unconfirmed stop received," though otherwise, "Refer to Drawer" must be used (and may be defamatory, if

---

[55] This is also considered above, Chap. 5, in the context of erroneous status opinions.
[56] Defamation is still tried by jury.
[57] Some dicta suggest otherwise: see *Flach* v. *London and South Western Bank Ltd.* (1915) 31 T.L.R. 334; *Plunkett* v. *Barclays Bank Ltd.* [1936] 2 K.B. 107. *Sim* v. *Stretch* [1936] 2 All E.R. 1237 says it is a question of fact in every case, for the jury. Other decisions are: *Jayson* v. *Midland Bank Ltd.* [1968] 1 Lloyd's Rep. 409 (jury found that the words "Refer to Drawer" were defamatory, if unjustified); *Szek* v. *Lloyds Bank Ltd.* (1908) *The Times*, January 15 (jury gave no tort damages for "Refer to Drawer"); *Cox* v. *Cox & Co.* (1921) *The Times*, March 18 (no damages for "N/S"—meaning "not sufficient."); *Davidson* v. *Barclays Bank Ltd.* [1940] 1 All E.R. 316 ("not sufficient" held to be capable of being defamatory); *Baker* v. *Australia and New Zealand Bank Ltd.* [1958] N.Z.L.R. 907 ("present again" defamatory); *Millward* v. *Lloyds Bank Ltd.* (1920) (unrep.) ("R/A"—return to acceptor of bill of exchange (a trader)—defamatory); *Frost* v. *London Joint Stock Bank Ltd.* (1906) 22 T.L.R. 760 (slip attached to unpaid cheque saying "Reason assigned" with handwritten words "not stated," not defamatory unless ordinary persons would so understand it. These cases are discussed in Paget, 241–243, though with no clear conclusion.
[58] See Holden, Vol. 1, 2–152.

unjustified). If a mistake is made, the damages will be reduced if there is a prompt and effusive apology to the customer and, more importantly, if the payee or his banker can be contacted, and the mistake explained so that no blame rests upon the customer.

The damages, in defamation, are either "special" losses flowing directly from the defamatory statement (*e.g.* the customer loses a contract with the payee) or are "general" (*i.e.* an amount needed to compensate the customer for loss to his reputation). The amount of damages is a jury question, but (whether in contract, or in tort) the damage to the customer's reputation will be the greater the smaller the cheque is, not the larger it is.[59]

In the case of contract, (tried by a judge, unless there is also a libel claim, **6.22** in which there may be application for a jury)[60] what the customer may recover depends on his losses, which will depend partly on who he is. In contract, those losses are recoverable which are of a sort which were foreseeable to the banker as likely to occur at the time the contract was entered. Because the matter is judged at the time of entry into the contract, the normal domestic (private) customer would find the proof of such losses difficult, and would generally recover only nominal damages for injury to his reputation, unless he can prove special circumstances of which the banker knew when the contract was entered ("special damage"). A trading customer, however, may recover greater ("substantial") damages for loss of proof to his reputation, this being a loss foreseeable when he opened the account.[61] But of course, the non–trader may sue in defamation, where this principle does not apply.

B. Bank's duty to obey countermand

The converse of the duty to honour a valid demand or mandate is the bank's **6.23** obligation to obey a countermand. Except in unusual cases[62] the authority of any agent may be revoked by his principal, even if the principal has agreed not to do this. When a bank pays on a cheque or other bill, it pays as agent for its customer, and its authority may be revoked by the customer-principal.[63] The customer's revocation of authority is generally referred to as a "countermand," but may be referred to as a "stop." If the bank disobeys the countermand, and pays on a stopped cheque, it would not strictly "incur" liability to the customer (unless it then dishonours other cheques on the ground of insufficiency of funds). Rather, it has no authority to debit his account for the payment thus made,[64] and the customer incurs no liability to the bank unless it pays on his mandate. If, however, the bank wrongly pays, it would (as any unauthorised agent) be subrogated[65] to the cus-

---

[59] *Marzetti* v. *Williams* (1830) 1 B. & Ad. 415: this is quite logical, though at first sight it seems odd.
[60] s.6(1), Administration of Justice Act 1933.
[61] See *Evans* v. *London and Provincial Bank* (1917) *The Times*, March 1; *Cox* v. *Cox & Co.* (1921) *The Times*, March 18; *Gibbons* v. *Westminster Bank Ltd.* [1939] 2 K.B. 882 (all on domestic customers.); *Wilson* v. *United Counties Bank Ltd.* [1920] A.C. 102; *Rolin* v. *Steward* (1854) 14 C.B. 595 (traders).
[62] *e.g.* for an irrevocable power given under the Powers of Attorney Act 1971 and in some cases under the Enduring Powers of Attorney Act 1985.
[63] This is stated in s.75 of the Bills of Exchange Act 1882.
[64] *Twibell* v. *London Suburban Bank* [1869] W.N. 127, and the cases discussed below, Chap. 7.
[65] See below, Chap. 14.

tomer's rights, if any, against the payee, and in many cases it may recover from the payee the money paid, as money paid by mistake of fact.[66]

Where persons have joint or joint and several liability, and their mandate to the bank allows for less than all to draw cheques (as may be the case in a partnership, or between trustees) and a cheque is drawn by one or more, any of the others may countermand the cheque.[67]

In order to be effective, the following conditions must apply to countermands: First, the bank, through its servants, must acually know of the notice of countermand, and constructive notice (arising by virtue of negligence) does not apply. In *Curtice* v. *London City and Midland Bank Ltd.*[68] the stop notice (in a telegram) was put into the bank's mailbox, but not picked up with the rest of the mail, and not read by any of the bank's staff until after the cheque in question had been paid. The plaintiff then drew a cheque for the whole of what he claimed to be the balance of his account, ignoring the debit, and when this was dishonoured he sued in debt.[69] It was clear that the bank had been negligent, and a question rose as to constructive notice. The court held that "There is no such thing as a constructive countermand in a commercial transaction of this kind"[70] and gave judgment for the bank. The court added that the bank might be liable in damages,[71] though the measure of damages might not be the same as in debt.

6.24   Secondly, as the banker has a duty to honour cheques if there are sufficient funds, etc., he is at risk if he obeys an unauthenticated notice, which may not be his principal's revocation. In the *Curtice* case, the court agreed that the bank was not bound to obey an unauthenticated telegram. Cozens-Hardy M.R. said, however, that the telegram might "reasonably and in the ordinary course of business, be acted upon by the bank, at least to the extent of postponing the honouring of the cheque until further inquiry can be made."[72] The same presumably applies to telephone stops. In cases like these, therefore, the bank may delay, and may mark cheques "Unconfirmed stop received," which is true and not defamatory if it should turn out that the stop is unauthorised. Generally banks will, and they certainly should, insist upon the customer's signed stop by following mail.

Thirdly, the stop must be sent to the branch at which the account is kept, and a stop delivered to another branch may be ignored by the bank.[73]

6.25   Fourthly, "an order must be unambiguous. If a master chooses to give an order to his servant that bears two meanings, he cannot find fault with his servant for having taken the meaning which it was not in fact intended to bear."[74] Thus, in *Westminster Bank Ltd.* v. *Hilton*[75] the plaintiff wired a stop order in respect of a post-dated cheque, giving the wrong cheque number, with the name of the payee and the amount of the cheque he wanted

---

[66] See below, Chap. 11.
[67] *Gaunt* v. *Taylor* (1843) 2 Hare 413 (partners).
[68] [1908] 1 K.B. 293.
[69] *i.e.* for money had and received.
[70] *Per* Cozens-Hardy M.R. at 298.
[71] *i.e.* in a contractual action, tortious ones being ruled out by *Tai Hing Cotton Mill Ltd.* v. *Liu Chong Hing Bank Ltd.* [1985] 2 All E.R. 947 (JC) [1986] A.C. 80, 519.
[72] [1908] 1 K.B. 293, 298.
[73] *London Provincial and South-Western Bank Ltd.* v. *Buszard* (1918) 35 T.L.R. 142. Contrast *Burnett* v. *Westminster Bank Ltd.* [1966] 1 Q.B. 742, discussed above, para. 6.09.
[74] *Per* Fletcher Moulton L.J. in *Curtice* v. *London City and Midland Bank Ltd.* [1908] 1 K.B. 293, 299.
[75] (1926) 43 T.L.R. 124.

stopped. The cheque with the number he gave had already been paid. When the payee presented the cheque which should have been stopped the bank assumed from the difference in number and from the date on the cheque (which was, it must be stressed, post-dated) that it was a replacement cheque, and paid it. The customer sued in negligence. The House of Lords, overruling the Court of Appeal, held that the bank had not been negligent, and was not liable. Lord Shaw[76] referred to the bank's conflicting duties: to pay, and to obey countermands. Given that possible conflict, the customer had to show that the stop reached the bank in time, and that the stop "was unequivocally referable to a cheque then in existence, and signed and issued by the customer before the notice to stop." If the cheque was dated after the date of stoppage, the bank might assume that the notice did not apply to it, unless the contrary was clearly brought home to it.

Fifthly, the customer must not have agreed not to countermand. This is done in respect of cheque cards, for example. The precise extent of this principle is unclear. It may be (on general agency principles) that the countermand is still an effective withdrawal of the bank's authority to pay, though the customer may be liable to the bank for damages for breach of contract, the amount of the damages being equal to the bank's loss if by reason of the breach it has no mandate to debit the account. Alternatively, it is possible that the use of the card constitutes a collateral contract between bank and payee, the bank being bound from the moment the cheque is drawn and delivered to the payee in reliance on the card, and the customer being under an obligation, from that moment, to indemnify the bank. If this is the case, the customer would have no right to order the bank not to pay, for in paying it is not carrying out his mandate but its own independent obligation to the payee, for which the customer has a contractual duty to indemnify the bank. Clearly the bank's reputation, and the whole convenient system of cheque cards would be in jeopardy if banks did obey countermands of such cheques, and it is inconceivable that they would be held liable to compensate the customer.

6.26

Sixthly, the countermand must be given to the bank before payment of the cheque, and presumably within a reasonable time before presentation for payment, so as to allow for communication of the stop to the appropriate staff within the branch in question. Except in the obvious case of payment of cash over the counter[77] difficult questions may arise as to when "payment" occurs for this purpose, and it may depend upon whether in the light of a given bank's administrative and technical procedures, or the procedures of the clearing system, an irrevocable process has been put in hand, whereby the payee is allowed to draw upon a credit, or a collecting bank is notified of the credit.[78]

Finally, the drawer (the bank's mandator) alone has power to countermand, but if the payee or holder of the cheque informs the bank that it has been lost or stolen, it is thought that the bank should seek the drawer's instructions, and refuse payment in the meantime (without good reason to the contrary) for if it makes payment without inquiry in these circumstances, it may not be in the ordinary course of business (or may be negli-

6.27

---

[76] At pp. 129–130.

[77] On an uncrossed cheque, or one specially presented.

[78] An extremely interesting case is *Momm* v. *Barclays Bank International Ltd.* [1977] 1 Q.B. 790. For general discussion, see Goode, *Payment Obligations in Commercial and Financial Transactions*.

gence) so that the bank is deprived of statutory protection[79] if it pays the wrong person.

C. Bank's duty to act upon notice of death

6.28　As with a countermand, notice of a customer's death revokes the bank's duty and authority to pay.[80] The notice must be actual, and not constructive, and must be more than a mere rumour, but a report from a reliable source (such as a newspaper, or relatives) should be acted upon. Banks may ask for sight of a copy of the death certificate, for noting in their records.

The effect of death on joint accounts[81] is considered elsewhere.

D. Bank's closing hours

6.29　The customer may demand repayment when the bank is open, and his countermands are effective if received then. When is a bank obliged to be open for the purpose? There are some statutory bank holidays, determined by the Banking and Financial Dealings Act 1971. Otherwise, opening hours may be determined by express agreement or by custom (acting so as to imply a term into the contract). General changes affecting all the clearing banks have in the past been made by notice given by the Committee of London Clearing Bankers.

Where a bank is bound to open at a certain time it may unilaterally extend opening hours (some banks thus open on Saturdays, though perhaps for limited purposes) and whether this becomes a term of the contract depends on what is expressly said. The extension of time could, in any case, be reversed by giving notice. A particular problem in extending opening hours is that banks are protected under section 60 of the Bills of Exchange Act 1882, or section 1 of the Cheques Act 1957 if they pay in the "ordinary course of business." Payment after advertised hours is not "ordinary" but there is a question whether the bank cannot by public advertisement extend hours so that for it the hours are then "ordinary." Payment within a reasonable time of advertised closing hours may be ordinary, for people may still be in the building, and so on. In *Baines* v. *National Provincial Bank Ltd.*[82] payment 5 minutes late was held to be acceptable.

---

[79] Under B.O.E. Act 1882, ss.60 or 80, or maybe s.1 of the Cheques Act 1957.
[80] s.75, B.O.E. Act 1882.
[81] Below, Chap. 12.
[82] (1927) 96 L.J.K.B. 801.

7. Paying Bank and Customer: Liability for Unauthorised Debits

Debits may happen by mistake, but much of this chapter concerns the liability of the bank for forgeries.

A. Duty to tell customer when forgeries discovered

In *Greenwood* v. *Martins's Bank*[1] it was said that the bank must inform the **7.01** customer if the bank becomes aware that forged cheques are being presented for payment. The duty is hypothetical not only in the sense that one can hardly imagine a bank failing to take appropriate action, but also in the sense that the question may equally be dealt with as a question of absence of mandate to debit the customer's account (whether it knows of the forgery, or not). Suppose, however, that the bank does not inform the customer and the forger defrauds the customer in some other business, unconnected with the bank. If there is a duty to inform, then failure to do so may make the bank liable in damages for losses elsewhere which might otherwise have been prevented.[2]

B. Liability for unauthorised debits

We have examined the bank's positive duty to observe its mandate and thus **7.02** to pay on cheques properly drawn.[3] The converse question is, when a bank pays the wrong person, or pays after a forgery, and so on, whether it may debit the customer's account in respect of the payment. The bank's mandate permits it to debit the customer's account where it has the customer's authority to do so. Bank mandate forms generally entitle the bank to pay on an authorised signature, and this has the effect of excluding implied authority. Thus, the only forms of authority justifying debits may be express actual authority (as where a cheque is received) or ostensible authority (that is, authority by estoppel). The dual nature of a cheque as bill of exchange and as mandate must be recalled here. One question is whether, where A is payee, and the bank pays the wrong person B (say, after a forged indorsement), the bank is liable to the true owner, A, for converting his bill. The other question (examined here) is whether, by paying B, the bank can debit its customer's account, and this arises whether or not it is liable to the true owner.

1. DRAWER'S FORGED SIGNATURE

Forgery may be of other details than the drawer's signature (*e.g.* the **7.03** amount)[4] but as the same principles generally apply, we shall tend to speak of signatures. Section 24 of the Bills of Exchange Act 1882 deals with forgeries, and unauthorised signatures, whether of drawer, indorser or others. The section is aimed primarily at the bill in its function as negotiable instru-

---

[1] [1933] A.C. 51, [1932] 1 K.B. 371, 381, see para. 7.15.
[2] The reverse of the situation in the *Greenwood* case.
[3] Above, Chap. 6.
[4] As in *London Joint Stock Bank Ltd.* v. *Macmillan and Arthur* [1918] A.C. 777.

ment, rather than as mandate, and applies whoever the drawee is, whether banker or not. According to section 24, the forged or unauthorised signature is "wholly inoperative" and confers no rights, in the absence of an estoppel. There is a proviso "that nothing in this section shall affect the ratification of an unauthorised signature not amounting to forgery." This suggests that forgeries cannot be ratified,[5] and if this is the case, it is a reason for distinguishing forgeries from unauthorised signatures.[6] It has been said[6a] that the "indoor management" rule in *Turquand's* case[7] does not apply to forgeries. That rule is that where there is a holding out, a company may not deny its officer's ostensible authority on the ground of matters contained in the Articles (about which everyone was supposed to know) if the matter is "procedural." On examination, the cases merely say that a company officer's own fraud cannot amount to a holding out of his authority by the company, and that *Turquand's* rule does not confer ostensible authority without a holding out. Forgery, as such, really has nothing to do with the matter, and it would not matter whether the officer was dishonestly fraudulent, or merely foolish, or even if he reasonably believed that he had authority.[8] Thus, apart from the question of ratification, there seems to be little reason to distinguish a case of a forgery from an unauthorised signature.[9] It seems difficult to distinguish forgery of a signature from an unauthorised signature (for banking purposes, at any rate) except by the introduction of a concept of dishonesty. If a forgery cannot be ratified, it must be because of a notion of public policy, which frowns on the ratification of a dishonest act. If one ignores the dishonesty of the act, then all that one need ask is whether a person has authority, (actual or ostensible) or not. If he has ostensible authority, his principal is bound. If he has not even ostensible authority, and signs or alters a cheque, it matters not for the civil law whether he is a forger, except where public policy intervenes (and there can be no sensible concern for mere lack of authority, but only for dishonesty). For the purposes of ratification, therefore, the principle may be simply that no dishonest act can be ratified, and forgery may consequently be defined sufficiently for present purposes as an unauthorised and dishonest act involving signature, addition to, or alteration of a bill or cheque or contract, done with intent to persuade someone else to accept it as genuine.

7.04   Considering the cheque or bill as mandate, rather than negotiable instrument, it is obvious that a forged drawer's signature cannot amount to express actual authority.[10] There is no statutory protection given to a bank for paying without its customer's (drawer's) authority, but the bank is protected if the signatory has ostensible authority to sign (*i.e.* if estoppel operates at the time of signature), or by the operation (subsequent to the signature) of estoppel. Estoppel is considered shortly.

---

[5] So stated in *M'Kenzie* v. *British Linen Co.* (1881) 6 App.Cas. 82.

[6] See further, to the same effect, *Morison* v. *London County and Westminster Bank Ltd.* [1914] 3 K.B. 356.

[6a] *Ruben and Ladenburg* v. *Great Fingall Consolidated* [1906] A.C. 439, 443; *Kreditbank Cassel GmbH Ltd.* v. *Schenkers* [1927] 1 K.B. 826, 835.

[7] *Royal British Bank* v. *Turquand* (1856) 6 E. & B. 327.

[8] But see Paget, 43–44, and 379–380.

[9] See the long discussion in Paget, 376–380.

[10] The proposition hardly needs authority, but see, *e.g.* *Greenwood* v. *Martin's Bank Ltd.* [1933] A.C. 51.

2. INDORSEMENT FORGED OR UNAUTHORISED

Similarly, if a bill is payable to a named payee or order, the bank has no
mandate to pay anyone else, and if it did so, it could not debit its customer's
account. This was clearly established in *Robarts* v. *Tucker*[11] and is now
stated in section 24 of the Bills of Exchange Act 1882. Here, however, the
bank has certain statutory protections,[12] which are discussed below.

7.05

3. DRAWER'S AGENT LACKS AUTHORITY

In the same way as with a forgery, the drawer-customer is not liable if an
agent of the customer exceeds his authority (actual, and ostensible).[13]
Again, there is no statutory protection, but if the person who signs is
known to be an agent and purports to sign as such, and the bank's mandate
permits it to honour his signature, there is actual or ostensible authority.
Actual authority may, however, have implied limitations, and the ostensible authority may at the same time be removed if the circumstances are
such as to place the bank "on inquiry." That is, if the bank is negligent in
failing to realise that the agent is exceeding his authority (for example,
where the principal's cheques are paid into the agent's private account) there
will be no ostensible authority (no estoppel).[14] Exactly the same principles
apply to a collecting banker: if sued in conversion by the true owner, ostensible authority of an agent is a defence, though negligence would remove
ostensible authority.[15] It is sometimes said, though unnecessarily, that the
bank has constructive notice of lack of authority: it is simpler to say that
there is no ostensible authority.

7.06

If the defendant bank is negligent so that it cannot rely on ostensible authority (based on estoppel) it cannot attempt to resurrect an estoppel by a
counter-assertion of negligence on the part of the plaintiff. Estoppel operates if there is (a) a statement of fact (or an omission to speak, where there is
a duty), (b) reliance upon the statement (or its omission) and (c) the person
relying suffers detriment from his reliance, or the circumstances are such
that it is inequitable to allow the other party to go back on what he has said
(or omitted to say). Initially, therefore, there must be a statement by the
customer, or a duty to speak. It is established clearly[16] in respect of both
agents[17] and employees[18] that the customer has no duty to his bank to
supervise his agents or employees, and that his failure to do so, however
careless it may be, gives rise to no liability in respect of his bank. There
were, in this context, dicta in *Morison* v. *London County and Westminster Bank
Ltd.*[19] which suggested the contrary. In that case, M's employee or agent

7.07

[11] (1851) 16 Q.B. 560; see also *Bank of England* v. *Vagliano Bros.* [1891] A.C. 107.
[12] Under the Bills of Exchange Act, ss.7(3), 59–60, 79–80, and the Cheques Act 1957, s.1.
[13] For an example, see *Lloyds Bank Ltd.* v. *Chartered Bank of India, Australia and China* (1928) 44
T.L.R. 534, [1929] 1 K.B. 40.
[14] *Ibid.*
[15] See, *e.g. Australia and New Zealand Bank Ltd.* v. *Ateliers de Construction Electriques de Charleroi*
[1967] 1 A.C. 86, [1966] 2 W.L.R. 1216 (said to be a case of implied authority, in which case
negligence could not affect the bank, but in fact a case of ostensible authority.); *Midland Bank
Ltd.* v. *Reckitt and Others* [1933] A.C. 1; *Reckitt* v. *Barnett, Pembroke and Slater Ltd.* [1929]
A.C. 176.
[16] Though see Paget, 393, 394.
[17] *Lloyds Bank Ltd.* v. *Chartered Bank of India, Australia and China* above, n. 13.
[18] *Tai Hing Cotton Mill Ltd.* v. *Liu Chong Hing Bank Ltd.* [1985] 2 All E.R. 947 (JC) [1986] A.C.
519, following *London Joint Stock Bank Ltd.* v. *Macmillan and Arthur* [1918] A.C. 777.
[19] [1914] 3 K.B. 356.

(the manager of a business) had authority to draw cheques for M's business, but he did so for his own purposes, paying the cheques into his own bank account. The frauds had gone on for a long while, and some or all were known to the plaintiff or his auditors. Indeed, an arrangement had been reached concerning some of the frauds and the employee was not dismissed despite his actions. Judgment was given for the bank, and according to Buckley L.J. "The position . . . was such that any suspicion [the bank] ought to have had would have been lulled to sleep by the action of Morison himself." This phrase "lulled to sleep" was seized on in subsequent cases by counsel defending banks, as a ground for an argument that negligence gave rise to an estoppel against the customer. But the argument was always rejected[20] and should now be regarded as unsustainable.[20a]

The position then, is that the bank may be protected if the agent (or employee) has an apparent mandate to sign, but that if the circumstances are suspicious (if the bank is negligent in not making inquiries) the agent's ostensible authority is removed, and though it may be restored by the operation of estoppel, estoppel will not operate merely because the employer or principal is negligent, but only from his statement or breach of duty. We have remarked already that this position may have to do with the "all or nothing effect" of estoppel, which would entirely debar the plaintiff's claim, and that a more satisfactory solution would involve the apportionment of the loss according to the degree of blame (*i.e.* a system of contributory negligence).[21]

4. INCHOATE INSTRUMENTS AND STATUTORY ESTOPPEL

7.08   Section 20 of the Bills of Exchange Act 1882 provides that where a simple signature on a blank paper is delivered by the signer, so that it may be converted into a bill, this operates as a prima facie authority to fill it up as a complete bill, for any amount, and the signer may be treated as drawer, acceptor or indorser. The same prima facie authority is given to the possessor of a bill wanting in any material particular.[22] The missing details must be filled up within a reasonable time, and "strictly in accordance with the authority given," but it is provided that this does not affect a holder in due course to whom the instrument is negotiated after completion.

This last provision is a form of statutory estoppel, enabling a "holder in due course" to sue a signatory even if the agent to whom the signatory gave the bill for completion exceeds his authority. This form of estoppel is not dependent on negligence or breach of duty or fault.[23] The provisions of section 29 of the 1882 Act apply to the holder in due course, so that (*inter alia*)

[20] In addition to the cases above (*Australia, Tai Hing, Macmillan*) see *Carpenter's Company* v. *British Mutual Banking Co. Ltd.* [1938] 1 K.B. 511; *A. L. Underwood Ltd.* v. *Bank of Liverpool and Martins* [1924] 1 K.B. 775; *Brewer* v. *Westminster Bank Ltd.* [1952] 2 All E.R. 650; (for cases before the Morison decision see, *e.g. Bank of Ireland* v. *Trustees of Evans' Charities in Ireland* (1855) 5 H.L.Cas. 389; *Swan* v. *North British Australasian Company* (1863) 10 Jur.(N.S.) 102 (though see *Re North British Australasian Company, ex p. Swan* (1860) 7 C.B. N.S. 400, 442, 447); *Vagliano Bros.* v. *Bank of England* [1891] A.C. 107, 115; *Farquharson Bros. & Co.* v. *King & Co.* [1902] A.C. 325; *Lewes Sanitary Steam Laundry Co. Ltd.* v. *Barclay & Co. Ltd.* (1906) 11 Com.Cas. 255; *Kepitigalla Rubber Estates Ltd.* v. *National Bank of India Ltd.* [1909] 2 K.B. 1010.
[20a] After the *Tai Hing* case, above, n. 18.
[21] Above, para. 3.18.
[22] *e.g.* the drawer may fill in his own name as the payee, if authorised to do so by agreement with the drawee: *Gerald Macdonald & Co.* v. *Nash & Co.* [1924] A.C. 625.
[23] *Barker* v. *Sterne* (1854) 9 Exch. 684, 687.

obviously there must be nothing suspicious on the face of the bill, and a holder in due course (unlike a mere holder for value under section 27 of the Act) must himself give value. One difficulty with section 20 is that the original named payee on a cheque cannot be holder in due course because it has been held that section 29 requires the bill to be "negotiated to"[24] a holder in due course, and this is not the case with the original named payee.[25] Clearly, the paying banker is rarely a holder in due course, though the collecting bank may be if the customer is overdrawn when the cheque is paid in.[26] In addition to that limitation, section 20 contemplates a bill which the signer knows to be incohate, and delivers "in order that it may be converted into a bill." It would not apply if, for example, the signer was merely in a hurry, and did not notice that what he signed was incomplete.[27] A further limitation applies to incomplete crossed cheques with the words "not negotiable" on them, for a holder of these takes subject to defects in the authority of anyone who completes the cheques.[28] But if the special statutory estoppel does not apply, the common law principles may, and they apply to others (such as the payee) than the holder in due course.[29] These common law principles also apply even if an incomplete bill is not delivered with the purpose mentioned in section 20.

5. MATERIAL ALTERATIONS: PAYMENT OF WRONG AMOUNT

Section 64 of the 1882 Act provides that any material alteration to a bill **7.09** made without the assent of all parties liable on it has the effect of avoiding the bill, except as against a party who has made, authorised or assented to the alteration, and subsequent indorsers.[30] But this does not affect a holder in due course, where the alteration is not apparent[31] and he may enforce payment of the bill according to its "original tenor." If, for example, the amount was altered by someone other than the drawer, the holder in due course may sue the drawer for the original amount, and could sue anyone who made the alteration or any subsequent indorser for the full (changed) amount.

As with section 20, the special protection given by this section applies only to the holder in due course, and the section is no protection for the paying banker unless he pays the correct (original) amount to a holder in due course. If he pays the wrong amount, he is certainly liable for the excess to his customer, the drawer, whose mandate was for the original amount.

[24] See s.29(1)(b).
[25] *R. E. Jones Ltd.* v. *Waring and Gillow Ltd.* [1926] A.C. 670.
[26] *Re Keever* [1967] Ch. 182: this can be so even if an order cheque is not indorsed to the bank: s.2, Cheques Act 1957.
[27] See *Smith* v. *Prosser* [1907] 2 K.B. 735 (handed over for safekeeping).
[28] s.81, B.O.E. Act 1882.
[29] *Lloyds Bank Ltd.* v. *Cooke* [1907] 1 K.B. 794; *London Joint Stock Bank* v. *Macmillan and Arthur* [1918] A.C. 777.
[30] Material alterations include: alteration of the sum payable; the date; the time of payment; the place of payment; adding a place of payment on a bill accepted generally, without the acceptor's consent; changing an inland bill into a foreign one; indorsing a particular rate of exchange not originally authorised by the bill; substituting a particular consideration, for the words "value received"; varying the rate of interest. See *Flanagan* v. *National Bank Ltd.* (1938) 72 ILT 63 (not a material alteration invalidating a promissory note to add signature after completion and issue of note: *Gardner* v. *Walsh* (1855) 5 E. & B. 83, followed); *Re Smith, ex p. Yates* (1857) 2 De G. & J. 191 (additional signature acts as indorsement).
[31] *i.e.* if it is of such a kind that it would be observed and noticed by an intending holder scrutinising it with reasonable care: *Woollatt* v. *Stanley* (1928) 138 L.T. 620.

The question arises, however, whether a banker has any mandate at all to pay any amount to someone who is not a holder in due course, when the drawer has not consented to the material alteration. While it is clear that under section 64 the bill is "avoided," this may mean, "as a bill of exchange" but not "as a mandate," or it may mean both. The cases generally suggest the latter, on the ground that the effect of the instrument is wholly changed by any material alteration, and becomes a different note.[32] If this is the case, then a bank has no mandate to pay any sum at all, other than to a holder in due course, following a material alteration to which the customer (drawer) has not assented.

It would seem that, like section 20, section 64 has, as between banker and customer, been affected by developments in the general common law of estoppel.

6. ESTOPPEL AT COMMON LAW

7.10 Estoppel may protect the bank from its customer's claim for breach of mandate, whether the claim arises from a forged or unauthorised drawer's signature, or a forged, unauthorised, missing or irregular indorsement. Where an indorsement is concerned, estoppel of the drawer will be rare, because the cheque generally leaves the drawer's possession before the indorsement is placed upon it, and the drawer is not responsible for it.[33] Generally, therefore, estoppel arises between bank and drawer (customer) in relation to the drawer's signature, his agent's authority, or in relation to alterations to the original details of cheques. Estoppel requires either a statement by the customer, or a duty to speak.

a. Misleading Statements

7.11 If the bank, suspecting an irregularity, asks the customer to confirm that all is well, and the customer does so, and the bank pays, then one may regard this confirmation either as a mandate to pay, or as a ratification, or one may say that an estoppel will arise in relation to the lack of authority.[34] An estoppel may affect cheques already drawn (on the ground of prejudice in catching, or suing and recovering from, the forger), and those to be drawn in the future (the prejudice being, obviously, that the bank pays them and increases its losses). In *Brown* v. *Westminster Bank Ltd.*[35] the customer was an elderly lady whose servant, C, had forged a number of cheques payable to himself. The bank noticed this, and drew her attention to the fact. At first, she said she frequently asked C to cash cheques for her. On other occasions, she did not deny drawing the cheques herself. Eventually, the bank became so concerned that a branch manager (the second at the branch in question to be concerned about the position) discussed the matter with the customer's

---

[32] See, *e.g. Master* v. *Miller* (1791) 4 T.R. 320, 5 T.R. 367; *Knill* v. *Williams* (1809) 10 East 431; *Hall* v. *Fuller* (1826) 5 B. & C. 750, 757; *Simmons* v. *Taylor* (1857) 2 C.B.N.S. 528, 539, 541, aff'd (1858) 4 C.B.N.S. 463; *Suffell* v. *Bank of England* (1882) 9 Q.B.D. 555. Contrast *Henfree* v. *Bromley* (1805) 6 East 309, and *Imperial Bank of Canada* v. *Bank of Hamilton* [1903] A.C. 49 (JC), where it was held that raised cheques were a mandate for the original sum (but the former case may be applicable only to holders in due course, and in the latter, the point was not in issue).

[33] But, of course, there are statutory defences mentioned above, para. 7.05 and dealt with below, Chap. 8.

[34] See *Vagliano Bros.* v. *Bank of England* [1891] A.C. 107, 114, 123.

[35] [1964] 2 Lloyds Rep. 187; followed in *Tina Motors Pty. Ltd.* v. *Australia and New Zealand Banking Group Ltd.* [1977] V.R. 205.

son (who held a power of attorney). He responded by suing the bank in respect of 329 forged cheques. The court exonerated the bank, holding that the customer was estopped from denying that the cheques were genuine, even in respect of cheques drawn before the bank first made inquiry (the bank relied on her statements, and accordingly took no action against C).

It seems clear that this principle would apply not only to forged signa- **7.12** tures, but to other forgeries or to material alterations. If, say, there is a material alteration of the amount payable, and the bank pays any sum to the original named payee (who is not a holder in due course) the bank would be liable. But if it queried the amount, and was reassured, it would have an ostensible mandate to pay (if reassured before paying) or an estoppel could subsequently arise (if reassured after paying).

It should be added that where an agent does not forge cheques, but acts outside his actual or ostensible authority (perhaps inadvertently) the principal may ratify, and a simple statement to that effect, or unequivocal behaviour indicating an intention to do so, will suffice, provided that the principal, through the agent or otherwise, has received valuable consideration.[36] There is then no need to prove reliance by the bank, or detriment, etc.[37] But ratification is impossible in some cases, of which, perhaps, forgery is one.[38] Again, an undisclosed principal cannot ratify.[39] In these cases, estoppel may be relied upon as an alternative, provided that in addition to the "ratification" there can be shown reliance, and detriment, etc.[40]

b. Estoppel arising from Duties owed by the Customer

Duties owed by the customer to his bank may also give rise to an estoppel, **7.13** and two such duties appear to be established (there may, perhaps, be more). Estoppel is a concept based on fault, and fault may be shown either by a representation, or by non-performance of a duty. The performance of the duty by the customer would enable the bank to avoid future losses, and perhaps to recover past losses from the forger. Non-performance by the customer of his duty may cause loss to the banker.

(i) Duty to tell of known forgeries. First, there is a duty to inform the **7.14** drawee bank of any known forgeries, whether in the signature or in other matters relating to the bill. This applies to anyone (customer, or not, and whether drawer, acceptor, indorser) who knows that his name (or some other detail in respect of which he has some liability) has been forged on a bill or cheque.[41] This is the true explanation of *Morison* v. *London County and Westminster Bank Ltd.*[42] to which reference has been made. It was clear that at a certain time, the employer (or his other agents, some auditors)

---

[36] *Per* Lord Tomlin in *Greenwood* v. *Martin's Bank Ltd.* [1933] A.C. 51, 57 "adoption, as understood in English law, requires valuable consideration." But it is thought that if consideration has moved from the payee of the cheque, that is sufficient, even if never actually received by the principal because of his fraudulent agent's act.

[37] For an example, see *London Intercontinental Trust Ltd.* v. *Barclays Bank Ltd.* [1980] 1 Lloyd's Rep. 241 (two directors should have signed, but only one did. The company ratified this).

[38] See para. 7.03 above.

[39] Below, para. 15.08.

[40] For an example of this, see *Spiro* v. *Lintern* [1973] 3 All E.R. 319.

[41] See *M'Kenzie* v. *British Linen Co.* (1881) 6 App.Cas. 82, 92, 101, 109; *Ogilvie* v. *West Australian Mortgage and Agency Corpn. Ltd.* [1896] A.C. 257, 270; *William Ewing & Co.* v. *Dominion Bank* [1904] A.C. 806. Paget, 393 (and 394, referring to the M'Kenzie case) says the duty exists if a person "has reasonable ground for believing that his name has been forged" but it is submitted that this clearly is not the case.

[42] [1914] 3 K.B. 356, above para. 7.07.

became aware of his employees forgeries. They did not inform the bank, and the forgeries continued. The bank was not liable for the debits. Knowing of the forgery, the customer had a duty to speak, and omitted to do so. In reliance on that the bank continued the account, and took no action against the employee. The customer, therefore, was estopped. The estoppel here did not give rise to ostensible authority at the time the agent or employee did the acts in question because there were suspicious circumstnaces which should have put the bank on inquiry. Rather, an estoppel subsequently arose from the customer's breach of duty, which might have caused the bank loss.

7.15   The (true) principle of *Morison*'s case is firmly established by *Greenwood* v. *Martin's Bank Ltd.*[43] where the customer's wife forged cheques on his account. He discovered this, but she gave him a false explanation, and refrained from informing the bank. Eight months later he discovered that the explanation was false, and said he would tell the bank. The wife committed suicide. The husband thereupon sued the bank in respect of the debits, but was held to be estopped from so doing, for he had a duty to speak. Ordinarily, if the bank itself was negligent in paying, no estoppel could arise, because the loss would be caused by the bank's actions, and not through the customer's fault. But here (as in *Morison*'s case) the bank was found to be negligent in paying. The House of Lords found, however, that though the cause of the original loss was the bank's negligence, the cause of the non-recovery from the forger (or inability to attempt recovery) was that the customer failed in his duty to inform the bank of the forgery. The same would apply to an unauthorised agent (as in *Morison*'s case). Lack of initial ostensible authority (because of the bank's negligence) meant in *Morison*'s case that the bank was the cause of its own original loss in paying. But the estoppel arose in the bank's favour because it lost the chance to proceed against the employee and to recover the money or prevent him from committing later frauds.[44] Even if the forger can still be sued, the bank has lost time, and perhaps the frauds would have increased to the extent that the forger can no longer repay, if caught, or he may have removed property, or himself, from the jurisdiction, and so on.[45] While one can comprehend the reasoning used, the idea of a type of negligence on both sides, first defeating estoppel and then resurrecting it, is a peculiar concept, and it is submitted that the introduction of contributory negligence would be more conceptually satisfying, and, since it allows for the apportionment of blame, more just.

There are dicta which suggest that a person may have a duty to inform the bank of forgeries of which they ought to know[46] but it is submitted that this is now insupportable, and it seems clear that only actual notice will suffice.[47]

---

[43] [1933] A.C. 51.

[44] See *Fung Kai Sun* v. *Chang Fui Hing* [1951] A.C. 489.

[45] Although some kind of prejudice to the bank or inequitable behaviour by the customer is generally required for estoppel—see *M'Kenzie* v. *British Linen Co.* (1881) 6 App.Cas. 82, 109, 111, 112; *Pacol Ltd.* v. *Trade Lines Ltd.*, [1982] 1 Lloyds Rep. 456—it does not matter that proceedings against the forger would not recover the money, if, say, he is bankrupt, or dead. See cases at n. 41 above (*M'Kenzie, Ogilvie, Ewing*). Contra, *Imperial Bank of Canada* v. *Bank of Hamilton* [1903] A.C. 49, 57.

[46] *M'Kenzie* v. *British Linen Co.* (1881) 6 App.Cas. 82, 92; *Morison* v. *London County and Westminster Bank Ltd.* [1914] 3 K.B. 356, *per* Buckley L.J. See also Paget, 393, 394.

[47] Below, para. 7.20.

(ii) Duty to draw cheques carefully. A second duty which the customer **7.16** owes to his bank, capable of giving rise to an estoppel, is the duty to draw cheques so as not to facilitate fraud. In *Young* v. *Grote*[48] a customer was held liable for the loss when he left blank signed cheques with his wife, who passed one to a clerk, who fraudulently altered the details on the cheque. This principle was accepted in *London Joint Stock Bank* v. *Macmillan and Arthur.*[49] Here, the customer was a partnership, and an employee had the task of filling in details of cheques and presenting them to partners for signature. One such cheque had no words and only the figures "2.0.0." A partner signed this, and the clerk thereafter filled in the words "one hundred and twenty pounds" and amended the figures to read "120.0.0." He presented the cheque and was paid in cash. The customer sued the bank over the debit. The House of Lords held the customer estopped, but denied any general duty in a customer to avoid negligent harm to his bank. The negligence, it was held, had to be "in the transaction itself, that is, in the manner in which the cheque is drawn."[50] The bank could not have been liable, for example, for negligence in employing the clerk, and (as recently reaffirmed in *Tai Hing Cotton Mill Ltd.* v. *Liu Chong Hing Bank Ltd.*)[51] negligence in the way the business is organised is insufficient to raise an estoppel. But the customer was bound to exercise reasonable care in drawing the cheque, so as to prevent the banker being misled. He must not, in drawing the cheque, facilitate fraud. If the cheque is drawn so as to "almost invite an increase in the amount by forgery if the cheque should get into the hands of a dishonest person, forgery is not a remote but a very natural consequence of negligence of this description."[52] It is clear that the House took the view that the customer was grossly negligent. But it is clear from *Tai Hing Cotton Mill Ltd.* v. *Liu Chong Hing Bank Ltd.*[53] that gross negligence outside of the manner in which the cheque is drawn is no defence to the bank. The trouble is that negligence is a matter of degree, ranging from the trivial to the gross. If a duty is admitted for any negligence, then the customer would hardly ever have any remedy because estoppel bars the whole action. It may have been this difficulty in drawing a line between degrees of negligence[54] which led the House to draw a line between kinds of negligent act, and to hold that the negligence must be confined to the manner in which the cheque is drawn. One can see a justification for this, inasmuch as the banker's liability arises from disobedience to the mandate, and the cheque itself is the mandate in question. The House of Lords was also very much influenced by the provisions of section 20 of the Bills of Exchange Act 1882, which is limited to omissions in the instrument itself. A better solution, however, would be to admit contributory negligence as a defence, in which case it might be freely admitted that there are degrees of negligence, and a distinction between kinds of negligent act would be unnecessary. In any case, the result of the decision is that where the customer is in breach of duty, he may be estopped

---

[48] (1827) 4 Bing. 253.
[49] [1918] A.C. 777. This case is often said to be responsible for reminding practitioners of the dual role of the cheque—negotiable instrument, and mandate—the former role having tended to obscure the latter.
[50] *Per* Lord Finlay at 795.
[51] [1985] 2 All E.R. 947 (JC), [1986] A.C. 519, below, para. 7.20.
[52] n. 49, above, at 789–790.
[53] Above, n. 51.
[54] As well, perhaps, as the bank's ability to spread the risk of losses through its system of charges to all customers.

from denying the authenticity of the details on the cheque. Apart from estoppel, there is another way to explain the effect of the decision.[55] This is, that the customer's breach of duty is an actionable breach of contract by the banker, for which the damages are losses naturally and directly flowing (*i.e.* the amount erroneously paid out).[56]

7.17 As to what the *Macmillan* case decided, the Privy Council has said[57] "their Lordships are in no doubt. The House held that the customer owes his bank a duty in drawing a cheque to take reasonable and ordinary precautions against forgery." It seems clear from *Young* v. *Grote*[58] that it is a breach of duty to sign and hand on blank cheques (except, perhaps, to agents of unimpeachable virtue), and also to fill in only the figures on a cheque, especially if the figures are so filled in that they can easily be amended. In cases other than those involving blank cheques, doubts occasionally arise because of those cases under section 64 of the 1882 Act, concerning material alterations. It will be recalled that it is generally said that the bank has no mandate (except to pay the original amount to a holder in due course) if there is a material alteration to which the customer-drawer has not consented. But as already said, an estoppel may arise despite the lack of mandate, and there is no reason in principle why estoppel should not apply to cases other than cases of blank cheques or "gaps," even though in the *Macmillan* case the House was at some pains to relate the facts there to a case under section 20 (incohate instruments) rather than under section 64 (materially altered instruments).[59] The point may be that one is much more likely to be considered blameworthy for leaving large gaps than for writing words or figures that can be altered, given the ingenuity of forgers. If the drawer has been negligent in so filling in the bill that a material alteration is facilitated, the loss should fall on the drawer, rather than the bank.

7.18 What amounts to negligence? It may be doubted that it is negligence to leave such a gap after a word like as "eight" that the letter "y" can be inserted.[60] A strong line was taken by Lord Shaw, in the *Macmillan* case, where he said that the customer, and not the paying banker, was responsible for any alterations bfore the cheque was presented to the banker (even by erasure and substitution).[61] This view, however, was not accepted in *Slingsby* v. *District Bank Ltd.*[62] where the gap was not in the figures, but in the payee's name. The customer made the cheque payable to "John Prust & Co." or order, with a gap between the payee's name and the word "or order." In that gap a fraudulent solicitor added the words "*per* Cumberbirch and Potts" (his firm's name) and succeeded in getting paid. This was held not to be a breach of the customer's duty of reasonable care.[63] If one looks at the words on the cheque alone, the decision might be (and has been) criti-

---

[55] Which appears in the judgment of Lord Finlay L.C., for example.

[56] Leaving gaps may also amount to contributory negligence, if a collecting bank is sued in tort: *Lumsden & Co.* v. *London Trustee Savings Bank* [1971] 1 Lloyds Rep. 114.

[57] In *Tai Hing Cotton Mill Ltd.* v. *Liu Chong Hing Bank Ltd.* [1985] 2 All E.R. 947, 954 (JC).

[58] Above, n. 48.

[59] Paget, 390 holds to the contrary that if in the *Macmillan* case a sum had been filled in, and then improperly raised, estoppel would not apply.

[60] So said by Bovill C.J. in *Société Général* v. *Metropolitan Bank Ltd.* (1873) 27 L.T. 849.

[61] This may be saying, that the customer is *ipso facto* negligent in not controlling the cheque.

[62] [1932] 1 K.B. 544; and see *Hall* v. *Fuller* (1826) 5 B. & C. 750, where the amount was altered, and the customer was not liable.

[63] In any case, the indorsement on the cheque was irregular and as this was before the Cheques Act 1957, the bank was liable on that ground.

cized. But it is submitted that a matter which must also be considered is the way in which the customer deals with the cheque, and that it is defensible to find that he is not in breach of his duty if he gives a cheque so drawn to an apparently worthy and trustworthy solicitor. The same may well be true of blank cheques.[64] In *Wood* v. *Clydesdale Bank Ltd.*[65] a deposit receipt was sent by a customer by registered letter overseas. It was stolen, cashed, and the customer's account debited. A Scottish court rejected as "fanciful" the view that by posting it, rather than handing it to the intended recipient, the customer was in breach of any duty to the bank.

It is thought, therefore, that the question reduces itself to one of fact in every case: whether the case involves forgery in a signature, or the leaving of gaps into which unauthorised additions are made, or the making of material alterations after the cheque is drawn, the customer has (according to the *Macmillan* decision) a duty not to facilitate the forgery, addition or alteration by the way in which he draws the cheque, and if he does not take "reasonable and ordinary precautions," an estoppel may arise. **7.19**

The "*Macmillan* defence" will not succeed if the alteration is "obvious or discoverable by the exercise of reasonable care, or where the state of the cheque raises suspicion of its having been tampered with and payment is made without inquiry."[66]

It has been held that no duty similar to that of the drawer is owed by an acceptor who signs a bill already drawn by the drawer and altered by the latter: in *Scholefield* v. *Earl of Londesborough*[67] it was said to be commercially unsound, for the acceptor could refuse to sign if the bill was not drawn so as to exclude all possibilities of fraud. Apart from that, there is no (necessary) contractual relationship between acceptor and bank. But in *Garrard* v. *Lewis*[68] the acceptor was estopped after signing a bill which was largely blank, with only the amount in figures in the margin, and it may be that the *Macmillan* principle applies if the bill is blank and is signed in that form by the acceptor.[69]

(iii) Other duties owed by the customer? In *Tai Hing Cotton Mill Ltd.* v. *Liu Chong Hing Bank Ltd.*[70] the Privy Council considered whether a customer owed any other duties than those discussed, and gave a firm negative answer to this question. It was argued that the law of tort had developed since the *Macmillan* and *Greenwood* cases. First, it was said that the *Macmillan* case was decided on the basis of principles of causation in tort now abandoned. This was rejected: *Macmillan* proceeded upon the basis that "the relationship between banker and customer is contractual and that its incidents, in the absence of express agreement, are such as must be implied into the contract because they can be seen to be obviously necessary."[71] Next, it was **7.20**

---

[64] Cf. *Orbit Mining & Trading Co. Ltd.* v. *Westminster Bank Ltd.* [1963] 1 Q.B. 794, where one of two directors signed blank cheques which he left with the other director, who paid them to his own account. The collecting bank was not negligent in these circumstances. Presumably, the company could not have recovered from the paying bank.

[65] (1914) S.C. 397.

[66] Paget, 384, citing *Scholey* v. *Ramsbottom* (1810) 2 Camp. 485.

[67] [1896] A.C. 514.

[68] (1882) 10 Q.B.D. 30.

[69] For a case where an acceptor was estopped in the normal way by including forged bills in advice given to his bank, see *Vagliano Bros.* v. *Bank of England* [1891] A.C. 107, below, para. 8.03.

[70] [1985] 2 All E.R. 947 (JC), [1986] A.C. 519.

[71] *Ibid.* 955. (All E.R.)

said that there might be a separate tortious duty, which the customer in this case had broken.[72] This also was rejected: "Their Lordships do not . . . accept that the parties' mutual obligations in tort can be any greater than those to be found expressly or by necessary implication in the contract."[73] As to the contractual action, based upon an implied term, the test of implication was necessity, and their Lordships could not agree that any implied term imposing a duty on the customer "a wider duty than that formulated in *Macmillan's* case" was necessary. On the contrary, "*Macmillan's* case itself decisively illustrates that it is not a *necessary* incident of the banker/customer relationship that the customer should owe his banker the wider duty of care."[74] There was, therefore, no defence for the bank arising from the customer's lack of supervision of a fraudulent employee, or from the customer's business methods, or from his failure to read and correct his bank statements. Their Lordships "fully understand" the comment of a judge below that "the banks must today look for protection."[75] In that case they could either seek to increase the severity of the terms of their business, or seek legislative protection. But it did not follow that because they may need protection, the "necessary incidents"[76] of the relationship with their customer should change. "The business of banking is the business not of the customer but of the bank. They offer a service, which is to honour their customer's cheques when drawn on an account in credit or within an agreed overdraft limit. If they pay out on cheques which are not his, they are acting outside their mandate and cannot plead his authority in justification of their debit to his account. This is a risk of the service which it is their business to offer."[77]

7. THE "DEFENCE" IN BREWER V. WESTMINISTER BANK LTD.[78]

7.21   In this case, two executors under a will had a joint account. One executor forged the other's signature to cheques, and the other sued the bank for breach of mandate. McNair J. held[79] that an action on the joint account could succeed only if brought by the joint account holders jointly, and that as one could not sue as plaintiff because of his own wrong, neither could sue. The superficial logic of this defence has not blinded other judges to the absurdity of the result, and the case has not been followed.[80] It now may be and should be regarded as wrongly decided. The bank is in breach of its mandate if it honours cheques signed by one only, even if not an apparent forgery, and any of the joint account holders may sue.

[72] For the facts of the case, see above, para. 3.12.

[73] The bank may sometimes be liable as constructive trustee, but the liability there is more difficult to establish than is breach of contract: see para. 10.22.

[74] *Ibid.*

[75] At 956 (in All E.R.): though, somewhat inconsistently, their Lordships went on to say that the risks were very small, or negligible, referring to *Kepitigalla's* case [1909] 2 K.B. 1010, above, n. 20.

[76] *i.e.* the implied terms arising out of the relationship.

[77] At 956. The ability to impose express terms was considered above, para. 3.10.

[78] [1952] 2 All E.R. 650.

[79] Relying on a dictum in *Hirschorn* v. *Evans* [1938] 3 All E.R. 491.

[80] See *Baker* v. *Barclays Bank Ltd.* [1955] 1 W.L.R. 822; *Welch* v. *Bank of England and Others* [1955] Ch. 508; *Jackson* v. *White and Midland Bank Ltd.* [1967] 2 Lloyds Rep. 68; *Ardern* v. *B.N.S.W.* [1956] V.L.R. 569; *Simos* v. *National Bank of Australasia Ltd. and Guelman* (3d. Party) (1976) 10 A.C.T.R. 4; *Catlin* v. *Cyprus Corporation (London) Ltd.* [1983] 1 All E.R. 809, [1983] Q.B. 759.

8. EFFECT OF PASSBOOK

We have observed[81] that the customer is not estopped merely by failing to **7.22** check on his bank statements, (or passbook) unless this is made expressly a term of the contract. Nor is the bank estopped, unless the customer relies upon and acts to his detriment upon the statement.

9. EFFECT OF PAYMENT TO THIRD PARTY

Payment to the third party, without the customer's mandate, does not pre- **7.23** vent the bank from recovering from the third party on the ground that the money was paid by mistake of fact.[82] No estoppel arises, even if the third party alters his position, because the bank owes him no duty of care, and because the bank's only representation, in paying, is that it believes the cheque to be valid or the signature genuine.[83]

---

[81] Above, paras. 3.16 *et seq.*
[82] Discussed below, Chap. 11.
[83] See, *per* Kerr J., in *National Westminster Bank Ltd.* v. *Barclays Bank International Ltd.* [1975] Q.B. 654. The subject is further considered below, Chap. 11.

8. The Paying Bank and Payment to the Wrong Party: Indorsements and Crossings

A. Introduction

8.01 A wrongful payment may be made as the result of forgeries of the drawer's signature, or where his agent lacks authority, or where there are material alterations to the bill, and so on. Those matters, concerning defects in the bill or cheque itself, were discussed in Chapter 7. In this Chapter, we assume that a cheque or bill is validly drawn, etc., but consider matters which generally arise because a valid order cheque needs indorsement, and where that indorsement has been forged, or is missing or irregular, so that the bank has not paid the true payee of the cheque, but has paid the wrong party. Additionally, we consider the effect of crossings upon cheques. There is some repetition here of matters dealt with in Chapter 18, concerning negotiable instruments, where some of the present matters are considered in the context of the whole Bills of Exchange Act 1882 and in this Chapter we attempt to summarize the position.

If a paying bank pays out on a cheque made out by its customer in favour of A, and the bank pays B who is not entitled to be paid, then the bank may commit two wrongs: (a) against its customer, for it has not obeyed his mandate to pay A, and (b) against the true owner of the cheque, A, who although he has no contract with the bank, may sue in the tort of conversion. Additionally, since payment by cheque is merely conditional payment, A may still hold the bank's customer liable to him, on the original debt. It will be seen that the bank has certain statutory protections, and that where this is so, it is protected simultaneously from its customer's claim for breach of mandate (the customer's debt to his payee being discharged, and the bank being entitled to debit his account), and from the claims of the true owner of the cheque.

If the bank is not protected as stated below, then if the wrongful payment does not discharge the instrument (as later described) an alternative possibility is for the bank to attempt to recover the money from the payee (as paid by a mistake of fact). That remedy is discussed elsewhere.[1]

B. Bearer cheques

8.02 No problem ordinarily arises with a bearer cheque, for first, a thief can give good title to an innocent person who becomes "true owner," and secondly, a bearer instrument entitles the bank to pay the holder (even if, unknown to the bank, he happens to be a thief). In the latter case, the cheque can be discharged under section 59 of the Bills of Exchange Act 1882. That provides that a bill is discharged by payment in due course, which means payment to the "holder" without notice that his title is defective. Section 2 of the Act provides that "holder" includes the bearer of a bill payable to bearer. Payment to the bearer of a bearer bill, therefore, discharges the bank's customer and the bill, and the bank is entitled to debit its customer's account, and can-

---

[1] Below, Chap. 11.

not be liable to the "true owner" (supposing that the bearer is not in fact true owner, but a thief). As an exception to this general rule, if the cheque is crossed, payment must (under section 79) be made to a banker, or the bank would be liable to the true owner (if the bearer is not true owner). But if payment is made to a banker, the bank and its customer are discharged, by section 80 of the Act. The transferability of a bearer cheque is unaffected by "not negotiable" crossings, so that what has already been said applies.

EFFECT OF S. 7(3) OF THE BILLS OF EXCHANGE ACT 1882

8.03

It should not be forgotten that certain bills which apparently need indorsement may be treated sometimes as bearer bills, with the effect that the bank is protected. This is the effect of section 7(3) of the 1882 Act, which allows a bill to be treated as if to bearer if the payee is fictitious or non-existent. A non-existent payee is one of whose existence the drawer did not know when he signed (even if, say, there is a real person of that name). A fictitious payee is one whom the drawer does not intend to receive payment. Thus, in *Clutton* v. *Attenborough*[2] a clerk dishonestly induced his employer to sign cheques drawn in favour of a Mr. Brett, by falsely telling the employer that money was owed to Brett. The employer did not know of a Mr. Brett (though there are persons of that name) and the cheque was held to be payable to a non-existing payee, and therefore was a bearer cheque. The clerk forged an indorsement from Brett to Attenborough, who was paid. The drawer then sued Attenborough, on the ground that he was not payee, and had been wrongly paid. But the cheque being payable to bearer, payment in due course discharged it (under section 59) Attenborough being a holder (under section 2). The argument in this case was between drawer and the person paid. But the drawer might have sued the bank, on the ground that the bank had no mandate to pay Attenborough, and the result would have been the same, for the bank would be entitled to pay to the holder of a bearer cheque.

Facts of the latter sort occurred in *Bank of England* v. *Vagliano*[3] where a clerk obtained his employer's acceptance of certain bills, which were apparently drawn by customers of the employer, and payable to persons known to the employer. These were, in fact, complete forgeries, by the clerk, who forged the payees' indorsements, and was paid. The employer sued his bank, alleging breach of mandate. But it was held that the "drawer" here was really the clerk, and that he did not intend the payees to be paid. The payees, therefore, were "fictitious," and the bill was to bearer, so that the bank properly paid the holder.

If, however, the payee is a real person, known to the drawer (as, say, his customer) but not intended (by the person inducing the drawer to sign, such as a clerk of the drawer) to be paid, then the standard rules apply, and the cheque remains an order cheque.[4] But in that case, supposing a forged or irregular indorsement, so that someone other than the named payee is paid, the bank may be protected from its customer's claim by provisions considered elsewhere[5] (which protect the bank from claims by the "true owner" as well as from the customer-drawer).

8.04

---

[2] [1897] A.C. 90.
[3] [1891] A.C. 107.
[4] *North and South Wales Bank Ltd.* v. *Macbeth* [1908] A.C. 137; *Vinden* v. *Hughes* [1905] 1 K.B. 795.
[5] Below, Chaps. 8, 18.

Section 7(3) does not apply except to a "bill" (which includes cheques). It has been held, however, that a bill payable to "Cash" or "Wages" may be a bill, even though no payee is named as required by section 3. It is treated as a direction to pay bearer.[6]

C. Order cheques

8.05   If, as is far more common, the cheque is made to A or order, then whether the cheque is discharged by payment to B depends upon whether the cheque has been properly transferred to B. Under section 31(3) this requires A's indorsement and delivery to B. A forged indorsement is, of course, ineffective, and that is stated by section 24. If there is no valid indorsement (as provided by section 32) because, for example, A has indorsed to X from whom a cheque is stolen by a thief who forges an indorsement to B, then the consequences stated above will apply (the bank has no mandate from A to pay B and is liable in conversion to the true owner). We have already observed that in relation to its customer, the bank may have some protection, arising (say) from estoppel, or from section 7(3) of the Act. So too, in relation to the third party, the bank is given some statutory protection, arising from sections 60, and 80 of the 1882 Act, and section 1 of the Cheques Act 1957.

SECTION 60 OF THE BILLS OF EXCHANGE ACT 1882

8.06   This section (which is also discussed elsewhere)[7] protects the bank if it pays a cheque ("a bill payable to order on demand [which] is drawn on a banker") "in good faith and in the ordinary course of business." If so, the bank is protected though it pays B who is not true owner because of forgery or unauthorised indorsement. Since the bank is deemed to have paid in due course, section 59 then applies, and the cheque is discharged, so that the customer's debt to the third party is also discharged, and the customer cannot complain of breach of mandate, and his account may be debited. Assuming good faith in the bank, the main question is as to what amounts to "the ordinary course of business." It has been held[8] that this is not the same as "negligence," so that a bank could be negligent yet still act in the ordinary course of business, and conversely could be careful yet act outside its "ordinary" course. In *Brighton Empire and Eden Syndicate* v. *London and County Bank*[9] the bank cashed an order cheque drawn by a customer, when an indorsement had been forged by an employee, whose handwriting was well known to the bank. Even if failure to recognise the handwriting was negligence, the court held that the bank was protected. Nevertheless, negligence must be an indication that the circumstances are not "ordinary" and even if this is wrong, it may go to "good faith." In the *Auchteroni*[9a] case Wright J. said[10] that where the circumstances were suspicious "the taker of the instrument is not acting in good faith if he shuts his eyes to the facts presented to him and puts the suspicions aside without further inquiry."

---

[6] *North and South Insurance Corpn. Ltd.* v. *National Provinicial Bank Ltd.* [1936] 1 K.B. 328; *Cole* v. *Milsome* [1951] 1 All E.R. 311; *Orbit Mining and Trading Co. Ltd.* v. *Westminster Bank Ltd.* [1963] 1 Q.B. 794.

[7] Below, Chap. 18.

[8] *Carpenters' Company* v. *The British Mutual Banking Company* [1938] 1 K.B. 511. This case also took the view that s. 19 of the Stamp Act 1853 no longer applied to cheques.

[9] (1904) *The Times*, March 24.

[9a] Below, para. 8.08.

[10] Quoting *London Joint Stock Bank Ltd.* v. *Simmons* [1892] A.C. 201.

(i) Paying an obviously suspicious person would be out of the ordinary **8.07**
course of business. In *Auchteroni & Co.* v. *Midland Bank Ltd.*[11] the question
involved a bill of exchange, rather than a cheque, and was whether there
was payment "in due course" under section 59. A fraudulent person presented the bill to the paying bank and was paid cash over the counter. The
court held that this was unusual, and infrequent, but not so unusual that it
deprived the bank of its protection under the section. Wright J. said, however, that payment to an obviously suspicious person (such as a tramp,
postman or office boy) would render the bank liable.

(ii) Payment after hours[12] might also be out of the ordinary course of
business, but a few minutes makes little difference, especially if the bank
pays to persons already in the building at close.[13]

(iii) Payment of an uncrossed cheque to a stranger who presents through
the post and asks for cash to be sent to him, would be suspicious, and not
"ordinary."

(iv) Payment "under advice" (by open credit) occurs when a branch at
which the account is not kept cashes cheques for a customer of the bank,
having been asked to do so. This is presumably within the ordinary course
of business.

Obviously, section 60 would not protect in case of payment of an
uncrossed cheque marked "not negotiable" since only the original payee
may be paid, such cheques being (perhaps) not transferable at all. But if the
cheque is crossed, then by section 81 it is still transferable and section 60
could apply, provided that section 80 is complied with and payment is made
to a banker.

Section 60 does not protect if the bill also suffers from other defects, such
as material alterations in the amount. In *Slingsby* v. *District Bank*[14] a fraudulent person altered the payee's name to include his own, and then indorsed.
The cheque was held to be materially altered, within section 64, and was
avoided by that section, so that section 60[15] could not protect the bank.
"This invalidity comes before any question of indorsement."[16]

SECTION 80

Further protection is given by section 80, (discussed elsewhere)[17] which **8.08**
applies to crossed cheques paid according to the crossing, "in good faith and
without negligence." If the bank pays a banker, or a specified banker or his
agent for collection, the bank is discharged, as is its customer the drawer
(but only if the cheque has come into the hands of the payee). Both are
placed in the same position as if the true owner had been paid, so that the
bank is not liable to the true owner or to its customer, and may debit the
latter's account, and the customer's debt to the true owner or others is discharged. The cheque must be paid "without negligence," but given payment to another banker, that would be rare.

Section 80 applies only to crossed cheques, and section 81 says that "not
negotiable" markings leave such a cheque still transferable. Thus, it may be

[11] [1928] 2 K.B. 294.
[12] Above, para. 6.29.
[13] *Baines* v. *National Provincial Bank Ltd.* (1927) L.J.K.B. 801.
[14] [1932] 1 K.B. 544.
[15] Or s.80.
[16] Scrutton L.J. at 559.
[17] Below, Chap. 18.

transferred by indorsement, but where an indorsement is bad or missing, section 80 still protects the bank.

The converse of section 80 is section 79, which provides that if the bank does not pay another banker the bank is liable to the true owner (and would be in breach of its mandate to its customer, who would still be indebted to whomsoever he gave the cheque). This applies even though the cheque is a bearer cheque (though the holder may then be true owner) and it has the effect of displacing section 60, for payment of a crossed cheque other than to another banker is clearly not then "in the ordinary course of business" under section 60.

SECTION 1 OF THE CHEQUES ACT 1957

8.09 This section (a) protects the bank from the true owner and its customer, and (b) discharges the instrument (so that the bank can debit its customer's account and he is not liable to the payee of the instrument) and applies in the following circumstances:

(i) to a banker acting in good faith and in the ordinary course of business

(ii) who pays a cheque drawn upon him, or any instrument issued by a customer which is a mandate for payment ("intended to enable a person to obtain payment from" the banker) or the banker's own demand draft (section 1 would include, for example, a postdated cheque)

(iii) where the cheque is not indorsed, or is irregularly indorsed (this probably includes forgeries, since by section 24 of the 1882 Act these have no effect and the instrument may be "not" indorsed or "irregularly" indorsed: but in any case, sections 60 and 80 apply).

It is sometimes said that this makes indorsements unnecessary. This should be treated with reserve. Indorsements are still necessary to transfer title from a payee A to the indorsee B. But if the bank complies with the section and pays C, who has no title, then the bank may debit the account of its customer, the drawer, the customer is discharged from any debt which he owed A and for which he gave the cheque, and the true owner B cannot sue the bank for conversion. Since the cheque is discharged, no party can be liable on it. B's remedy is as true owner, against C. Rather than saying that indorsements are unnecessary, it is better to say, therefore, that provided the bank acts in the ordinary course of business, indorsements need not be checked by it. But if C wishes to become holder, so as to be able to sue the drawer or prior indorsers if the cheque is not paid, indorsements are still needed.

8.10 Section 1 was felt to be necessary because of the sheer volume of cheques received by the banks, so that checking indorsements became impractical.

The question then is, what amounts to acting "in the ordinary course of business." What is said in relation to section 60, above, would apply here also, so that paying a crossed cheque to someone other than a banker would not be protected. Additionally, however, the Committee of London Clearing Bankers have (in a Memorandum of September 23, 1957) laid down certain rules of practice. It is extremely likely that if a bank fails to comply with these, it does not act "in the ordinary course of business."

In relation to paying banks, the rules provide that indorsements will generally not be examined on cheques or other instruments, whether presented through the clearing system or specially presented. "House debits" (where the branch in question pays its customer A and debits its customer

B) are similarly treated. The exceptions, where indorsements should be examined, are (i) instruments which are combined cheque and receipt forms, but only if marked with a bold outline letter "R" on the face of them, (ii) travellers' cheques, (iii) bills of exchange (not being cheques), (iv) promissory notes, (v) cheques and other instruments cashed at the counter (including those cashed under open credits).

Where indorsements are to be examined, sections 32–35 of the Act applies so that:

(i) a simple signature written on the cheque or on an allonge (attached continuation sheet) will suffice,[18]

(ii) a cheque payable to two or more persons may be indorsed by one if he has the authority of the others: but otherwise, all must indorse.

(iii) if the payee or indorsee is wrongly designated (*e.g.* "Mr." instead of "Mrs.") or his name is mis-spelt (*e.g.* "O'Shea" instead of "Shea") then the indorsement is to be in the incorrect form (followed, if the party thinks fit, by his correct signature.[19]

(iv) the bank may ignore a conditional indorsement (*e.g.* "Pay A if he does X").[20]

Other rules on indorsements, many deriving from custom, are far too numerous and complicated to mention here.[21]

D. Crossings on cheques

Crossings are considered in this work in the context of negotiable instruments[22] but we provide here a summary of the rules. It will be remembered that crossings affect primarily the paying banker, and that section 79 requires the paying bank to pay another banker, in which case by section 80 the banker and his customer is treated as if they have paid the true owner. **8.11**

(i) If the paying banker pays the true owner of the cheque, no problem can arise. The risk is that he pays the wrong person, with the complications mentioned above.

(ii) On a bearer cheque, the holder (if innocent) is very likely to be true owner, for title to a bearer bill may be transferred free of equities merely by delivery, provided that the holder is a bona fide purchaser for value and without notice of any defect in his transferor's title. But the holder may be a thief, and section 79 applies to bearer cheques also, requiring the bank to pay another banker.

(iii) Crossings have no effect whatsoever on bills of exchange other than cheques (which means, of course, that the bank is not protected by section 80).

(iv) The drawer and any holder may cross the cheque. **8.12**

(v) The crossing is a material part, and by section 78 may not be deleted by a subsequent holder, though the drawer may alter his mandate to the bank by writing "pay cash" and initialling the amendment.[23] This alteration of the mandate probably would not protect the bank from a "true owner"

[18] s.32(1).
[19] s.32(4).
[20] s.33.
[21] Reference might be made to Thomson's *Dictionary of Banking*, under the entry for "Indorsement." To give one of hundreds of examples: if the payee is "Mr. John Brown" an indorsement "Mr. John Brown" is not acceptable (he should indorse "John Brown").
[22] Below, Chap. 18.
[23] *Smith v. Union Bank of London* (1875) L.R. 1 Q.B.D. 31.

since the Act does not contemplate the "opening" of a cheque in this way,[24] but the bank would probably be entitled to an indemnity from its customer, and it can debit his account. The Committee of London Clearing Bankers has recommended to banks that no opening of cheques be recognised unless the full signature of the drawer by appended to the alteration, and then only when presented for payment by the drawer or his known agent. (Banks may often accept an initialling, in practice.)

(vi) A "not negotiable" addition to a crossing on cheques is authorised by section 76 of the 1882 Act, and according to section 81 this leaves the cheque transferable but not fully negotiable, in the sense that the transferee takes subject to equities. A "not negotiable" marking (whether with or without a crossing) on other bills of exchange makes them not transferable so that only the original payee may be paid. A "not negotiable" marking on an uncrossed cheque probably has the same effect: the cheque is not transferable.

(vii) The words "account payee only" and similar expressions sometimes used on crossed cheques are not recognised by the Act of 1882, and do not prevent the cheque from being transferable by the original payee to another. They are a direction to the collecting bank as to how it deals with the money after it receives it[25] and the effect of that is that if the collecting bank receives payment for another than the named payee, it may be negligent so that the protection of section 4 of the Cheques Act 1957[26] is not available. But the words do not affect the paying banker, which may safely pay the collecting banker. If the words appear without a crossing, they are not in themselves equivalent to a crossing, and the paying bank might pay the holder.

[24] *Smith and Baldwin* v. *Barclays Bank Ltd.* (1944) L.D.A.B. 370, 375.
[25] *Akrokerri (Atlantic) Mines Ltd.* v. *Economic Bank* [1904] 2 K.B. 465; *A. L. Underwood Ltd.* v. *Bank of Liverpool and Martins* [1924] 1 K.B. 775.
[26] Below, Chap. 18.

9. The Collecting Bank: Its Customer, and Third Parties

In this short chapter we deal with some particular matters involved in the relationship between a customer and a bank which collect a cheque for that customer, and between the bank and third parties who claim rights over the cheque in question. Many of these matters may be dealt with in Chapter 18, concerning Negotiable Instruments, and accordingly, only a summary is given here.

A. Collecting bank and its customer

9.02

(i) We have observed elsewhere the effect upon the banker's obligation to honour cheques of the customer's paying an uncollected cheque into the account.[1]

(ii) The words "not negotiable" on a crossed cheque have in themselves no bearing upon a collecting banker. The cheque is still transferable (section 81) and it is not negligence to collect such a cheque.[2] A bill of exchange or an uncrossed cheque, marked "not negotiable" should not be collected for any but the original named payee, for the cheque or bill is not transferable, and there is no protection from the true owner.

(iii) The words "account payee" or "account payee only" are an indication to the collecting bank as to how it is to deal with the proceeds of the collection, and it will be negligence to collect the cheque for any other account than that of the named payee. This reply should be given to the presenting customer. Naturally, this will be of concern only if an indorsee is not the true owner, in which case the bank may be protected by section 4 of the Cheques Act 1957, but only if it acts without negligence.

(iv) A cheque or bill payable on demand must be presented for payment within a reasonable time after issue.[3] In other words a cheque may become "stale."

(v) If a cheque is given to a collecting bank, it must be present for collection within a reasonable time. This means that where the paying bank is in the same town, the collecting banker should present the following business day after receipt.[4] If the paying bank is elsewhere then the cheque should either be presented or forwarded on the following business day.[5] If the banker fails to present the cheque within the time allowed, he is liable to his customer for any loss.[6]

(vi) Cheques today are normally presented through the clearings, and a collecting bank which is a non-clearing bank may forward to another branch, or to an agent of the bank, and those persons have the same time for presentation, after they receive the cheques.[7]

9.03

---

[1] Above, Chap. 6, para. 6.11.
[2] Paget, 347–384.
[3] s.45, rule 2, B.O.E. Act 1882.
[4] *Alexander v. Burchfield* (1842) 7 Man. & G. 1061: *Forman v. Bank of England* (1902) 18 T.L.R. 339.
[5] *Hare v. Henty* (1861) 10 C.B.N.S. 65, *Heywood v. Pickering* (1874) L.R. 9 Q.B. 428.
[6] *Lubbock v. Tribe* (1838) 3 M & W 607.
[7] *Prideaux v. Criddle* (1869) L.R. 4 Q.B. 455, Paget 372.

(vii) A bank may specially collect by special presentation to another bank (not through the clearings) but the paying bank may hold the cheque until the day after receipt and pay then.[8] By custom, a bank may present by post.[9]

(viii) If a bank delays in presenting so that there are insufficient funds available to meet a cheque drawn by his customer, the bank will be liable if it dishonours the cheque.[10]

(ix) If a cheque drawn by one customer is paid in by another customer, and it is crossed, the payee customer's account should be credited, rather than cash paid (according to section 79 of the 1882 Act). But the bank may make a "house debit," debiting the account of the drawer, crediting the account of the payee, and effectively paying him cash. There is no obligation to do this, for as agent for collection the bank would have the normal time allowed (the following business day).[11] If the cheque is not crossed, the bank ought to pay the customer as it would pay any other holder: *i.e.* on demand.

9.04 (x) Section 60 of the 1882 Act protects a bank paying a cheque in the ordinary course of business, if an indorsement is forged, etc., and the customer is not the true owner. But it seems that this does not apply to a bank which is both collecting and paying bank.[12] However, the bank may still be protected as paying bank by section 80, and as collecting or paying bank by sections 1 and 4 of the Cheques Act 1957.

(xii) If a cheque is dishonoured, the banker must inform his customer as soon as reasonably possible, (so that he can given notice of dishonour to the drawer and others) and will be liable for any losses arising from the delay. The bank itself may give notice of dishonour (as agent) but rarely does. The usual practice is to return the cheque to the customer. Notice of dishonour must be given by the customer in a "reasonable time"[13] and this means (a) where they reside in the same place (postal district, perhaps)[14] it must be sent so as to arrive on the day following dishonour, and (b) otherwise must be sent on the day following dishonour if there is a post then (otherwise sent by the next post). If, however, bank or branch A acts as clearing agent for bank B, then each person in the chain has the same time: so that A has the time allowed to inform B, and B has the time to inform its customer, who has the time allowed to give notice to the drawer, etc.[14a]

B. Collecting bank and third parties

9.05 (i) At common law, the bank is liable to the true owner of a cheque or bill if it pays another. Its liability is in tort, in conversion. This is a "strict liability" tort, inasmuch as innocence, or the taking of care, does not protect at common law. Contributory negligence, however, is a defence.[15] Liability now arises under the Torts (Interference with Goods) Act 1977.

(ii) If the cheque is a bearer cheque the presenter is "holder" and the bank

---

[8] *Bailey* v. *Bodenham* (1864) 16 C.B.N.S. 288.

[9] s.45, rule 8, B.O.E. Act 1882.

[10] *Forman* v. *Bank of England*, (1902) 18 T.L.R. 339.

[11] *Boyd* v. *Emmerson* (1834) 2 Ad. & El. 184.

[12] *Carpenter's Co.* v. *British Mutual Banking Co. Ltd.* [1938] 1 K.B. 511, esp. 533.

[13] s.49, rule 12, B.O.E. Act 1882.

[14] See *Hamilton Finance Co. Ltd.* v. *Coverley Westray Walbaum and Tosetti Ltd.* [1969] 1 Lloyds Rep. 53.

[14a] s.49, rule 13, B.O.E. Act 1882.

[15] *Lumsden & Co.* v. *London T.S.B.* [1971] 1 Lloyds Rep. 114, s.47, Banking Act 1979.

is protected, even if the holder is a thief. Under section 59 payment in due course protects the bank by discharging the cheque. Liability is most likely to arise when an order cheque has a missing or forged indorsement, being presented by a person not entitled. Indorsements on order cheques being necessary to transfer title, the "holder" is not in fact holder and the bank is not discharged by payment.

(iii) If the bank is also paying bank (both the drawer and payee are its customer) it may be protected by section 80 of the 1882 Act (crossed cheques) or by section 1 of the Cheques Act 1957.[16] It is not protected by section 60 of the 1882 Act.[17]

(iv) The collecting bank may also be protected from a third party if it can show that the party is not "true owner." In this context, the most likely case is that the collecting bank itself is true owner (or rather, if different, "holder in due course," for such a person takes free of all prior claims, including those from any other "true owner"). For this to be the case it is insufficient that it be the holder for value. It must be "holder in due course" under section 29 of the 1882 Act, and it may achieve this status in two ways: first, if its customer is indebted to it at the time he pays in the cheque (in which case, under section 27 it has a lien, and is holder for value who gives value within section 29).[18] Secondly, the bank may allow the customer to draw against uncleared effects, and this is a giving of value which makes it holder in due course. This is more fully discussed elsewhere.[19] In these cases, the bank may be "holder" (so as to be holder in due course) even though the cheque is not indorsed to it: this is the effect of section 2 of the Cheques Act 1957.

(v) The standard protection, however, formerly arose under section 82 of **9.06** the 1882 Act, which provided a "no negligence" defence. That section has been repealed and replaced by section 4 of the Cheques Act 1957, by virtue of which, if a bank pays in good faith and "without negligence," for a "customer" it may be protected. That is, prima facie it is liable, but there is a "no-negligence" defence. What amounts to negligence is the all important question, and this is considered below.[20] There may be negligence on opening the account and in its subsequent conduct, and the question is largely as to what steps the bank must make by way of inquiry. The meaning of "customer" is considered in Chapter 2.

(vi) As already noted,[21] collecting a "not-negotiable" crossed cheque for someone other than the original payee is not negligence, since this does not affect the transferability of the cheque, but collecting an uncrossed cheque marked "not negotiable" (or "Pay A only") would clearly be impermissible, since only the original payee (A) can be paid, the bill being not transferable.

(vii) As already noted,[22] collecting an "account payee (only)" cheque for other than the named payee is negligence, unless inquiry is made.

(viii) The section applies even if a bank received money into an over-

---

[16] Above, para. 7.08 *et seq.*
[17] Above, n. 12.
[18] *Re Keever*, [1966] 2 Lloyds Rep. 475; *Barclays Bank Ltd.* v. *Astley Industrial Trust Lrd.* [1970] 2 Q.B. 527.
[19] Below, Chap. 18.
[20] Below, Chap. 18.
[21] Above, para. 9.02.
[22] Above, para. 9.02.

drawn account, or where at the time the cheque is presented, it credits the account to cash. Formerly, in those cases, it received payment for itself, and the old section 82 did not apply.[23] But section 4 does apply in those circumstances. Nevertheless, one must distinguish the case where the cheque is collected for crediting to the customer's account, and where the cheque is bought by the bank, for in the latter case it is not collected for a customer, and section 4 does not apply.

9.07   (ix) Although under section 4 of the Cheques Act 1957 the bank may establish a "no-negligence" defence, that section does not refer to the "ordinary course of business" (unlike section 1, applying to paying banks). Nevertheless, failing to comply with the ordinary course of business must often amount to negligence, though the two things are not necessarily the same.[24] In this context, then, the ruling of the London Clearing Banks on September 23, 1957 is important. That ruling concerns the cases in which indorsements are still required. Just as paying banks which fail to comply may be acting outside the ordinary course of business, so may a collecting bank which fails to comply be guilty of "negligence." The cases in which indorsements are still necessary, therefore, are as follows: (a) if the payee's name is mis-spelt or he is incorrectly designated, and there are circumstances to suggest that he is not the person to whom payment is intended to be made (failure to inquire would, in any case, surely amount to negligence); (b) if the cheque or other instrument is collected for an account other than that of the ostensible (original named) payee, indorsement will be required (so called "third party" cheques). This does not apply if the cheque has been specially indorsed to the customer who presents the cheque for his account (*i.e.* if payable to A, and A has indorsed to B who presents it). It can be seen that this is, in fact, a very major exception to the rules about indorsement, and that it is quite false to say that there is a general rule that indorsements are not required (that is more true for paying banks). Since the question of indorsements arises only if the original payee does not present the cheque, then whenever he does not, indorsements are still needed; (c) instruments payable to join payees must be indorsed if to be credited to an account to which all are not parties; d) combined cheque and receipt forms marked "R" must be indorsed, as must bills of exchange, promissory notes, travellers cheques and instruments payable by banks abroad (this fourth class also applies to paying banks).

In all those classes of case, therefore, the collecting bank must ensure that the instrument is properly endorsed, or it will be liable to the true owner unless (being also a paying bank) it has the protection of section 1, or section 80 of the 1882 Act, or unless it is a holder in due course.

---

[23] *Capital and Counties Bank Ltd.* v. *Gordon* [1903] A.C. 240.
[24] Above, para. 7.06.

10. Banks and Some Elements of Trusts[1]

A. Introduction

Although the relationship between banker and customer is primarily one of **10.01** debtor and creditor a bank may become affected by rights which third parties have over funds held by the customer in an account. Those third party rights may be legal, where, for example, an express legal assignment of the funds is made. Alternatively, the customer may hold funds in trust for another. The bank may become concerned with the trust in several ways. First, if a particular fund is expressly a trust fund, mere knowledge of this fact does not, of course, necessarily affect the bank's ability to obey the customer's instructions, because it is not notice of a trust, but notice of a breach of trust, which is significant. Where, however, two or more trustees are appointed jointly, the bank must (unless otherwise expressly authorised) act on their joint signatures, and not on the signature of one alone.[2] It is a general principle that unless otherwise authorised by the trust deed, trustees must act unanimously[3] and only the joint signatures can give the bank a mandate to pay.[4] Secondly, a bank may be affected by a "Quistclose trust" where funds are paid into an account for a particular purpose, and this may prevent the bank from using the funds for its own purposes. Thirdly, in various cases, the bank may become a constructive trustee, having notice of the trust and breach of trust, in which it has become involved. Fourthly,[5] a fund may be subject to the equitable proprietary remedy of tracing, where the customer has been wrongly paid money by a person with whom he had a fiduciary relationship, and where the fund may be recovered from the customer or his bank, provided that the bank still has the fund, and did not receive it in good faith and for value (*e.g.* into an overdrawn account).[6]

In this chapter we consider primarily the effect which certain trusts bind- **10.02** ing a bank's customer may have upon a bank as constructive trustee, and then briefly consider developments in relation to the Quistclose trust.

B. Constructive trusts and constructive notice

When it is said that a bank is subject to a constructive trust, it means that the **10.03** bank's actual or constructive notice of a breach of trust or of fiduciary duties by another has, taken in conjunction with certain acts of the bank, caused

---

[1] See *Goodhart & Jones* (1980) MLR 489; *Smith* (1977) Crim.L.R. 395; *Williams* (1985) Legal Studies 183; *Ong* (1985) Otago L.R. Vo. 5, No. 2 p. 219; *Hayton* (1985) 27 Mal.L.R. 313; *Harpum* (1986) 102 L.Q.R. 114, 267, 267.

[2] *Stone* v. *March* (1826) Ry. & Mood 364, 369–370; *Innes* v. *Stephenson* (1831) 1 M. & R. 145, 147; *Bowstead on Agency* (14th ed.), 155.

[3] Though not with charitable trusts.

[4] This seems to apply notwithstanding s.14, Trustee Act 1925 which can allow a single trustee (or two trustees in a trust for sale of land) to give a good discharge.

[5] In fact, some of the constructive trust cases are co-extensive with the availability of tracing.

[6] Similarly, although it is not a question of trust, the (legal) personal remedy of money had and received (considered below, Chap. 11) may be available. Here there is no defence of receipt for value, although if the funds are received through the collection of a cheque (or other bill of exchange) the bank may be holder in due course (since an overdraft makes it holder for value) and entitled to the fund in its own right.

the bank to be considered as having become "involved" in the breach, with the result that the bank itself comes under a liability. That liability may be (i) to the same extent as the defaulting trustee, or (ii) to the extent of the bank's involvement, or (iii) either of the above, mitigated by a principle of contributory negligence on the part of the beneficiary—plaintiff.

The "trust" need not be formal, but there must be at least a fiduciary duty between the so-called trustee and the property of another. For this purpose, for example, the relationship between company directors and the company property is fiduciary (as it is for tracing).[7]

There is a tendency to say that the bank is liable if it is "knowingly" party to a breach of trust. It is not, however, always necessary that it be a "party" and the word "knowingly" refers to "notice," which, in this context, may be express, or constructive.

1. ACTUAL (EXPRESS) NOTICE OF TRUST FUNDS

10.04 If an account is headed with the name " . . . trust account," then obviously the bank has actual notice of the existence of a trust. But even an account headed "police account" was held in *Re Gross* to amount to proof that the bank had notice of the fiduciary nature of the account.[8] As already stated, however, mere knowledge that an account is a trust account or that funds paid in are trust funds, imposes no liability on a bank, and the bank may receive trust funds for its own benefit without incurring liability provided that it receives as a bona fide purchaser without notice of any breach of trust. The bank is a purchaser if it has given value, as where the funds are received into an overdrawn account. If the bank gave no value, then it can have no title to set up against the customer or beneficiary. Notice of breach of trust makes the bank liable (at least) to return what it has received, even if it gave value. Obviously, the receipt of known trust funds entitles the bank to receive as "bona fide" purchaser only if the funds are received into a trust account or an ordinary account known to be used for trust purposes by the trustees. If, for example, known trust funds are received into a trustee's personal account, the bank cannot combine accounts. Similarly, if the trust funds are received into the trust account, they cannot be combined subsequently with a debit in a non-trust account.[9]

In relation to dispositions of the trust fund from the account on the customer's order, the bank has an obligation to obey its customer's orders, and (as shortly described) would not be liable unless it had notice of breach of trust. The important question, therefore, is what amounts to "notice" of breach of trust?

2. THE BARNES V. ADDY (TWOFOLD) CLASSIFICATION

10.05 The most widely accepted form of classification of constructive trusts is derived from the well-known decision in *Barnes* v. *Addy*.[10] This establishes a twofold classification of liability. The first arises from the knowing receipt and dealing with a trust fund ("knowing receipt") and the other arises from

---

[7] See, *e.g. Sinclair* v. *Brougham* [1914] A.C. 398; *Chase Manhattan Bank N.A.* v. *Israel-British Bank (London) Ltd.* [1981] Ch. 105.

[8] *Re Gross, ex p. Kingston* (1871) 6 Ch. App. 632.

[9] *Re European Bank, Agra Bank Claim* (1872) 8 Ch. App. 41, 44. *cf. Union Bank of Australia Ltd.* v. *Murray-Aynsley* [1898] A.C. 693 where the bank did not know that the funds were trust funds.

[10] (1874) 9 Ch. App. 244, 251–252.

the giving of knowing assistance to a dishonest trustee ("knowing assistance"). According to the traditional exposition of this classification both the guilty acts and the guilty knowledge[11] differ between the two categories. In other words, the acts involved in "knowing assistance" may be any act which assists the trustee, except the act of receiving the funds,[12] and the "mental state" or type of fault required for knowing assistance is something like dishonesty, or morally reprehensible behaviour, or lack of probity to such a degree that the bank might be said to have become a "party" to the dishonesty. Knowing receipt does not require this degree of fault, but requires "lack of probity." Once the distinction is made between knowing receipt and knowing assistance, the extent of the liability differs: in knowing receipt cases, the bank is liable to account only for the funds which it receives or deals with in breach of the trust, while in the more serious knowing assistance cases the bank's liability extends to all the losses to the trust fund caused by the dishonest trustee, whether or not the funds came into the hands of the bank.

In short, on the traditional exposition, knowing receipt differs from knowing assistance in definition (as to the acts in question, and as to the "mental stage" or type of fault) and in consequences (whether liable for what is received only, or for all losses to the fund.)[13]

3. TYPES OF FAULT

At the present time, there is disagreement as to what amounts to fault such as to attract equity's attention. A variety of "states of mind" or types of fault were described in *Baden Delvaux & Lecuit* v. *Societe General S.A.* (a knowing assistance case).[14] Five categories of fault are described here: but the last of these refers to negligence, and might easily be divided (for the sake of discussion) into "gross" and "mere" negligence to create six categories of case. Accordingly, the categories are: **10.06**

(i) actual notice or knowledge, where the bank knows of the facts and is aware of the breach of trust,

(ii) wilfully shutting one's eyes to the obvious (not inquiring for fear of finding distressing facts),

(iii) wilfully failing to make such inquiries as a reasonable man might make,

(iv) inferred notice, where the bank knows of the facts, from which an honest and reasonable man could infer that there had been a breach of trust, but the bank has failed to do so,

(v) a failure to inquire, in circumstances amounting to gross negligence, somewhere between fraud and negligence,

(vi) a failure to inquire, in circumstances amounting to negligence of the sort that would suffice for the ordinary tort of negligence.

The distinction between the fourth case, and the last two cases in this classification is that in the fourth, there is no duty to inquire. The bank is assumed to know of the facts, and its error lies in its failure to consider them. In the last case, however, there is a duty to inquire. Either of the last

---

[11] "Knowledge" and "mental state" are misnomers, if negligence will suffice.
[12] Though subsequently parting with it will suffice.
[13] For a reasonably straightforward recent case see *Rolled Steel Products (Holdings) Ltd.* v. *B.S.C.* [1984] B.C.L.C. 466, [1985] 3 All E.R. 52, [1986] Ch. 246.
[14] [1983] B.C.L.C. 325. The actual decision was affirmed by the Court of Appeal (unrep. 1985).

two cases given may be described as "constructive notice," with the others being forms of actual notice, wilful blindness or failure to appreciate. It is the existence of the last two classes which give rise to the term "constructive trust."

4. BANK'S DUTY TO OBEY MANDATE

10.07 One major difficulty with the application of doctrines of constructive notice to banks is that if there is a duty to inquire, this must, at least to a certain degree, be set against the bank's duty to obey (promptly) its customer's instructions, failure to do which will make it liable to the customer for breach of contract.

It is clearly established that if the bank has no notice (actual, or constructive) of the existence of a trust it may treat the monies as the absolute property of the customer, and is not liable if in good faith it does so.[15] This principle is asserted by numerous cases. It is a necessary principle, for the bank has a duty to obey its customer's instructions, and to pay on his cheques on demand. The practice of banking would be excessively difficult if the banker was required to investigate its customer's title to the money, and it is established, therefore, that he should not refuse to pay on the ground that the funds might belong to others.[16]

This particular conflict was recognised in *Gray* v. *Johnston*.[17] There, Lord Cairns said

> "On the one hand, it would be a most serious matter if bankers were to be allowed, on light and trifling grounds—on grounds of mere suspicion or curiosity—to refuse to honour a cheque drawn by their customer, even although that customer might happen to be an administrator or an executor. On the other hand, it would be equally of serious moment if bankers were to be allowed to shelter themselves under that title, and to say that they were at liberty to become parties or privies to a breach of trust committed with regard to trust property, and, looking to their position as bankers merely, to insist that they were entitled to pay away money which constituted a part of trust property at a time when they knew it was going to be misapplied . . . the result of those authorities is clearly this: in order to hold a banker justified in refusing to pay a demand of his customer, the customer being an executor, and drawing a cheque as an executor, there must, in the first place, be some misapplication, some breach of trust, intended by the executor, and there must, in the second place . . . be proof that the bankers are privy to the intent to make this misapplication of the trust funds."[18]

---

[15] *Thomson* v. *Clydesdale Bank Ltd.* [1893] A.C. 282; *Union Bank of Australia Ltd.* v. *Murray-Aynsley* [1898] A.C. 693; *Bank of New South Wales* v. *Goulburn Valley Butter Co. Pty.* [1902] A.C. 543.

[16] *Calland* v. *Loyd* (1840) 6 M.7 W. 26; *Tassell* v. *Cooper* (1850) 9 C.B. 509; *Fontaine-Besson* v. *Parr's Banking Co. and Alliance Bank Ltd.* (1895) 12 T.L.R. 121; *Szek* v. *Lloyds Bank* (1908) *The Times,* January 15; *Plunkett* v. *Barclays Bank Ltd.* [1936] 2 K.B. 107; *John Shaw (Rayners Lane) Ltd.* v. *Lloyds Bank Ltd.* (1945) 5 L.D.A.B. 396; *Stoney Stanton Supplies (Coventry) Ltd.* v. *Midland Bank Ltd.* [1966] 2 Lloyd's Rep. 373.

[17] (1868) L.R. 3 H.L. 1.

[18] Contrast *Re Gross, ex p. Adair* (1871) 24 L.T. 198, 203; *Re Wall, Jackson* v. *Bristol and West of England Bank Ltd.* (1885) 1 T.L.R. 522, which was approved in *John Shaw (Rayners Lane) Ltd.* (1944) 5 L.D.A.B. 396.

5. LEADING AND MISLEADING CASES

Impetus was given to the idea that mere negligence would suffice, by *Selangor United Rubber Estates Ltd.* v. *Cradock (No. 2)*[19] where a man devised an illegal scheme to use company funds to buy shares in the company. The District bank had given him a bridging loan in the meantime, and another bank had handled and met cheques by which payments were made. Knowing assistance was alleged against the banks and others, and the District bank and others (but not the bank which merely handled cheques) were held liable for the full extent of the trust fund's losses, Ungoed-Thomas J. held that for knowing assistance, a crime need not be committed, if the parties were dishonest, knowing the act was morally reprehensible. Inconsistently, perhaps, he went on to hold the District bank liable, for its bridging loan had assisted, and it knew of circumstances from which a reasonable banker would have concluded that the payment was to finance a share purchase. This hardly seems to make the bank party to dishonesty, but rather made it liable—in the more serious case of knowing assistance—for what seems to be a form of negligence.[20] On the other hand, knowing receipt was not alleged, and the bank received the trust funds for its own benefit, the account being overdrawn because of the bridging loan. As shortly described, it may be that a form of constructive notice based upon gross negligence may not be inappropriate in a knowing receipt case where the bank benefits. On this ground, on a finding of gross negligence the bank might have been found liable, for knowing receipt (for the funds which it handled, and no more) having had a duty to inquire. The other bank was not liable, because it had been assured by the company's solicitor (when it handled the cheques) that they were for internal book-keeping reasons, and it was justified in assuming that this was correct, and in not making further inquiries. **10.08**

Similarly, in *Karak Rubber Co. Ltd.* v. *Burden (No. 2)*[21] a bank was held liable for knowing assistance, in circumstances where the bank's branch manager was held to be grossly negligent. The circumstances here were so strange that it seems arguable that the bank manager turned a blind eye to them, or at least, he knew the facts, and failed to draw the proper inferences, and perhaps the decision is justifiable on that ground. But this is not the basis of the decision, and it is by no means clear that the bank was party to any dishonesty. **10.09**

These cases suggest, therefore, that in relation to the most serious class of liability—knowing assistance, where liability for all of the trust fund's losses is sought to be established—constructive notice (classes (v) and (vi) of the cases discussed in para. 10.06 above) would suffice. It now seems reasonably clear, however, that these cases should no longer be regarded as good law. This conclusion arises mainly from the decision of the Court of Appeal, in *Belmont Finance Corpn. Ltd.* v. *Williams Furniture Ltd. (No. 2)*[22] where both knowing receipt and knowing assistance were alleged. Knowing receipt was proved, but not knowing assistance, because this required the defendant "to be in some way a party to the dishonesty." Even actual knowledge of what had happened did not amount to complicity in the scheme, if all that the defendant did was to receive the money. The Court of

[19] [1968] 2 All E.R. 1073.
[20] See Paget, 225 for severe criticism of the burden upon the bank.
[21] [1972] 1 All E.R. 1210. See also [1971] 3 All E.R. 1118.
[22] [1980] 1 All E.R. 393 (see also [1979] Ch. 250 for the earlier proceedings).

Appeal stressed that for knowing assistance actual dishonesty had to be shown, not merely misfeasance or breach of trust. What is said in the *Selangor* case about moral reprehensibility must be understood in this light.

According to Goff L.J. (referring to the two classes of *Barnes* v. *Addy*)

> "namely, receiving trust funds in such a way as to become accountable for them, and knowing participation in a dishonest and fraudulent design on the part of the trustees. The second of those ways does depend on fraud or dishonesty, but the first does not, and in saying that fraud was essential, we were dealing only with the second class of case, and with the argument of Belmont's counsel, which we rejected, that even there fraud is not a necessary part of the action."

That the "*Selangor* view" of knowing assistance is no longer good law is also suggested by *Re Montague's Settlement*[23] where Megarry V-C dissented (in a knowing receipt case) from the view expressed in the *Baden Delvaux* case, and held that "knowledge" required a "want of probity which justifies imposing a constructive trust." If this is so for knowing receipt, *a fortiori* for knowing assistance. Megarry V-C's dictum was followed by Alliott J. in *Lipkin Gorman* v. *Karpnale Ltd*[24] (in a knowing assistance case).[25] Alliott J. there said:

10.10
> "In my view, want of probity is a key aspect in the approach the court should take . . . There are, of course, differences in the court's approach to the two types of constructive trusteeship. In knowing receipt, fraud is irrelevant. The recipient will be liable if, with want of probity on his part he had actual or constructive notice that the payer was misapplying trust money and that the transfer to him was in breach of trust. In knowing assistance, the stranger to the trust must be proved subjectively to know of the fraudulent scheme of the trustee when rendering assistance, or to shut his eyes to the obvious, or to have wilfully and recklessly failed to make such inquiries as a reasonable an honest man would make.
>
> When (as in this case) the alleged constructive trustee is a bank, the court's approach must reflect the established contractual duties of a bank. In this context counsel for the bank made five propositions to me, as follows: 1. The bank is entitled to treat the customer's mandate at its face value except in extreme cases. 2. The bank is not obliged to question any transaction which is in accordance with the mandate, unless a reasonable banker would have grounds for believing that the authorised signatories are misusing their authority for the purpose of defrauding their principals or otherwise defeating his true intention. 3. It follows that if a bank does not have reasonable grounds for believing that there is fraud, it must pay. 4. Mere suspicion or unease do not constitute reasonable grounds and are not enough to justify a bank in failing to act in accordance with a mandate. 5. A bank is not required to act as an amateur detective. Those propositions were well supported by authority . . . and I accept them."

10.11
It would seem clear, therefore, that in knowing assistance cases something approaching complicity in the dishonest behaviour is required, but

[23] Unreported, (1986).
[24] June 10, 1986, FT.
[25] See also *Consul Development Pty. Ltd.* v. *D.P.C. Estates Pty. Ltd.* (1975) 132 C.L.R. 373.

that even in knowing receipt cases, lack of probity is required. Alliott J. makes reference to the first three categories of fault expressed in *Baden Delvaux* and it seems that he intends to exclude the other categories. It is not entirely clear from *Lipkin Gorman* whether "lack of probity" can ever be equated with gross negligence, but on the whole, it seems not. (One might, however, think of the distinction drawn in manslaughter cases between "criminal" negligence, warranting criminal sanctions, and tortious negligence: surely in the former case, one lacks probity?). Even where inquiry is necessary, it has been said that the bank need not behave as if it were a detective agency,[26] and need not follow every lead (it could offend an honest customer and drive him away), and to some extent the bank must be entitled to assume that the answers it receives (if they are sensible) are honest.[27] Certainly, a powerful argument may be made[28] that in no cases should "mere negligence" (class (vi)) be sufficient, for mere negligence of that sort is a common-law conception, not to be equated with equity's conception of reckless disregard for the rights of others (*i.e.* class (v) gross negligence) which arose in the context of dealings with real property, where a good purchaser would investigate title and make inquiries.

There is some discussion of "lack of probity" in *Carl Zeiss Stiftung* v. *Herbert Smith & Co. (No. 2).*[29] According to Sachs L.J. **10.12**

> "It does not, however, seem to me that a stranger is necessarily shown to be both a constructive trustee and liable for a breach of the relevant trusts even if it is established that he has such notice. As at present advised, I am inclined to the view that a further element has to be proved, at any rate in a case such as the present one. That element is one of dishonesty or of consciously acting improperly, as opposed to an innocent failure to make what a court may later decide to have been proper inquiry. That would entail both actual knowledge of the trust's existence and actual knowledge that what is being done is improperly in breach of that trust—though, of course, in both cases a person wilfully shutting his eyes to the obvious is in no different position than if he had kept them open . . . these cases tend quite strongly to the conclusion that negligent, if innocent, failure to make inquiry is not sufficient to attract constructive trusteeship."

And according to Edmund Davies L.J.

> "It may be objected that . . . reference to 'unjust enrichment,' 'want of probity' and 'the demands of justice and good conscience' merely introduces vague concepts which are in turn incapable of definition and which therefore provide no yardstick. I do not agree. Concepts may defy definition and yet the presence in or absence from a situation of that which they denote may be beyond doubt. The concept of 'want of probity' appears to provide a useful touchstone . . . It is true that not every situation where probity is lacking gives rise to a constructive

---

[26] See dicta in *Baden Delvaux and Lecuit* v. *Société Générale*, C.A. above, n. 14, referring to *Marfani & Co. Ltd.* v. *Midland Bank Ltd.* [1968] 2 All E.R. 573.

[27] See also *John Shaw (Rayners Lane) Ltd.* (1944) 5 L.D.A.B. 396.

[28] See Harpum, *loc. cit.* n. 1, above, citing *Ware* v. *Lord Egmont* (1854) 4 De G.M. & G. 460, 473; *Bailey* v. *Barnes* [1894] 1 Ch. 25, 34–35; *Oliver* v. *Hinton* [1899] 2 Ch. 264, 274; *Jones* v. *Smith* (1841) 1 Hare 43, 56; *West* v. *Reid* (1843) 2 Hare 249, 259; *Hudston* v. *Viney* [1921] 1 Ch. 98, 104; *Thomson* v. *Clydesdale Bank Ltd.* [1893] A.C. 282, 290.

[29] [1969] 2 Ch. 276; see also *Competitive Insurance Co. Ltd.* v. *Davies Investment Ltd.* [1975] 1 W.L.R. 1240.

trust. Nevertheless, the authorities appear to show that nothing short of it will do. Not even gross negligence will suffice."

10.13 If, however, want of probity is required for knowing receipt, and want of probity differs from complicity in fraud, (required for knowing assistance) where is the line to be drawn? One possibility would be to apply to knowing assistance cases the test drawn in criminal cases, where dishonesty is shown by a two-stage test: first, did the accused think that what he did was morally wrong? If so, he is dishonest. If not, did the accused think that people generally would think that what he did was wrong? If so, he is dishonest. Otherwise, he is not dishonest.[30] It may be that this test should be the appropriate test in judging the actions of the alleged constructive trustee. If so, then liability for all of the losses of the trust fund may lie whenever the bank dishonestly does an act which assists the dishonest trustee in causing loss to the trust fund.

Alternatively one might attempt to distinguish between knowing receipt and knowing assistance cases on the basis of the *Baden Delvaux* classifications, so that[31] knowingly assisting (liability for all the losses of the fund) requires any of classes (i) to (iii) of the type of fault mentioned and knowing receipt requires any of classes (i)-(iv) of the six classes mentioned.

6. CASES WHERE THE BANK BENEFITS FROM THE TRANSACTION

10.14 Notwithstanding what has already been said, a number of cases appear to hold that constructive knowledge (in the sense of gross negligence in failing to inquire) is sufficient if the bank itself benefits from the transaction (the usual case being where it applies funds to an overdraft).[32] Thus, if a trustee (whether known to be, or not) who is overdrawn, pays money into his account under pressure from his banker (or gives a security) the banker will be liable if either he knows that the trust money is used for the purpose, even if he does not realise the impropriety, or if the circumstances were such as to arouse suspicions and where he fails to make inquiries.[33]

10.15 In *Gray* v. *Johnston*[34] Lord Westbury referred to the banker's duty to honour mandates, and his duty not to set up this party rights against his customer, but continued:

"But then it has been very well settled that if an executor or a trustee who is indebted to a banker, or to another person, having the legal custody of the assets of a trust estate, applies a portion of them in the payment of his own debt to the individual having that custody, the

---

[30] See *Ghosh* [1982] Q.B. 1053. This catches "Robin Hood" or the anti-vivisectionist animal thief, who may believe that his acts are morally correct, but knows that people generally do not think so.

[31] Proposed by *Harpum, loc.cit.* n. 1, above.

[32] See *John* v. *Dodwell & Co.* [1918] A.C. 563; *Foxton* v. *Manchester and Liverpool District Banking Co.* (1881) 44 L.T. 406; *A-G* v. *De Winton* [1906] 2 Ch. 106; *British America Elevator Co. Ltd.* v. *Bank of British North America* [1919] A.C. 658; *Reckitt* v. *Barnett, Pembroke and Slater Ltd.* [1929] A.C. 176; *Midland Bank Ltd.* v. *Reckitt* [1933] A.C. 1. *Contra, Coleman* v. *Bucks and Oxon Union Bank* [1897] 2 Ch. 243, where Byrne J. says that knowledge or reasonable suspicion on the bank's part of breach of trust, etc., is required. These cases are discussed in Paget, 90–91, where they are put on the ground of "benefit" to the banker.

[33] See the cases previous note, and *Jameson* v. *Union Bank of Scotland* (1913) 109 L.T. 850; *Imperial Bank of Canada* v. *Begley* [1936] 2 All E.R. 367. Contrast *Thomson* v. *Clydesdale Bank Ltd.* [1893] A.C. 282, 292.

[34] (1868) L.R. 3 H.L. 1, 14.

individual receiving the debt has at once not only abundant proof of the breach of the trust, but participates in it for his own personal benefit."

And again, Lord Cairns said,[35] having recognised the conflict of duties which might face the banker,

"if it be shewn that any personal benefit to the bankers themselves is designed or stipulated for, that circumstance, above all others, will most readily establish the fact that the bankers are in privity with the breach of trust which is about to be committed."

A recent "benefit" case is *Neste Oy* v. *Lloyds Bank P.L.C..*[36] A bank learned that its customer had decided to cease trading and to appoint a receiver. Before the receiver was appointed, the bank received a payment, which it credited to the customer's bank account, and which it wished to combine against other debts of that customer. The bank knew no more than the fact of the receivership and cessation of trading, and that some of the payments from the plaintiff were in advance of expenditure incurred by the customer. It would have been allowed to combine accounts, had there been no reason to make inquiry, but it was held that it should have inquired as to the circumstances of the receivership. This would have revealed that the funds concerned were the subject of a trust in favour of the receivers. The bank, therefore, had knowingly received trust funds. **10.16**

The first question is how one should categorise the degree of fault of the bank. It is difficult to see any "lack of probity" here, and the case seems to be an example of pure constructive liability, applicable because of the benefit to the bank, and its knowledge that some funds were advance payments. It is doubtful that mere knowledge of a receivership would lead to any duty to inquire, if funds were received before the receivership, and not known to be advance payments. What seems very debatable is whether the bank was so seriously at fault that its behaviour could be characterised as "gross" negligence.

A second question is when the duty to inquire would arise in such a case. It could arise on receipt of the funds, or at the time of the attempted combination. At the time of receipt, however, there may or may not be a debt on another account giving rise to the right to combine. If there is no such debt, why should the bank inquire, unless, perhaps, it contemplates allowing an overdraft on the strength of the funds received? If, on the other hand, the account is overdrawn at the time of receipt, that is when the right to combine arises, even if only later exercised, for it may be "exercised" at any time.[37] But it hardly seems reasonable to expect a banker, who has no intention of combining, to make inquiry at that stage. This suggests inquiry at the time of exercising the right of combination, not at the earlier time of receipt of funds. If, however, the statutory set-off provisions in the Insolvency Act 1986 apply[38] it would seem unlikely that the operation of the statute could be impeded by any duty to inquire. The relevant time for inquiry, therefore, may be the time at which the funds are received, and if this is the case for statutory set-off, it may be so for combination. The receipt of the funds may have encouraged the banker to allow the overdraft **10.17**

---

[35] At p. 11.
[36] [1983] 2 Lloyds Rep. 658.
[37] It is, after all, only an accounting position.
[38] Below, Chap. 28.

on the other account (or to allow it to be increased), and it may be wrong to judge the matter at the time of combination. But there is no easy answer.

7. A DIFFERENT (TRIPARTITE) CLASSIFICATION

10.18   What seems reasonably supportable from the authorities mentioned is that:

(a) there is a distinction between cases where one attempts to make the bank liable for the whole of the loss to the trust fund and those where the bank is merely to be liable for those funds which it has received or which have passed through its hands;

(b) knowing assistance requires that the bank be a party to the dishonesty. The decisions in the *Selangor* case, and in the *Karak Rubber* case, are insupportable. Both were knowing assistance cases where it was not shown that the bank was "party" to dishonesty;

(c) even in cases of knowing receipt, a lack of probity may be required and negligence, therefore, (even, probably, gross negligence) is insufficient. This conclusion is closely connected with the bank's contractual duty to its customer to obey the mandate;

(d) there may be a difference in "benefit" cases, where gross negligence may prevent the bank from retaining the benefit concerned;

(e) "mere" negligence, of a tortious standard, is insufficient as between bank and stranger-plaintiff, though it would seem that as between parties in a contractual relationship (bank and customer-plaintiff) mere negligence will suffice. This is simply because the bank has a contractual duty of reasonable care to its customer. Thus, it is established that where an agent acts on behalf of a principal (the customer), the agent's apparent authority (which depends on estoppel) is removed by negligence on the bank's part.

10.19   (f) the question arises, whether one may distinguish between cases depending on the kind of acts done ("receiving" as against "assisting"). If, for example, a bank which receives money subsequently pays it out again, it commits acts of "assistance" which, depending on the "mental" state, may make it party to the dishonesty and liable for all losses. Surely mere "receipt" may be just as dishonest, and in many cases just as apt to lead to further losses to the trust fund as any other kind of act, and it seems pointless to differentiate liabilities on the basis of acts done rather than on the basis of purpose, motive, knowledge or fault. If this is correct, the standard nomenclature is somewhat deceptive. The question is, what type of liability is one attempting to impose: if for the whole of the loss to the fund, the case is one of "knowing assistance"; if merely for the funds received or dealt with, it is a case of "knowing receipt." The standard terminology seems to refer to a definition of what has to be done to establish the liability in question, whereas in fact any act of assistance or receipt will establish either kind of liability depending on the degree of fault involved. One can become a party to theft merely by dishonestly receiving stolen funds, and so it should be with liability for constructive trust.

If these propositions are supportable, then (particularly if one accepts the application of the criminal definition of dishonesty) one may simply say[39] that:

(a) liability for all losses of the fund is established by dishonestly doing any act which contributes to any loss to the fund. (Ordinarily, the bank will be liable only for the funds which have passed through its hands. If the

---

[39] This analysis is similar to that proposed by *Harpum, loc.cit.* n. 1, above.

plaintiff seeks to establish the additional liability, he should be put to a high degree of proof, and should be required to show complicity in the fraud, by proof of dishonesty on the bank's part.) This might be referred to as "dishonest assistance";

(b) liability for funds which have passed through the bank's hands is established

either

(i) by gross negligence, where the bank receives a benefit from the transaction in question (the bank's duty should be highest, for the possibility of benefit is a temptation to turn a blind eye, and it should have to justify the retention of the benefit where the circumstances are such that it would be grossly negligent if an honest and reasonable man did not inquire). This might be referred to as "negligent receipt of benefit."

or

(ii) by behaviour falling short of dishonesty but still amounting to a lack of probity, where the bank receives no benefit. (The bank's duty to obey its principal may be said to outweigh any duty to strangers to inquire.) This might be referred to as "improperly dealing inconsistently."

The same ideas may be expressed in terms of the Baden Delvaux classifications:

(a) dishonest assistance (liability for all losses of the fund) requires classes (i) to (iii) of the six categories.

(b) improperly dealing inconsistently (liability for what passes through the bank's hands) requires any of classes (i)-(iv).

(c) negligent receipt of a benefit (liability for what passes through the bank's hands) requires any of classes (i)-(v) of the six classes mentioned earlier (*i.e.* it includes gross negligence).

(d) But mere negligence of a tortious standard is always insufficient (as regards stranger-plaintiffs).

8. DEFENCES TO LIABILITY

10.20 Clearly, the primary defence is that the bank has acted in good faith and (in benefit cases) without gross negligence. But assuming a prima facie liability is established, a defence similar to that of contributory negligence may be available to the bank.[40] This may apply even between stranger plaintiffs and the bank, for the principle may be that a court of equity may hold it to be inequitable to grant relief to a plaintiff who has behaved in a way which is "totally inadequate."[41]

9. THE REMEDY OF TRACING

10.21 Tracing is a proprietary remedy available to the beneficiary of a trust fund to recover his property. In the present context, there are two significant limitations on its availability: first, it is unavailable against a bona fide purchaser for value, and secondly, it is not available against a person who, hav-

---

[40] So held in *Lipkin Gorman* v. *Karpnale Ltd.*, above, n. 24, where the plaintiff was customer of the bank.

[41] See *International Sales and Agencies Ltd.* v. *Marcus* [1982] 3 All E.R. 551, where the defence in s.9(1) of the European Communities Act 1972, now in s.35 C.A. 1985, was held not to apply to liability based on constructive trusts—and, in any case, the receipt of gratuitous payment was not a "dealing" within the section (nor had the defendant acted in good faith).

ing received money for a principal, has, in good faith, passed the money on according to his principal's instructions. It seems clear that the question of "bona fides" in tracing cases is no more than an alternative way of posing the questions already considered in the preceeding discussion: that is, what amounts to fault. In other words, liability as constructive trustee in the "improperly dealing inconsistently" or "negligent receipt of benefit" cases is co-extensive with the availability of the remedy of tracing in the sense that if the equitable remedy of tracing is not available, one cannot be a constructive trustee under these heads.[42]

10. CONTRACT AND TRUST

10.22 In *Tai Hing Cotton Mill Ltd.* v. *Liu Chong Hing Bank Ltd.*[43] the Privy Council was concerned to insist that as between banker and customer the liabilities of the one to the other should be co-extensive. Accordingly,

> "their Lordships believed it to be correct in principle and necessary for the avoidance of confusion in the law to adhere to the contractual analysis."[44]

In the *Lipkin Gorman* v. *Karpnale Ltd.*[44a] (which involved a customer's claim against the bank) Alliott J. accepted that

> "it is undesirable to seek remedies outside the contract when the parties are clearly in a contractual relationship. I have been referred to, and accept, the passage in the Tai Hing case [1985] 2 All E.R. 947 at 957. But the fact remains that all bankers and their customers are in contractual relationship and there has been no complaint that the courts have considered on a number of occasions whether or not the bank has become a constructive trustee of a customer's money. I consider that the correct approach is that, in given circumstances, breach of contract on the part of the bank will render it liable as a constructive trustee."

This, it is submitted, is undeniably correct, though, as Alliott J. went on to say "It is important that there should be consistency between the two approaches." This is a somewhat odd remark, since Alliott J. excluded even gross negligence for liability for constructive trust, and it is clearly the case that a bank may be liable in contract for "mere" negligence towards its customer. The learned judge rejected the argument of counsel that the plaintiffs could not succeed on the basis of constructive trust if they failed in contract, and do not need to succeed on that basis if they succeed in contract. "In my view this is too disjunctive an approach."

It is not, however, clear what advantages there would ordinarily be for a customer be in sueing a bank for constructive trust, rather than for breach of contract. In cases such as *Lipkin Gorman*, the question may be reduced to one of mandate. If the bank has a mandate, it may debit the customer's account, and otherwise it should not. The mandate gives at least apparent authority to a fraudulent agent[45] but that apparent authority may be removed if the bank is negligent in not knowing of limitations on the auth-

---

[42] See also *Hayton*, (1985) 27 Mal.L.R. 313.
[43] [1985] 2 All E.R. 947, [1986] A.C. 519.
[44] At 957 (All E.R.).
[44a] Above, nn. 24, 40.
[45] A partner of a firm of solicitors, in that case.

ority of the partner.[46] In other words, constructive notice of want of authority removes apparent authority. In this context, constructive notice seems to mean "mere negligence." This being so, it would seem simpler to rely upon contractual principles.[47]

C. Quistclose trusts[48]

If A pays money to B for a specific purpose, known to B (or of which he has **10.23** constructive notice), the money is "clothed with a trust" for that purpose, and may not be appropriated by B for his own, or other uses. In *Barclays Bank Ltd.* v. *Quistclose Investments Ltd.*[49] money was paid into a company's bank account so that (as the bank knew) the company would be able to meet a dividend payment. When the company went into liquidation, the bank claimed a right of combination for debts which the company owed to it. But the House of Lords held that the company held the money on trust for the recipients of the dividend payments, and if that purpose failed (as it did here on liquidation) the primary trust was replaced by another trust (a "resulting" trust) in favour of the person who paid the money in. This is an unhappy rule, so far as banks are concerned, for the right to combine or to set-off is a reason for allowing companies to continue with a debt on one account, if money is available elsewhere.[50] Under this rule, however, the payer of money can defeat the bank's priority merely by ensuring that the bank knows of the purpose of payment. On the other hand, third party finance for companies suffering from difficulties is made easier if the third party knows that the bank or receiver or liquidator may not take the money if the company fails before it is paid out.

The principle of the Quistclose trust was expanded considerably in *Re Northern Developments (Holdings) Ltd.*[51] where it was decided that a "purpose" expressed with a great deal of vagueness, might still be effective to create a trust. Northern was the parent company of K. Co., which was experiencing difficulties. In a rescue attempt, a group of banks put up a fund which they paid into Northern's account for the purpose of K's unsecured creditors only. K went into receivership and the banks and K's other creditors were held to be entitled to the money, rather than Northern, or its bank. It would seem that a trust "for all our trade creditors," or "for all our creditors except you, our bank" would be effective.

In *Carreras Rothmans Ltd.* v. *Freeman Mathews Treasure Ltd.*[52] the plaintiff **10.24** employed the defendant as an advertising agency, and the defendant would contract with third party advertising media. Each month the plaintiff paid the defendant money equal to the defendant's fee plus money paid by the defendant to the third parties in the last month. When the defendant got into difficulties, the plaintiff started to pay money into a special account to be used for the sole purpose of settling invoices submitted by the third parties. This was held to create a Quistclose trust, and the liquidator of the defend-

---

[46] See, *e.g. Reckitt* v. *Barnett Pembroke and Slater Ltd.* [1929] A.C. 176; *Colonial Bank* v. *Cady and Williams* (1890) 15 App.Cas. 267.
[47] For another case which could have been decided on contractual principles, see *Rowlandson* v. *National Westminster Bank Ltd.* [1978] 3 All E.R. 370.
[48] See *Millet* (1985) LQR 269, and *Goodhart & Jones* (1980) MLR 489. See also *Re Kayford* [1975] 1 All E.R. 604.
[49] [1970] A.C. 567.
[50] For combination, see Chap. 13, below.
[51] (Unrep.)
[52] [1985] Ch. 207, noted [1986] 1 JIBL N–25 and [1985] All E.R. Review, 316.

ant company was not entitled to the money. The liquidator argued that repayment to the plaintiff offended against the principle of *pari passu* distribution, but the court said that this applied only to assets owned beneficially by the company, and that assets subject to a trust were not the company's assets. The liquidator also argued that the agreement created a charge on the company's book debts in favour of third parties, and was void for non-registration under section 395 of the Companies Act 1985. The court, however, held that either the arrangement did not constitute a charge, but was only a trust, or if it was a charge there was also a trust, and the trust could be enforced even if the charge could not be enforced. A further complication was that at the date of liquidation, the plaintiff owed one month's payments. The liquidator claimed this, but the plaintiff resisted because the money would have gone not to the third parties, but to creditors generally. Nevertheless, the liquidator was entitled to the money. Thus, money as yet unpaid but owing went free of the trust, while money actually paid into the special account was subject to the trust.

Quistclose trusts, like other trusts, may arise from constructive notice, and it is thought that the same principles as discussed earlier would apply, depending on whether the bank intends to benefit from receipt of the money (constructive notice may affect it) or is alleged only to have disposed of the funds to the wrong source.

D. Duties where bank is trustee of funds

10.25 It is an interesting question whether the principle of *Foley* v. *Hill* applies where the bank itself is trustee of funds, which is to say, where funds are given to it so that it may act as trustee. This must be distinguished from cases where a customer is trustee of funds deposited, and from constructive trusts, in which cases the bank is liable only if it knows (or maybe ought to know) of the customer's breaches of trust. The Quistclose trust, already considered, is an example of the present problem, and we have seen that monies deposited to a customer's account for a specific purpose may be impressed with a trust, so that they are not available on the customer's insolvency to the customer's creditors. It would seem to follow, similarly, that the monies would not be available on the insolvency of the bank, for the bank's creditors. The question arose in *Space Investments Ltd.* v. *Canadian Imperial Bank of Commerce Trust Co. (Bahamas) Ltd.*[53] where at first instance it was held that trust creditors of a bank ranked in priority to the unsecured creditors of that bank, on the bank's insolvency. The Privy Council reversed this decision. Having pointed out the general rule (from *Foley* v. *Hill*) applying to ordinary depositors, Lord Templeman discussed the special rules applicable to bank trustees. First, the funds might be wrongly misappropriated by the bank. In that case, the equitable remedy of tracing had the effect of creating an equitable charge for the beneficiaries, over all the assets of the bank, and this charge took priority over the unsecured creditors. But equity gave no similar protection where the bank exercised powers conferred by the trust instrument, in good faith. In this case, some of the settlements of which the bank was trustee empowered the bank (as trustee) to deposit with itself (as banker) monies which it had received in trust. The effect of that was that just as with ordinary deposits, the monies received as banker were held beneficially by the bank, on a

[53] [1986] 3 All E.R. 75 (JC).

debtor-creditor relationship with the beneficiaries. The beneficiaries had no rights to any asset (or in all the assets) of the bank. The bank continued to have obligations as trustee, but in respect of the proper management of the account, not in a proprietary respect of the money transferred to its general banking business. This reasoning seems to be of general application, wherever monies are deposited in trust with a bank not for a specific purpose, but for general investment. But it may not apply to the Quistclose trust, where monies are deposited with the bank for the specific purpose of being paid to other persons. On the other hand, in none of the modern "Quistclose cases" was a bank the insolvent party, and it would seem that unless the "purpose" is to be effected immediately the funds are received, the bank has the right to apply those funds generally in the meantime. If it has the right to do so then, there being no breach of trust to cause an equitable charge to affix to the bank's assets, the reasoning of the *Space Investments* case seems to be applicable. The result of this, therefore, is that even if a bank receives funds as trustee, unless it is in some way prohibited from dealing with the funds as banker, the beneficiary has no right over the assets of the bank, although the bank retains obligations as trustee properly to manage the account, and not to misappropriate the money in breach of trust. Whether or not one can say that in relation to the deposit the relation is one of debtor-creditor, the result is the same.

115

11. Remedies to Recover Money

11.01 There are two actions to recover money paid. One of these is known as a tracing, and this is a "proprietary" action.[1] The other is known as a personal action, or as the "action for money had and received" or for "money paid by mistake of fact." We have space here to consider only the latter remedy, although reservation of title (Romalpa) clauses (which depend to some extent upon tracing) are considered elsewhere.[2]

The personal action: money paid by mistake[3]

INTRODUCTION

11.02 Through an administrative error on the bank's part, or because of forgery on a cheque or an unauthorized signature, a bank may wrongly pay money to a payee who is unauthorized by the bank's customer, and the bank may, if not protected (say, by estoppel, or by statute), be liable to the customer or to the true owner of a cheque. The bank may, therefore, wish to recover the money wrongly paid from the person paid.[4] In addition to this, a bank may be the recipient of money wrongly paid, and the question of its liability arises.

Common examples of mistakes, some at least of which are sufficient to allow recovery, would be: (a) if payment is accidentally made on a countermanded cheque; (b) if payment is made on a cheque where the drawer's signature is forged; (c) if payment is made in the belief that the drawer has sufficient funds in his account (whether the money is recoverable in this case is considered below); (d) if payment is made to the wrong person (*e.g.* if there are two Smiths with accounts at the bank); (e) if money is overpaid (double credits seem to be quite common); (f) if payment is made by a confirming bank to the beneficiary of a letter of credit, where the bank believes wrongly that the documents are correct.

11.03 The personal remedy depends on the action for "money had and received."[5] One circumstance in which this action is available is where money is paid by mistake of fact: this is one of the clearest examples in English law of a remedy given to prevent unjust enrichment.[6] There has been much discussion of the basis of the action (whether contractual, tortious, equitable, etc.)[7] but this seems unnecessary to pursue here.[8]

---

[1] See *Scott* (1966) 7 W.A.L.R. 463; *Goode* (1976) 92 L.Q.R. 360, 528; *Pearce* (1976) 40 Conv.(NS) 277; *Khurshid and Matthews* (1979) 95 L.Q.R. 78; and generally Goff and Jones, *The Law of Restitution* (2nd ed., 1978).

[2] Below, Chap. 23.

[3] Generally, see Goff and Jones, *The Law of Restitution.*

[4] If a bank wrongly pays, acting as agent, the customer may sue the payee: *Turvey* v. *Dentons (1923) Ltd.* [1953] 1 Q.B. 218.

[5] In the older forms of action, the plaintiff would demand repayment of money said to have been "had and received by the defendant to the plaintiff's use."

[6] See *Kelly* v. *Solari* (1841) 9 M. & W. 54.

[7] See Goff and Jones, *op. cit.*, Paget, 283 *et seq.*

[8] *Cf. Bank Russo-Iran* v. *Gordon Woodroffe & Co. Ltd.* (1972) 116 Sol.Jo. 921 where the point is made that the existence and effect of the right is not determined by the proper law of the contract, since it is not a contractual right.

1. CONDITIONS FOR RECOVERY OF MONEY

If money paid by mistake is to be recoverable by way of the action for **11.04** money had and received, the following conditions must apply:

(a) Payment to the payee must not be made under mandate from the customer so that a debt is created between bank and customer.[9] If for example, the payee is the wrong person (*e.g.* not the true owner of a cheque), the money could be recovered, but not if there is an insufficiency of funds. At first sight it is difficult to see why the existence of a mandate is crucial, for the bank in either case pays as agent either with actual or (in many cases) (*e.g.* payment on a countermanded cheque, where payee does not know of the countermand) with ostensible authority, and payment with either form of authority is sufficient to discharge a liability of the customer to the payee. The real difference between the two situations seems to be that payment under mandate (actual authority) creates a debt between bank and customer, so that the bank has some kind of remedy for the payment, whereas payment without mandate leaves the bank remediless against the customer unless it can recover the money from the third party payee. If it is understood that the personal action is based upon the avoidance of unjust enrichment, a principle based on the existence of a mandate is somewhat easier to comprehend.

(b) the mistake must be one of fact, not of law[10]

(c) the mistake must cause the payment—*i.e.* the mistake must not be so trivial that the bank would have paid anyway, and the payer must not intend the payee to have the money anyway. This is sometimes expressed by saying that the mistake must be fundamental, though for payments thought by the payer to be made under obligation, there seems to be no such requirement.[11] Since the mistake must cause the payment, it is the payer's mistake which matters, not that of the payee.[12]

(d) It is sometimes said that the payer must pay believing that it is legally **11.05** obliged to do so, and that a voluntary payment is insufficient. This may often be so, but is not necessarily the case, and a payment not made to discharge a liability, but made under a fundamental mistake, may be recoverable.[13] In *Morgan* v. *Ashcroft*[14] the court explained that a mistake in a voluntary payment would often be insufficiently fundamental (a bookmaker's overpayment was irrecoverable). This would seem to be the true principle, in the light of *Kerrison* v. *Glyn Mills Currie & Co.*,[15] where a payment not made to discharge a liability was recoverable.[16] If this is the case, then the true question seems to be merely, did the mistake cause the pay-

---

[9] *Barclays Bank Ltd.* v. *W. J. Simms, Son & Cooke (Southern) Ltd.* [1979] 3 All E.R. 522, [1980] Q.B. 677.

[10] Below, para. 11.13. Note, however, the special equitable action described below, para. 10.14.

[11] *Barclays Bank Ltd.* v. *W. J. Simms, Son & Cooke (Southern) Ltd.* above, n. 9. Mistake must be "vital or material." Causation is stressed in *R. E. Jones Ltd.* v. *Waring and Gillow Ltd.* [1926] A.C. 670; *Edler* v. *Auerbach* [1950] 1 K.B. 359.

[12] *Westminster Bank Ltd.* v. *Arlington Overseas Trading Co.* [1952] 1 Lloyds Rep. 211; *Secretary of State for Employment* v. *Wellworthy (No. 2)* [1976] I.C.R. 13; *Barclays Bank Ltd.* v. *W. J. Simms, Son & Cooke (Southern) Ltd.* above, n. 9.

[13] *Aiken* v. *Short* (1856) 1 H. & N. 210, suggests this.

[14] [1938] 1 K.B. 49.

[15] (1911) 17 Com.Cas. 41, discussed below, para. 11.11.

[16] See also, *Larner* v. *L.C.C.* [1949] 2 K.B. 863.

ment, in the sense that without it, the payment would not have been made, so that by reason of the mistake the payee has been unjustly enriched.

11.06   (e) Although the only mistake which matters is that of the payer, it is often said that the mistake must be "between" payer (bank) and payee.[17] The meaning of this is obscure, perhaps especially in relation to banks. It is easy enough to understand if the wrong person is paid: that is clearly a mistake between payer and payee. But if, say, the drawer countermands, or if the bank pays wrongly believing its customer to have sufficient funds, can it be said that this is a mistake between payer and payee, or only between customer and bank? In *Barclays Bank Ltd.* v. *W. J. Simms, Son & Cooke (Southern) Ltd.*[18] (a countermand case) both of these were held to be a mistake between payer and payee, although it is also, of course, between bank and customer (drawer). The bank believed itself obliged to obey the mandate. It would seem that any payment which the bank believes itself obliged to make is a mistake between itself and payee[19] but that other mistakes may be included. In *R. E. Jones Ltd.* v. *Waring and Gillow Ltd.*[20] J, being deceived by B, paid W & G at B's request, in return for a contractual right expected from W & G. The money was recoverable, though J was in no sense obliged to pay. What then does it add to the understanding of the principles involved to say that the mistake must be between payer and payee, given that it is conceded that the payee need not know of the mistake? It is respectfully submitted that nothing is added, and that it is sufficient if a mistake is made which is of sufficient seriousness that it can be said that but for that mistake no payment would have been made by the payer to the payee. This makes it a mistake between payer and payee.[21]

In summary, it appears that there are only three requirements for recovery, these being (i) that the payment must not be made by the bank under mandate so as to create a customer-bank debt relationship, (ii) that the mistake must be of fact, not of law, and (iii) that the mistake must cause the payment to be made.

2. RESTRICTIONS ON THE RECOVERY OF MONEY

11.07   Payments will not be recoverable if any of the three conditions mentioned above are not fulfilled, and also in the following cases:

(i) If the payment is to an agent who has passed the money to his principal before learning of the mistake, only the principal, and not the agent can be sued.[22] That the principal is unidentified, or that the bank thinks it has paid A, when it has paid B, makes no difference, and if the bank has paid honestly, etc., it is not liable.[23] The agent must have had no notice of the plaintiff's claim before he disposes of the money, he must not act as principal during the transaction, and must have received the money bona fide

---

[17] See the discussion below of *Barclays Bank Ltd.* v. *W. J. Simms, Son & Cooke (Southern) Ltd.*, above, n. 9, and *Chambers* v. *Miller* (1862) 13 C.B.N.S. 125.

[18] Above, n. 9.

[19] *Aiken* v. *Short* above, n. 13. *Weld-Blundell* v. *Synott* [1940] 2 K.B. 107.

[20] [1926] A.C. 670.

[21] Paget, 296 comes close to this, but then adds "But the mistake must be between the parties . . ."

[22] *Buller* v. *Harrison* (1777) 2 Cowp. 565, *Rahimtoola* v. *Nizam of Hyderabad* [1958] A.C. 379; *Continental Caoutchouc and Gutta Percha Co.* v. *Kleinwort Sons & Co.* (1904) 90 L.T. 474; *Thomas* v. *Houston Corbett & Co.* [1969] N.Z.L.R. 151; *National Westminster Bank Ltd.* v. *Barclay's Bank International Ltd. & Ismail* [1975] Q.B. 654.

[23] *Gowers* v. *Lloyds and National Provincial Foreign Bank Ltd.* [1937] 3 All E.R. 55.

(with no knowledge, for example, of any other wrongdoing). If these conditions are not fulfilled, the agent is liable as is the principal.[24]

(ii) Money cannot be recovered if the payer is estopped from asserting his entitlement to it. In this context, the rule is that estoppel requires (a) a representation made to the payee, or some breach of duty owed to him by the bank, (b) the payee's reliance on this representation or omission, to his detriment or so that it is inequitable for the payer to claim to recover,[25] (c) that the payee is himself not at fault.[26] Examples of the third case could be where the defendant must have realised the mistake (*e.g.* because of a large, unexpected and unexplained credit to the account), or where he has induced the representation by concealing material facts[27] or where a cheque comes into his hands under suspicious circumstances (*e.g.* offered at an unusually deep discount).[28]

Much of the difficulty in this area arises from the rule often referred to as the rule in *Cocks* v. *Masterman*,[29] which holds that the representation which gives rise to the estoppel must be *other than the payment itself.* The mere fact of wrongful payment is neither a representation nor a breach of duty sufficient to give rise to an estoppel. But if the money credited to an account is notified to (say, by bank statements) and then spent by the recipient who has then insufficient funds to repay without hardship, recovery may be impossible. In *Lloyds Bank Ltd.* v. *The Hon. Cecily K. Brooks*[30] the bank overpaid the defendant's account, and sent her statements showing the exaggerated balance. She relied on this, and spent more money than she would otherwise have done. This was irrecoverable by the bank. This would not have been the case had the overcrediting have been of such an amount that the customer must have realised the mistake. In *United Overseas Bank* v. *Jiwani*[31] the defendant, who had been credited in error, failed to prove that he had altered his mode of living as a result, but had he done so, he would have succeeded. In *Avon CC.* v. *Howlett*[32] the defendant was overpaid by his employer while on sick leave. Representations were made to him in the form of pay slips showing his supposed entitlement. He showed that he had spent some of the money, and the court accepted that it would be inequitable to demand all of the money back. Since estoppel has an "all or nothing" effect, the employer was able to recover none of the money, even that part of the sum overpaid which had not yet been spent. It is clear, then, that the mere fact that the recipient spends money received wrongly, even if paid to him as the result of negligence on the part of the payer, is insufficient to establish any right in the payee to retain, though there may be some circumstances in which some form of negligent behav-

11.08

---

[24] *National Westminster Bank Ltd.* v. *Barclay's Bank International Ltd. & Ismail* [1975] Q.B. 654. Paget, 302 appears to think that the principal is not liable if the agent is liable, but there is no authority for this.

[25] Where someone is overpaid, that is hardly a detriment. But it may be inequitable to call on them to repay once they have spent the money: *Avon C.C.* v. *Howlett*, below n. 32.

[26] Though this may be regarded merely as an example of a case where denial is not inequitable.

[27] See *George Whitechurch Ltd.* v. *Cavanagh* [1902] A.C. 117, 145.

[28] See *National Westminster Bank Ltd.* v. *Barclay's Bank International Ltd. & Ismail* [1975] Q.B. 654. In *Secretary of State for Employment* v. *Wellworthy Ltd. (No. 2)* [1976] I.C.R. 13 it is suggested that even negligence by the defendant debars him: *sed quaere.*

[29] (1829) 9 B. & C. 902.

[30] (1950) 6 L.D.A.B., 161.

[31] [1976] 1 W.L.R. 964.

[32] [1983] 1 All E.R. 1073.

iour (other than solely in relation to the payment) amounts to a representation.[33]

11.09   (iii) *Cocks* v. *Masterman* also establishes that money cannot be recovered
from the holder of (a) a negotiated (b) negotiable instrument, (c) with an
intrinsic defect, where (d) he has been paid (for example, from the holder of
a negotiated bill of exchange with a forged indorsement). The principle here
is sometimes said to depend on estoppel, but if so it is an easier form of
estoppel to establish than that just described. Here, (a) the payment itself is
sufficient to establish a representation, and (b) it may be the case that the
payee need not actually have altered his position in reliance. Some dicta suggest that it is sufficient if he might suffer detriment, and others suggest that
it is sufficient if the payment has been made, apparently on the theory that if
the payee is to be able to sue other parties on the instrument, he would have
to give notice of dishonour, and if he gets paid, and then has to repay, this
would cause delay, and the delay is itself a detriment which may affect his
position. More recent dicta suggest that as with ordinary estoppel, there
must actually be detriment or it must be inequitable to call for repayment.[34]
In *Barclays Bank Ltd.* v. *W. J. Simms, Son & Cooke (Southern) Ltd.*[35] Goff J
agreed what was said by the Privy Council in the *Imperial Bank of Canada* v.
Bank of Hamilton[36]; that the reason for the rule is the possibility of prejudice
when notice of dishonour is required, and that if no notice has to be given to
anyone, or if it is given in reasonable time without loss, the "easier estoppel" principle of *Cocks* v. *Masterman* will not apply. It may be, then, that the
only special advantage of negotiable instruments is that receipt of payment
itself is a representation.[37] But this "easier" principle will not apply if the
instrument is not a negotiable instrument (*e.g.* if it has a forged drawer's signature, it is not a bill, and not negotiable)[38] or if the mistake is not about
some defect intrinsic to the instrument itself (*e.g.* if it is only about funds in
the account)[39] or if the payee is the original payee (because the bill cannot
have been negotiated to him). In these cases, therefore, the payee could only
rely on the strict form of estoppel described earlier, and if he cannot establish that, he must repay the money.

3. LEADING CASES

11.10   In *R. E. Jones Ltd.* v. *Waring & Gillow Ltd.*[40] B bought goods on hire-
purchase from W & G. B falsely told J that B was an agent for motor manu-
facturers and got J to agree to pay £5000 in return for an appointment as agent

---

[33] *Kelly* v. *Solari* (1841) 9 M & W. 54; *Barclays Bank Ltd.* v. *W. J. Simms, Son & Cooke (Southern) Ltd.* above, n. 9. There are dicta in *R. E. Jones Ltd.* v. *Waring & Gillow,* above, nn. 11,
20 which do suggest that the defendant's alteration of position in itself may debar recovery,
but this seems insupportable—thought Paget, 308 treats the matter as being still in doubt.

[34] The principles referred to are derived from *Cocks* v. *Masterman* (1829) 9 B & C. 902; *Mather*
v. *Lord Maidstone* (1856) 18 C.B. 273, 294; *London and River Plate Bank* v. *Bank of Liverpool*
[1896] 1 Q.B. 7; *Imperial Bank of Canada* v. *Bank of Hamilton* [1903] A.C. 49; *National Westminster Bank Ltd.* v. *Barclays Bank International Ltd. and Ismail* above, n. 24; *Barclays Bank Ltd.*
v. *W. J. Simms, Son & Cooke (Southern) Ltd.* above, n. 9.

[35] Previous note.

[36] Above, n. 34.

[37] *Contra,* Paget 311–313.

[38] *National Westminster Bank Ltd.* v. *Barclays Bank International Ltd. and Ismail* [1975] 1 Q.B.
654. This case also disposed of the false principle that the banker has a duty to know his customer, which had been argued so as to raise an "ordinary" estoppel.

[39] *Ibid.*

[40] [1926] A.C. 670.

for the car manufacturer. Because J were reluctant to pay B, B told J to pay the money to W & G. J gave B a cheque for W & G and B gave the cheque to W & G to pay off his debt to them. W & G returned to B goods which they had seized when B defaulted. Now J sued W & G for the money and W & G were required to repay. Although J had been negligent, there was no representation (other than payment) by J on which W & G had relied to their detriment, so that J was not estopped. Two points may be expressly made: i) it would be different if W & G were holders for value, since J as drawer would then be liable to them on the cheque. But W & G were not holders for value because no consideration had been given by them, the payees, to the drawer W & G, they being the only two parties to the cheque, and ii) although this was a negotiable instrument, the mistake was extraneous to the instrument, and in any case, it had not been negotiated and there were no prior parties, and there was no possible detriment to anyone by delay.

In *Kleinwort, Sons & Co.* v. *Dunlop Rubber Co.*[41] D owed money to Kramisch. Kramisch told D to pay part of this to Kleinwort, and equitably assigned £3000 of the debt to B, (and told D to pay this to B). By mistake, however, D paid the £3000 to Kleinwort.[42] B sued D, and was successful, and D then sued Kleinwort to recover the money. Kleinwort argued that at the time they were paid, they had already let Kramisch exceed an overdraft with them, and had put the £3000 to that account, and had continued the account, so that they had acted in reliance on the payment, to their detriment. Mere receipt to an overdrawn account in good faith would be a defence to an equitable tracing action, but by the personal action the money was recoverable by D because only estoppel could assist Kleinwort, and the jury had found that Kleinwort had not altered their position to their detriment. (They had made further advances, and it might have been thought that this would have been enough, but the jury's finding indicated that they would have done so anyway.) But even if they had so acted, there would have to be some representation other than the payment itself. The principle concerning negotiated bills did not apply, the defect being extrinsic to the cheque.

In *Kerrison* v. *Glyn Mills Currie & Co.*[43] K paid money by mistake to the account of a customer at G.M.C. (the customer then owing a greater sum to G.M.C.). G.M.C. made no further advances on the strength of the payment in. K then claimed the money from G.M.C., who asserted that they had a right of combination (referred to as a "lien") in respect of the payment, but the court excluded that right, the money not being the customer's. G.M.C. were required to repay. Again, a tracing remedy would have been defeated when the bank took for value. Additionally, it should be observed that although the action is personal, it is available (as here) against not only the customer to whose account it is credited, but against the bank which receives the money for him. Thus, on the one hand the bank is considered to receive the money as agent for the customer, and not in its own right as purchaser for value, (as it would be regarded in respect to tracing) but on the other hand the bank is subject to a personal, non-proprietary action, on the grounds that it (albeit as agent) is the recipient of the funds. These distinctions are very curious.

In *National Westminster Bank Ltd.* v. *Barclay's Bank International Ltd. &*

11.11

---

[41] (1907) 97 L.T. 263. (H.L.).
[42] For Kramisch's overdrawn account, so that it is really a payment to Kleinwort.
[43] (1911) 81 L.J.K.B. 465, 17 Com.Cas. 41.

Ismail[44] Ismail, in Nigeria bought a cheque drawn on an account at the plaintiff bank, but before paying for it Ismail sent it to his own bank (Barclays) in London for collection. Barclays collected it, and Ismail then paid for it in Nigeria. The bill was then found to be a complete forgery. The plaintiff sued Barclays and Ismail. Ismail argued for an estoppel on the grounds that the plaintiff owed him a duty of care[45] and that he had acted to his detriment in reliance on the fulfilment of this duty. Both Barclays and Ismail were held liable. No representation had been made to Ismail, other than by payment, and no duty was owed to him. Barclays were liable, because they had not paid Ismail, but if they had done so, only Ismail would have been liable. The "easier" rule about negotiable instruments did not apply, because the forgery meant that this was not even a bill.

11.12   In *Barclays Bank Ltd.* v. *W. J. Simms, Son & Cooke (Southern) Ltd.*[46] payment was made on a cheque contrary to the drawer's countermand and the paying bank was able to recover the money.[47] This is relatively straightforward, but there was some discussion also of the case where a bank pays believing that the customer has sufficient funds, when he has not. In *Chambers* v. *Miller*[48] the bank discovered such a mistake immediately after paying, and attempted to stop the payee from leaving the bank. The court held that they were liable for assault and false imprisonment.[49] The judgment is given in terms of the effect of the mistake, on the assumption that if the money is irrecoverable, the bank was liable. The court said that the mistake was between drawer and payer, not between payer and payee. Thus, property in the money passed to the payee, and he could not be detained. In the present case, Robert Goff J. disagreed with the reasoning in *Chambers* v. *Miller*, holding that the mistake there was capable of being a mistake between payer and payee. The real reason for the decision, said the learned judge, was that the cheque is a good mandate, and a request for an overdraft, which the bank accepts by paying. The customer's debt to the payee is discharged. As the payee gave the customer consideration, the money is irrecoverable. Paget[50] agrees that the mistake in *Chambers* v. *Miller* was between payer and payee but argues that if it was, the presence or absence of a mandate is, because of that very fact, irrelevant, as the money is still paid by mistake. Paget also argues that the existence of consideration between customer and payee is no concern of the bank's, and that money paid by mistake as to adequacy of funds should be recoverable. It is submitted that Paget is correct as to the consideration point. Additionally, if a bank pays on a countermanded cheque or on an insufficiency of fund it has, in either case, at least ostensible authority (and, in the latter case, actual authority) and payment with either form of authority should discharge the customer's liability to the payee. It is nevertheless thought that the argument of the learned editor of Paget ignores the element of unjust enrichment, and the purpose of the remedy. The distinction made by Goff J. between cases of mandate and no mandate may be justified by the principle of avoiding unjust enrichment.

---

[44] [1975] Q.B. 654.
[45] To know their own customer's signature.
[46] [1979] 3 All E.R. 522 (Robert Goff J.), [1980] Q.B. 677.
[47] See also *Southland Savings Bank* v. *Anderson* [1974] 1 N.Z.L.R. 118.
[48] (1862) 13 C.B.N.S. 125, 32 L.J.C.P. 30.
[49] This, one would think should be so whether or not the bank has a legal remedy to recover the money.
[50] At 332–3.

Where a party is paid by mistake and the bank had a mandate (*e.g.* payment on insufficient funds) a debt is created between bank and customer by reason of the payment. The bank may then debit the customer's account and there is no reason to recover from a third party. The customer is not detrimentally affected, because his liability to the third party is discharged. Where there is no mandate (*e.g.* countermand not obeyed), then even if (as submitted here) the payment discharges the customer's liability to the payee, non-recovery would enrich the customer inasmuch as the bank has no remedy against him. By way of compromise, the money is recoverable from the payee, who may then, as before, sue the customer for the debt. Another reason for rejecting Paget's argument is that if it is correct, the bank would be able to sue both the customer (in a mandate case, a debt would be created), and the payee. Robert Goff J.'s opinions as to case of insufficiency of funds were stated *obiter*, but it is submitted that it would be correct to deny the bank recovery on the principle that there is a mandate (whether or not the customer's debt to the payee is discharged.)

4. MISTAKE OF FACT, AND MISTAKE OF LAW

In *Kelly* v. *Solari*[51] Lord Abinger said that money paid by mistake of law **11.13** was irrecoverable. The distinction between a mistake of fact and one of law is notoriously difficult (if not impossible) to make, and many have suggested that the distinction should be abolished. In our view, the present state of the law as shown in the cases is ridiculous and scandalous, and we make no attempt to bring order from chaos, since we believe it to be both impossible and pointless.[52] In *Kiriri Cotton Co. Ltd.* v. *Dewani*[53] the principle concerning mistake of law was said to be subject to an exception, where the defendant was responsible for causing the mistake.

There appears to be an exception in cases arising out of the administration **11.14** of estates, where, for example, an executor wrongly pays persons not entitled in law to receive any part of the estate. This money is recoverable.[54]

---

[51] (1841) 9 M. & W. 54.

[52] The reader must turn to other works for a full exposition: some of the confusing judicial statements have been as follows (they are paraphrased): This property is not subject to the Rent Acts (fact)—*Solle* v. *Butcher* [1950] 1 K.B. 671. The Rent Acts bind the Crown, so that this Crown tenant is protected (law)—*Territorial & Auxiliary Forces Assn.* v. *Nichols* [1949] 1 K.B. 35. A certain statute exists, affecting a landlord's right to rent (law)—*Sharp Bros. & Knight* v. *Chant* [1917] 1 K.B. 771. A statement about the powers of a company, under a private Act of Parliament (fact)—*Kitson* v. *Commercial Bank*. The law of a foreign state is XYZ (fact) *Andre & Cie S.A.* v. *Ets. Michel Blanc* [1977] 2 Lloyds Rep. 166 (in this case Lord Denning, with whom the majority disagreed, said that the distinction between fact and law was illusory, and should be abandoned). We owe you £X while you are away from work (fact)—*Avon C.C.* v. *Howlett*, above, n. 32. There is a legally enforceable option between us, or between me and another (fact) *Taylor Fashions Ltd.* v. *Liverpool Victoria Trustees Co. Ltd.* [1981] 1 All E.R. 897. There is a contract between us and we are liable under it to you (fact)—*AIP Co. Ltd.* v. *Texas Commerce International Bank Ltd.* [1981] 1 All E.R. 923. Goff J. says "where one party has represented to the other that a transaction between them has an effect which in law it does not have" this is factual and can give rise to an estoppel. We are liable (law); we will pay you money (promise, not fact)—*China Pacific S.A.* v. *Food Corpn. of India* [1980] 3 All E.R. 556. Payments under this separation agreement are free of any deduction of tax (law) *Ord* v. *Ord.* [1923] 2 K.B. 432. Whether under a statute a landlord has an obligation to pay for repairs is a question of fact—*Brikom Investments* v. *Seaford* (*per* Ormrod L.J. "these dichotomies are dangerously neat and apt to mislead. Representations of fact shade into representations of law . . . ") Whether under a statute a tenant was protected (fact)—*Keen* v. *Holland* [1984] 1 All E.R. 75.

[53] [1960] A.C. 192.

[54] *Re Diplock* [1948] Ch. 465, aff'd [1951] A.C. 251.

This may not apply, for example, to a company liquidation.[55] The recipient is not liable unless the personal representative is sued first, or is protected by insolvency or otherwise. Nor is the recipient liable if he is a bona fide purchaser for value, without notice.

5. COMBINATION, AND SET–OFF, AND MISTAKE

11.15 If money is wrongly paid to a customer's account, and is recoverable from him by action, it is also recoverable from the bank, even if it takes for value (*e.g.* paying into an overdrawn account). The reason is simply that the money is not the customer's, so that the bank cannot exercise its rights of set-off or combination, whether on the customer's insolvency, or otherwise.[56]

6. SUMMARY OF THE PERSONAL ACTION

11.16 Money paid by a bank under a mistake of fact may be recovered by the payer if:

(i) the payment is not made by the bank under a mandate which creates a debt between customer and bank; and (ii) the mistake is of fact, not of law; and (iii) but for the mistake the payment would not have been made; provided that:

(a) an agent is not liable if he has paid the money to his principal without knowledge of the claim;

(b) recovery is not possible if the defendant is entitled to refeb to an estoppel, by reason of representation (or duty), reliance, and detriment or inequitableness;

(c) recovery may not be possible if the payment is under a negotiated negotiable instrument with an intrinsic defect, (in which case payment alone is a representation, and it may be the case that no actual detriment need be suffered in order to establish an easier form of estoppel).

7. COMPARISON WITH PROPRIETARY ACTION

11.17 A proprietary action (tracing) may be available instead of the personal action of money had and received. The proprietary action is advantageous (i) in terms of interest which can be claimed, (ii) in terms of actions against companies acting *ultra vires* if the action starts before liquidation commences (a personal action is not available on an *ultra vires* debt) and (iii) especially advantageous if the recipient who still holds the money is bankrupt. A personal remedy is available against the bankrupt, but only as an unsecured creditor, unless the trustee holds an identifiable chattel belonging to the plaintiff, in which case conversion (or money had and received for the value of the chattel) lies.

Tracing depends on the initial existence of a fiduciary relationship, and the personal action does not. In practice, however, a fiduciary relationship exists if a person is erroneously paid money.

The action for money had and received, however, has a special advantage to a plaintiff claiming against a bank holding the funds and claiming a right

---

[55] *i.e.* not being an administration of an estate—see *Butler* v. *Broadhead* [1975] Ch. 97, but see *Re J. Leslie Engineers Co. Ltd.* [1976] 1 W.L.R. 292.

[56] *Admiralty Comrs.* v. *National Provincial and Union Bank of England Ltd.* (1922) 127 L.T. 452; *Kleinwort, Sons & Co.* v. *Dunlop Rubber Co.* (1907) 97 L.T. 263, *Kerrison* v. *Glyn Mills Currie & Co.* (1911) 81 L.J.K.B. 465, 17 Com.Cas. 41.

of set–off or combination against the recipient, its customer, for the action is effective against the bank on the ground that the money does not belong to the customer and cannot be taken by the bank. The remedy of tracing is lost if the fund comes into the hands of a bona fide purchaser for value without notice, and if a bank receives funds for the account of an overdrawn customer, the bank receives for value. It seems, therefore, that for the purpose of the proprietary remedy the bank is (sometimes) considered to be purchaser, but for the purpose of the personal remedy the bank is always considered to receive merely as agent for the customer. This is a peculiar distinction, but seems well established. Whichever remedy is in question, the bank's liability ceases if as agent it pays the money to its principal, when it has no notice of the plaintiff's claim.

On the other hand, if the money comes into the hands of some third party as purchaser (*e.g.* if the customer has some existing liability to the recipient) then the proprietary remedy is defeated (if the recipient has no notice, etc.), but the personal remedy is defeated only if the bank had a mandate to pay, regardless of the discharge of the debt owed to the payee.

12. Some Aspects of Joint Accounts

A. Operation of the account

12.01　If the parties do not expressly allow the bank to act on one signature, both must act jointly in signing cheques.[1] We have observed the false notion that both must join in any action against the bank, which would result in neither being able to sue if one forged a cheque so that the bank paid without a mandate.[2] It would seem that any joint party may countermand[3] subject to the terms of the mandate.

Liability may be either joint, or joint and several (separate), but bank mandates are always in joint and several form. An account is not joint and several merely because the mandate states that either or both parties may sign cheques.[4] At one time joint liability had the consequence that if A and B were jointly liable to C, and C sued A, this "exhausted" the rights of C, who could not thereafter sue B. But this is not now the case, and C may subsequently sue B.[5] Remaining advantages of joint and several liability are:

(i) if liability is only joint, the estate of a deceased party is relieved from liability on his death, because the survivor inherits the debt (just as he inherits any credit).[6] But this does not occur if liability is joint and several.

(ii) if one of the joint parties has a separate account of his own, combination (or, on bankruptcy, statutory set off under section 323 of the Insolvency Act 1986) is possible against credits in that separate account in respect of debts in the joint account[7] because the party is separately liable for the joint debt.

(iii) In relation to partnership joint accounts, there is yet a further advantage, for if there is only joint liability, then when the bank seeks to sue a bankrupt partner for partnership debts, the bank may claim only after non-partnership (private) creditors of the bankrupt have been satisfied. But if liability is joint and several, the bank ranks as a private creditor on the separate claim.

B. Death, bankruptcy of a party

12.02　Whether the bank is entitled to pay cheques after the death of one joint account party depends on whether the bank's debt is owned by the creditors as joint creditors, or as tenants in common, and in the case of joint ownership, whether the ownership is beneficial or not.

In the (unusual) case of tenants in common, ownership of the debt would pass to the personal representatives of the deceased, and they alone would have authority to deal with the debt (following normal probate or administration procedures).

12.03　In the normal case of joint ownership, the doctrine of "survivorship" applies, and causes sole legal title to vest in the survivor. Normally, also,

---

[1] *Husband* v. *Davis* (1851) 20 L.J.C.P. 118.

[2] Above, para. 7.21.

[3] *Gaunt* v. *Taylor* (1843) 2 Hare 413.

[4] *Hirschorn* v. *Evans* [1938] 2 K.B. 801.

[5] Civil Liability (Contribution) Act 1978.

[6] Though perhaps the Law Reform (Miscellaneous Provisions) Act 1934 causes rights of action to survive: Williams, Joint Obligations (1949) p. 72.

[7] Not the other way around, unless there is a contractual set-off clause.

the parties would be joint beneficial owners, so that on death of one the other is both legal and beneficial owner by survivorship, in which case the bank is entirely free to deal with the survivor. In some cases, however, the joint account may be for mere reasons of convenience, and though both parties are the joint legal owners, one of them may hold his legal title in trust for the other (*i.e.* he is not joint beneficial owner, there being only one beneficial owner) so that on that other's death the legal title is held by the survivor in trust for the heirs of the deceased. On a normal joint account, the presumption (regardless of whether under the mandate one or both must sign) would be that property is jointly owned, legally and beneficially, so that the bank may pay the survivor, who can give a good discharge for the debt.[8] Even if the survivor is merely legal owner, and another has beneficial title, this will not ordinarily concern the bank, unless it knows of breach of trust, or (in a case where it receives a benefit) has constructive notice. Otherwise, the survivor, as sole trustee, can give a good receipt and the bank is unaffected by any unknown wrongdoing of his.

If the mandate allows payment notwithstanding the death of one signatory, this can be relied upon as evidence of joint beneficial ownership, giving rise to survivorship (in other respects, the mandate ceases on death of the party concerned). In any case, the mandate should make the question of survivorship and beneficial ownership clear. If there is a clause providing for payment to the survivor, then the bank should pay the survivor only, and not the executors, or it is in breach of contract to the survivor. In *McEvoy* v. *Belfast Banking Co. Ltd.*[9] the bank paid the executors, and the survivor (the son of the other named account party) sued. The bank won, but only because the son failed to show that he was party to the contract with the bank. Had he done so he would have succeeded, even though the property was held by the executors in trust for him, for the bank would have disobeyed his mandate.[10]

If a cheque is received signed by the deceased party only, this should be **12.04** returned unpaid, marked "Drawer deceased." If signed by both parties, and the survivor is entitled to the contents of the account (as just described), the cheque may be honoured. If there is more than one survivor, a fresh mandate is taken. Since the point of taking joint and several liability is to preserve rights against the deceased's estate, the effect of *Clayton's case*[11] is eliminated by stopping an overdrawn account, or by terms in the original mandate.

It may be added that bankruptcy does not have the same effect as death (*i.e.* there is no survivorship), and if one of the joint account holders becomes bankrupt, the bank should act in relation to a credit account just as if a single account holder is bankrupt (*i.e.* acknowledging the rights of the trustee in bankruptcy to the undivided debt)[12] and where there is an over-

---

[8] For discussion of these principles, see *e.g. Husband* v. *Davis*, above, n. 1; *Marshall* v. *Crutwell* (1875) L.R. 20 Eq. 328; *Williams* v. *Davies* (1864) 3 Sw. & Tr. 437; *Re Bishop* [1965] Ch. 450. See also Cullity, (1969) 85 L.Q.R. 530.

[9] [1935] A.C. 24.

[10] As it was, the bank was strongly criticized by the House of Lords, which said that it should have interpleaded, or refused to pay. Interpleading involves the bank itself taking out a summons against the other parties as defendants, under Ord. 17, R.S.C.

[11] Below, Chap. 13.

[12] See below, Chap. 28, for bankruptcy.

drawn account, this may be combined with a credit account if possible, or otherwise is stopped to prevent the operation of *Clayton's case*. A new mandate may be taken from the solvent party, and a separate account opened for him.

13. The Banker's Lien, Right of Appropriation, and Combination of Accounts

The banker's lien, his right of appropriation, and the right of combination **13.01** may be considered separately, but often work in tandem. By way of preliminary definition, the lien is a right to retain an indebted customer's property while the bank has it, and to sell it to satisfy the debt. The right of appropriation is the banker's right, if not instructed otherwise, to appropriate funds to whichever account he chooses. The right of combination is a right to combine separate accounts where, say, one is overdrawn and the other is in credit, so as to take account of the overall state of indebtedness of customer to bank and vice versa. All of these rights are subject to contrary agreement, but otherwise arise by operation of law. The right to combine may be confused by some with the lien, and worse, is often referred to as "set-off", though this terminology runs the risk of confusion with the quite separate right of equitable set-off (which seldom concerns bankers), and also with contractual or statutory set-off. Contractual set-off, indeed, may be regarded as an extension by contract of the rights of combination, and statutory set-off is an extension of combination which arises by statute on bankruptcy or liquidation of the customer.[1]

A. The banker's lien

1. LIENS AND PROPERTY OTHER THAN CHEQUES

The lien is relatively uncomplicated here, and is described below. A com- **13.02** mon example would be the lien over shipping documents which would arise in a documentary credit transaction where a seller of goods presents documents to a nominated bank in return for some form of payment. The nominated bank has a lien in relation to its customer, the issuing bank, and the issuing bank has a lien when it receives the documents, in relation to its customer, the buyer (if he has not yet put the bank in funds.)

2. LIENS AND CHEQUES (OR OTHER BILLS)

In the context of bills or cheques given to the banker for collection, there are **13.03** four main reasons for considering liens: first, while the banker has the cheque it gives him security for non-payment of a debt, and when the cheque is collected other rights—those of appropriation and of combination—may arise, so that the banker can (sometimes) either appropriate the proceeds received to an overdrawn account, or appropriate them to a credit account and later combine accounts. Secondly, the existence of a lien may add to the protection which a banker has from an action for conversion brought by one claiming to be the "true owner," by making the banker a holder in due course. Thirdly, by making him holder in due course or by

---

[1] Formerly, under s.31, Bankruptcy Act 1914, now s.323, Insolvency Act 1986, and Insolvency Rules 1986, r. 4.90.

bringing him within other statutory cases the banker may have a title good against a trustee in bankruptcy or liquidator of his customer. Fourthly, if the indebted customer does not indorse a cheque deposited for collection, the lien may make the bank holder for value so that it may sue the customer or the parties to the cheque if the cheque is dishonoured (whereas this is not so if there is no lien).

13.04 It is important to realise that in the normal case where a bank receives a cheque from an indebted customer for collection, three separate rights may be involved. These are, first, the lien itself, or right to retain the cheque; secondly, the right (generally, but not necessarily connected with the lien) whereby the bank may realise the lien by collecting payment and appropriating the proceeds to whichever account the bank chooses; and thirdly the right not necessarily connected with the lien to combine accounts (if, say, the proceeds are paid into a credit account). The lien itself is, in a sense, the least useful, since the bank ordinarily has a duty to present the cheque for collection within a reasonable time, and thus generally cannot retain cheques.[2] It appears odd to speak of a right to retain while the bank has a duty to present quickly for collection, but it seems that there is a lien while it has the cheque. This is decided by *Re Keever*,[3] where the bank was held to be a holder in due course by reason of its lien (which made it first a holder for value). When the cheque or bill is cleared "it ceased to be a negotiable instrument and also ceased to be in the possession of the bank. Any lien of the bank on the cheque must thereupon have come to an end."[4] Hence, in the ordinary course of events, with cheques deposited for collection, the right of appropriation of the proceeds is more important than the lien itself, though the right of appropriation arises from the lien, which causes the bank to be a holder for value of the cheque,[5] so that unless otherwise instructed it may apply the proceeds as it sees fit (so long as one of the customer's accounts is credited).[6]

It is clear that a customer has the right to appropriate payments in to a particular debit item unless it is otherwise agreed. The important question is whether, where a customer appropriates, there can still be a lien? The question is important, for if the answer is in the negative, the bank could not by virtue of the lien be a holder for value or holder in due course. If the banker's lien is conceived of as carrying with it a right to realise the lien (by collection) for the banker's benefit, then it would seem that there is no sense in which the bank has a lien: it cannot collect for its own benefit. If this is correct, then if there is no right to appropriate, and no right, therefore, to realise the lien, then there can be no lien. Perhaps, however, one might still say that the bank is, regardless of the lien, a holder for value. Section 2 of the Cheques Act 1957, for example, refers to a banker "who gives value for, or has a lien on" a cheque. The same might apply to the question of whether it is a holder in due course.

---

[2] See *Hamilton Finance Co. Ltd.* v. *Coverley, Westray, Walbaum and Tosetti Ltd. and Portland Finance Co.* [1969] 1 Lloyds Rep. 53, 72.

[3] [1967] Ch. 182. See also *Barclays Bank Ltd.* v. *Astley Industrial Trust, Ltd.* [1970] 2 Q.B. 527.

[4] [Buckley L.J. in *Halesowen Presswork & Assemblies Ltd.* v. *Westminster Bank Ltd.* [1971] 1 Q.B. 1. at 46.

[5] See s.27(3), B.O.E. Act 1882.

[6] For a case demonstrating the advantage of the right of appropriation over the right to combine accounts, see *Re William Hall (Contractors) Ltd.*, [1967] 2 All E.R. 1150, below, Chap. 27.

In short, (i) there is a lien although there is a duty to present quickly, (ii) **13.05** the lien is lost when the cheque is presented for collection but there may be a right then to appropriate the proceeds to such accounts of the customer as the bank chooses, (iii) there may be circumstances where there is no duty to present quickly and where the lien is more obvious, as when bills not yet matured are deposited for collection on maturity, and so on, (iv) an appropriation by the customer probably destroys the lien even while the bank has the cheque, but the bank may still be a holder for value (and holder in due course).

3. HOW THE LIEN ARISES

The banker's lien is often referred to as an "implied pledge"[7] to distinguish **13.06** it from an ordinary lien which gives merely a right to retain, but not to sell. A banker's lien carries the right to sell.[8] Securities or assets, the subject of an "ordinary" lien can be realised only by obtaining judgment for the debt and by executing the judgment against the securities. Both pledges and banker's liens carry the right to sell. Both the pledge and the lien are legal rights, and both depend on possession. The pledge, however, is the creation of an agreement, whereas the lien arises by operation of law.[9] Like pledges, liens are not registerable as bills of sale (when the property is that of an individual) or under the Companies Act 1985 (for a company's property).[10] The banker's lien extends to a banker acting as agent for a remitting banker.[11]

4. OVER WHAT SECURITIES DOES THE LIEN ARISE?

In the leading case of *Brandao* v. *Barnett*[12] it was said that "Bankers . . . have **13.07** a general lien on all securities deposited with them as bankers by a customer, unless there be an express contract, or circumstances that show an implied contract, inconsistent with lien."[13] We must consider the meaning of "all securities," "deposited with them as bankers,"and inconsistent circumstances or agreements.

(a)"all securities." It seems that this must be qualified, to mean "paper securities"[14] so that, for example, gold coins deposited for sale by the bank would not be subject to the implied pledge, though conceivably they are subject to an ordinary lien. Negotiable and other securities are included, and there seems to be no reason to exclude any class of document (such as deeds to land).[15] The lien has extended to share certificates[16] an order for payment

---

[7] *Brandao* v. *Barnett* (1846) 3 C.B. 519, 531.

[8] *Brandao* v. *Barnett*, previous note, *Rosenburg* v. *International Banking Corpn.* (1923) 14 Ll L.Rep. 344, 347.

[9] The reference in s.27(3) of B.O.E. Act 1882 to "lien by contract" is a reference to a pledge.

[10] For liens see the wording of s.395, C.A. 1985.

[11] *Re Parker, ex p. Froggatt* (1843) 3 Mont D. & DeG 322; *Prince* v. *Oriental Bank Corpn.* (1878) 3 App. Cas 325. For the lien of an advising/confirming bank in a documentary credit transaction, see *Aschkenasy* v. *Midland Bank Ltd.* (1934) 50 T.L.R. 209; 51 T.L.R. 34.

[12] Above n. 7.

[13] *Ibid.*, at 806.

[14] *Davis* v. *Bowsher* (1794) 5 Term Rep. 488.

[15] *Contra*, Paget 406.

[16] *Re United Service Co. Johnstone's Claim* (1870) 6 Ch. App. 212.

of money to a particular person[17] a species of deposit receipt[18] an insurance policy[19] and bills of exchange.[20] In *Wylde* v. *Radford*[21] Kinderesley V.-C. said "what is intended is such securities as promissory notes, bills of exchange, exchequer bills, coupons, bonds of foreign governments, etc . . ." The court held that deeds to land were not intended to be included, but it would seem better to regard this as a decision on the parties' intention on the particular facts of the case.[22]

13.08   (b) 'deposited with them as bankers." The question of what constitutes the "business of banking" is examined elsewhere.[23] Whatever a banker's business may be, the securities must come to him in the course of it. In particular, goods or securities deposited with him by way of safe deposit are (for some reason) generally not so regarded.[24] But even there, it depends on whether the banker does things with the securities (other than holding them for safe-keeping) which are in the course of his normal business and if, for example, he holds bonds, and is to present them for payment, or to collect interest upon them then these are things which bankers normally do.[25] It would be otherwise, however, if interest on shares, etc. is merely arranged by the customer to be paid to the bank which happens to hold the share certificates, etc.[26] Of course, banks may take express pledges, or charges, over any goods or securities.

(c) Inconsistent agreements. Liens arise by operation of law, and will not arise if there is an inconsistent agreement or circumstances implying that the lien is not intended to arise. One effect of a lien over a cheque deposited for collection, for example, is that the bank has a right of appropriation of the cheque or its proceeds to whichever account the bank chooses, and that if there is no right to appropriate, there is no lien. The right to appropriate (and the lien) exists even if there is an agreement to keep accounts separate (*i.e.* if there is no right to combine accounts). But some agreements may suggest not only that accounts are to be kept separate, but also that the debit on an account should not be reduced. Thus, there may be an agreement to "freeze" the amount of an overdraft, or a loan may be made for a fixed period of time, so that an appropriation to that account reducing the debit would seem to be a breach of the agreement for credit. Here, then, the same agreement which "separates" the accounts may be an agreement not to appropriate except to the current account. We must say, then, that while in principle appropriation is a distinct right from combination, in practice, the two (and, therefore, the lien) may be simultaneously excluded.[27] However, merely taking the cheque for collection is not in itself "inconsistent," for even though the bank may be the agent of the customer (and subject, for example, to a duty to present the cheque in a reasonable time) the bank (as

---

[17] *Misa* v. *Currie* (1876) 1 App Cas. 554.
[18] *Jeffreys* v. *Agra and Masterman's Bank* (1866) L.R. 2 Eg. 674.
[19] *Re Bowes, Earl of Strathmore* v. *Vane* (1886) 33 Ch.D. 586.
[20] *Davis* v. *Bowsher* (above, n. 14); *Giles* v. *Perkins* (1807) 9 East 12; *Re Firth, ex p. Schofield* (1879) 12 Ch.D. 337; *Dawson* v. *Isle* [1906] 1 Ch. 633. See *Re Keever*, below, para. 13.19.
[21] (1863) 33 L.J.Ch. 51, 53.
[22] See *Re London and Globe Finance Corpn.* [1902] 2 Ch. 416, 420.
[23] Above, Chap. 2.
[24] *Leese* v. *Martin* (1873) L.R. 17 Eq. 224; *Currie* v. *Misa*, above n. 17.
[25] So, it may be said, is safe-keeping!
[26] See Paget, 410–411, commenting on a dictum in *Re United Service Co. Johnstone's Claim* (1870) 6 Ch. App. 212.
[27] See *Halesowen Presswork and Assemblies Ltd.* v. *Westminster Bank Ltd.* [1971] 1 Q.B. 1 (frozen account); *Re Keever, ex p. Cork* v. *Midland Bank Ltd.* [1966] 2 Lloyds Rep. 475.

we have seen) may also have its own rights over the cheque (as a holder for value, etc.).[28]

The existence of a consensual security is treated as being inconsistent with **13.09** a lien arising by operation of law. Thus, a pledge, charge or mortgage destroy an existing lien, or prevent one from arising.[29] If, therefore, a consensual security is given for a specific debt and is later discharged by repayment, the customer is entitled to the return of the property even if he is still otherwise in debt to the banker.[30] But if he does not ask for its return, and the property is left in the hands of the banker in the course of his ordinary business, a lien may later arise.[31] Paget argues that if a consensual security relates to a specific debt, A, then a lien might arise over the same asset in respect of another debt, B, even if B exists at the same time as A.[32] No case establishes this, and in principle the notion of a single asset simultaneously subject to a consensual and a non-consensual security for different debts appears suspect.

It is, however, clear that if there is a consensual security for a specific **13.10** debt, and the asset in question is realised, then the balance of the proceeds, if any, after satisfaction of the secured debt, is subject to the right of combination. Thus, even if the banker cannot by virtue of a lien appropriate the proceeds to the overdrawn account, he may combine the overdrawn account with that into which he pays the proceeds, with the same result.[33]

5. OVER WHOSE PROPERTY DOES THE LIEN ARISE?

It would seem that the bank may take an ordinary lien from anyone entitled **13.11** to possession, but that its general lien (or implied pledge), with the right of sale, will be defeated by a prior legal right: thus, only the legal owner of the property can cause the general banker's lien to arise.[34] Thus, if the banker receives a cheque or money for the account paid by mistake to its customer, the cheque or proceeds are returnable to the true owner (the payer) and are not subject to a lien or to combination.[35] If there is an equitable owner of the property, then on general principles, the bank's legal lien would defeat his rights, but if the bank knows of prior equitable rights, (other than a floating charge) it cannot insist upon a lien. A floating charge, however, does not prevent subsequent dispositions, charges, etc., and knowledge of this would not prevent a lien from arising. In *Siebe Gorman & Co. Ltd.* v. *Barclays Bank Ltd.*[36] a bank consented to an assignment of bills of exchange held by it for collection, relying on its peculiar fixed charge over present and future book debts. The assignee was held to have been misled by the bank's consent (he would have thought the bank's charge was a "normal" floating charge), and the bank could not rely on its charge. The bank then relied on its lien, which had existed before the assignment. However, the account had been continued and *Clayton's case* operated so that payments in and out discharged the original debt almost entirely. Since the bank knew of the

[28] See also *Currie* v. *Misa*, above n. 17; *Sutters* v. *Briggs* [1922] 1 A.C. 1, 18.
[29] See *Re Bowes*, above n. 19 and *Jones* v. *Peppercorne* (1858) John 430.
[30] *Wilkinson* v. *London and County Banking Co.* (1884) 1 T.L.R. 63.
[31] *Re London and Globe Finance Corpn.* [1902] 2 Ch. 416.
[32] Paget, 409.
[33] *Re Bowes*, above, n. 17; *Jones* v. *Peppercorne*, above n. 29 *Re London & Globe Finance Corpn.*, above n. 31.
[34] See *Cuthbert* v. *Robarts, Lubbock & Co.* [1909] 2 Ch. 226, 233.
[35] *Admiralty Comrs.* v. *National Provincial and Union Bank of England Ltd.* (1922) 127 L.T. 452.
[36] [1979] 2 Lloyds Rep. 142.

assignment, and had consented to it, the lien was ineffective against the assignee for "new" debts arising after the time of the assignment.

It follows that there can be neither a lien over assets nor any combination of accounts if the assets or moneys are to the bank's knowledge held on trust, or constructive trust, or if there is a Quistclose trust.[36a]

If the customer is not legal owner of a security, the bank may, nevertheless, gain rights over the security if it is represented by a negotiable instrument and the bank is holder in due course.

6. LIENS OVER MONEY, AND LIENS FOR CONTINGENT LIABILITIES

13.12   Where there is a lien over a security which has been realised (*e.g.* by collection of a cheque) the right of a banker to the proceeds is as owner (to the extent of the customer's indebtedness) and as owner he may appropriate the proceeds to whichever account of the customer he pleases. Indeed, even in the absence of lien, it is correct to regard the bank as owner of the money, because it is established that the relation of banker and customer is that of debtor-creditor, and that there is no enforceable right in a customer to money until he makes a demand for it.[37] The customer's right, until he makes demand, is to have a correct statement of the state of accounts between himself and the banker. Thus, the banker must appropriate the proceeds to an account of the customer: if to an overdrawn account, the debit balance is reduced; if to a credit account, the bank retains its separate right to combine. If the customer demands repayment, the bank may, in the absence of contrary agreement, first combine. Although, therefore, some dicta refer to a lien over money paid in to a banker, these dicta are misleading, and ought, perhaps, to be references to the right to combine.[38] In *Halesowen Presswork & Assemblies Ltd.* v. *Westminster Bank Ltd.*[39] the argument concerned statutory set-off, but there was some discussion of the existence of a "lien" over the proceeds of a cheque. Buckley L.J. said[40] that "The money or credit which the bank obtained as the result of clearing the cheque became the property of the bank, not the property of the company. No man can have a lien on his own property and consequently no lien can have arisen affecting that money or that credit . . . a banker has a general lien on all securities deposited with him . . . [but] . . . The term "securities" . . . does not . . . extend to the banker's own indebtedness to the customer."[41] The case clearly recognizes the right to combine accounts, and that, it is now clear, is the only right other than appropriation on receipt, against the proceeds of a cheque. This must be the case if it is accepted that the banker-customer relationship is debtor-creditor, for by definition a chose in action cannot be the subject of a possessory right, such as a lien. The lien exists while the bank has the cheque, and carries with it a right of appropriation, but when the proceeds are received, it is replaced by a right of combination if the appropriation is to a credit account. Buckley L.J. said that the pro-

---

[36a] Discussed above, Chap. 10.

[37] *Foley* v. *Hill* (1848) 2 H.L.Cas. 28; *Joachimson* v. *Swiss Bank Corpn.* [1921] 3 K.B. 110—"The proceeds . . . are not to be held in trust for the customer, but the bank borrows the proceeds and undertakes to repay them." (*per* Atkin L.J. at 127).

[38] For such dicta, see *Misa* v. *Currie* (1876) 1 App. Cas 554, 565, 569, 573, and Paget, 411.

[39] [1971] 1 Q.B. 1, C.A. [1972] A.C. 785, HL.

[40] *Ibid.,* C.A., at 46.

[41] See also *Viscount Dilhorne* [1972] A.C. 785, at 802. Contrast Lord Denning's judgment in the C.A. p. 33, where his Lordship does refer to "a lien over a cheque . . . or its proceeds." He says, however, that it "is no true lien", but a right of combination or set-off.

ceeds of a cheque become the bank's property. This is so whether or not there is a lien (the bank merely being debtor, not trustee), but if there is a lien, it carries with it the additional right of appropriation to the account of the banker's choice.

The problem of a (so-called) lien over an account has arisen in a particular **13.13** context: that of contingent liabilities. Suppose that a banker discounts or accepts bills for a customer. The banker may wish to retain a balance on current account to meet the contingent liability on the bills. In the absence of any agreement, has he any right (by reason of a lien) to do so? The authorities demonstrate that there is no such "lien" (better called, a right to retain). On demand, the customer must be repaid.[42] If, however, the customer becomes bankrupt or goes into liquidation, the bank may immediately prove for even contingent liabilities,[43] and at this time the right to statutory set-off may be asserted against the customer-indorser.[44] This is not a right of lien.[45]

7. THE BANK AS HOLDER FOR VALUE

If a bank receives a bill or cheque for collection, it may be discounting (buy- **13.14** ing) the bill, or forwarding it as agent, or forwarding it on its own behalf (as holder for value or in due course). It is possible (and common) for a bank to be at the same time agent of the customer in forwarding the bill (for, unless it buys the bill, it has a duty to do so, within a reasonable time)[46] and holder for value.[47] The reason that the bank is holder for value (and probably holder in due course) is that section 27(3) of the Bills of Exchange Act 1882 states: "Where the holder of a bill has a lien on it arising either from contract or by implication of law, he is deemed to be a holder for value to the extent of the sum for which he has a lien." We have seen that there is a lien if the customer is indebted to the bank, and if the bill is delivered in the course of the business as banker (*e.g.* for collection). Thus, unless the bank has the bill for an unusual purpose[48] then if there is a lien, it is a holder for value. The significance of this is, of course, that as a holder for value it can sue the parties to a dishonoured cheque even if the cheque (given to it for collection) is not indorsed to the bank[49] and that it may be holder in due course which will give it a perfect title both to sue, and by way of defence to an action in conversion brought by a "true owner."

It is a largely academic question whether, if the bank is holder for value it **13.15** loses its lien. This is academic because even if the lien is lost, the bank obtains another right, like ownership, which is as effective as the lien in relation to the three rights (to the lien, to appropriate and to combine accounts). Paget[49a] argues that the bank is owner, and that the lien is lost. It

---

[42] *Jeffryes* v. *Agra & Masterman's Bank* (1866) L.R. 2 Eq. 674; *Bower* v. *Foreign and Colonial Gas Co. Ltd.*, *Metropolitan Bank, Garnishees* (1874) 22 W.R. 740; *Baker* v. *Lloyds Bank Ltd.* [1920] 2 K.B. 322. For dicta to the contrary see *Bolland* v. *Bygrave* (1825) 1 Ry. & M. 271, NP.

[43] s.30, Bankruptcy Act 1914, and see definition of "bankruptcy debt" and "debt" in ss.382(1) and 382(3), Insolvency Act 1986.

[44] Under s.31, Bankruptcy Act 1914 (or s.323, Insolvency Act 1986).

[45] See *Baker* v. *Lloyds Bank Ltd.*, above, n. 42.

[46] See above n. 2.

[47] Which will normally make the bank holder in due course, under s.29, B.O.E. Act 1882. On the "dual capacity," see *Barclays Bank Ltd.* v. *Astley Industrial Trust Ltd.* [1970] 2 Q.B. 527.

[48] Such as in *Westminster Bank Ltd.* v. *Zang*, below, n. 50.

[49] s.2, Cheques Act 1957.

[49a] pp. 412–413.

is submitted, however, that a holder in due course is not necessarily owner of the bill: it depends on the intention with which the bill is given to him, and in most cases the customer does not intend to transfer ownership (unless a bill is discounted to the bank). As holder in due course the bank can sue all parties, and would have a defence against the "true owner." It is unnecessary to say that it is the owner, and, therefore, as against the customer, it is correct to talk of the bank's rights to retain and to appropriate arising under the lien, though if a question arose as to the bank's rights to retain against a third party, such as a liquidator or "true owner," one needs to refer to the bank as holder in due course. In other words, if the customer has a defective title, he can create no lien, but the bank may have a special title as holder in due course arising from the nature of negotiable instruments, and the effect is the same as if there is a lien.

If a bank has a lien, but redelivers a dishonoured cheque to the customer (*e.g.* so that he can sue) this destroys the lien. If it is returned to the bank so that it can sue, then no new lien arises even if the customer indorses the cheque, because the bank is given possession not in the course of its business as banker but so that it can sue.[50] In *Westminster Bank Ltd.* v. *Zang*[51] the argument centred on the question whether the bank had given value, since, if it had, it could sue on a cheque given to it for collection even if the cheque was not indorsed to it—by section 2 of the Cheques Act 1957. When it received back the dishonoured cheque, it could not be holder in due course since it knew of the dishonouring. At most it could be holder for value from its customer. It was not a holder for value by reason of lien, because there was none. It was held to have given no value. Since the lien arises by operation of law, it cannot be maintained by contract, as by redelivery of a security to the customer for a specific purpose (*e.g.* as agent for the bank). It would have to be expressly taken as a pledge, and released by Trust Receipt.

13.16   We have seen that the lien exists if at the time the cheque is received, the customer is indebted to the bank and the customer does not appropriate. A question arises whether there is a lien if an account (not being overdrawn) is credited to cash before the cheque is cleared. If in such a case the cheque is dishonoured, the account can be debited again, regardless of whether the bank receives as agent for collection, or for value, and whether the cheque is indorsed by the customer, or not. But if the account is overdrawn at the time, or will be after the debit, the bank may wish either to allow or increase the overdraft or to sue the customer or the drawer on the cheque. Even if the customer has not indorsed, it can sue, provided that it takes for value or where there is a lien. This occurs by virtue of section 2 of the Cheques Act 1957.[52] Is it, then, a holder for value by virtue of lien because it credited to cash? It was formerly thought that it was: this is said in *Capital and Counties Bank Ltd.* v. *Gordon.*[53] A reflection of this view appears in section 4(1)(b) of the Cheques Act 1957. The *Gordon* case concerned the bank's defence against the true owner: for this purpose it now matters little if the bank is holder for value or not, because of section 4 of the Cheques Act 1957. But the answer may still affect the bank's right to sue on the cheque, and may affect other matters, such as the garnishing of the account. The

---

[50] *Westminster Bank Ltd.* v. *Zang* [1966] A.C. 182.

[51] Previous note.

[52] For an example of such a case, see *Midland Bank Ltd.* v. *Reckitt* [1933] A.C. 1, and *Barclays Bank Ltd.* v. *Astley Industrial Trust Ltd.* [1970] 2 Q.B. 527.

[53] [1903] A.C. 240. See also *Sutters* v. *Briggs* [1922] 1 A.C. 1, 14.

modern view appears clearly to be that merely crediting to cash does not make the bank holder for value: it neither gives value thereby (the credit entry may be reversed), nor has it a lien thereby. This was established in *A. L. Underwood Ltd.* v. *Bank of Liverpool: Same* v. *Barclays Bank Ltd.*[54] It may be different, however, if the bank allows the customer to draw against uncleared effects. Although this does not create a lien, it may amount to the giving of value.[55]

8. GARNISHEE ORDERS AND LIENS

R.S.C. Ord. 49, r. 1, allows the court to attach debts owed to the judgment debtor, and to order the garnishee to pay "any debt due or accruing due to the judgment debtor." A "debt due" is one for which the creditor could immediately and effectually sue.[56] Moneys represented by bills of exchange are attachable when the bill matures[57] so that cheques (payable on demand) are affected by the order. If, however, a bank has a lien over bills, etc., deposited with it, these are unaffected by the terms of the order, simply because the creditor could not sue for a debt. Similarly, if the bank has collected the cheque, the proceeds are subject to the right to combine, and the debt due is that calculated by looking at the overall state of accounts.[58] In any case, cheques received after the garnishee order are not subject to it, as any debt must be owed at the time of the order.[59] If a bank credits the account to cash before the cheque is cleared, the decision in *Jones & Co.* v. *Coventry*[60] suggests that the amount credited is affected by the garnishee order. The sum in the case was held not to be affected, being specially protected while it had the character of retirement pay, by the Army Act 1881, s.141. The court held that the retirement pay warrant in question was not negotiable, so that the bank was not holder for value, and that no debt existed until the warrant was paid by H.M.P.G. Until then, (after the attachment) it retained the protected character of retirement pay. This suggests that had it been, say, a cheque, it would have been subject to the attachment. It is difficult to see why this should be so. The credit entry is reversible if the cheque is dishonoured, and in the interim the customer could not sue for the debt, unless there was an express agreement to allow him to draw against uncleared effects. It would seem that *Jones & Co.* v. *Coventry* reflects the earlier view already mentioned, that in such cases the bank has given value, so that the credit does reflect a debt due to the customer on his demand (and that, in collecting, the banker collects for himself). After the *Underwood* case it would seem that the credit entry is simply reversible, despite the garnishee order, so that the account reflects the true state of indebtedness between customer and bank.

13.17

If the account is overdrawn at the time it is credited, and the cheque is dishonoured, exactly the same applies. The only special advantage which flows in such a case from the lien is that the bank gives value and may sue

13.18

[54] [1924] 1 K.B. 775; and see *Westminster Bank Ltd.* v. *Zang*, above, n. 50.
[55] See *Underwood* case, previous note, at 804, 805.
[56] *Glegg* v. *Bromley* [1912] 3 K.B. 474.
[57] *Hyam* v. *Freeman* (1890) 35 Sol. Jo. 87.
[58] *Tapp* v. *Jones* (1875) L.R. 10 Q.B. 591, holding that debts before the attachment can be set off, but not those arising after, and that the order does not affect debts not yet due; *Stumore* v. *Campbell & Co.* [1892] 1 Q.B. 314.
[59] *Webb* v. *Stenton* (1883) 11 Q.B.D. 518; *Heppenstall* v. *Jackson & Barclays Bank Ltd.* [1939] 1 K.B. 585.
[60] [1909] 2 K.B. 1029.

the customer. This right to counterclaim has been held to create a right of set-off which is covered by R.S.C. Ord. 18, r. 17, giving the bank a reply to the garnishee order.[61]

9. LIENS IN BANKRUPTCY

13.19   In bankruptcy or liquidation, there is a right of statutory set-off.[62] But a bank may also assert the separate common-law right to a lien, and this will give it the same priority against the trustee or liquidator as it had against the customer. In *Re Keever, a Bankrupt, ex p. Cork* v. *Midland Bank Ltd.*[63] a bank received a cheque for collection on the day before a receiving order was made, not knowing of an act of bankruptcy. The bank received the proceeds on the day the receiving order was made, and it claimed that it was entitled to apply the proceeds to the customer's overdrawn account. Under the 1914 bankruptcy scheme, the title of the trustee in bankruptcy related back to the first available act of bankruptcy, and the trustee claimed that the cheque, and its proceeds, belonged to him. However, section 45 of the Bankruptcy Act 1914 protected "Any contract, dealing, or transaction by or with the bankrupt for valuable consideration" if before the receiving order and without notice of an act of bankruptcy. It was held that the "dealing" was the receipt of the cheque (which was before the receiving order), and that it was for valuable consideration because the bank had a lien. A separate ground in the bank's favour was that it was a holder for value within section 27(3) of the Bills of Exchange Act 1882, and a holder in due course within section 29, and its title was unimpeachable by the trustee. Neither principle, however, applies if the cheque is not received until after the date of the receiving order.[64] Under the new bankruptcy scheme established by the Insolvency Act 1986, bankruptcy commences on the day of the bankruptcy order (section 278) and property vests in the trustee when (later) appointed (section 306) but his appointment relates back to the commencement (section 307), and covers all property vested in the bankrupt at the commencement (section 283) subject to some exceptions (sections 283(2–4)). The trustee's title is subject to the rights of others, whether they are secured or not (section 283(5)). He may seize property of the bankrupt disposed of or paid by the bankrupt in the period between the petition and the vesting order, unless ratified by the court (section 284), but he may not do this for property received before the bankruptcy order if the person who receives the property does so in good faith for value and without notice of the petition (section 284(4)). It would seem, therefore, that the principle of *Re Keever* is still relevant, since it helps to show "value," and the title of another, but that now the making of the bankruptcy order (rather than the receiving order, as before) is the last stage at which a lien may arise.

13.20   It is specifically provided in section 284(5) that if a bankrupt incurs a debt to a banker or other person by making a payment after the bankruptcy order (*e.g.* by drawing on his account) this shall be deemed to occur before the bankruptcy order (and hence is not subject to the trustee's rights) unless the bank had notice of the "bankruptcy" (presumably the petition) before

---

[61] See *Hale* v. *Victoria Plumbing Co. Ltd.* [1966] 2 Q.B. 746.
[62] s.31, Bankruptcy Act 1914, or s.323, Insolvency Act 1986 (replacing the former).
[63] [1967] Ch. 182.
[64] *George Barker (Transport) Ltd.* v. *Eynon* [1974] 1 W.L.R. 462.

the debt was incurred.[65] This would seem to mean that, (a) the banker can prove for that debt, and (b) a lien or right to appropriate or to combine accounts could arise over it (or that statutory set-off under section 323 applies). Subject, to this, no lien can arise for debts incurred after the bankruptcy order.

B. The rights of appropriation

1. GENERALLY

Funds may come to the banker's hands by way of a cash deposit, or by way of receipts from the collection of a cheque, or from a telegraphic or electronic transfer, or, maybe, from the realisation of securities held by the customer. Where the customer has more than one account, then in every case, unless it was otherwise agreed in the original mandate, the customer has the right to appropriate the funds to whichever account he pleases.[66] This is the case even if one account is in debit and another is not. Similarly, the customer has the right to appropriate within a particular account, so that he may demand that a particular payment to meet a particular cheque which has been or is to be drawn should be applied to that purpose.[67] In *W. P. Greenhalgh & Sons* v. *Union Bank of Manchester*[67a] court proceeded on the basis of an equitable assignment to the payee, entitling the payee to sue. This is very unusual, except perhaps if there is a trust, in which case the payee-beneficiary may have a complaint against the bank, as trustee.

13.21

We have observed that (at least where there is a duty to present the cheque quickly) it is probably the case that if there is no right to appropriate, there can be no lien, since a lien should carry with it some right of realisation for the benefit of the bank. But what matters for the purpose of right to combine is not what account the customer specifies, but whether he specifies some particular debit item for which he is paying in the cheque or money. Thus, if all that happens is that there is an appropriation by the customer to a given account, then the bank should appropriate funds to that account, but there is nothing to stop it thereafter combining accounts, with the same effect as if it had originally appropriated to the account of its choice. Naturally, the existence of a contrary agreement or any sort of trust would defeat the bank's right to combine, for that right may not be exercised in those circumstances.

The customer's right to appropriate funds so as to discharge a particular individual debit item implies necessarily that one must not consider for all purposes that the overall debt on an account, or on multiple accounts, is a single undivided debt. The account must for this purpose be regarded as a series of individual debts making up the greater debt, and the customer may appropriate his payment to any of the individual debts. This might be significant in the unlikely case that a security were taken for a particular debt, and the customer appropriated his payment in so as to discharge that debt.

13.22

---

[65] Or if it is not practicable for the trustee to obtain repayment—though this will not apply to bankers.

[66] *Simson* v. *Ingham* (1823) 2 B. & C. 65, 72; *Deeley* v. *Lloyds Bank Ltd.* [1912] A.C. 756; *Re Footman Bower & Co. Ltd.* [1961] Ch. 443.

[67] *Farley* v. *Turner* (1857) 26 L.J. Ch. 710; *W.P. Greenhalgh & Sons* v. *Union Bank of Manchester* [1924] 2 K.B. 153.

[67a] Previous note.

13.23   The rules as to appropriation between customer and banker may be summarised as follows:

(i) unless otherwise agreed, the customer has a right to specify to what account, or what debit item his payment will be applied.[68]

(ii) the customer may show his intention by a course of dealing or by other circumstances indicating his intent to the banker[69] but a mere private act such as making an entry in his own books is insufficient.[70]

(iii) if the customer does not specify, then the banker may do so.[71]

(iv) the banker may appropriate to a statute-barred debt (which exists still, but is merely unenforceable by action).[72]

(v) once the banker has credited a given account the appropriation is final[73] (though he may later be able to exercise the rights of combination, or contractual or statutory set-off). There have been suggestions that it was final only when communicated to the debtor[74] but it is thought that (partly because of the rule next described) an appropriation would be made, and would be final, when a payment is credited in the bank's books to an account, and when the customer is informed or when, under the bank's own rules, the credit is treated as irreversible.

(vi) if on a current account there is no specific appropriation by banker or customer to a specific debit item then a *default rule* applies.

2. THE DEFAULT RULE: CLAYTON'S CASE

13.24 If neither customer nor banker specifically appropriates a payment, and it is merely credited to the account, there is a presumption that (a) the first sum paid in is the first to be drawn out, or (b) the payment in is appropriated to the first undischarged debit item on the account so that that debit item is (wholly or partly) discharged. This "default rule" is usually referred to as "the rule in *Clayton's case*."[75] There is some authority that the rule in *Clayton's case* applies only to a banking account.[76] The rule is merely a presumption, which may be displaced by evidence of some contrary intention. But it seems that the contrary intention must be express: in *Deeley v. Lloyds Bank Ltd.*[77] a bank had a mortgage, as security for an overdraft. They heard that their customer had given a second mortgage to someone else, but continued the account. The Court of Appeal took the view that the bankers must have intended to appropriate to the unsecured debts, because they would not have wished to discharge the secured debt and loose the security, but the House of Lords held that the rule in *Clayton's case* applied. An express appropriation, therefore, would seem to be required, failing which the default rule will apply when the account is credited. According to *Deeley's* case, the express appropriation may be shown by "ruling off" (stopping) the account, and opening a separate account for subsequent transactions.

[68] *Simson v. Ingham* (1823) 2 B. & C. 65, and cases above, nn. 66–67.
[69] *Marryatts v. White* (1817) 2 Stark 101; *Burn v. Boulton* (1846) 2 C.B. 476; *Nash v. Hodgson* (1855) 6 De G.M. & G. 474, 486, 487.
[70] *Manning v. Westerne* (1707) 2 Vern. 606.
[71] *Simson v. Ingham*, above, n. 68.
[72] *Mills v. Fowkes* (1839) 5 Bing. N.C. 455; *Williams v. Griffith* (1839) 5 M. & W. 330.
[73] *Deeley v. Lloyds Bank Ltd.* [1912] A.C. 756.
[74] See *Simson v. Ingham* (1823) 2 B. & C. 65; *London and Westminster Bank v. Button* (1907) 51 Sol.Jo. 466.
[75] *Devaynes v. Noble, Clayton's Case* (1816) 1 Mer. 529, 572.
[76] *Re Diplock* [1948] Ch. 465, 555.
[77] [1912] A.C. 756.

The facts of *Clayton's case* were that Clayton had an account with a bank- **13.25**
ing partnership. One of the bank's partners died, and at that time the bank
owed Clayton a certain sum, for which the deceased partner was jointly
liable, his debt becoming "fixed" at that time. However, Clayton and the
bank continued to operate the same account, so that more than the original
debt was paid in and drawn out. The bank then failed, and Clayton
attempted to sue the estate of the dead partner. But it was held that the payments through the account, which exceeded the original debt, had discharged that debt, and the "new" debts on the account were no
responsibility of the dead partner, being incurred after he ceased to be
partner. In this case the bank was debtor, but it is the same if the customer is
debtor, where it is normally of significance.

The rule is often significant for banks, and three particular cases may be
mentioned.

First, if money is advanced on a security, the security may be security for
a given debt, and if money passes through the account, the debt will be discharged, and the security rendered ineffective. This may be overcome if the
security is not for a specific advance, but for "all monies" to be advanced,
for as long as there is a debt, it is covered by the security. Even so, where
the bank learns of a second mortgage or security being given over the same
assets to another creditor, the bank may not normally take priority over that
second creditor[78] once it knows of his right, so that although its all monies
security is not discharged by payments in and through the account, the
priority of the security is affected by such payments. The old debt will be
discharged, and replaced by new debt, and the security over the new debt,
while still valid, will rank behind the second mortgagee's security because
his debt is prior in time.[79]

Secondly, if, as in *Clayton's case* itself, a partner or other joint account **13.26**
holder dies, or becomes bankrupt, or if in some other way his liability is
"fixed," then that fixed debt may be reduced by the operation of the rule,
leaving the bank with a remedy for the new debt only against the remaining
debtors.[80]

Thirdly, where a guarantee is determined, so that the liability of the guarantor becomes fixed, payments through the principal debtor's account may
discharge the debt for which the guarantor is liable, even though the total
amount of debt (new debt) remains the same. If a guarantor guaranteed a
certain sum, for example, the guarantor's liability becomes fixed on the first
occasion that the debtor's debt reaches the amount in question, and thereafter the guarantor's liability is reduced by the operation of *Clayton's case*.
This may be avoided if the guarantor does not guarantee a specific sum, but
guarantees all debts of the debtor, with a limitation on the amount. In this
way, there is no time at which his liability becomes fixed.[81]

These are only specific instances of the many cases in which the rule **13.27**
requires some caution on the part of bankers. It may be added that there are
some occasions on which the rule is peculiarly beneficial to bankers. One
such occasion concerns floating charges. By section 245 of the Insolvency

---

[78] Unless it has a right to "tack" on further advances: see below, Chap. 24, in relation to mortgages of land.
[79] As in *Deeley* v. *Lloyds Bank Ltd.* [1912] A.C. 756.
[80] For an example, see *Royal Bank of Scotland* v. *Christie* (1841) 8 Cl. & Fin. 214.
[81] To make it perfectly clear, liability is often expressed to be "continuing" but this would
seem to add nothing. On guarantees, see below.

Act 1986[82] such charges may be invalid where liquidation occurs within (*e.g.*) twelve months of the date of creation of the charge, except to the extent that the charge is given for consideration. If a bank to which a company is indebted takes a floating charge for past advances, this charge may be affected by subsequent liquidation, and is invalid to the extent to which it represents "old" debt. But if the account is continued, a position may quickly be reached by virtue of *Clayton's case*, by which the old debt is replaced by "new" debt, so that the security is saved. A second situation of advantage may occur in relation to advances for wages and salaries. In case of the customer's bankruptcy or liquidation, some debts (the most important of which, here, are wages and salary debts) are given preference in the distribution of the assets.[83] So too, if money is advanced to the customer for the purpose of paying such debts, and if it is used for such purposes, these advances enjoy preferential status. The preference, however, is given only for debts arising four months before the bankruptcy. The rule in *Clayton's case* assists the bank's administration here, inasmuch as "old" debts may effectively be transferred out of the account merely by transferring payments in each month, equal to the amount of the debit four months ago. The payments in are automatically appropriated to the old debts, which are thus "transferred" to the current account, from which the payments in came. This, though not perhaps legally necessary, assists in the bank's supervision of the state of accounts.[84] Even if there is no separate Wages account, the effect of *Clayton's case* may, in a particular case, be that a non-preferential debt in the current account is paid off first.[85]

3. WHERE THE DEFAULT RULE DOES NOT APPLY

13.28   The rule in *Clayton's case* does not apply in the following cases:

First, between trustee and beneficiary. Where a trustee pays money belonging to a beneficiary into the trustee's own account, thus mixing it with his own funds, and subsequently withdraws funds for his own purposes, there is a presumption that the funds withdrawn are not the trust funds, but the trustee's own funds.[86] This rule protects both the beneficiaries, and the trustee (from possible breach of trust). If, on the contrary, *Clayton's case* applied, it might be that the first funds paid in would be set against the first withdrawals, and the beneficiaries' money would be affected. However, if funds belonging to two beneficiaries are paid into the account, and part of the trust moneys are drawn out, the rule does apply between the two beneficiaries to determine whose money was withdrawn.[87]

13.29   Secondly, the rule does not apply to separate accounts at the bank, even if they are at the same branch.[88] But in some cases the accounts, although apparently separate, may be operated together in such a way that they are in reality a single account, and the rule can then apply.[89]

[82] The successor of s.322, C.A. 1948 and s.617, C.A. 1985.
[83] Even above floating charges, though not fixed charges.
[84] For Wages accounts, see below, Chap. 28 (preferential creditors).
[85] See *Re Primrose (Builders) Ltd.* [1950] 1 Ch. 561.
[86] *Re Hallett's Estate* (1880) 13 Ch.D. 696.
[87] *Re Stenning, Wood* v. *Stenning* [1895] 2 Ch. 433.
[88] *Bradford Old Bank Ltd.* v. *Sutcliffe* [1918] 2 K.B. 833; *Re Yeovil Glove Co. Ltd.* [1965] Ch. 148.
[89] *Re E. J. Morel* (1934) Ltd. [1962] Ch. 21, discussed below, at n. 9, and Chap. 27.

Thirdly, the rule does not apply to a stopped account, where payments in and out do not take place. The rule applicable to stopped accounts[90] is no more than an instance of a specific contrary appropriation by the banker. By "ruling a line" under the old account, and starting a new one, he shows as clearly as may be that he makes an appropriation other than to the old debits. It may be necessary to distinguish stopped accounts from the type of account where credits are allowed, though new debits would not be permitted, and where the rule would apply. Some might refer to these as "frozen" accounts.

Fourthly, the rule does not apply if there is an express contrary agreement, or express reservation of the right of appropriation by the banker at the time of payment, since it is merely a prima facie presumption of fact rebuttable by clear evidence of some other intended method of appropriation.[91] Thus, in *Westminster Bank Ltd.* v. *Cond*[92] a customer's account was guaranteed. Demand was made of the guarantor, and this would normally "fix" his liability, so that continuation of the debtor's account would cause the old debt to be discharged (as, according to the guarantor, had happened here). The guarantee form, however, contained (as most now do) a term that the bank might continue the account without discharging the guarantor's liability, and this was held to be effective. Similar terms often appear in securities and the like, even as between banker and principal debtor, and may also appear in joint accounts so as to protect against death, retirement or bankruptcy of a joint account holder. Bankers seem reluctant to rely upon such terms, however, and the general practice is to stop the account and to open a new one. This is presumably an uncertainty arising from the terms in which the *Deeley* case was decided,[92a] but it seems to be unnecessary. There was no such term in the *Deeley* case, and all the House of Lords decided was that where, without more, a bank credited an account with a payment in, the rule in *Clayton's case* applied, and was not displaced by an argument that it could not have been intended because it was disadvantageous to the bank. Stopping the account is no more than an express contrary appropriation, and if that is effective, so should be any other express contrary appropriation made by a contractual term.

13.30

Fifthly, the rule applies only to current accounts, on which there is a "running" balance, and does not apply between parties where there have been separate transactions.[93]

C. Combination of accounts (banker's set-off)

1. GENERALLY

Combination (or "consolidation") refers to the right of a bank to set one account off against another of the same customer in order to determine the total state of indebtedness between customer and bank. It is frequently called set-off, but must be distinguished from equitable set-off (where one person's legal claim against the other may be set-off in a judgment (usually at the discretion of the court) instead of by way of a separate action). With combination, the bank does not assert a separate claim, and merely asserts

13.31

---

[90] From *Deeley* v. *Lloyds Bank Ltd.* [1912] A.C. 756.
[91] *Cory Brothers & Co.* v. *Mecca Turkish S.S. (Owners), The Mecca* [1897] A.C. 286.
[92] (1940) 46 Com. Cas 60.
[92a] Above, nn. 77, 90.
[93] *Cory Brothers 7 Co.* v. *Mecca Turkish S.S. (Owners), The Mecca* [1897] A.C. 286.

that its liability to the customer, taking both accounts into consideration, is less than he says it is. Combination also differs from contractual and statutory set-off. Some cases have referred to it as a right of lien, though clearly it is not a lien since by definition there cannot be a possessory right over a chose in action[94] and there cannot, therefore, be any lien over the content of a bank account. Buckley L.J. has explained the right in these terms, "the situation is not, in my judgment, a situation of lien at all. A lien postulates property of the debtor in the possession or under the control of the creditor. Nor is it a set-off situation, which postulates mutual but independent obligations between the two parties. It is an accounting situation, in which the existence and amount of one party's liability to the other can only be ascertained by discovering the ultimate balance of their mutual dealings. . . . "[95] We shall refer to the right simply as "combination."

13.32   The leading case is *Garnett* v. *McKewan*[96] in which a customer had drawn cheques on an account in credit held at one branch of the bank, at a time when he was overdrawn on an account held at another branch. Without notice to him, the bank combined the balances, and dishonoured the cheques. It was held that the bank was entitled to combine the accounts, and that they might, therefore, dishonour cheques for insufficiency of funds. Despite the clear authority of this case, in *W. P. Greenhalgh & Sons* v. *Union Bank of Manchester Ltd.*[97] Swift J. held that if a customer had two accounts, this implies an agreement to keep them separate. Swift J.'s views were rejected by the Court of Appeal and by the House of Lords in the *Halesowen Presswork* case.[98] In the Court of Appeal, Lord Denning said that on the contrary "You have to find an agreement to keep them separate. The mere opening of two accounts does not do it."[99] The effect of the principle is nicely summarized by Mocatta J., in *Barclays Bank Ltd.* v. *Okenarhe*[1] as follows:

> "As regards the case in which the customer has separate running current accounts at each of two branches of a bank, it is plain that the general principle is that the bank is entitled to combine the two accounts. There is clear authority for this in the case of *Garnett* v. *McKewan*. The learned Barons, in giving their judgments in that case, emphasised, of course, as one would have expected, that there was no right of combination in relation to accounts maintained with a banker by one person but in two different capacities; for example, one account might be a personal account of the customer and the other might be a trust account. Further, it was made clear by Baron Bramwell that the right to combine did not arise if there was an agreement between the customer and the banker that the two accounts should be kept separate, or if such an agreement should be implied from their conduct. Furthermore, in the case the learned judges dealt with what, at first sight, might seem the apparent anomaly that the customer cannot without

---

[94] Above, para. 13.12.
[95] *National Westminster Bank Ltd.* v. *Halesowen Presswork and Assemblies Ltd.* [1970] 3 All E.R. 473, 488, approved in the H.L. [1972] 1 All E.R. 641, 646, 653.
[96] (1872) L.R. 8 Ex. 10. See also *Re European Bank, Agra Bank Claim* (1872) 8 Ch. App. 41. decided on the same day in a different court.
[97] [1924] 2 K.B. 153.
[98] Above, n. 95.
[99] [1971] 1 Q.B. 1, 35.
[1] [1966] 2 Lloyd's Rep. 87, 95.

the specific agreement of the bank draw on account A a sum in excess of his balance on that account but which is less than the combined balance at account A and account B. That limitation on the customer's rights, in other words, the inability of the customer without specific agreement to combine to accounts, is explained as necessary to business efficacy. It would make the task of the banker impossible if every branch was expected to know the state of a customer's account at every other branch."

It is clear, therefore, that the rights arise by operation of law, and not by agreement, and that no notice needs to be given to the customer: "it might be proper or considerate to give notice to that effect, but there is no legal obligation on the bankers to do so. . . . The customer must be taken to know the state of each account. . . . "[2] Both *Garnett* v. *McKewan* and the *Okenarhe* case show that the accounts may be at different branches of the bank.

As with liens, there is no right of combination for contingent liabilities.[3] **13.33**

Combination is possible for any account, unless there is an express or implied agreement not to combine. Thus, certainly in the case of a loan account for a fixed period, and perhaps in the case of a frozen or other account, there may have been an agreement not to call the loan in, or to keep the frozen account separate from the current account. (A frozen account is merely one in respect of which there is an agreement by the bank not to call in the amount owing if certain conditions—such as the maintenance in credit of a new current account—are fulfilled.) In *Buckingham* v. *London & Midland Bank Ltd.*[4] it was found that where there was a loan account (secured) and a current account, the course of dealing between bank and customer was such that the right to combine without notice did not exist. That is to say, it was impliedly agreed otherwise.[5]

If there is an agreement not to combine then that agreement will end on **13.34** the customer's bankruptcy, when the banker-customer relationship is terminated[6] (at the same moment, the right of statutory set-off comes into existence).[7] Similarly, the bank may terminate the banker-customer relationship by reasonable notice in cases other than insolvency, and then combine accounts.[8]

If there are multiple accounts, it is probable that a bank must take a view over all the accounts, and combine all, if any, and not in any particular order. Thus, it probably cannot combine a debit account No. 1 with a credit account No. 2, leaving untouched a debit account No. 3 where No. 3 is a preferential debt in case of the customer's insolvency.[9] The result of this would be that the credits would be apportioned rateably against the

[2] *Garnett* v. *McKewan*, above, n. 96, at p. 13.
[3] *Jeffryes* v. *Agra & Mastermans Bank* (1866) L.R. Eq. 674; *Bower* v. *Foreign & Colonial Gas Co. Ltd.*; *Metropolitan Bank, Garnishees* (1874) 22 W.R. 740.
[4] (1895) 12 T.L.R. 70, and see also *Bradford Old Bank Ltd.* v. *Sutcliffe* [1918] 2 K.B. 833.
[5] See the discussion in the *Halesowen Presswork* case, above n. 95 and see in *Re E. J. Morel* (1934) Ltd. [1962] Ch. 21, where Buckley J. held the same in relation to a frozen account.
[6] *National Westminster Bank Ltd.* v. *Halesowen Presswork and Assemblies Ltd.* [1970] 3 All E.R. 473 (C.A.), rev'd [1972] 1 All E.R. 641 (H.L.).
[7] Below, Chap. 27.
[8] See *Joachimson* v. *Swiss Bank Corpn.* [1921] 3 K.B. 110; *Prosperity Ltd.* v. *Lloyds Bank Ltd.* (1923) 39 T.L.R. 372; *Buckingham* v. *London & Midland Bank Ltd.*, above n. 4.
[9] *Contra*, see *Re E. J. Morel* (1934) Ltd. [1962] Ch. 21, [1961] 1 All E.R. 796, disapproved in *Re Unit 2 Windows Ltd.* [1985] 3 All E.R. 647.

non-preferential and preferential debts in proportion to the respective amounts of the debts.[10]

2. CUSTOMER'S RIGHT TO COMBINE?

13.35 The customer has no right to insist upon combination, as by presenting a cheque at one branch where he has an insufficiency of funds, and to demand that the bank pay it because of funds in an account kept elsewhere, although of course, the bank can combine such accounts as a reason to refuse to pay. This "apparent anomaly"[11] was established in *Garnett* v. *McKewan*, and was put on the ground of business efficacy, since the bank could not be expected to know the state of a customer's account at every other branch, whereas the customer can be expected to know the state of his various accounts.[12] There seems to be no reason, however, why a customer cannot insist upon the combination of accounts kept at one branch, if it has not been agreed that they be kept separate.[13]

If a customer has two current accounts, and draws a cheque generally (*i.e.* not referring to a particular account)[14] there may be a duty on the bank to combine, since the bank must investigate all the accounts held by the customer at the bank.[15] But this could not be the case if the accounts are at separate branches.

A third case in which a bank is bound to combine is on terminating the relationship of customer and banker, if the customer has more than one account, and one is in debit.[16]

Finally, if for some reason a bank does not take steps to combine accounts on bankruptcy or winding-up, the mandatory provisions of section 323 of the Insolvency Act 1986 will compel it to do so by way of statutory set-off of mutual debts.

3. ACCOUNTS IN DIFFERENT RIGHTS

13.36 Combination is not possible for funds held in different rights by the customer, to the bank's knowledge. For example, the funds may be known to be trust funds, in which case the account may not be combined with another debit account.[17]

It follows from this that a bank has no right to combine a partner's private account with the partnership account, even though the partner's liability on

---

[10] Contrast the situation in *Re William Hall (Contractors) Ltd.* [1967] 2 All E.R. 1150, discussed below, Chap. 27.

[11] Above para. 13.32, (*Okenarhe* case) and see *Woodland* v. *Fear* (1857) 7 E. & B. 519; *McNaughten* v. *Cox & Co.* (1921) *The Times*, May, 11.

[12] See also *Direct Acceptance Corpn. Ltd.* v. *Bank of N.S.W.* (1968) 88 W.N. (Pt. 1) (N.S.W.) 498.

[13] See *Mutton* v. *Peat* [1900] 2 Ch. 79.

[14] Rare nowadays, because of the use of printed cheque forms with account numbers on them.

[15] See Chorley, 70.

[16] Paget, 146, observing that the bank must give notice in order to close. A banker may, however, close an account by exercising the right of combination, and no notice is needed for this.

[17] See *Halesowen* case, above n. 95, *Okenarhe* case, above n. 1. *Re European Bank, Agra Bank Claim*, (1872) 8 Ch. App. 41, 44, *Union Bank of Australia Ltd.* v. *Murray-Aynsley* [1898] A.C. 693. Here, the bank did not know the funds were trust funds. See also *Stumore* v. *Campbell & Co.* [1892] 1 Q.B. 314 (Quistclose trust); *Barclays Bank Lltd.* v. *Quistclose Investments Ltd.* [1970] A.C. 567; money paid by mistake of fact; *Kerrison* v. *Glyn, Mills, Currie & Co.* (1911) 81 LJKB 465; *Scottish Metropolitan Assurance Co.* v. *P. Samuel & Co.* [1923] 1 K.B. 348; joint debts: *Watts* v. *Christie* (1849) 11 Beav. 546; *Re Willis, Percival & Co., ex p. Morier* (1879) 12

the partnership account is joint.[18] If, however, a bank takes (as is usual) a joint and several mandate from the partners, then the debt is not merely a joint debt of the partners as partners, but also a separate personal debt of each individual, and the private account may be combined with the partnership account.

Ch.D. 491. This may be overcome by a course of business showing an agreement to the contrary, or by an express term allowing set-off—*Vulliamy* v. *Noble* (1817) 3 Mer. 593, 618; *Muggeridge* v. *Smith & Co.* (1884) 1 T.L.R. 166.

[18] *Watts* v. *Christie* (1849) 11 Beav. 546.

14. Subrogation and Subordination

A. Subrogation

14.01 The idea of subrogation "embraces more than a single concept in English law. It is a convenient way of describing a transfer of rights from one person to another, without assignment or assent of the person from whom the rights are transferred and which takes place by operation of law in a whole variety of widely differing circumstances."[1] The essence of the doctrine is often explained by saying that one person may stand in the shoes of another in relation to a third party, generally to avoid unjust enrichment. That is to say, but for subrogation, A would have no enforceable rights against C, but because B has rights against C, and because of some relation between A and B and C, A may be able to stand in B's shoes and enforce A's claim against C as though A were B. This avoids C's unjust enrichment. A common example of subrogation is the right of an insurer who pays a loss to stand in the shoes of the insured in respect of the insured's right of action against any party responsible for the loss. The rights gained by A in this way may be either personal or proprietary: for example, he may be able to sue C in debt, or he may be able to enforce against C a security held previously by B. But his rights may be no greater than those held by B, no matter the extent of A's claim.

1. SUBROGATION AND SECURITIES

14.02 If C is indebted to B, who holds a mortgage or charge as security for the debt, and if at C's request A advances money so as to discharge the mortgage, A has a personal right of indemnity from C, but will also be subrogated to B's rights as mortgagee, so that A will have a proprietary right. Equity regards the mortgage as being kept alive in equity for A's benefit, and not discharged by the payment, even though as a legal mortgage between B and C (if it was such) it is discharged.[2] The example given is an example of contractual subrogation: that is to say, of subrogation arising pursuant to a contractual agreement between A and C to advance money to B. It may seem somewhat misleading to refer to the right of subrogation as "contractual," since it will arise even if the parties say nothing about it, and it might well be regarded as arising by operation of law.[3] However, and although the point is academic, some dicta suggest that it should be deemed to arise by way of an implied term in the agreement between A and C.[4]

2. SUBROGATION AND MARSHALLING

14.03 The equitable doctrine of marshalling holds that if creditor 1 has a separate security over different assets, a and b, and creditor 2 then takes a second security over asset b, and if creditor 1 realises asset b before he realises asset a, then after creditor 1's security rights have been satisfied by payment out of assets, creditor 2 will be subrogated to creditor 1's security rights over

---

[1] *Orakpo* v. *Manson Investments Ltd.* [1978] A.C. 95, 104 (*per* Lord Diplock.)

[2] *Butler* v. *Rice* [1910] 2 Ch.277; *Ghana Commercial Bank* v. *Chandiram* [1960] A.C. 732.

[3] If not, and if it is based on contract, why is it not simply an equitable mortgage or charge, and why has subrogation anything to do with it?

[4] See *Orakpo* v. *Manson Investments Ltd.* [1978] A.C. 95, 104, 120.

asset a. This is not to say that creditor 1 must have any concern about creditor 2. Creditor 1 may realise whichever of the assets he chooses, and is entitled to be satisfied in full if he is fully secured. But if a secured asset remains, or part of the proceeds of a secured asset remain, creditor 2 is entitled to stand in the shoes of creditor 1 in respect of that asset or its proceeds, even if his original security was over another asset taken by creditor 1.[5]

3. SUBROGATION AND SURETIES OR GUARANTORS

If A, being a surety or guarantor for C's obligation to B, pays off C's debt or performs the obligation (or part of it) A has a right to be reimbursed or indemnified by C, and in addition A is subrogated to B's security rights against C to the extent of his payment. A is also entitled to assert B's claims against A's co-guarantors. If A's liability under the guarantee (and thus, the amount he pays) did not cover the whole of B's claim, then A acquires a proportionate interest in the securities and the claims against the co-guarantors. It is immaterial that when A contracted, he was unaware of the existence of the securities, and indeed, he is entitled to security taken after the guarantee. To this extent, A receives a windfall.[6] **14.04**

If B has been fully paid, there will be no objection to this, but where he has been only partially paid, he may object to sharing his security with the guarantor, and to the guarantor's claims against the co-guarantor. It is, therefore, common for bank guarantees to contain a term excluding the right of subrogation until such time as B (the bank) has been fully paid.[7]

A guarantor or surety for a debt which in bankruptcy or liquidation is preferential, and who pays the debt, will by subrogation achieve the same priority that the creditor would have had.[8]

A particular instance of the right of subrogation by a surety exists in relation to a bill of exchange, where a drawer or other person liable upon the bill (an indorser) when it is dishonoured seeks to be subrogated to securities provided by the acceptor to the holder. A buyer of goods, for example, may have provided a security to his bank and the seller draws a bill upon that bank and discounts the bill with the bank upon recourse terms (thus putting himself in the position of surety). If the buyer fails, the bank may either have recourse to its securities or to the seller, and in the latter case the seller has recourse to the securities.[9] **14.05**

There are at least two limitations upon the principle of subrogation in cases such as that just mentioned: first, the surety must have paid the bill, or declared his willingness to do so.[10] Secondly, the securities in question must

[5] *Wallis* v. *Woodyear* (1855) 2 Jur. N.S. 179; Goode, *Commercial Law*, 755.
[6] *Deering* v. *Lord Winchelsea* (1787) 2 B. & P. 270; *Aldrich* v. *Cooper* (1803) 8 Vest. Jun. 382; *Craythorne* v. *Swinburne* (1807) 14 Ves. 160; *Mayhew* v. *Cricket* (1818) 2 Swans. 185; *Stirling* v. *Forrester* (1851) 3 Blig. 575, 590; *Yonge* v. *Reynell* (1852) 9 Hare 819; *Forbes* v. *Jackson* (1882) 19 Ch.D. 615; *Ghana Commercial Bank* v. *Chandiram* [1960] A.C. 732. The principle is given statutory expression in the Mercantile Law Amendment Act 1856, s.5. See *Ellinger* (1986) J.B.L. 399 and the Australian cases there cited.
[7] Sometimes, indeed, even other separate rights of the guarantor against the debtor are subordinated to the bank's rights.
[8] *Re Lamplugh Iron Ore Co.* [1927] 1 Ch. 308.
[9] The matter was conclusively settled in *Duncan, Fox & Co.* v. *North and South Wales Bank* (1880) 6 App.Cas. 1,22. See also *Aga Ahmed Isphany* v. *Crisp* (1891) 8 T.L.R. 132 (J.C.); *Jowitt & Sons* v. *Union Cold Storage Co.* [1913] 3 K.B. 1.
[10] *Re Howe, ex p Brett* (1871) L.R. 6 Ch. App. 838, 841; cf. *Re a Debtor* [1976] 2 All E.R. 1010; *Buckeridge* v. *Mercantile Credit Ltd.* (1981) 147 C.L.R. 654.

have been given by the debtor (or co-surety where his securities are in question) so as to cover the debts related to the bills in question (as well, perhaps, as other debts).[11] This is a question of construction of the contract, and is generally easy to establish in the case of the principal debtor. But with other parties, such as alleged co-sureties, there can be no subrogation if the party creating the security did not intend to be liable to the party claiming subrogation (if he is not really a co-surety). Thus, in *Scholefield, Goodman & Sons Ltd.* v. *Zyngier*[12] the surety (Z) had guaranteed Z & Co.'s liability to a bank (including liability on bills). Another person (the plaintiff) drew bills on Z & Co., which were accepted but not paid, having been discounted with the bank. The bank made claims under another transaction against Z, who met the claims and demanded the vacation of the mortgage. The drawer, however, claimed that as co-surety with Z he was entitled to subrogation in respect of Z's security. The Judicial Committee held that the drawer's claim must fail, because Z had not warranted payment to the drawer. On the contrary, all Z had done was to guarantee to the bank that a party liable on the bill would pay it, and the drawer was a party liable on the bill. Z and the drawer were not in equal positions: had Z paid the bill Z could have had recourse against the drawer. In other words, Z was not in truth a "co-surety" with the drawer, not having intended to be liable to the drawer on these bills.

4. SUBROGATION AND AGENTS

14.06 If an agent borrows money from a bank (A) for a principal (C), and the agent has no authority to borrow, the agent is liable[13] but the principal is not. If, however, the money is applied in satisfaction of the principal's debts to another (B), then the bank is subrogated to B's rights against the principal, and may sue him notwithstanding the agent's want of authority. Thus, in *B. Liggett (Liverpool) Ltd.* v. *Barclays Bank Ltd.*[14] a bank, contrary to its mandate, honoured a company's cheques signed by one director only. The cheques were drawn in favour of trade creditors, who received payment. The company sued the bank, which would have been liable but for the principle of subrogation, which enabled the bank to be subrogated to the trade creditors whose debts were paid, thus avoiding unjust enrichment of the company.[15]

We have observed[15a] the rule that where a bank pays without mandate from its customer it may recover money from a third party under a personal action based on payment by mistake even if the payment is such as to discharge the third party's debts. This avoids unjust enrichment of the customer whose debt is discharged. An alternative and perhaps more logical solution might be to allow the bank to stand in the shoes of the third party to recover from its customer, despite the lack of mandate. That is, the bank would recover for the amount of the third party's debt which has been discharged, not for any debt owing directly from customer to banker. The *Liggett* case seems to support this principle.

[11] *Duncan, Fox & Co.* v. *North and South Wales Bank* (1880) 6 App.Cas. 1.22.
[12] [1985] 3 All E.R. 105, [1986] A.C. 562 (J.C.)
[13] On a warranty of authority.
[14] [1928] 1 K.B.48.
[15] See also *Re Cleadon Trust* [1939] Ch. 286 (company secretary acted outside his authority in borrowing for company—subrogation possible).
[15a] Above, Chap. 11.

In many cases of this sort, the principal will ratify, but if he does not, and **14.07** if the payment can be identified as having gone to pay an authorised debt (and this will often be a simple matter where an unauthorised cheque is in question) subrogation is possible. The question arises whether the principle in *Clayton's case* applies, in order to identify the destination of payments. While there seems to be no decided case, there is no reason why the rule should not apply, as it does for the remedy of tracing. Thus, if an unauthorised advance is made to a customer's account, the rule would help to show to what debit that advance was applied.

Until the law on director's powers is reformed, subrogation may be of considerable use where directors of a company act *intra vires* the company but outside their own powers. After the decision in *Rolled Steel Products (Holdings) Ltd.* v. *British Steel Corpn.*,[16] however, directors acting with a secret improper purpose should be regarded as having ostensible authority to bind the company, so that the right of subrogation is unnecessary. The question may arise, however, whether subrogation is available if the bank is aware of the secret improper purpose (when there is no ostensible authority). Subrogation is an equitable principle, and he who comes to equity must come with clean hands. It seems, however, that subrogation may be available, for it is based on the principle of avoidance of unjust enrichment, and the company is not prejudiced (having merely exchanged one creditor for another).[17] But it may be otherwise if the directors are acting in an underhand or morally reprehensible fashion, and the bank knows this.

5. SUBROGATION AND CONTRACTS ULTRA VIRES A COMPANY

Until the law on *ultra vires* transactions is reformed, different principles **14.08** apply where the dealing with a company (for example, a loan) is not authorised by the objects clause.[18] Again, the lending bank is entitled to subrogation in respect of the loan itself.[19] Additionally, if the bank had taken securities for the loan, and assuming that the company has power to give securities for lawful debts, the bank subrogated in respect of the debt may enforce its own security.[20] But the normal rule that the lender is subrogated in respect of securities held by the creditor whose debt is paid, is displaced with an *ultra vires* loan. The lender is entitled neither to the securities, nor to any priority enjoyed by the creditor whose debt is paid over the other creditors of the company. In short, if it has no security of its own, the bank claims merely as an unsecured creditor.[21] Thus, in *Re Wrexham Mold and Connah's Railway Co.*[22] a company had three classes of secured debentures, ranking between themselves in a certain order, and the company borrowed money from a bank (exceeding the company's borrowing powers) so as to be able to pay interest arrests to the first-ranking debenture holders. Neither the security held by those creditors, nor their preferential ranking, could be relied upon by the bank.

[16] [1984] BCLC 466, [1986] Ch. 246.
[17] *B. Liggett (Liverpool) Ltd.* v. *Barclays Bank Ltd.* [1928] 1 K.B. 48, where the bank knew that a single director had no authority.
[18] True *ultra vires*, as opposed to cases where the directors act without authority, or exercise express powers for an improper purpose.
[19] *Neath Building Society* v. *Luce* (1889) 43 Ch.D. 158.
[20] *Cunliffe Brooks & Co.* v. *Blackburn and District Benefit Building Society* (1884) 9 App.Cas. 857, affirming (1882) 22 Ch. D. 61.
[21] *Re Wrexham Mold and Connah's Quay Railway Co.* [1899] 1 Ch. 440.
[22] Previous note.

Subrogation is not available if the loan is used to repay share capital, as this is not regarded as payment of a debt of the company.[23]

6. MENTALLY DISORDERED PERSONS

14.09 If it should happen that a bank advances money to a mentally disordered customer who has no contractual capacity, subrogation may provide a remedy if the money is used to pay for a lawful debt, such as meeting necessary outgoings of the customer's estate.[24]

7. INFANTS

14.10 According to section 1 of the Infants' Relief Act 1874 all contracts with persons under 18 years of age "for the repayment of money lent or to be lent" are "absolutely void." Mortgages are also void.[25] This is the case even if the bank advances money so as to pay for necessaries. If, however, the money advanced is actually applied to a lawful debt, such as a purchase of necessaries, then the bank is subrogated to the rights of the lawful creditor.[26]

8. STATUTORY SUBROGATION

14.11 This occurs in case of an individual or company insolvency, and is considered elsewhere.[26a] The principle is that on insolvency there are preferential creditors, and that a person who pays the debts of those preferential creditors may stand in their shoes, and becomes a preferential creditor himself.

B. Subordination Agreements

14.12 "Subordination is a transaction whereby one creditor (the subordinated creditor) of the borrower agrees not to be paid until another creditor (the senior creditor) is paid in full."[27] The subordinated creditor may be an ordinary creditor or a preferential creditor, surrendering his preference, or he may be a secured creditor under a fixed charge, surrendering his priority to the holder of a floating charge. It is unclear to what extent subordination agreements are affected by the *pari passu* provisions of bankruptcy law, requiring equal treatment of unsecured creditors. The *pari passu* principle[28] seems designed to prevent creditors from obtaining unfair advantages over other stranger creditors. It appears to be necessary to distinguish between a mere private contractual subordination (affecting only the parties to the contract) and a full subordination agreement (purporting to affect others). There can be no objection in principle to the former, but there is to the latter. If creditor 1 agrees with creditor 2 that the latter will take priority over the former, this priority should not be asserted against the debtor or his trustee or liquidator. There is, first, a practical reason, that the liquidator

---

[23] *Cunliffe Brooks & Co.* v. *Blackburn and District Benefit Building Society* (1884) 9 App.Cas. 857, affirming (1882) 22 Ch. D. 61. Tracing may be available.

[24] *Re Beavan, Davies, Banks & Co.* v. *Beavan* [1912] 1 Ch. 196; *Lloyd* v. *Coote and Ball* [1915] 1 K.B. 242. Interest and commission are not recoverable.

[25] *Nottingham Permanent Benefit Building Society* v. *Thurstan* [1902] 1 Ch. 1, aff'd [1903] A.C. 6.

[26] *Re National Permanent Benefit Building Society* (1869) 5 Ch. App. 309, 313; *Lewis* v. *Alleyne* (1888) 4 T.L.R. 560.

[26a] Below, Chap. 28.

[27] Wood, *Law and Practice of International Finance*, p. 403.

[28] Discussed below, Chap. 28.

may then be obliged to consider the validity of the contract between the two creditors. Secondly, there may, in addition, be a third creditor not party to the agreement, who must rank equally with creditor 1, and who would, therefore, stand ahead of creditor 2 by virtue of an agreement to which he was not party. There seems to be nothing to stop creditor 2 denying to creditor 3 the priority of creditor 3, but this entails denying the priority of creditor 1. The liquidator would not know who to pay first even if creditors 1 and 2 have no dispute. It would seem, therefore, that the *pari passu* principle cannot be displaced in relation to non-contracting parties by a full subordination agreement.

Suppose, however, that creditor 1 assigns his debt to another. The **14.13** assignee has the same priority as the assignor and can assert his assignment against a liquidator, who must consider the validity of the contract. If creditor 1 is preferential, he could assign his preferential debt to creditor 2 in return for an assignment of creditor 2's non-preferential debt. Problems would, however, arise if the amounts of the debts differ, as an assignment of part of a debt is equitable in nature and the equitable assignee could not give a good discharge to the liquidator.

In order to avoid such problems, it may be agreed as a mere private matter between creditors that distributions received by the subordinated creditor should be handed over to the senior creditor for application to the senior debt. If this is done, then it would seem right that the subordinated creditors should be subrogated to the claims of the senior creditors which the former have paid.[29] It should be observed that "seniority" refers to the position between the creditors: so far as the liquidator is concerned, the "senior" creditor may still rank equally with the subordinated creditor: subrogation would not affect the priority of the subordinated creditor in the liquidator's eyes.

The *pari passu* principle does not apply to secured creditors, and subordi- **14.14** nation agreements between them were accepted as valid in *Re Woodroffes (Musical Instruments) Ltd.*[30] where a fixed charge which would have had priority over a floating charge was expressed to be subject to the floating charge. The order of priority was as follows: (i) the floating chargeholder to the extent of the claim of the fixed chargeholder, (ii) the preferential creditors, (iii) the floating chargeholder for the balance of its claim, and (iv) the fixed chargeholder. It is clear that as against the preferential creditors, the nature of the floating charge was unchanged, but by virtue of a term in the fixed charge, the floating charge holder took priority as between the chargeholders. It is not certain if one should regard this as a case of subordination at all, in the sense that the floating chargeholder gained no rights against preferential creditors. There was no dispute between fixed and floating chargeholders as to their priority *inter se*, and the floating chargeholder "stood ahead" of the preferential creditors (if he did) only to the extent of the debt secured by the fixed charge. It can make no difference to preferential creditors how the chargeholders arrange matters between themselves, so long as those arrangements do not alter the sums of money payable to preferential creditors. Suppose that the question has to be considered by a liquidator: it is submitted that he should (unless he receives a direction by a court as did the receiver in *Re Woodroffes*) pay first the fixed chargeholder,

---

[29] Wood, *op.cit.*, 411.
[30] [1985] 2 All E.R. 908, [1986] Ch. 366.

then the preferential creditor, then the floating chargeholder. It would be otherwise if the liquidator or receiver had the consent of the fixed charge-holder (as also seemed to be the case in *Re Woodroffes*). The liquidator should take these steps even if the agreement between the chargeholders has the effect of an assignment, for unless the cross-assignment is of debts of equal amounts, they will be equitable in nature, and only the legal owner can give a good discharge. The written consent of the legal owner, or the court order, solves this problem.

On the whole, therefore, it seems that subordination of the rights of creditors between themselves is unobjectionable, but that a subordination so as to affect third parties not party to the agreement is not possible, except (in the case of debts with priority) by way of legal assignment (of the whole of the debts).

SUBORDINATION AGREEMENTS AND BOND ISSUES

14.15   Disregarding the problems which may arise in insolvency, as to third parties, a question may arise whether on an issue of debentures or bonds the issuing company may subordinate the rights of a class of bondholders to other creditors. Here we may consider only the two parties: the senior creditors and the subordinated creditors. Bonds may be traded, and come into the hands of new holders. This in itself causes no problems, for the terms of the bonds being known, the transferees can have no greater rights than the original holders. The real problem is to determine how the original holders can be subordinated to other parties unknown to the original holders, who enter a different relationship with the issuer and at a later time. In fact, English law has long recognised a principle by which this effect can be achieved and whereby parties entering a contract at different times and ignorant of the identity of other contracting parties may be held to a con-tractual relationship with the other parties.

In *Clarke* v. *Dunraven*[31] a yacht club organised a regatta, inviting competitors to apply to enter the race subject to certain rules. The entries for the race might have been made at different times, and competitors did not necessarily know of the identity or existence of other competitors. Nevertheless, a contract was held to exist between the parties. This principle explains how the members of an unincorporated association may be bound *inter se* by the rules of the association[32] and also how members of a company are bound *inter se* by the articles of the company.[33] There is a principle, therefore, by which where through a single co-ordinator different parties agree to bind themselves by common rules, each of the parties may be bound to the other parties though they enter the contract at different times and in ignorance of the identity of the others.

If, therefore, a bond issue is structured so that it subordinates those entering the agreement, the issue may operate not merely as a contract between the company issuer and bondholder, but between bondholder and subsequent borrowers entering a relationship with the company with reference

[31] [1897] A.C. 59.
[32] *Hybart* v. *Parker* (1858) 4 C.B. (N.S.) 209; *Gray* v. *Pearson* (1870) L.R. 5 C.P. 568; *Evans* v. *Hooper* (1875) 1 Q.B.D. 45.
[33] *Rayfield* v. *Hands* [1960] Ch. 1.

to the terms of the subordinated bond issue. In order to bring the issue clearly within the principle of *Clarke* v. *Dunraven*, the bonds should specify that their terms constitute a contract between bondholders and subsequent borrowers, as stated.

15. Agents[1]

15.01 Banks are not infrequently asked to act as agents, and this practice will increase given the new types of business being undertaken nowadays by banks. For this reason, some discussion of the rules of agency is essential. A further consideration is that customers, whether individuals, clubs, partnerships, corporations or others frequently, and sometimes necessarily (with corporations) employ agents to act on their behalf, and the limits of the agent's authority become an essential question for the bank.

A. Types of authority

15.02 As a matter of terminology, an agent (A) is merely someone who has authority to act on behalf of another (his principal) (P) so as to be able to produce a change in the legal relations between the principal and a third party (C).[2] A's authority may be actual or ostensible.

1. ACTUAL AUTHORITY

Actual or "real" authority may be *express* (where P has clearly and expressly given authority to A) or *implied* (where P intends A to have authority, but has not expressed the fact in so many words, it being understood between them). Partners, and managing directors of companies, for example, have a considerable degree of implied authority to bind their principles, though the precise extent of their authority may never have been discussed with or regulated by the principal. In cases like those, where the authority is implied in relation to a class of agent (all managing directors, for example) the implied authority may be referred to as "usual" or "customary." It still arises from the fact that P actually does intend A to have the authority in question, and P may intend this in relation to a class of agents, or to a particular agent acting on a special occasion. What C knows is immaterial, for actual authority is a question between P and A. If authority is not implied as "usual" it may be implied on the ground of business efficacy in a particular case. In either case, an express prohibition by P ends actual authority, but not necessarily ostensible authority.

2. OSTENSIBLE AUTHORITY

15.03 Even if A has no actual authority, circumstances may arise in which there has (by words or conduct) been a representation or "holding out" by P (not by A)[3] or by P's other authorised agents[4] who has thereby made it appear to C[5] that A has P's authority to act, and if C relies upon this, and acts to his

---

[1] See *Fridman's Law of Agency*, (5th ed.) (1983); Markesinis & Munday. *Outline of the Law of Agency*, (2nd ed.) (1986).

[2] *John Towle & Co.* v. *White* (1873) 29 L.T. 78.

[3] *Att.-Gen. for Ceylon* v. *Silva* [1953] A.C. 461; *Armagas Ltd.* v. *Mundogas S.A., The Ocean Frost* [1986] 2 All E.R. 385 (H.L.), [1986] A.C. 717.

[4] *Freeman & Lockyer* v. *Buckhurst Park Properties (Mangal) Ltd.* [1964] 1 All E.R. 630, [1964] 2 Q.B. 480.

[5] This distinguishes ostensible authority from actual authority, for here it matters what C is led to think.

detriment or so that it would be inequitable for P to deny A's authority, P may be estopped from doing so. In that case it may be said that A has authority by estoppel, or more simply, that he has "ostensible" or "apparent" authority.[6] Ostensible authority may operate so that P is estopped from denying that there is a certain relationship between him and A: for example, A may be an ordinary director of P (a company) but P may so act that it seems that A is managing director. In this case, P is estopped from denying the relationship, and as a consequence is estopped from denying that A has the implied authority which goes with the position of managing director, so that A may do whatever an ordinary managing director could do. Alternatively, it may be known what the relationship between A and P is, (*e.g.* that he is an ordinary director) but P may act so that on a given occasion it appears that the extent of A's special authority is greater than it actually is (*e.g.* that he has authority to borrow).[7] Commonly, A is in a position in which a person would usually have authority (would have implied actual authority), and because he is in that position he has ostensible "usual" authority, even if, as it happens, he has been expressly prohibited from doing the "usual" thing (has no actual authority). Thus, the fact that people usually have actual authority in a given position may lead to ostensible authority. Similarly, if P gives A authority, known to a third party, C, but P imposes some secret limitation on A's authority, known to P and A, but not C, then A will still have ostensible authority, though no actual authority.[8] Similarly, if A was known to have authority, but unknown to C it has been revoked, A still may have ostensible authority.[9] This is a problem often troublesome to retiring partners.[10]

Being based on estoppel, which depends on C's reasonable reliance on a **15.04** holding out by P, ostensible authority cannot exist if C knows or ought to know of limitations on A's authority *i.e.* if C has actual or "constructive"[11] notice of limitations. It may be said that if the circumstances are such that a reasonable man would inquire from P as to A's authority, C is "put on inquiry." This just means that if C does not inquire, A has no ostensible authority, and if A turns out not to have actual authority, P is not bound.[12] A frequent sort of case is where A, who clearly has P's authority to act in a general way (he may, for example, have a power of attorney) uses his authority for some transaction which C can or ought to see is for A's private benefit. In this type of case, A's authority may be expressed by P in quite general and extensive terms, but is still subject to the generally implied limitation that A must act for P's benefit: that is the only actual authority which P gave to A.[13] In acting for his own benefit, A exceeds his actual authority, and C can rely only upon ostensible authority, but only if he is not put on inquiry. As a general rule, it is always suspicious if any agent appears to benefit from his position, since everyone should know that authority is not generally given for this purpose. Thus, if stockbrokers deposit signed blank

---

[6] We use any of these words as if absolutely synonymous.
[7] Ostensible authority in relation to partners is very important, and is examined below, Chap. 16.
[8] *Manchester Trust* v. *Furness* [1895] 2 Q.B. 539.
[9] *Drew* v. *Nunn* (1879) 4 Q.B.D. 661.
[10] Below, Chap. 16.
[11] Where he ought to know.
[12] Some cases were examined above, when considering forgery, in Chaps. 7, 8.
[13] Of course, A may have actual authority to act for his own benefit, an example being under the Enduring Powers of Attorney Act 1985, considered below, para. 15.15.

share transfer forms as security for advances for a bank, the bank ought to inquire whether this use of assets belonging to others is within their authority.[14] So too, if A uses his authority to draw on P's account to pay off a private debt,[15] or to reduce his personal overdraft at a bank[16] the bank or creditor should make inquiry, and cannot rely upon ostensible authority if they do not.[17]

15.05 In *Armagas Ltd.* v. *Mundogas S.A., The Ocean Frost*[18] the House of Lords held that in the absence of any representation by P that A had authority, A had no ostensible authority, and C could not rely on A's own assertion of authority. Similarly, since the misrepresentation of A was outside his ostensible authority, P could not be liable for that. The House pointed out that ostensible authority to enter a particular transaction (as against transactions in general) would be very rare and unusual, since *ex hypothesi*, C knows there is no general authority. It contradicted common sense to say that it made any difference just because A says he has gone back to P and obtained actual authority.

Ostensible authority cannot exist if C does not know that A is acting for P (*i.e.* for any principal).[19]

If the reforms of company law discussed elsewhere[20] are carried out, all directors of companies will have ostensible authority to bind the company, unless an outsider has actual knowledge of a lack of authority. At present, ostensible authority may not arise if there are prohibitions in the company's Articles, unless the prohibition can be removed by internal procedural steps,[21] since all are taken to know of the Articles.

3. AUTHORITY BY NECESSITY

15.06 In rare cases, even though A has no actual or ostensible authority, he may be said to have "authority by necessity." This may occur if he is lawfully in possession of P's property, and an emergency arises[22] in which it is not

---

[14] *Colonial Bank* v. *Cady & Williams* (1890) 15 App.Cas. 267 (the brokers could, of course, have had authority to do this, but where they themselves might be benefiting, inquiry should have been made).

[15] *Reckitt* v. *Barnett, Pembroke & Slater Ltd.* [1929] A.C. 176 (P's cheque was used to pay for a car which defendant dealers knew was for A's own use).

[16] *Midland Bank* v. *Reckitt* [1933] A.C. 1.

[17] See also *Daun* v. *Simmins* (1879) 41 L.T. 783 (C, a trade creditor, should have known that a house was "tied" and that A could not deal with C in purchasing alcohol). See also *Overbrooke Estates Ltd.* v. *Glencombe Properties Ltd.* [1974] 3 All E.R. 511 where A's (an auctioneer) catalogue said that P gave him no authority to make representations about P's property. P was held not to be bound by A's representations. Other well-known cases are: *Biggerstaff* v. *Rowatt's Wharf Ltd.* [1896] 2 Ch. 93; *Hely-Hutchinson* v. *Brayhead Ltd.* [1968] 1 Q.B. 549, 573; *Rama Corporation* v. *Proved Tin and General Investments Ltd.* [1952] 2 Q.B. 147; *Houghton & Co.* v. *Nothard, Lowe & Wills Ltd.* [1927] 1 K.B. 246, aff'd [1928] A.C. 1; *Kreditbank Cassel GmbH* v. *Schenkers Ltd.* [1927] 1 K.B. 826; *British Thomson-Houston Co. Ltd.* v. *Federated European Bank Ltd.* [1932] 2 K.B. 176; *British Bank of the Middle East* v. *Sun Life Assurance Co. of Canada (UK) Ltd.* [1983] B.C.L.C. 78 (H.L.) [1983] 2 Lloyd's Rep. 9; *B. Liggett (Liverpool) Ltd.* v. *Barclays Bank Ltd.* [1928] 1 K.B. 48; *Rolled Steel Products (Holdings) Ltd.* v. *British Steel Corpn.* [1984] B.C.L.C. 466, [1986] Ch. 246; *Waugh* v. *H.B. Clifford & Sons Ltd.* [1982] Ch. 374; *Sorrell* v. *Finch* [1977] A.C. 728.

[18] [1986] 2 All E.R. 385 (H.L.), [1986] A.C. 717.

[19] *McLaughlin* v. *Gentles* (1919) 51 D.L.R. 383; *contra: Watteau* v. *Fenwick* [1893] 1 Q.B. 346. This last case is generally thought to have been wrongly decided.

[20] Below, Chap. 17.

[21] The rule in *Turquand's* case, referred to below, para. 15.29 (n. 44) and 17.07.

[22] *cf. Sachs* v. *Miklos* [1948] 2 K.B. 23 (no emergency, but merely for A's convenience).

possible to ask for P's instructions,[23] and where A acts in good faith,[24] and does what is reasonably necessary to save P's property or to secure P's interests, and (probably) where A and P were not strangers, but had some pre-existing, and probably contractual relationship.[25] Suppose A is a carrier, asked to deliver tomatoes to a particular place. When he arrives at the place, P's other agent does not appear to collect the goods, and A has no means of contacting that agent, or P. If the goods are not promptly sold, they will perish, A's van not being refrigerated. In those circumstances, A would probably have necessary authority to sell the tomatoes, so that he would not commit any wrong by doing so, and so as to make P contractually liable to C if the tomatoes are of unmerchantable quality.[26]

B. Ratification

Further, if A acts without authority (actual, or ostensible) then P may ratify what A does (confirm and adopt it) so as to bind P. Although it may appear that ratification has nothing to do with authority, because P binds himself subsequently to A's unauthorised actions, the theory is that ratification is retroactive, and subsequently confers authority on A (so that, for example, he cannot be sued, even for breach of warranty of authority).[27] Ratification can be implied from the circumstances, and need not be express.[28] The ratification can be effective even though C has purported already to revoke, unless his contract was made subject to ratification.[29]   **15.07**

In order for ratification to occur, there are a number of conditions. First, the whole and not only part of the contract must be ratified (P cannot blow hot and cold at the same time). Secondly, unless a fixed time was agreed by A and C, it must occur within a reasonable time after the transaction.[30] Thirdly, P must be aware of all the material facts at the time of ratification: he cannot be held to ratify in ignorance. (As an exception to that, he may, of course, waive his right to know, and it seems he would be bound as long as there is no fraudulent agreement between A and C.)[31] Fourthly, when A contracts, it must be on the basis that he is acting for a principal (*i.e.* the principal must not be undisclosed). Fifthly, when A contracts, P must exist and have contractual capacity. Finally, P must have the power to ratify. We shall examine here only the last three of these matters.

1. UNDISCLOSED PRINCIPAL CANNOT RATIFY[32]

A principal is undisclosed if A does not say, and C does not know, that A acts for another. The undisclosed principal cannot subsequently ratify. A reason for this rule is, perhaps, that if P is bound, so is C, so that C would be liable to someone of whose existence he was unaware, and who did not   **15.08**

[23] *Sims & Co.* v. *Midland Ry. Co.* [1913] 1 K.B. 103, 112.
[24] *Prager* v. *Blatspiel, Stamp & Heacock Ltd.* [1924] 1 K.B. 566.
[25] *Jebara* v. *Ottoman Bank* [1927] 2 K.B. 254.
[26] *Springer* v. *Great Western Ry. Co.* [1921] 1 K.B. 257; *G.N.R. Co.* v. *Swaffield* (1874) L.R. 9 Ex. 132; *China-Pacific S.A.* v. *Food Corpn. of India* [1982] A.C. 939.
[27] *Boston Deep Sea Fishing & Ice Co. Ltd.* v. *Farnham* [1957] 3 All E.R. 204; *Risbourg* v. *Bruckner* (1858) 3 C.B.N.S. 812.
[28] *The Bonita, The Charlotte* (1861) Lush. 252.
[29] *Bolton Partners* v. *Lambert* (1888) 41 Ch.D. 295; *Watson* v. *Davies* [1931] 1 Ch. 455.
[30] *Metropolitan Asylums Board Managers* v. *Kingham & Sons* (1890) 6 T.L.R. 217.
[31] *Marsh* v. *Joseph* [1897] 1 Ch. 213.
[32] Undisclosed principals are further discussed below.

authorise the transaction. In *Keighly, Maxsted & Co.* v. *Durant*.[33] A bought wheat from C, not mentioning P, at a price greater than authorised.[34] P said to C that he would take the wheat, but A did not pay C, who sued P. P was not liable, because at the time of contracting A did not disclose P's existence. Although ratification is impossible, estoppel may produce a result which is very similar. Whereas ratification requires no more than P's assent to the prior transaction to bind P, estoppel requires (a) a representation by P (*i.e.*, in this context, his assent), (b) reliance by C on that representation, (c) circumstances in which it is inequitable for P to assert that A was an undisclosed agent (generally expressed by saying that C must act to his detriment). Thus, in *Spiro* v. *Lintern*[35] P's wife acted without authority in agreeing to sell a house to C, but afterwards P treated C as the new owner, and C spent money on legal fees and on architect's fees relating to the house. When P repudiated the agreement, C sued. Ratification was impossible, because at the time of contracting P's existence (as owner) had not been disclosed to C. But the conduct of P[36] amounted to a representation that there was a binding obligation between the parties, and as C had acted to his detriment in incurring expenses, etc., P was bound. If, therefore, A acts without authority, P is not bound, but (a) may subsequently ratify if his existence was disclosed at the time of the contract, or (b) may subsequently be estopped if he makes a representation upon which C relies to his detriment.

2. AT THE TIME A CONTRACTS, P MUST EXIST AND MUST HAVE CONTRACTUAL CAPACITY, AND BE CAPABLE OF ASCERTAINMENT

15.09 Thus, if P is an infant, an enemy alien,[37] or of unsound mind at the time of the contract, he cannot subsequently ratify even if his incapacity has ceased. Similarly, A cannot act for an unascertainable class of principals.[38]

The rule in question produces difficulties in connection with companies. A promoter may, for example, decide to form a company to exploit a particular contract, and may wish to secure finance in advance. But he cannot act for the company, which does not yet exist, and when it comes into existence, it cannot ratify.[39] In order to bind the company, it must be adopted as a fresh contract by the company when formed, and that requires consideration, or to be done by deed. The promoter may, of course, accept personal liability under the contract, but frequently he will not wish to do so (he is forming a limited liability company to avoid risks), and even if he did, it may be that he has insufficient assets of his own for security (perhaps there is a benefit in the offing which has been promised to the company, when formed, but that is not the promoter's asset). The promoter can contract, on terms that his liability ceases if either the company enters a similar contract, or does not do so within a certain time. The contract for finance might be made on terms that it is assignable if the company adopts the contract, but will terminate if the company does not adopt within a specified period. In

---

[33] [1901] A.C. 240.
[34] *i.e.* A had no actual authority, and obviously an undisclosed agent cannot have ostensible authority.
[35] [1973] 3 All E.R. 319.
[36] And his agents—the estate agent and his solicitors.
[37] *Boston Deep Sea Fishing & Ice Co. Ltd.* v. *Farnham* [1957] 3 All E.R. 204.
[38] *Watson* v. *Swann* (1862) 11 C.B. n.s. 756.
[39] *Kelner* v. *Baxter* (1866) L.R. 2 C.P. 174.

the case of a bank, however, a letter of intent to lend—not contractually binding—will normally be sufficient.

At common law, if a promoter entered a contract on behalf of an unformed company, the company and not the promoter was bound, and he might show that the contract was for the company simply by signing "X Company Ltd., by A."[40] In other words, if the parties do not intend the agent to be bound, he is not bound. This is still the case, but by statute, A will now be bound if he purports to contract for the company or as its agent when it is unformed, unless expressly agreed to the contrary.[41] It has been held that merely signing "for and on behalf of" the company does not amount to an agreement to the contrary, and A would be bound.[42] It is simple, cheap and quick to incorporate, and generally a promoter should be advised to do so first, and for the company then to contract for its finance with the bank (with a prior letter of intent from the bank, as indicated).

3. P MUST HAVE THE POWER TO RATIFY, BOTH AT THE TIME A ACTS AND AT THE TIME OF RATIFICATION

Someone who is still an infant clearly cannot ratify what he could not originally authorise, and so on. This type of problem has tended to arise particularly in respect of companies,[43] whose ability to act has (until abolished by the new legislation discussed below)[44] been limited by the company documents. If an agent acts in a way in which the principal himself has no power to act, then ratification is impossible.[45] The proposed abolition of the restrictions on a company's power to act will remove many of the difficulties previously encountered.[46]

15.10

C. Subrogation

This is discussed elsewhere[47] but its effect may be that if, for example, C lends money to A on P's behalf, but A exceeds his authority, then if the money is actually applied to pay off existing lawful debts owed by P to another creditor, the lender may be subrogated to (allowed to stand in the position of) that other creditor to the extent of the debt paid off, and may

15.11

---

[40] *Newborne* v. *Sensolid (Great Britain) Ltd.* [1954] 1 Q.B. 45.

[41] S.36(4), C.A. 1985, formerly in s.9(2), European Communities Act 1972.

[42] *Phonogram Ltd.* v. *Lane* [1982] Q.B. 938.

[43] Though it could arise in other cases, as between two agents in a chain.

[44] In Chap. 17, below.

[45] *Foss* v. *Harbottle* (1843) 2 Hare 461; *Simpson* v. *Westminster Palace Hotel Co.* (1860) B H.L.Cas. 712; *Spokes* v. *Grosvenor Hotel* [1897] 2 Q.B. 124. Previously, the result of this has been that (a) a breach of the company's Memorandum of Association could not be ratified: *Ashbury Ry. Carriage and Iron Co.* v. *Riche* (1875) L.R. 7 H.L. 653, and Pennington, 591, (b) any action or agreement which entails future breaches of the company's Articles could not be ratified (the Articles must be changed by a general meeting, on a special resolution): *Irvine* v. *Union Bank of A/Asia* (1877) 2 App. Cas. 366; *Boschoek Proprietary Co. Ltd.* v. *Fuke* [1906] 1 Ch. 148; *Salmon* v. *Quin and Axtens Ltd.* [1909] 1 Ch. 311, aff'd [1909] A.C. 442, but (c) any other past breach could be ratified by those in the company who had power to authorise the act in the first place (a past breach of the Articles could be ratified by the company in general meeting by ordinary resolution, unless the articles themselves say that ratification is to be by special resolution). If the breach of the Articles directly and personally affected a member's rights, ratification by the company was impossible. See generally, Pennington, 591 *et seq.*

[46] For that reason, s.35, C.A. 1985 is not considered here.

[47] Above, Chap. 14.

sue P for that amount. The same would apply if P's bank debits his account on a cheque wrongly drawn by A.[48]

D. Extent of authority

15.12   A written mandate avoids arguments as to the extent of the authority, but it should be observed that (depending on the detail gone into) it may exclude implied powers (on the basis that if the parties have troubled to spell something out, they have not intended what is not stated).[49] This is not a hard and fast rule, but a guide to the parties' intention. We have seen, therefore, that a power to draw cheques does not include a power to overdraw the account.[50] Where, on the contrary, powers are not so spelled out in great detail, the courts may imply whatever powers are reasonably incidental to the authority given[51] especially if it is "usual" in a given sort of case.[52] Deeds are, however, construed more strictly than other classes of documents, and powers are rarely implied.[53]

If P gives authority which is ambiguous, and A reasonably interprets it in one fashion, differently to P, P cannot deny that A has authority.[54] It may, however, be reasonable for A to seek clarification, if there is an obvious ambiguity or one which a reasonable man would notice, and if time and circumstance allows for P to be contacted.[55]

E. Appointment of agents

15.13   Authority can generally be conferred orally,[56] though in a few cases writing is necessary for appointment,[57] and in relation to payments by cheque from a current account, banks will always demand a written mandate (even if they are to pay the customer himself, for they need his signature). Agents acting for companies may be appointed orally or in writing, and may act in the same way as agents for natural persons, using the company seal where deeds are required.[58] An agent appointed orally can sign a document so as to make the company liable for deceit in respect of representations about the credit of another.[59]

It is also possible to appoint an agent by power of attorney. This is a deed. A deed must be written, complete on execution[60] signed by the maker (the donor, or principal, in agency terms), sealed[61] and attested (witnessed) by one witness. Consideration is not needed for a deed. Under the Powers of Attorney Act 1971, the signature and sealing may be by another person if in

---

[48] *B. Liggett (Liverpool) Ltd.* v. *Barclays Bank* [1928] 1 K.B. 48.

[49] *Expressio unius est exclusio alterius* (to express one thing is to exclude others).

[50] Above, para. 2.16.

[51] *Ashfordshire Council* v. *Dependable Motors Pty. Ltd.* [1961] A.C. 336, 341.

[52] *Wiltshire* v. *Sims* (1808) 1 Camp. 258.

[53] *Jonmenjoy Coondoo* v. *Watson* (1884) 9 App. Cas. 561; *Danby* v. *Coutts & Co.* (1885) 29 Ch.D. 500; *Jacobs* v. *Morris* [1902] 1 Ch. 816.

[54] *Ireland* v. *Livingston* (1872) L.R. 5 H.L. 395.

[55] *European Asian Bank A.G.* v. *Punjab & Sind Bank* [1983] 3 All E.R. 508, 517–518.

[56] *Heard* v. *Pilley* (1869) L.R. 4 Ch.App. 548 (agent appointed to buy land could be appointed orally, though could only contract in writing).

[57] *e.g.* under s.64, C.A. 1985 (signatures on prospectuses).

[58] s.36(1), C.A. 1985.

[59] *U.B.A.F. Ltd.* v. *European American Banking Corpn.* [1984] 2 All E.R. 226, [1984] Q.B. 713.

[60] See *Powell* v. *London and Provincial Bank* [1893] 2 Ch. 555 where a deed containing blanks filled in after execution was invalid.

[61] A circle on the page, or a piece of coloured paper will do, though a company must use its common seal (s.36(1)(a), C.A. 1985).

the donor's presence and by his direction[62] (*e.g.* if he cannot write, being disabled)[63] but in this case, two witnesses must attest.[64] The Act allows photocopies of the deed, certified by the donor or a solicitor or stockbroker to be used as sufficient proof of the existence and contents of the power.[65] Powers of attorney may be special (for limited purposes) or general (without limitations, or at least, very wide). A simple form of deed is provided by the Powers of Attorney Act 1971[66] conferring general powers (to do anything which the donor can lawfully do by an attorney).[67] The power of attorney must be stamped within 30 days of execution, or within 30 days of its receipt in the United Kingdom, if made abroad.

The advantages of powers of attorney are, in general, twofold: first, if an agent is to have authority to act by deed, he must be appointed by deed.[68] A legal conveyance of land, for example, must be made by deed. Secondly, authority given by other means may be revocable, even if the principal has contracted not to do so (though he may be in breach of contract if he revokes).[69] In addition, it may be revoked by the donor's death, bankruptcy, or mental incapacity. If, however, the appointment is made by power of attorney, and is given either to secure a proprietary interest of the donee, or to secure the performance of an obligation owed to him, then it cannot be revoked so long as the interest or obligation continues, whether by revocation by the donor or by his death, incapacity, bankruptcy or winding-up.[70] This is very valuable, so far as banks are concerned, for such a power is commonly taken in connection with certain equitable mortgages, and gives the bank a power to sell the property mortgaged, without recourse to the courts. Where a bank has a security, this may be considered as the "proprietary interest" in question, or else one may regard the debt for which the security and power of attorney were taken as the "obligation" the performance of which is secured. Even if powers are not given by way of security (in which case they may be revoked) it is provided that the donee incurs no liability if when he acts he did not know of the revocation[71] and that any third party who does not know of the revocation is unaffected, and any transaction between him and the donee relying on the power is unaffected.[72] **15.14**

If given as a security, the power of attorney is not revoked by mental incapacity of the donor, but otherwise it may be revoked by that circumstance. If, however, a special form of power of attorney is made under the Enduring Powers of Attorney Act 1985, it may endure despite incapacity. This will avoid the need for application to the Court of Protection for the appointment of a receiver. Obviously, only an individual can execute such a document. An "enduring power" may be created by following certain for- **15.15**

---

[62] Deeds could be made this way at common law: *Ball* v. *Dunsterville* (1791) 4 T.R. 313.
[63] s.1(1).
[64] s.1(2).
[65] s.3.
[66] s.10(1) and Sched. 1.
[67] Except for duties as a trustee or personal representative and some other cases. Even so, trustees have some rights to delegate.
[68] *Berkeley* v. *Hardy* (1826) 5 B. & C. 355.
[69] See below, para. 15.43: termination. Even at common law, revocation is impossible if the authority is to secure an interest which A has.
[70] s.4.
[71] s.5(1).
[72] s.5(2).

malities. The document must say that the donor intends it to continue despite subsequent mental incapacity, and it must incorporate certain explanatory information, and state that the donor has read this, or had it read to him. The attorney may be only an adult individual, or trust corporation, and may not be an undischarged bankrupt. Joint or joint and several attorneys may be appointed. The authority may be general, or limited. If expressed to be general, the donee may do whatever the donor could lawfully do by an attorney.[73] While an ordinary agent may not benefit himself, the donee of an enduring power may benefit himself to a limited extent (unless the instrument says otherwise).[74] While the donor is mentally capable, the enduring power operates as an ordinary power of attorney, except that the attorney may not disclaim his role other than by giving written notice to the donor. When the donor becomes incapable the attorney's authority is suspended, and he must apply to the Court of Protection for registration of the instrument, giving notice ordinarily to the donor and specified relatives, if any. As soon as he applies, he has limited power to act so as to maintain the donor, to prevent loss to his estate, and to maintain himself and others as previously mentioned. The court may (whether application for registration is made or not) authorise other actions. Relatives may object to registration, but if the court decides to register the power the attorney's full powers are restored, and the power cannot be revoked by the donor. The attorney must give notice to the court, if he intends to disclaim. If for any reason the power is invalid or is revoked, etc., then the attorney is protected, and transactions with third parties are valid, unless those concerned know of the invalidity.[75] In favour of a purchaser, validity is conclusively presumed for transactions within 12 months of registration or where within 3 months after the purchase is completed the purchaser makes a statutory declaration that he had no reason to doubt the attorney's authority.[76]

The ordinary provisions of the 1971 Act apply (except as modified) to the 1985 Act, so that a certified photocopy of the power may be relied on,[77] but where the power has been registered, the 1985 Act provides[78] that a document purporting to be an office copy of the registered instrument is evidence of its contents and of the fact that it has been so registered.

F. Duties of agents to principal

15.16 The provisions of the Unfair Contract Terms Act 1977 (U.C.T.A.) apply to agencies. Section 3 applies between contracting parties if one is a consumer (does not act in the course of a business, while the other does)[79] or if there are written standard terms, and prevents any contractual term which excludes liability, or permits the rendering of no contractual performance, or of one substantially different from that reasonably expected, unless the term is reasonable. Section 2 applies even if there is no contract, where the agent is "negligent" (defined by section 1(1)(a) as the breach of any com-

---

[73] s.3.
[74] s.3(4). He may do what the donor might reasonably be expected to do to meet his needs (he may be the donor's spouse, or other relative, for example).
[75] s.9.
[76] s.9(4).
[77] 1985 Act, s.7(4).
[78] s.7(3).
[79] s.12.

mon law duty to take reasonable care or exercise reasonable skill, but not any stricter duty). Any clause excluding liability for economic loss (including a clause defining duties) is enforceable only if reasonable. These sections apply only to business liability.[80] These provisions may prove to be of considerable importance to banks, given the new roles being undertaken by banks, in relation to investment advice, dealings in securities, and so on. The Act does not apply to insurance contracts, but this refers only to the insurer's liability stated in the insurance, and not to the liability of any insurance agent.[81] The Act does not apply to "any contract so far as it relates to" the following: the creation, transfer, or termination of an interest in land, or intellectual property (copyrights, etc.), the formation or dissolution of a company or partnership or unincorporated association or to the company's constitution or its members rights and obligations, the creation or transfer of securities or of any right or interest in securities.[82] It seems that these exclusions may be intended to apply to terms in the contracts between principal and third party, rather than to any liability of the intermediaries, though to take an example, a contract by a bank to sell shares for a customer seems strictly to come within the literal meaning of the words "a contract so far as it relates to the transfer of securities." It may be arguable that the Act was not intended to apply to such dealings because (a) of the commercial risks involved ordinarily in securities dealings, or (b) because securities dealings are regulated by the Companies Act or by the Stock Exchange and others, but this argument seems more relevant to principals than to intermediaries, especially given the nature of the duties imposed upon them, and it may well be that dealings of intermediaries in relation to the matters mentioned are subject to the operation of the Act.

The duties of an agent to his principal include the following: **15.17**

First, to carry out his agreed tasks with reasonable skill and diligence, (and without exceeding his authority).[83] What is reasonable depends on the exact relationship between A and P, and is greater if A is paid, or if he holds himself out as having special skills.[84] This duty is, of course, owed by a bank to any customer, even if not acting as agent for him in any matter, and a similar duty is (in effect) owed by a collecting bank to the owner of a stolen cheque, since the defence to an action to conversion depends on showing lack of negligence in handling the cheque.[85] Where a bank is acting as agent, its duties depend on what it has undertaken to do, and otherwise may be implied from the circumstances. If paid, it must obey instructions and use reasonable efforts to see they are carried out[86] though not if they are unlawful or contrary to public policy.[87] It is clear that ordinary practice of banks is important in deciding what it is impliedly bound to do: "A man who employs a banker is bound by the usage of bankers."[88] A common example of the liability of a bank occurs in the collection of cheques for its customer, P, when it may be liable to him for negligent loss or unreasonable

---

[80] s.1(3).
[81] Sched. 1, para. 1(a).
[82] Sched. 1, para. 1(b–e).
[83] *Fray* v. *Voules* (1859) 1 E. & E. 839.
[84] *Beal* v. *South Devon Ry. Co.* (1864) 3 H. & C. 337.
[85] For the bank's duty in collecting cheques, see above, Chap. 9.
[86] *Turpin* v. *Bilton* (1843) Man. & G. 455.
[87] *Cohen* v. *Kittell* (1889) 22 Q.B. 680.
[88] Per Willes J. in *Hare* v. *Henty* (1861) 10 C.B.N.S. 65, 77. See also, *e.g. Schioler* v. *Westminster Bank Ltd.* [1970] 2 Q.B. 719 below, para. 19.17.

delay in clearing the cheque.[89] This being a duty of reasonable care, any attempt to exclude liability for breach may be particularly affected by the U.C.T.A. For breach of this duty, an agent may be liable either in contract, where paid, or in tort, and his principal may decide on what cause of action to sue.[90]

Secondly, an agent cannot normally delegate the performance of his functions[91] but he may delegate if it is necessary for proper performance,[92] or if custom sanctions it, or if there is statutory power to do so, or if unforeseen emergencies arise making it necessary. The principal may give actual authority to delegate.[93]

15.18   Thirdly, an agent may not have a conflict of interest between himself and his principal. That is to say, the agent's best efforts must always be directed towards his principal's interests, and not his own.[94] It is clear that what concerns the courts is not only the taking of some advantage from the situation, but the potential for conflict: that is, the rule is based not on actual wrongdoing but on possible wrongdoing, and the agent breaks his duty if he places himself in a position where his principal's interests and his own might be in conflict. (The duties later mentioned may be regarded as an instance of this duty.) Even someone who has ceased to be an agent may continue to have the duty towards his ex-principal.[95]

15.19   In particular, the agent must not make any secret profit, or advantage from his position, or take any bribe.[96] There is no objection to the agent earning profits, and it would be surprising if any customer did not expect his bank to profit in some way from advice given, but he expects the profit to come from declared charges made to him, the customer. The point is really twofold: first, if the agent acts for a principal, then profits belong to the principal, not the agent[97]; and secondly, if the agent is to gain a profit from another source, this may affect (or may reasonably be thought by the principal to affect) the impartiality of the agent. If, therefore, the agent is to profit from or gain an advantage from some other source than his principal, arising out of his agency or association with the principal, it must not be secret, but all the facts concerning the profit or advantage must be declared to and approved by the principal, who thus gives up his proprietary rights

---

[89] Discussed above, Chap. 9.

[90] *Esso Petroleum Co. Ltd.* v. *Mardon* [1976] Q.B. 801; *Batty* v. *Metropolitan Realisations Ltd.* [1978] 2 All E.R. 445; *Midland Bank Trust Co. Ltd.* v. *Hett, Stubbs and Kemp* [1979] Ch. 384; *Ross* v. *Caunters* [1980] Ch. 297.

[91] *Delegatus non potest delegare*: see *e.g. John McCann & Co.* v. *Pow* [1975] 1 All E.R. 129 (estate agent not entitled to appoint sub-agent); contrast *Solley* v. *Wood* (1852) 16 Beav. 370 (country solicitor could appoint town agent).

[92] So that, for example, administrative, rather than decision-making powers may be delegated to solicitors, accountants, and so on. See *Quebec & Richmond Ry. Co.* v. *Quinn* (1858) 12 Moo P.C. 232; *Allam & Co. Ltd.* v. *Europa Poster Services Ltd.* [1968] 1 All E.R. 826.

[93] The exceptions are stated in *De Bussche* v. *Alt* (1878) 8 Ch.D. 286.

[94] *Keech* v. *Sandford* (1726) Sel Cas Ch. 61; *Aberdeen Ry. Co.* v. *Blaikie Bros.* (1854) 1 Macq. 461; *Ritchie* v. *Couper* (1860) 28 Beav. 344; *Parker* v. *McKenna* (1874) L.R. 10 Ch. App. 96; *Reid-Newfoundland Co.* v. *Anglo-American Telegraph Co. Ltd.* [1912] A.C. 555; *Boardman* v. *Phipps* [1967] 2 A.C. 46.

[95] *Allison* v. *Clayhills* (1908) 97 L.T. 709.

[96] *Boston Deep Sea Fishing & Ice Co.* v. *Ansell* (1888) 39 Ch.D. 339; *Industries & General Mortgage Co.* v. *Lewis* [1949] 2 All E.R. 573.

[97] *Reading* v. *Att.-Gen.* [1951] A.C. 507 (this is regardless of any loss to the principal).

to profits earned, and confirms his trust in the agent's impartiality.[98] If A takes a secret profit, then P may dismiss him without notice,[99] claim the secret profit or bribe as his own[1] or sue A or the party who bribed him for damages for any loss suffered by P[2], refuse to pay A any commission on the transaction in question (not on others); and rescind a connected contract within a reasonable time of discovering the truth.[3] In some circumstances, A and the party who bribes him may commit a criminal offence.[4]

Particular difficulties may arise, given the varied nature of the modern banking business. One department of a bank may act for a corporate customer whose shares are marketed by the bank, while another department advises investors. Each department must, therefore, advise customers of any profits gained from the other, and of the relationship with the other.[5] It is uncertain how general the advice may be. The Securities and Investment Board, (S.I.B.) and Self Regulatory Organisations (S.R.O's) may make rules as to what is disclosed[6] but these cannot alter the common law of agency to a principal's disadvantage, though the rules can extend the rights of investors by giving them a right of damages if the rules are broken. It may be that despite these rules, anything but the most explicit warning clearly notified to the customer of a possible conflict may amount to a breach of the duty, and may expose banks to the risks of liability to account to the customer concerned for the profits made, and also to substantial bad publicity. **15.20**

Fourthly, an agent has a duty to keep secret any confidential information acquired as agent. He is allowed neither to disclose it to others,[7] nor to use it for his own benefit. If he does use any confidential information for profit, the profit belongs to P.[8] A bank, of course, has a duty of confidence to all of its customers. In the case of companies, there are statutory prohibitions on "insider dealing"[9] which impose wide restrictions on the ability of persons with insider information (unpublished price-sensitive information) acquired directly or from others to use that information and to deal in the company's securities. These duties have proved a source of difficulty for banks and other financial institutions, and this may increase given the new range of conglomerate activities.

A particular difficulty arises because of a fifth duty, which is to avoid a conflict of interest between two principals. According to *Fullwood* v. *Hurley*[10] "If and so long as the agent is the agent for one party, he cannot engage to become the agent of another principal without the leave of the first prin- **15.21**

---

[98] *Boardman* v. *Phipps* [1967] 2 A.C. 46, 111; *Bentley* v. *Craven* (1853) 18 Beav. 75; *Salomons* v. *Pender* (1865) 3 H. & C. 639.

[99] *Bulfield* v. *Fournier* (1895) 11 T.L.R. 282.

[1] *Barker* v. *Harrison* (1846) 2 Coll. 546; *Thompson* v. *Meade* (1891) 7 T.L.R. 698; *Burdick* v. *Garrick* (1870) 5 Ch.App. 233; *Reading* v. *Att.-Gen.* [1951] A.C. 507.

[2] Either the profit or damages, but not both; *Mahesan* v. *Malaysia G.O.C.H.S.* [1979] A.C. 374, J.C.; and see also *United Australia Ltd.* v. *Barclays Bank Ltd.* [1941] A.C. 1.

[3] *Oliver* v. *Court* (1820) 8 Price 127 (13 years not too long).

[4] Under s.1 of the Prevention of Corruption Act 1906.

[5] The corporate customer may not object, but the recipient of investment advice might.

[6] Under the Financial Services Act 1986.

[7] *Weld-Blundell* v. *Stephens* [1920] A.C. 956.

[8] *Peter Pan Manufacturing Corpn.* v. *Corsets Silhouette Ltd.* [1963] 2 All E.R. 402; *Lamb* v. *Evans* [1893] 1 Ch. 218.

[9] Company Securities (Insider Dealing) Act 1985.

[10] [1928] 1 K.B. 498.

cipal with whom he has originally established his agency."[11] One department of a bank say, for example, be involved in investment advice, while
another is involved with corporate customers. If the corporate department
learns of matters which may either increase or decrease that customer's
share values (*e.g.* prospective takeover, or imminent announcement of dis-
astrous losses) then what is the duty of the investment advice department to
its customers? The bank, as a single corporate institution, is bound to give
the best advice possible to its customers, but its situation here involves it in
an impossible conflict of duties. Attempts are being made to resolve this
conflict by erecting "chinese walls" which are simply internal arrangements
whereby different persons work for different departments, and are prevented by administrative rules and means from meeting and exchanging
information. Problems may still arise in respect of senior personnel of
banks, who may simultaneously hold directorships in other companies. If
they have knowledge obtained from the other company, the effect of which
matters to the bank's future policies, it is difficult to accept that they can or
will refrain from using that information when deliberating upon bank
policy (this assumes that as honourable men they do not expressly reveal it
to others in the bank). It may be, also, that knowledge of senior officials
may be imputed to the banks, even if it is not expressly revealed to others in
the bank, and if the bank "knows" the information it may be at fault in failing to reveal it to others.

15.22   The main difficulty is that if the chinese walls work at all, they will
merely prevent the wrongful exchange of information, eliminating that
source of complaint from the customer from whom the information came
(*i.e.* in relation to the fourth duty). They do not eliminate the complaint of a
customer seeking investment advice that the bank held useful information,
and did not reveal it to him (the first, and fifth duties). Suppose that a customer asks about investment in a particular company, and the bank through
senior officials "knows" that the company (another customer) is about to
make an announcement of large losses. While the bank may rightly say to
such a customer that it has a duty not to reveal confidential information, the
problem here is that the real breach of duty arose when the bank allowed
itself to get into a position where its duties to two different customers came
into conflict. It may be that it cannot thereafter avoid a breach, by reference
to duties of confidence. This problem is well known, for example, to solicitors, whose duty it is to refuse to act for two clients whose interests conflict.
It may be that the only effective solution is for different businesses to take
place in different bank-owned companies formed for the purpose, together
with chinese walls to prevent the exchange of information, though whether
that is effective in relation to senior management sitting on the boards of
more than one company is uncertain. It seems to be accepted that an agent
may act for two principals if the consent of both is obtained, but it would
seem that for this to be effective full information would have to be provided
to them. In the case of a securities marketing department, or an investment
advice department, for example, it may be necessary to comply with strict
contractual rules about giving notice and to give notice to each customer
that the bank acts or may act in another capacity for customers whose shares
or securities are involved, and about which advice is given, and that the

---

[11] See *North and South Trust Co.* v. *Berkeley* [1971] 1 All E.R. 980 where a dual agency was held
wholly unreasonable, despite a long standing practice at Lloyds.

bank may be required not to reveal information about that customer, and even to give advice which another department of the bank knows to be quite false. If this advice is in small print, it may be unreasonable under the Unfair Contract Terms Act 1977, and if it is clearly brought to the customer's attention, it may not attract much custom to the bank. Quite possibly, the problem is insoluble. This may, however, be too gloomy a prospect, and it may be that the courts will take a more benevolent view than that expressed here. It may be said again that rules promoted by the S.I.B. or S.R.O's cannot change the common law of agency so as to reduce the protection given to principals.

G. Rights of agents, against principal

A has a right to be paid as agreed and when agreed. Where the agreed sum is **15.23** payable on completion, then if he is guilty of a serious breach in performance, he has not substantially performed, and earns nothing.[12] If he is guilty of a minor breach of contract, (*i.e.* if he substantially performs, or does not break a term called a "condition" or fail to fulfil some express condition to payment) the agreed sum is earned, but P may generally deduct the amount of damages before paying, or pay the whole, and sue for damages. If no sum is agreed, then (if it is understood that A will be paid) he may charge a reasonable sum for the value of the work that he has done.[13] What is reasonable is a question of fact. If the amount of payment is left expressly to P's discretion, then A cannot object if P gives him none, or very little.[14] If A is to be paid in a certain event (*e.g.* on completion of a sale) and it does not occur (*e.g.* because P, the vendor, changes his mind) no payment is due, however much work A may have done, there being no implied term requiring P to assist A or not to act so as to prevent him from earning the sum. For example, where the event on which A is to be paid involves P's consent to a transaction with C, P is at liberty to refuse consent.[15] But a term may be implied that P will not break a contract with another so as to deprive A of his commission.[16]

If in the performance of his tasks as agent, A reasonably and properly incurs expenses, losses or liabilities, he is entitled to be indemnified by P.[17]

Until paid, or indemnified, A has a lien on P's property. In the case of a bank, the lien may carry with it a right to sell certain property.[18]

H. The agent, and third parties

The general rule is this: A is merely a middleman, and has no rights against **15.24** C, nor obligations to C, arising from any contract which he makes for P.

---

[12] *Mason* v. *Clifton* (1863) 3 F. & F. 899; no *quantum meruit* lies for a reasonable sum: *Sumpter* v. *Hedges* [1898] 1 Q.B. 673.

[13] *Way* v. *Latilla* [1937] 2 All E.R. 759.

[14] *Re Richmond Gate Property Co. Ltd.* [1965] 1 W.L.R. 335.

[15] *Luxor (Eastbourne) Ltd.* v. *Cooper* [1941] A.C. 108.

[16] *Alpha Trading Co.* v. *Dunnshaw-Patten Ltd.* [1981] Q.B. 290.

[17] See *Brooks Wharf & Bull Wharf Ltd.* v. *Goodman Bros* [1937] 1 K.B. 534; *Hichens, Harrison, Woolston & Co.* v. *Jackson & Sons* [1943] A.C. 266.

[18] Above, Chap. 13. and see *Chelmsford Auctions Ltd.* v. *Poole* [1973] Q.B. 542 (auctioneer's lien); Brokers generally have no lien, but an insurance broker may have one under s.53(1) of the Marine Insurance Act 1906.

1. A'S RIGHTS AGAINST C

15.25 Since A is a middleman, he generally cannot sue C.[19] But in the following cases he may sue C:

(i) if A is intended by C to have rights, he may have them.[20]

(ii) if A acts for an undisclosed principal.[21]

(iii) if A is an auctioneer, he can assert a lien and sue C for the price of the goods sold.[22]

(iv) if A is a factor, he can sue C on the contract.[23]

(v) if A purports to act as agent for a named principal but then declared himself to be principal before suing C, he may sue.[24] It is otherwise if P's identity is made a material element so that C excludes any other principal.[25]

(vi) if A purports to act as agent for an unnamed principal, he may generally sue C.[26]

2. A'S LIABILITY TO C

15.26 A is generally a middleman, and not liable to C.[27] This is the case (so far as the contract is concerned) even if A has no authority[28] (though A may be liable on a warranty of authority). But in the following cases he may be liable:

(i) If A expressly agrees with P or C that he will be liable (he makes himself a party to the contract, as principal).[29] It has been held, however, that where C obtains judgment against either A or P this bars a subsequent action against the other.[30] But this probably is not now the case, because the Civil Liability (Contribution) Act 1978 enables one joint contractor to be sued even after an action against the other.

(ii) If P does not exist or has no capacity, A is liable unless he agrees otherwise, and in the case where P is an unformed company, the agreement otherwise must be express.[31]

(iii) If A signs a contract in his own name, and not as agent, he may sometimes be liable.[32]

(iv) If A signs a bill of exchange in his own name, and not as agent, he is liable. In some cases, where P is already bound (maybe by A's signature) a subsequent signature by A will make him liable as indorser.[33]

---

[19] *Fairlie* v. *Fenton* (1870) L.R. 5 exch. 169; *Repetto* v. *Miller's Karri & Jarrah Forests Ltd.* [1901] 2 K.B. 306.

[20] *Short* v. *Spackman* (1831) 2 B. & Ad. 962.

[21] Below, paras. 15.31 *et seq.*

[22] *Chelmsford Auctions Ltd.* v. *Poole* [1973] Q.B. 542.

[23] *Drinkwater* v. *Goodwin* (1775) 1 Cowp. 251.

[24] *Bickerton* v. *Burrell* (1816) 5 M. & S. 383; *Rayner* v. *Grote* (1846) 15 M. & W. 359.

[25] *The Remco* [1984] 2 Lloyds Rep. 205.

[26] *Schmaltz* v. *Avery* (1851) 16 Q.B. 655.

[27] *Wakefield* v. *Duckworth & Co.* [1915] 1 K.B. 218; *Royle* v. *Busby & Son* (1880) 6 Q.B.D. 171; *Teheran-Europe Co. Ltd.* v. *S.T. Belton (Tractors) Ltd.* [1968] 2 Q.B. 53 (same rule if foreign princpal).

[28] *Lewis* v. *Nicholson & Parker* (1852) 18 Q.B. 503.

[29] *International Ry. Co.* v. *Niagara Parks Commission* [1941] A.C. 328; *The Swan* [1968] 1 Lloyds Rep. 5; see *Reynolds* (1969) 85 L.Q.R. 92, (1978) 94 L.Q.R. 224. Where P is foreign and especially where credit is expended by C, this may be weak evidence that A is also to be liable: *Teheran-Europe Co. Ltd.* v. *S.T. Belton (Tractors) Ltd.* [1968] 2 Q.B. 53.

[30] *Debenham's Ltd.* v. *Perkins* (1925) 133 L.T. 252.

[31] Above, para. 15.09.

[32] *Hancock* v. *Hodgson* (1827) 4 Bing. 269. See below, para. 15.38.

[33] These matters are discussed below, paras. 15.36 *et seq.*

15.27 (v) If A makes false statements he may sometimes be liable. The statement may be fraudulent (made not believing it to be true), negligent (made without reasonable care), or innocently false (neither of the previous two). Liability in fraud (Deceit) does not depend on the existence of contract. Thus, if P actually authorises it, and P but not A is fraudulent, only P is liable in Deceit. If A also is fraudulent, he also is liable in Deceit. If A has ostensible authority (*e.g.* acting in the course of a known agency, doing the class of thing for which he is employed) P will be vicariously liable in Deceit for A's fraud, even if P has not actually authorised the statement and does not know of it. A is, of course, also liable.[34] If P does not actually or ostensibly authorise it, and A does not know it is false, then neither P nor A are liable in Deceit, whatever P knows. P's liability in the tort of negligence depends on the same principles, though he could be additionally liable if he had been negligent in employing an incompetent agent. Whether P authorises acts or not, if A is negligent, A may be liable in the tort of negligence, but not under the Misrepresentation Act 1967 (which applies only to contracting parties). Whenever P actually or ostensibly authorises a statement, he is liable to C in contract for damages in the ordinary way if it is false and is a term of the contract. If P actually or ostensibly authorises misstatements, then if by A's misrepresentation (fraudulent, negligent, or innocent) C contracts with P, C can rescind the contract and recover from P, and C has the normal remedies against P under the Misrepresentation Act 1967. If A has neither actual or ostensible authority[35] then P is entirely unaffected by any misstatement of A, and A alone is liable (in tort, if fraudulent, or negligent, but not at all if innocent and not a party to the contract). Whenever by A's fraud P profits, the profit is C's. If A's fraudulent misrepresentation is as to the character or credit of P or another, A is not liable in Deceit unless he signs, and P is not liable unless he signs.[36] But they may be liable in the tort of negligence or in contract, as already stated.[37]

15.28 (vi) If A exceeds his authority, he may be liable on a warranty of authority. This does not require A to be party to any contract, or to have any ostensible authority, and it is not clear upon what principle the liability depends, but it clearly exists. It may be expressed like this: whenever A purports to act upon the authority of P, and has not actual authority, A is liable on a warranty of authority (not on the contract) if P does not perform and C suffers loss, because A has warranted (expressly, or impliedly) his authority to act for P.[38] A is liable even though the transaction entered between C and P does not amount to a contract.[39] He may also be liable where he tells C that another person, X, has authority to bind P (*i.e.* where A warrants X's authority).[40] It would seem[41] that A is liable even if he has ostensible authority so that, in law, P is bound and could be sued by C. There is good reason for that, since P may have expressly forbidden A to act on the

---

[34] See *Armagas Ltd.* v. *Mundogas S.A.* above, n. 3.
[35] As in the *Armagas* case, n. 3 above, or in *Overbrooke Estates Ltd.* v. *Glencombe Properties Ltd.* [1974] 1 W.L.R. 1335.
[36] Statute of Frauds Amendment Act 1828 (Lord Tenterden's Act) discussed above, paras. 5.04, 5.05.
[37] *Banbury* v. *Bank of Montreal* [1918] A.C. 626.
[38] *Collen* v. *Wright* (1857) 8 E. & B. 647.
[39] *Firbank's Executors* v. *Humphreys* (1886) 18 Q.B.D. 54.
[40] *Chapleo* v. *Brunswick Permanent Building Society* (1881) 6 Q.B.D. 696.
[41] See, *e.g. Cherry and McDougall* v. *Colonial Bank of Australasia Ltd.* (1869) L.R. 3. P.C. 24.

ground of P's inability to perform. On the other hand, since ratification has retroactive effect, A is not liable if P ratifies his acts.[42]

15.29   A common instance of A's liability may occur with a company, when the company itself has no authority to act (under its Memorandum) so that A can have no authority, or when the directors or individual who acts have no authority.[43] Persons dealing with companies have previously been deemed to know the contents of the Memorandum and Articles, and where there was a prohibition in those, this removed the possibility of ostensible authority, unless the prohibition was of a procedural nature.[44] Ostensible authority could also be restored in some cases by the operation of section 35 of the Companies Act 1985, where either the company, or the directors, act outside their powers, and it is thought that the same rule would then apply so that the directors are liable on the warranty.[45] Under the proposed new legislative regime[45a] the company will have authority to do most acts, and individual directors will have ostensible authority, in which case the company will generally be bound, though the possibility of the directors' liability on a warranty of authority presumably remains.

15.30   The following points may also be made: first, if A does not believe he has authority, he is fraudulent, and is also liable in Deceit. Secondly, A may escape liability if he warns C that he doubts the extent of his own authority.[46] Thirdly, A may escape liability if he has a reasonable exclusion clause, though maybe only a "warning" is reasonable. Fourthly, constructive notice of lack of authority operates between C and P,[47] but not between C and A, so that C cannot be accused by A of negligence if C believes A's express or implied assertion of authority. Fifthly, A's liability is strict, so that he is liable even though he had authority which has been terminated by the death or mental incapacity of P, about which A does not know. He is liable because he warrants, not because he is negligent.[48] Finally, liability is imposed only for losses flowing from A's lack of authority, and on a contractual basis.[49]

15.31   (vii) If A does not disclose that he is acting as agent for any principal, P is an "undisclosed principal" and A can sue C and vice versa. (If P's existence

---

[42] *Risbourg* v. *Bruckner* (1858) 3 C.B.N.S. 812; *Buron* v. *Denman* (1848) 2 Exch. 167.

[43] *Weeks* v. *Propert* (1873) L.R. 8 C.P. 427; *Chapleo* v. *Brunswick Permanent Building Society* (1881) 6 Q.B.D. 696 (directors warranted authority of Secretary); *West London Commercial Bank* v. *Kitson* (1883) 12 Q.B.D. 157 (1884) 13 Q.B.D. 360 (unauthorised directors signed bill as agents, and not liable on bill: but liable on a warranty). Contrast *Rashdall* v. *Ford* (1866) L.R. 2 Eq. 750 (powers in Memorandum held to be a question of law, and no liability except for warranty of fact).

[44] Then, under the rule in *Royal British Bank* v. *Turquand* (1855) 5 E. & B. 248, 6 E. & B. 327 there might still be ostensible authority, and the directors might be liable on the warranty even though the company is still bound: *Cherry and McDougall* v. *Colonial Bank of Australasia Ltd.* (1869) L.R. 3 P.C. 24.

[45] s.35 does not validate transactions entirely, but only disallows the company, as against the other party, from relying on lack of authority or power as a defence: in fact, therefore, the agent still has no actual authority.

[45a] Discussed below, Chap. 17.

[46] *Halbot* v. *Lens* [1901] 1 Ch. 344; *Lilly, Wilson & Co.* v. *Smales, Eeles & Co.* [1892] 1 Q.B. 456.

[47] Above, para. 15.04.

[48] *Yonge* v. *Toynbee* [1910] 1 K.B. 215 (solicitors acted for client who, unknown to them, had been declared insane. They were liable to a person sued by and later suing their client for whom they acted in the action); *Collen* v. *Wright* (1857) 8 E. & B. 647.

[49] *Simons* v. *Patchett* (1857) 7 E. & B. 568.

is disclosed he need not be named, and A is not then liable.)[50] Further, (by what many consider to be a peculiar rule of English law) when C discovers P's existence, C can choose (make an "election") to hold either A or P liable, and to sue the chosen party. (This depends on A having acted within his actual authority, for there can be no question of "ostensible" authority where P's existence has not been revealed. If A exceeded his actual authority, P cannot ratify, but may sometimes be estopped.)[51] Once C has unequivocally made his election it is final, and he may not change his mind.[52] If the breach is non-payment by P, and if in fact P has before any action by C put A in funds to pay C, only A will be liable to C, even if A is paid before P is disclosed.[53] This is odd, and may be incorrect, though it is the rule where P is disclosed. In a similar way, P is entitled to disclose his existence, and sue C (but not A). If he does so, he is subject to rights of set-off acquired by C against A before the disclosure.[54] P, however, cannot set-off against C any sums owed to him by A.[55]

If P, being refused a loan by his bank, uses an associate, A, to persuade the bank to make a term loan to A, and after signing A announces that he is acting for P, is the bank bound to honour the loan?[56] The rule as to the undisclosed principal is subject to an important limitation, namely, that A alone is liable on the contract or able to sue upon it if at the time of contracting he described himself as principal or in some other way indicated that there was no undisclosed principal—that is, if the possibility of any undisclosed principal was expressly[57] or impliedly[57a] excluded by A. The same would apply if C makes it clear that he intends to deal with A only, and that he excludes any other principal. Indeed, there is no reason why C should not exclude a class of principal, or even an individual principal. Such an exclusion occurred in *Said* v. *Butt*[58] where P had argued with C (theatre owners) and knew they would not sell him a ticket for the first night of a play. He sent A, a friend, to buy him a ticket (without disclosing P's existence) but when P turned up. he was refused admission, and he sued C. The court held that C had reserved the right to sell first-night tickets to specially selected persons, and this indicated that the personality of the other contracting party was material to him, so that he excluded (impliedly) anyone but the actual purchasers from the contract. Arguably, C had not clearly

15.32

[50] *The Santa Carina* [1977] 1 Lloyds Rep. 478: see Reynolds (1983) 36 C.L.P. 119.
[51] Above, para. 15.08.
[52] *Scarf* v. *Jardine* (1882) 7 App.Cas. 345; *Clarkson Booker Ltd.* v. *Andjel* [1964] 2 Q.B. 775 (bringing an action against a party is prima facie evidence of election, but can be rebutted. Obtaining judgment is final.
[53] *Armstrong* v. *Stokes* [1872] L.R. 7 Q.B. 598, not following *Heald* v. *Kenworthy* (1855) 10 Ex. Ch. 739.
[54] *Browning* v. *Provincial Insurance Co. of Canada* (1893) L.R. 5 P.C. 263; *Rabone* v. *Williams* (1785) 7 T.R. 360n. But see *Cooke & Sons* v. *Eshelby* (1887) 12 App.Cas. 271 (no set-off unless P is estopped).
[55] *Irvine & Co.* v. *Watson & Sons* (1880) 5 Q.B.D. 414.
[56] The converse is not uncommon: a bank acts for other undisclosed banks in arranging the loan.
[57] See *Finzel, Berry & Co.* v. *Eastcheap Dried Fruit Co.* [1962] 1 Lloyds Rep. 370, 375; *Dunlop Pneumatic Tyre Co. Ltd.* v. *Selfridge & Co. Ltd.* [1915] A.C. 847, 864; *U.K. Mutual S.S. Assurance Assn.* v. *Nevill* (1887) 19 Q.B.D. 110.
[57a] *e.g.* by his description of himself as principal; *Humble* v. *Hunter* (1848) 12 Q.B. 310. But see *Drughorn Ltd.* v. *Rederiaktiebolaget Trans-Atlantic* [1919] A.C. 203 (no implied exclusion of P unless A's description of himself inconsistent with P's intervention).
[58] [1920] 3 K.B. 497. See also *Archer* v. *Stone* (1898) 78 L.T. 34 (C asked A if acting for P, and A untruthfully said not. Contract voidable for misrepresentation).

showed that he did not intend to deal with P, but at least the decision illustrates the principle that C may exclude whom he wishes. Similarly in *Nash* v. *Dix*[59] P (a committee of Roman Catholics) wished to buy a Congregational chapel from C, who refused to sell to P. P made a bargain with A, whereby he would buy, and re-sell to P. A contracted with C, but when C discovered P's existence, he repudiated his contract with A, and A sued. The court held C liable to A, but here A had not contracted as agent. He intended to buy as principal, and to resell. But it seems clear that if he had acted as agent, the action would have failed, as in *Said* v. *Butt*.

15.33   On the other hand, in *Dyster* v. *Randall & Sons*[60] C (as P knew) would not sell land to P, and P employed A to buy the land and then claimed to hold C liable. The court held C liable. It is doubtful that the case is correctly decided, for P knew that C did not wish to deal with him, but if it is correct, it may represent a special rule applicable to tangible or real property. If, as in *Nash* v. *Dix*, A can buy property as principal and resell to P, whatever C wishes, this is because C has no right to impose "proprietary" conditions (affecting the property itself) on the alienation of tangible property which he disposes of to someone who is not his agent.[61] If this is so, then it is equally futile to prevent the direct purchase of tangible property through an agent, rather than by way of purchase and resale.[62] But choses in action are treated differently: in *Said* v. *Butt*, the right in question was a chose in action (a right to visit the theatre.) It is established law that choses in action may be "personalised" or made non-transferrable at the time the chose is created.[63] This "personalisation" may be achieved expressly, or may be inherent or implied from the nature of the chose. The chose, therefore, cannot be assigned if the creator of the chose has prohibited it, and this distinguishes choses in action from tangibles or real property.[64] This is clear for assignments, and it is submitted that *Said* v. *Butt* shows that the same rule applies in relation to undisclosed principals. If, when C creates the chose in action, he intends (objectively, so that A or P ought to know this) the rights so created to belong to A alone, and to no other, then the rights so created may neither be assigned to nor claimed by an undisclosed principal.[65] The question posed earlier was whether this applies to transactions with banks, such as term loans. It is submitted that it clearly would, where P has already been rejected by the bank. The situation is the same as in *Said* v. *Butt* or *Nash* v. *Dix*. In other cases, it seems likely that the credit assessment process which banks undertake before lending makes it obvious that the personality of the other contracting party is a material element in the contract, and impliedly excludes others, either as undisclosed principals, or as assignees. It is thought also that if assignment of rights by a borrower is prohibited, this impliedly excludes the possibility of an undisclosed principal.

(viii) If A deals with property belonging to C, even believing it in good faith to be P's, then A is liable to C in conversion, even if he has passed the proceeds to P.[66] Banks may thus be liable when they collect for X or pay to

---

[59] (1898) 78 L.T. 445.
[60] [1926] Ch. 932.
[61] It may be a breach of contract, but the sale is effective.
[62] Lawrence J. in the *Dyster* case referred to this futility.
[63] Bills of exchange may be made non-transferrable in this way: s.8(1), B.O.E. Act 1882. So may bus tickets, or any chose in action.
[64] It may still be the case that *Dyster* v. *Randall & Sons* is wrongly decided.
[65] *Greer* v. *Downs Supply Co.* [1927] 2 K.B. 28.
[66] *Consolidated Co.* v. *Curtis & Son* [1892] 1 Q.B. 495; *Hollins* v. *Fowler* (1875) L.R. 7 H.L. 757.

X on cheques belonging to C.[67] Banks are not liable under tracing, or for money paid by mistake, if they have in good faith passed the money on to their principal or at his order.[68]

I. Summary of P's liability to C

Where P is disclosed he is liable if A contracts on P's authority (actual or ostensible) or if P ratifies, or is estopped, or if subrogation operates. He is not liable if he has paid A to pay C.[69] Where P is not disclosed, he is liable if (i) A contracts with actual authority (ostensible authority is impossible) or if P is subsequently estopped, (and possibly subrogation operates), and (ii) if neither A nor C expressly or impliedly excludes the possibility of an undisclosed principal. In tort the same principles as to authority seem to apply[70] so that P is liable if A has actual or ostensible authority.

15.34

J. Dispositions of P's property by A

No-one may sell what he does not own (*Nemo dat quod non habet*). But A may sell P's property in the following cases (which we merely mention here).[71]

15.35

(i) if he has actual authority.

(ii) if he has ostensible authority.

(iii) if P ratifies.

(iv) if P is subsequently estopped.[72]

(v) if A is apparently owner at the time of the sale, a form of estoppel operates in relation to sales of goods.[73]

(vi) if A is a factor and C is a bona fide purchaser without notice of A's lack of authority to sell.[74]

(vii) if A sells in market overt.[75]

K. Signatures of agents

The rules as to the signatures of agents acting for companies are generally the same as those for other types of agent.[76] It was formerly thought that where Lord Tenterden's Act[77] required the signature of the person to be charged with a fraudulent misrepresentation as to another's credit, that a company could not be charged unless it signed by appending its seal, but this is not the case, and the signature of any ordinary agent will suffice.[78] The company's seal is needed on deeds[79] unless the deed is to be executed

15.36

---

[67] Unless specially protected, as by ss.60, 80, B.O.E. Act 1882, or the Cheques Act 1957.

[68] Above, para. 11.07.

[69] *Wyatt* v. *Marquis of Hertford* (1802) 3 East 147; *Heald* v. *Kenworthy* (1855) 10 Exch. 739; *Irvine & Co.* v. *Watson & Sons* (1880) 5 Q.B.D. 414. As noted above, this has been said to apply also to undisclosed principals, but that may not be correct.

[70] *Armagas Ltd.* v. *Mundogas S.A., The Ocean Frost*, above, n. 3.

[71] Reference might be made to Goode, *Commercial Law*, for discussion of points (v)-(vii) below in the text.

[72] See *Spiro* v. *Lintern*, above, para. 15.08.

[73] Sale of Goods Act 1979, s.29(1).

[74] Factors Act 1889.

[75] Sale of Goods Act 1979, s.22(1).

[76] See ss.36–37, C.A. 1985, particularly.

[77] Above, paras. 5.04–5.05.

[78] *U.B.A.F. Ltd.* v. *European American Banking Corporation* [1984] 2 All E.R. 226 (C.A.), [1984] Q.B. 713, explaining *Hirst* v. *West Riding Banking Union Co. Ltd.* [1901] 2 K.B. 56, and applying what is now s.36(1)(b), C.A. 1985.

[79] s.36(1)(a), C.A. 1985.

abroad[80] and this is a distinction between companies and other principals (who may, by deed, appoint agents to execute deeds.)

Generally, an agent may sign in several ways:

15.37 First, he may simply use his own name. If in so doing he discloses P's existence, and states to C that he contracts for P alone, then it is difficult to see why he should be held liable to C on an ordinary contract. Some older cases[81] suggest that he may be liable, because of the "parole evidence rule" by which a person was bound by what he signed, and was unable to adduce parole evidence (oral evidence) to vary or contradict the effect of the written contract. Nowadays, however, the parole evidence rule is almost defunct, and it is thought that the true explanation of the cases is that because both P and A may (if so intended) be liable on the contract, then if A signs in his own name, he may be liable even if he discloses P's interest, if A does not (orally or in writing) expressly exclude his own liability. Signing in his own name, that is, is a strong indication that he accepts personal liability, even if P is also liable.[82] If, therefore, A signs in his own name and says he signs as agent, he is not liable[83] but if he merely adds words describing himself as an agent, this may be insufficient to exclude his own liability on the contract, for he could be taken to be describing his occupation, rather than asserting that on this particular occasion he acts for P as his agent.[84] It is a question of fact, but "A, P's agent" may be insufficient, while "A, signing as P's agent", or "A, for P" is clearly sufficient.

15.38 In relation to deeds, the rule is that P cannot be sued unless his name appears on the deed as a party, and the deed is executed in his name, or A acts as his trustee.[85] But if A is appointed by power of attorney, he can sign in his own name and P may be bound.[86] A may be bound if, as above, he does not show the acts as agent.[86a]

A special rule applies to bills of exchange, signed in A's name. The doctrine that C may sue an undisclosed principal on discovering his existence does not apply to bills of exchange, so that P cannot be liable to C unless P's name appears on the instrument.[87] It is not enough for A orally to say that he acts for P, for the bill may be negotiated to another, who may not know of P, and cannot sue P when he discovers the circumstances. In other words, the parole evidence rule still applies to bills of exchange. Accordingly, section 26 of the Bills of Exchange Act 1882 provides that if a person signs a bill using his own name and does not show that he signs as agent, he

---

[80] s.38, C.A. 1985.
[81] *Higgins* v. *Senior* (1841) M. & W. 834; *Magee* v. *Atkinson & Townley* (1837) 2 M. & W. 440. Parole evidence is, inconsistently, allowed to show that A is liable: *Hutchinson* v. *Tatham* (1873) L.R. 8 C.P. 482 (A signed "as agents" but trade custom allowed to be shown by which A became personally liable after a time).
[82] See *Parker* v. *Winlow* (1857) 7 E. & B. 942; *The Swan* [1968] 1 Lloyds Rep. 5.
[83] *Universal Steam Navign. Co. Ltd.* v. *J. McKelvie & Co.* [1923] A.C. 492 (A not liable when signed in own name "as agents"); *Gadd* v. *Houghton* (1876) 1 Ex. D. 357 (A not liable when contract said "we have sold to you on account of X").
[84] See cases previous two notes and *Sika Contracts Ltd.* v. *B. L. Gill and Closeglen Properties Ltd.* (1978) 9 B.L.R. 11 (A signed in own name and added "Chartered Civil Engineer". This merely described his occupation, and he was liable).
[85] *Re International Contract Co., Pickering's Claim* (1871) L.R. 6 Ch. App. 525; *Schack* v. *Anthony* (1813) 1 M. & S. 573; *Harmer* v. *Armstrong* [1934] Ch. 65 (trustee).
[86] s.7(1), Powers of Attorney Act 1971.
[86a] See above, n. 32.
[87] See the cases above, nn. 81–85.

is personally liable on the bill. As with ordinary contracts, this applies even if P's name is on the bill and A uses words describing himself as P's agent, but not showing that on this particular occasion he signs as agent. The difference from ordinary contracts is that there the parole evidence rule may be displaced, but with bills of exchange it is insufficient that C knows that A signs as agent: it must appear on the instrument. While strictly this rule seems unnecessary between the original payee, C, and A, (the parole evidence rule being generally defunct) the words of section 26 seem to make it clear that the parole evidence rule survives between C and A, and not merely between indorsees from C, and A. In summary, therefore, unless P's name appears on the bill he is not liable, and unless A's signature shows that on this occasion he signs as agent for P then A is liable, whatever may be agreed orally between A and C.

Secondly, the agent may sign "per procurationem" (on behalf of **15.39** another). Examples of this (all of which appear to achieve the same effect) are "A, per pro P", or "A, pp. P", or "A, for B", or "A, for and on behalf of B", or "A signing as B's agent." If a person signs bills of exchange in this fashion, it indicates that he has only a limited authority, and P is bound only if A acts within his actual (express or implied) authority.[88] There is, in other words, no question of ostensible authority with such a signature on a bill of exchange. But this rule does not apply generally (other than to bills of exchange). It applies to bills because they may be negotiated, and the subsequent holder cannot generally know if A was held out by P to C as having ostensible authority. If it was a general defence, then ostensible authority could rarely, if ever, have applied to companies, because invariably persons contracting for companies sign *per procurationem*.

Thirdly, the agent may sign with P's name, and there is no objection to this if he has authority and does not pass himself off to C as P. (Even passing himself off as P may not always matter, if it is not for a dishonest purpose. It would matter with cheques, where the recognition of P's signature is important to the paying bank, but the practice there is that P authorises the bank to pay A and the bank takes A's signature.) If, of course, A has no authority, and passes himself off as P, a signature in this form is forgery, and the forgery is ineffective to pass rights, unless P is estopped. Section 24, B.O.E. Act 1882,[89] states this general forgery rule in the context of bills of exchange.

Fourthly, as long as there is no dishonest intent, in England and Wales **15.40** anyone is allowed to use whatever name they wish, in signing or contracting. A may, therefore, sign in an assumed or trade name. This general rule is stated in relation to bills of exchange, by s.23, B.O.E. Act 1882. Unless the assumed or trade name is one known by C to be used by P, it would seem that such a signature would be considered to be A's signature, and the rules previously considered would then apply (so that A is bound on a bill, if he does not sign "[assumed name] for P", and so on).

Before proceeding, it is as well to observe that any party who signs a bill of exchange, whether as drawer, acceptor or indorser, may attract liability merely by reason of the signature. Even if, therefore, the principal is bound as drawer or acceptor by the bill, through his agent's signature, it is still

---

[88] s.25, B.O.E. Act 1882.
[89] Discussed above, para. 7.03.

possible for the agent to be bound in another capacity, as indorser. The fact that P is bound does not prevent A from being bound.

RELEVANT CASES

15.41   In *Chapman* v. *Smethurst*[90] a promissory note was signed by the managing director (M.D.) of a company "S Ltd., S, M.D." As is quite usual, all except his signature "S" was by rubber stamp. Held, this indicated a clear intent that the company and not S was to be bound. It is not, therefore, necessary to say "For", etc. The signature showed that on this occasion, A contracted as agent.

In *Elliott* v. *Bax-Ironside*[91] two directors accepted a cheque "accepted payable at the W. Bank, I and M directors, F. Ltd." The drawer asked them to indorse it upon the back, where they signed "F. Ltd., I and M directors." The argument concerned the latter signatures alone, and it was held that they were liable for two distinct reasons: first, because these signatures merely described their occupations, and did not say that on this occasion they signed as agents[92] and secondly, because the company was already liable by the signature on the front, and there could be no possible reason to sign on the back other than to accept personal liability, regardless of the form of the signature. This, it is submitted, makes good sense.

In *Rolfe Lubell & Co.* v. *Keith*[93] the M.D. accepted two bills of exchange "For and on behalf of the company, signed K, director." He was asked for the personal indorsement of two officers of the company, and on the back he and the secretary signed in exactly the same form. He was held liable because the words were (i) contrary to the agreement to be personally liable, and in any case (ii) superfluous if they did not mean to impose personal liability. If, therefore, the principal for whom the agent has signed is bound, or intended to be bound, by a signature on one part of the bill, it may be taken to be an invariable rule that a signature by the agent elsewhere, whatever its form, binds the agent.

15.42   *Bondina Ltd.* v. *Rollaway Shower Blinds Ltd.*[94] A bank's printed cheque form contained the company's printed name, and a printed line of figures containing the number of the cheque, the branch of the bank, and the number of the account, and a cheque was signed by two directors, who added their names only (*i.e.* "W, M"). The court held that by signing the cheque, the signatories adopted all the writing on it, including the company's name and account number. "The effect of this is to show that the cheque is drawn on the company's account and not on any other account . . . It shows plainly . . . that the drawer of the cheque was the company . . . " and not W. or M.[95]

---

[90] [1909] 1 K.B. 927.
[91] [1925] 2 K.B. 301.
[92] It is thought that in the light of the previous case, this is insupportable.
[93] [1979] 1 All E.R. 860.
[94] [1986] 1 All E.R. 564 (C.A.). Strictly, the court merely gave leave to defend on the ground that there is an arguable case, but it states the law clearly, and the view expressed can hardly be thought not to be binding.
[95] At p. 566, *per* Dillon L.J. The court followed *H. B. Etlin Co. Ltd.* v. *Asselstyne* (1962) 34 D.L.R. (2d.) 191, and distinguished *Bank of Nova Scotia* v. *Radocsay* (1981) 125 D.L.R. (3d.) 651 and *Glatt* v. *Ritt* (1973) 34 D.L.R. (3d.) 295.

L. The termination of an agency relationship

First, A may renounce or give up his authority. If he has contracted not to **15.43** do so, he is in breach of contract. In relation to the Enduring Powers of Attorney Act 1985, there may be certain restrictions on his ability to renounce.

Secondly, as an agency is no more than the granting of authority by P to A, the revocation of that authority is effective, even if P has agreed not to do so (he may, however, be in breach of contract). Revocation is impossible in the cases described already in connection with powers of attorney.[96] It is also impossible, even if not given by power of attorney, where the authority is given by contract so as to secure some interest of A[97] or if A has started performance and incurred liabilities for which he is entitled to be indemnified by P.[98] Revocation may not affect third parties[99] since, if they know of the previous authority, A will continue to have ostensible authority, until C has actual or constructive notice of the revocation.

Thirdly, the death[1] or mental incapacity[2] of P or of A may (even if unknown to the other) revoke the authority, but P's death or incapacity will not do so if a power of attorney is given as security, or in cases affected by the Enduring Powers of Attorney Act 1985.

Fourthly, P's bankruptcy may revoke the authority, unless a power of attorney is given as security. A's bankruptcy does not revoke the authority given by P, but is a ground for P's revocation, and notice of the bankruptcy would put C on inquiry as to whether A continued to have authority.

Fifthly, the authority may be revoked if the agency becomes illegal, as where A or P is an enemy alien on the outbreak of war, or if otherwise the contract is frustrated.[3]

Sixthly, an authority may be given for a specified time (which expires) or purpose (which is achieved). An example is an authority limited to P's absence from the country.

---

[96] Above, paras. 15.13–15.15.
[97] *Clerk* v. *Laurie* (1857) 2 H. & N. 199, 200; *Gaussen* v. *Morton* (1830) 10 B. & C. 731; *Smart* v. *Sandars* (1848) 5 C.B. 895.
[98] *Read* v. *Anderson* (1884) 13 Q.B.D. 779.
[99] There are specific provisions in relation to powers of attorney.
[1] *Campanari* v. *Woodburn* (1854) 15 C.B. 400 (P's death).
[2] *Yonge* v. *Toynbee* [1910] 1 K.B. 215 (P's insanity).
[3] *Marshall* v. *Glanvill* [1917] 2 K.B. 87 (A drafted into armed services).

16. Partnerships[1]

A. Introduction

16.01 Whether they know it or not, two or more persons who are in business[2] in common with a view of profit, and who have not adopted a company structure are, in law, partners.[3]

In opening a bank account for the firm, the account (and the mandate) may be in the firm's name (a partnership account) or the names of the partners (a joint account). In the former case, the bank will require some evidence of the existence of a partnership (such as sight of the articles of partnership) though the signatures of all partners on the mandate form is in any case sufficient to bind the signatories as if they were partners. Hence, whatever the name of the account, all partners are asked to sign. If this is not done, the others are bound if they are partners and the account is opened in the partnership name for the partnership business (but there is not implied authority to open an account other than in the firm's name).[4] In any case, the bank will wish to obtain the protection given in relation to indorsements, etc., by the Cheques Act 1957, and it will make what checks it reasonably can as to the identity and credit, etc., of the partners. The mandate may limit the authorised signatories to specified partners, and for reasons later stated always declares that the liability of the partners is to be joint and several.

16.02 Various names may be given to partners. In relation to outsiders, the basic distinction is between partners and "limited partners," the latter being created by virtue of the Limited Partnership Act 1907. They must be registered, and their liability is limited to the amount of capital contributed. If part of that capital is withdrawn, the partner stays liable for the original amount. The limited partner may advise the others, but must not take part in the management or deal with outsiders, or he is fully liable for liabilities incurred while he does so. He cannot prevent new partners from entering the partnership, or withdraw from the partnership except by assigning his share to someone else with the consent of the other partners (the assignee becomes a limited partner). At least one partner must have unlimited liability (must be a "general" partner). Limited partnerships are a way for persons to invest in a firm without acquiring the unlimited liability which is otherwise a characteristic of a partnership. More commonly, perhaps, a retiring partner may not withdraw the whole or any of his capital, but will wish to continue to share in the profits, while limiting his future liability.

A "general" partner means an ordinary partner: one who is active as a partner. He may be contrasted with a limited partner or with a "dormant" partner, which in common parlance may be a synonym for a registered limited partner or, more usually, merely a partner who no longer takes an active part in the business. A "salaried" partner takes not a share of the profits but a set income, and a "junior" partner is merely a newcomer to the firm who may be expected to prove himself before becoming a "full" or "senior" partner. The junior partner may not play a major role in manage-

---

[1] See generally *Underhill's Principles of the law of Partnership*, (12th ed.)
[2] This includes every trade, occupation or profession: s.45.
[3] Partnership Act 1890, s.1(1).
[4] *Alliance Bank* v. *Kearsley* (1871) L.R. 6 C.P. 433.

ment, and may often be salaried. Unlike the limited partner, the application of these terms to a partner reflects an agreement between the partners as to their rights *inter se*. Except for the limited partner, the terms have no relevance so far as outsiders are concerned. We may repeat what has been said: in relation to outsiders, the liability of partners is a matter of the general law; while between themselves, the partners may by contract allocate to themselves whatever rights and duties they choose. Unless otherwise agreed all the partners have equal rights in management,[5] although entitlement to capital or income is determined by other rules. Each has an equal vote. No change in the nature of the business is possible unless by unanimous consent. No new partner may be admitted unless by unanimous consent. No existing partner may be expelled against his will. These rules, however, are subject to contract, and often the agreement will provide for majority vote, or for decisions to be taken by senior members, and so on.

All partners have a duty of utmost fairness and good faith to their co-partners in all partnership matters. All the duties of agents previously examined[6] apply, so that the partner may not have an undeclared conflict of interest, or make secret profits, etc.[7] Partners have a right to inspect the books of the partnership or to nominate agents (such as an accountant) to do so.[8] No partner is entitled to remuneration, but he is entitled to an equal share of the profits.[9] Partners are entitled to an indemnity for payments made or liabilities incurred for the firm's business or for the preservation of its property.[10] If, therefore, one partner alone is sued, the others must contribute (this is a general right of jointly liable parties).[11]

16.03

It is essential to recall that all of the rights or duties here discussed are, as between the partners, subject to contrary agreement.

B. Partners, and principles of agency

In contract, the liability of partners to outsiders is joint, (unless the partners agree to joint and several liability) and each partner is liable for the debts and obligations of the firm incurred while he is a partner.[12] It follows that the liability of each member of the partnership is unlimited. Failure of the partnership business may, therefore, lead to personal bankruptcy. Although a partnership is not a "person" in the same way as a corporate person, a partnership may sue and be sued in the firm's name. That is to say, an action brought against the firm in the firm's name is an action against all the members of the partnership.[13] Partners may alternatively be sued in their individual names, and since the Civil Liability (Contribution) Act 1978, the bringing of an action against one party jointly liable does not "exhaust" the action, and failure to recover from one party does not debar a subsequent action against the other partners. (The same has always been possible if liability is joint and several). Banks' mandate forms always provide for the joint

16.04

---

[5] ss.24–35 of the 1890 Act.
[6] Above, Chap. 15.
[7] See *Thompson's Trustee in Bankruptcy* v. *Heaton* [1974] 1 All E.R. 1239; *Bentley* v. *Craven* (1853) 18 Beav. 75, and see ss.29–30 of the 1890 Act.
[8] s.24(9) of the 1890 Act; *Bevan* v. *Webb* [1901] 2 Ch. 59.
[9] s.24(1) of the 1890 Act.
[10] s.24(2) of the 1890 Act.
[11] Generally on the relations of partners *inter se* see Underhill, *op. cit.*, Chap. 3. Here we are primarily concerned with their relations with third parties, and with their property rights.
[12] s.9 of the 1890 Act. In tort, they are jointly and severally liable: s.12 of the 1890 Act.
[13] R.S.C. Ord. 81(1).

and several liability of partners, for two positive reasons: first, where a partner is bankrupt this entitles the bank to proceed against his personal property equally with his personal creditors (otherwise, the bank is postponed to the claims of the personal creditors)[14] and secondly, if there is a debit balance on the firm's account, the bank will obtain the right of combination in respect of credit balances on the partner's personal account, since the partner is personally liable for the debt.

16.05 The general concern of an outsider (C) is to know whether an individual (A) may bind the partnership (P). Section 5 of the 1890 Act says that every general partner is an agent of the firm for the purpose of the partnership business, and while acting in the usual business of the partnership, has authority to bind the firm. On ordinary principles of agency law, this means that if A has no actual authority because the other partners have imposed an express prohibition on his acts, P is still bound by acts of A in the usual course of P's business, unless either C does not know or believe A to be a partner,[15] or C knows of the prohibition.[16] That is to say, A has ostensible authority except in the cases mentioned. There cannot be ostensible authority, except (i) for acts done in relation to the partnership business, (ii) in the usual way, and (iii) where A purports to act as partner.[17] This last rule to some extent displaces the ordinary principle of the undisclosed principal. Ordinary rules of agency otherwise apply.

Although A may not in fact be a partner, on ordinary principles he may be held out by the firm to be a partner, and the firm will then be bound by his acts in the normal way. A may not hold himself out as a partner, so as to bind the firm.[18] He may, however, hold himself out as a partner so as to bind himself to C for the firm's debts, etc., as if he had been a partner: he is a partner by estoppel.[19] A is then bound by what P does, although P, the firm, not having held him out, is not bound by what A does. Holding out may occur if communicated to C by another party with the firm's, or A's authority.[20]

16.06 A general partner's implied powers include the following: he may draw cheques,[21] sell and buy goods, employ staff, and give a good discharge (receipt) for monies received from debtors. He may not borrow for the firm (or give security).[22] These powers are more extensive if the partnership is a commercial or trading one (*i.e.* if its principal operations are buying and selling, as opposed, say, to a professional partnership, such as a firm of accountants, or solicitors).[23] In that case, A may also draw, make, sign,

[14] See below, para. 16.23 *et seq.*
[15] s.5.
[16] s.8.
[17] ss.5, 7. *Watteau* v. *Fenwick* [1893] 1 Q.B. 346 suggests that P is bound although A does not disclose that he is a partner. This contradicts the clear words of s.5 and has been widely criticized.
[18] *Armagas Ltd.* v. *Mundogas S.A., The Ocean Frost.* [1986] 2 All E.R. 385 [1986] A.C. 717 (HL). For other holding out cases, see above, paras. 14.03–14.05.
[19] s.14 of the 1890 Act.
[20] *Martyn* v. *Gray* (1863) 14 C.B. N.S. 824.
[21] But not other bills of exchange: *Backhouse* v. *Charlton* (1878) 8 Ch.D. 444. In some firms, this may be inconsistent with the usual course of the partnership business, and would be prohibited.
[22] *Higgins* v. *Beauchamp* [1914] 3 K.B. 1192.
[23] See *Higgins* v. *Beauchamp* [1914] 3 K.B. 1192 for the distinction.

indorse, accept, transfer, negotiate or discount negotiable instruments,[24] contract and pay debts on the firm account, borrow money on the firm's credit,[25] and pledge goods or securities for the business.[26] Implied powers do not extend to commencing litigation[27] or arbitration proceedings or authorising the use of the firm name for the purpose, to executing deeds, to giving guarantees for the firm (unless there is a trade custom), or to accepting property in lieu of a money debt owed to the firm. Naturally, these implied powers may be extended by agreement with the other partners, or they may be restricted, but as already noted, a restriction will not remove the ostensible authority of the partner to perform the acts in question in any case where he would have implied actual authority but for the restriction. Because there is no implied power to borrow, except in a trading partnership, a bank's mandate form should expressly authorise the making of advances on the signatures of those specified in the mandate as general signatories. This express actual authority removes the need for argument concerning implied actual, or ostensible, authority. For the same reasons the mandate will authorise the signatories to give security over the partnership property, though it is in any case common practice to obtain the signatures of all the partners to such a transaction, as this avoids any argument that the transaction was not in the ordinary course of the partnership business. But if there is no written authority and the signatures of all partners are not obtained, all are bound nevertheless provided that the partnership is a trading partnership, and that no terms of any mandate are contravened, and that the borrowing is for and in the ordinary course of the business of the partnership. As stated, the provisos become irrelevant if the signatures of all partners are obtained. Infant partners may bind the partnership and its assets (though they cannot give securities over their personal assets for their own debts, or for those of the firm). Special complications may arise in the case of land. If legal title is in partners A, B, and C, and if a legal mortgage is to be taken, this must be made by deed, so that A, B and C are bound by a legal mortgage only if they sign the deed or if an agent is authorised by deed. Even so, if A signs a purported legal mortgage which fails for this reason, B and C's equitable interests may be effectively mortgaged in equity if A was authorised (actually, or ostensibly). Similarly, A may pledge deeds of title to partnership property (creating an equitable mortgage) or may pledge negotiable instruments (creating a legal pledge of this personal property). If, however, legal title to land is held by one partner, A, (in trust for the others) then A may give an effective legal and equitable title (supposing, as already stated, that he has authority of some sort).

So far as the law of tort is concerned,[28] the relation between A and P **16.07** resembles that of employee-employer. That is to say, the firm is liable in tort if it has authorised the act (actually, or ostensibly), but even if it has not done so, it may be liable if the partner was acting in the course of the part-

---

[24] Though except in favour of a holder for value without notice of the manner of acceptance, he may not bind the firm by accepting a bill of exchange in blank, or as an accommodation party: *Hogarth* v. *Latham & Co.* (1878) 3 Q.B.D. 643.

[25] *Lane* v. *Williams* (1692) 2 Vern. 277.

[26] *Ex p. Bonbonus* (1803) 8 Ves. 540; *Re Clough* (1885) 31 Ch.D. 324; *Re Bourne, Bourne* v. *Bourne* [1906] 2 Ch. 427.

[27] *Arbuckle* v. *Taylor* (1815) 3 Dow. 160.

[28] Liability is joint and several: s.12.

nership business.[29] Thus, if A has actual or ostensible authority to take securities, but does so fraudulently, in his own name, the firm is liable because A does the kind of thing for which he has authority, but in an improper manner or fashion.

16.08   If a partner lies about the credit of another partner or the firm, the firm is liable in Deceit only if the representation is in writing and signed by those to be made liable.[30] This is the effect of Lord Tenterden's Act.[31] The firm may, however, be liable in the tort of negligence, or in contract if the representation is incorporated into the contract as a term. But the firm is not liable in negligence under section 2(1) of the Misrepresentation Act 1967 unless it would be liable in Deceit.[32] Lord Tenterden's Act does not apply if the partner misrepresents his own credit. It has been said that the signature of the firm's name is not sufficient to make the firm liable.[33] But if the name is used with authority, this may not now be so.[34]

Where the bank's money is misapplied, the position is dealt with expressly by section 11 of the Partnership Act 1890. If a partner acts within the scope of his ostensible authority and receives the bank's money as a partner and misapplies it, the firm is liable.[35] The firm is bound, therefore, if the money is paid for the partnership business, with no notice of any prohibition, etc.[36] The firm is similarly liable if money is received by the firm itself and subsequently misapplied by the partners.[37]

C. Withdrawal of authority

16.09   Where A authorises B to act on his behalf, A may generally withdraw his authority (even if he has contracted not to do so).[38] Thus, in relation to bank mandates, any single partner has the power to withdraw his authority and thus to revoke the mandate. It follows that any partner may countermand a cheque, even if not signed by him; and whatever the original mandate said, he may insist at any time on his own signature appearing on cheques, etc. Mandates are, of course, automatically cancelled on the dissolution of the firm, when the fact of that dissolution is or ought to be known to the bank (when it has at least constructive notice of withdrawal of authority).

D. Change in composition of firm

16.10   If there is a change in the composition of the firm, by retirement,[39] death[39a] or addition of a new partner, or if a partner becomes bankrupt[40] or an enemy alien (or the partnership is otherwise illegal),[41] the partnership is

[29] *Hamlyn* v. *John Houston & Co.* [1903] 1 K.B. 81; *Mara* v. *Browne* [1896] 1 Ch. 199, 208; *Arbuckle* v. *Taylor* (1815) 3 Dow. 160; *Lloyd* v. *Grace, Smith & Co.* [1912] A.C. 716; *B.N.S.W.* v. *Owston* (1879) 4 App.Cas.270.
[30] *Williams* v. *Mason* (1873) 28 L.T. 232 (one partner signed: the other was not liable).
[31] Discussed above, paras. 5.04–5.05.
[32] *U.B.A.F. Ltd.* v. *European-American Banking Corpn.* [1984] 2 All E.R. 226, [1984] Q.B. 713.
[33] *Swift* v. *Jewsbury* (1874) L.R. 9 Q.B. 301.
[34] After *U.B.A.F. Ltd.* v. *European-American Banking Corpn.* above, n. 32.
[35] s.11(*a*).
[36] See *Harman* v. *Johnson* (1853) 2 E. & B. 61.
[37] s.11(*b*). See *Rhodes* v. *Moules* [1895] 1 Ch. 236.
[38] See above, para. 15.43.
[39] s.32(*c*).
[39a] s.33(1).
[40] s.33(1).
[41] s.34.

automatically dissolved. It may thereafter be replaced by a new partnership if the remaining or new partners continue to work together. The old partnership will not be dissolved if the partnership agreement provides to the contrary. It is important that partnership agreements provide for this, for an agreement applicable to A, B, and C would not necessarily apply to the remaining partners B and C, where A leaves the partnership. The old agreement might, however, be impliedly adopted if the remaining partners continue to act in accordance with its terms.[42] A further undesirable consequence is that on the dissolution of the partnership the retired partner, or estate of a deceased partner, would be entitled to demand repayment of that partner's share of the capital, which might have a detrimental effect on the business. Further, on the dissolution a valuable asset—the goodwill—would simply vanish as an asset of the firm. A bank mandate given by A, B and C should also make provision for A's leaving the partnership, and may permit the bank to continue to act on the signature of the other parties. The bank will, however, ordinarily take a new mandate from the remaining parties, and certainly will do so if a new member is admitted to the partnership.

Third party guarantees or securities (whether given to the firm, or for the firm's debts) may also be invalidated by a change in the composition of the firm (whether or not the firm is dissolved) unless the guarantee contains contrary terms.[43]

E. Deceased and surviving partners

The death (when known) of a partner who has signed a cheque revokes the authority of the paying bank to pay on that cheque, and it should[44] be returned to the surviving partners for signature. The estate of the deceased partner remains liable for anything done while the deceased person was a partner. But even if the partnership is not dissolved on the death (because of a prior agreement) the estate of the deceased partner is not liable for debts, etc., arising thereafter merely because of continued use of the partner's name in the firm name, and notification to creditors of the fact of death is not needed to protect the estate against further liability.[45] A personal security given by a partner cannot be charged with advances made after the death of the partner, for death revokes his authority, and the property will pass to another. On the death of a partner, his rights to the partnership assets pass to his personal representatives[46] but these rights are no greater than the deceased partner had (except that his death may result in dissolution, and a right to have the assets distributed).

Because the deceased partner's estate is not liable for fresh debts, and because the rule in *Clayton's case*[47] may have the effect of discharging the past liability (for which the partner remains responsible) if the original account is continued, it is general practice where accounts are in debit to rule off the old account and to open a new account, even if there is a term in the mandate excluding the operation of the rule. If this is not done, and the rule in *Clayton's case* operates to reduce the debt, then a personal security

16.11

---

[42] The Act so provides where a fixed term expires and the partnership is continued: s.21(1); see *Brooks* v. *Brooks* (1901) 85 L.T. 453.

[43] See s.18. For Guarantees, see below, Chap. 20.

[44] In law: but it seems that some banks may pay, judging the risk to be slight.

[45] s.14(2), and s.36(3).

[46] s.20 of the 1890 Act.

[47] Discussed above, paras. 13.24 *et seq.*

given by the deceased partner may also become ineffective except to the extent of the remaining debt, if any.[48]

16.12   If dissolution occurs the surviving partners have some residual authority to bind the estate of the deceased. They (or a single survivor) have implied power to do whatever is necessary to wind up the affairs of the partnership, and this includes the power to mortgage the firm's property where necessary.[49] They may, therefore, continue a partnership bank account for a period and a new mandate is necessary only if new partners are to be admitted or if there is otherwise to be a change in the authorised signatories (the same applies if the partnership is not dissolved by the death). Further, in the absence of any evidence to the contrary, a person dealing with the survivor(s) may assume that a mortgage is made in the proper course of winding up. There is no duty to inquire.[50] On this principle, even if on dissolution the deceased partner's liability is reduced by the operation of *Clayton's case*, the survivor(s) may still charge partnership property (a share of which belongs to the deceased) so as to bind the estate of the deceased in respect of debts incurred after the death.[50a] The deceased partner is not personally liable, but the security over partnership property to which his estate is entitled is effective against his estate.

The bank has no duty to inquire as to the state of indebtedness between survivor and deceased, and payments may, therefore, safely be made to the survivors. This would not be the case if the bank had actual notice of the state of accounts and additionally had some reason to think that the survivors would not account. (The mandate is subject to that limitation).[51]

If the old partnership is dissolved by death but the survivors form a new partnership (perhaps simply by continuing the business in common with a view to a profit) then strictly a new mandate is required. As shortly stated, the partnership assets must then be distributed, with a share going to the estate of the deceased unless his representatives otherwise agree. Debts of the old partnership may be called in by the bank, but this need not be done if the business is prosperous. New securities should be taken unless the old securities provide for their continuation in these circumstances—*i.e.* "despite any change in the composition of the firm." Wording such as that clearly binds those partners party to the original agreement, but new partners should be asked to sign a fresh agreement. If new security agreements are taken there may be a notional repayment and fresh advance, so that the consideration is not past.

F. Mental disorder of a partner

16.13   This does not necessarily dissolve a partnership, unless the other partners so decide, and apply to the court for dissolution[52] but notice of the fact countermands the authority of the remaining partners, and the bank should not pay on cheques signed by the partner unless otherwise agreed. If the

---

[48] See *e.g., Royal Bank of Scotland* v. *Christie* (1841) 8 Cl. & Fin. 214.

[49] s.38 of the 1890 Act.

[50] *Re Bourne, Bourne* v. *Bourne* [1906] 2 Ch. 427.

[50a] *ibid.*

[51] It would seem unnecessary to invoke the doctrine of constructive trust (discussed above, Chap. 10).

[52] Under ss.94 and 96 of the Mental Health Act 1983.

partnership is dissolved, the case resembles that of a deceased partner (the account is stopped, etc.). The partner is not bound by contracts made by third parties with the firm if the third party is aware of the mental disorder and the disorder is such as to make him incapable of contracting (the contract is voidable, not void). If the disorder is not known to the third party and there is no reason to know of it the partner still has ostensible authority to bind the firm. Where a partner is thought to be of unsound mind the other partners may apply for an interim injunction to restrain him from acting until such time as the matter is fully disposed of. This may be vital to prevent much damage being done in the meantime.

G. Retiring partners[53]

Retiring partners remain liable for anything done while they were partners,[54] unless a novation[55] occurs. It is common for insurance to be taken out against the possibility of unexpected liability, either by the retiring partner or by the firm. In relation to creditors who have previously dealt with the firm, the retiring partner has been held out as partner, and will be liable for new partnership debts (and the firm could be bound by the partner's acts for the business) until the creditor is given notice of the retirement.[56] Persons who are "apparent" members may be treated by third parties as members until the third party has notice of the change.[57] In *Tower Cabinet Co. Ltd. v. Ingram*[58] a partner retired. The third party had not dealt with the firm before and the only evidence of the retired partner's partnership was his name which appeared on some old notepaper used by the other partner without authority. The court held that the retired partner was not "apparently" a partner, in these circumstances. It must be "apparent," therefore, because of some act done by the partner himself (*e.g.* trading as a partner, or allowing the notepaper to be used). Notification to existing creditors may be done individually, and by additionally placing an advertisement in the *London Gazette*. The latter alone is sufficient for new creditors of the firm, even if the partner's name is by his authority used as part of the firm's name.[59] Provided that proper notification has been given, this is not a holding out either by him or the firm that he is a partner. But if the partner's name is not removed from the firm's stationery, this is a holding out by the firm which confers ostensible authority on the retired partner to bind the firm (though it will not impose liability upon him unless he knew of the fact, and did not object).

Retirement of a partner dissolves the firm, unless otherwise agreed. The retired partner is liable for old debts, but no new ones, and as with a dead partner the account is ruled off, etc. The remaining partners have authority to bind the partnership for winding-up purposes.

16.14

---

[53] See especially ss.14, 17(2), and s.36 of the 1890 Act.
[54] s.17(2). See *Court* v. *Berlin* [1897] 2 Q.B. 396.
[55] See new partners, below, and s.17(2).
[56] s.36 of the 1890 Act.
[57] s.36(1).
[58] [1949] 2 K.B. 397. The partner did not "knowingly" allow himself to be represented as a partner.
[59] *Re Fraser, ex p. Central Bank of London* [1892] 2 Q.B. 633; *Newsome* v. *Coles* (1811) 2 Camp. 617.

H. New partners

16.15   New partners are not liable for anything done before they become partners, unless a "novation" occurs, by which the firm's creditors agree to accept the promise of the new partner to assume liability in consideration for discharging a retiring partner, or for some other consideration. A new mandate should be taken when the bank learns of a new partner. This is done so as to bind that partner, and in case there is to be any change in signatories. In the latter event or with a joint account mandate, all partners must sign the new mandate, though this is unnecessary if the new partner is not to be a signatory, and signs a new mandate in the name of the firm.

The firm is dissolved unless otherwise agreed, and if it is dissolved the old account is stopped in the normal way, and a new mandate taken from all partners.

I. Partnership property

16.16   The partners are joint owners of all property brought into or acquired by the firm, except that on the death of a partner his interest passes to his personal representative.[60] Partnership property is that bought for the firm's business or on its account, and according to section 21 of the 1890 Act, where partnership money is used for the purpose the property purchased is deemed to be partnership property unless a contrary intention appears.[61] Occasionally, there may be difficulty in distinguishing partnership from personal property of individual partners,[62] and it is wise for partners to retain written memoranda explaining their intentions.

There are a number of occasions on which it may be important to consider whether property belongs to the individual or the firm: first, on a dissolution of the partnership the property has to be distributed,[62a] and the asset and any increase in the value of the asset, belongs to the owner.[63] The same applies to the proceeds of sale if at any time the property is sold. If on the death or bankruptcy of a partner, creditors of the firm or personal creditors of a partner find it necessary to proceed against the assets of the firm or partner, the rule (circumvented by joint and several liability) is that partnership creditors may proceed first against partnership property and personal creditors may proceed first against personal property. Again, partnership land is treated not as real property, but as personality.[64] A disposition by will of "My personal property" would include a share in partnership land. Various statutes may also refer to "personal" property.

Partners may assign their share in the assets of the firm (or their right to profits) to an outsider or another partner. The assignee takes no other rights.[65] This enables a partner to mortgage his share of the partnership assets. This is rarely done by way of security for bank advances to partners personally, (though mortgages as security for advances to the firm itself are common).

16.17   Unless otherwise agreed, a partner is not entitled to a share of the partnership assets (its "capital") while the business continues. The assets are avail-

[60] s.20 of the 1890 Act.
[61] See *Wray* v. *Wray* [1905] 2 Ch. 349.
[62] See, *e.g. Miles* v. *Clarke* [1953] 1 All E.R. 779.
[62a] s.39.
[63] *Robinson* v. *Ashton* (1875) L.R. 20 Eq. 25.
[64] s.22.
[65] s.31 of the 1890 Act.

able for distribution (unless otherwise agreed) only on a dissolution of the partnership. Thus, if a partner owes money personally, and judgment is obtained against him, execution against the firm's assets is not available.[66] The partner's interest can, however, be charged by a charging order.[67] As stated, dissolution may occur by a change in the composition of the firm (death, retirement, new partners) which may dissolve the partnership, as may bankruptcy. This may lead to a distribution of the assets and the firm may be deprived of a significant amount of its capital. Dissolution will not occur, however, if the partners have previously agreed to the contrary, and this is an important reason for doing so. (The need for dissolution, before his share is recoverable, may lead a discontented partner to apply to the court for a dissolution, as later discussed). Because creditors of the firm have first claim against the partnership assets, and because it is often agreed that events such as death, or bankruptcy will not dissolve the partnership, a bank in considering the assets of a personal customer who is a partner rarely gives weight to the partnership assets. If, on the contrary, the customer is the partnership itself, the bank will give weight to the personal assets of the partners, for their liability is not limited to the assets of the partnership except by special agreement with the creditor, or except where the partner is a limited partner.[68]

Partnerships may give a mortgage or charge over the firm's property, book debts, etc., and partners may, of course, give a mortgage of their personal property for the firm's debts. It is, however, impossible at present[69] for a partnership or the partners to give a floating charge over their assets. A fixed charge may be taken over future book debts[70] but care must be taken that the charge is properly drawn as a fixed charge[71] for if the intended charge is floating, it will be completely ineffective.

16.18

The main rules as to entitlement to capital and profits are as follows (capital refers to the entitlement of a partner on a distribution which occurs on a dissolution of the firm):

(i) The basic rule is that unless otherwise agreed (expressly or impliedly) capital and capital gains, and profits are shared equally[72] (after payment of debts).

(ii) However, when partners enter a firm they may or may not contribute capital. It may be agreed that there is no capital "contribution," and instead some partners may contribute expertise. If not express, this generally amounts to an implied agreement displacing the basic rule, so that on dissolution capital is not shared equally, but would be shared between those who made the financial contribution. Their rights on dissolution are prima facie related to the size of that contribution, whatever it may be. Alternatively, the parties may expressly agree to unequal distribution, or to the distribution of particular amounts.

(iii) Even if there are different capital rights because of different contributions, the profits would probably be shared equally during the continuance of the partnership, because the expertise contributed would probably

---

[66] s.23(1): *Peake* v. *Carter* [1916] 1 K.B. 652.
[67] s.23(2) and the making of an order is a ground to seek dissolution: s.33(2).
[68] For priorities between partnership and personal creditors, see below, paras. 16.23 *et seq.*
[69] For technical reasons arising from the Bills of Sale Acts 1878–1891.
[70] See the *Siebe Gorman* case, discussed below, Chap. 20.
[71] See *Re Brightlife Ltd.* [1987] 2 W.L.R. 197.
[72] s.24(1) of the 1890 Act.

(impliedly, if not expressly) be accepted as equal for the purpose of profit-sharing.

(iv) As with profits, losses during the continuance of the partnership are (unless otherwise agreed) shared equally, but if profits are unequal, losses will be shared the same way.[73]

(v) Each partner is entitled to an indemnity from his other partners for expenses incurred for the business.[74]

16.19 (vi) If, on dissolution, there is insufficient to repay each partner his agreed amount of capital (i.e. there is a capital deficiency) the deficiency is divided and shared not according to capital but according to profits (it is treated as a loss, as in (iii) above), each party contributing the required amount. If, however one partner is insolvent and cannot contribute the full amount which this would require, the amount which he should, but does not contribute is divided between the remaining partners according to their rights to capital, not profits. They need not "contribute" this, but it is deducted from their shares.[75]

(vii) Similarly, if there is a capital surplus on dissolution the surplus is divided according to profits.

(viii) If the partnership was intended to last for a fixed term or purpose and a partner has paid a premium (lump sum) in order to be admitted, then if the partnership is dissolved early or before the purpose is achieved, the court may order repayment of the whole or part of the premium, unless the partner in question agreed otherwise, or dissolution occurs because of his improper behaviour.[76]

16.20 (ix) Goodwill (i.e. the "reputation" of a business, leading to customer loyalty) is regarded in law as an asset[77] (frequently the most valuable asset of a firm), which is often valued and sold separately with the other assets. Until the goodwill is sold, any partner has the right to restrain others from doing anything to reduce the value of the goodwill.[78] Thus, a partner attempting to set up another competing business with the same name may be restrained[79] (while the partnership continues, this may be regarded as an aspect of the fiduciary duties owed by one partner to another: on dissolution, it may be regarded as a proprietary right of the partners). As with other assets, the rights of a deceased partner to goodwill vest in his personal representatives. Once goodwill is sold to a purchaser, the purchaser alone has the right to represent that he is carrying on the business. The vendor may compete, but cannot canvass or solicit customers of the sold business, and it would be an infringement of goodwill to set up business in the same effective business area in the same business using the same name (even if the name of the sold business is the personal name of the vendor). If the name of the sold business includes the personal name of the vendor(s) there is a danger that by allowing their names to be used they are allowing themselves to be held out as partners. Notification ought, therefore, to be given to cus-

---

[73] s.44.

[74] s.24(2). See *Matthews* v. *Ruggles-Brice* [1911] 1 Ch. 194.

[75] This is the "rule in *Garner* v. *Murray*" [1904] 1 Ch. 57.

[76] s.40.

[77] See *Trego* v. *Hunt* [1896] A.C. 7, 24 for the definition.

[78] *Gillingham* v. *Beddow* [1900] 2 Ch. 242. In exceptional cases goodwill is deemed to belong individually to each partner so that it need not be sold on dissolution, as with a solicitor's practice: see *Arundell* v. *Bell* (1883) 52 L.J.Ch. 537. Doctors in general practice may not sell goodwill: National Health Service Act 1977, s.54.

[79] This affects the valuation of the goodwill: *Re David & Matthews* [1899] 1 Ch. 378.

tomers and an advertisement placed in the *London Gazette*, and it is frequently agreed as a term of sale that the purchaser will display on the premises and on stationery for a period a notice "under new management" and so on. If goodwill is not sold, each of the old partners may canvass the old customers and each can use the old firm's name, for these proprietary rights belong to them all.

(x) Interest is not payable on capital,[80] but if a partner advances sums over and above his capital contribution it is payable at the rate of 5 per cent. unless a different rate is agreed.[81]

J. Bankruptcy of a partner

If a partner is insolvent, but not all partners are insolvent, the position bears **16.21** many similarities to that of a dead partner. The partnership is dissolved, unless otherwise agreed. If it is dissolved, the other partners may continue the business in order to wind it up. The partner's estate is not liable for debts incurred after the bankruptcy, and an overdrawn account should be ruled off to prevent the operation of the rule in *Clayton's case*. Neither the bankrupt nor his trustee in bankruptcy may take part in management. A cheque signed by a bankrupt partner should be returned for further signature. In case of a capital deficiency occuring, that loss is shared amongst the remainder according to their capital entitlement. The assets of the partnership are available to personal creditors only if the partnership is dissolved.

A solvent partner may pay off liabilities of the firm as they arise and may, accordingly, wish to claim against the insolvent partner(s). The general rule is that the solvent partner cannot prove in competition with the firm's creditors against either the partnership assets or personal assets of the insolvent partner(s).[82] There are the following exceptions to the general rule:

(i) If there are no partnership creditors (the solvent partner has paid them **16.22** all off) or if the personal estate of the insolvent partner clearly has insufficient assets for the partnership creditors to resort to it, (they must ordinarily claim after the personal creditors)[83] then the solvent partner may prove equally with the personal creditors.[84] This is allowed because no harm can be done to any partnership creditors and the solvent partner is in fact a personal creditor.

(ii) If the solvent partner's claim arises from the fraud of the bankrupt which has not been condoned.[85]

(iii) If the bankrupt has carried on a distinct trade which has become indebted to the partnership in the ordinary course of business.

(iv) If a partner has been discharged from liability for the partnership debts (*e.g.* by lapse of time, under the Limitation Act 1980, or by obtaining his discharge in bankruptcy) and subsequently becomes a creditor of the firm, he may prove against the firm's assets.[86]

---

[80] s.24(4).
[81] s.24(3).
[82] *Nanson* v. *Gordon* (1876) 1 App.Cas. 195; *Re Blythe, ex p. Blythe* (1881) 16 Ch.D. 620.
[83] Next section, below, para. 16.23 *et seq.*
[84] *Re Slaney, ex p. Young* (1814) 2 Rose 40; *Re Sheath, ex p. Watson* (1819) 4 Madd. 477; *Re Head, ex p. Head* [1894] 1 Q.B. 638.
[85] *Bury* v. *Allen* (1844) 1 Coll. 589.
[86] *Re Atkins, ex p. Atkins* (1820) Buck 479.

K. Bankruptcy of a partnership

16.23   The partnership is not a corporate entity, but the Insolvency Act 1986 and the Insolvent Partnerships Order 1986 (I.P.O.) permits partnerships to be wound up as though they were unregistered companies (without necessarily involving the bankruptcy of the partners).[87] Winding up cannot be voluntary,[88] and a petition for winding up may be made by a creditor or by a partner, if the partnership has ceased to carry on its business or is dissolved, or is unable to pay its debts, or if it is "just and equitable" to do so.[89] The partnership may be proved unable to pay its debts,[90] but is deemed unable to pay its debts if (i) a creditor owed £750 serves a written demand on the partnership at its principal place of business (or to a partner) requiring the partnership to pay, and it does not pay within three weeks (or give the creditor security, etc., to his satisfaction),[91] or (ii) a notice of an action for a debt against a partner for a partnership debt is served and within three weeks the partnership does not make a satisfactory agreement,[92] (iii) if execution against it is unsatisfied, or (iv) if its liabilities exceed its assets.[93]

   The rules about commencement of the winding up apply as for companies,[94] so that after the presentation of the petition, any dispositions of the partnership property is void unless ratified by the court. This is further discussed elsewhere.[95] On learning of a petition, any bank account should be stopped, whether the account is that of the firm or of any partner.

16.24   The Insolvent Partnerships Order 1986 provides that the partnership property is to be applied first to the expenses of winding up the partnership, and the separate property of the partners is applied first to their separate bankruptcy expenses.[96] Similarly as to the partnership property of an insolvent partnership, and the separate property of an insolvent partner, the partnership property is applied first to the partnership debts, and any residue is divided amongst the separate estates of the partners according to their interest in the capital of the partnership (and it then becomes available for the personal creditors). Personal property of the partners is available first for the personal creditors and any residue may be applied to partnership debts.[97] All partnership debts rank equally amongst themselves. There are important exceptions to the general rule just stated:

   (i) the most important exception is that if the partnership creditor has a separate contract for the same debt with an individual partner he may claim against both the partnership and the partner for the total amount owed. This was previously stated in the relevant Act[98] and although it is not now stated, the rule appears unchanged, so long as the debt is "separate."[99] This desirable result may be achieved by taking a separate guarantee of the part-

---

[87] The I.P.O. applies Part V of the Act to partnerships. The choice is (a) to wind up the partnership alone, or (b) to bankrupt partners alone, or (c) to do both together.
[88] s.221(4).
[89] s.221(5).
[90] s.224(1)(d).
[91] s.222.
[92] s.223.
[93] s.224.
[94] s.221.
[95] Below, Chap. 28, esp. para. 28.78 *et seq.*
[96] I.P.O., Art. 9.
[97] I.P.O., Art. 10.
[98] In Sched. 2, art. 19 of the 1914 Bankruptcy Act.
[99] Within art. 10(2).

nership liabilities, or, more commonly, simply by providing for joint and several liability in the mandate.[1]

Other exceptions are as follows, and since the Insolvent Partnerships **16.25** Order 1986 does not alter "any rule of law" relating to priority[2] these are presumably still effective:

(ii) if there are no partnership assets the partnership creditors may claim equally with the personal creditors. (Hence, it may be advantageous to write off insignificant assets).[3]

(iii) A partnership creditor who was the petitioning creditor in the personal bankruptcy may claim equally with the personal creditors.[4]

(iv) If a partner has fraudulently used partnership property for his own use without the knowledge of the other partners, the firm or its receiver may claim for the value of that property as a debt, equally with personal creditors.[5]

(v) If a creditor was defrauded by any partner and the firm is liable, the creditor may choose whether to claim against the partnership or personal assets (but not both).[6]

(vi) If a partner carries on a separate business with separate capital and that business is debtor to the partnership, the partnership creditors may claim against that other business.[7] (But if two or more partners in firm A have a separate partnership (B), the creditors of B are treated as separate creditors, and cannot claim first against A).[8]

(vii) If a bank or other creditor has advanced money to a firm and as **16.26** security a partner has given his own separate property, the bank may, if it chooses, first claim against the partnership assets, and if the debt is unsatisfied it may then sell the security to obtain the balance (any surplus, in the normal way, belongs to the partner or his trustee in bankruptcy). Alternatively, the bank may simply sell the security at once, if it is valuable enough. (If the security is taken over certain partnership property, the bank may first claim against any unsecured partnership assets and then, if the debt remains unsatisfied, realise the security).

The foregoing primarily affects the position of outsiders as regards the partners. As between the firm and the individual partners, the position is generally as follows:

(i) if the firm owes the partner money and the firm is bankrupt (in which case the partner is ordinarily (but now, after the I.P.O., not necessarily) bankrupt) the partner (or his creditors) may not claim against partnership property until the partnership creditors are satisfied.

(ii) conversely, if the partner owes money to the firm, the firm may not claim against the partner until the personal creditors of the partner are paid (exceptions (iii), (iv), and (vi) above would apply).

(iii) if the firm owes money to one partner A, and A is not bankrupt but the other partners (B and C) are bankrupt, then A may claim equally with the other partnership creditors against B and C (this being allowed because

---

[1] *Re Jeffry, ex p. Honey* (1871) 7 Ch.App. 178.
[2] Art. 10(7).
[3] *Ex p. Elton* (1796) 3 Ves. 238; *Re Budgett, Cooper v. Adams* [1894] 2 Ch. 557.
[4] *Ex p. Ackerman* (1808) 14 Ves. 604.
[5] *Read* v. *Bailey* (1877) 3 App.Cas. 94.
[6] *Re Kent County Gas Light & Coke Co. Ltd.* [1913] 1 Ch. 92.
[7] *Re Petheridge, ex p. Cook* (1831) Mont. 228.
[8] I.P.O. Art. 10(9).

those other creditors may always sue A and are not disadvantaged by A's equal status with them).

L. Postponement of bank's rights

16.27 If a lender makes a loan to a person or firm on the basis that the rate of interest is to vary with the profits, and the borrower is adjudged bankrupt, the lender may not recover anything in respect of the unpaid interest until the claims of the other creditors of the borrower have been satisfied.[9] This treatment of the lender almost as if he were a partner in the enterprise applies only to the proof in insolvency: there is nothing to stop such a lender taking security and realising that security.

M. Dissolution[10]

16.28 Dissolution may occur without reference to the court, as follows: A partnership agreed to last for a fixed term,[11] or until a specific purpose is achieved, or a given event occurs, is dissolved on expiry of the term or achievement of the purpose or if the purpose becomes impossible, or the event occurs. A partnership for an indeterminate time (called a partnership of will) may be ended by notice (*i.e.* any partner can resign or retire).[12] The articles of partnership may, however, provide that the partnership may be ended or its composition changed only by "mutual agreement," in which case unilateral resignation may be impossible[13] (and, of course, the articles may say that resignation is permitted, but shall not dissolve the partnership). Retirement, death, bankruptcy, the admission of a new partner, and illegality (*e.g.* if a partner becomes an enemy alien) dissolve the partnership unless otherwise agreed. If a partner has been guilty of misrepresentation in entering the contract, the contract is voidable at the option of the other partners. If a partner is the subject of a court order charging his partnership assets with a personal debt, the other partners have the option to dissolve the partnership.

16.29 If none of these occur, s.35 of the 1890 Act allows an application to the court, which may dissolve the partnership if a partner becomes permanently incapable of carrying on (*e.g.* through ill health, or mental incapacity); if another partner (not the petitioner) is guilty of conduct (such as dishonesty) prejudicial to the firm's business; if another partner wilfully or persistently breaks the partnership agreement in such a way as to destroy the fiduciary relationship; if the business can be carried on only at a loss; or if the court considers it to be "just and equitable." The last ground may be used if there is a managerial "deadlock" where (say through hostility) the partners cannot reach agreement on important matters, or if a majority attempt to "freeze out" a partner by refusing to co-operate with him, while not agreeing to a dissolution and distribution of assets, or if the majority use their powers unfairly and oppressively. As a partnership must be based on trust and confidence, the destruction of that state of affairs will generally lead to the court ordering the dissolution of a partnership, and this is the more true the smaller the partnership is.

---

[9] s.3, specifically preserved by Art. 10(7) of the I.P.O. 1986. The same applies to a vendor of the goodwill of a business in consideration for a share of the profits.
[10] ss.32–38 of the 1890 Act.
[11] See *Abbott* v. *Abbott* [1936] 3 All E.R. 823.
[12] s.26(1).
[13] *Moss* v. *Elphick* [1910] 1 K.B. 846.

As already stated, dissolution does not affect existing liabilities, and limited trading may continue for a period for the purpose of winding-up. The partners retain authority to bind the firm so far as matters necessary for the winding-up are concerned.

If the partnership is insolvent, then winding up on a petition by a partner (as a contributory) is possible.[14]

---

[14] Above, para. 16.23.

17. Company Customers[1]

A. Introduction

17.01 We make no attempt to give an exhaustive account of company law, but only of those aspects which are of most importance to the traditional business of banking. Our assumption is that the proposals put forward by Dr. Prentice will,[2] in one form or another, become law, and for that reason, we assume the abolition of the *ultra vires* rule.

17.02 When companies are registered, they must have a registered office, where certain documents or registers may be required to be kept, or where writs may be served. The place of registered office determines the nationality of the company, and the law of the place of its incorporation determines the company's capacity to hold property, incur liabilities, enter contracts, and so on. Like a natural person, the company may reside elsewhere. Generally, the company is resident wherever its main centre of control or management is, and this may affect tax liability.

All companies must be registered with a "registered name." They may not use names too similar to those of already registered companies, and if they do, the registrar of companies will not register them. They may not use certain names, such as those suggesting a relationship with government. Restrictions on the use of words such as "bank" or "banking" were imposed by the Banking Act 1979 but are modified by the Banking Act 1987. Public companies must have as part of their name the words "public limited company" or the abbreviation "p.l.c.," and private limited companies must have the word "Limited" or the abbreviation "Ltd."[3] A business name such as "Smith & Smith" with or without an "& Co." may, therefore, belong either to an unlimited liability company, or to a partnership (which has unlimited liability). It is perfectly permissible for a company to trade under a name other than that by which it was registered, but the registered name and an address for service of writs must be stated legibly on all business letters, written orders for goods or services to be supplied to the business, invoices and receipts issued in the course of the business and written demands for payment of business debts. The registered name and an address for service must also be displayed in a prominent position in any premises where the business is carried on, so that customers may easily read it.[4] The company name must also appear on the outside of every office or place where its business is carried on, in legible letters, subject to fine.[5] If the name is not mentioned on business letters, notices, bills of exchange, promissory notes, endorsements, cheques and orders for money or goods purporting to be signed by the company, and in all its bills of parcels, invoices, receipts and letters of credit, it and its officers may be fined.[6] The company's place or registration and registered number and address of registered office must be shown on all business letters and order

---

[1] See Pennington's *Company Law*, (5th ed.), Gower's *Principles of Modern Company Law*, Northey & Leigh's *Introduction to Company Law*, (3rd ed.)
[2] Below, para. 17.08.
[3] For Welsh companies, Welsh equivalents are provided.
[4] Business Names Act 1985. The penalty is a fine.
[5] s.348, C.A. 1985.
[6] s.349, C.A. 1985.

forms of the company.[7] If any officer signs or authorises signature on behalf of the company any bill of exchange or promissory note or endorsement or cheque or order for money or goods, and the company's registered name[8] does not appear, the officer may be liable to the holder or other party unless the company performs its obligations.[9] The omission of "Ltd."[10] or "&" from a company's name[11] is enough to establish liability. The use of "Co." instead of "Company" is acceptable.[12] If, however, a bill is drawn on a company and the drawer writes the wrong name, and the bill is accepted by a director for the company, the drawer whose fault it was may not sue the director, though any other holder might do so.[13] The same would apply to other kinds of orders or contracts. If a bank incorrectly prints the incorrect name on a company's cheque form, the signatories may be liable to the holder, but the bank may be liable to compensate the signatories.[14]

B. Banks and companies

Although our assumption is that the law will soon be changed, company **17.03** law has previously been bedevilled by the concept of *"ultra vires."* This referred to legal limitations on the power of the company to perform certain acts, so that if done, these acts could produce no legal consequences (they were "void"). When a company was formed it was required to register two documents with the registrar of companies: the Memorandum of Association, and the Articles of Association.[15] These were both public documents, in the sense that registration of them was deemed to give notice of their contents to the public. The Memorandum deals with the basic form and structure of the company: whether it is public or private, limited or unlimited, and so on. In particular the Memorandum was required to state the company's "objects," which is to say, its field of endeavour, or the kind of business which the company was to conduct (was it a bank, or a farming business, or an accommodation agency, and so on). The Memorandum also stated the company's powers: whether it could borrow or give security, and so on. The source of all the company's powers was the Memorandum, and if not express, some powers might be implied if reasonably incidental to the carrying out of the objects. Even if there was a power (say, to borrow) there might be a restriction on the power (say, to borrow not more than a given sum). If not expressly or impliedly allowed by the Memorandum, the company had no power to act, and any unauthorised act was *ultra vires*, and void. Unlike a natural person, then, the company could do only what its

---

[7] s.351, C.A. 1985.
[8] Not a trading name, even when those could be registered under the Registration of Business Names Act, 1916, now abolished: *Maxform SpA.* v. *B. Mariani & Goodville Ltd.* [1979] 2 Lloyds Rep.385.
[9] s.349(4), C.A. 1985.
[10] *British Airways Board* v. *Parish* [1979] 2 Lloyds Rep. 361.
[11] *Hendon* v. *Adelman* (1973) 117 Sol.Jo. 631.
[12] *Banque de L'Indochine et de Suez S.A.* v. *Euroseas Group Finance Co. Ltd.* [1981] 3 All E.R. 198.
[13] *Durham Fancy Goods Ltd.* v. *Michael Jackson (Fancy Goods) Ltd.* [1968] 2 All E.R. 987, [1968] 2 Q.B. 839.
[14] *Hendon* v. *Adelman* (1973) 117 Sol.Jo. 631: the name was "L. & R. Agencies Ltd." which the bank printed as "L.R. Agencies Ltd."
[15] This may continue to be the case, but the Memorandum may not require a statement of the company's objects: this may, perhaps, be filed annually with the company's accounts.

Memorandum authorised it to do (though the Memorandum might be changed to allow for new objects).[16]

17.04   This *ultra vires* rule was intended to protect creditors, who would know in their dealings with the company that their money was at risk only in the fields of endeavour specified in the Memorandum. In practice, however, it was the creditor who suffered. If, for example, a creditor supplied goods to a company which was acting *ultra vires*, the creditor could not sue for the price. If a bank advanced money to a company with no power to borrow, the bank might not be able to recover the money. In order to avoid the problem, it became the practice for companies to be formed with a Memorandum drawn in the widest possible form, stating long lists of objects and powers, and in addition, often attempting to give the directors the power to decide what the objects of the company might be. These devices, and others, were of doubtful effect.

17.05   In addition to the problem of the Memorandum, which governed what the company itself might do, the Articles of the company govern other matters, such as the powers of the directors (as agents of the company), whether any matters were reserved to the general meeting of shareholders, the types of shares and the rights attaching to them, and what the administrative rules of the company were. Companies may adopt the articles provided in Table A of the Companies Act 1985. The articles may be altered by special resolution.[17] As with the Memorandum, all persons were deemed to know of the registered Articles, so that if any matter was prohibited by them, any person dealing with an agent of the company would be deemed to know that that agent had no power to act in the manner proposed, and the company would not be bound. Since this is a matter of the authority of the company's agents, ratification[18] was possible (though not with true *ultra vires*, where the company itself has no power to act, for a principal who has no power to act cannot authorise his agent to do those acts).[19] It might be that the directors were in breach of the articles in the sense that they used powers for a purpose for which the powers were not given. If that wrongful purpose was known to the person dealing with the company, the directors would not have even ostensible authority, and clearly, they have no actual authority.[20] But if the directors had some secret wrongful purpose, unknown to the other party, the company would be bound in the normal way by the ostensible authority of the directors.

17.06   The rule that ostensible authority of an agent might be removed by "deemed" knowledge of prohibitions in the Articles was mitigated by a rule known as the "rule in *Turquand's* case"[21] or as the "indoor management rule." This related to procedural matters, and was to the effect that where something might be done by the directors if certain procedures were followed, the outsider was not bound to inquire to determine whether those procedures had been followed. (In *Turquand* itself the directors could issue bonds if authorised by a resolution of a general meeting of the company.

---

[16] See s.4–6. The change could, in some circumstances, be challenged by dissenters in the company.

[17] s.9, C.A. 1985.

[18] See above for ratification, para. 15.07.

[19] See Chap. 15 on agency.

[20] *Rolled Steel Products (Holdings) Ltd.* v. *B.S.C.* [1984] B.C.L.C. 466, [1986] Ch. 246.

[21] *Royal British Bank* v. *Turquand* (1856) 6 E. & B. 327; See *Dey* v. *Pullinger* [1921] 1 K.B. 77, for an example of its application.

This was not done, but the outsider was not affected). He could not enforce any transaction if he knew that they had not been followed, but otherwise he could rely on the ostensible authority of those acting. This rule applied only to outsiders, and not to members of the company. This rule is a special development of the rules of ostensible authority,[22] inasmuch as (unusually) the agent can himself hold out his authority to an outsider on the ground that the procedures in question have been followed.[23] As with all cases of ostensible authority, this rule did not apply if the third party knows facts which could reveal to a reasonable person in his position that the correct procedures have not been followed. If, for example, a particular quorum of the Board was required, and the bank knew that one of the directors (without whom there was no quorum) had voted on the matter when he had some interest which, under the Articles, prevented him from voting, then the bank had constructive notice of the defect in the authority of the Board (which had failed to authorise itself by following the proper procedures).[24] The rule did not apply to matters on the face of them inconsistent with the articles,[25] nor to insiders, such as directors or shareholders of the company.[26]

In addition to the protection of *Turquand's* case, the Articles themselves **17.07**
might provide that a breach of their provisions should not affect any third party dealing with the company in good faith.

The rules as to the Memorandum and Articles were widely criticised, and in 1972, Parliament responded to a directive of the European Community, requiring the reform of the *ultra vires* rule, with a curiously limited provision. This measure, in section 9(1) of the European Communities Act 1972, and subsequently in section 35 of the Companies Act 1985, did not abolish the rule. It provided that in favour of a person dealing in good faith with the company (though not in favour of the company) a transaction decided upon by the directors should be deemed to be within the powers of the company, and of the directors. Much of this was obscure: what was a "transaction"; could the directors delegate; what amounted to a "decision" of the directors; what was "good faith" (if, for example, a bank had once seen the Memorandum and Articles, could it rely on the provision)?[27] As a result of mounting criticism, proposals drafted by Dr. Dan Prentice were published in 1986 concerning the reform of the *ultra vires* rule. These proposals (which are to be warmly welcomed) are to the following effect:

C. The Prentice proposals

The doctrine of *ultra vires* assisted no-one, and should be abolished, so that **17.08**
with specific prohibitions, a company will be able to do any act whatsoever. No person will have constructive notice of the contents of the Memorandum or Articles of Association. An individual director (not only the managing director) will have an enhanced ostensible authority to bind the company. Only actual notice and "understanding" of the director's lack of

---

[22] Discussed above, para. 15.03.
[23] Contrast *Armagas Ltd.* v. *Mundogas S.A., The Ocean Frost* [1986] 2 All E.R. 385, [1986] A.C. 717 (H.L.).
[24] See *Victors Ltd.* v. *Lingard* [1927] 1 Ch. 323.
[25] *Howard* v. *Patent Ivory Manufacturing Co.* (1888) 38 Ch.D. 156.
[26] *Morris* v. *Kanssen* [1946] A.C. 459.
[27] On s.35, see *International Sales and Agencies Ltd.* v. *Marcus* [1982] 3 All E.R. 551; *TCB Ltd.* v. *Gray* [1986] Ch. 621.

authority would give the company any defence. An exception would exist in relation to officers or directors of the company, who may be affected by constructive notice: *i.e.* the type of knowledge which may reasonably be expected of a person carrying out the functions of that director or officer. If a third party has notice the company may still ratify, but if the notice is that the transaction falls outside the company's objects, the ratification is to be by special resolution. Companies will not be required to register an objects clause, but must instead file an annual activities and business statement (probably as part of the annual return), though to comply with the E.E.C.'s Second Directive on Company Law this will be deemed (at least for public companies) to be part of the Memorandum.

By way of summary, therefore, under the old law there were three general questions for any lender dealing with a company: first, did the company itself have the power to act, in the sense that what is done is expressly or impliedly permitted by the Memorandum, being in pursuit of the company's objects. If not, ratification was impossible[28] but section 35 of the Companies Act 1985 was relevant and might protect a party dealing with the company. Secondly, if a transaction is entered with the authority of the Board of Directors, did the Board have authority to enter the transaction? It would have ostensible authority at least, unless prohibited by the Articles. If prohibited, a third party might be protected still by ostensible authority, if the directors acted with a secret wrongful purpose. If the fault was procedural, *Turquand's* rule might give the directors ostensible authority, on their own holding out. In any case, section 35 of the Companies Act 1985 might protect the other party, and the company could ratify the transaction. The third question was whether the individual(s) who purported to arrange the transaction had the authority to do so, as agents of the company. They might have actual, or ostensible authority. Section 35 of the Companies Act 1985 was irrelevant to this question, but a lack of authority might be ratified by others in the company who had authority.

17.09   Under the new proposals, however, (if they become law) it seems that only the last two questions remain. The company may do all that a natural person might do, with the statutory exceptions.[29] Even where an absolute (as against procedural) prohibition is actually known to the third party, the company may still ratify, and in "procedural" cases, *Turquand's* rule may protect the third party.

It will become unnecessary, therefore, for banks to inspect the Memorandum of any company to determine if the company may borrow money and give security. This may be presumed. It has been a general practice of banks to take copies of the Memorandum and Articles of corporate customers. This would seem no longer to be necessary. It may be that having seen the Articles, the bank would be held to have actual notice of its contents, and that might be positively disadvantageous in dealings with the Board of directors. The bank may safely deal with an individual director, or may act on a resolution of the Board of Directors, unless the bank has actual notice of a prohibition in the Articles. The bank is not required to make any judgment as to whether a transaction is for the company's objects, or for its benefit[30] and it would seem that directors (or the Board of directors) do not

---

[28] Above, para. 17.05.

[29] It may not marry, hold public office, etc.

[30] Though this might become an issue in case of liquidation, for deciding such matters as transactions at an undervalue or preferences.

exceed their ostensible authority by agreeing to enter a transaction which appears to the other contracting party not to be for the benefit of the company.

Previously, an individual might actually be appointed as managing direc- **17.10** tor, and would then have all the authority which a managing director usually has, to bind the company. It would be safe to advance money to the company on his agreement, and to take securities from the company on that authority, and the bank was unaffected by prohibitions in the Articles of which it does not have actual notice. An individual might be held out by the company or its Board of directors as managing director, or as otherwise having authority, and the company would then be bound by his ostensible authority.[31] It may be observed here that only the managing director (whatever he is called) has implied actual authority to borrow or give security. That is not an authority given to an ordinary director. Nor is it a power given to the company Secretary, who has power to enter into contracts of an administrative kind (hiring cars for staff, or purchasing stationery, or hiring staff)[32] but no power to hold out an ordinary director as having authority,[33] or to borrow money[34] or to start litigation on the company's behalf.[35] Similarly, the company accountant has very few implied powers, but he may acknowledge debts on behalf of the company so as to bind the company to pay them (*i.e.* his acknowledgement is proof of the existence of the debt).[36] Under the new regime, all directors will have ostensible authority to bind the company, but the position of other officers (such as the Secretary) remains unaltered.

D. When the company is not bound

The company is not bound if those who act for it have no actual (express or **17.11** implied) or ostensible authority, or if there is no ratification. Dicta in *Ruben v. Great Fingall Consolidated*[37] suggest that even where there is ostensible authority to confirm a transaction, the company is not bound by a forged document, but this is contrary to general principles, and the true explanation of the case appears to be that the agent there (the Secretary, who forged the directors signatures to a security for a loan to him, personally, and applied the company seal without authority) was not held out in any way as having authority to confirm the transaction.

E. Liability of agents of the company

The general rule, as with all agents, is that the agent is not bound by the **17.12** contract. To this rule there are a number of exceptions, several of which have been considered (concerning express agreements, non-existing or incapable principals, the form of signatures on deeds and other contracts, the making of false statements, the warranty of authority, the undisclosed principal, and liability in conversion).[38] In addition to those the following apply:

[31] See above, para. 15.03.
[32] *Panorama Developments (Guildford) Ltd. v. Fidelis Furnishing Fabrics Ltd.* [1971] 2 Q.B. 711.
[33] *Houghton & Co. v. Nothard, Lowe & Wills Ltd.* [1927] 1 K.B. 246.
[34] *Re Cleadon Trust Ltd.* [1939] Ch. 286.
[35] *Daimler Co. Ltd. v. Continental Tyre & Rubber Co. (G.B.) Ltd.* [1916] 2 A.C. 307.
[36] *Jones v. Bellgrove Properties* [1949] 2 K.B. 700.
[37] [1906] A.C. 439.
[38] Above, para. 15.24 *et seq.*

(i) it is common for a director separately to guarantee the company's liability, and he is then liable on this separate contract;

(ii) if he signs a bill or cheque or order for money or goods, etc., and the name of the company does not appear on the document, he will be liable if the company does not pay.[39]

In addition, there are a number of special insolvency provisions, some of which may affect directors as directors, rather than as agents.

(i) The company's memorandum may provide that the liability of the directors, or of the managing director, shall be unlimited.[40] If it does, section 75 of the Insolvency Act 1986 provides that in addition to their liability (if any) to contribute as an ordinary member, the directors shall be liable to contribute as if members of an unlimited liability company, but not if they ceased to be directors more than a year before winding up, or for liabilities incurred after they cease to be members, or where the court thinks it unnecessary to require a contribution.

(ii) The directors (or others) may be civilly and criminally liable for fraudulent trading or wrongful trading.[41]

17.13 (iii) Certain disqualified persons acting as directors or in company management may be personally liable.[42]

(iv) Liability may be imposed under section 212 of the Insolvency Act 1986, for misfeasance and breach of fiduciary duty.[43]

(v) If a public company carries on business without the certificate from the registrar of companies and allots shares, and anyone thereby suffers loss, the directors are jointly and severally liable to that person.[44]

(vi) If a company's members falls below two and the company carries on business for more than six months thereafter the remaining member is jointly and severally liable with the company for its debts thereafter.[45]

(vii) If the directors commit independent torts (such as negligent or fraudulent misrepresentation) they may be liable personally (just as they may be liable on a warranty of authority).

(viii) Under section 76 of the Insolvency Act 1986[46] where a company is being wound up and the company has in the previous year expended capital to redeem or purchase its own shares and has insufficient assets now to pay its debts and liabilities and the cost of winding up, the person from whom the shares were redeemed or purchased may be liable to contribute up to the amount of the payment he received, and the directors are jointly and severally liable with him. Those so made liable may apply to the court for an order directing others to contribute, if the court thinks that just and equitable.

F. Other special statutory rules

17.14 A variety of rules affecting companies may impinge upon banks. These are too numerous to consider here, and we deal only with some of the most important rules (unaffected by the Prentice proposals).

[39] Above, para. 17.01.
[40] ss.306–307, C.A. 1985.
[41] Below, paras. 28.40 et seq.
[42] Below, para. 28.43.
[43] Below, para. 28.44.
[44] s.117(8), C.A. 1985, below para. 28.38.
[45] s.24, C.A. 1985, below para. 28.39.
[46] Formerly s.504 of the Companies Act 1985.

1. FINANCIAL ASSISTANCE FOR SHARE PURCHASES

The Companies Act 1985 prohibits[47] public companies or their subsidiaries **17.15** from directly or indirectly giving financial assistance (by any means which reduces the company's net assets) to anyone to help purchase shares in the company, or to discharge his liability for purchases already made. Private companies may do so, if they give the assistance out of distributable profits (but not if they are part of a group with a public company in the chain of ownership above the private company in question). The public company may give assistance if it is given in good faith in the best interests of the company, and if it is "an incidental part of some larger purpose of the company," and not merely in order to enable the purchase of shares. To avoid doubt a number of transactions are expressly declared[48] to be valid, such as ordinary dividend payments, bonus share allotments, authorised redemptions or purchases of shares by the company[49] reductions of capital confirmed by the court under section 137, certain insolvency transactions,[50] the lending of money as part of the company's ordinary business, the provision of money to employees as part of an employees' share scheme to enable them to buy fully paid shares, and loans to employees other than directors by way of a trust under which they hold the shares beneficially. A public company may do the last three of these only if its net assets are not thereby reduced, or if the assistance is given out of distributable profits. If these rules are broken, it is a criminal offence and the assistance is "unlawful."

It is possible that the bank may become involved if the funds provided are either held by the bank or advanced by the bank by way of loan or overdraft. The difficulty in paying out the company's funds arises because of the rules relating to constructive trust. The effect of those rules[50a] is that as the directors of the company are acting in breach of fiduciary duty in ordering the payments, the bank may become liable to compensate the company if the bank knows (and perhaps, sometimes, if it ought to know) of the purpose of the payment. If the bank knowingly makes an advance to the company for the purpose, that advance may be irrecoverable by the bank from the company, being made with knowledge of an unlawful purpose.

2. GUARANTEES AND LOANS GIVEN TO OR FOR DIRECTORS

Frequently a bank's customer will be the director of a company (and the **17.16** director may itself be another company) or a person connected with a director. If the bank proposes to make an advance to the director, it may call for a guarantee to be given by some other person, and the director may suggest the name of his company. Alternatively, the bank may hold company funds, which a company proposes to lend to the director. Transactions such as these are affected by rules in the Companies Act 1985, (ss.330–347) restricting loans and guarantees given by the company to or for the directors of that company. The effect of the rules may be that the guarantee is void, and the bank may be liable as constructive trustee if it knowingly pays out company money for the purpose of the loan.

Transactions are prohibited in relation to directors and some also extend

---

[47] In ss.151–158.
[48] In s.153.
[49] Under s.s. 159–181, C.A. 1985.
[50] Under ss.425, 582, 601.
[50a] Above, Chap. 10.

to "connected persons."[51] The latter are (a) directors' families; (b) companies with which the director is associated (if he controls over 1/5 of the equity or voting power); (c) the trustee of a trust whose beneficiaries include the director or members of classes (a) or (b) above; (d) a partner of the director or of any person in classes (a) or (b) or (c) above. "Director" includes a shadow director,[52] which means a person in accordance with whose directions the board is accustomed to act.

Subject to exceptions later mentioned, some transactions are prohibited for all companies, and more for "relevant companies."

17.17   No company may (a) make a loan to a director, or to a director of a holding company, (b) give a guarantee, indemnity or security for a loan made by anyone to such a director, (c) have assigned to it any rights or liabilities which contravene (a) or (b) above or the rules in relation to relevant companies, below, or (d) take part in "back to back" deals (*e.g.* where Company A lends to Company B's directors and Company B lends to Company A's directors; or where Company A lends to the directors of Company B on favourable terms if Company B puts business with Company A; or any arrangement where Company A benefits from Company B or its holding or subsidiary company in return for the loan to the directors of Company B).

"Relevant companies" are public companies or a company which is part of a group any member of which is a public company. In addition to the foregoing prohibitions, no relevant company may (a) make a loan or quasi-loan to a director, or to a director of a holding company, (b) make a loan or quasi-loan to a connected person of such a director, (c) give a guarantee, indemnity, or security for a loan or quasi-loan to a director or connected person, (d) enter a credit transaction[53] as creditor for a director or connected person, (e) give a guarantee, etc., for a credit transaction made by a third party for a director or connected person. A "quasi-loan" is a transaction which is in substance a loan, although it may not at first resemble one.[54] That is to say, it occurs where A agrees to pay (or pays) a sum to B for C, or where A agrees to reimburse (or reimburses) B for C, and where C agrees to (or does) reimburse A. An example would be the provision by the company to a director of a company credit card, which the director uses to buy goods, later reimbursing the company.

17.18   If there is a breach of these rules, the transaction is voidable by the lending company, but not by the other party. The lending company loses its rights if restitution of money or other assets is impossible or the company has been indemnified for its losses, or a third party who has acquired rights bona fide and for value would be affected. If, say, a cheque is made payable to a director, the bank may not know that the purpose is by way of loan and unlawful, and the avoiding of the transaction between company and director would not be allowed to affect the bank's debiting of the company account and paying of the director. (In addition, directors and connected persons may be liable to account to the company for gains or to indemnify it for losses, and there may be criminal offences committed). If, therefore, Company A gives to a bank a guarantee for an advance by the bank to Company

---

[51] See s.346.
[52] s.330(5).
[53] For definition see s.331(7).
[54] See s.331(3).

B, where B is a director of A,[55] the guarantee is voidable by A, and the taking of it would be a criminal offence by the bank.

There are important exceptions to the provisions mentioned, and these include the following: **17.19**

(i) loans or quasi loans or guarantees, etc., by a relevant company to another member of its group of companies are not bad merely because a director of one group member is "associated" with another member. "Association" may mean that the director is a connected person. That alone, therefore, does not prevent inter-group lending. Thus, if X is a director of Company A and controls 2/5 of the equity shares of Company B, X is "connected" to B, and but for this exception, A could not lend to B (a person connected with a director of A), but the exception permits it. If, however, Company A is a director of Company B which "holds" Company C, then C cannot lend to A, because A is a director, and not merely "associated."[56]

(ii) quasi-loans by a relevant company to a director or to the director of a holding company are permitted if less than £1000 and to be repaid in two months or less.

(iii) Credit transactions and guarantees, etc., by relevant companies for a director or connected person are permitted if they do not exceed in the aggregate £5000.

(iv) All transactions by all companies in favour of holding companies are valid. Thus, if Company A is a director of Company B and holds Company B, loans by B to A are allowed, and B may guarantee loans by C to A.

(v) Credit transactions by relevant companies in the course of their ordinary business and on a normal commercial basis are permitted.

(vi) Funds or credit, etc., supplied to meet expenses incurred by the director in performing his duties are permitted, with a maximum (for relevant companies) of £10,000. Either the approval of a general meeting is needed, or the loan is to be on terms that it is repayable within six months if approval is not given by the next annual general meeting.

(vii) Loans, etc., by moneylending companies in the ordinary course of business, on normal commercial terms, up to £50,000 in aggregate (for each director) are permitted. If made for the purpose of a home purchase by the director they may be on more favourable terms than ordinary. The monetary limit mentioned does not apply to a recognised bank.

(viii) Loans to the director, or the director of a holding company not exceeding £2500 are permitted.

---

[55] B not being a holding company of A, as later mentioned.
[56] The fourth exception below, permits C to lend to B.

Section Three
Negotiable Instruments
Anu Arora

18. Negotiable Instruments

PART A: NEGOTIABLE INSTRUMENTS

Negotiable instruments are a class of documents used in the commercial world and whilst the functions of these documents may vary, they are invariably connected with financial obligations. Since in many transactions negotiable instruments take the place of cash, they have, in return, been given many of the characteristics of cash; *i.e.* (i) they are easily transferable and (ii) the recipient has confidence that he is receiving or will receive full value. As with cash, a person giving value for a negotiable instrument and receiving it in good faith gets a good title to the instrument, even though the transferor's title is defective, *e.g.* it has been stolen or obtained by fraud. The transferee, therefore, gets an unfettered right to sue on the promise contained in it. A negotiable instrument, however, is not legal tender. **18.01**

Terminology and purposes served by negotiable instruments

Where an original debtor (A) owes money to another (B) but does not wish to pay cash, he may himself instruct a third party (C), who is his debtor, to make payment to B of the whole or part of the amount C owes to A. A may send a bill of exchange to B entitling B to call upon C to pay to B the whole or part of the sum originally owed by C to A. When C pays B, he discharges his debt to A to the extent of the payment made to B. **18.02**

The person who drew up the document ordering C to pay B is known as "the drawer" of the bill; B to whom the payment is to be made, is known as "the payee"; and C to whom the instruction is given to make the payment to B, is known as "the drawee." C will usually be the banker with whom A has an account in credit and in that case the bill of exchange may take the form of a cheque.

The person holding a bill of exchange or cheque may wish to use it to make a payment to some other person. Thus, B may wish to use the bill or cheque to make a payment to X, who then may want to use it to make a payment to Y. The steps taken to achieve this will depend on the instruments given by A to C. If A has not named B in the document but directed C to pay whoever is "the bearer" of the document, then he has created a "bearer instrument" and mere delivery of it by B to X with the intent to pass ownership will be enough to give X a valid title. In turn X could similarly pass title to the instrument to Y merely by delivering it to him.

If, however, A's order to C reads "pay B or order" or simply "pay B," A has created an order instrument, and if B wishes to transfer it to X he must "indorse" the instrument by writing his signature on the back. If B merely writes his signature, this is known as an "indorsement in blank" and converts the instrument into a bearer instrument. Then, X can pass title to the instrument to Y by mere delivery with intent to transfer ownership. If B, in addition to his signature on the back of the instrument, directs that payment shall be made to "X or order" or "to X," the indorsement is a "special indorsement" and if X in turn wishes to transfer the instrument to Y he must himself indorse it, either specially or in blank. **18.03**

The document sent out by A may not merely direct C as to whom payment is to be made, but also state when payment is to be made. Thus, C may be ordered to pay the bearer (or B or order) "on sight or demand" (*i.e.* as soon as the document is produced to him). These documents are called "sight" or "demand" bills of exchange. A cheque (by definition) must always be payable on demand. Alternatively, A may order C to pay the amount only on a stated date or after the lapse of a specified time (*e.g.* 90 days from the date when A issued the bill to B, or 90 days after sight (*i.e.* after B presents the bill to C for his signature). In the case of these time bills, B may require an assurance that the amount represented by the document will be paid and may look for such an assurance some time before the date on which C is required to pay. In that case B will seek to obtain C's acceptance; this is an acknowledgement by C that he is liable to pay when the document matures (namely, when the time for payment arrives).

18.04　　When a negotiable instrument is transferred to a person who obtains the full benefits of negotiability, the instrument is said to be "negotiated." When, however, the instrument is transferred in circumstances in which the transferee merely obtains whatever title his transferor has, or a defective title, *e.g.* where a cheque is marked "not negotiable," the instrument is said to be transferred. The terms have sometimes been confused and not always used in their proper form. When the Bills of Exchange Act 1882, however, refers to the word "transfer" to mean transfer by "delivery", *i.e.* transfer of possession, or "delivery" and "indorsement," the instrument is said to be negotiated, so that here the word means "transferred".

When the Act refers to a situation where the recipient of the instrument gets the full benefit of negotiability, the document is said to be negotiated to a "holder in due course." A "holder in due course" takes the "bill free from any defect of title of prior parties, as well as from mere personal defences available to prior parties among themselves and may enforce payment against all parties liable on the bill."[1]

Section 81 of the Bills of Exchange Act 1882, provides that "where a person takes a crossed cheque which bears the words not negotiable he should not have and shall not be capable of giving a better title to the cheque than that which the person from whom he took it had." The word negotiable in this context is being used as equivalent to "negotiable to a holder in due course." The cheque is still transferrable.

18.05　　The word "issue" under the Act means "the first delivery of a bill or note, complete in form to a person who takes it as a holder, *e.g.* where the drawer of a cheque "delivers" it to the payee. "Delivery" is defined in the Act as the "transfer of possession, actual or constructive from one person to another." The word "holder" is defined as "the payee or indorsee of a bill or note who is in possession of it, or the bearer."[2]

A bank on which a customer draws a cheque or other instrument, and which pays in accordance with the mandate is the "paying bank." When a customer delivers a cheque or other instrument to his bank to obtain the sum of money payable under that instrument, the bank acting for the customer is known as the "collecting bank."

Where payment is refused on a bill of exchange or cheque the instrument is said to be "dishonoured." In the case of a bill of exchange the "dishonour" may be by non-acceptance or by non-payment.

---

[1] s.38.
[2] s.2.

Definition and conditions for incurring liability

DEFINITION

A bill of exchange is defined under the Bills of Exchange Act 1882,[3] as:

18.06

> "an unconditional order in writing, addressed by one person to another, signed by the person giving it, requiring the person to whom it is addressed to pay on demand or at a fixed or determinable future time a sum certain in money to or to the order of a specified person, or to bearer."

The significance of this section is reinforced by section 3(2) of the Act which provides:

> "An instrument which does not comply with these conditions, or which orders any act to be done in addition to the payment of money, is not a bill of exchange."

An instrument which is invalid as a negotiable instrument because of some formal defect in its issue is not necessarily devoid of all legal effect. A conditional instrument may be valid and lawful evidence of the debt or the legal rights it invokes. Moreover, it may be that the rights embodied in that instrument are assignable although the transferee will not enjoy all the rights granted on the negotiation of a negotiable instrument.

It is essential to examine the definition contained in section 3(1) of the Act, not merely for its own sake, but because the succeeding provisions of the Act in effect provide a commentary on it.

UNCONDITIONAL ORDER

A bill according to the provisions of the Bills of Exchange Act is an "unconditional order," with the result that instruments which require as a condition of payment the signing of a receipt by the payee on the front or reverse of the document are not negotiable instruments. In *Bavins and Sims* v. *London and South Western Bank*[4] the plaintiff received an instrument in the form of a cheque which read: "Pay to . . . provided the receipt form at the foot is duly signed and dated."

18.07

The instrument was stolen from the plaintiff, and an indorsement forged on it and the receipt form signed. In an action by the plaintiff against the collecting bank it was held that the instrument was not a cheque within the definition of the Bills of Exchange Act, because it was not an unconditional order.

Where, however, the condition or requirement embodied in the cheque is not to be fulfilled by the drawee bank, but is simply a direction addressed to the payee, the order to the bank to make payment is unconditional for the purposes of the Act. In *Nathan* v. *Ogden*[5] a cheque drawn in the ordinary form contained a clause requiring a receipt on the back of the cheque to be signed by the payee. One of the questions before the court was whether the document was in law a cheque. The court held that the condition requiring the payee's signature on the receipt was addressed to the payee alone, and

---

[3] s.3(1).
[4] [1900] 1 Q.B. 270.
[5] [1905] 94 L.T. 126.

not to the bank; consequently the instrument was in law a cheque. Similarly, in *Thairlwall* v. *The Great Northern Railway Company*[6] a dividend warrant contained a note that it would not be honoured after three months of the date of issue. The court held that the instrument was a cheque and the note did not make the order conditional, since the words were merely a definition of what was considered a reasonable time within which the warrants were to be presented for payment and was in any case only a direction to the payee to present that cheque within that time and not a condition for the bank to fulfil.

18.08   It is the order to the drawee of a bill or cheque which "must be unconditional," but ambiguity can arise as to whether the receipt form is for the attention of the payee or for the bank or the drawee to observe. Only if the receipt forms part of the drawer's mandate to the bank does the instrument become conditional. An instrument may be valid although it indicates that a particular account of the drawer is to be debited and it is common for a cheque to contain such an indication for example, through the words "number 1 account" or "business account" or by some similar term in the body of the cheque.

A cheque may further provide that the instrument must be presented for payment within a certain period and a provision of such a nature does not make the instrument conditional, but once the period during which the instrument is to be presented for payment has expired, the payee cannot as against the drawer insist on payment of the cheque, although the debt represented by it still remains owing. The debt represented in a cheque is payable on demand at any time within six years of its issue, but banks usually refuse to pay cheques considered to be stale, *i.e.* cheques not presented for payment within six months after the date of drawing.

AN ORDER

18.09   A bill or cheque must be "an order" in that it must be expressed in imperative terms, although mere terms of courtesy will not make it precative. In *Little* v. *Slackford*[7] an instrument in the form "You will oblige your humble servant . . . ," was held to be a mere request and not a demand on the bank.[8]

IN WRITING

The instrument must be "in writing" to be a bill or cheque and the Bills of Exchange Act,[9] provides that writing includes print, so that a cheque prepared on a typewriter would be valid, although in practice this is discouraged by some banks because of the ease with which typewritten cheques can be fraudulently altered. A customer who writes a cheque by hand would probably facilitate fraud by drawing cheques in lead–pencil, and in such a case a bank would probably return it unpaid.

---

[6] [1910] 2 K.B. 509.
[7] (1829) 1 Mood. & M. 171.
[8] See also *Ellison* v. *Collingridge* (1850) 9 C.B. 570, where the words "fifty three days after the date, credit Messrs. P & Co. or order . . . " were held to amount to a mandate.
[9] s.2.

ADDRESSED BY ONE PERSON TO ANOTHER

18.10 A bill or cheque must be "addressed by one person to another" so that there must be one person as drawer, and another, the bank, as drawee. It is possible to have one or joint drawees, but not drawees in the alternative. The head office and branches of a bank constitute one legal entity, and for this reason an instrument drawn by one branch of a bank on another branch is not a cheque, because it is not addressed by one person to another. Such an instrument is a bankers draft, which is a form of promissory note to which statute has extended the special rules relating to cheques.

SIGNATURE

18.11 A bill or cheque, to be a valid instrument, must be signed by the person issuing it (the drawer) or a person authorised by him. The instrument is not complete until the drawer has signed it, so that a cheque form which is otherwise complete is not a valid cheque until signed by the drawer or his agent. Under the Act[10] it is possible for an agent or official of an organisation to be vested with the power to draw cheques on behalf of the organisation. In the case of large companies and corporations it may be possible, after giving an indemnity to the bank, to draw instruments in the form of cheques which bear a printed facsimile reproduction of the signature of one of its officials.

PAYABLE ON DEMAND, OR AT A FIXED OR DETERMINABLE TIME IN FUTURE

18.12 A cheque must be payable on demand although the body of the cheque need not expressly state that the instrument is so payable. The Bills of Exchange Act 1882,[11] provides that a bill of exchange is payable on demand when it is expressed to be so payable, or is payable at sight, or on presentation or when no time for payment is expressed. It follows that a post-dated cheque is not a cheque, not being payable on demand (though it is a valid bill).

A bank is bound, these days, to pay a post-dated cheque presented on or after the date which it bears, even though it has refused payment of the same cheque beforehand, and in such circumstances the bank incurs no liability. In *Whistler* v. *Forster*[12] it was held that a holder for value can recover from the drawer on a post-dated cheque payable to "A. B. or order," and the instrument is to be taken to have been drawn according to the date appearing on the face of it. Similarly, in *Austin* v. *Bunyard*[13] the plaintiff received an indorsed cheque from the payee but without knowledge that when it was drawn it was post-dated. The court held that the plaintiff was entitled to recover against the defendant, the drawer, the amount of the post-dated cheque which was a valid instrument.

18.13 When a post-dated cheque is sent to a bank for collection before the date it bears, the bank may either present it for payment immediately, but in that case the drawee bank will return it unpaid, or the collecting bank may advise its customer that it is holding the instrument for his instructions, or the arrival of the due date. If the collecting bank lets its customer draw against the cheque, the bank becomes a holder of it for value, and can sue on

---

[10] s.91(1).
[11] s.10(1); see also *Korea Exchange Bank* v. *Debenhams (Central Buying) Ltd.* (1929) 123 S.J. 163.
[12] (1863) 14 C.B. (N.S.) 248.
[13] (1865) 6 B. & S. 687.

the cheque after the date for payment has arrived or on dishonour. As post-dated cheques are recognised as bills by the Bills of Exchange Act, they cannot be said to be irregular or incomplete by reason of the post-dating (though they are not cheques).

SUM CERTAIN IN MONEY

18.14 A bill or cheque may be drawn or negotiated for any sum of money but it must be for a certain sum, which normally is expressed both in words and figures, although there is no provision to this effect in the Act. In *Cohen* v. *Boulken*[14] a cheque drawn for 7,680 francs was held to be for a certain sum of money although it was required to be paid according to the rate of exchange prevailing when that cheque was presented. In *Barlow* v. *Broadhurst*[15] an instrument drawn "Pay B after deducting what he owes me" was held not to be a cheque since without looking beyond the wording of the instrument it was not possible to ascertain the amount which was to be paid to the payee. Where there is a discrepancy between the words and figures in a cheque the sum denoted by the words is payable.[16] In practice banks usually return such cheques unpaid except in some instances where the amount claimed on the cheque is the amount in figures and that is the smaller amount.

PAYABLE TO A SPECIFIED PERSON OR HIS ORDER OR BEARER

18.15 Finally, for a cheque to be valid it must be payable to a specified person or his order or to bearer. The payee is the person to whom the drawer primarily intends and directs payment to be made, but it rests on the payee to decide whether he will present the instrument for payment or negotiate it, and in the latter case there must be an intention to transfer the property, coupled with the delivery of the instrument. In *Chamberlain* v. *Young*[17] the court held that an instrument which was made payable to " . . . order" the blank never having been filled in must be construed as meaning that it was payable to "my order," *i.e.* to the order of the drawer.

At one time cheques drawn payable to "wages or order," or "cash or order" were considered as being payable to bearer, but section 7(3) cannot extend to instruments in this form since the instruction "Pay cash" or "Pay wages" relates to what is to be paid or the purpose for which the payment is to be used and not to the identity of the payee. In *Orbit Mining and Trading Company Ltd.* v. *Westminster Bank Ltd.*[18] the court held that an order to a bank in the form "Pay cash or order" is not a cheque but merely a mandate. Harman L.J. said:—

> "Clearly cash is not a specified person and I do not think that unless made expressly in favour of the bearer it is enough to argue that 'cash or order' in the end as a matter of construction means bearer, and I agree with the judge below that the mandate to pay bearer must be expressed and not implied."

[14] (1920) 36 T.L.R. 769.
[15] (1820) 4 Moore C.P. 471.
[16] s.9(2).
[17] [1893] 2 Q.B. 206.
[18] [1963] 1 Q.B. 794.

The court rejected the view taken earlier[19] that the words "or order" on a **18.16** "pay cash or order" instrument were to be disregarded, with the result that the instrument was by implication a bearer instrument. A pay cash document means no more than that if the amount of the instrument is paid to the person intended to receive it the drawer cannot claim it back from the bank and the person who holds the pay cash instrument is not treated as the nominee of the drawer.

A bill is payable to bearer when it explicitly says "pay bearer," or when the last or only indorsement is an "indorsement in blank," *i.e.* at the back of the bill is a simple signature of the indorser without the indication of any person to whom the bill is to be transferred.[20] Section 7(3) also provides that the bill can be treated as payable to bearer "where the payee is a fictitious or non-existing person."

The situation where the payee of a bill is fictitious or non-existing

Section 7(3) of the Bills of Exchange Act provides that where the payee of a **18.17** bill is a fictitious or non-existing person, the bill may be treated as payable to bearer. The significance of the section is realised when one examines section 24 of the Act which provides that a forged indorsement is a nullity, and no one can acquire a good title to a negotiable instrument through such an indorsement. Consequently, a person who takes the instrument after the indorsement was placed on it cannot sue parties prior to the indorsement, *i.e.* he cannot sue the acceptor or drawer.

In the case of an instrument payable to a fictitious or non-existing payee, there must be an indorsement if the instrument is to be transferred and that indorsement must necessarily be forged. A non-existent or fictitious payee cannot pay the instrument into his non-existent or fictitious account, and so the only way the instrument can be turned to account is by indorsing it for value to a third party. However, section 24 prevents the transferee from suing parties prior to the forged indorsement and in order to circumvent this difficulty it was provided that an instrument made payable to a fictitious or non-existing person should be regarded as payable to bearer. Consequently, the forged indorsement can be ignored, since forged indorsements are irrelevant to transferring title to bearer instruments and the drawer and acceptor can be made liable to a holder in due course. The drawer or acceptor will, therefore, bear the loss arising out of the instrument having been paid.

The effect of section 7(3) was discussed in the leading case of *Bank of Eng-* **18.18** *land* v. *Vagliano Brothers*.[21] The plaintiffs in that case were a firm of merchants in London who banked with the Bank of England, and were in the habit of accepting bills which were drawn payable at the Bank. Among the firm's foreign correspondents was one Vucina, who, in the course of business habitually drew bills on Vaglianos in favour of Petridi and Co., a firm in Constantinople. A clerk of Vagliano forged a series of bills purported to be drawn by Vucina on Vaglianos in favour of Petridi & Co. and in order to obtain Vaglianos acceptance of the forged bills he also forged corresponding letters of advice purporting to come from Vucina. When Vaglianos had

---

[19] *North & South Insurance Corpn. Ltd.* v. *National Provincial Bank Ltd.* [1936] 1 K.B. 328.
[20] s.8(3).
[21] (1891) A.C. 107.

accepted the forged bills, they were misappropriated by the clerk and indorsed by him with a forgery of Petridi & Co.'s, signature. On the bills maturing, the clerk presented the bills at the Bank of England, and the Bank having been advised of the acceptance of the bills by Vaglianos, paid them over the counter to the fraudulent clerk and then debited Vaglianos account. When the fraud was discovered, Vaglianos brought an action to determine whether the Bank was entitled to debit their account with the amounts paid out. The House of Lords held that as Vaglianos had accepted the bills and had advised the bank that they had done so they could not contend that the payments by the Bank were unauthorised. The majority of the members of the House of Lords were of the opinion that the case should be decided as one within section 7(3) of the Bills of Exchange Act.

18.19   Lord Herschell held firstly, that Petridi & Co. were under the circumstances fictitious payees within the meaning of the Act, and secondly, the Bank was entitled to treat the bills as payable to bearer and payment by the Bank over the counter to the person who presented them was hence payment which discharged the bills.[22]

The *Bank of England* v. *Vagliano* case left doubt on certain matters namely, whether the real or fictitious character of the payee could depend on the intention of the person who actually drew the bill, whether the intention of the other parties to the bill should be taken into account in determining the character of the payee; and finally whether the character of the payee as real or fictitious should be linked with the presence or absence of a real transaction in connection with which the bill was issued.

18.20   In *Clutton* v. *Allenborough*[23] it was held that a cheque drawn to the order of a fictitious or non-existing person may be treated as payable to bearer within section 7(3) although the drawer had drawn the cheque in the belief and with the intention that it should be payable to the order of a real person. In that case a clerk in the accounts department of the appellants, by fraudulently representing to them that work had been done on their account by a person called B, induced them to draw cheques payable to the order of B. The cheques when signed by the appellants were handed to their accounts department for transmission to the payees. The clerk then obtained possession of the cheques, indorsed them to B's name and negotiated them to the respondents who gave value and took the cheques in good faith. The cheques were paid to the respondents by the appellant's bankers, and when the appellants subsequently discovered the fraud, they brought an action against the respondents to recover the amount of the cheques as money paid under a mistake of fact. The House of Lords in dismissing the appeal said that although the cheques were drawn in favour of a person named B, and there might be a person of that name in existence, the payee of the cheques was nevertheless fictitious because the name (B) had been provided by a person who wished to commit a fraud on the appellants. Since they knew no one of that name they could not have intended the payee to be a real identifiable person. The House, therefore, held the *Vagliano* case to be directly applicable and the cheques payable to bearer.

---

[22] Lords Bramwell and Field were of the opinion that the payees were not fictitious. There was a real firm of Petridi & Co. in existence, and their name had been inserted as payees. Since the intention of the forger (*i.e.* the bills were not to be paid to Petridi & Co.) could not affect the existence of the payee, the payees as a real and existing firm could not be a fictitious payee.

[23] [1897] A.C. 90.

In *Vinden* v. *Hughes*[24] a cashier filled in a number of cheque forms with the names of customers of his employer as payees and obtained the employer's signature as drawer. He then forged the signatures of the payees by way of an indorsement and discounted the cheques to an innocent third party, who obtained payment from the drawer's bankers. It was held that on the facts of the case the payees could not be regarded as fictitious or non-existing, because at the time the cheques were drawn, the drawers intended identifiable persons namely, certain of their customers to be the payees in the belief that the drawer owed the sums represented by the cheques to those persons. The *Bank of England* v. *Vagliano* case was distinguished, there being in that case no drawers in fact since the drawers' signature was forged, and the use of the name of Petridi & Co. as payees was a mere fiction. There, the House was not dealing with the case of a drawer of the bill who intended identifiable payees to receive payment. It appears, therefore, that the intention of the drawer of a bill is relevant, but not the intention of the acceptor, nor the knowledge of the acceptor that the payee is fictitious.

18.21

Lord Herschell in the *Vagliano* case said:—

18.22

> "In order to establish the right to treat a bill as payable to bearer, it is enough to prove that the payee is in fact a fictitious person, and that it is not necessary if it be sought to charge the acceptor to prove in addition that he was cognizant of the fictitious character of the payee."

The importance of the rule that a bill payable to a fictitious or non-existing payee may be treated as payable to bearer arises from the fact that it enables any forged indorsement purporting to be that of the payee to be disregarded. However, the decision in *North & South Wales Bank Ltd.* v. *Macbeth*[25] deprives the *Vagliano* case of most of its practical value in the case of cheques, since it will rarely happen that a person who signs a cheque as drawer will do so without intending it to be payable to an identifiable payee. In that case one White fraudulently induced Macbeth to draw a cheque in favour of "Kerr or order." Kerr was an existing person known to Macbeth, and Macbeth, although misled by White as to the use to which he would put the cheque, fully intended that Kerr should receive the money. White in obtaining the cheque, forged Kerr's indorsement and paid the cheque into his account with the appellant bank. On discovering the fraud, Macbeth brought an action against the bank to recover the money collected by it on the ground that the bank was guilty of conversion by collecting a cheque to which its customers had no title. The bank contended that the payee was a fictitious person within section 7(3) of the Act, and that the cheque was, therefore, payable to bearer. The House of Lords held that the subsection did not apply, because the drawer of the cheque, Macbeth, intended that a real person known to Macbeth, namely Kerr, should receive the amount of the cheque and so it could not be said that the payee of the cheque was fictitious.

Section 7(3) therefore comes in operation where the payee is fictitious or non-existent and, as has been shown, this may arise in one of two ways, namely:–

18.23

(a) he may be so because no such person exists or no particular person was intended by the party sued, for example in *Vinden* v. *Hughes* where a fraudulent clerk induced the plaintiffs to draw cheques payable to "G.

---

[24] [1905] 1 K.B. 795.
[25] [1908] A.C. 137.

Brett" under the belief that he owed money to a person known as "G. Brett," but the drawer had no particular person in mind, or

18.24 (b) he may be so because such a person does exist, but that person was not intended as payee by the person who drew the bill, for example, in the *Vagliano* case the payee of the bills of exchange involved, Petridi & Co., existed but were not intended by the person who drew the bill to be the recipients of the amounts of the bills. The position that arose was that (so far as the clerk was concerned) Petridi & Co. were fictitious payees, and since he was the person who fabricated the bills and not the firm whose signature he forged as drawers, Vucina & Co., the relevant intention as to who should receive payment of the bills was that of the clerk and not that of the nominal drawers.

In (a) above, both the drawer and the acceptor can be sued by a holder in due course in reliance on the estoppels created by section 55(1)(b) and 54(2)(c) of the Bills of Exchange Act. By section 55 the drawer of a bill by drawing it is precluded from denying the existence of the payee and his capacity to indorse the bill. The acceptor, by section 54(2)(c) is similarly precluded from denying the existence of the payee and his capacity to indorse the bill. The payee does not in fact exist and the effect of the estoppels is, therefore, that the drawer or acceptor must have intended that anyone to whom the bill was delivered would be able to indorse it with the payee's name, even though that was not the indorser's real name.[26]

18.25 In situation (b) above, it is possible for the drawer to be estopped because he does not intend an existing identifiable person to be the payee, but for the acceptor to intend the real named payee (and not someone else) should receive the amount of the bill (namely, the position Vaglianos were in since they intended the real Petridi & Co. to receive payment). In that case the acceptor is not estopped by section 54(2)(c) from denying that the bill is a bill payable to bearer, although the drawer is estopped under section 55(1)(b). The acceptor can, therefore, only be sued on the bill under section 7(3), when according to the decision in *Vagliano's* case it is the state of mind of the person who actually fabricated the bill (*i.e.* the clerk) which is material.

18.26 However, even in this situation, where the acceptor intended an existing person to be the payee, but the drawer did not, a subsequent bona fide holder of the bill for value claiming through a forged indorsement of the payee's signature still has a title to the bill against the drawer by reason of the estoppel of the drawer under section 55(1)(b), and the holder can, therefore, claim the value of the consideration given by the drawer to the acceptor for accepting the bill as money had and received by the acceptor to the use of the person now entitled to the bill as against the drawer. This is a common law[27] claim made outside the bill, but the right is preserved under the present legislation by section 97(2) of the Act.

The result is that the only circumstance where the holder of a bill drawn in favour of a fictitious person can rely on section 7(3) of the Act (and not recover by relying, either on the rules of estoppel binding the drawer and acceptor, or alternatively suing for money had and received) is where the bill is payable to a real person although the drawer did not intend that per-

---

[26] See *Minet* v. *Gibson* (1791) 3 T.L.R. 481.
[27] See *Tatlock* v. *Harris* [1781] 3 T.R. 174; and *Vere* v. *Lewis* [1789] 3 T.R. 182.

son to receive payment, and additionally, the acceptor did not know of the drawer's intention and did not receive any consideration from the drawer or any subsequent indorser of the bill (*i.e.* he accepted the bill for the drawer's accommodation).

Inchoate instruments

An inchoate instrument is a bill of exchange, cheque, or a promissory note **18.27** which contains one or more, but not all of the necessary elements to constitute it a bill, cheque or a promissory note. Consequently, where an acceptance is written on an instrument in the form of a bill which does not contain the name of a drawer or payee and is addressed to no named drawee, the instrument is as yet neither a bill, nor a note. It may, however, be completed in accordance with the conditions of section 20 of the Act, and if the instrument then purports to be addressed to the person who has signed it as acceptor, it is valid as a bill.[28] If the name of the drawee is not inserted and there is no drawer but the instrument is otherwise complete, it is a valid promissory note made by the person who signed it initially.[29]

There are a number of requirements which have to be satisfied in order to **18.28** take advantage of section 20. In the case of a blank or inchoate instrument, it is essential that the drawer has either actually delivered the instrument to another person with authority to complete it, or that his agent or servant has been given the instrument for that purpose.

In *Baxendale* v. *Bennett*[30] and *Smith* v. *Prosser*[31] it was held that in neither case were the defendants liable where they had given blank acceptances on instruments, with limited authority to complete the instruments. The instruments were subsequently completed by unauthorised persons and negotiated to the plaintiffs who had given value. It was held that in neither case was the defendant liable. Brett L.J. in *Baxendale* v. *Bennett* said the defendant incurred no liability by reason of negligence, since he owed no duty of care to the plaintiff.

A bill which is incomplete at the time of issue is to be treated, when com- **18.29** pleted in accordance with the section, as though it had never been incomplete. The bill or instrument must be filled in accordance with the authority given, so that if a drawer or acceptor hands over an incomplete bill with instructions to fill it up immediately, these instructions must be complied with strictly; in any other case the document must be completed within a reasonable time.[32] Alternatively, the drawer or acceptor of any instrument may hand it over with instructions that the instrument is not to be completed until a specified later date or only on fulfilment of certain conditions; in such a case if the person to whom the instrument is delivered completes the instrument contrary to the instructions, the drawer or acceptor is not liable.[33] The signatory may also specify the maximum amount for which the instrument may be completed. If the holder of an incomplete bill draws

[28] *Haseldine* v. *Winstanley* [1936] 2 K.B. 101.
[29] *Mason* v. *Lock* [1939] L.T. 696.
[30] [1878] 3 Q.B.D. 525.
[31] [1907] 2 K.B. 735.
[32] *Griffiths* v. *Dalton* [1940] 2 K.B. 264.
[33] *Smith* v. *Prosser* [1907] 2 K.B. 735.

it for a larger sum than that specified the party facilitating the fraud may be responsible.[34]

Bramwell L.J., said in *Baxendale* v. *Bennett*:—

"Where a man has signed a blank acceptance, and has issued it, and has authorised the holder to fill it up, he is liable on the bill whatever the amount may be, though he has given secret instructions to the holder as to the amount for which he shall fill it up, he has enabled his agent to deceive an innocent party, and he is liable."

18.30 A person who becomes a party to an incomplete instrument prior to its completion must observe strictly the limits of the authority conferred upon him for completion. An instrument which has been completed beyond the terms of the authority can only be enforced against the signatory who gave the authority if the instrument falls within the provisions of section 20(2). To enable a holder to benefit under this proviso two conditions have to be satisfied namely, the instrument must have been completed before it was negotiated to him and secondly, he must be a holder in due course. A payee of a bill cannot be a holder in due course and is not protected by the proviso, even though the instrument does not come into his hands until after its completion.[35]

Section 20 is supplemented by sections 12 and 15. Section 12 provides that:—

"Where a bill expressed to be payable at a fixed period after date is issued undated, or where the acceptance of a bill payable at a fixed period after sight is undated, any holder may insert the true date of issue or acceptance, and the bill shall be payable accordingly. Provided that (1) where the holder in good faith and by mistake inserts a wrong date, and (2) in every case where a date is inserted, if the bill subsequently comes into the hands of a holder in due course the bill shall not be avoided thereby, but shall operate and be payable as if the date so inserted had been the true date."

The section does not apply as between the immediate parties where a wrong date is inserted, even in good faith, if in fact this date is contrary to a prior agreement as to the date from which the bill is to run. Consequently, a bill completed by the payee with the wrong date is unenforceable against the drawer and acceptor, even though the error is in favour of the party sued on the bill.[36]

Apart from the completion of the instrument under sections 20 and 12, a drawer or indorser may make an addition to it under section 15 of the Act, which permits any holder to add the name of a "referee in case of need." Such a person is one named in the bill or by an indorsement on it, to whom the holder may present the bill if the drawer or acceptor dishonours the bill, or if presentation for acceptance or payment cannot be made, and that person may then accept or pay the bill for the honour of the drawee or acceptor and enforce the rights of a holder against it. In practice with modern speedy communication references in case of need are not now provided for in bills.

[34] *Young* v. *Grote* [1827] 4 Bing. 253.
[35] *Herdman* v. *Wheeler* [1902] 1 K.B. 361.
[36] *Foster* v. *Driscoll* [1929] 1 K.B. 470.

Conditions for incurring liability on a bill

Section 23 of the Act provides that no one is liable as drawer, indorser, or **18.31** acceptor of a bill who has not signed it. A signature may actually be written by an agent. However, a signature is not of itself sufficient to render a person liable on a contract on a bill. For the purposes of incurring liability on a bill the signature must be accompanied by delivery of the instrument.

Section 21(1) provides: "Every contract on a bill, whether it be the drawer's, the acceptor's or an indorser's, is incomplete and revocable, until delivery of the instrument in order to give effect thereto."

The Act also says: "Delivery means transfer of possession, actual or constructive, from one person to another."[37]

Thus, the drawer will not be liable to the payee of a cheque until he has handed the cheque over to him, the acceptor will not be liable to the payee, until either he has signed and handed back the bill or signed the acceptance and given notice that he has done so, and an indorser will not be liable until he has signed and handed over the instrument to the indorsee.

Forged signatures

Section 24 provides that forgery is a defence to a person sued on a bill, **18.32** cheque or promissory note even as against a person who is (that is, but for the forgery would be) a bona fide holder for value or a holder in due course. The section deals with forged or unauthorised signatures and lays down the principle that a forged signature is a nullity whether the forgery be of the drawer, acceptor or indorser.

Section 24 deals merely with a forged or unauthorised signature (section 64 deals with the effect of forgery in other parts of the instrument). The Bills of Exchange Act does not define the term "forgery" and in *Kreditbank Cassel* v. *Schenkers*[38] it was held that in interpreting the Bills of Exchange Act the court should apply the Forgery Act 1913. In *Re London & Globe Finance Corporation Ltd.*[39] it was said that forgery requires the making of a false document with intent to deceive. Thus, forgery may take the form of creating a false document without authority or it may take the form of creating a false document by exceeding the authority conferred (*e.g.* where an agent with a limited authority draws cheques for sums larger than those authorised). An unauthorised signature is one where the agent either by mistake or negligence goes beyond his authority in drawing the instrument.

Whether the signature is forged or unauthorised the basic rule is that the signature is a nullity, *e.g.* a forged signature is ineffective in passing title and the bank which pays the cheque cannot debit the customer's account. The payee, even if a holder in due course, cannot compel the drawer to make payment but if he has received payment he can be compelled to restore the money. Similarly, if the drawee's signature is forged on an acceptance, the drawee cannot be sued or if the indorsee's signature is forged he cannot be sued on the indorsement.

The holder suing on the bill can sue all the indorsers whose names appear **18.33** on the bill after the forged signature but then there is a break in the succession of valid transfers. The person whose name has been forged and any

[37] s.2.
[38] [1927] 1 K.B. 826.
[39] [1903] 1 Ch. 728.

indorsers before him, together with the acceptor and drawer cannot be sued on the bill.

A person or bank who makes payment on the forged indorsement may find itself liable to the rightful owner who can insist on a second payment being made to him.

There are two kinds of forgery which must be examined here, namely, where the signature of the drawer is forged at the inception of the bill, etc. First, an instrument drawn, whether to bearer or to order, on which the drawer's signature is forged is not a bill at all and is a complete nullity. Secondly, a bill may be valid at its inception, but the holder's title to it will be invalid if an indorsement is forged on it.

18.34   In the former case, it is clearly settled that an instrument on which the drawer's signature is forged is not a bill of exchange and no one may sue him on it. Lord Halsbury in *Bank of England* v. *Vagliano Brothers*[40] said:

> "I have designedly avoided calling these instruments [*i.e.* instrument on which the drawer's signature was forged] bills of exchange, they were nothing of the kind."

An instrument sham in its inception may, however, by the addition of a genuine signature become a negotiable instrument by estoppel. Section 54 estops the acceptor from denying the genuineness of the drawer's signature and section 55(2)(b) estops an indorser from denying the genuineness of the drawer's, acceptor's or any previous indorser's signature, in each case as against a "holder in due course." An instrument on which the drawer's signature is forged will only become a bill by estoppel if the genuine signature of the party sued is placed on it subsequent to the forgery.

18.35   Secondly, however, a bill may start off as a valid instrument but the title of the claimant may be invalid if an indorsement is subsequently forged on it. In such a case section 55 states that an indorser of a bill is precluded by his indorsement from denying to a holder in due course the genuineness of his signature and the signatures of any previous indorsers. The person who would otherwise be a holder in due course normally cannot recover the proceeds of the bill from the person whose signature was forged or from a party to the bill prior to the forged indorsement, and any payment made by that party can be recovered as paid under a mistake of fact, subject to the defence of estoppel by payment. The rights available to a holder in due course are limited to rights of recourse against indorsers subsequent to the forged signature, so a subsequent valid indorsement does not make the instrument fully negotiable in the sense that all prior parties are made liable. However, an acceptor is liable on his acceptance to a holder claiming through a forged instrument:

(i) where, at the time of the acceptance, the acceptor knew of the forgery and intended that the bill should be put into circulation by a forged indorsement[41]; and

(ii) where the payee is a fictitious or non-existing person and consequently, the holder does not need to make title through the indorsement since by section 7(3) of the Act the instrument is payable to bearer.

18.36   Section 24 states that the section will not apply if the party against whom it is sought to retain or enforce the bill is precluded from denying forgery or want of authority. Where a signature is forged it cannot be ratified for two

[40] [1891] A.C. 107.
[41] *Beeman* v. *Duck* (1843) 11 M. & W. 251.

reasons: first, that the ratification would protect the forgery and, therefore, be against public policy, and secondly, the ability to ratify a transaction only operates where the person who carries out the transaction purported to act on behalf of the principal whose signature he inserts on the instrument. The forger does not do this since he pretends himself to be the very person whose signature he forges.[42]

Nevertheless, the person whose signature has been forged may represent the forged signature to be his own and induce subsequent holders for value to take the instrument upon the supposition that the signature is genuine. He is then estopped from setting up the fact that it is a counterfeit and so he may become liable on it.[43]

Even mere non-disclosure of the forgery may result in an estoppel where there is a duty of disclosure on the person who raises the estoppel, *e.g.* as in the instance of a customer in relation to his banker.[44]

18.37

A bill may be forged in other ways than by the forgery of the signature of a party to the bill. For example, where the amount of an existing bill is increased subsequent to its issue or negotiation. This involves uttering a forged document. However, such a forgery does not necessarily invalidate the bill completely and if the forgery is not apparent, a subsequent holder in due course may under section 64(1) enforce the instrument in its original form.[45]

The capacity of parties to a bill

A person who has placed his signature on a bill will normally incur liability on that instrument. However, he may not incur any liability, or only a limited liability if he belongs to a class of persons on whom the law confers limited capacity. The question of capacity is dealt with under section 22 of the Bills of Exchange Act, which provides that as a general rule capacity to incur liability on a bill of exchange is co-extensive with capacity to contract.

18.38

INFANTS

Most contracts made by infants are void and section 1 of the Infants Relief Act 1874 makes absolutely void contracts for repayment of money lent or to be lent, contracts for goods supplied or to be supplied other than necessaries and accounts stated.

An infant is, however, bound to pay a reasonable price for goods and services suitable to his station in life and his needs, and in the case of goods they must be suitable to his requirements at the time of delivery. Contracts of a continuous nature, for example, leases are binding on an infant unless he repudiates them during infancy or within a reasonably short time afterwards. Thus, unless the payment is for necessaries an infant can plead his own incapacity against an innocent assignee.

The Bills of Exchange Act 1882,[46] confirms the common law to the extent that capacity to incur liability to a bill is co-extensive with capacity to contract. An infant may sue on a bill[47] but he cannot be made liable on a bill or other negotiable instrument as drawer, acceptor or indorser even though

[42] *Brook* v. *Hook* [1871].
[43] *Leach* v. *Buchanan* (1802) 4 Esp. 226.
[44] *Greenwood* v. *Martins Bank* [1932] 1 K.B. 371.
[45] *Kwei Tek Chao* v. *British Traders and Shippers Ltd.* (1954) 2 Q.B. 459.
[46] s.22(1).
[47] *Warwick* v. *Bruce* (1813) 2 M. & Sel. 205.

the plaintiff is a holder in due course and the transaction is one on which the infant could have been sued namely, the supply of necessaries.[48]

18.39   A holder in due course has no special additional remedy against an infant who is party to a bill, but he is in the same position as any other holder for value. Section 22(2) of the Bills of Exchange Act 1882 provides:

> "Where a bill is drawn or indorsed by an infant or corporation having no capacity or power to incur liability on a bill, the drawing or indorsement entitles the holder to receive payment of the bill, and to enforce it against any other party thereto."

Where, however, an instrument is drawn after the infant has attained his majority in satisfaction of a promise which arose during his minority the question of liability, if any, involves two different statutes, *i.e.* the Infants Relief Act 1874, and the Betting and Loans (Infants) Act 1892.

The Infants Relief Act 1874[49] provides:

> "No action shall be brought whereby to charge any person upon any promise made after full age to pay any debt contracted during infancy whether there shall or shall not be any new consideration for such promise or ratification after full age."

18.40   However, in *Smith* v. *King*[50] this was interpreted as holding that the former infant is liable to a holder of a bill or other negotiable instrument issued in payment of a debt contracted during infancy, unless the holder has notice of the purpose for which the instrument was issued. In *Belfast Banking Co.* v. *Doherty*,[51] it was held that a holder in due course of the bill could recover on an instrument accepted by an infant. The court restricted the application of section 2 of the Infants Relief Act to the original parties to the bill and any holders of the bill with notice of the purpose for which it was accepted. The judge said on a true reading of section 2, as between the parties to a new promise, no action would lie because in such a case the consideration is illegal, but where the new promise is contained in the form of a negotiable security the rights of a bona fide transferee for value are not affected.

Section 2 of the Infants Relief Act 1874, unlike section 1 does not provide that the contract is absolutely void but merely that "no action shall be brought on it" and section 29(2) of the Bills of Exchange Act enacts that an illegal consideration for the issue of a bill is no defence against a holder in due course. The court also thought it fair to restrict the protection of an infant once he has become an adult, at least against innocent parties who could not, without difficulty discover that the bill was given in connection with a litigation originally incurred during his infancy. The court based this conclusion on the general principle that the position of a holder in due course should be unassailable.

The Betting and Loans (Infants) Act 1892,[52] states:

> "If any infant who has contracted a loan which is void in law, agrees after he comes of age to pay any money which in whole or in part represents or is agreed to be paid in respect of any such loan, and is not a new advance, such agreement, and any instrument negotiable or other,

---

[48] *Re Soltykoff* [1891] 1 Q.B. 431.
[49] s.2.
[50] [1892] 2 Q.B. 543.
[51] (1879) 4 L.R.Ir. 124.
[52] s.5.

given in pursuance of or to carry into effect such agreement or otherwise in relation to the payment of money representing or in respect of such loan, shall, so far as it related to money which represents or is payable in respect of such a loan, and is not a new advance, be void absolutely as against all persons whomsoever."

Byles[53] states that under this section an instrument made after an infant attains his majority is absolutely void in the hands of any holder, even a holder in due course, if the original contract in respect of which it was given was void.[54]

CORPORATE INCAPACITY

In order for a corporation to be liable on a contract, it is necessary that its constitution should either expressly or impliedly vest in it a power to enter into contracts of that kind, and that the contract must be entered in such a form as to bind a corporation. Section 22 of the Bills of Exchange Act 1882 enacts "nothing in this section shall enable a corporation to make itself liable as drawer, acceptor or indorser of a bill of exchange unless it is competent to do so under the law . . . "   **18.41**

However, the rule in respect of corporate capacity applies only to statutory corporations and corporations formed under general Acts, *e.g.* the Companies Act 1985 and Building Societies Acts, but not chartered corporations.

Under the Companies Act 1985,[55] any transaction decided on by the board of directors of a company is deemed to be within the company's capacity, and within the powers of its board in favour of any person dealing with the company in good faith. Such a person is not obliged to inquire about the scope of the company's objects or the powers of the board of directors and is considered to have acted in good faith unless the contrary is proved. A third party who, therefore, enters into a contract bona fide with a company may rely on any resolution passed by the board of directors relating to that contract. Questions of corporate capacity are further discussed in Chapter 17.

SOVEREIGN AND DIPLOMATIC IMMUNITY

Sovereign and diplomatic immunity of foreign ambassadors and corporations will defeat the rights of a holder in due course unless the immunity is waived, or the case falls within one of the qualifications introduced in the Diplomatic Privilege Act 1964 or the State Immunity Act 1978. The doctrine of sovereign immunity prior to 1978 was derived largely from international law as interpreted by judicial decisions (see *Trendtex Trading Corporation* v. *The Central Bank of Nigeria*)[56]   **18.42–18.44**

The rule in the *Trendtex* case has been given statutory approval by the State Immunity Act 1978. The Act provides that a state is immune from the jurisdiction of the courts of the U.K. except as provided by the statute. The Act then enumerates the circumstances in which a sovereign, a state, a constituent territory of a federal state or a separate entity exercising sovereign authority will lose their immunity. By section 3(1) it is enacted that a state is

[53] *Byles on Bills of Exchange*, ed. Megrah and Ryder, (S. & M., 25th ed., 1983), p. 52.
[54] *Hutley* v. *Peacock.*
[55] s.35.
[56] (1977) 1 All E.R. 881.

not immune where proceedings relate to a commercial transaction entered into by the state, or an obligation of the state which has to be performed wholly or partly in the United Kingdom. Section 3(3) of the Act defines a commercial transaction as being a contract for the supply of goods or services, any loan or other transaction for the provision of finance, or any undertaking of indemnity or guarantee relating to such a transaction or any other transaction or activity into which a state enters otherwise than in the exercise of sovereign authority.

Consideration

18.45 At common law a person who wishes to enforce a contractual promise must show that he provided valid consideration for that promise. The law, therefore, recognises and will enforce bargains where some value, however small,[57] has been provided in exchange for the promise. In *Dunlop Pneumatic Tyre Co. v. Selfridge*[58] consideration was said to be "the price for which the promise is bought."

The Bills of Exchange Act in part adopts the common law rules, and in part qualifies them. Section 27 adopts the common law rule and provides that consideration for a contract on a bill may be constituted by "any consideration sufficient to support a simple contract," but it qualifies the common law because section 27(1)(b) goes on to provide that consideration for a bill of exchange may also be "an antecedent debt or liability."[59] This is an exception to the common law rule that consideration must not be past. Moreover, section 27(2) enables not merely immediate parties to the contract to take the benefit of the consideration but it provides that "the holder is deemed to be a holder for value as regards the acceptor and all parties to the bill who became parties prior to such time." This is an exception to the doctrine of privity of contract.

18.46 As between the immediate parties to the contract, *i.e* between the drawer and acceptor, payee and drawer, indorser and indorsee, valid consideration must have been given if the plaintiff is to sue for breach. In such cases consideration may be executory (*e.g.* the drawer of a cheque draws a cheque in return for a promise to supply goods or services) or executed (*e.g.* where the drawer gives a cheque on the actual delivery of goods).

Section 27(2) provides that a person is liable on a bill if consideration was given by the person suing on the bill, or if it had been given by a party through whom the person suing is claiming. The section provides that "where value has at any time been given for a bill the holder is deemed to be a holder for value . . . " Thus it is not necessary for the holder of a bill who sues on it to show that he provided consideration to the defendant. It is sufficient that consideration was provided by anyone in the holder's chain of title provided the defendant became a party to the bill before any such consideration was given. Consequently, the plaintiff will succeed although he gave no consideration for the bill. For example, B draws a bill on A, who accepts it gratuitously. C gives B value for the bill and indorses it to X as a gift. X can sue A although X gave no consideration for the bill and A received nothing for his acceptance. X can also sue B, but X cannot sue C,

---

[57] *Chappell and Co. Ltd.* v. *Nestle Co. Ltd.* [1960] A.C. 87.
[58] [1915] A.C. 847.
[59] See *Elkington* v. *Cooke* (1914) 30 T.L.R. 670 and *Ayres* v. *Moore* [1940] 1 K.B. 278.

as C did not become a party prior to the giving of value. Chalmers states the rule as follows:

> "The holder of a bill who receives it from a holder for value, but does not himself give value for it, has all the rights of a holder for value against all parties to the bill except the person from whom he received it."

Section 27(3) provides that a holder of a bill who has a lien on it, whether by operation of law or by contract, is a holder for value to the extent of the law. A lien is a right either to retain or to realise someone else's property in order to pay off debts owed by that person to the person enjoying the lien. Banks are entitled to exercise a general lien over securities belonging to a customer which a bank holds until all amounts owed to it by the customer are paid to the bank.[60] The lien extends to all documents under which money will or may become payable to the customer, including negotiable instruments.

A bank cannot claim a lien over securities delivered to it by its customer **18.47** for a specific purpose (*e.g.* safe custody) and a bank cannot exercise a lien over securities which belong to a third party, except negotiable instruments provided the bank takes the security for value and good faith. In *Barclays Bank Ltd.* v. *Astley Industrial Trust Ltd.*[61] it was held that a bank which had allowed the customer to draw against uncleared cheques was a holder for value. The lien is further discussed above, in Chapter 13.

A party to a contract who cannot sue on it except by pleading the illegality of the consideration to establish his case cannot succeed in his action and the whole contract is contaminated[62] by the illegality. Moreover, the illegal consideration under a transaction which gives rise to the debt in question may be raised as a defence by the debtor against an innocent assignee of the debt. Thus, salaries of public offices may not, on grounds of public policy, be assigned, and indebtedness tainted by maintenance or a design to defraud the revenue authorities is void and an assignee of such a contract cannot sue on it.

In the case of a holder for value of a bill of exchange the position is simi- **18.48** lar; it is of no consequence whether the consideration which moves from him is illegal or merely void, for in neither case does the holder give value in the eye of the law and he cannot, therefore, recover on the bill. However, on transfer by such a person the position is different in the two cases. Where B obtains a bill from A for an illegal consideration and transfers it to C who gives value, C cannot recover from A if he knows of the manner in which B obtained the instrument, but he can recover from A if he was unaware of the illegality. In *Woolf* v. *Hamilton*[63] a cheque was given by the defendant in payment of bets on horse races lost by him and indorsed by the payee to the plaintiff for value with notice of the consideration for which it was given. The court held the plaintiff could not maintain an action on the cheque as it must be deemed to have given for an illegal consideration. A person who takes such a security for value knowing the consideration for which it was given, takes it with notice that it was given for an illegal consideration and therefore cannot recover upon it. The court added, however, that the

---

[60] *Brandao* v. *Bartnett* (1846) 12 Cl. & Fin. 787.
[61] [1970] 2 Q.B. 527.
[62] *Simpson* v. *Bloss* (1816) 7 Taunt. 247.
[63] [1898] 2 Q.B. 337.

illegality of the wagering consideration would have been immaterial if the plaintiff were a bona fide holder without notice of the consideration, and so as a holder in due course would be able to sue both the issuer and other parties to the cheque. The decision of the court in *Woolf* v. *Hamilton* illustrated the rule laid down by section 38(2) of the Act which lays down that a holder in due course holds the bill free from any defect of title of prior parties.

18.49   Among contracts illegal at common law are contracts which violate rules of morality, contracts involving trade with the enemy in time of war and contracts impeding the proper course of justice. In *Jones* v. *Merionethshire Building Society*[64] the relatives of the defaulting secretary of a building society gave promissory notes for the amount of his defalcations on the implied agreement that he should not be prosecuted. It was held that the building society could not sue on the instruments, as they were given for a consideration illegal on grounds of public policy. In order to recover in such cases the holder of the instrument must be a " holder in due course," which the building society was not.

18.50   However, if B obtains a bill from A for a consideration which is not illegal but merely void, and B transfers the bill to C for value, C by giving value himself, cures the want of value between A and B and can recover from A even though he knew that the consideration given by B was void. In *Lilley* v. *Rankin*[65] the defendant gave a cheque to X in payment of a gambling transaction. X indorsed the cheque for value to the plaintiff who had knowledge of the circumstances. It was held that the plaintiff could recover on the cheque as the consideration was merely void by virtue of the Gaming Act 1845 and not illegal as in *Woolf* v. *Hamilton*.

Section 29 of the Bills of Exchange Act provides that if an illegal consideration has been given for the acceptance, issue or subsequent negotiation of a bill it does not affect the title of a subsequent holder in due course (see *Bank für Gemeinwirtschaft Aktiengesellschaft* v. *City of London Garages Ltd.*[66]

The acceptor

18.51   The acceptor is merely the drawee, after he has undertaken liability on the instrument. The Act defines acceptance as the signification by the drawee of his assent to the order of the drawer.[67] It must be written on the bill and normally, an acceptance is written across the face of the bill and consists of the drawee's signature, the word "accepted" and the date. The date will be important if the bill is payable a fixed period after sight, but it may be inserted later. In order for the acceptance to be valid, it must not state that the debt may be discharged in any manner other than by the payment of money.[68]

The basic rule is that only the named drawee can accept a bill. A person who writes an acceptance on the bill otherwise than as drawer or acceptor will incur liability as an indorser. However, if the drawee dishonours the bill by refusing to accept or giving a qualified acceptance which the holder refuses to accept, the bill must be "protested" for non-acceptance. Any person not a party to the bill may accept it "supra protest".[69] Hence acceptance

[64] [1892] 1 Ch. 173.
[65] (1886) 56 L.J.Q.B. 248.
[66] [1971] 1 W.L.T. 149.
[67] s.12.
[68] s.17(2)(b).
[69] s.65.

for honour was allowed in order to salvage the commercial standing of the drawee who failed to accept the bill.

An acceptance may be general or qualified.[70] A general acceptance is an **18.52** unqualified assent to drawer's order. A qualified acceptance, however, departs from the terms of the drawer's order, *e.g.* where the drawee's acceptance is conditional, partial, local or qualified as to time or place. A holder may refuse to take a qualified acceptance and treat the bill as dishonoured for non-acceptance, but a holder who takes a qualified acceptance must secure the agreement of the drawer or indorsers. If he fails to do so, they are released from their obligations on the bill, except when the qualification is only as to amount and they are notified of it.

Section 18 deals with problems relating to acceptance and provides:

(i) a bill may be accepted before it has been signed by the drawer, or is in some other respect incomplete. Such a document is an inchoate instrument but even if it is never completed the person thus putting his name to the document may be liable;

(ii) a bill may be accepted when overdue or after it is dishonoured, for non-payment. In such a case the bill will be payable on the same day.

Both time and demand bills can be presented to the drawee for acceptance but section 39 sets out three circumstances where acceptance is essential, namely;

(a) when the bill is payable at some fixed period after sight because acceptance is necessary in order to calculate the date of maturity;

(b) when the bill expressly provides that it must be accepted; and

(c) when the bill orders payment to be made at some place other than the place of business or residence of the drawee.

Section 41 provides that the bill will be properly presented for acceptance **18.53** if it is presented by the holder or his agent to the drawee or his agent at a reasonable hour on a business day before the bill becomes overdue. If there are joint drawees, who are not partners, the bill must be presented to all of them unless one has been appointed to accept the bill, as their agent.

Presentment is excused and the bill treated as dishonoured by non-acceptance when the drawee is dead, or is a fictitious person, or a person unable to contract by the issue of a bill. Presentation is also excused when, with the exercise of reasonable diligence, it cannot be effected, and when, although a presentment is defective, acceptance is refused for some other reason. The fact that the holder believes that the bill will be dishonoured on presentment does not, however, amount to an excuse and he must still present it in those cases where it is essential.

Section 43 provides that a bill is dishonoured by non-acceptance if it is presented in accordance with the Act, and an acceptance is either refused or cannot be contained, or when presentment is excused, if no acceptance is forthcoming. Section 42 provides that, where a bill is presented and is not accepted within the customary time, which in the United Kingdom is twenty-four hours (excluding non-business days), then the person presenting it must treat it as dishonoured by non-acceptance. If he fails to do so, he loses his right to sue the drawer and indorsers.

When a bill is dishonoured by non-acceptance and there is no acceptance for honour, the holder at once has "a right of recourse" against the drawer

---

[70] s.19.

and indorsers, *i.e.* a right to sue them on their guarantee liability, and he need not wait to see if the bill will be paid when he presents it for payment.

The holder in due course

18.54 The liability of a party to a bill is contractual, and the position of the holder is, therefore, dependent on whether he or his predecessor in title has given consideration for the instrument. A holder who has not given value for the bill cannot claim against any person who became a party to the bill without receiving consideration unless consideration has been given by an intermediate party. This is in accordance with the general rule that a bill being a simple contract, consideration is necessary to support it. However, it must be borne in mind that, first, every party is presumed to have received consideration so that proof of the contrary rests on him, and secondly, that a holder who has not given value himself will have the benefit of the fact that a previous holder has given valuable consideration. In such a case he himself will be deemed to be a holder for value as regards parties prior to the one who gave value. For example, B draws a bill payable to himself upon A, who accepts it gratuitously; C gives B value for B's indorsing the bill to him, and C further indorses the bill to D by way of a gift. D can sue A on the bill although D gave nothing for the bill and A received nothing for his signature, and this applies even though D knew that A had accepted the bill gratuitously. D can also sue B who received value from C, but D cannot sue C, as C did not become a party prior to the giving of value for the bill by himself. The rule applicable is that the holder of a bill who receives it from a holder for value but does not himself give value for it has all the rights of a holder for value against all parties to the bill, except the person from whom he received it. A holder for value, on the other hand, will either have given value, or be able to rely on the fact that value was given by an earlier party to the bill. A holder for value has a complete title to the bill, although he may not personally have given consideration for it and his title can only be impeached by proof of a defect in his title namely, that the issue or transfer of the bill was void or voidable. For example, if the issue or any transfer of the bill had been obtained by fraud, a holder for value obtains no benefit from the mere fact that he has himself given value for the bill or that he takes through one who has given value. To take free from the defect of title, the holder for value must also be a holder in due course and a holder for value, as such, may not be a holder in due course, either because he is the payee of the instrument, or because he took a bill which suffered from some formal irregularity or because he did not act in good faith.

18.55 In the holder in due course is concentrated the highest efficacy of a bill of exchange due to the fact that it is a negotiable instrument. Subject to certain exceptions, the holder in due course is unaffected by any defect in the title of any previous holder, or by an omission on the part of any previous holder to carry out the steps necessary to preserve the rights of recourse of a holder against prior parties. Nevertheless, it cannot be said that the position of a holder in due course is impregnable, *e.g.* he cannot claim against an apparent party to the bill whose signature was unauthorised or forged, nor can he claim through such an apparent party against parties prior to that apparent party. A holder who derives title through a holder in due course has, generally, the rights of a holder in due course, but this is not the case if he was a party to any fraud or illegality affecting the bill before it came into the hands of a holder in due course through whom he derived the title (see section 29(1) of the Bills of Exchange Act.)

CAPACITY TO BE A HOLDER IN DUE COURSE

18.56 To be a holder in due course the holder of the bill must have taken the bill in such circumstances as to constitute him a holder within the definition of section 2 of the Act. For example, a person in possession of an unindorsed bill payable to the order of someone else is not a holder, though he may have given value for the bill and he cannot sue on the bill in his own name.

There is one class of holder within the meaning of the Act who falls outside section 29(1) of the Bills of Exchange Act. It has now been settled, after some doubt that the original payee of a bill cannot be a holder in due course although he is, of course, a holder and can be a holder for value. The House of Lords in *R.E. Jones* v. *Waring and Gillow*[71] took the view that the expression "holder in due course" cannot include the original payee of the cheque.

18.57 Section 29(1)(b) enacts that a holder in due course must have had the bill "negotiated" to him and since the section uses the word "negotiated," and not "issued or negotiated" it becomes necessary to determine the meaning of negotiation. Section 31(1) enacts: "A bill is negotiated when it is transferred from one person to another in such a manner as to constitute the transferee the holder of the bill," and since a holder is defined by section 2 as including the "payee or indorsee," section 29(1) could be satisfied by a transfer to the payee, and he therefore could become a holder in due course. Those who oppose this line of argument rely on section 31(3), which provides that "a bill payable to order is negotiated by the indorsement of the holder completed by delivery" and since the original payee does not become a holder by indorsement he cannot be a holder in due course.

The word "negotiated" in section 29(1) seems broadly to mean the same as "transferred," and the House of Lords, ignoring the effect of sections 29(1) and 31(1) construed the word "negotiated" in accordance with section 31(3), thus producing the result that a payee of an order bill can never be a holder in due course. The decision in *Waring and Gillow* has been accepted as correct in subsequent cases without question.[72]

THE COMPLETENESS AND REGULARITY OF THE BILL

18.58 A holder of a bill may be a holder in due course only if the bill is :omplete and regular on the face of it (and this includes the back) when he takes it. If the bill itself conveys a warning of possible defects because of its own formal irregularity, the rule of the overt market, *caveat emptor*, applies and the holder however honest can acquire no better title than that of his transferor. Consequently, the holder takes at his own risk a blank acceptance, or a bill which has been torn and the pieces pasted together if the condition of the instrument shows that a prior holder may have cancelled it. However, this situation has to be contrasted with that where the appearance of the bill is consistent with an accidental tearing.[73]

---

[71] [1926] A.C. 670.
[72] *Ayres* v. *Moore* [1940] 1 K.B. 278; *Arab Bank* v. *Ross* [1952] 2 Q.B. 216.
[73] *Ingham* v. *Primrose* (1859) 7 C.B. (N.S.) 82.

18.59   The effect of section 29(1) was discussed in *Arab Bank Ltd.* v. *Ross*[74] where the plaintiff's bank sued as holders in due course of two promissory notes made by the defendant in favour of "Fathi and Faysal Nabulsy Company" which were indorsed on the reverse "Fathi and Faysal Nabulsy." The court, on appeal, held that the indorsements were sufficient to pass title to the bank, but the bank did not become a holder in due course because the indorsements were irregular, in that they did not set out the name of the indorser, the company, in full.

The need for regularity was expressed by Lord Denning:

> "A bill of exchange is like currency. It should be above suspicion. Completeness and regularity must be determined by looking only at the bill itself; both sides must be in apparent order, and an irregularity in the indorsement will deprive a subsequent holder of the rights of a holder in due course . . . "

There is an exception to this rule of regularity namely, where a bill is indorsed by a person for the purpose of making himself liable on the bill (for example, to guarantee its payment). The signature of such persons raises the question whether the bill is complete and regular and whether there can be a holder in due course. In this type of situation two questions arise generally namely:–

(i) the indorsements are placed chronologically in the wrong order;

(ii) the indorsements appear on the bill in the wrong order and the question arises whether they are intended to create liability on the part of the indorser.

18.60   Both these questions have been examined by the courts. In *Macdonald & Co.* v. *Nash & Co.*[75] the payee's indorsement was placed on the bill after the indorser had indorsed it, but because the payee's indorsement was placed above the indorser's signature the indorsement in blank appeared in the proper place. The House of Lords held that a bill to the drawer's order, indorsed by a third party before any indorsement by the drawer in his capacity as payee, was a bill of exchange, although incomplete, and it could be completed by the drawer afterwards indorsing his signature at any time, including a time after the defendant had indorsed the bill to make himself liable on it to the drawer.

A holder in due course who, therefore, takes a bill which is not complete and regular on the face of it can in these circumstances become a holder in due course under section 20 if he fulfils the conditions under that section.

The House of Lords did not overrule *Jenkins* v. *Coomber*[76] and *Shaw* v. *Holland*[77] where it had been held that the defendants who had indorsed the bills as sureties were not liable because at the time of the indorsement the bills were not complete and regular on the face because they lacked the drawer's indorsement.

18.61   The second situation which arises is whether a backer is liable on a bill to a subsequent holder if the indorsements are formally irregular. In *Yeoman Credit Ltd.* v. *Gregory*[78] the payee's indorsement was below the drawer's signature and was a restrictive indorsement under which no title to the bill

---

[74] [1952] 2 Q.B. 216.
[75] [1924] A.C. 625.
[76] [1898] 2 Q.B. 168.
[77] [1913] 2 K.B. 15.
[78] [1963] 1 W.L.R. 434.

was intended to pass. The court held the fact that the indorsement by the plaintiffs was restrictive and subsequent in time to the defendants' indorsements and, added below the defendants' indorsement, did not prevent the bill being complete and regular on its face. Regard must be had to the intention of the parties as established by extrinsic evidence. However, the court, having established the general rule held that in the particular case the defendant was not liable because there had not been due presentment of the bill on the dates when the bills fell due for payment. The court cited with approval the judgment of Wright J. in *National Corporation Sales* v. *Bernardi*[79]:

" . . . on general principles, evidence, in my judgment, is admissible to explain the intention with which a signature is added on the back, since the order of the indorsements as they principally appear on the back is not conclusive."

OVERDUE BILLS AND NOTICE OF DISHONOUR

A holder in due course must have taken the bill he holds before it became overdue and without notice of any prior dishonour which had taken place.[80] **18.62**

When a bill is overdue it can be negotiated within the limits of the Bills of Exchange Act namely, it remains transferable but it cannot be negotiated so as to confer a title on a subsequent holder free from defects affecting it when it became due. On the other hand, where a party takes a bill which has previously been dishonoured by non-acceptance with knowledge of that fact, he cannot be a holder in due course, but if a bill payable on demand is taken by A before it has been in circulation for an unreasonable time, although it has in fact already been presented for payment and dishonoured, A can still be a holder in due course if he does not know that this has happened.

THE NECESSITY FOR VALUE AND GOOD FAITH

A holder in due course must himself have given value or derive title **18.63** through a prior holder in due course, and he cannot take the benefit of the fact that he takes through a holder for value who was not a holder in due course. For example, A gives value for a bill with notice of a defect in the prior title and A indorses the bill to B, who takes it gratuitously but without knowledge of the defect. B cannot be a holder in due course. The conditions for holding in due course cannot be split up among successive holders and value and good faith must proceed from the same person to constitute a holder in due course. However, once this has happened, the benefits of a holder being a holder in due course are enjoyed by subsequent holders of the bill, and they, therefore, take free from defects which do not affect him.

In order to be a holder in due course, it is essential that the holder should act in good faith. Section 90 of the Act provides that a thing is done in good faith where it is in fact done honestly, whether it be done negligently or not. It is, therefore, a question of the state of mind of the person who takes the instrument at the time he takes it. A party who has not taken the bill in good faith whether he gives value or not will not, therefore, be able to retain it

[79] [1931] 2 K.B. 188.
[80] s.36(5).

and he will obtain no better title than the person who negotiates it. Thus, in *Clarke* v. *Shee*[81] Lord Mansfield said:

> "Where money or notes are paid bona fide and upon a valuable consideration, they shall never be brought back by the true owner, but where they come mala fide into a persons hands, they are in the nature of a specific property, and if their identity can be traced and ascertained, the party has a right to recover."

18.64   A person who buys a bill from a person whom he realises is not its true owner cannot be a holder in due course, and similarly, a person who wilfully shuts his eyes to the existence of a defect of title which is apparent cannot be such a holder. Once the taker of the instrument has a suspicion that something is wrong with the bill, he is put on inquiry. In *Jones* v. *Gordon*[82] Lord Blackburn examined the meaning of good faith and stated:

> "If the facts and circumstances are such that the jury, or whoever has to try the question, comes to the conclusion that he was not honestly blundering, but that he must have had a suspicion that there was something wrong, and that he refrained from asking questions, not because he was an honest blunderer, but because he thought in his own mind 'I suspect there is something wrong and if I make further enquiry it will be no longer my suspecting it but my knowing it, and then I shall not be able to recover.' I think that is dishonest."

The two important points which arise out of Lord Blackburn's judgment are:

(i) If a man suspects something is wrong with a negotiable instrument, that is enough to prevent him from taking it in good faith. The suspicion need not be accurate, provided it is near the truth.

(ii) If a man admits that he was careless in not discovering a defect in the title to the bill, he is entitled to be treated as having acted in good faith, but when a man says he was careless, the court may conclude that he was not in fact merely careless, but did suspect something to be wrong and wilfully closed his eyes to it. In that case he has not acted in good faith.

18.65   It is more difficult to determine the question whether the doctrine of constructive notice can be applied to negotiable instruments, and here, two issues have to be looked at: (i) whether the person taking the instrument knows of facts which would make a reasonable businessman suspicious and (ii) even if he had no knowledge of such facts, whether he was grossly negligent in not discovering the defect and whether in consequence he must be treated as having acted in bad faith.

On the former point, the courts approved a direction given to the jury in *Gill* v. *Cubitt*,[83] namely, that they were to find a verdict for the defendant, acceptor, if they thought the plaintiff, holder, took the bill "under circumstances which ought to have excited the suspicion of a prudent and careful man." This ruling was followed in *Down* v. *Halling*[84] and had it been adhered to it would have created an objective standard for judging a holder's good faith, and the standard of behaviour of a reasonable business man would have determined whether a holder was a holder in due course.

---

[81] (1773) 1 Cowp. 197.
[82] (1877) 2 App.Cas. 616.
[83] (1824) 3 B. & C. 446.
[84] (1825) 4 B. & C. 330.

However, the courts rejected this line of reasoning in favour of a subjective test, and the relevant question is not whether the person who took the instrument ought reasonably to have suspected a defect in the title to it, but whether he must in fact have suspected it in the light of the reasonable knowledge he actually possessed.

In *London Joint Stock Bank Ltd.* v. *Simmons*[85] it was contended on behalf of **18.66** the plaintiffs that the bank was under a duty to inquire as to the title of the person with whom it dealt, or alternatively as to the authority he possessed to deal with the instruments on behalf of his principal. The bank having failed to do this could not be a holder in due course since it had not acted in good faith. The House of Lords, however, rejected this reasoning and said there were no circumstances known to the bank to cause it to entertain suspicions, and so the bank was entitled to retain and realise the securities having taken the instruments in good faith and for value. The theory of constructive notice has thus been rejected. In *Raphael* v. *Bank of England*[86] it was said that for the purposes of section 29 constructive notice is not sufficient. Notice means actual notice, although it need not be specific or complete and so knowledge of the suspicious facts or a suspicion of something wrong combined with a wilful disregard of the means of knowledge will amount to notice.

Once a holder for value of the instruments has notice that the person from **18.67** whom he took them was not the unincumbered owner but had only a qualified, conditional, or voidable interest, then such a holder, however honestly he may have acted in taking the instruments, will acquire a limited interest equivalent to that which the person with whom he dealt could lawfully transfer. If, however, the holder for value deals with an agent, whom he believes has full authority to deal with the particular instruments and of whom he has no suspicion that his powers may be restricted, the holder is entitled to retain the instruments as owner, notwithstanding any fraudulent act of the agent committed on his principal.

Finally, the situation of the holder who is grossly negligent in taking the bill from the transferor remains to be dealt with. In *Snow* v. *Peacock*[87] a banker changed a £500 Bank of England note for a stranger, without any further inquiry than merely asking his name. He was held liable in conversion, to the person from whom the note had been unlawfully obtained. Best C.J. said:–

> "The party's caution should increase with the amount of the note which he is called upon to change. A man may change a £20 note without asking a single question, but would that be right as to one of several thousands?"

The transferee's title would, therefore, be affected by a failure to take due **18.68** caution if the circumstances indicate that inquiry was called for. This is consistent with the subjective test of good faith which now prevails. If a man takes a negotiable instrument honestly believing that he is acquiring a good title to it, even though that belief is negligent he does acquire a good title unless he is so grossly negligent that he does not follow up suspicions which he must have entertained.[88]

---

[85] [1892] A.C. 201.
[86] (1855) 17 C.B.N.S. 161.
[87] (1826) 3 Bing. 406.
[88] *Goodman* v. *Harvey* (1836) 4 A. & E. 870.

It is, therefore, not sufficient to establish negligence or carelessness, however serious, on the part of the holder of a bill to deprive him of the status of a holder in due course. He must have appreciated from the circumstances that the title of his transferor was suspect and he must have failed to satisfy himself by inquiry that his suspicions were groundless.[89]

THE TITLE OF THE HOLDER IN DUE COURSE

The general rule is that if a person's title to a bill is defective, the person to whom he transfers it will obtain no better title to the instrument than he himself has, and the true owner of the bill can therefore enforce his rights, notwithstanding any ineffective transfers of the title by other persons. Thus, if someone forges an indorsement of a bill to a person who believes the indorsement to be genuine, the indorsement is a nullity and the true owner may recover the bill and enforce it himself.[90]

18.69 If, however, the holder for value of a negotiable instrument takes it with actual notice that the person with whom he is dealing has only a limited interest, however honestly he may have acted in so doing, he cannot acquire a greater interest in it than that which the person with whom he dealt could lawfully confer.

If an indorser is induced to indorse it by mistake, the negotiation of the bill is void, and the indorsee obtains no title to the bill despite his good faith. But if an indorsement is merely voidable by the transferor (*e.g.* if it is induced by misrepresentation or undue influence) the title of a subsequent holder in due course is unimpeachable, and this applies also to any person who acquires the bill for value subsequent to the voidable indorsement without notice of the indorser's right to avoid it.

Defects of title from which the holder in due course takes free

18.70 A holder in due course of a bill of exchange, in addition to having all the rights and powers of a holder, is provided by the Act with certain additional protection. Section 38(2) of the Act provides that where the holder is a holder in due course:

> "he holds the bill free from any defect of title of prior parties, as well as from mere personal defences available to prior parties among themselves and may enforce payment against all parties liable on the bill."

Defects of title are enumerated, although not exhaustively, in section 29(2) of the Act which provides:–

> "In particular the title of a person who negotiates a bill is defective within the meaning of this Act when he obtains the bill, or the acceptance thereof, by fraud, duress, or force and fear, or other unlawful means, or for an illegal consideration, or when he negotiates it in breach of faith, or under such circumstances as amount to a fraud."

The expression "personal defences" in section 38(2) refers to such defences as set-off and counterclaim, and probably covers defences such as omission of the duties of presentation. The operation of the section may be exemplified as follows: A, the holder of a bill, indorses it to B, who is a person who cannot be made liable on a bill (namely, a minor or a member of a

[89] *Raphael* v. *Bank of England* (1855) 17 C.B. 161; *Venables* v. *Baring Bros.* [1892] 2 Ch. 527.
[90] *London Joint Stock Bank Ltd.* v. *Simmons.*

foreign embassy who enjoys diplomatic privilege). The bill is stolen from B by C, who forges B's indorsement and disposes of the bill to D, who fulfils the conditions to be a holder in due course. D indorses the bill to E, and E to F, who is also a holder in due course. F can sue D and E on the dishonour of the bill, and it makes no difference if E obtained the bill from D by fraud. But F cannot sue A or B, who became parties to the bill before the forgery of B's indorsement, which is, of course, a nullity.

The list of defects in section 29(2) of which the holder in due course takes free is not exhaustive; the section states "in particular" that the title of a transferor is defective when affected by fraud, duress or one of the other specified defects. The holder in due course will be able to enforce the instrument despite these defects, although if duress, fraud or illegality is proved, he will have to prove positively that he took the bill in good faith and without notice of such defects. Duress is a common law concept, and is supplemented by the equitable doctrine of undue influence which renders a contract voidable if a party is induced to enter into it by the improper influence of the other. The fact that undue influence is not mentioned specifically in section 29(2) does not mean that a party who obtains the transfer of a negotiable instrument by such means acquires an unimpeachable title, although a subsequent holder in due course may do so. The words "or other unlawful means" in section 29(2) probably covers undue influence. Similarly, the section makes no mention of a transfer procured by misrepresentation, and once again it is clear that the words "or other unlawful means" covers misrepresentations and that a subsequent holder in due course would take free from such a defect. **18.71**

The wording of sections 29 and 38 is in fact confusing, because section 29 refers to defects in the title of a person who negotiates a bill, whereas section 38(2) speaks of a holder in due course taking free of any defect of title of prior parties and subsection (3) of defects in the holder's title. These modes of reference must be assumed to refer to the same thing and the difference in wording referring either to the transferor's defective title or a holder in due course acquiring free from all defects of title must be considered insignificant.

By section 30(2) the Act provides that every holder is prima facie deemed to be a holder in due course, but if it can be proved or admitted that the acceptance, issue or subsequent negotiation of a bill was affected by fraud, duress or force and fear, or illegality the burden of proof is shifted and the holder who sues on the bill must prove that value has been given in good faith for the bill subsequent to the fraud or illegality. **18.72**

Defects of which the holder in due course does not take free

The holder in due course can ignore many defects in title to an instrument, but there are a number of situations where his claim to the instrument or to rights arising from it can be defeated. In each of these cases, other than forgery, it is not the whole title of the holder in due course which is invalid, but his right to sue one or more particular parties to the instrument and so his normal rights as a holder in due course have to be qualified accordingly. These defects which affect a holder in due course may be divided into those which arise under the law relating to negotiable instruments and those which arise otherwise. **18.73**

1. DEFECTS UNDER THE LAW OF NEGOTIABLE INSTRUMENTS

18.74   (a) A party who expressly negatives liability by signing *sans recours* cannot be sued although title can be traced through him.

(b) A person whose signature has been forged or is unauthorised incurs no liability even to a holder in due course, unless that person is precluded from alleging forgery or want of authority.[91]

(c) A holder in due course cannot sue a person who can plead the defence of *non est factum* but it seems that a title can be obtained through such an invalid signature.[92]

(d) Where an overdue bill is negotiated it can only be negotiated subject to any defect of title affecting it at its maturity, so no person can give or acquire a better title than that which the person from whom he took it had, *e.g.* no one can take an overdue bill as a holder in due course.

(e) Where a bill that is not overdue is dishonoured before the date it becomes due, any person who takes it with notice of the dishonour takes it subject to the defect of title and, therefore, not in good faith. However, if the holder takes without notice of any defect or the fact of dishonour he will be a holder in due course and he takes free from the defect.

(f) A former holder in due course is not protected against defects arising after he negotiates the bill if he later re-acquires it after maturity even though in ignorance of the defect but he is protected against defects which arose before he first acquired the bill.

(g) A holder in due course is not protected against a failure to give notice of dishonour by non-payment of a demand bill by section 48(1) of the Bills of Exchange Act.

(h) A holder in due course is not protected against failure to give notice of dishonour by non-payment of a demand bill by section 48(1) of the Bills of Exchange Act.[93]

2. OTHER DEFECTS

18.75   These relate to the incapacity or the immunity from suit of the party whom the holder seeks to make liable on the bill.

(a) Infants and statutory corporations contracting *ultra vires* incur no liability on negotiable instruments although title to such an instrument can be traced through their signatures and acts in negotiating the instrument.

(b) Sovereign and diplomatic immunity of foreign ambassadors and corporations prevents a holder in due course from suing them as parties to the instrument unless the immunity is waived, or the case falls within one of the statutory qualifications. Again the fact that a sovereign power or a person or body which enjoys sovereign or diplomatic immunity cannot be sued on the instrument does not prevent a holder deriving a title to it through them and his title is in no way impaired by the immunity of a prior party.

The rights and liabilities of the parties to a bill of exchange

18.76   The various parties who may incur liability on a bill of exchange are
(1) the drawer;
(2) the drawee; who may become

[91] s.24, Bills of Exchange Act 1882.
[92] *Ayres* v. *Moore* [1939] 4 All E.R. 351.
[93] *Roscoe* v. *Hardy* (1812) 12 East 434.

(3) the acceptor; —— *18.51*

(4) the payee (in an order bill), or the bearer. The payee may later become

(5) the indorser;

(6) the quasi-indorser;

(7) the transferor by delivery, or the bearer of a bill who transfers it.

Sections 53–58 of the Act deal with the precise liability of the parties. It is the circumstances and the scope of the liability incurred by these parties that will be examined in this section of the chapter.

THE DRAWER

The drawer is, normally, responsible for bringing a bill of exchange into existence. As with all parties, he must sign and deliver the bill before he incurs any liability on it. Until the bill is accepted he is primarily liable on it, and if the instrument is of a nature that is never accepted, *e.g.* a cheque, the drawer remains primarily liable throughout. **18.77**

If the bill is accepted, then the acceptor becomes primarily liable, and the drawer in effect becomes the guarantor for the acceptor. Consequently, the drawer is only liable to pay on the bill if the acceptor fails to pay and the holder has taken proper steps to bring this guarantee liability into existence. Section 18(1) of the Act provides that a bill can be accepted before it is signed by the drawer. In such a case the drawer never becomes primarily liable on the bill and his liability throughout is that of guarantor.

Section 55(1)(a) of the Act deals with the liability of the drawer and imposes on him an undertaking that the bill will be accepted and paid on proper presentation, and if it is dishonoured by the acceptor, he (the drawer) will be liable to pay the holder, or to compensate any indorser who has been compelled to make payment provided proper proceedings are taken on dishonour. In *Starke* v. *Cheesman*[94] it was held that the act of drawing a bill implies a promise from the drawer to pay it, if the drawee does not. Moreover, an indorsement by the drawer does not give him a new character as indorser, or divest him of any liability to which as drawer of the bill he would have been subject, and he remains the ultimate debtor.

Where, however, the acceptor fails to pay on a bill of exchange accepted by him the bill is not a debt. In *Henry* v. *Burbidge*[95] the court held that an acceptance constitutes a promise to pay, but where the acceptor fails to make payment, there arises against the drawer by law, a promise to pay the bill if the acceptor fails to do so. **18.78**

Section 55(1)(b) states that the drawer is precluded from denying to a holder in due course the existence of the payee and his capacity to indorse it. However, section 7(3) provides that where the payee is fictitious or a non-existing person the bill is payable to bearer. This means that parties subsequent to the forged indorsement of the fictitious or non-existing payee may sue the acceptor or drawer. The fact that the drawer may not attempt to deny the existence of the payee prevents the drawer making any attempt to escape liability on the ground of the payee's non-existence.

Even if the payee is in existence, the drawer cannot raise, as against the holder in due course the lack of capacity in the payee to indorse the bill.[96] The infancy of the payee is, therefore, no answer, in an action by the indor-

---

[94] (1699) Carth. 509.

[95] (1837) 3 Bing. N.C. 501.

[96] *Grey* v. *Cooper* (1782) 3 Doug.K.B. 65.

see of a bill of exchange against the drawer. The estoppel under this section does not prevent the drawer disputing the genuineness of the payee's indorsement, however, unless the indorsement was already on the bill when the drawer signed it and he knew it to be a forgery.

THE DRAWEE

18.79 The drawee is strictly not a party to the bill and incurs no liability on the bill until he accepts it. Thus, banks which never accept cheques do not incur liability on them to the payee or the holder. However, a drawee who refuses to accept a bill may be sued for breach of a separate agreement with the drawer or payee although he cannot be sued on the bill itself.

THE ACCEPTOR [18-51]

18.80 If the drawee accepts the bill he becomes primarily liable to make payment on it. Section 54(1) provides that by the acceptor accepting a bill he undertakes to make payment on that bill according to his acceptance. Where, therefore, the bill has been altered so as to increase the amount payable after acceptance, the acceptor will only be liable to pay the original amount. Moreover, the acceptor is under no obligation to see that the bill is in such a state as to preclude possible alterations.[97]

By section 54(2)(a) the acceptor is precluded from denying to a holder in due course:

(i) the existence of the drawer;

(ii) the genuineness of the drawer's signature. This is an exception to the rule under section 24 that a forged signature is a nullity;

(iii) the capacity and authority of the drawer to draw the bill;

By section 54(2)(b) the acceptor is precluded from denying to a holder in due course:

(a) the capacity of the drawer to indorse an order bill, but not the genuineness or validity of the indorsement; and by section 54(2)(c) the acceptor is precluded from denying to a holder in due course:

(b) the existence and capacity of the payee to indorse the bill in the case of a bill payable, or in purported payment of a bill, to a named payee or his order but not the genuineness or validity of his indorsement.

Since the acceptor cannot deny the genuineness of the drawer's signature, the courts have consistently held that in an action against the acceptor of a bill of exchange the authenticity of the drawer's signature need not be proved.[98] In *Jenys* v. *Fowler*[99] and *Sanderson* v. *Collman*[1] the court held that the acceptor of a bill cannot, in an action against him by an indorsee, dispute the handwriting of the drawer because he is estopped by his acceptance from denying its authenticity.

18.81 In *Beeman* v. *Duck*[2] a bill of exchange purporting to be drawn by B. & W. (a really existing firm), payable to their order and to be indorsed by them, was accepted by the drawee with that indorsement on it. The court held that where the name of a real person is forged as that of the drawer and payee, a drawee who accepts the bill in ignorance of the forgery is estopped from

---

[97] *Schofield* v. *Londesborough* (1896) A.C. 514.
[98] *Wilkinson* v. *Lutwidge* [1925] 1 Stra. 648.
[99] (1733) 2 Stra. 946.
[1] (1842) 4 Man. & G. 209.
[2] (1843) 8 Q.B. 473.

denying the validity of the drawer's signature, but not the forged indorsement of the payee although in the same handwriting. This case in fact goes further than the wording of section 51(2) which precludes an acceptor from denying the genuineness of the drawer's signature.

In an action against the acceptor of a bill of exchange by a holder in due course, it is no defence that the drawers who had drawn the bill payable to themselves and indorsed it, were infants or under any other incapacity when the bill was drawn.[3]

Similarly, in an action by a bona fide indorsee against the acceptor of a bill of exchange payable to the drawer's order, the defendant is estopped from pleading that the drawer indorser was an undischarged bankrupt.[4]

The acceptor of a bill of exchange, payable to the order of a drawer which is a corporation, cannot deny the capacity of the drawer to draw or indorse such a bill. In *Halifax* v. *Lyle*[5] the court said the law was that the acceptor of a bill, payable to the order of another, cannot be permitted to deny the capacity of the person who draws it or the person who indorses it as payee to carry out either of these acts effectively.

Where a bill is made payable to a fictitious person to the knowledge of the acceptor and is indorsed by the drawer, the acceptor cannot impugn the holder's title on the ground that the indorsement is fictitious.

THE PAYEE

If the payee, or an indorsee under a special indorsement transfers the bill for value without indorsing it, then section 31(4) provides that the transferee gets whatever rights the transferor had to the bill, together with the right to demand an indorsement from the transferor. Such an indorsement only operates from the time it is actually written on the bill so that if the transferee learns of defects of title prior to the indorsement he will be bound by these defects.

18.82

THE INDORSER

By section 55(2) of the Act the indorser of a bill undertakes that on due presentment it will be accepted and paid and that if it is dishonoured he will compensate the holder provided the requisite steps by way of notice of dishonour and protest (in the case of foreign bills) are taken. In other words the indorser guarantees acceptance and payment of the bill to the holder, and he also guarantees parties to the bill subsequent to himself that he will reimburse them if the holder enforces his right of recourse against them.

18.83

Sections 55(2)(b) and (c) provide that the indorser is precluded from denying to a holder in due course:

(i) the geniuneness and regularity in all respects of the drawers signature and all previous indorsements; and

(ii) is precluded from denying to the immediate or subsequent indorsee that the bill was at the time of his indorsement a valid and subsisting bill and that he had a good title.

In *MacGregor* v. *Rhodes*[6] the declaration charged that P drew a bill of

---

[3] *Tayler* v. *Croker* (1802) 4 Esp. 187.
[4] (1846) 1 Q.B. 473.
[5] (1849) 18 L.J.Ex 197.
[6] (1856) 6 E. & B. 266.

exchange payable to his own order and indorsed it to the defendants, who indorsed it to the plaintiffs and that the bill was dishonoured.

The defendants admitted that they indorsed the bill to the plaintiff but sought to deny that P had indorsed it to them. The court held that the fact of the indorsement to the plaintiffs would be conclusive evidence of the validity of P's indorsement to the defendants, and would estop them from showing that what purported to be P's indorsement was a forgery. It was further held that when a man indorses a bill he undertakes that, if the drawee or acceptor fails to pay it, the indorser will do so and he cannot deny that the payee has made the order.

QUASI-INDORSER

18.84   In addition to the liability of an indorser section 56 of the Act provides that a quasi-indorser is someone who signs the bill without actually being the drawer or indorser. He does, however, incur the liability of an indorser to a holder in due course. He does not sign the bill to transfer title to it but to guarantee payment. The liability of the quasi-indorser is that of guarantor or "banker" and the bill is made commercially more attractive.

TRANSFEROR BY DELIVERY

18.85   By section 8(3) a bill is payable to bearer if it states on its face that it is payable to bearer, or on which "the only or last indorsement is an indorsement in blank."

Section 58 of the Act deals with liability arising from the delivery of a bearer bill. It provides that where the holder of a bill payable to bearer negotiates it by delivery without indorsing it, he is called a "transferor by delivery." A transferor by delivery is not liable on the instrument except in exceptional circumstances, *e.g.* where the transferor impliedly gives an indemnity against loss.[7] Section 58(3) does, however, provide that a transferor by delivery warrants to his immediate transferee (if he gave value) that the bill is what it purports to be (*i.e.* it is not a forgery), that he has a right to transfer it, and that at the time of transfer he had no knowledge of any facts which rendered it valueless.

The liability of a transferor by delivery is less extensive than an indorser, since an indorser's liability is not limited to his immediate indorsee for value. Further, an indorsee will be liable on a genuine bill when it is dishonoured but a transferor by delivery will only be liable if he had knowledge at the time of transfer which rendered the bill valueless.

A holder of a bill payable to order who transfers it by mere delivery is not a "transferor by delivery" and he will be liable to the holder to give a proper indorsement when required.[8] Finally, it should be noted that a drawer or indorser who negatives his liability by signing *sans recours* is bound by the warranties given by the "transferor by delivery" under section 58(3).

Negotiation

18.86   The rules relating to the negotiation of a bill of exchange are set out in sections 31–38 of the Bills of Exchange Act 1882. Section 31 provides that a bill is negotiated when it is transferred from one person to another in such a

---

[7] *Turner* v. *Stones* (1843) 12 L.J.Q.B. 303; *Woodland* v. *Fear* (1857) 26 L.J.Q.B. 202.
[8] s.31(4), Bills of Exchange Act 1882.

way that the transferee becomes the holder of the bill. The definition section[9] states that the "holder" means the payee or indorsee of a bill or note who is in possession of it, or the bearer. A bearer instrument is negotiated by delivery. This includes any bill which is expressly drawn to bearer, or one which was drawn to the order of a specified person but has since been indorsed "in blank." An order instrument is negotiated by indorsement and delivery. The word "delivery"[10] is defined as "transfer of possession, actual or constructive, from one person to another." However, not all transfers amount to negotiation, e.g. where the instrument is handed over for safe keeping.[11] It is, therefore, essential that a transfer of a bearer instrument is accompanied by an intention to transfer title to the transferee.

A bill specially indorsed is payable to the order of the person named in the indorsement, whether or not the words "or order" are added. A person who transfers an order bill for value without an actual indorsement is merely assigning the bill. The transferor, therefore, takes subject to equities. A subsequent indorsement of the bill will only operate as a negotiation from the time of indorsement. A bill can only be negotiated by the holder. In the case of an order bill, he will be the payee or the person specified as indorsee in the last indorsement. The holder's signature will suffice provided it is written with the intention to indorse the bill.

The indorsement is usually written on the back of the bill, but if there is **18.87** insufficient space for further indorsements, a slip of paper may be attached[12] on which further indorsements may be written. A holder may not, however, have a good title to an instrument, e.g. the thief of a bearer bill or one indorsed in blank, has no title to it but since it is a bearer bill and the thief, the bearer he is, therefore the holder. A holder in due course who acquires the bill from a person whose title to the bill is defective, may however acquire a valid title. Moreover, a bill payable to bearer must be coupled with an intention to pass title, for negotiation to be complete.

The absence of an intention to negotiate the bill is a personal defence as between previous parties; it does not affect the title of a holder in due course.

Section 21(2) of the Act provides that if a bill is in the hands of a holder in due course, a valid delivery of the bill by all parties prior to him, so as to make them liable is "conclusively presumed." Section 2 provides that delivery (transfer) may be actual or "constructive." Thus, there can be a transfer of possession without the instrument actually changing hands, e.g. where a person holding the instrument as owner agrees to transfer ownership to someone else and continues to hold as an agent for that person, or if a person who holds the bill as an agent agrees to hold the same bill as an agent for another person.

INDORSEMENT

There are a number of statutory requirements which must be satisfied if an **18.88** indorsement is to operate as part of the negotiation. The indorsement must be written on the instrument itself and signed by the indorser or his agent,[13] e.g. where one partner in a firm signs on behalf of his co-partners. Usually,

[9] s.2, Bills of Exchange Act 1882.
[10] Ibid.
[11] Lombard Banking Ltd. v. Central Garage and Engineering Co. [1963] 1 Q.B. 220.
[12] Called an "allonge."
[13] s.91(1), Bills of Exchange Act 1882.

the indorsement is written on the back of the instrument itself but there are cases which have held that an indorsement on the face of it would be valid.

PARTIAL INDORSEMENTS

18.89 Section 32(3) of the Bills of Exchange Act 1882, provides that an indorsement if it is to operate as a negotiation of the instrument, must be an indorsement of the entire bill. Thus if A is the holder of a bill for £1,000 and he purports to indorse £500 of it to X, retaining £500 for himself; or if A purports to indorse the bill £500 to Y and as to £500 to Z, these indorsements do not amount to a valid negotiation of the bill. If X, Y, and Z have given value they acquire only equitable interests in the bill as assignees and so will take subject to any defects of title affecting A. They will have no title to the instrument as holders, and so the acceptor or prior parties may safely pay the whole amount of the bill to A.

Where in an order bill a payee or indorsee is given a wrong name, or his name is mis-spelt, he may indorse the bill in the wrong name or spelling, adding if he thinks fit, his own signature.[14]

KINDS OF INDORSEMENT

18.90 An indorsement may take one of three forms, namely: (i) indorsement in blank, (ii) special indorsement and (iii) restrictive indorsement. An indorsement in blank consists merely of the indorser's signature and such an instrument is payable to bearer. A special indorsement "specifies the person to whom or to whose order the bill is to be payable." No particular form of words is necessary but the form is likely to use the words "pay X or order" followed by the signature of the indorser. It is immaterial whether or not the words "or order" are included.

The Act recognises that the indorsee under a special indorsement is in effect a new payee and the provisions of the Act relating to a payee apply with the necessary modifications to an indorsee under a special indorsement.[15] This, basically, means that the indorsee must be indicated with reasonable certainty, that a bill may be indorsed to two or more indorsees jointly, or to one of two indorsees in the alternative, or to one or more of several indorsees. These rules do not infringe the rules against partial indorsements since the whole bill is indorsed by the indorser. In the case of alternative indorsees one person gets the right to the entire bill, and in the latter case the group as a whole gets a right to the entire bill. Where the indorsee is a fictitious or non-existing person, the bill will be payable to bearer, and any later forged indorsements can be ignored.[16]

If the indorsement merely uses the words "Pay Order" followed by the signature of the indorser, then by section 8(4) this is equivalent to "Pay X or order" and X can in his turn indorse.

18.91 The Act provides that any holder may convert an indorsement in blank into a special indorsement, by writing an order to pay a specific person over

[14] s.32(4), Bills of Exchange Act 1882.
[15] s.34(3).
[16] *Bank of England* v. *Vagliano* A.C. 107.

the signature of the indorser. The bill will then require indorsement by the person whose name has been inserted, if it is to be further negotiated. The indorsee in turn may indorse in blank or specially.

Section 35 provides that there is a restrictive indorsement where the terms of the indorsement prohibit further transfer of the instrument as such, *e.g.* when the indorsement states "Pay X only," or when it clearly indicates that it is not intended to transfer ownership in the instrument, but merely to give the transferee authority to deal with the instrument for some limited purpose, *e.g.* 'Pay X for the account of Z," where X would receive payment and hold the proceeds as an agent for Z.[17] The section contains other examples of restrictive indorsements but it should be emphasised they are merely illustrations. Such an indorsement gives the indorsee the right to receive payment and to sue any party whom the indorser could have sued, but it gives the indorsee no power to transfer his rights "unless expressly authorised."

DURATION OF NEGOTIABILITY

Section 36 of the Act provides that when a bill is originally negotiable it continues to be negotiable until it is either restrictively indorsed or "discharged by payment or otherwise." The words "or otherwise" cover discharge by cancellation, renunciation, etc. **18.92**

If a bill payable at a fixed or determinable future time is negotiated after that date, the bill can only be negotiated subject to defects of title.[18] Since the date for payment has passed, anyone finding the instrument in circulation after that date has notice that something abnormal has happened. The same rule applies where the bill is overdue and has been in circulation for an unreasonable length of time or if the bill is negotiated after dishonour.

Except in the case of a time instrument where an indorsement clearly bears a date after the maturity of the instrument, every negotiation is presumed to have taken place before the bill was overdue.

Section 37 deals with special circumstances, *e.g.* "where a bill is negotiated back to the drawer, or to a prior indorser, or to the acceptor," any such party may "re-issue and further re-negotiate the bill, but he is not entitled to enforce payment of the bill against any intervening party to whom he was previously liable." Thus, for example where X gives a cheque to Y to settle a debt for £100. The cheque is passed through several people to Z, who himself owes £100 to X. Z may hand the cheque to X in settlement of his debt, but X can put that cheque into circulation yet again by handing it in payment of a debt, to A. **18.93**

Where A, an indorser of a cheque, has indorsed back to him the same cheque after it has passed through the hands of intermediate parties (*e.g.* B and C) section 37 provides that A may re-issue the bill to D, but if the bill is dishonoured and D exercises his right of recourse against A, A cannot exercise a right of recourse against B and C by virtue of his second indorsement, since if A were permitted to do this, B and C would have a right of recourse against A because of his original indorsement.

[17] *Bute (Marquess)* v. *Barclays Bank* [1955] 1 Q.B. 202.
[18] s.29(1)(a), Bills of Exchange Act 1882.

However, section 37 provides that a bill can only be re-issued subject to the Bills of Exchange Act, in particular sections 59–64.

Dishonour and notice of dishonour

18.94   A bill of exchange may be dishonoured either by non-acceptance or by a failure to make payment on maturity. A bill may be dishonoured when it is properly presented for acceptance and acceptance is either refused or cannot be obtained or when presentment for acceptance is excused and the bill is not in fact accepted. The bill will be treated as dishonoured for non-acceptance if the drawee becomes bankrupt, dies, is a fictitious person, does not have the capacity to draw a bill or fails to accept within a reasonable time.

The holder will have an immediate right of recourse against the drawer and indorsers of the bill and is discharged from his obligation to present the bill for payment on maturity. If the drawee gives a qualified acceptance, the holder may elect whether or not to treat the bill as dishonoured.

A bill is dishonoured by non-payment either when the instrument is presented for payment and payment is refused or when the time for payment has passed and the instrument is still unpaid. The holder of the bill again has an immediate right of recourse against the drawer and indorsers.

If the instrument has passed through the hands of a number of indorsers, the holder may elect to sue, any or all of them jointly. Alternatively, the holder may elect to sue the indorser who transferred the bill to him. That indorser may then sue any indorsers prior to him until the chain of indorsers flows back to the original indorser and the drawer, and he can then sue the acceptor. Moreover, an indorser who has been held liable to the holder can sue any one or more of the indorsers prior to him, or sue all of them jointly.

18.95   When a bill has been dishonoured for non-acceptance or non-payment the holder must, in order to protect his cause of action, give notice of the dishonour to the drawer and indorsers if they are not to be discharged from their liability. The drawer and indorsers are discharged from liability not only on the bill but also for the consideration received.

The Bills of Exchange Act 1882, section 48, provides that the drawer and indorsers will remain liable although there has been a failure by the holder to give notice, firstly, where a holder in due course takes a bill after the transferor has failed to give notice of this failure and, secondly, where a bill has been dishonoured by non-acceptance and notice of the dishonour has been given, the holder need not give notice of a subsequent dishonour by non-payment unless in the interval the bill has been accepted.

18.96   The notice of dishonour is not required to be formal or in a specific form of words. The notice may be given either in writing or personally, and in any terms which identify the bill and indicate whether it has been dishonoured for non-acceptance or non-payment. Thus, merely returning the bill to the drawer or indorser is sufficient. Notice of dishonour must, however, be given within a reasonable time. If the parties live in the "same place," notice must reach the holder or indorser the day after the dishonour of the bill, or, if they live in different places, notice must be sent off on the day following the dishonour. The rules relating to notice of dishonour provide that the notice must be given by or on behalf of the holder, or by an indorser or on his behalf. An indorser can rely on the notice given by the holder, but in order to ensure that he will be indemnified, any indorser who may be held liable can give notice to the drawer and prior indorsers. However, notice given by the holder will be effective for all subsequent holders and any prior indorsers entitled to sue the holder. The same rules apply to an indorser who gives notice of the dishonour.

The obligation to give notice of dishonour is dispensed with if it is actually impossible, or if the right to be notified has been waived. Section 50(2) dispenses with the notice if, after the exercise of reasonable diligence, notice cannot be given.

NOTING AND PROTEST

18.97 When a foreign bill is dishonoured notice of dishonour must be given, as in the case of an inland bill (*i.e.* a bill which is drawn and payable within the United Kingdom on a person resident there) but the bill must also be "protested" in order to preserve the holder's right of recourse against the drawer and indorsers. The holder must employ a notary who will re-present the bill to the drawee or acceptor. The notary will note that the bill was re-presented and note the answer given when he presents the bill and date, and initial the bill. After the instrument has been noted it will be "protested." This will take the form of a document which contains a copy of the bill which is signed by the notary after he has set out the demand made (*i.e.* acceptance or payment of the bill) and the answer given by the drawee or acceptor.

An inland bill does not have to be noted or protested to preserve any right of recourse.

ACCEPTANCE AND PAYMENT FOR HONOUR

18.98 A person who is not a party to the bill may either accept or pay a dishonoured bill to save the "honour" of those involved in the default. An acceptance for honour will be valid if the bill has been protested for dishonour and is not overdue. In addition, the holder must consent to the bill being accepted for honour and the acceptance must be written on the bill and indicate that it is an acceptance for honour.[19]

An acceptor for honour is liable to the holder and to all persons who have become parties to the bill after the party for whose honour it was accepted.

Damages for dishonour

18.99 The measure of damages when a bill is dishonoured is dealt with in section 57, and it provides that the damages awarded shall be liquidated, *i.e.* damages which are ascertained or ascertainable before the trial by mathematical calculation. The section summarises the rights of various parties to sue other parties to the bill for damages for dishonour. It provides:

(1) the holder can sue any party whether the acceptor, the drawer or an indorser for the full amount of the bill, together with any expenses and interest;

(2) a drawer, who is compelled to make payment on the bill, may sue the acceptor for the amount of the bill, together with any expenses and interest; and

(3) an indorser who is compelled to pay the amount of the bill may sue the acceptor, the drawer and any prior indorser for the amount of the bill, together with any expenses and interest.

[19] s.65, Bills of Exchange Act 1882.

The amount which is recoverable for dishonour is the amount on the face of the bill and, if the bill specifies, interest from the date of presentment for payment or from the date of maturity. This payment of interest is separate from any award of interest the court might make.

The expenses of noting and protesting a bill, where protest is necessary, are recoverable.

Payment and discharge of a bill of exchange

18.100   The Bills of Exchange Act 1882, provides five methods by which a bill may be discharged and it is proposed to deal with these individually. By section 59(1) of the Act: "a bill is discharged by payment in due course by or on behalf of the drawee or acceptor . . . " A plea of payment should be supported by proof of payment in money, and if satisfaction of the bill otherwise than by a money payment is alleged, it must be proved that the party to whom payment was made agreed to treat satisfaction of the bill in that alternative form as equivalent to a payment in money.[20]

Section 59(2) expressly provides for the case where payment is made in full by a drawer or indorser, but does not deal with the case of part payment. Chalmers[21] suggests that part payment of a bill in due course operates as a discharge *pro tanto*, but the holder may refuse part payment. Byles,[22] however, takes the view that in any event of a bill remaining in the hands of a holder after a payment in part or in full by the drawer or indorser, there can be little doubt that a subsequent holder in due course can sue the acceptor for the entire amount of the bill.

18.101   The payment must be made at or after maturity. A transfer of the bill to the acceptor before maturity does not operate as a discharge of the bill since there cannot be payment by anticipation, for example, A the holder of a bill, obtains payment from the acceptor before maturity, and hands the bill to the acceptor who negotiates it to B. Whether or not B is ignorant of the premature payment of the bill, he can recover on the bill against all prior parties whose names remain on the bill.[23]

The payment must be made to the holder or some authorised person on his behalf, and the payee or indorsee must be the holder.[24] If a bill which is payable to the order of A is stolen, and the thief forges A's indorsement on the bill and disposes of the bill to B, B or a person deriving title under him may present the bill for payment on maturity and obtain payment from the drawee or acceptor. The bill is not thereby discharged, as the payment is not made to the "holder" of it, namely A. An exception to this rule is provided by section 60 of the Act so that a bank which pays a cheque in such circumstances is discharged from further liability if the bank acts in good faith and in the ordinary course of business. However, if in the above circumstances a bill indorsed in blank is stolen and the thief presents it to the acceptor for payment on maturity, the bill is discharged by payment if the acceptor pays in good faith, for the thief is the holder (*i.e.* the bearer) of the bill despite his own lack of title to it.

---

[20] *Camidge* v. *Allenby* (1827) 6 B. & C. 373; *Glassock* v. *Balls* (1889) 24 Q.B.D. 13.
[21] Smout, *Bills of Exchange* (Stevens, 13th ed.), p. 200.
[22] *Byles on Bills of Exchange* ed. Megrah and Ryder, (S. & M., 25th ed.), p. 130.
[23] *Burbridge* v. *Manners* (1812) 3 Comp. 193.
[24] s.2, Bills of Exchange Act 1882.

The payment must have been made in good faith and without notice of **18.102** any defect in the holder's title. Where the acceptor pays a bearer bill which he knows has been obtained from A by fraud, the bill will not be discharged and the acceptor will remain liable on it. However, when a holder who has a defective title to a payment receives payment in due course, he will not necessarily have to refund the money to the true owner of the bill.[25]

Finally, the payment must be made by or on behalf of the drawee or acceptor. As the drawee or acceptor is the party primarily liable on the bill, payment by another party will not serve to discharge the bill as a whole and relieve the other parties from liability.[26]

There is, however, one case in which payment by a party other than the drawee or acceptor will discharge a bill, namely, in the case of an accommodation bill, and section 59(3) provides: "Where an accommodation bill is paid in due course by the party accommodated the bill is discharged."

In *Harmer* v. *Steele*[27] a bill was accepted by three joint acceptors and paid by one of them at maturity. The court held the bill was discharged and could not be re-negotiated and it was immaterial that the acceptor who paid the bill accepted it for the accommodation of the other two.

Secondly, a bill may be discharged by the acceptor becoming the holder **18.103** of it. The Act provides: "When the acceptor of a bill is or becomes the holder of it at or after its maturity, in his own right, the bill is discharged."

The rule stated in section 61 is a deduction from the general principle that a present right and liability united in the same person cancel each other out. "There is no principle" says Best C.J. "by which a man can be at the same time plaintiff and defendant."

If the acceptor becomes the holder through a person with a defective title he will not have acquired the bill in his own right within the meaning of the section unless he is holder in due course.[28]

A bill of exchange may be discharged by renunciation.[29] In the case of bills of exchange the liability of the acceptor or other party, remote or immediate, may be discharged by an express renunciation of his rights against them by the holder, and whether or not consideration is given for the renunciation. However, renunciation must be "at or after maturity," and renunciation before maturity will not discharge a bill. The renunciation must be of the holder's rights against the "acceptor," for although renunciation of his rights against another party may discharge that party and all succeeding indorsers, it will not discharge the prior parties from liability. A record of a mere intention to renounce is insufficient for this purpose; there must be an actual renunciation.[30] A renunciation must be in writing[31] although the written renunciation can be addressed to a third party or the world in general.

In order to discharge the bill as a whole, a renunciation must be of the **18.104** rights against the acceptor, but if the individual liability of any party is to be renounced, the renunciation must comply with subsection (2) which refers

---

[25] *London and River Plate Bank Ltd.* v. *Bank of Liverpool Ltd.* [1896] 1 Q.B. 7.
[26] s.59(2), Bills of Exchange Act 1882.
[27] (1849) 4 Ex. 1.
[28] *Nash* v. *De Freville* [1900] 2 Q.B. 72.
[29] s.62(1), Bills of Exchange Act 1882.
[30] *Re George* (1890) 44 Ch.D. 627.
[31] *Rimault* v. *Cartwright* (1924) 93 L.J.K.B. 823.

to the "liabilities of any party" being renounced by the holder, as opposed to the renunciation of the holder's right under subsection (1). The renunciation must be "in like manner" to that set out in subsection (1) but the question this difference in wording raises is whether the return of the bill to any other party is a waiver of the holder's rights against that party and against all other parties, because an action cannot be brought by the holder of a bill unless he is actually in possession of the bill. In *Westminster Bank Ltd.* v. *Zang*[32] the Court of Appeal was of the opinion that by handing the cheque in question back to the payee the bank which held it on presentation for payment lost its lien over it.

A bill may be discharged by cancellation.[33] The Act does not provide what amounts to cancellation but it must be "apparent" in order to be operative, so that some unmistakable method should be employed,[34] and, furthermore, it must be intentional.

Section 63(3) deals with cancellation by mistake and provides that such a cancellation, whether done unintentionally or under a mistake, is inoperative, but the burden of proof lies on the party alleging that the cancellation is ineffective.[35]

18.105   Finally, a bill may be discharged by alteration.[36] Thus, if A while a holder of a bill, alters the amount and then indorses it to B who indorses it to C, and B and C are aware of the alteration, C cannot enforce the bill against any party antecedent to A, but he can recover its amount from A and B. However, an alteration by pure accident is not within the above provision. In *Hong Kong and Shanghai Banking Corporation* v. *Lo Lee Shi*[37] Lord Buckmaster in delivering judgment said sections 64(1) and (2) apply only to alterations effected by the will of the person by whom or under whose directions they are made, and it does not apply to an alteration resulting from a pure accident. It is not reasonable to assume the parties would contemplate that the document would be cancelled by a mouse eating part of it, or a lighted cigarette burning it or any other means by which accidental disfigurement can occur.

The effect of an alteration in an indorsement on a bank was dealt with by the court in *Bank of Montreal* v. *Exhibit and Trading Co.*[38] where the indorsement of a promissory note payable to "Gooderich Organ Co." was altered by the addition of the word "limited" to the indorser's signature. The note was then indorsed and negotiated to a holder in due course. The court held the alteration was not apparent, and the company therefore could not be sued as an indorser on the bill.

By section 64(2) the alteration must be material if it is to discharge the bill, and the test of this is whether the alteration affects the rights or liabilities of any of the parties to the bill. The onus of proving non-materiality is on the person claiming under the bill that an accidental error is not a material alteration.

---

[32] [1966] A.C. 182.
[33] s.63(1), Bills of Exchange Act 1882.
[34] See *Ingham* v. *Primrose* (1859) 7 C.B. (N.S.) 82 . . . where the court held that merely tearing the instrument is not sufficient cancellation.
[35] *Warwick* v. *Rogers* (1843) 5 Man. & G. 340.
[36] s.64(1), Bills of Exchange Act 1882.
[37] [1929] A.C. 181.
[38] [1906] 11 Com.Cas. 250.

Special rules relating to cheques

CROSSED CHEQUES

A crossing is an instruction to a bank to pay a cheque either to any bank col- **18.106** lecting it if the crossing is general, or to the bank named in the crossing if it is special.[39] Consequently, a crossed cheque should not be paid by the paying bank in cash across the counter to anyone who may happen to present it. The relationship of the bank with its customer is governed by the contract between the parties, but a crossed cheque may also be used by the customer-drawer as a means of instructing the collecting bank on how the cheque should be presented, although it should be realised that a variety of other persons, apart from the drawer, may add to or adopt the crossing on a cheque.[40] The purpose of crossings is to minimise the risk of loss if the cheque is lost or stolen, especially if the cheque is sent through the post. As the paying bank will refuse to pay such cheques over the counter, the thief or person finding a crossed cheque must either have a bank account or arrange for someone with a bank account to receive payment so that proceeds fraudulently collected can be traced. If the cheque is specially crossed, he must additionally have an account at the bank named in the crossing.

TYPES OF CROSSINGS

General and Special Crossings

The forms of crossings are set out in section 76 of the Bills of Exchange Act **18.107** 1882, and they are divided into two main types. A general crossing, consisting of two transverse lines across the face of the cheque, merely requires that the cheque should be presented for payment by a bank, whilst the "special" crossing consists of transverse lines between which the name of a specified bank is written and that bank alone is to receive payment. Section 76(1)(a) and (b) governs general crossings and the law relating to special crossings is enacted in section 76(2).

The crossings, whether general or special, should appear on the face of the cheque, and it would seem that a crossing on the back of the instrument giving a slight impression on the face of the cheque is not enough, since the crossing must be visible on the front of the cheque.

The question of who may cross a cheque or add to a crossing is dealt with by section 77, which provides that the drawer of the cheque may cross it specially or generally, or if the cheque is uncrossed the holder may cross it either generally or specially, or convert a general into a special crossing or add the words "not negotiable" to a special or general crossing. Paget[41] suggests the holder need not be a holder for value, nor a lawful holder, so that a thief in possession of a bearer cheque is a holder for the purposes of crossings. This would clearly not be so if the thief crossed a cheque drawn to the payee or order unless the cheque had been indorsed in blank by the payee.

When a cheque is crossed specially the banker to whom it is crossed may **18.108** again cross it specially to another banker for collection; this will occur where the first banker is employing the second as his agent for the purposes

---

[39] s.75, Bills of Exchange Act 1882.
[40] s.77, *ibid.*
[41] *Law of Banking*, ed. Megrah and Ryder, (Butterworths, 9th ed., 1982).

of collecting the proceeds. In no other case may a cheque be crossed more than once.

An authorised crossing under the Bills of Exchange Act is a material part of the cheque, and it is unlawful, except as authorised by the Act, for anyone to obliterate or add or alter the crossing.[42] However, the drawer of a crossed cheque, especially when using cheque forms printed with a crossing, may open the crossing by writing words such as "open cheque" or "pay cash" over the crossing and adding his signature.[43] This is because the cheque form does not become a cheque before the drawer completes it. If the bank pays the amount of the cheque to someone other than the true owner of it on the strength of such an "opening," it may debit the drawer's account unless it later appears that the crossing was opened by a person other than the drawer of it at the time it was opened. In order to safeguard the position of the banks, the committee of London Clearing Bankers in 1912 resolved that such cheques are not to be paid in cash, unless the full signature of the drawer is added to the opening, and even then payment is only to be made to the drawer or his known agent.

18.109   Where the drawee bank disregards a crossing, for example where payment is made over the counter, or in the case of a special crossing if payment is not made to the named banker, the collecting bank is liable in conversion to the true owner of the cheque for any loss[44]; and the paying bank is guilty of a breach of duty to its customer, which Chorley[45] submits will disentitle the bank from debiting its customer's account with the amount of the cheque. The term payment is not defined for these purposes and in *Meyer and Company* v. *Sze Hai Tong Banking and Insurance Co. Ltd*[46] it was held that if the drawee bank gives its own cheques in exchange for crossed cheques presented for payment, that, in law, amounts to payment and the bank is in breach of its duty to the customer. The remedy under section 79(2) is given to the "true owner" of the cheque and although the term, once again, is not defined, it refers to the person who would be entitled to sue on the indorsement as its holder, had it not been avoided by the material alteration, or if it has not been avoided by the person who is entitled to possession of it.

The making of a payment contrary to the crossing amounts to negligence on the part of the paying bank.

If, however, a paying bank pays contrary to the crossing on an instrument which at the time of presentment does not appear to be crossed, or if the crossing has been obliterated and the paying bank acts in good faith and without negligence, the bank is not responsible and does not incur any liability. The bank is then placed in a position as if it had paid the cheque to the true owner. A holder in due course is, furthermore, protected if a crossing has been obliterated or altered so that it cannot be noticed on ordinary inspection. In favour of the holder in due course the cheque is then treated as if it were not crossed under the Bills of Exchange Act 1882.[47]

---

[42] s.79, Bills of Exchange Act 1882.
[43] *Orbit Mining and Trading Co. Ltd.* v. *Westminster Bank Ltd.* [1962] All E.R. 565.
[44] s.79(2), Bills of Exchange Act 1882.
[45] *Law of Banking*, (S. & M., 6th ed., 1974), p. 100.
[46] [1913] A.C. 847.
[47] s.64(1), Bills of Exchange Act 1882.

"Not Negotiable" Crossing

The "not negotiable" crossing is provided for in the Bills of Exchange Act **18.110** 1882,[48] and the effect of the words does not deprive the cheque of its transferability but it does deprive the instrument of its negotiability in that no one can become a holder of it in due course. An indorsee or holder who takes the cheque honestly and for value cannot acquire any better title or any better rights than any prior party to the cheque or its proceeds, than the transferor himself. In *Great Western Railway Company* v. *London and County Banking Company*[49] the Court of Appeal giving judgment examined the "not negotiable" crossing and held section 81 does not mean:

> "that the person to whom the payee of the cheque gives a crossed cheque marked "Not Negotiable" shall not become the transferee of the cheque, but merely that he shall not take a better title than that which the person from whom he took it had. The transferability of the cheque is not affected by the words "Not Negotiable" but only its negotiability."

Consequently, the appellant company to whom a cheque obtained fraudulently and marked "not negotiable" had been indorsed was a holder of the cheque, but it could not be a holder in due course.

Although the House of Lords allowed the appeal against the decision of the court the passage cited is generally accepted as correct on the effect of the "not negotiable" crossing. Similarly, in *Universal Guarantee Property Ltd.* v. *National Bank of Australasia*,[50] it was recognised and accepted by the court that the words "not negotiable" do not prevent the cheque from being negotiated but it does mean that the holder of the cheque cannot have and is not capable of giving a better title to the cheque than that of the holder from whom he obtained it.

The words "not negotiable" have no effect unless combined with a **18.111** general or special crossing, and a cheque bearing these words without a crossing is not a crossed cheque; consequently, the drawee bank cannot insist on it being presented through a bank for payment, and it incurs no liability under section 79 if it pays such an instrument over the counter. The words "not negotiable" on their own in a cheque without a crossing have no express statutory effect in hindering the negotiability of the instrument. However, in *Hibernian Bank* v. *Gysin and Hanson*[51] the question was whether a bill of exchange drawn "to the order of the Irish Casing Company Ltd. only" and crossed "not negotiable" could be transferred to the plaintiffs who claimed to be holders of the bill and brought an action against the acceptor when the instrument was dishonoured by non-payment. The court held the crossing "not negotiable" and the word "only" prohibited the transfer of the bill altogether, and so the plaintiffs could not recover since they were not holders of the bill. It would seem that the inclusion of the words "not negotiable" in a cheque otherwise than as part of a general or special crossing would have the same effect.

The words "not negotiable" do not have to appear within the transverse lines, so long as they appear on the face of the cheque.

---

[48] s.81.
[49] [1901] A.C. 414.
[50] [1965] 1 W.L.R. 691.
[51] 1 K.B. 483.

"Account Payee" Crossing

18.112   The words "account payee" or "account payee only" are frequently used in cheques although they are not expressly authorised by the Bills of Exchange Act, and it has been suggested that they invalidate the cheque or the crossing under section 78. However, Paget[52] suggests that the words "account payee" do not constitute an addition of the nature section 78 was intended to deal with, and these words are merely a memorandum of the instruction to the collecting bank that the proceeds of the cheque are not to be collected for any account other than that of the named payee without full inquiry. In *National Bank* v. *Silke*[53] it was held that such an addition to the crossing does not prevent the cheque from being transferable. The fact that the Court of Appeal affirmed the judgment in favour of the bank reinforces the view that the court did not consider the negotiability of the cheque to have been affected in any way.

It is advisable for a drawer to combine the words "Account payee" with "Not negotiable" in the crossing, for if the latter words are omitted and the cheque is indorsed in blank and then stolen, a holder in due course could compel payment.

18.113   The words "Account payee" merely put the collecting banker on inquiry by signifying the account to which the proceeds from the cheque are to be placed, and consequently, if the collecting bank receives payment to the credit of anyone else other than the customer without making sure that the payee consents to make payment to him, the bank is liable in negligence and loses the protection granted to it under section 4 of the Cheques Act 1957. If, however, the collecting bank does make reasonable inquiries it will be protected by section 4 of the Cheques Act. Consequently, in *Bevan* v. *National Bank Ltd.*[54] it was held that the bank had not acted negligently in collecting an "account payee" cheque for a person other than the named payee after making reasonable enquiry.

In *House Property Co. of London Ltd.* v. *London County and Westminster Bank*[55] the court examined the meaning of the words "account payee" and said that the words did not mean or refer to the account of whoever as the result of the negotiation of the cheque may have become the owner of it; the word "Payee" meant the person named as payee in the cheque or the person to whom it was issued if it was originally in bearer form, and, as the bank had failed to inquire whether its customer was the person to whom the cheque was issued, it was negligent.

18.114   A much more recent development has been the addition of the words "only" after the words "Account payee" and the question is what effect, if any, does the word "only" have? Paget considers that if the drawer, by adding the words "only," intends to restrict the negotiability of the cheque it is doubtful whether he succeeds, because such words are not prescribed by the Bills of Exchange Act 1882.[56] He considers the words "Account payee only" are a mere variant of "Account payee," and so the collecting bank is under the same duty in both cases. If any meaning is to be given to the additional word "only," then it must be treated as requiring the paying bank to make payment to the payee by means of the bank clearing. If the

---

[52] *Law of Banking*, ed. Megrah and Ryder, (Butterworths, 9th ed.) p. 209.
[53] [1891] 1 Q.B. 435.
[54] [1906] 23 T.L.R. 65.
[55] (1915) 84 L.J.K.B. 1846.
[56] *Law of Banking*, ed. Megrah and Ryder, (Butterworths, 9th ed.) p. 212.

collecting bank collects for anyone other than the named payee, the drawee bank acquires an implied right to an indemnity from the collecting bank. This is because the collecting bank is more likely to be in a position to know whether its customer, for whom the cheque is collected, is authorised by the named payee to receive payment, but as this indemnity is also required in the case of an "Account payee" crossing as well as "Account payee only" the effect is the same. In *Universal Guarantee Property Ltd.* v. *National Bank of Australasia*[57] the Judicial Committee treated the two crossings "Account payee" and "Account payee only" as synonymous, and implied that they are merely variations of the same restriction, *i.e.* the words should place the collecting bank on enquiry but they do not restrict the negotiability of the instrument. A transferee of such a cheque can be a holder in due course, even though he is not the named payee. In *Sutter* v. *Briggs*[58] the court merely concluded that whether a cheque so marked has any further significance than one marked "Account payee" remains to be seen.

Crossings by a Collecting Bank

18.115 The collecting banker may be a holder of a cheque and may then exercise the powers of crossing cheques, such as converting a general into a special crossing, or crossing an open cheque generally. Under section 77(5) the bank is given, in the case of a specially crossed cheque, the power to cross it again to another banker for collection, and under section 77(6) the bank can cross specially an uncrossed or generally crossed cheque.

Cheques may be presented for payment crossed at two different offices, a branch and the head office of the same bank where the cheque is transmitted from the bank branch to the head office for purposes of convenience in collecting. This second type of crossing clearly does not fall within the provisions of the act and it can be challenged as to whether it qualifies as a crossing, because for most purposes the head office and its branches constitute only one bank. On the other hand it may be contended that two crossings naming the same bank may be treated as a single crossing. Because of the present arrangements for clearing cheques, two crossings naming the same collecting bank will only be possible if the cheque is cleared specially and not through the general clearing.

18.116 The position where one bank employs another to collect cheques as its agent has been provided for in section 77(5). Paget raises the question of when a bank receives a specially crossed cheque for collection on behalf of a customer who has no title to it because the payee's indorsement has been forged, and the named bank specially crosses the cheque to a second bank for collection and that second bank on receiving the proceeds transfers the amount to the first bank. The true owner of the cheque then sues the second bank employed as an agent for collection, claiming that it was guilty of conversion of the cheque.

In such a case the second agency bank appears to be protected by the fact that it collects on behalf of its customer, namely, the first bank. This was the situation in *Importers Co.* v. *Westminster Bank Ltd.*[59] where Atkins L.J., said: " . . . it seems to me that if a non-trading bank regularly employs a clearing bank to clear its cheques, the non-clearing bank is a customer of the clearing bank." The second bank is also protected by section 77(6) and the

[57] [1965] 2 All E.R. 98.
[58] [1922] 1 A.C. 1.
[59] [1927] 2 K.B. 297.

subsection applies not only to cheques crossed generally but also to uncrossed cheques.

In *Gordon* v. *London City and Midland Bank Ltd.*[60] it was held that no protection could be given to a bank which receives cheques from a person who had no title to them and then deals with them in a manner amounting to conversion before crossing them. The bank cannot escape liability for conversion by subsequently crossing the cheques. Collins, M.R., said, referring to the effect of s.77(6), " . . . that is a facility given for the purpose of affording additional protection during the process of collection after the crossing of the cheque."

The liability of paying and collecting banks in conversion

18.117 When a bank pays, collects or transmits a cheque bearing a forged or unauthorised indorsement, at common law it is guilty of a conversion and is liable to the true owner of the cheque for the amount for which it was drawn. This liability still exists, but is now subject to the statutory defences available to the bank. A conversion is a wrongful interference with goods (including documents) by taking, using or destroying them inconsistently with the owner's right to possession. There must be some act of the defendant which amounts to a repudiation of the owner's rights of ownership or the exercise of some dominion over the subject matter which is inconsistent with that right.

In all cases involving the payment of money by a bank, the bank's liability for conversion of the instrument is independent of any question of its right to debit its customer with the amount paid. The bank may be both liable in conversion to the true owner of the instrument and disentitled to debit its customer at the same time, in which case it stands to bear a double loss. Where the document converted is a negotiable instrument, the damages are its face value.

The person to whom the right of action in conversion is available is called the "true owner" of the bill, cheque, etc., in the Bills of Exchange Act 1882, but no definition is given of this term in the Act. It would appear to mean the holder of the instrument who can prove a defect in the title of the person whom he sues. Where a cheque or bill has been wrongfully taken or detained from the holder or dealt with in a manner inconsistent with his rights and prejudicial to him his remedy is to bring an action for conversion against any one or more of the persons who have taken, detained or dealt with the instrument. Except for suing for money had and received as an alternative to conversion there is no other form of action available to the holder.

18.118 The essential feature of the plaintiff's case in an action for conversion is that at the relevant time he was entitled to the subject matter. Consequently, in *Smith* v. *Union Bank of London*, where a cheque which had become payable to bearer by the payee's indorsement was stolen and negotiated to a holder in due course on whose behalf the defendant bank collected the cheque, it was held that the holder in due course and not the person from whom the cheque was stolen was the true owner at the time of the defendant bank's alleged conversion, and so the bank was not liable to the plaintiff.

[60] [1920] 1 K.B. 242.

A difficulty arises where a bill or cheque is drawn payable to an agent in his own name or under his official designation, but for amounts due to and intended to be received by his principal. Where a cheque is made payable to a person under his official denomination and for a debit which is really due to his principal, the court will probably hold that the principal was the true owner of the cheque and that anyone taking or dealing with such a cheque will be liable to the principal in conversion.

Generally, the view taken by the courts is that, for an action in conversion, the plaintiff must be entitled to immediate possession of the chattel at the date of the conversion in order to be entitled to sue. However, in *Marquis of Bute* v. *Barclays Bank Ltd.*[61] McNair J. held that in order to claim in conversion it is sufficient if the plaintiff can prove that at the time of the alleged conversion he was entitled to immediate possession. It is not necessary to establish that he is the legal owner of the thing alleged to have been converted provided he has a right to acquire ownership, by calling for an immediate vesting of the legal title in himself, which a principal can always do. In the case of a cheque, the plaintiff's right to such a vesting of the legal title depends on the intention of the drawers as expressed in the instrument. In the present case, where the cheque was payable to a named agent "for the Marquis of Bute," the additional words were an essential part of the description of the payee as such, an agent, and the Marquis therefore had a legal right to the cheque and could sue for its conversion. In *International Factors Ltd.* v. *Rodriguez*,[62] the plaintiffs and a company entered into an agreement under which the plaintiffs agreed to purchase all the company's book debts and the company agreed in return to assign them to the plaintiffs for 98½ per cent. of the full amount of the debts. It was expressly agreed that if any payment in respect of an assigned debt was paid directly to the company it would hold the full amount paid in trust for the plaintiffs. The company received four cheques totalling £11,370 towards payment of debts which were subject to the agreement, and arranged for these to be paid into the company's bank account. It was held on appeal, that the plaintiffs were entitled to sue in conversion because the agreement gave them a right to immediate possession of the cheques since it imposed on the company an obligation to hand over immediately to the plaintiffs any cheque which came into its possession, and it created a trust which arose immediately the cheques were received by the company. The court approved the *Marquis of Bute* case and said it is of assistance to the plaintiffs because it shows that the fact that the cheques were made out in favour of the company is not a sufficient answer to the plaintiffs claim that they were entitled to the cheques in equity. The court was satisfied that conversion had been established.

18.119

The protection of the paying bank

A cheque is a mandate of the customer to its bank, which is under a duty if certain conditions are satisfied, to obey the drawer's instructions and pay the cheque to the holder who presents it, or to his bank. If the cheque is payable to bearer, the bank can debit its customer with the amount of the cheque if it pays in good faith any person who presents the cheque, whether in fact he is entitled to the payment or not. If such a payment is made in due

18.120

[61] [1955] 1 Q.B. 202.
[62] [1979] 1 All E.R. 17.

course it amounts to a valid discharge under the Bills of Exchange Act 1882.[63]

At common law the drawee bank could only debit its customer's account where, in the case of an order cheque, it was presented by the payee or by a person to whom it had been negotiated by indorsement. The paying bank is, however, now protected by sections 60 and 80 of the Bills of Exchange Act 1882, and section 1 of the Cheques Act 1957, if it pays a cheque to someone who has no title to it. Nevertheless, if the bank pays the cheque inconsistently with the drawer's order, for example, contrary to a crossing, it is still unable to debit the drawer's account and it may be liable to the true owner of the cheque.

Protection under section 60 of the Bills of Exchange Act 1882

18.121   Under section 60 the paying bank is protected if it pays a cheque in good faith and in the ordinary course of business to a person other than the true owner of it, where the defect in the title of the person who receives payment is the forgery of an indorsement on the cheque. The section applies both to crossed and uncrossed cheques, and, apparently, even though the paying bank has been negligent in making the payment, provided that it has acted in good faith and in the ordinary course of its business. The effect of section 60, therefore, is that if a bank pays a cheque on the assumption that all indorsements on it are valid, but one or more indorsements are in fact forgeries, the bank is put in the same position as if the indorsements had been valid, provided of course the bank acts in good faith and in the ordinary course of business. It is important to note that the protection given by the section is confined to "forged or unauthorised indorsements;" irregular but genuine indorsements are not provided for under section 60 of the Bills of Exchange Act, although section 1 of the Cheques Act 1957 provides the bank is "deemed to have paid . . . in due course" in such circumstances.

The term payment is not defined by the Bills of Exchange Act 1882, or under any other statutory provision for the purposes of negotiable instruments. The decision of the courts in *Meyer and Company Ltd.* v. *Sze Hai Tong*[64] has already been looked at for this purpose. In *London City and Midland Bank* v. *Gordon*[65] a cheque drawn on one branch of a bank was paid in at another and appeared as an item in balancing the accounts between the two branches; the branch on which it was drawn was held to have paid it within section 60. However, an intimation by the paying bank that the cheque will be paid, known as notifying its fate, in answer to an enquiry by another bank, is not treated as payment.

18.122   Section 60 of the Bills of Exchange Act only protects the paying bank if it has acted in "good faith" and "in the ordinary course of [its] business." The question which has caused debate is whether a bank can claim the protection of Section 60 if it acts negligently. The section does not specifically provide that a bank must act without negligence, and so it appears that negligence is not incompatible with good faith. Milnes Holden[66] strenuously argues that

---

[63] s.59(1), Bills of Exchange Act 1882.
[64] [1913] A.C. 847.
[65] [1903] A.C. 240.
[66] *History of Negotiable Instruments in English Law*, (Pitman, 1st ed.), p. 227.

this view is mistaken, and that the absence of negligence is an essential pre-requisite to the protection of the paying bank.

The view taken by Holden, however, was furthermore rejected in the Court of Appeal decision of *Carpenters Company* v. *British Mutual Banking Co. Ltd.*[67] The plaintiffs, in that case, were trustees of a charitable company and kept an account in this connection with the defendant bank. The plaintiffs' clerk misappropriated the funds of the company by obtaining the signature of the trustees to cheques payable to tradesmen. He then forged the payees' signatures by way of indorsement and paid the cheques into his own account also with the defendant bank. Branson J. found that the defendant bank had paid the cheques in good faith and in the ordinary course of business, and was therefore protected by section 60 notwithstanding its negligence in collecting the cheques on behalf of the plaintiffs' clerk. The judges of the Court of Appeal were divided on the issue whether negligence by the paying bank precludes the protection of section 60. Mackinnon L.J. said:

> "A thing that is done not in the ordinary course of business may be done negligently; but I do not think the converse is necessarily true. A thing may be done negligently and yet be done in the ordinary course of business."

This view was also accepted by Slesser, L.J. who said: "Negligence does not necessarily preclude the protection of Section 60 . . . "

However, Greer L.J. did not agree with the view that a bank could be protected by section 60 where it had been guilty of negligence. He took the view that a bank could not argue: "when acting negligently, that it was acting in the ordinary course of business."

It is generally thought that the view of the majority in *Carpenter's* case is more acceptable, so that provided a bank acts "in the ordinary course of business" in paying a cheque, it is protected by section 60 even though it is guilty of negligence. But a bank which pays in obviously suspicious circumstances will nevertheless lose the protection of section 60 if it pays the instrument without a proper inquiry, because payment would not then be made in the ordinary course of business. The courts have not defined what will amount to such obviously suspicious circumstances that the paying bank will lose the protection of section 60 and so each case will be decided on its individual facts taking into account the customary course of business of the banking community as a whole. In *Bank of England* v. *Vagliano Brothers*[68] Lord Halisbury, in discussing the question of paying a bill or uncrossed cheque for a large amount over the counter commented: **18.123**

> "I do not know what is the usual course among bankers, and I should doubt whether in such a matter it would be possible to affirm that any particular course was either usual or unusual in the sense that there is some particular course to be pursued when circumstances occur necessarily giving rise to suspicion . . . "

In *Auchteroni and Company* v. *Midland Bank Ltd.*[69] the court held the bank was justified in paying over the counter a bill for £876.9s. but it was suggested that a different course might have been adopted if a bill for a larger amount was presented by an office boy or a tramp. In *Baines* v. *National* **18.124**

[67] [1938] 1 K.B. 511.
[68] [1891] A.C. 107.
[69] [1928] 2 K.B. 294.

Provincial Bank Ltd.[70] a cheque was paid at 3.05 p.m. (five minutes after closing time). The court held the payment to be good and said that the time limits within which a bank may conduct business are largely for the bank's own convenience. The payment after closing hours, although unusual, was sufficiently within the ordinary course of business.

It is submitted that cheques encashed by customers at branches other than the one where their account is kept is within the ordinary course of business, if cheques are presented by the customer personally, but it is doubtful if it applies to those presented by third parties unless the customer's authorisation of payment is given expressly.

Where the indorsement of cheques is required by a paying bank which, since the passing of the Cheques Act 1957, does not include those paid in for the credit of the account of the payee, the cheque must purport to be indorsed by or under the authority of the proper person if the paying bank is to have the protection of section 60. If an irregularity in the indorsement is overlooked or disregarded by the paying bank, it will have difficulty if it seeks to rely on the protection afforded by the section. An important question is whether the term indorsement includes the signature of the payee of a cheque prior to payment in cash by the drawee bank. This signature is called an indorsement but it is doubted whether in law it amounts to an indorsement, and if this is the case the paying bank would be deprived of its statutory protection when paying open cheques across the counter. It is argued that section 2 of the Bills of Exchange Act 1882, provides that the term indorsement means an indorsement completed by delivery, and the same section provides that "delivery" means "transfer of possession, actual or constructive, from one person to another," hence, it is to be concluded that indorsement takes place only when a cheque is negotiated from one person to another.[71]

18.125   The basis of the protection of a bank against forged indorsements has been stated to be the impossibility for it to know whether the signatures of persons indorsing order cheques drawn by its customer are genuine or not. There is a duty on the part of the bank to know the signatures of its customers in their capacity as drawers of cheques, but not to know or generally to question the genuineness of other persons' signatures. The deception of a bank by a forgery of such other signatures does not necessarily involve breach or negligence, and so the bank can debit the customer's account with the amount of the cheque it has paid. Where a bank, in paying an order cheque with a forged indorsement, acts in such a way as to deprive itself of the protection of section 60 it bears the loss of the amount paid and it also becomes liable to the true owner of the cheque. The bank is not entitled to charge its customer with the amount paid on the forged indorsement and it is also liable to the true owner, if he is a person other than a customer in trover or conversion. Neither the right to possession of the cheque nor the property in it is divested out of the true owner by the forgery of the indorsement. The payment by the bank is merely to a possessor, and unless it operates to discharge the cheque, the receipt and retention of the cheque by the paying bank constitutes conversion.

Where a cheque is duly paid or discharged an action for conversion will not lie, but to constitute valid payment on a forged indorsement under sec-

---

[70] (1927) 96 L.J.K.B. 801.
[71] *Keene* v. *Beard* (1860) 8 C.B.N.S. 372.

260

tion 60 it must be in accordance with the section. The effect of section 24 is that a forged indorsement is inoperative and it does not pass any title or give a discharge so that a person in possession under a forged indorsement is neither the payee, an indorsee nor the bearer of the cheque, and payment to him does not discharge the bank except where section 60 operates and the bank is thereby deemed to pay the cheque in due course.

However, in order to be protected under section 60 the paying bank has to satisfy one further requirement. The protection is limited to "the banker on whom it [the cheque] is drawn" and the question is: how liberally will the courts interpret this? Holden[72] suggests that where a cheque is encashed by one branch of a bank at the request of another branch of the same bank there is only one bank involved, and provided that the paying branch acts in good faith and in the ordinary course of business, the bank is protected. Where, however, two banks are involved in paying the cheque and the bank which pays the person who presents the cheque obtains the authorisation of the bank on which it is drawn to make payment, the relationship between the banks is that of principal and agent, the encashing bank being the agent of the drawee bank. In this case encashment by an unauthorised agent is equivalent to payment by the drawee bank itself and, therefore, section 60 would apply to protect the encashing bank as well as the drawee bank.

18.126

In *Carpenters' Company* v. *British Mutual Banking Co. Ltd.* it was held that where the same bank acts as the collecting and paying bank, it must satisfy both section 60 of the Bills of Exchange Act 1882 (as the paying bank) and section 4 of the Cheques Act 1957 (as the collecting bank). The latter section requires proof that the bank was not negligent.

Protection under section 80 of the Bills of Exchange Act 1882

Section 80 provides that where a bank on which a crossed cheque is drawn pays it in good faith and without negligence, the bank paying the cheque is placed in the same position and has the same rights as if payment of the cheque has been made to the true owner. If conduct amounting to a departure from the ordinary course of business within section 60 is *ipso facto* negligence on the part of the bank, then it would also amount to negligence under section 80, and debar the bank from protection under that section. Further, a bank which pays a cheque bearing a forged indorsement contrary to the requirements of the crossing it bears cannot set up a defence under section 80.

18.127

In order to procure the protection of section 80 payment must be made in case of a general crossing to a bank, and in the case of a special crossing to the bank named in the crossing.

DISCHARGE UNDER SECTION 80

Where payment of a cheque bearing a forged indorsement is made strictly in accordance with sections 60 and 80, the payment is technically a payment in due course. It not only discharges the drawee bank from liability to the true owner of the cheque but if the cheque has been either constructively or actually delivered to the payee, the payment also discharges the drawer from liability on the cheque itself and for the debt represented by the cheque

18.128

---

[72] *Law and Practice of Banking*, (Pitman, 2nd ed.), pp. 248–249.

under the transaction for which it was drawn. In *Charles* v. *Blackwell*[73] it was held that the payee cannot sue the drawer on the cheque or in respect of the underlying transaction after the cheque has technically been paid by a paying bank which is protected by section 60. The test is whether the paying bank has discharged its obligations to the drawer of the cheque, since the paying bank acts under the mandate given by the drawer. The payee has no recourse against the drawer where the cheque is paid lawfully (although to the wrong person), and the drawer is discharged by the payee's acceptance of an instrument in conditional satisfaction of the debt owed to him, which if it is paid according to law, discharges the drawer from liability. In this situation the loss must fall on the payee. But this reasoning only applies if the cheque is at some point in the possession of the payee. If it is never in his possession so that he does not accept it in conditional satisfaction of his debt the paying bank may be protected under section 80, but the drawer is still liable to the debt.

Protection under section 1 of the Cheques Act 1957

18.129   The protection which section 1 of the Cheques Act 1957 offers is additional to that conferred by sections 60 and 80 of the Bills of Exchange Act 1882. Consequently, the paying bank is entitled to rely on all or any of these provisions if sued by the true owner of a cheque. The two latter sections apply where the bank pays cheques bearing forged or unauthorised indorsements which prima facie appear regular but which in fact bear a forged or unauthorised indorsement. In addition to the protection afforded by these sections, section 1 of the Cheques Act 1957 gives protection to the paying bank if it pays a cheque in good faith and in the ordinary course of business, which is not indorsed or is irregularly indorsed. However, it is questionable whether the protection extends to payments made across the counter to a person other than the payee himself, so that the paying bank is apparently only protected if it makes payment to the payee (if the cheque is uncrossed), or to another bank. By a circular issued by the Committee of London Clearing Banks in 1957, an indorsement is still required for purposes mentioned in it, and this includes cheques cashed or exchanged across the counter. A paying bank which departs from this practice may find it difficult to establish that it paid the cheque in the ordinary course of business and it would then be unable to obtain the protection of section 1 of the Cheques Act, *e.g.* if it pays someone not entitled to payment. If, however, the person who presents the cheque is the payee or is entitled to the cheque the paying bank would not require the protection of the section and would not be liable to the drawer or anyone else by paying the cheque without it being indorsed or being irregularly indorsed.

18.130   The protection given by section 1 of the Cheques Act is required because normally cheques are presented for payment by a collecting bank and the paying bank has no means of discovering whether the collecting bank's customer is the payee of the cheque or a third party in whose favour the payee should have indorsed it. But the protection extends to cases where the third person's title to the cheque is void or voidable and the cheque has not been indorsed at all or the indorsement, although genuine, is irregular in form. Section 1 would also seem to extend to forged indorsements if they are irregular in form but only so as to protect the paying bank against the

[73] (1877) 2 C.P.D. 151.

irregularity. The bank must rely on sections 60 and 80 of the Bills of Exchange Act 1882 for protection against the consequencies of a forged indorsement.

The protection of the collecting bank

18.131

The collecting bank is now protected by section 4 of the Cheques Act 1957, and unless a bank can bring itself within the conditions of the section it is liable in common law for conversion or for money had and received, if the person from whom it receives cheques for collection has no title or a defective title to them. The collecting bank is, therefore, afforded a means of avoiding claims for liability in conversion to which it would otherwise have no defence. It should, however, be noted that the Cheques Act 1957 was enacted to extend the protection afforded to banks by section 82 of the Bills of Exchange Act 1882, in respect of crossed cheques to cover the collection of uncrossed and unindorsed or irregularly indorsed cheques and certain other instruments as well; no other change in the law was intended and so it is, therefore, necessary to look at cases under section 82 of the Bills of Exchange Act 1882, in order to understand the effect of the present law contained in section 4 of the 1957 Act.

COMPONENT OF THE DEFENCE

18.132

The protection given under section 4 of the Cheques Act 1957 applies to a banker, *i.e.* an authorised institution under the Banking Act 1987. On the other hand, a customer is a person who has an account with a bank for however short a time, and does not include someone for whom the bank merely performs the service of paying cheques over the counter.

In order to invoke the protection of section 4(1), the collecting bank must act in good faith and without negligence. These requirements are distinct; a thing is done in good faith when it is in fact done honestly, whether it is done negligently or not. However, section 4 of the Cheques Act 1957 requires the bank also to act without negligence and the onus of proving the absence of negligence is on the bank seeking to rely on the defence afforded by the section. The bank must in its defence set out all the facts and matters it relies on to establish that it did not act negligently, especially any enquiries the bank had undertaken as to the customer for whom it acted, and the cheque it collected.

18.133

There is generally no contractually binding relationship between a collecting bank and the true owner of a cheque it collects, giving rise to a duty on the part of the bank. The only contractual obligation imposed on the bank is towards its own customer, and the bank's duty to the true owner arises in tort but is moderated by the statutory defence available to the bank, which reduces its liability to one for negligence. The negligence consists in a failure to take proper care to protect the interests of the true owner, wholly apart from the interests of the customer for whom collection is made. The standard of care owed to the true owner has been modified from time to time.[74]

---

[74] See *Commissioners of Taxation* v. *English, Scottish and Australian Bank Ltd.* [1920] A.C. 683; see also *A. L. Underwood Ltd.* v. *Bank of Liverpool and Martins* [1924] 1 Q.B. 775; *Orbit Mining and Trading Co.* v. *Westminster Bank Ltd.* [1963] 1 Q.B. 794.

A somewhat modified test was formulated by Lord Warrington in *Lloyds Bank Ltd.* v. *E.B. Savory and Co.*[75] in which it was stated:

"The standard by which the absence, or otherwise, of negligence is to be determined must in my opinion be ascertained by reference to the practice of reasonable men carrying on the business of bankers, and endeavouring to do so in such a manner as may be calculated to protect themselves and others against fraud."

In the more recent case of *Marfani* v. *Midland Bank Ltd.*[76] Diplock L.J. said:

"What the court has to do is to look at all the circumstances at the time of the acts complained of, and to ask itself: were those circumstances such as would cause a reasonable banker, possessed of such information about his customer as a reasonable banker would possess, to suspect that his customer was not the true owner of the cheque."

Generally, therefore, where there is something on the face of the cheque or in the attendant circumstances or the quality and behaviour of the customer for whom the cheque is collected which should put the bank on enquiry, the bank is in breach of its duty to the true owner of the cheque if it fails to make proper enquiries. It is no defence to suggest that if proper precautions had been taken, the enquiry would or might still have revealed nothing suspicious. In *Lloyds Bank* v. *Savory* it was held that a precaution does not cease to be necessary merely because, although generally effective, in the particular circumstances of the case it would have revealed nothing suspicious or extraordinary.

ILLUSTRATIONS OF NEGLIGENCE BY COLLECTING BANKS

18.134   The courts have held various acts or omissions on the part of the bank to amount to negligence within section 4 of the Cheques Act 1957. These decisions serve as an indication whether the circumstances or transactions amount to negligence.

Prior to the Act, the bank was put on enquiry by irregularities in the indorsement which customers paying cheques into their accounts for collection were required to insert so as to make the cheque payable to bearer. The collecting bank could not ignore any discrepancy between the name of the payee as written in the body of the cheque and the purported indorsement.[77]

The words of section 4(1) of the Cheques Act 1957, making the bank liable for negligent acts refer only to the act of collection but it has been held that the obligation on the collecting bank to take care applies from the beginning of its relationship with the customer for whom it collects the cheque. The bank is not only concerned with the customer's apparent respectability, but also with all matters relating to him which may be relevant to the possibility of his using his account to obtain payment of cheques to which he has no title. The bank is obviously under an obligation to see that everything is apparently in order when it receives the cheque for payment

---

[75] [1933] A.C. 201.
[76] [1964] 1 W.L.R. 956.
[77] *Bavins Jnr. & Sims* v. *London and South Western Bank* [1900] 1 Q.B. 270.

and presents it for collection. If the circumstances in which the customer came into possession of the cheque should cause the bank to entertain suspicions as to his title to it, the bank must clear up those suspicions by making all proper enquiries before it presents the cheque for payment. The responsibility imposed on the bank was illustrated in the case of *Lloyds Bank Ltd.* v. *Savory & Co.*, where bearer cheques intended to be paid into the account of the employers were paid into his personal account by an employee of a firm of stockbrokers, who instructed the sums to be transferred to his wife's account held at another branch of the same bank. On discovery of the frauds the drawers brought an action against Lloyds Bank for money had and received. The defence pleaded by the bank that it had acted with due care failed on it being shown that it had not undertaken a full enquiry into the circumstances as laid down in the bank rule book on opening the wife's account at the other branch to which the cheques in question were credited as to her husband's employers or as to her husbands' occupation. This failure to enquire was coupled with the payee bank's branch to enquire how the husband came to have possession of the cheques before instructing them to credit his wife's account.

The problem raised by the decision in *Savory's* case is: how far should the **18.135** collecting bank go when making enquiries? Lord Buckmaster indicated that in similar circumstances it may be reasonable to make enquiries with regard to a daughter or housekeeper of the customer or prospective customer in order reasonably to prevent fraud. The case marks one of the extreme limits to which the courts have extended the duty of care in the collection of cheques.

Lord Blanesborough, in his dissenting judgment in the *Savory* case, touched on the point where the customer's employment, and the employment of the husband of a female customer, might admittedly be changed on the day after the account was opened, and whether any useful purpose would be served in inquiring about them.

In *Orbit Mining and Trading Co. Ltd.* v. *Westminster Bank* Harman L.J., referring to the *Savory* case, said: " . . . it cannot at any rate by the duty of the bank continually to keep itself up to date to the identity of a customer's employer." It would be otherwise if for example, a customer known to be the secretary, or director or employee of a company paid into his account through the branch credit system cheques payable to his company and indorsed by him on the company's behalf. In such a case the bank must enquire how the customer came by the cheque which normally would be collected by his employer's (company) bank on its behalf. The cheques in *Savory's* case were bearer cheques and it could be argued that where such cheques are paid into a customer's account for collection the bank must always ask for an explanation how he came by them if they are for a substantial amount.

A more flexible view of the enquiries a bank must make on opening a cus-   **18.136** tomer's account was taken recently by the Court of Appeal in *Marfani and Co. Ltd.* v. *Midland Bank Ltd.* The Court of Appeal accepted that the bank had acted according to the current practice of bankers in obtaining and relying on the reference of another customer as to the employer's respectability and that the bank was not negligent in failing to ask for further evidence of the employee's identity or to enquire as to his employment. This was so, even though the other customer's reference was received after the bank had collected the cheque in question but before it allowed the employee to draw against it. The court established a new standard for the enquiries a bank should make. Diplock L.J. said:

> "What the court has to do is to look at all the circumstances at the time of the acts complained of, and to ask itself were those circumstances such as would cause a reasonable banker, possessed of such information about his customer as a reasonable banker would possess, to suspect that his customer was not the true owner of the cheque."

The court referring to the *Savory* decision said the case was decided in the light of social conditions of the 1920's when banking facilities were less commonly used and suspicion might more commonly be aroused. It was decided according to the expert evidence available at that time and the case is an illustration of the general principle "that a banker must exercise reasonable care in all the circumstances of the case."

18.137   The court was further of the view that it did not constitute any lack of reasonable care if before opening an account for a customer, the bank refrained from making enquiries which would probably fail to lead to the detection of the customer's dishonest purpose, if he were dishonest, and which would only offend him if he were not. The *Marfani* case recognised that negligence is to be measured by varying current professional banking standards, and every case must be considered on its merits. The court also recognised that if the defendant bank exercised sufficient care, it was only just sufficient, and the decision should not encourage any relaxation of the rules that the banks had established. In *Lumsden and Co.* v. *London Trustee Savings Bank*[78] Donaldson J. held the bank was negligent in not fully establishing the customer's credentials when the account was opened, the bank having trusted the customer because he said he had professional qualifications and appeared respectable.

The duty to enquire is a continuous one, and arises every time a transaction occurs which is apparently out of harmony with the description of the customer's business or occupation given by him or is otherwise inconsistent with the normal manner of conducting his account (see also *Nu-Stilo Footwear Ltd.* v. *Lloyds Bank Ltd.*[79]

The implication of this decision is that the bank must at all times be cognisant through all its officers, present and future, who may be concerned with collecting cheques for any customer, of information about the customer which the bank obtained at the time the account was opened. It is to be treated as having this knowledge for all time, whether it was in fact aware of it at the time of collecting or not.

18.138   The strict attitude of the courts is illustrated by its decision in *Baker* v. *Barclays Bank Ltd.*[80] In that case Baker and Bainbridge were trading in partnership under the name "Modern Confections." Bainbridge misappropriated nine cheques amounting to about £1,160 payable to the partnership. He indorsed the cheques and handed them to one Jeffcott, an insurance agent, who paid them into his account at Barclays Bank for collection. Jeffcott further paid in cheques payable to Bainbridge personally who had indorsed them. The bank manager "on enquiry" was assured that Jeffcott was paying in cheques for his friend Bainbridge who was the sole proprietor of Modern Confections and who had just begun in business and was using

---

[78] [1971] 1 Ll.Rep. 114.
[79] [1956] 7 Legal Decisions Affecting Bankers 121.
[80] [1955] 1 W.L.R. 822.

Jeffcott's bank account temporarily before opening one of his own. The manager was satisfied with the explanations and never asked to see Bainbridge. In an action for conversion by the other partner, Baker, the bank was held to have been negligent in not making further and fuller enquiries. Devlin J., gave two reasons for his decision namely, that the bank was not protected by section 82 of the Bills of Exchange Act 1882 because the explanation given by Jeffcott to the bank manager was not one which should have satisfied him, and, as Bainbridge was not a customer of the bank but was using another customer's account, the bank manager should have made enquiries about Bainbridge personally. Secondly, the bank was not a holder of the cheques in due course because Bainbridge was guilty of fraud in his dealings with the cheques and the bank did not sustain the burden of proving that it had given value for them.

This decision seems to be in line with the case in *Motor Traders Guarantee Corporation Ltd* v. *Midland Bank Ltd.*,[81] where it was held that a breach of the bank's "own rules is not conclusive proof of negligence, nor is a customer even entitled to demand literal performance of them," and the court rejected the view that if the named payee on an indorsed cheque is a limited company, the bank is necessarily put on enquiry as to the title of its customer to whom the cheque has apparently been indorsed.[82]

18.139

In the *Baker* case it seems to have been accepted that the standard of care to be shown by a collecting bank will become more exacting if the amount of the individual cheques and the number of indorsed cheques passing through the account is substantial or increasing.

The banker's duty of care and inquiry operates when the first large cheque which is indorsed in favour of a customer is presented for collection, but the bank's duty may be less stringent where a number of small cheques, indorsed in favour of its customer, are presented for collection over a considerable period of time. In *Crumplin* v. *London Joint Stock Bank Ltd*[83] the court gave judgment in favour of the bank that the circumstances did not call for special inquiry, but the judge stated that in his opinion the case was "very near the line." It can only be a question of fact in each case whether the payment into an account for collection of a second or third (or even subsequent) small cheque should give rise to suspicion, so that if the collecting bank does not make the inquiries as to its customer's title, it will lose the defence under section 4 of the Cheques Act 1957. Furthermore, the bank cannot assume that a transaction by its customer is legitimate simply because it is similar to other such transactions which have occurred over a substantial length of time. The conclusion to be reached from an examination of the recent decisions of the courts is that banks are always required to take reasonable precautions, and in determining what precautions are called for in a particular case, the current prevailing practices of the banking community are taken into account. The courts are not bound by the standards set by the banks for themselves, but will work out with the benefit of hindsight what a reasonable and competent banker would have done in the circumstances.

Particular questions arise in connection with the possible negligence of a collecting bank which collects cheques drawn payable "to A for B" to "A

18.140

---

[81] [1937] 4 All E.R. 90.
[82] *London and Montrose Shipbuilding & Repairing Co. Ltd.* v. *Barclays Bank Ltd.* (1926) 31 Com. Cas. 61.
[83] (1913) 30 T.L.R. 99.

on behalf of B" or "to A for the account of B." Probably the most important decision in this area is the 1955 case of *Marquis of Bute* v. *Barclays Bank Ltd.*[84] where the plaintiff employed one McGaw as manager of certain sheep farms on the Island of Bute. Payment warrants, made payable to "Mr. D. McGaw, Kerrylamont, Rothesay, Bute" but immediately after were added in parenthesis the words "for the Marquis of Bute," were paid to McGaw by the defendant bank. The Marquis claimed the amounts of the warrants in an action for damages for conversion.

McNair J. rejected all three defences raised by the bank, and held that to claim in conversion the claimant need only establish that at the material time he was entitled to the immediate possession of the subject matter which the plaintiff in this particular case could do. In any event the test as to true ownership is the intention of the drawer, and the Department of Agriculture, knowing that the subsidies were due to the plaintiff, had indicated their intention in the words in parenthesis.

18.141   The duty on the bank to inquire is not removed by the fact that an agent who draws cheques on his principals' account has a power of attorney, under which he draws cheques payable to his own order (see *Midland Bank Ltd.* v. *Reckitt and Others*[85]). However, there is no absolute rule that inquiry must be made in cases of this kind and in *Penmount Estates Ltd.* v. *National Provincial Bank Ltd.*[86] the bank succeeded in its defence that it had not been negligent. In that case cheques payable to a principal were sent to his solicitor who forged the principal's indorsement and paid the cheques into his practice account. The court held the collecting bank was not guilty of negligence in crediting the cheque to the solicitor's account since it was normal that a solicitor should pay into his account money belonging to his clients.

The second defence raised in the *Bute* case was that the Marquis was estopped from denying that he had intended the warrants to be received and collected by McGaw. McNair J., rejecting this defence, said that the estoppel argument could succeed only if the documents were in a form that could reasonably be understood as an unequivocal representation that McGaw was entitled to the proceeds of the warrants. A warrant in payment of Hill sheep subsidies issued by the Department of Agriculture in Scotland when presented through a branch of a bank in Barnsley was not such a representation.

CONTRIBUTORY NEGLIGENCE

18.142   In *Lumsden & Co.* v. *London Trustee Savings Bank*[87] the plaintiffs brought an action for the conversion of certain cheques. The court recognised and accepted the view advanced by Milnes Holden that the Law Reform (Contributory Negligence) Act 1945 applied not only to actions for negligence, but also to other torts including the tort of conversion, so that if the plaintiffs are contributorily negligent in facilitating a fraud the damages recoverable by them must be proportionally reduced. In the *Lumsden* case the plaintiffs' damages were reduced by 10 per cent. because the court held that while the bank was negligent in not fully establishing its customer's credentials when his account was opened, the plaintiffs had also been negligent in

[84] [1955] 1 Q.B. 202.
[85] [1933] A.C. 1.
[86] (1945) 89 Sol.Jo. 566.
[87] [1971] 1 Ll.Rep. 114.

leaving spaces on the cheques in question which allowed unauthorised additions to be made to the payee's name.

The decision has now been given statutory force by section 47 of the Banking Act 1979, which enacts:

"In any circumstances in which proof of absence of negligence on the part of a banker would be a defence in proceedings by reason of s.4 of the Cheques Act 1957, a defence of contributory negligence shall also be available to the banker notwithstanding the provisions of s.11(1) of the Torts (Interference with Goods) Act 1977."

The Torts (Interference with Goods) Act 1977 had abolished the defence of contributory negligence in tort except actions for negligence and so the Banking Act 1979 has merely restored the position before the 1977 Act was passed. The position is not completely restored, however, because if the drawer sues the paying bank for conversion the 1977 Act still applies and the paying bank cannot plead the defence of contributory negligence.

Prior to the *Lumsden* case and the Banking Act 1979, the courts did not recognise any duty or obligation on the part of the customer to take precautions to reduce fraud.

The collecting bank as a holder for value

18.143 The Bills of Exchange Act 1882 and the Cheques Act 1957, provide the collecting bank with statutory protection over and above that given to a holder in due course, and although these may operate concurrently to confer protection, the bank may find itself without statutory protection and thus totally dependent on its position as a holder for value or a holder in due course. The position of the bank as holder for value was discussed in the *Capital and Counties Bank* v. *Gordon*[88] and more fully in *A.L. Underwood Ltd.* v. *Barclays Bank Ltd.*[89] In the latter case the bank argued that it had received payment of the cheques as a holder in due course. It was shown the bank had credited Underwood's account immediately on receiving the cheques for collection, and it was further shown that there was no agreement with Underwood that he should be allowed to draw against the cheques before they were paid by the drawee banks. The Court of Appeal, affirming the first instance decision, gave judgment for the plaintiff. Atkins L.J. said:

"... it [is] sufficient to say that the mere fact that the bank in their books enter the value of the cheques on the credit side of the account on the day on which they receive the cheques for collection does not, without more, constitute the bank a holder for value. To constitute value there must be in such a case a contract between banker and customer ... that the bank will before receipt of the proceeds honour cheques of the customer drawn against the cheques ..."

In practice a contract of the kind evisaged by Atkin L.J. will rarely exist, and banks in fact usually provide by their conditions of business that customers may not draw against uncleared cheques.

18.144 The question of an agreement to allow a customer to draw against uncleared cheques was again raised in *Westminster Bank Ltd.* v. *Zang*[90] where the bank claimed to be a holder for value of a cheque which had, when paid

[88] [1903] A.C. 240.
[89] [1924] 1 K.B. 775.
[90] [1966] A.C. 182.

in, reduced a substantial overdraft. The House of Lords rejected the bank's argument that there was an implied agreement to reduce the overdraft immediately by the amount of the cheque, and the Court held that the bank had not established itself as a holder for value of the cheque.

Viscount Dilhorne dealt with the point of the implied agreement to permit drawings against uncleared effects. He considered that the reduction of the overdraft could have been "value," but in this case there was in fact no effective reduction, in view of the fact that the bank charged interest on the amount of the cheque until it was cleared and said: "In these circumstances it is hard to see that by crediting it to the account and reducing the overdraft the bank gave value for it."

18.145   He further held that no implied agreement could be read into the circumstances of the case, in view of the fact that the printed words on the credit slip negatived such an agreement, and no evidence was given that cheques drawn by the customer were honoured in consequence of the uncleared cheques being paid in. It must now be assumed that a bank can establish a claim to be holder for value of a cheque paid in for collection only by proving an agreement or by showing that the cheques were in fact honoured specifically against the uncleared effects. On this point Salmon L.J. in the Court of Appeal in the *Zang* case said:

> "In my judgment this court [referring to the Underwood case] certainly did not lay down that in no circumstances could a bank become holders for value save by an express or implied contract to honour cheques drawn against the uncleared cheques. An obvious way of becoming a holder for value is to give value by honouring a cheque drawn against an uncleared cheque, whether or not there is an antecedent contract to do so. Whether the bank has honoured a cheque drawn against uncleared effects is a matter of fact . . . "

On this reading of the law, value is given by the bank only if it can be shown that cheques drawn by the customer were paid which would have been dishonoured had the cheques in question not been paid in.

18.146   An example is seen in *Barclays Bank Ltd.* v. *Astley Industrial Trust Ltd.*[91] where Milmo J. distinguished the *Zang* decision as being on materially different facts; in particular there was no question (unlike this case) of the bank having a lien on the cheques paid in. The bank claimed to be holders for value in respect of the full amount of the customer's overdraft including the amounts drawn pending collection of the cheques paid into the company's account. The bank succeeded on all of its contentions. Milmo J. expressly rejected the defendants' argument that the bank could not be at once an agent for collection of a cheque and a holder for value of that cheque. The language used in section 2 of the Cheques Act 1957 negatives this proposition, since it presupposes that a banker who has been given a cheque for collection may, nevertheless, have given value for it. It is, furthermore, a common occurrence for a banker to allow credit to a customer against an uncleared cheque. Milmo J. accepted the view that if a banker holds a cheque merely as the customer's agent for collection, then it cannot also be a holder for value and even less a holder in due course. He further rejected the argument that the fact of the bank charging interest on the uncleared effects

[91] [1970] 1 All E.R. 719.

prevented it from being holders for value. However, in view of Viscount Dilhorne's opinion in the *Zang* case this last finding is questionable.

PART B: INNOVATIONS IN MONEY TRANSFER METHOD

Credit transfers and direct debits

The last 20 years has seen a revolution in the development of alternative **18.147** methods of transferring money payments from one person to another, and from one place to another. The traditional methods of transferring money, namely, cash, cheques, bills of exchange and bankers drafts, will undoubtedly continue to be used for many years yet as a means of settling payment obligations, but the innovations of the last 20 years have made a considerable leap towards the cashless society. Whilst the fully automated systems of money transfers (CHAPS in the United Kingdom on a national basis, and SWIFT on an international basis) have been operational over the past few years, a number of partially automated systems, namely, the credit transfer and direct debit systems, have been in operation for some time now and are of considerable importance. The number of payments made through the credit transfer and direct debit systems has been increasing steadily and, consequently, some pressure has been removed from an over-burdened cheque clearing system. Basically, however, like cheques and bills of exchange, the credit transfer and direct debit method of payment is a paper-based system of money transfer.

DEFINITION OF OPERATIONS

Since the credit transfer and direct debit systems are purely the development **18.148** of the banking community there are no statutory definitions, but any definition must take account of the operational nature of the system.

A credit transfer is the transfer of funds from one bank to another under a mandate given by the payer to the paying bank. Conversely, the direct debit payment is the transfer of funds from one bank to another under a general mandate given by a debtor to his creditor where the transfer is effected by the creditor initiating a payment by the debtor's bank to his own or by collection from the debtor's bank to the creditor's bank.

In the monthly review of the Federal Reserve Bank of New York[92] "a debit transfer" is described as:

> "one in which an item containing a request or order for the payment of money is received by the banking system from a depositor who is to receive payment if the item is honoured by the drawee after receipt: and a credit transfer is one in which the first impact on the banking system is the receipt by the paying bank from its depositor of an order to pay money, to the debit of his account, and to the credit of an identified account in the same or another bank, which is also identified."

The credit transfer system enables a person to make payments through **18.149** his bank, either to other customers of the same bank or those of other banks. Furthermore, a person without a bank account can avail himself of

---

[92] Clarke, "The Payment System", May 1970, Vol. 52, p. 109. See also Arora on "Recent Developments in Money Transfer Methods, L.M.C.L.Q. 1980, pp. 416–432; see Wilcox in Journal of the Institute of Bankers (1969–70) Vol. 90–91, p. 12.

the system. Generally, the credit transfer system has no advantages over the cheque system for a person with a bank account. It is, however, valuable to a person not possessing a bank account who wishes to avoid sending cash or postal or money orders through the post. Any such person may now go into any bank and by filling up a transfer form and paying cash over the counter ensure payment is made to the credit of the payee's bank account. The system is more advantageous to enterprises which have to make a large number of payments regularly for varying amounts to different payees. In these circumstances a company can make payments of wages and salaries to its employees and amounts owing to its creditors by sending instructions to its bank with details of the intended transfers accompanied by a single cheque for the total amount to be transferred.

18.150   The payee, on the other hand, will no longer receive a cheque which his bank has to present for collection, but instead obtains payment by the amount transferred to his bank being credited to his account, and he will simply be informed by his bank that this has been done. The credit transfer system may also be used by a customer who wishes to make a payment to the credit of his own account, either at the branch where he has his account or at another branch of the same bank.

Direct debiting is a term used to describe payments which are made by a bank out of its customer's account to a third person who instructs the bank to transfer the amount involved to his own bank, but this will, of course, only be done if the customer of the paying bank gives it an appropriate mandate for the purpose. The payment is, therefore, initiated by the payee and because of the possibility of fraud the banks will extend direct debiting facilities only to payees of high financial standing who can be relied on to act properly. The banks require the payee to indemnify them for any loss occasioned by improper or unauthorised use of the system, and for this reason the system cannot be used by individuals.

The main differences between the two services are:

(1) Credit transfers are initiated by the payer (debtor) whereas direct debits are made on the instruction of the payee (creditor).

(2) In the case of credit transfers the payer need not necessarily be a customer of the bank, but in a direct debit the payer must have an account out of which the payment is made.

(3) In the credit transfer system no restrictions are placed on the payees to whose accounts payments may be made, but only a limited class of payees may initiate direct debits.

THE HISTORY OF CREDIT TRANSFERS AND DIRECT DEBITS

18.151   A Giro system for the direct transfer of money between bank accounts has existed for over 90 years in Europe, where it was developed by the co-operative banks alongside the traditional payment facilities provided by the commercial banks. In Britain the pressure for the introduction of a credit transfer system gradually increased as the banks wished to attract more customers. Wilcox[92] calculated that only one in four, or at the most two in five people held bank accounts in the 1950's, and thus there was considerable scope for the banks to attract further customers, especially those making small payments regularly. Finally, in order to avoid a serious loss of deposits, following the introduction of the National Giro system by the Post Office in 1968, the commercial banks were forced to consider favourably the introduction of the credit transfer system. The interest expressed by the Radcliffe Committee[93] in a low-cost national system for transferring money and credit, and its recommendation that unless the banks provided such a service the Post Office should do so, gave immediate impetus. In November 1969 the banks committed themselves to extend and develop a system of credit transfers.

Credit transfer were not an entirely new concept, since the banks had run a standing order service since the nineteenth century to facilitate the payment of fixed amounts at regular intervals and also a traders' credit system by which firms paid their employees salaries by transfers to the credit of the employees' bank accounts. In 1961 these facilities were extended to all kinds of payments and to persons who were not customers of a bank. The credit transfer vouchers used in connection with such payments are cleared through the Bankers' Clearing House in London. Unlike the credit transfers there was no continental precedent for the direct debiting service and on its introduction it was unique to the United Kingdom. It came into operation as an addition to the credit clearing service in 1970.

THE PROCEDURE FOR CREDIT TRANSFERS

18.152 When payment is made by credit transfer the payer initiates the transfer of funds by giving written instructions for it to his bank on a credit transfer form. There is no prescribed wording for the form but it must clearly authorise the paying bank to make a payment to the credit of the account of a specified person with the same or another bank. The credit transfer form must consequently have appropriate spaces for details of the payee's name, his bank account number, the name of his bank and the branch where the account is kept and, finally, the amount to be transferred. Each bank has its own standard credit transfer form and as yet no standardisation has been achieved between the banks. Where more than one payment is to be made, the debtor may list the details of each payment in a separate schedule and a separate credit transfer form must be made out for each transaction. A cheque for the total amount is then drawn by the payer (debtor) payable to the paying bank to cover all the transfers, or if the payer has no account at the paying bank he may be required to pay it an equivalent amount. On receipt by the paying bank the credit transfer forms are then passed through the credit clearing bank in London. The clearing of credit transfers is regulated by "The Bankers' Clearing House Credit Clearing Rules," which provide that a clearing is to be held each working day for the exchange of Bank Giro Credits between the London Clearing Banks. Rule 3 of the Credit Clearing Rules excludes the following articles from the clearing, namely:

(a) re-directed credits (*i.e.* those which originally have been delivered to the wrong collecting bank);

(b) credits bearing more than one amount;

(c) credits with attachments (*e.g.* documents relating to the transaction in connection with which the payment is made);

(d) outsize credits (credit transfer forms larger than those currently accepted, *i.e.* more than seven inches by four inches in dimension);

(e) dividend and interest counterfoils.

18.153 The credit transfer forms are then sorted into bundles to be presented to each collecting bank and are then delivered to the Clearing House or

---

[93] Report of the Committee on the Working of the Monetary System, Cmnd. 827.

directly to the collecting bank by 10.30 a.m. The dockets accompanying the bundles of credit transfer forms should list the amount of each credit transfer. The total of all dockets should be agreed between the paying and collecting banks on the day of delivery, but adjustments can be made late in case of errors. Rule 6 (b–h) of the Credit Clearing Rules lays down the procedure where there is an error on the dockets, where the docket is sent to the wrong collecting bank or where a credit transfer listed on a docket cannot be found. The banks agree on any differences arising from these causes by 9.30 a.m. the following day. Wrongly delivered vouchers must also be returned by the following day. The presenting bank must check all errors noted on returned dockets and must notify the collecting bank of any adjustments which it agrees. A final agreement of "In" and "Out" totals (including wrongly delivered vouchers returned on the previous day) must be reached by 9.45 a.m. on the next following working day. Final settlement takes place on the same working day at 11.00 a.m. by inclusion of the balances to be transferred between the paying and collecting banks in the town clearing. The credit transfer is finally credited to the payee's account by the collecting bank on the day after the receipt of the credit transfer voucher by it.

DIRECT DEBITS

18.154   In order to make payments by the direct debit system, the creditor or initiator (which is always a company) has first to obtain the written consent of his bank and the Committee of the London Banks Clearing House to its initiating direct debits. The application is made initially to the head of the initiator's own bank, and when approval has been given by the bank final approval is normally given automatically by the Clearing House Committee. All companies using the direct debit system are given an identification number which must be included in the details of all debits which they initiate. If the debit is for a fixed amount payable periodically and there is a standing order of the debtor already in existence for its payment, the consent of the debtor to the conversion of the standing order into a direct debit mandate must be obtained. Where there is no standing order, the creditor (initiator) must obtain a direct debiting mandate from its debtor authorising his bank to honour debits initiated by the creditor, and this must be sent to the debtor's bank. The form must contain the debtor's signature and must indicate the name of the creditor (initiator), the amount to be debited (where fixed or variable) and the dates upon which payments are to be made (if they are periodic). If the sum to be debited is to be ascertained by the creditor (e.g. a monthly debit for goods supplied to the debtor during that month or an earlier period), a similar authority must be obtained from the debtor, but the wording of the form is more general.

18.155   In all cases the creditor (initiator) must sign an undertaking to indemnify all the banks involved in the direct debiting scheme against claims which may arise from debits initiated by the initiator which are erroneous or unauthorised. The payee is entitled to payment under a direct debit when payment falls due by one of two alternative methods:

(1) If the payee is linked by computer to the computer bureau operated by Bankers Automated Clearing Services Ltd., a company of which all clearing banks are members, he delivers to the computer bureau a computer magnetised wire-recording of the particulars of the debits to be made (namely, the

payer's respective account numbers, the paying and receiving bank branches and their respective sorting code numbers and the respective debtors account numbers and the amount of the debit). The bureau's computer digests the information on the initiators computer tape and prepares corresponding tapes directed to each paying banks which confirm details of debits to be made against their customers account. These are delivered to the paying banks within one to two days after the initators computer tape is received by the bureau, and the debits are effected by the paying banks on the following day. The bureau also notifies the initiators banks head office of the total amount to be credited to the initiator's account, and this is done on the same day as the debits are made by the paying banks. The bureau also delivers legible print-outs of debits and credits passed through it to the paying and collecting banks' London Head Offices for transmission to the branches where the debtors and the initiators accounts are kept, and a copy of the print out is also sent to the initiator itself; or

(2) The alternative method is for the payee to send a direct debit voucher **18.156** containing particulars of the debit (including the payer and initiators names and their respective bank branches) to the London Head Office of the payer's bank, together with a credit transfer form for the total amount of such debits, so that this amount may be credited to the payee's account at the branch of the bank where its account is kept. The credit transfer is then passed through the credit clearing on the day following the receipt of the debit voucher by the paying bank, then the debit voucher is sent on to the branch of the paying bank where the payer's account is kept on the same day. The payer's account is debited and the initiator's account credited on the following day.

If a debit is dishonoured by the branch of the payer's bank where his account is kept, the branch must notify the branch of the initiator's bank where its account is kept by 12 noon on the day following the receipt of the debit voucher by the payer's branch, and the debit voucher is then returned to the initiator's branch. The payer's bank recovers the amount of the debit (which has already been paid by its head office) by passing an unpaid claim through the cheque or debit clearing in the same way as if the dishonoured debit were a dishonoured cheque. The clearing banks have not yet established specific rules about these matters, but apply the General Clearing Rules relating to the cheque clearing by analogy.

THE LAW RELATING TO CREDIT TRANSFERS

The Bank Giro services have been developed entirely by the banking com- **18.157** munity and are not established or regulated by statute. Consequently, the law relating to them must be derived by applying the general principles of common law and equity to the relevant banking practice.

THE LEGAL CHARACTER OF CREDIT TRANSFERS

The most important problem in the field of credit transfers is to establish the **18.158** exact stage at which payment can be said to have been made to the payee, and in this connection the primary question is: when does the payment become both effective and irrevocable? The earliest possible moment that this could happen is when the payer hands the completed credit transfer voucher to the paying bank, together with the necessary cash if he is not a customer of the bank. If it could be said that a mere instruction of the payer operates as a transfer of the funds involved to the payee by way of a legal assignment of the paying banks indebtedness to the payer, the payment would become irrevocable immediately and the payee would be entitled to sue the paying bank for the amount involved. This would differ from the operation of a cheque which merely operates as a mandate by the payer to pay a certain sum of money, and does not take effect as an assignment of a corresponding part of the drawer's credit balance at the drawee bank.[94]

A credit transfer form does not contain a direct order by the payer to the paying bank for payment and of the amount involved, nor an acceptance of that order by the bank, and so it cannot be said that there is a direct relationship between the paying bank and the payee similar to the relationship between the acceptor and the payee of a bill of exchange. Consequently, the payee cannot sue the bank for breach of contract if it does not fulfil its mandate by effecting the transfer. Indeed, the payee is not normally aware of the credit transfer until his bank notifies him that payment has actually been made.

18.159   It may be argued alternatively that the initiation of the credit transfer constitutes a transfer of funds to the payee if it can be shown that the paying bank becomes a trustee for the benefit of the payee of the appropriate amount out of the payer's credit balance or that the payee becomes an equitable assignee of that part of the payer's credit balance even though no express or implied trust in favour of the payee arises.

There is no express trust in favour of the payee in a credit transfer transaction, since neither the payee nor his bank at any stage employs words creating a trust. An implied trust must therefore be deduced from the nature of the transaction and the surrounding circumstances if one is to exist at all. In the case of an implied trust, however, there must be compelling evidence of an intention to create such a trust, and the courts will not infer such an intention from the payer's mandate to transfer funds.[95] In *Re Nanwa Gold Mines Ltd.*[96] and more recently in *Barclays Bank Ltd.* v. *Quistclose Investments Ltd.*[97] and *Re Kayford Ltd.*,[98] however, it was held that if money is put into a separate account for the specific purpose of being returned to the person who provided it in the event of certain conditions not being fulfilled, the money is held on trust for those persons.

18.160   In most cases of credit transfers the payer is a customer of the paying bank, and no question of the bank holding the money to be transferred under the credit transfer in a separate account arises. The amount is simply debited to the payer's current account when the transfer is made. Although money credited by the bank to the payer's account is to be used for the specific purpose indicated by the payer in the credit transfer form he delivers to his bank, it will not be possible to imply a trust of any part of the credit balance in favour of the payee from that fact. It is also suggested by Professor Pennington[99] that no trust arises even in the case of a payer who is not an account holder and who puts the bank sufficiently in funds to make one specific payment. The purpose of the payer's instruction in both situations is merely to require his bank to transfer money to the payee out of its own

[94] s.53(1), Bills of Exchange Act 1882.
[95] *Lister & Co.* v. *Stubbs* (1890) 45 Ch.D.I., and *Mossley* v. *Cressey's Co.* (1865) L.R.L.Eq. 405.
[96] [1955] 1 W.L.R. 1080.
[97] [1968] 1 All E.R. 613.
[98] [1975] 1 W.L.R. 279.
[99] *Commercial Banking Law*, (Macdonald & Evans) p. 284.

resources, and not to establish an immediate trust of earmarked funds on behalf of the payee, because the amount paid is in no way earmarked as being held on behalf of the payee.

Alternatively, even if no trust arises when a credit transfer is initiated, the question arises whether the delivery of the credit transfer voucher by the payer to the paying bank effects an assignment of funds in the hands of that bank. Since the credit transfer form is merely a mandate to the paying bank, like a cheque, it seems almost certain that the acceptance of the credit transfer form and the mandate by the bank does not constitute an assignment of any part of the payer's credit balance with the bank. Nevertheless, the possibility of the credit transfer taking effect as a legal or equitable assignment must be examined.

By section 136(1) of the Law of Property Act 1925, in order for there to **18.161** be a legal assignment, two requirements have to be satisfied, namely:

(i) that there must be a document signed by the assignor containing an absolute assignment of a legal chose in action which includes a credit balance on a bank account, and

(ii) that notice in writing of the assignment must be given to the debtor by the assignee.

Whether a credit transfer is to be paid for by the paying bank debiting the payer's account with its amount or by the payer putting the paying bank in funds to make the transfer, the second requirement of a legal assignment cannot be satisfied unless the payee actually knows of the intended transfer and gives the bank formal notice of it. The initiation of the credit transfer alone cannot amount to a legal assignment of any part of the payer's credit balance, because this would only be possible when the transfer has been completed and the payee's account has been credited, and at that stage it would of course be purposeless. In *Curran* v. *New Park Cinemas & Others*[1] it was held that a mere direction by a creditor to his debtor to pay the debt to a third person who knows nothing of the matter could not amount to a legal assignment, and the creditor could not be treated as an agent of the third person to notify an intended assignment on his behalf.

Equitable assignments, on the other hand, may be more informal, but **18.162** even so not every mandate to make a payment amounts to an equitable assignment of funds held by the mandatory. In *Scott* v. *Porcher*[2] and *Morrell* v. *Wootten*[3] it was held that an instruction to pay amounted to no more than a mandate to the mandatory which conferred no right or interest on the third person and that it made no difference that the mandatory held funds for the purpose. In *Williams* v. *Everett*[4] the court additionally dealt with the question of whether an intended payee who has been notified by a bank that it has been instructed by an intending payee to credit his account with the amount concerned has any rights against the bank. It was held that the intended payee could sue the bank for money had and received only if he could establish privity of contract between himself and the bank, and there was no such contractual relationship in this case, because there had been no agreement entered into between them. A mere notification by the bank to the intended payee of the instructions of the payer did not constitute an offer, nor does the acknowledgement by the payee of the receipt of the noti-

---

[1] [1951] 1 All E.R. 295.
[2] (1817) 34 L.T. 735.
[3] (1852) 16 Beau. 197.
[4] (1811) 14 East. 582.

fication amount to an acceptance. There is a dictum in *Greenhalgh and Sons* v. *Union Bank of Manchester*[5] which conflicts with this analysis, but the statement went further than the facts of the case necessitated and there was no supporting authority for it. In the *Greenhalgh* case, moreover, there was an express assignment by the payer to the payee of an amount the bank was to receive on his behalf from a third party.

18.163   The next question that arises is where notification by the payer to the payee that the paying bank has been instructed to make a credit transfer constitutes the intended payee an assignee of the relevant funds. In *Morrell* v. *Wootten* the court said:

> "Where a person, having money in the hands of another, directs him to pay it to a third party . . . if the holder or depositee consents to do so, and the direction is communicated to the third person, the thing is complete and the payee can enforce the payment of the money but it is absolutely necessary that the order should be communicated to the intended payee."

The statement, however, was *obiter* since on the facts the payee had not been informed of the proposed transfer of the money involved. It is generally accepted that a mere mandate to pay does not constitute an equitable assignment of the funds, whether the payee is notified of the mandate by the intending payer or not.[6]

The discussion, so far, has been based on a situation in which the payer requests payment by credit transfer and notifies the payee, either himself or through the bank. Exceptional circumstances may arise where the payee requests or authorises payment of a debt by credit transfer and the debtor consequently instructs the paying bank to pay by this method. A question of this nature arose in *William Brannelt's Sons & Co.* v. *Dunlop Rubber Co.*[7] where the court held that there was evidence of an equitable assignment of the purchase price of the goods to the bank with notice to the purchasers, and the bank could, therefore, recover the purchase price from the purchasers as an equitable assignee. It was said that a mere fact that a creditor of X, with his consent, calls on a person who is indebted to X to make payment of his debt directly to the creditor may be sufficient to constitute an equitable assignment. Lord Macnaughten said: "The language [of an equitable assignment] is immaterial if the meaning is plain. All that is necessary is that the debtor should be given to understand that the debt has been made over by the creditor to some third person."

The same rule was applied in *Re Kent and Sussex Sawmills Ltd.*[8] and *Greenhalgh & Sons* v. *Union Bank of Manchester*.[9]

THE TIME WHEN PAYMENT IS MADE

18.164   If there is no transfer of funds by the initiation or notification of a credit transfer the question which then arises is whether payment is made as between the payer and payee when the transfer form is delivered by the paying bank to the collecting bank through the clearing, or only when the balance of credit transfer transactions for the day is agreed by both banks, or

[5] [1924] 2 K.B. 153.
[6] See *Roderick* v. *Gundell* (1852) 1 De G.H. & G. 763.
[7] [1905] A.C. 454.
[8] [1947] Ch. 177.
[9] [1924] 2 K.B. 153.

alternatively when following the agreement of the balance between the banks, the collecting bank credits the payee's account. In *Sibree* v. *Tripp*[10] and *Camidge* v. *Allenby*[11] it was established that the point of time when payment of a debt is made, either absolutely or conditionally depends upon the intention of the parties, and in order to ascertain those intentions the terms of the transaction must be looked at as a whole. In the case of credit transfers two situations may arise:

(1) there are two banks involved in the transfer, one bank acting as the paying and the other as the collecting bank; or

(2) only one bank acts for both the payer and payee.

In the majority of cases the paying bank and the collecting banks are separate, and the transfer is made through the credit clearing system. In such a case, on the first working day after the credit transfer voucher is delivered to the paying bank by the payer, it is presented to the collecting bank concerned through the Clearing House in London. Payment is not effected at this point because the credit transfer vouchers may still be withdrawn by the paying bank or rejected by the collecting bank because they are wrongly delivered (*i.e.* to the wrong collecting bank), and as yet no funds have been transferred as between the banks. On the second day the banks agree on the totals to be paid under the credit transfers delivered between them on the previous day. The difference is then paid out of the credit balance at the Bank of England held by the bank which is the net debtor. This process is the same as for the cheque clearing, with one difference, namely, that the bank delivering the credit transfer vouchers must pay for every item delivered since it has already received the money from its customers or debited their account. Unlike a cheque, a credit transfer cannot subsequently be dishonoured. In the light of *Mardorf Peach & Co. Ltd.* v. *Attica Sea Carriers Corpn. of Liberia*[12] and *Momm* v. *Barclays Bank International Ltd.*[13] where credit transfers were paid directly between the banks and not through the clearing, it would appear that payment is made under a credit transfer which passes through the clearing when the collecting bank takes delivery of the credit transfer form and accepts the paying bank's implied statement of intention to pay. In the *Mardorf* case, charterers hired a ship under an agreement which required payment to be made regularly and punctually in advance. Payment fell due on a Sunday, and on Monday the owners gave notice of their intention to withdraw the vessel. The charterers gave their bank instructions to make an immediate payment. The bank made out a "payment order," and on issuing the payment order the charterer's bank made an entry crediting the owner's bank with the appropriate sum. The payment order was taken by hand to the owner's bank and delivered at about 3 p.m. On receipt of the order an entry was made by the owner's bank in its *intra* bank account, debiting the charterer's bank with the appropriate sum, and the owner's bank began to process the "payment order," in order to collect payment from the Bank of England where the charterers' bank had an account; it normally took 24 hours before the owner's account was credited by the owner's bank. When the owners were informed by their bank that payment had been received from the charterers they gave instructions to their bank to refuse acceptance of the payment and to return the

18.165

---

[10] (1846) 15 M. & W. 23.
[11] (1827) 6 B. & C. 373.
[12] [1976] 2 All E.R. 249.
[13] [1976] 3 All E.R. 588.

payment order to the charterer's bank. The owner's bank complied with this request, and at the same time the ship owners gave notice to the charterers purporting to withdraw the ship under the charterparty. The Court of Appeal held that since the banks regarded the payment order as equivalent to cash the payment for the hire by the charterers took place when the payment order was handed to the collecting bank (the owner's bank) and accepted by them without objection. The court said that the subsequent processing of the order which took place within the receiving bank before the amount was credited to the owner's account was merely an internal banking matter which did not affect the legal position of the party making the payment or the party receiving. This was followed in *Momm & Others* v. *Barclays Bank International Ltd.* where the court followed the decision in the *Mardorf* case and held that payment was complete when the defendant bank decided to accept the H bank's instructions to credit the plaintiffs and the computer processes were set in motion, because the defendants would not have accepted countermanding instructions from the H bank once the computer process had been set in motion.

18.166   However, notwithstanding these decisions, it is submitted that in the case of credit transfers cleared through the Credit Clearing payment is made, not when the receiving bank takes delivery of the credit transfer form and thereby accepts the paying bank's intention to pay, but, when the net amount to be paid by one bank to the other as a result of the day's business is agreed between them, because until then the collecting bank can return wrongly-delivered transfer forms and exclude them from the settlement and the paying bank can request the return of such wrongly-delivered forms. The final stage of a credit transfer occurs when the collecting bank credits the payee's account. However, it is submitted that payment becomes irrevocable at the time of settlement between the bank, and not when the payee's account is credited. This is borne out by the *Mardorf* and *Momm* cases cited above. Furthermore, the cases which have decided that payment of cheques through the clearing is effective and irrevocable when the paying and collecting banks agree the net payment to be made between them on settlement of the day's presentations support a parallel result with regard to the credit clearing. In *Pollard* v. *Bank of England*[14] the plaintiffs had an account with a branch of the defendant's bank and the defendants discounted a bill for the plaintiffs. On the morning when the bill became payable a credit note was issued to the plaintiffs by the defendant clerk. After closing hours it was discovered that the acceptor had insufficient funds to meet the bill and, moreover, payment of the bill had been stopped. The defendant bank requested the defendants to take the bill back as unpaid. The court held the plaintiffs were entitled to be credited by the defendant's bank with the amount of the bill, since there was nothing to show that the credit given by the defendant for the bill was provisional and subject to revocation. In *Parr's Bank Ltd.* v. *Thomas Ashby & Co.*[15] a cheque was presented through the clearing house by the plaintiff bank to the defendant bank. The clearing house rules then in force required the drawee bank to return an unpaid cheque on the day of presentation. Instead, the defendant bank returned a cheque one day late, but the plaintiff, acting on the assumption that the cheque had been paid, honoured a bill accepted by its customer.

---

[14] (1871) R.L. 6 Q.B. 623.
[15] (1898) 14 T.L.R. 563.

The court held that the plaintiff bank was entitled to recover the sum paid from the defendant bank on the ground that its delay in returning the dishonoured cheque amounted to a representation that the cheque had been paid and that the plaintiff bank had acted upon this representation.

If there is only one bank acting for both the payer and payee, the credit **18.167** transfer will not be made through the clearing system and therefore different rules apply. In *Gibson* v. *Minet*[16] and *Rekstin* v. *Severo Sibirsko A.O.*[17] analogous problems were discussed by the court. In *Gibson* v. *Minet* the plaintiff kept an account with the defendants, a London bank. The plaintiff delivered to X. & Co., who held an account with the same bank, a letter directing the defendants to hold £400 out of its account at the disposal of X. & Co. The letter was handed to the defendants, who made a note of the instruction on the debit side of the plaintiff's account. The plaintiff subsequently countermanded the direction, but the defendants, on the instruction of X. & Co., debited the plaintiff's account and placed the £400 to the credit of X. & Co.'s account. It was held that the plaintiff could recover the amount transferred because it had not been transferred before the plaintiffs direction to make the payment was revoked. Thus, it is implicit that, for a payment to be made from one account to another at the same bank, there must be an entry in both accounts, namely, that the payer's account must be debited and the payee's account credited before the authority given by the payer is revoked. A similar conclusion was reached in *Rekstin* v. *Severo Sibirsko A.O.* in which it was held that payment between accounts at the same bank had not been effected, because although the payer's account had been debited, the payee's account had not been credited until after a garnishee order had been served on the bank attaching the payer's account. It was also suggested in that case that payment would not have been completed until the payee had actually been notified that a transfer had been made to his account, but this was repudiated as a ground for the decision in *Momm* v. *Barclays Bank International Ltd.*

It is submitted that if this requirement of notification to the payee of the crediting of his account were accepted by the court, it would detract from the practicality and reliability of the credit transfer system, and would produce a disparity of the rules governing the effectiveness of and irrevocability of the transfer, depending on whether it was between accounts held with the same bank or different banks.

DEFECTS IN THE PAYEE'S TITLE

There may be defects in the payee's title to a payment made by a credit **18.168** transfer which give rise to claims by the payer against the payee or against the paying or collecting banks after the payment has been completed. There are four types of defects which may arise; namely:

(i) *That the Instruction for the Credit Transfer was Forged or Unauthorised*

In the case of credit transfers the signature of the payer appears on the **18.169** instrument as a mandate to his bank to make the transfer, and if the signature is forged or unauthorised the principle laid down in *Orr* v. *Union Bank of Scotland*[18] is applicable by analogy and the payer's bank cannot debit the drawer's account. Furthermore, the forger or unauthorised signatory will

[16] (1791) 1 H.B. 47.
[17] [1933] 1 K.B. 47.
[18] (1854) 1 Macq. (H.L.) 513.

be liable to the paying bank in deceit or for breach of warranty of authority and also to the payer if his account has been wrongly debited and he suffers loss in consequence.

If the payer's agent has a limited authority to sign credit transfer forms on behalf of his principal, and he exceeds those limits, the signature is unauthorised and the principal is not normally bound by it. The position of the parties may, however, be modified by an application of the rules of estoppel. If the principal has so acted by words or conduct as to lead the paying bank or any other person to believe either that he has appointed the agent to act on his behalf when he in fact has not done so, or that the agent has a more extensive authority than is really the case, the principal will be estopped from denying the apparent scope of the agents authority to the paying bank or any other person who acted to his or its detriment in reliance on the principal's representation. If, however, a paying bank receives a limited mandate from its customer to effect credit transfers signed by a third person on the customer's behalf (*e.g.* by a company customer in respect of credit transfers signed by a director) and the bank gives effect to a credit transfer which is manifestly outside that mandate (for example, in payment of a personal debt of the signatory), then the signature is equivalent to a forgery and the bank has no authority to debit the customer's account. The bank will, however, have a claim against the agent for the tort of deceit or for breach of warranty of authority.[19]

(ii) *That the Transfer was Made under a Mistake of Fact.*

18.170 The appropriate action by which the customer or the paying bank may recover money paid under a credit transfer signed by an agent in excess of his authority is an action for the recovery of money paid under a mistake of fact, and is identical to the action brought to recover money paid under cheques or bills of exchange bearing a forged signature. In *Barclays Bank Ltd.* v. *W. J. Simms & Cookes (Southern) Ltd.*[20] the question arose of whether a bank which pays a cheque which has been countermanded by its customer can recover the amount paid from the payee as having been paid under a mistake of fact. The court held that the bank is prima facie entitled to recover the money from the payee unless he has changed his position in good faith. Unlike forgery, however, in many cases where the bank pays out on an unauthorised signature of a credit transfer form, it may have acted negligently, and the question is whether this affects its rights of recovery. In *Kelly* v. *Solari*[21] it was held that money paid under an impression of the truth of a fact which is untrue can be recovered, however careless the party paying it may have been. Byles,[22] however, has suggested, as regards bills of exchange and cheques, that any fault or negligence of the party or the person who pays a bill will disable him from recovering its amount from the recipient. However, in *Price* v. *Neal*[23] and *Smith* v. *Mercer*[24] (as explained in *London & River Plate Bank* v. *Bank of Liverpool*)[25] it appears that if the plaintiff had conducted himself so as to lead the holder of a bill to believe that the plaintiff considered the signature to be genuine the plaintiff cannot

[19] *Collen* v. *Wright* (1857) 8 E. & B. 647.
[20] [1979] 3 All E.R. 522.
[21] (1841) 9 M.K.W. 54.
[22] p. 122.
[23] (1762) 3 Burr. 1354.
[24] (1815) 6 Taunt. 76.
[25] [1896] 1 Q.B. 7.

afterwards recover a payment made to the holder. This is a quite distinct ground from negligence for refusing the payer or the paying bank a right of recovery. This principle would appear to apply to payments under credit transfers, but it is questionable whether negligence would preclude recovery, particularly in view of the recent decision of Goff J. in *Barclays Bank Ltd v. Simms Sons & Cooke (Southern) Ltd*.[26]

18.171

By law, a contract induced by mistake is void although the types of operative mistake are narrow. By analogy to contract, two types of mistake may occur in credit transfer transactions. Firstly, the payer may sign a credit transfer form by mistake, believing it to be an entirely different kind of document. The payer will then be able to recover the amount paid if he can successfully plead *non est factum*. It would appear the paying bank has no effective mandate from the payer to debit his account in such a case, and must thus seek recovery from the collecting bank or the payee by suing them for money paid under a mistake of fact.

Whatever the nature of the action brought by the payer or the paying bank, however, section 4(1) (together with other sections) of the Cheques Act 1957 provides that where a collecting bank in good faith and without negligence collects payment under an instrument issued by a person to enable another to obtain payment from a bank, and the collecting bank receives payment for a customer who has no title or a defective title to the instrument, the bank does not incur any liability to the true owner of the instrument. This provision clearly seems to extend to credit transfers, and so provide protection for the collecting bank if it is sued by the payer under a credit transfer or by the paying bank.

Secondly, a relevant mistake may be made because the payer makes a payment by credit transfer under the belief that he is under a liability to pay the amount transferred to the payee when in fact he is not. In order that the payer or the paying bank may recover the payment, the mistake must be such that the payer believes he was legally liable to make the payment,[27] or at least the payment would not have been made if the payer or his bank had known the truth (*Simms* case). Alternatively, if the payer makes the payment under mistake as to the identity of the payee, he may recover the amount transferred.[28] However, in these circumstances the payer in fact assents to the issue of the mandate under which the paying bank makes the transfer, and the paying bank would therefore undoubtedly be entitled to debit the payer's account unless it actually knew of the mistake which vitiated the payment.

(iii) *That the Transfer was Induced by a Fraudulent or Innocent Misrepresentation or was Otherwise Voidable in Equity (e.g. for Undue Influence of Non-disclosure in Situations where Good Faith by the Payee is a Requisite).*

If the payer is induced by a false representation made by the payee to sign a credit transfer form without realising that the representation was false, the payer and the paying bank may recover the payment from the payee unless the payer ratifies the payment after becoming aware of the falsity of the representation. Recovery from the collecting bank is not possible, however, if

18.172

[26] [1979] 3 All E.R. 522.
[27] *Kelly* v. *Solari* (1841) 9 M.K.Q. 54.
[28] *Cundy* v. *Lindsay* (1878) 3 App.Cas. 450.

it received the transfer in good faith.[29] Moreover, the collecting bank is also protected by sections 4(1) and 5 of the Cheques Act 1957 in the same way as a credit transfer vitiated by mistake.

(iv) *That the Transfer was Made for an Illegal Consideration or in Connection with an Illegal Transaction.*

18.173   The consideration provided on the issue, acceptance or negotiation of a bill of exchange or cheque must not be illegal or arise from an illegal transaction. A holder of a bill of exchange or cheque must show that he did not know of the illegality if he is to enforce his rights.[30] A bank which pays or collects a cheque given for an illegal consideration has the same protection at common law and under the Bills of Exchange and the Cheques Acts as in the case of a cheque obtained by mistake or misrepresentation. In the case of a payment made by credit transfer which is affected by illegality, the consequences are the same as in the case of bills or cheques, except that there is no possibility of the payee or anyone else claiming the protection given to a holder in due course.

Consequently, the payer and the paying bank can recover the payment from the payee and also from the collecting bank to the extent that the payee has not drawn against it,[31] but a third party to whom the amount paid is passed cannot be pursued if he acted in good faith.[32] Furthermore, if sections 4(1) and (2) of the Cheques Act 1957 apply to credit transfers, the collecting bank is also protected against personal liability to reimburse the amount collected if it acted in good faith and without negligence.

18.174   The discussion so far has dealt with the rights of the payer to recover money paid to the payee under a forged or unauthorised credit transfer or under a transfer vitiated by mistake or misrepresentation, and it has been assumed that the full amount transferred may be recovered from both the payee and the collecting bank except where the collecting bank has a special defence to plead. The question arises, however, whether the payer can recover the full amount paid from the collecting bank if it has no special defence but has paid out the whole or part of the amount received by it in good faith on the instructions of the payee. In *National Westminster Bank Ltd v. Barclays Bank International Ltd*[33] the court held that unless the collecting bank knew of the vitiating factor the payer could recover from the collecting bank only that part of the amount received by it which it had not paid out to the payee or on his instructions. This is because the collecting bank is in the same position as an agent who has received money on behalf of his principal to which the principal is not entitled; if the agent has paid the money to his principal, he is no longer liable to restore it to the person from whom it was received.[34] Where the collecting bank has paid part of the sum collected under a forged or unauthorised transfer or a transfer vitiated by mistake or misrepresentation, the collecting bank is only liable to return the balance of the amount received which it still holds when a demand is made on it by the payer or the paying bank.

---

[29] *Babcock* v. *Lawson* (1879) 4 Q.B.D. 394.
[30] *Wool* v. *Hamilton* [1898] Q.B. 337.
[31] *National Westminster Bank* v. *Barclays Bank International* [1975] Q.B. 654.
[32] *Bank Fir Gemeinwirschaft A.G.* v. *London & City Garages* [1971] 1 W.L.R. 149.
[33] [1975] Q.B. 654.
[34] *Kleinwort Sons & Co.* v. *Dunlop Rubber Co.* [1907] 97 L.T. 263, 265.

THE LAW GOVERNING DIRECT DEBITS

In order to obtain payment under a direct debit other than one made **18.175** through the computer bureau operated by Bankers Automated Clearing Services Ltd., the payee will send to the payer's branch bank a direct debit voucher and a credit transfer form signed by him, the agent of the payer. The credit transfer is put through the credit clearing in the same way as any other credit transfer and so the same rules as to the effectiveness and irrevocability of payment apply. This payment is made at the time of the daily settlement between the paying and collecting banks, or if one bank holds the accounts of both payer and payee, payment is made when it has been entered on the accounts of both parties.

If payment of a direct debit is made through the computer bureau operated by Bankers Automated Clearing Services Ltd. it will be cleared in the way described above, and the daily balance of direct-debits cleared by this method is settled separately by the bankers without entering either the credit or debit (cheque) clearing. The paying and receiving banks are notified daily of the previous day's balances of direct debits payable between them mutually, and after the head offices of the banks have agreed the totals, a transfer ticket is issued by the bank with a net balance against it instructing the Bank of England to transfer that amount from its account at the Bank to the other bank's account, and a transfer is then made between the respective accounts of the banks kept at the Bank of England. In other words, the settlement is a bilateral one between the two banks.

A person who has authorised another to initiate direct debits on his **18.176** account can revoke his original mandate to the initiator and his bank at any time by giving notice of his intention to revoke to his bank and to the holder of the mandate. The authorisation to initiate direct debits may be revoked at any time before payment is made under it, and revocation is possible even though the initiator has given the payer's bank the ten days notice required by the terms of his mandate before the payment can be initiated. Direct debits notified to the paying bank subsequent to the revocation will be returned unpaid, and if the paying bank does make payment, it cannot debit its customer's account because the customer has revoked its authority to do so. However, the paying bank will be able to recover from the payee amounts wrongly paid. The revocation of an authority to initiate a direct debit may involve the payer in liability for breach of contract as between himself and the initiator, but the revocation is nonetheless effective as far as the paying bank is concerned.

The paying bank is entitled to reject a direct debit because the payer has insufficient funds to meet the order, without any possibility of an action against the bank for wrongful dishonour.

DEFECTS IN THE INITIATOR'S TITLE

There is generally less risk of payment being made improperly by direct **18.177** debits than by credit transfers because payment can only be made in accordance with the written mandate given by the payer to the paying bank authorising the payee to draw against the payer's account. The mandate will specify the payee, the amount to be debited (if not variable) and the time of payment (if periodic). Any mistake or other defect affecting the initiator's right to payment will not relate to the nature of the mandate by which the payer authorises the debiting of his account, but to the underlying transaction between himself and the initiator. The paying bank's mandate to honour debits presented to it and the authority given by the payer to the banks in general to concur in debit transactions will only rarely be subject to question since the giving of the mandate is a unilateral voluntary act which is unlikely to be influenced by mistake or misrepresentations, and the likelihood of forgery or mistake as to its intrinsic character when signed by the paying bank's customer is remote.

In the operation of direct debits there is unlikely to be a significant risk of forgery of the direct debit vouchers or unauthorised use of computerisation facilities in an initiator's name, since the only person who can receive the benefit of the transfer of funds by direct debit is the person named in the mandate given by the payer as authorised to initiate debits. However, there are occasions when fraudulent third parties could benefit from a forgery, for example, if company A legitimately draws sums by direct debit from company B, which authorises it to do so, and the funds transferred are credited to a separate account by A's bank. An employee of company A then fraudulently draws sums out of this account and obtains further funds from B by signing further direct debit vouchers purporting to be issued by company A in order to cover up his forgery. In this case the paying bank has no mandate to debit the payer's account since the direct debit voucher was not signed on behalf of company A but was a forgery concocted by its employee for his own purposes. In this situation company B and its bank would be entitled to recover the money paid from the collecting bank as money paid under a mistake of fact from company A and also from its bank, except to the extent that the bank had in good faith paid out the amount collected by it.[35]

18.178   The commonest type of fraud which may be perpetrated by means of the direct debit system will be when the initiator makes an unauthorised debit on the payer's account. This can only occur when there is a general mandate for the payment of variable sums which consequently does not specify the amount or the dates of the debit. In this situation the paying bank would be protected by its mandate from the payer and it would be entitled to debit the payer's account. To some extent, this is guarded against by the requirement that the initiator should notify the payer ten days before initiating a debit against his account, but in a case of fraud by the initiator he would obviously omit this step. In this situation the payer would be able to recover the amount paid from the initiator as money paid under a mistake of fact or in restitution in an action for fraud, and he could also recover from the collecting bank so far as it had not paid the money out in good faith; in this situation the payer's position would be the same as if the payment had been made by cheque. He would have no claim against his own bank if it made the payment in good faith, however, since it would be protected by the authority given by the payer in his mandate.

Electronic money transfers: an examination of the methods of electronic transfer of funds and the legal issues

18.179   The aim of this article is to examine the methods of electronic transfer of funds and their legal implications (see Arora "Electronic Fund Transfers," *Company Lawyer* (1986) Vol. 7, No. 2, pp. 195–201 and Elinger, "Giron

---

[35] *National Westminster Bank Ltd.* v. *Barclays Bank International Ltd.* [1975] Q.B. 654.

system and Electronic Transfers of Funds," L.M.C.L.Q. (Feb. 1986), pp. 178–218).

Truncation of Cheque Presentation

Presently, there are some four or five different clearing systems for the payment of cheques, credit transfers, standing orders, direct debits and B.A.C.S. Many of the payments made by these various methods can originate from and be directed to anywhere in the country, and because on the whole the clearing systems are based on the physical presentation to the paying bank of the instrument evidencing the right to payment, it may take up to four days for the payment process to be completed. This undoubtedly results in a waste of time and resources; there are limits to the economies that can be achieved when inter-bank cheque clearing is based on the physical movement of paper.

18.180

The banks, therefore, need to solve the problems of and arising from the physical movement of paper in the clearing process. To a limited extent this has already been achieved by a process known as truncation, which involves the capture of relevant data to enable payment to be made to the payee's account, and simultaneously for the drawer's account to be debited, without the physical movement of paper. At present this can only be done when the drawer and payee of a cheque have accounts at different branches of the same bank; a cheque drawn on the branch of another bank still has to be physically presented for clearing.

A problem with the cheque truncation system is that of capturing the relevant data for electronic transmission. This may be resolved in one of two ways, firstly, in a partially truncated system cheques could be remitted to the clearing department for data collection with cheques being retained at a central location; the cheque is not then sent on to the branch where the drawer has his account. Secondly, in a fully developed system the data collection would be carried out at the collecting branch with cheques being retained at that branch. In the latter case, the branch to which the cheque is presented for collection will truncate it by capturing the relevant information on computer tape, which is sent to the bank's head office so that the details of the accounts which have to be credited/debited may be entered on the records of the drawer's and payee's accounts.

If cheque truncation were fully implemented for inter-bank payments there would be an instant reduction in the volume of paper handled within the clearing system, and eventually with full automation it would be possible to provide for the payment of cheques, credit transfers and other instruments by appropriate payment messages being sent through CHAPS. The data necessary for electronic payment of money (namely, the payer's name and account number, bank and branch codes, together with the payee's name and account number with his bank and branch codes, and the amount of the payment) could be truncated at one of two following stages:

18.181

(i) since the cheque already has magnetic inkprints giving details of the bank and branch codes and account number on which payment is to be made, the cashier at the counter of the collecting bank may key into the computer additional information, (for example the amount of the cheque, the payee's account and other details) so that its computers can transmit the information and receive payment; or

(ii) the same information as is keyed in by the cashier when the cheque is paid in for collection, may be encoded later at the branch of the collecting bank, so that it never leaves the branch of the bank which received it for collection.

18.182 If fully implemented the process of cheque truncation may be completed by the cashier at the counter of the collecting bank when the cheque is paid in. The cashier will pass the cheque through the document reader machine which transmits the data on the cheque to the bank's computer. The cashier will also key in any further information necessary and each transaction will be given its own individual reference number. A complete record of the transaction in question is then transmitted electronically to the paying bank, including the individual reference number. Where the paying bank refuses payment, for example, if the account on which the cheque is drawn has insufficient funds, the paying bank will be able to refuse payment by sending a reverse payment message to the collecting bank by using its own computer terminal. The reference number given to each individual transaction can be used in these circumstances to identify the transaction in question.

There are several advantages to the introduction of cheque truncation on a wider basis. It would remove the need for several separate listings, the physical movement of paper at the clearing house, returning wrong deliveries or sending a dishonoured cheque to the collecting branch. The major task of handling paper would disappear, resulting in a speedier and more economical method of payment. More importantly, the delay of four days before payment is made under the present clearing of cheques and credit payments would no longer exist resulting in a "paper-based" system of payment which is more competitive with the totally automated systems of payment, *e.g.* point of sale.

The truncation process could be extended to other instruments which have presently to be presented physically for collection, for example, credit transfer forms, but this in the first instance would require the standardisation of credit transfer vouchers.

THE LEGAL ISSUES

18.183 Any discussion of a system of cheque truncation will raise a number of legal issues. The discussion arises largely out of the fact that under a system of cheque truncation the collecting bank will no longer physically present the cheque for payment. Instead, the collecting bank will transmit relevant data from the cheque to the paying bank which will make payment on receipt of the data from the collecting bank without actually having seen the cheque. A discussion of a system of cheque truncation must, therefore, necessarily deal with:

(i) the extent to which the banks must comply with their obligation to physically present the cheque for payment;

(ii) the extent to which the existing law and banking practice will protect a bank against a customer who objects to a cheque truncation system being used; and

(iii) against defects of title which are discovered subsequently, in particular, defects on the face of the instrument which might have been discovered had the cheque been physically presented to the paying bank.

At present, the collecting bank is under a duty to its customer, who pays in a cheque to the credit of his account to collect it by the method normally employed as expeditiously as possible.[36] This involves the physical presentation of cheques by the collecting bank. Whilst the electronic transmission of data would obtain payment for the customer more rapidly, the bank would technically be in breach of its obligation to physically present the cheque for payment, unless the customer actually authorises it to use an alternative method of presentation, *e.g.* by a system of cheque truncation.

Similarly, paying bank is under an obligation to its customer (implied from long established banking practice) to pay cheques only on physical presentation, and if payments were made without actual presentation to another bank whose customer had a good title to the cheque, there would technically be a breach of duty on the part of the paying bank. It is, therefore, questionable whether the bank could debit its customer's account as of right. At the most, the bank would be subrogated to the rights of the payee. Consequently, if the payee had no enforceable claim against the drawer, the bank would acquire no rights against its customer.[37]

A bank must, therefore, obtain the express consent of its customer if it is **18.184** to operate a system of complete or partial truncation of cheques.

On the assumption that no special arrangements are made by the collecting or paying banks with their customers to employ a system of cheque truncation, a number of consequences are likely to flow under the existing law, namely:

(1) The Bills of Exchange Act 1882,[38] provides that a "bill must be duly presented for payment." The consequence of not physically presenting the cheque would be that the drawer and indorsers (if any) would be discharged from liability on the cheque, unless physical presentation had been waived.[39] However, any contractual rights which the payee or indorsee of the cheque had against the drawer or his immediate indorser would be preserved.

(2) It would appear that a cheque paid through the transmission of data under a system of truncation without physical presentation by the collecting bank would still be paid in due course under the Bills of Exchange Act 1882.[40] The Act defines payment in due course as "payment made at or after maturity of the [cheque], to the holder thereof in good faith and without notice that his title to the bill is defective." The definition does not require the physical presentation of the cheque for payment to have been made in due course, provided all other physical requirements are satisfied, *i.e.* payment is made after the issue date by the paying bank in good faith and without notice of any defect in the title of the holder. The payment is therefore made in due course, although the cheque is never physically presented and although the paying and collecting banks are technically in breach of their obligation to the customer. If, however, a cheque is collected on behalf of a person who has no title to it and who does not qualify as its holder at the time of payment, the paying and collecting banks will only be protected against liability if they can rely on the statutory protection given to them.

(3) It would appear that a paying bank may not be protected under section 60 of the Bills of Exchange Act 1882, where a cheque paid as a result of data

[36] *Hare* v. *Henty* (1861) 30 L.T.C.P. 302.
[37] *Liggett* v. *Barclays Bank Ltd.* [1928] 1 K.B. 48.
[38] s.45.
[39] s.46(2)(e), Bills of Exchange Act 1882.
[40] s.57, Bills of Exchange Act 1882.

transmitted through a system of cheque truncation is subsequently discovered to be tainted by a forged or unauthorised indorsement because the cheque will not have been paid "in the ordinary course of business." The words require a cheque to be paid in conformity with existing banking practice and until such time as a system of cheque truncation is regarded as part of general banking practice it is unlikely that a paying bank will be able to rely on section 60 for protection if it turns out to have paid a cheque bearing a forged or unauthorised indorsement.

18.185 (4) Section 80 of the Bills of Exchange Act 1882, however, would appear to protect the paying bank if it pays a crossed cheque in "good faith and without negligence" and payment is made to another bank. In order not to be negligent the paying bank has to conform to relevant banking practices at the time the cheque is paid, whether or not the practices have been recognised by the law. In this instance the paying bank would not be negligent in making payment of a cheque from data transmitted by the collecting bank, provided the method of payment was in conformity to banking practices at that time. Although the section only specifically applies to crossed cheques, it will in reality apply to all cheques presented through the clearing system under a system by which the collecting bank will cross the cheques presented to itself.

(5) It is likely that a collecting bank would be able to rely on section 4 of the Cheques Act 1957, if under a system of truncation it collected payment on instruments which were subsequently discovered not to belong to the customer on whose behalf the instrument was collected. The section merely requires the collecting bank to receive payment "in good faith and without negligence" and the same rules are likely to apply as in the case of the paying bank under section 80 of the Bills of Exchange Act 1882. Consequently, if a collecting bank receives payment of a cheque under a system of truncation after the system is used and has become accepted as normal banking practice, the true owner of the cheque could not complain that the collecting bank had acted negligently. Section 4 of the Cheques Act 1957 applies to both crossed and uncrossed cheques.

Although the existing law may adequately protect both the paying and collecting banks, there is the possibility that banks may technically be in breach of their duties to their customers in using a truncation system, and unless he had previously consented to its use, any customer may object. Secondly, the courts may hold that the introduction of a truncation system without prior consent of their customers may deprive both the paying and collecting banks from their statutory protection. It may, therefore, be necessary to pass legislation to deal with some of the points raised in this discussion.

Clearing house automated payments system (CHAPS)

18.186 In order to satisfy the demand by business and professional customers of banks for a rapid payments system, the United Kingdom banks in 1980 decided to work towards the introduction of an electronic interbank system for making guaranteed sterling payments from one clearing bank (known under the system as a settlement bank) to another for same day settlement. This system, known as the Clearing House Automated Payments System (CHAPS), became operational in 1984, and now functions on a nationwide basis through the head offices of each clearing bank being connected by computer terminals to its principal country branches. The system was introduced initially with a minimum payments limitation of £10,000 and a maximum limit of £100,000. The maximum limit was removed gradually in stages, so that only the minimum payment restriction now remains. It is eventually planned to extend the CHAPS system to non-clearing banks and large companies through subscription, and they like the branches of the clearing banks will then have the facility of making payments through their nominated clearing banks under the CHAPS system.

Whilst both the Banker's Automated Clearing Services (BACS) and Town Clearing systems do contribute towards meeting the demands of commerce and industry for fast and efficient methods of transferring money, neither of these systems provides for a national system of same day paper-free transfers. The banks, therefore, proposed and introduced the Clearing House Automated Payments System (CHAPS) in February 1985. The CHAPS system facilitates the electronic transfer of funds between accounts of the customers of the 13 banks which are members of the system (the settlement banks), and it will also eventually provide a computer link between the head office of each participating bank and its branch offices nationally. It will, therefore, be possible to make a same day payment from any connected branch of a clearing bank to any other connected branch of the same or another clearing bank.

The stated objectives of the CHAPS system are: (i) to enable same day **18.187** sterling payments to be made with speed; (ii) to enable the settlement of balances to be effected between the clearing banks for the total payments passing between them on the same day as the payments are made; this is done at the same time as the settlement of balances on the cheque and the credit transfer clearing, namely, at 4.30 p.m. each day, and because of this individual CHAPS payments cannot be initiated later than 3 p.m. each day; and (iii) to provide instantaneous information about payments made and received to the head offices, branches and participating customers who are involved.

The CHAPS system operates to make same day electronic payments from one participant bank to another by the use of separate computer terminals maintained at the head offices of each of the settlement banks and certain of their branches. These are connected through a central concentrator with the computer terminals of the head offices and other settlement banks by land lines belonging to British Telecom and through a central packet switching unit maintained by it to ensure that messages reach the intended destination. The computer terminals at the head offices of each settlement bank feed instructions through the concentrator, known as the gateway, which acts as a routing device for the transmission of instructions to the other settlement banks. At present, there is no single centralised computer into which the head offices of the participant banks can feed information so that the computer itself effects payment and credits or debits customer accounts. Although a payment instruction sent to the head office of a paying bank cannot be countermanded or recalled once it has entered the system, the instruction will not in fact be released for transmission until it is checked and authenticated by a senior member of the staff of the paying bank. The payment is then transmitted to the head office of the receiving bank whose own computer will immediately credit the payment to the payee's account; simultaneously the receiving bank's computer will transmit the information contained in the payment instructions to its branch where the payee's account is held so that a print-out made by the terminal at that branch may be sent to the payee.

18.188   The payment instruction comprises the name of the payee, the amount of the payments, the special sorting code number of the payee's bank and the branch to which payment is to be made, and the payee's account number. Similar information must be given about the payer's own account so that the account may be debited on the computerised record of the accounts of the paying bank's customer and also so that the payee can be informed. In this connection the payer may include in the payment instruction certain additional information for the benefit of the payee about the reason for payment or the transaction to which the payment related.

CHAPS embodies a settlement mechanism, as well as a payment facility. Consequently, at the end of the CHAPS settlement day, the head offices of the settlement banks agree on the net balances of the day's payments between themselves, and they then electronically notify the Bank of England of the amount to be credited or debited to each settlement bank's account kept with the bank as the banker's bank.

18.189   At present, the machinery for the electronic transfer of funds between banks is operated wholly within the banking system, and instructions by customers to their banks to make a CHAPS payment is communicated by them in writing or by telephone. It is eventually planned to extend the CHAPS system further by the introduction of the Electronic Funds Transfers at Point of Sale (EFT/POS) system in retail and business premises, with the result that a customer of the connected business will be able to pay for goods and services by giving direct instructions to his bank to debit his account for a specified amount and simultaneously to credit the retailer's account with an equivalent amount.

The point of sale system will operate in the same way as a CHAPS terminal and will itself be linked with a terminal of the payee's bank, and through it with the CHAPS system. A customer of the connected shop who is making a payment through the EFT/POS system will produce a payment authorisation card issued by his own bank and key in on the retailer's terminal his personal identification number given to him by his own bank. This enables the terminal to verify the customer's identity and to ascertain whether his account is sufficiently in credit. Assuming these preliminary matters are satisfactory, the instruction will then be processed and transmitted like the normal CHAPS payment, except that it will proceed in the reverse order through the receiving bank to the paying bank. The net effect, however, will be exactly the same as if the shop's customer had initiated the payment instruction through his own bank. Whilst the EFT/POS system may be designed to function in a variety of different ways with each system, resulting in slightly different legal relations between the parties involved, the basis of EFT/POS is that the retailer will treat the payment as being made (at least conditionally) when the bank responds by accepting the instruction. The transfer of funds would be made by the customer's bank to the credit of the retailer's account with his bank or through CHAPS or other alternative settlement mechanism.

18.190   It is eventually intended to extend the CHAPS system itself so that non-settlement banks and corporate customers of the settlement banks can be connected to the system by their own computer terminals being linked with CHAPS directly, or through their respective sponsoring banks. This will enable non-settlement banks and large companies to initiate payment messages themselves and to transfer funds directly from their accounts with their respective branches to accounts held with other settlement banks. Such transfers will be treated for the purpose of the daily settlement of CHAPS transactions as though they were transfers effected by the payer's sponsoring banks.

THE LEGAL ISSUES

The electronic funds transfer systems will, to a considerable extent, involve the same or similar risks to the participating banks as incurred when acting on a conventional payment authorisation (*e.g.* as embodied in a cheque or credit transfer instruction). In this section of the article it is proposed to examine the legal problems which may arise and the extent to which these problems may be resolved by the existing law.

18.191

No doubt the existing law will resolve many of the problems which may arise from the nature of an electronic transfer of funds, but the courts may have to adapt the law to the new payments methods. Any legislation will have to accommodate technological developments which are likely to occur in the future.

The legal issues which may call to be resolved in connection with electronic fund transfer systems are likely to include the following:

(i) *No Payment is Authorised by the Customer*

A bank is only entitled to debit its customer's account if it conforms to the mandate given to it by a customer. If, therefore, a bank pays on a cheque which is forged or bears an unauthorised signature the bank does not act on the customer's mandate or make the payment on its customer's behalf and it cannot therefore debit his account.[41] In *Catlin* v. *Cyprus Finance Corporation (London) Ltd.*[42] Bingham J. held that a bank owes a joint obligation in debt to the joint account holders. However, it also owes a further contractual duty to each account holder separately when honouring cheques, namely, a bank which undertakes to honour cheques or other instruments which are properly drawn by the account holders accepts an express contractual obligation to conform to the customer's mandate and the bank will exceed that mandate if it allows one of the account holders to draw on the account without the consent of the other.

18.192

The bank is, however, protected if the customer asserts that a forged signature on a cheque or other instrument is his when in fact it is not or when it is improperly authorised. The customer would be estopped from denying the signature as being his or that the instrument is unauthorised.[43] In *Greenwood* v. *Martins Bank*[44] it was established that the customer is under a duty to inform the bank immediately of any forgery of cheques drawn on his account of which he becomes aware, and if he fails to inform the bank he cannot compel the bank to re-credit his account with the amount paid out on the forged cheques.

These cases, however, impose only a limited duty on the customer which enables the bank to raise an estoppel against him preventing the customer from pursuing an action against the bank for recovery of amounts debited against the customer's account. The traditional view has been that the cus-

18.193

---

[41] *Orr* v. *Union Bank* (1854) 1 Hacq. H.L. 513.
[42] [1983] 1 All E.R. 809.
[43] *Brown* v. *Westminster Bank Ltd.* [1964] 2 Lloyds Rep. 187.
[44] [1932] 1 K.B. 371.

tomer's duty is to draw cheques with care so as not to facilitate alteration, and to report any known forgeries of cheques. In *Kepitagalla Rubber Estates Ltd.* v. *National Bank of India Ltd.*[45] it was held that a customer was under no general duty to take precautions to prevent persons who have access to his cheque books from forging cheques, and that if such forged cheques are drawn on the customer's account, he is under no duty to check that cheques have not been debited which he has not himself authorised. There is no more an extensive duty of care to prevent the theft or misapplication of cheque forms, and the forgery of the customer's signature on them. There is thus no duty of care to check statements of account.

This was reaffirmed by the Privy Council in *Tai Hing Cotton Mill Ltd.* v. *Lui Chong Hing and Bank and others*[46] where it was held that a bank customer is under no obligation to exercise care in the operation of his current account so as to prevent forgery or unauthorised or altered cheques being presented to the bank, and he is under no obligation to take steps to detect possible forgeries or unauthorised withdrawals from his account, but is obliged to notify the bank of any forgeries or unauthorised drawing he actually discovers.

18.194   If the bank's customer is a company whose directors have either been improperly appointed or who have continued to act in that capacity when their appointment has expired and continue to draw cheques in the company's name, the bank will be protected.[47]

In the case of a payment through CHAPS, the risk of fraudulent alteration or authorisation of an instruction are fewer (there being no instrument or document in circulation), since a written instruction will be completed either at the bank's premises or be delivered personally by the customer. Nevertheless, there may be some possibility that the mandate may be forged.

(ii) *The Customer's Instructions to Transfer Funds are Ambiguous*

18.195   An instruction to make payment by CHAPS will necessarily contain some essential information relating to the transfer instructions, *e.g.* the name of the payer and payee, their respective banks and branches and account numbers, and the amount to be debited or credited. If the customer's instructions are ambiguous (*e.g.* as to the amount to be transferred, or the name of the payee, or the account to which payment is to be made) the bank is protected if it carries out the instructions in good faith and on a reasonable interpretation of the customer's instructions. In *Westminster Bank Ltd.* v. *Hilton*[48] it was said that if a principal gives an order to an agent in such uncertain terms as to be susceptible of two different meanings and the agent bona fide adopts one of them and acts upon it, the principal cannot repudiate the act as unauthorised because he in fact meant something different.

The fact that the transaction between the customer and the payee which gives rise to the customer's instructions to the bank is vitiated by fraud, misrepresentation or other negating factor does not affect the validity of the instructions given to the bank. The bank is protected if it makes payment without knowledge of any such event.

---

[45] [1909] 2 K.B. 1010.
[46] [1985] 2 W.L.R. 317.
[47] *Mahony v. East Holyford Mining Co.* (1875) L.R. 7 H.L. 869.
[48] (1926) 43 T.L.R. 124.

(iii) *Payment is Authorised for a Different Amount than That Paid out of the Customer's Account*

18.196

A payment which has been completed in the daily settlement may be recovered in one of two ways, namely, it may be possible for the payer to recover the amount paid from the payee, or by the paying bank to recover the amount paid under a mistake of fact from the receiving bank or the payee.

The payer can recover the amount paid from the payee if the transaction between the payer and payee is void (*e.g.* payment is made for an illegal consideration) or voidable (*e.g.* for fraud or misrepresentation) or where consideration has wholly failed, the payer can recover the amount as money had and received.

The rights of the paying bank to recover money from the receiving bank are dependent on the payment operation itself, and not on the underlying contract of sale. Thus, the paying bank can recover the money where the payment was made on a forged or altered bill of exchange or cheque on the grounds of money paid under a mistake of fact.[49] Where a customer's account is debited through a mistaken transfer of funds using an automated payments system, there is no reason why the existing law cannot be relied upon to recover the payment.

(iv) *Delay in Transmitting*

18.197

The obligation of the paying bank is to act expeditiously in carrying out the customer's mandate by presenting a cheque or other instrument for payment.[50] The question arises whether this rule can apply to a payment made through CHAPS, a same day payment facility. In a fully automated system of payment delays can arise, *e.g.* due to mechanical failure or pressure of work or instructions to transfer funds being received too late in the working day for payment to be transmitted on the same day. The contractual terms on which the banks agree to provide the CHAPS facility will undoubtedly deal with the consequences of delays and liability for loss caused due to delays in making payment.

At present, settlement banks protect themselves against instructions notified to the bank within an hour before the CHAPS system closes at 3.00 p.m. not being processed on the same day.

WHEN IS PAYMENT MADE AND WHAT AMOUNTS TO AN EFFECTIVE COUNTERMAND OF THE PAYMENT INSTRUCTION?

18.198

The question of what amounts to payment raises two distinct questions, namely:

(a) when is payment made or completed between a payer and payee; and

(b) when is payment made or completed between the paying and receiving banks.

PAYMENT BETWEEN THE PAYER AND PAYEE

18.199

The question of whether payment has been made finally has usually arisen when a debt has been settled otherwise than in currency or legal tender (for example, by cheque, promissory note or by a bank note issued by a private

---

[49] *National Westminster Bank Ltd.* v. *Barclays Bank Ltd.* [1975] Q.B. 654.
[50] *Hare* v. *Henty* (1861) 30 L.T.C.P. 302.

bank). The dispute between the payer and the payee may be over whether the payment was final or was only conditional, so that if the payee failed to recover the amount payable under the instrument given to him, he could still sue the payer in debt. The legal presumption is that payment by an instrument given by the payer (such as a cheque), or an instrument issued or accepted by a third party (such as a bill of exchange or a letter of credit), is only taken by the payee as conditional payment[51] and payment is only complete and final when the payer or the third person delivers legal tender or makes funds immediately and unconditionally available to the payee.

PAYMENT BETWEEN THE PAYING AND COLLECTING BANKS

18.200   Payment is made between two banks when the banks finally agree on the net balance payable by the one bank to the other on settlement of business between the accounts maintained by the banks at the Bank of England.

When payment is made by means of a cheque presented through the cheque clearing, payment is therefore made between the banks when the "In" and "Out" totals of the day's business are agreed between them, and the Bank of England makes, or is bound to make, a transfer of the net difference to the credit of one bank's account and to the debit of the other bank's account with it.[52] When the paying bank reserves the right to dishonour the cheque or other instrument, payment between the bank is complete only when settlement is effected between them, and if the cheque or instrument is dishonoured the paying bank has the right to recover the amount paid from the collecting bank.[53] Payment is not made finally by the drawer to the payee or holder until the expiration of the time within which the cheque may be dishonoured by the branch of the drawer's bank at which his account is kept, *i.e.* under paragraphs 12(a) and (b) of the General Clearing Rules, 12 noon of the day following that on which the cheque is received at that branch after presentation through the clearing.[54] It follows that payment of a cheque is made as between the paying and collecting banks under the General Clearing Rules at a different time to when final payment is made between the payer and the payee. When payment is made between banks otherwise than through an established clearing system, by the crediting and debiting of their respective accounts with the Bank of England the payment is completed as between the banks and their respective customers when the receiving bank decides to accept payment in the form tendered by the paying bank and credits the payee's account accordingly. Thus, when a payment instruction is sent by the paying to the receiving bank by telegraphic transfer[55] or when it takes the form of a payment order or a statement by the paying to the receiving bank that it may draw on funds credited to it by the paying bank with itself or with another bank, payment is complete when the receiving bank accepts the instruction, regardless of any internal book keeping which must be done before pay-

---

[51] *Gunn* v. *Bolckow, Vaughan & Co.* (1875) 10 Ch.App. 491; *W. T. Alan & Co. Ltd.* v. *El Basr Export and Import Co.* [1972] 2 Q.B. 189.

[52] *Pollard* v. *Bank of England* (1871) L.R 6 Q.B. 623.

[53] *Banque del Indochine et de Suez S.A.* v. *J. H. Rayaner (Mincing Lane) Ltd.* [1982] 2 Lloyds Rep. 476.

[54] *Barclays Bank p.l.c.* v. *Bank of England* [1985] 1 All E.R. 385.

[55] *The Brimmes* [1974] 3 All E.R.; *Momm* v. *Barclays Bank International Ltd.* [1976] 3 All E.R. 588.

ment is credited to the payee's account.[56] If, therefore, an immediately effective payment message is accepted by the receiving bank, the paying bank cannot revoke it and the payer cannot revoke his mandate for making the payment unless the right to do so is expressly reserved by the payment message, order or statement.[57] In the normal situation, where such a reservation is not made, payment is final and effective both between the paying and receiving banks and between the payer and the payee when the receiving bank accepts the payment message, order or statement and credits the payee's account. If, however, the payment instruction is conditional or the value date of the payment is deferred so that the receiving bank does not have free and immediate disposal of the full amount, *e.g.* where the amount is available but only at a loss of interest to the collecting bank,[58] payment is not complete on the receiving bank accepting the instructions from the paying bank.

On the assumption that these rules apply to the effectiveness and finality of electronic transfer of funds, payment must be said to be complete as between the payer and payee when the payer no longer has the right to revoke the payment. **18.201**

A payment instruction made through CHAPS may be altered, abandoned or cancelled at any time prior to it being released through the gateway. Although payment is not made until the payment instruction is transmitted through the CHAPS gateway and acknowledged by the receiving bank, the paying bank cannot amend or countermand the payment once it is transmitted through the gateway.

A payment which is not acknowledged by the receiving bank lapses and is not taken into account in the day's final settlement of the net balances between the banks. A payment which is not acknowledged will have to be transmitted again through CHAPS and acknowledged by the receiving bank. The payment will therefore have been made once the receiving bank acknowledges receipt of payment.

(v) *Where the Payment is Tainted by Fraud*

In order to avoid loss by fraud adequate steps will have to be taken to prevent an unauthorised payment being made, or alternatively an authorised payment being altered in an unauthorised manner. The question of whether it is the bank or its customer who is obliged to take steps to prevent fraud, will undoubtedly depend on the terms of the contractual agreement between the parties, but also on which party is in a position to take active steps to prevent or deter fraud. Thus, for example, the bank will be responsible for the fraudulent conduct of its employees and it is unlikely that the bank will be permitted to exclude or restrict liability for the fraudulent conduct of an employee.[59] The bank will also be liable for the fraudulent conduct of any independent contractors it engages to carry out the whole or part of a transaction. **18.202**

However, a bank will not be liable for the fraudulent conduct of a third party who obtains access to the bank's terminals or facilities for his dis-

---

[56] *Mardorf Peach & Co. Ltd.* v. *Attica Sea Carriers Corpn. of Liberia* [1976] 2 All E.R. 249.
[57] *Royal Products Ltd.* v. *Midland Bank Ltd.* [1981] 2 Lloyds Rep. 194.
[58] *A/S Awilco of Oslo* v. *Fulvia S.p.A. di Navigazione of Caglari (The Chikuma)* [1981] 1 L.W.R. 315.
[59] *Lloyd* v. *Grace & Co.* (1912) A.C. 716.

honest purposes, provided the bank acted with reasonable care and provided an adequate security system.

The customer's obligations not to facilitate fraud have already been examined.

Where a bank customer has its own CHAPS terminal (*e.g.* a non-participating bank or a company which has a CHAPS terminal linked directly to its own bank's gateway) to transmit instructions through its gateway, the participating bank will not be liable for the negligence or fraud of employees of the non-participating bank or company, providing the participating bank acts with reasonable care and skill.

(vii) The Bank's Duty of Confidentiality

18.203   The bank owes a duty to keep matters relating to the customer's account and details of transactions in respect of the account in confidence. There are certain exceptions to this rule (*e.g.* where disclosure would be in the public interest and where disclosure is required by compulsion of law.

Computer terminals are capable of storing a considerable amount of information which may add to problems of privacy and security. The *Tournier* case[60] establishes the law on breach of confidentiality and will extend to electronic payments.

Whilst a same day automated payments system will have a considerable effect on the payment mechanism, it appears that the existing law on the legal problems that may arise in making payment will adequately cover any legal problems in connection with the automated transmission of money.

---

[60] *Tournier* v. *National Provincial & Union Bank of England Ltd.* [1924] 1 K.B. 461.

Section Four

Guarantees and Securities

19. Undue Influence, Mistake, Misrepresentation, and Duties to Inform or Disclose to Customers and Third Parties

The questions considered in this chapter are general ones, inasmuch as they help to define the nature of the relationship between banker and customer, but they are dealt with at this stage because they tend specifically to arise in the context of real securities and guarantees.

A. Undue influence

Many guarantors (including sureties) enter their commitments in good faith **19.01** but without expecting that they will ever be called upon to honour them, and when faced with the shock of the bank's demand, some respond by asserting that they should have been told more, or given some kind of warning, and that the bank has taken advantage of them. In addition, many guarantors may be family members, and some of them may be the victims of deceit or of pressure by the debtor whose debt they guarantee. There are, then, two main types of allegations: (a) that the bank itself has used undue influence against the guarantor, or (b) that the bank's debtor has used undue influence against the guarantor, and that the bank has in some fashion become caught up in the situation, and is to blame for it, or at least is deprived of any advantage from it.

1. UNDUE INFLUENCE, GENERALLY

Equity will set aside contracts or gifts on the ground that a party has **19.02** behaved unconscionably and has obtained a benefit by reason of the exercise of undue influence over another party.[1] This principle may affect banks in dealing with guarantors or sureties, since the bank obtains a benefit from them, and they seem to obtain little in return from the bank.

Where a "stronger" party obtains some contractual or other benefit from a "weaker" party, it is sometimes presumed that the relationship between the two is of a kind which requires the stronger party to prove that the benefit received by him was not received by the exercise of undue influence: such relationships exist, for example, between parent and unemancipated child,[2] or between solicitor and client.[3]

Such a relationship is not presumed between principal and agent,[4] or between husband and wife.[5]

If a relationship giving rise to the burden of disproving undue influence is

---

[1] *Allcard* v. *Skinner* (1887) 36 Ch.D.145.
[2] *Bullock* v. *Lloyds Bank* [1955] Ch. 317.
[3] *Wright* v. *Carter* [1903] 1 Ch. 27. Other examples of such presumed relationships are guardian and ward, fiance and fiancee, trustee and beneficiary, religious adviser and disciple, doctor and patient.
[4] *Re Coomber* [1911] 1 Ch. 723.
[5] *Howes* v. *Bishop* [1909] 2 K.B. 390; *Bank of Montreal* v. *Stuart* [1911] A.C. 120; *Mackenzie* v. *Royal Bank of Canada* [1934] A.C. 468.

not presumed, such a relationship may yet be *affirmatively proved to exist* in any given case, if it is shown that the relationship between the parties is of a fiduciary nature, in the sense that the weaker party reposes such a trust in the other party that the latter is in a position to take unfair advantage of the former.[6] The relationship need not be one of "domination."[7]

19.03   Where such a relationship between two parties is presumed or proved, so that a burden to disprove undue influence arises, a finding that the transaction was unconscionable, in the sense of being in fact influenced by "undue" influence, may be rebutted by appropriate evidence. The party who benefits from the transaction can discharge his burden by showing that the transaction was the result of the exercise by the weaker party of "the free exercise of independent will."[8]

Generally speaking this is done by showing that the weaker party had competent[9] independent advice, say, from a lawyer. But even this may not save the transaction, if the influence is particularly strong, and the weaker party does not follow the independent advice.[10] Obviously, the advice must be received before the transaction is entered, and not when the party is already bound.[11] It is doubtful whether in some cases the burden can be discharged merely by advising the weaker party to seek independent legal advice (which is not in fact obtained), but this must depend on the strength of the "influence" exerted by the stronger party.[12] If that influence is strong, so that the weaker party totally trusts the stronger party, any suggestion to seek independent counselling may simply be disregarded. In other words, the undue influence extends to such a suggestion. Similarly, the signing of disclaimers by the customer may be ineffective. A statement by him that he does not rely on the bank would be ineffective (in those very rare cases) where he was under the bank's influence when he signed it.

The burden of proof is not discharged by showing that the benefit is obtained not by the stronger party personally, but by someone else. If, for example, a religious superior obtains a benefit not for herself but for a religious order, the burden still remains.[13] However, it is now clear that undue influence is not presumed, and cannot be proved to exist, unless the transaction in question is one which is "manifestly disadvantageous" to the weaker party. This was decided by the House of Lords in *National Westminster Bank P.L.C.* v. *Morgan*[14] where the Morgans faced the loss of their jointly owned house to a building society, and a bank entered urgent refinancing arrangements with the husband for his business liabilities, these arrangements being secured by a legal charge over the house (executed by husband and wife). When, later, the bank sought possession, which the wife resisted on the ground of undue influence exerted on her by the bank, the

---

[6] See *Tate* v. *Williamson* (1866) L.R. 2 Ch. App. 55 (financial adviser to undergraduate): *Inche Noriah* v. *Shaik Allie bin Omar* [1929] A.C. 127 (adviser to elderly person): *Lloyds Bank Ltd.* v. *Bundy* [1975] Q.B. 326 (bank and elderly surety).

[7] *Goldsworthy* v. *Brickell* [1987] 1 All E.R. 853, following *Tufton* v. *Sperni* (1952) 2 TLR 516.

[8] *Inche Noriah* v. *Shaik Allie bin Omar* [1929] A.C. 127, 136.

[9] See case in previous note: the adviser must be in possession of the facts.

[10] *Wright* v. *Carter* [1903] 1 Ch. 27; *Powell* v. *Powell* [1900] 1 Ch. 243; *Re Coomber* [1911] 1 Ch. 723, 730.

[11] *Mackenzie* v. *Royal Bank of Canada* [1934] A.C. 468, 474–475.

[12] This is suggested by the decision of the discussion of the Court of Appeal in *National Westminster Bank P.L.C.* v. *Morgan* [1983] 3 All E.R. 85.

[13] *Allcard* v. *Skinner* (1887) 36 Ch.D. 145.

[14] [1985] 1 All E.R. 821, [1986] A.C. 686.

House of Lords (reversing the Court of Appeal) held that no undue influence could exist unless the transaction was manifestly disadvantageous to the person influenced. This transaction was not of that kind, because in fact it saved the home from the building society which was going to repossess it. The court rejected a general principle of relief where there was "inequality of bargaining power."[15] This was a relevant feature, but not a sufficient one. Such general principles should be left to Parliament.[16]

It is not entirely clear what "manifestly disadvantageous" means. The House did not agree[17] that there could be unfair advantage taken where the transaction provides "reasonably equal benefits for both parties."[18] Clearly, on the special facts of her case, Mrs. Morgan received a reasonably equal benefit. But what of the wife who simply mortgages her share of the home in order to secure her husband's business overdraft? There may be no direct benefit to her, and the transaction resembles a gift by her to the bank,[19] but on the other hand the wife has an interest in the success of the husband's business, and the continuation of the overdraft is an indirect benefit to her. On the one hand, she now runs the risk of loss of the house, which was not the case before. On the other, she may be said to receive a "reasonably equal benefit" from the prospect of her husband's continued success. Is such a transaction "manifestly" disadvantageous to her? What then, of the company director, who is asked to guarantee the company's overdraft? The success of the company is, of course, of vital interest to the director. Surely this transaction cannot be regarded as manifestly disadvantageous. It may, in these cases, be otherwise if the wife or director is misled by the husband or other directors as to the purpose of the loan, since then the benefit expected by them is not that which is obtained. **19.04**

There is talk, sometimes, of "conflict of interest" as the ground for challenge, which is to say, that the bank's duty conflicts with its interest.[20] This is unnecessary, since if there is a "duty," there is a burden to disprove undue influence, in which case any "conflict" is irrelevant.

There is a defence to undue influence known as the defence of "laches" and this may apply if it is "practically unjust" to set aside the agreement in question.[21] This may occur if one party has acted so as to waive his rights, or by his conduct he has placed the other party in a situation in which it would not be reasonable to place him if the remedy were afterwards to be asserted. **19.05**

Two things, therefore, are needed to show undue influence: (i) a relationship where one party is presumed or proved to be in a position to take unconscionable advantage of another, and where this has not been rebutted, and (ii) a manifestly disadvantageous transaction (without which the advan-

---

[15] Put forward in *Lloyds Bank Ltd.* v. *Bundy* [1975] 2 Q.B. 326, 339 by Lord Denning M.R. Counsel in Morgan did not rely on that principle and Lord Scarman (at 830 in the All E.R. report) says "in my view he was right not to do so."

[16] *Ibid.*, 830.

[17] Disagreeing with Slade L.J. in the Court of Appeal, [1983] 3 All E.R. 85, 92.

[18] See Tiplady, 48 M.L.R. 579, 583, criticising this.

[19] Even though consideration is given, nominally, by the bank giving accommodation to the husband: this consideration "moves" to the husband, which is sufficient in law for a contract.

[20] *e.g.* in *Lloyd's Bank Ltd.* v. *Bundy* [1975] Q.B. 326.

[21] *John, Taupin & Others* v. *James, Dick James Music Ltd. and others* [1986] S.T.C. 352.

tage is not "unconscionable"). But the agreement will not be set aside if it is "practically unjust."

2. THE BANK AS STRONGER PARTY, EXERTING UNDUE INFLUENCE

19.06 It may sometimes be alleged that the bank itself exerted the undue influence. In *Williams* v. *Bayley*[22] a son gave to his bank some promissory notes on which he had forged his father's endorsements. The bank arranged a meeting of the three parties and made it clear to the father and son that the latter would be prosecuted unless some arrangement was reached. The father, in despair, said "What be I to do? How can I help myself? You see these men will have their money." Then, in consideration for the return to him of the notes, (and the implied dropping of any prosecution) he agreed to give the bank a security for the son's debt. In these disgraceful circumstances, the mortgage was set aside. On the other hand in *Lloyds Bank Ltd.* v. *Suvale Properties Ltd.*[23] a married couple who had themselves defrauded the bank may have been threatened with prosecution[24] to persuade them to give securities for their overdraft, and the Court of Appeal[25] suggested that this would not have been harsh and unconscionable so as to render the securities void. It is debatable whether any reliance should be placed upon this principle. The crime of blackmail[26] involves the making of an unwarranted demand with menaces with a view to a gain. A demand for security on the threat of prosecution is clearly a demand with menaces, and the bank has a view to a gain. All that would protect it is an argument that the demand is not "unwarranted." It is unwarranted unless the person who makes the demand does so "in the belief (a) that he has reasonable grounds for making the demand; and (b) that the use of menaces is a proper means of reinforcing the demand."[27] While the demand itself (for repayment) is reasonable, the question would seem to be whether the threat of prosecution is believed (by the bank official who utters it) to be a proper means to reinforce the demand. The dividing line between a proper and an improper threat is poorly defined, but it is a subjective question, so that it depends on what a jury accepts that the bank official in question thought. However, the case just mentioned is an indication that in civil proceedings on the security, the courts may hold threats by a bank against the wrongdoer himself to be reasonable. Perhaps if head office instructed managers that threats of this kind were a proper means of enforcement, individual convictions would be unlikely, as it would be difficult to prove that subjectively the individual thought that his threat was unwarranted. The whole subject is, however, fraught with dangers for banks.

---

[22] (1866) L.R. 1 H.L. 200.
[23] (Unreported) (1981) C.L.Y. 271. The fraud was "cross-firing"—*i.e.* two persons draw corresponding cheques on different banks or on different branches of the same bank. Since there is a delay in clearing, the credit in each account is temporarily augmented, and in the meantime each of the two customers borrows against the uncleared effects.
[24] They alleged this, but it was not proved.
[25] See the judgment of Oliver L.J.
[26] Under s.21 of the Theft Act 1968. This is an indictable offence, and carries a maximum term of imprisonment of 14 years. The bank would not be criminally liable for what its branch manager did—see *Tesco Supermarkets Ltd.* v. *Nattrass* [1972] A.C. 153—but the individual manager could be liable, and the contract would be voidable.
[27] *Ibid.*, s.21(1).

A well-known case of a different kind is *Lloyd's Bank Ltd.* v. *Bundy*[28] in   **19.07**
which the defendant was an elderly farmer who had guaranteed his son's
overdraft of £1500 with the bank, and who had charged his farm (worth
£10000) as security. He was also a customer of the bank. The son's business
ran into difficulties, and the bank called for further security, and the father
agreed to increase the guarantee, and the security, to £6000. On this
occasion, the father discussed the matter with his solicitor, who advised a
commitment of only £5000, but the father did not take that advice. The
son's business deteriorated further, and a newly appointed assistant
manager told the son that further steps must be taken. He said that his father
would help. The assistant manager went to the farm, with the forms to
increase the guarantee and charge up to a figure of £11000. The documents
were executed immediately by the father, on being told that otherwise the
bank could not support the business. The Court of Appeal held that the
father had relied on the bank and had placed confidence in it, as the bank
knew. He had been a customer for years, and his reliance was clear. (It also
appeared, when he gave evidence, that he had some difficulty in understanding all that went on.) In these very unusual circumstances[29] it was
found that the relationship between the parties was such that a burden was
placed on the bank to disprove undue influence, and that it had not done so.

The unusual nature of the case was emphasised in *National Westminster
Bank P.L.C.* v. *Morgan*[30] in which the bank manager had also visited the
Morgan's home. Mrs. Morgan was told by the manager about the meaning
and effect of the agreement, and she clearly relied on that. She made it clear
that she had no confidence in her husband's business abilities. He was
"hovering around," in and out of the room, and the atmosphere was tense.
The Court of Appeal concluded that if the wife relied on the bank, this
reliance imposed a "fiduciary" duty on the bank to advise the wife to seek
independent legal advice. The House of Lords rejected this. The mere fact
of reliance did not take the transaction outside the normal course of a
banker-customer relationship. The relationship between the parties must,
on the contrary, have "crossed the line" between mere reliance to a position
where the banker exercised a "dominating influence," and on the facts of
this case, that had not occurred.[31] Thus, the notable characteristics of Mr.
Bundy's case would seem to be (a) that he was a customer of long standing,
who had come over the years to trust the bank and to rely greatly on it for
advice, and (b) that he was very elderly and perhaps not fully able to comprehend all that was happening, and (c) that he had been specially influenced
by previous transactions relating to the guarantee and security between him
and the bank,[32] and (d) that he was obviously very concerned for his son.

---

[28] [1975] Q.B. 326.
[29] Each member of the court emphasises the unusual nature of the case, and is at pains to stress
that undue influence will rarely succeed. Lord Denning based his decision on a wider principle of unequal bargaining power, but this has now been rejected by the House of Lord in
National Westminster Bank P.L.C. v. *Morgan* [1985] 1 All E.R. 821, [1985] A.C. 686.
[30] Previous note, and above, para. 19.03 .
[31] The influence, however, need not be "dominating," as long as one takes unconscionable
advantage of the other: *Goldsworthy* v. *Brickell*, above n. 7.
[32] For other cases, see *Williams and Glyn's Bank Ltd.* v. *Barnes* [1981] Com.L.R. 205; *Burmah
Oil Corpn. Ltd.* v. *Bank of England, The Times,* July 4, 1981.

Although *Morgan's* case demonstrates that normally between banker and customer there is no relationship of trust and confidence such as to give rise to the burden of disproving undue influence, there may be a "special relationship" for the purpose of making the bank liable in the tort of negligence, to a person to whom the bank gives advice.[33]

3. THE BANK'S INVOLVEMENT IN UNDUE INFLUENCE EXERTED BY ANOTHER

19.08   A different possibility is that the bank may be caught up or involved in questionable acts of the debtor. This may happen if the bank asks the party who exerts the influence himself to procure the guarantee or security from the third party. Thus, in *Bank of Montreal* v. *Stuart*,[34] Mrs. Stuart had given guarantees and securities to the bank. The negotiations as to these had been carried on by a Mr. Bruce, who was a director and secretary of the debtor company, and solicitor to the bank, and also legal adviser to Mr. Stuart, the debtor company's president. Mrs. Stuart challenged the guarantees, etc. In court, Mrs Stuart admitted that she acted of her own free will. The court held that this merely showed how long lasting her husband's influence was, that Mrs. Stuart was under her husband's influence, and that Mr. Bruce knew this, or certainly ought to have known it. Mr. Bruce, therefore, owed Mrs. Stuart a duty to advise her. She would probably have rejected that advice, in which case he ought to have insisted to the husband that she have independent legal advice. If this was not done, Mr. Bruce should have retired from the business altogether, and should have told the bank why he did so. Thus, Mr. Bruce was involved in the undue influence, and the bank was also involved because "The bank left everything to Mr. Bruce and the bank must be answerable for what he did . . . "

Two important principles emerge from this case:

(i) If a person (such as Mr. Bruce) knows or ought to know that a third party is under the influence of another, the person with that knowledge is under a duty to advise the third party to seek independent legal advice, and if it is not done, the person in question should not act in the transaction. Thus, if a bank knew that a wife is under her husband's influence, or if it knows of a relationship where undue influence is "presumed," it should behave accordingly. The bank's knowledge involves it in the affair, and it behaves unfairly if it seeks to take advantage of the known weakness of the third party.[35]

(ii) Whatever its knowledge, if the bank uses as its agent to procure the guarantee or security the debtor or another person (such as Mr. Bruce) who is involved in the undue influence, the bank will be unable to enforce the security.

---

[33] See *Woods* v. *Martins Bank Ltd.* [1959] 1 Q.B. 55; *Hedley Byrne & Co. Ltd.* v. *Heller & Partners Ltd.* [1964] A.C. 465; *W. B. Anderson & Sons Ltd.* v. *Rhodes (Liverpool) Ltd.* [1967] 2 All E.R. 850; *Box* v. *Midland Bank* [1979] 2 Lloyds Rep. 391; *Shea*, [1986] J.I.B.L. 20, above, Chap. 5.

[34] [1911] A.C. 120.

[35] Another example is *Lancashire Loans Ltd.* v. *Black* [1934] 1 K.B. 380 where a young person just come of age guaranteed a parent's debts.

In *Kingsnorth Trust Ltd.* v. *Bell*[36] the plaintiffs proposed to lend to Mr. **19.09** Bell, and required the consent of Mrs. Bell. The plaintiffs' solicitors asked Mr. Bell's solicitors to arrange for the documents to be signed, and Mr. Bell's solicitors gave him the documents, which he took away for his wife to sign. He misled her as to the purpose of the loan. The Court of Appeal held that he had procured her signature by undue influence, and that as the plaintiffs had (through the two solicitors) entrusted to the husband the task of obtaining the execution of the relevant document, the plaintiffs could be in no better position than the husband. It would presumably be different had the plaintiffs' solicitors prohibited Mr. Bell's solicitors from passing on the forms to Mr. Bell. Again, in *Avon Finance Co. Ltd.* v. *Bridger*[37] a finance company had obtained a security from the debtor's elderly parents, and had appointed the debtor to procure their signatures. The plaintiff lender perhaps thought[38] that the parents would have independent legal advice, but this made no difference. The court also referred to the fact that the plaintiffs should have been aware that the son would have influence over his parents. These decisions were distinguished in *Coldunell Ltd.* v. *Gallon*[39] in which elderly parents were asked to give a charge to money-lenders. The solicitors for the lenders wrote directly to the parents, advising both to seek legal advice. Neither letter was received, having (apparently) been intercepted by the son, who turned up next day with the documents. An independent solicitor explained the consent form to the mother, who signed it, and the father signed the charge. The debtor son was present, and he hurried the proceedings along. The independent solicitor noted that the son was unhappy that the form was explained to the mother. The Court of Appeal declined to set the transaction aside. The son had not acted as agent for the money-lender in obtaining the charge. In cases such as *Avon Finance Co. Ltd.* v. *Bridger* the creditors had left it to the principal debtor to obtain execution of the document, whereas the transaction here was to be completed by the plaintiffs' solicitors, and those solicitors had, without any negligence, posted the documents directly to the parents. It is unclear what would have been the position if the son had lived with the parents, and the bank had known this. Perhaps then the possibility of interception should have been foreseen, and sending through the post might have been negligence.

In order to avoid involvement in the exercise by another of undue **19.10** influence against the guarantor or surety, the bank should (a) post the documents to the third party, at least where the danger of interception is unknown, or to solicitors for that party, or (b) post the documents to the debtor's solicitors (*e.g.* if the debtor says that those solicitors also act for the wife) with an express prohibition against their being handed on to the debtor to take away for signature, or (c) visit the guarantor or surety or call him or her in to the bank. After the decision in *National Westminster Bank P.L.C.* v. *Morgan* the last of these possibilities is unlikely, except in most unusual circumstances, to entitle the guarantor to allege that direct undue influence has been exercised by the bank. (Bank forms generally contain a

---

[36] [1986] 1 All E.R. 423.
[37] [1985] 2 All E.R. 281.
[38] Either because the son told them so, or because they had communicated with solicitors who had previously acted for the parents.
[39] [1986] 1 All E.R. 429, [1986] Q.B. 1184.

place for the solicitors to witness the taking of the guarantee and might confirm that independent legal advice has been given.)

B. Whether the bank has a duty to explain the terms of the documents

19.11   It is common, and perhaps usual, for banks to explain the terms of security documents, and guarantees, to those who execute them, particularly if the latter are not businessmen. In *O'Hara* v. *Allied Irish Banks*[40] Harman J. held that a bank has no duty to explain the terms and legal effect of guarantees to a stranger guarantor, that is, to one who is not a customer of the bank. However, in *Cornish* v. *Midland Bank P.L.C.*[40a] a customer gave a charge to the bank, and was given only a very brief and erroneous explanation of the effect of the charge. On later contesting this charge, she alleged (amongst other things)[41] that the bank was in breach of a duty to her to explain the agreement. Only Kerr L.J. dealt with this. He agreed that *O'Hara* was irrelevant to a case involving a customer. In his Lordship's view, evidence of standard banking practice was necessary and would be relevant in determining the bank's duty of care. He said that at any rate in relation to customers, banks may well be under a duty, in accordance with standard practice, to proffer an adequate explanation to persons about to sign a document in the nature of a guarantee. Had it been necessary to determine the question, he would have "inclined to the view that in the circumstances of this case the bank owed a duty to explain the nature and effect of the document." He felt that evidence of banking practice would support the view that bankers themselves recognise that "their proper professional standards would not be consistent with mere silence on their part in such situations."

In the absence of other authority, it is unclear if this *obiter dictum* represents the law. In *Saunders* v. *Anglia Building Society*[42] the House of Lords seemed to take the view that in the absence of misrepresentation literate persons of sound mind who sign documents the legal nature of which they broadly understand are bound by their contract. According to Lord Hodson "There is no burden on the opposite party to prove want of care." On the other hand, the court there was particularly concerned with contracts which might become void, since that would affect innocent third parties (whereas breach of the present duty would at most lead to the contract being voidable, which would not affect third parties.) If there is a duty, it must arise from the fact that the customer relies on the bank for advice, and the bank knows or ought to know this, and ought to say something. This may be thought to be coming dangerously close to the idea repudiated by the House, in *Morgan's* case.

19.12   If there is any duty, it may be that the bank can refuse to give advice, on the (very true) ground that security documents are legally complex, and that the customer should seek legal advice as to the meaning of the terms elsewhere. It is submitted that this should be sufficient. As Kerr L.J. said

---

[40] *The Times*, February 4, 1985.
[40a] [1985] 3 All E.R. 513.
[41] She also alleged misrepresentation (successfully), undue influence (unsuccessfully), and a breach of duty in the conduct of the account (unsuccessfully).
[42] [1970] 3 All E.R. 961.

"mere silence" may not be sufficient, but such a warning should be. If the customer refuses to take independent advice, it is submitted that the bank would have discharged its duty, if, indeed, there is one.

Cornish v. *Midland Bank P.L.C.* involved a domestic house and a private debt. If there is a duty in such a case, it may be queried if there is a similar duty in the case of a company mortgage, though probably there would be a similar duty with guarantees by directors of a company (not being a company themselves) of the company's debts. It would seem very doubtful if there is any duty where the meaning of a form has been explained previously to the customer.

A serious problem, if there is a duty, is as to the amount of detail a bank must go into. We make an attempt elsewhere in his book to explain the whole meaning of a bank guarantee form, and this is difficult enough, leaving alone the accompanying charge (if there is one). It is impossible in practice for the bank official to explain every term in detail. Only the main terms, therefore, can be explained. In relation to guarantees it would seem that the bank might explain the following:

(i) whether the guarantee is limited, and to what amount,

(ii) that the guarantee is continuing, and secures not only the present debt but the fluctuating debit balance of the overdrawn account, (or whatever is the case),

(iii) the method by which the guarantor terminates his liability for the future.

(iv) As this is commonly misunderstood, it should be carefully explained that such a notice to terminate will not affect accrued liabilities.

(v) It may be explained that the bank will keep the guarantee for a period of time (six months to two years) after any apparent discharge, to avoid problems with insolvency.

(vi) Since the bank can generally call for repayment from the debtor on demand, thus fixing the liability of the guarantor, it is thought that this must be explained, since there is a strong likelihood that otherwise the guarantor will believe that a positive default by the debtor is required.

(vii) It may be necessary to say that the bank need not proceed against the debtor, but is entitled to sue only the guarantor.

If there is any duty to explain, this may be sufficient, though in special **19.13** cases, other explanations may be needed: thus, with a guarantor of an infant's account, it may be explained that the guarantor is liable even though the infant is not. And with multiple guarantors, it may be explained that one may be discharged without discharging the others, and so on. A sensible precaution would be for banks to either write guarantees in "plain English" or to prepare a short written explanation of the guarantee, thus ensuring that accurate and uniform explanations are given by all members of staff, who would merely need to read through the explanation in the customer's presence.

In relation to accompanying charges, it is thought that it would be sufficient to explain that this covers the liability under the guarantee already explained, and that the guarantor must repay the debt when the debtor is in default, unless the debtor does so, and that on default, the bank may take possession of the charged property and sell it. If the bank is to insure, this would need explanation. Perhaps if the mortgage is a first mortgage the bank should explain that it will keep the title deeds or land certificate, and should explain about the costs of registering the charge, if any.

19.14   In all cases, it will be recalled that banks are bound by a duty of secrecy to the debtor-customer, and that without his permission they may not disclose details of the conduct of his account, or of the amount of his debt.[43] If, however, he is liable to the full extent of the guarantee given, the bank may say that the guarantee is being fully relied on. A question arises whether (in a case where there has been previous difficulty with the account) a bank should now expressly explain to the guarantor-customer that it is unable to disclose details of the account without permission of the customer, thus putting the idea of querying it into his head. This (or something like it) again is a practice which is often adopted in practice[44] and accordingly, there may be a duty to do it.

In *Midland Bank P.L.C.* v. *Perry* (*The Times*, May 28, 1987) a bank took a security from a husband and his wife. The wife was subject to undue influence from the husband, but the bank did not know this. The wife signed at a meeting with the bank. As the bank had not itself used undue influence, and did not know of the husband's influence, and had not used him as the bank's agent, the security was not void for undue influence. The first instance judge, however, gave damages against the bank on the ground that the bank had failed to explain the transaction adequately to her, and, in particular, had not made it clear that the charge attached to her beneficial interest in the property, so that the bank was negligent. If this is correctly decided, then it seems that there is indeed a duty on the bank to explain the terms of security documents. It seems very odd, however, that it was necessary to tell the wife that the charge attached to her beneficial interest. What, one might ask, did she think she was mortgaging? It is a pity that there was no appeal to the Court of Appeal against this finding, but only on the ground of undue influence (the court dismissed that appeal). The result of the case, at any rate, is that the house could be sold, but the wife had to be compensated in damages for her lost share.

C. Duty to avoid misrepresentation

19.15   The contract of guarantee and the charge is a contract like any other, and subject to the ordinary remedies if there is a misrepresentation. These remedies include rescission, and damages for negligence. A misrepresentation of any part of the guarantee material enough for the customer to have relied upon the representation as one of the reasons for entering the contract will entitle the customer to rescind the contract.[45] Although the representation may concern the legal effect of the terms of the document, it is deemed to be a mistake of "private right" and not a mistake of law, and to be the equivalent of a mistake of fact.[46]

In *National Westminster Bank P.L.C.* v. *Morgan*[47] the bank manager erroneously told Mrs. Morgan that the charge secured only the refinancing of the mortgage, and not the husband's business liabilities. In fact, of course, those were covered by the "all moneys" charge. However, the courts did not treat this as a misrepresentation, because at the time the manager said

---

[43] There are many cases; see, for example, *Hamilton* v. *Watson* (1845) 12 Cl. & Fin. 109; *National Provincial Bank of England* v. *Glanusk* [1913] 3 K.B. 335, see below, para. 19.21.

[44] The bank may call a tripartite meeting for the purpose.

[45] *Stone* v. *Compton* (1838) 5 Bing. N.C. 142; *Mackenzie* v. *Royal Bank of Canada* [1934] A.C. 468, P.C.; *Cornish* v. *Midland Bank P.L.C.* [1985] 3 All E.R. 513. Above, para. 19.11.

[46] *Solle* v. *Butcher* [1950] 1 K.B. 671, 695.

[47] Above, n. 14.

this, he (and the bank) did not intend to rely on the charge for the business liabilities. It would seem that because that was his intention, his statement was not a misrepresentation, but had the effect of acting as a contractually binding variation of the contract. The branch manager in this case had been instructed to arrange the mortgage for this limited purpose, so he clearly had authority to vary the written terms of the contract.[48] A clerk would presumably not have such authority, and such a statement by a clerk, therefore, would amount to a misrepresentation, and would have entitled Mrs. Morgan to rescind the contract, or to sue for damages. Clearly, a bank could not avoid rescission by subsequently deciding to give the charge the effect which had been misrepresented, since the contract would already have been entered into under a misrepresentation. The bank could not waive its own misrepresentation in that way.

A bank may become involved in allegations of undue influence if it gives **19.16** guarantee forms to a debtor who takes them away to have them signed by a guarantor.[49] The same should happen if the debtor misrepresents some fact to the guarantor. But in *Carlisle and Cumberland Banking Co.* v. *Bragg*[50] where this occurred, the jury found that the debtor was not the agent of the bank to obtain the signature, and was not liable for it. Thus, the debtor was a mere messenger, rather than an "agent." If the *Carlisle* case is still correct on this point, the difference may be that misrepresentation is a matter of the agent's express or apparent authority to make statements which will bind the bank, while undue influence has more to do with a practical risk, not connected with a question of authority, that the bank has not sufficiently disassociated itself from a relationship of undue influence. Even if, therefore, one should for purposes of misrepresentation distinguish mere messengers from agents,[51] it is, nevertheless, debatable whether the jury's finding in the *Carlisle* case was correct. The misrepresentation was that the bank forms were in fact insurance papers, and surely this particular bearer of the forms had apparent authority at least to say what the forms were. What is said above, relating to the avoidance of undue influence, should be sufficient to protect the bank.

If, however, a bank clerk is entrusted to obtain G's signature, and the clerk explains the terms wrongly to G, the clerk has apparent authority at least to bind the bank, and the bank could not enforce the guarantee.[52] This perhaps emphasises the desirability of banks either drafting the guarantee forms in clearer language, or else providing a brief summary in plain English, which their officials can use.

D. Whether there is a duty to warn the customer concerning the conduct of the customer's account

In *Schioler* v. *Westminster Bank Ltd.*[53] a Danish woman resident in the United **19.17** Kingdom but still domiciled in Denmark maintained an offshore bank account for (at least in part) the purpose of lawful tax avoidance. She was forwarded dividends from an overseas company from time to time, and as

[48] See the judgment at p. 825, letter (b), in the All E.R. report above, n. 14.
[49] Above, para. 19.08.
[50] [1911] 1 K.B. 489. The case was overruled (in relation to the ground of *non est factum*) by *Saunders* v. *Anglia Building Society* [1970] 3 All E.R. 961, [1971] A.C. 1004.
[51] See Paget's *Law of Banking*, (9th ed.), 504.
[52] *Cornish* v. *Midland Bank P.L.C.* [1985] 3 All E.R. 513.
[53] [1970] 2 Q.B. 719.

long as those did not come into the U.K. she avoided paying tax. The bank knew this, and why she had opened the account. Such business, indeed, plays a very large part in offshore banking. On one occasion, however, the overseas company sent a dividend warrant expressed in foreign currency, and in accordance with its normal practice the bank sent the warrants into the United Kingdom for conversion into sterling. This made the plaintiff liable to pay tax, and she sued the bank, alleging that the bank had a duty in these circumstances to take instructions from her before doing an act which the bank knew would cause her loss. The bank replied that it had followed its normal practice, and that this was the only way in which it could have collected the warrant for the customer's account, and that in the absence of positive instructions to the contrary, had no such duty as alleged. While the court felt sympathy for Mrs. Schioler, it concluded that in the absence of any authority on the matter, the bank had not acted improperly, and had no such duty as alleged. Thus, a bank acting according to its normal practice may have no duty to contact the customer and to warn him or seek instructions, even if the bank proposes to do an act which it knows will cause the customer financial loss of a kind which the whole purpose of establishing the account was to avoid. One can see that where a bank has established procedures, and a customer joins the bank, the customer is not normally entitled subsequently to argue that the standard procedures should be put aside for the customer. But where the bank knows as it did in this case, that the whole purpose of opening the account is to avoid the loss in question, this seems much less apparent. Surely the bank was under a duty to explain its procedures at the outset, or if it did not, then to contact Mrs. Schioler at the time the problem arose? But the law is otherwise.

19.18   A problem with a joint account arose in *Cornish* v. *Midland Bank P.L.C.*[54] Mrs. Cornish and her husband[55] borrowed £2000 on the security of a mortgage. Mrs. Cornish was required to become a customer of the bank. Shortly after, she left her husband, (who remarried) and went abroad. The bank knew all of this. Later it increased the amount of the advances to the ex-husband, so that he became indebted to the bank in excess of £16000. When the property was sold, there was little left for Mrs. Cornish, who sued the bank, alleging negligence. One of Mrs. Cornish's arguments was that the bank owed her a duty in conducting the account, so as not to conduct it in such a way as to cause her loss. It is not clear what she thought the bank might have done, but the obvious way would have been for the bank either to refuse new advances to the ex-husband, or to seek instructions from Mrs. Cornish. It did neither. Little is said by the court about this argument, since Mrs. Cornish won her case on the ground of misrepresentation. It seems, however, that the court concludes that liability under this head would have arisen only from the original breach of duty, arising out of the misrepresentation. That is, there was no separate and independent duty to refuse advances, or to seek advice, and the bank would have been entitled to behave in accordance with the mandate and with its normal practice. This, it is submitted, is the correct conclusion. Mrs. Cornish could have given notice to the bank that she wished to terminate her liability for further advances, but she did not do so. In the absence of such notification, the bank were surely entitled to assume that their security was still good, and since in

---

[54] Above, n. 40[a].

[55] Their married name was Humes. On divorce, Mrs. Humes reverted to her maiden name, Cornish.

terms it covered further advances, they should (but for the misrepresentation) have been entitled to make those. It would have been not the bank, but Mrs. Cornish, who was "negligent" in this respect.

In short, therefore, there seems to be no duty in conducting an account to avoid actions which the bank knows will avoid loss to the customer, even if the purpose of opening the account was to avoid losses of that kind, provided that the bank complies with any express mandate, and acts in accordance with its normal practice or with the practice of bankers generally It would do no harm (to banks) if their mandate forms, guarantee forms, and charge forms expressly stated this. It might help to avoid subsequent disputes (though possibly, and perversely, it might act as a challenge to the judiciary to apply the Unfair Contract Terms Act 1977).

E. Non est factum

This is a defence of extremely limited application which may be raised in cases of mistake induced (normally) by fraud. A may be induced to enter a contract by B's misrepresentation as to the nature of a document (he may, for example, be told that he is witnessing a will, or that a guarantee is an insurance form, and so on). If B has ostensible authority from C to explain at least the nature of the documents to A, then the misrepresentation makes the contract voidable, which means that A has a right to rescind the agreement with C. But the right to rescind is lost in certain cases: by waiver (affirmation by A), by lapse of time (perhaps not in a fraud case), if it is impossible to restore the status quo, or if the rights of an innocent third party would be affected by rescission. For this reason, A may seek to rely upon the law of mistake instead, to allege that the contract is not voidable, but totally void from the start. This would mean, for example, that an innocent third party could usually acquire no rights. Precisely because of that, however, the doctrine, known as *non est factum* (literally, "it is not his doing") is hedged around with qualifications, and is of very limited effect. It must be remembered, however, that as between A and C, in the example given, where B is C's agent, A may still rescind the contract for misrepresentation by C's agent, B. In the usual case, unless A affirms, only an assignment by C to D (an innocent party) of the security right would prevent A from rescinding for misrepresentation.

The defence of *non est factum* is available to A in the following circumstances, and there is a heavy burden of proof upon A to establish each point:

(1) The contract which A enters must be of a "nature altogether different" from that which A believes it to be. That is, it must be a fundamentally different thing. If A believes he is signing as a witness, that would be fundamentally different from signing as a mortgagor. But if A believes he is signing an assignment of a leasehold by way of gift to X, and it is an assignment by way of sale to Y, this is not a fundamental difference, for A knows the document involves a disposition of the property.[56] It seems that if A does not care or have any positive belief about what he signs, he could have no defence.[57]

(2) The defence is available only to those who are "permanently or temporarily unable through no fault of their own to have without explanation

19.19

---

[56] See *Saunders* v. *Anglia Building Society* above, n. 50; *Howatson* v. *Webb* [1907] 1 Ch. 537, affd. [1908] 1 Ch. 1.

[57] See *Gillman* v. *Gillman* (1946) 174 L.T. 272.

any real understanding of the purport of a particular document, whether that be from defective education, illness or innate incapacity."[58] Normally, therefore, literate persons of full mental capacity may not raise the defence. Thus, where an elderly widow was deceived as to the contents of a document, which she did not read because her glasses were broken, she was unable to reply on the defence.[59]

(3) A must not be negligent, and (even if one's glasses are broken) it is negligent to sign a document without reading it, where this would have revealed its true nature to a person of ordinary capacity.[60]

The doctrine of *non est factum*, therefore, is of very limited application.

F. Mistake and rectification

19.20   Mistake is sometimes a defence to an action upon a contract. Generally, it will have no effect unless the bank knows of the other's mistake, or where both parties understand the documents in one sense, but on its face, it bears another meaning. The latter often happens where standard documents are used without amendment, in special circumstances. In this kind of case, the document may be rectified to correspond with the true intentions of the parties.[61]

G. Whether the bank must disclose to third party sureties the affairs of the debtor

19.21   The debtor (D) is the bank's customer, and it will be recalled that the bank owes him a duty of confidence, not to reveal details of the conduct of his account to others. It is now clear that this is the appropriate principle, although the older cases tend to speak (with the same result) in terms of the absence of any duty in the bank (B) to reveal facts to a guarantor or surety (G.)

In *Hamilton* v. *Watson*[62] the House of Lords held that a bank had no duty to inform a substitute surety that the bank had, on the death of a surety, previously asked the debtor for payment or fresh security, and had obtained neither.[63] The contract was not *uberrimae fidei*, and the surety should have asked, if he wished to know. Unfortunately, a dictum in the case seems to say that B need not tell G matters which might not naturally occur between B and D.[64] From time to time, arguments have been put to the court that the situation between B and D is so "unusual" and unexpected, that B should disclose to D. But it has been said that even if the bank knows of suspicious transactions by D, so that he may be using the account for purposes not contemplated by G, there is no duty to tell G.[65] In *Royal Bank of Scotland*

---

[58] *Per* Lord Reid, in *Saunders* v. *Anglia Building Society* [1971] A.C. 1004, 1016.

[59] *Ibid.*

[60] *Saunders* v. *Anglia Building Society* [1971] A.C. 1004.

[61] *Joscelyne* v. *Nissen* [1907] 2 Q.B. 86.

[62] (1845) 12 Cl. & Fin 109.

[63] D died, insolvent, and G was liable on the guarantee.

[64] At 118, *per* Lord Campbell.

[65] *National Provincial Bank of England* v. *Glanusk* [1913] 3 K.B. 335. D was G's agent, using the account for improper purposes. In fact the bank had no suspicions about this. See also *Cooper* v. *National Provincial Bank Ltd.* [1945] 2 All E.R. 641 (D's husband was an undischarged bankrupt with power to draw on the account, and D had stopped about a dozen cheques. No duty to tell G. See also *Westminster Bank Ltd.* v. *Cond* (1940) 46 Com.Cas 60; *c.f. The Commercial Bank of Australia* v. *Amadio* (1983) 57 A.L.J.R. 358, 361.

v. *Greenshields*[66] the court stated that the bank need not disclose unless (i) it is asked a specific question, or (ii) the bank misleads G, by volunteering half the truth, or (iii) in the bank's presence G makes a statement or gives some indication which demonstrates that he entirely misunderstands D's position. This, however, appears to be inaccurate, and is qualified by *Lloyds Bank Ltd.* v. *Harrison*[67] where D had had business troubles which caused the bank to insist that for six months he reduce his stock and should not increase his liabilities. The court, holding that this need not be disclosed by B to G, emphasised (a) how impractical it was to expect bankers to disclose everything they may know about the past history of the account, and (b) that the bank owed a duty of confidentiality to the customer, D.

It is submitted, therefore, that notwithstanding occasional dicta, and statements in the *Greenshields* case, the bank may not disclose details of the account even if it is asked directly by G, or if G shows that he misunderstands the position, or even, probably, if the bank has misled G with half the truth. If G is misled, this may already be a breach of the duty of confidence. The breach should not be made worse. G should be told that he may have been misled, and that the bank is to ask D for permission to explain in detail. The proper course in such cases would be for the bank to ask D to allow the bank to reveal the information to G, or else for the bank to decline to take the guarantee from G. Often banks arrange tripartite meetings where, with D's permission, the facts may be revealed. If, at these meetings, D says something which does not correspond with what the bank knows to be true, then unless D's approval for disclosure has previously been gained, the bank should, it is submitted, be entitled to say that the information just given does not correspond with that on the bank's records, and should invite D to correct the statement, or to allow the bank to elucidate. If he will not agree, the bank must decline to take the guarantee.[68]

19.22

H. Effect of estoppel

Estoppel may produce a contractual variation similar to that apparently achieved in *Morgan's* case.[69] In *Amalgamated Investment and Property Co. Ltd.* v. *Texas Commerce Bank*[70] G guaranteed the debts of one company (D) to whom a bank was to advance money. Subsequently, by agreement, the money was advanced to a different company, X, which advanced it to D.[71] The bank assumed that the guarantee covered this situation, though it did not in fact do so since D was indebted to X, and not to the bank, and G had guaranteed D's debts to the bank. Robert Goff J., at first instance, found as a fact that while G had not caused the mistake, he was responsible for its continuation. In these circumstances, in which G was blameworthy, an estoppel arose, so that G could not deny that the legal affect of the guarantee was to make G liable under it, as both parties had assumed. It would be otherwise if G was not at fault, since the mere fact that the parties assumed that the contract had a different meaning than it had in law could not change its

19.23

---

[66] (1914) S.C. 259.
[67] (1925) 4 L.D.A.B. 12.
[68] Paget, *op. cit.*, 502 suggests that when questioned by the customer, the bank must answer "the occasion justifying disclosure or the customer's authority for such disclosure being implied in the introduction of the surety." A more cautious approach may be justified.
[69] Above, para. 19.15.
[70] [1981] 1 All E.R. 923, aff'd on misleading grounds in [1982] Q.B. 84.
[71] X was the bank's subsidiary, set up to avoid certain Bahamian restrictions.

meaning.[72] The case demonstrates, therefore, that where A misleads B or causes the continuation of B's mistake as to the legal affect of a contract already entered into by them, A is estopped[73] from denying that the agreement has the effect which both (or B alone) thought it to have. If, of course, A misled B before the contract was concluded, the law of misrepresentation might operate, or if there is no misstatement of fact, the contract could be avoided by B for mistake caused by A.

---

[72] See *Taylor Fashions Ltd.* v. *Liverpool Victoria Trustees Co. Ltd.* [1981] 1 All E.R. 897; *Keen* v. *Holland* [1984] 1 All E.R. 75. It is respectfully submitted that the discussion in the Encyclopedia at E(2066) is, accordingly, misleading.

[73] Supposing that it is inequitable for A to resile from what he has said.

20. Guarantees[1]

While banks naturally prefer real securities, guarantees are extremely **20.01** important. They are widely used in dealings with limited companies which have insufficient assets for real securities, being taken from the directors or associates, who are then unable to hide behind the limited liability of the company. They are commonly taken in dealings with groups of companies, from others in the group. They are by no means uncommon with individuals who are unable to offer other security. A familiar example is in the guaranteeing of a young customer's overdraft by a parent of the customer.

"Guarantors" and contracts of guarantee may be distinguished from "sureties" and from contracts of suretyship. A surety may be regarded as one who gives a real security for another's debt. Bankers prefer him also to give a guarantee for that makes him personally responsible for the debt, whereas the taking of the security alone leaves the banker with recourse to the security alone. The ideal situation, therefore, is a surety who also gives a guarantee. A guarantee alone merely creates a personal obligation between bank and guarantor. Sometimes cash deposits are taken from the guarantor, on terms that he is not to withdraw this, and so that the bank has an immediate right of recourse against the deposit if the guarantee is determined in any way. This may help to ensure that the guarantor is not a "man of straw." In addition, references may be taken up concerning the guarantor's financial position.

For convenience and brevity, we shall refer to the bank's customer (the debtor) as D, to the guarantor (or surety)[2] as G, and to the bank as B.

A. Guarantees and indemnities

It may be necessary to distinguish a guarantee from an indemnity.[3] With a **20.02** guarantee, G agrees with B that if D does not meet a legally binding obligation owed by D to B, then G will meet it. Thus, G's liability is "secondary" or "collateral," in the sense that it is dependent on D's obligation, and he is liable only on D's default.[4] If D is not liable (say because he is an infant, and the debt is unenforceable against him)[5] G is not liable.[6]

With an indemnity, G agrees with B that he will meet a legally binding obligation which G thereby undertakes (D may or may not owe a legally binding obligation to B). G's liability is "primary," and does not depend on D's obligation, nor on D's default. G is himself liable, and it is misleading to say that he guarantees D's obligations, for in fact he undertakes his own sep-

---

[1] For guarantees given by banks, see Vol. 2 (performance bonds).
[2] Even if he is an indemnifier, as explained below.
[3] See *Davys* v. *Buswell* [1913] 2 K.B. 47.
[4] The reason is sometimes said to be that G is entitled to be subrogated to B's rights, and if B has no right against D, B can have no rights against G. But it appears simpler to say that this is the case because that is what G and B have agreed.
[5] As in *Coutts & Co.* v. *Browne-Lecky* [1947] 1 K.B. 104.
[6] See also *Gaskell Ltd.* v. *Askwith* (1929) 45 T.L.R. 439 (D not liable on promissory note taken by B from D in breach of Moneylenders Act 1927).

arate obligation to B. If, say, D were an infant, and not liable on the debt, G would still be liable to B.[7]

20.03 It is often difficult to distinguish the two, and in practice, bankers and their customers use the terms "guarantee" and "indemnity" as if they were synonymous.[8] But it may be important to separate them for the following reasons: first, because a guarantor is liable only if D is liable, but this is not so with an indemnity. Secondly, the guarantor is liable only to the extent that D is liable, but not so with an indemnity. Thirdly, a guarantor is liable only if D defaults, but an indemnifier is liable for his own actions. Fourthly, section 4 of the Statute of Frauds (1677) requires that guarantees should be evidenced in writing[9] but there is no similar requirement for indemnities. Hence, the latter may be oral, or may arise by implication, as, for example, between principal and agent, where the agent is entitled to indemnity for expenses properly incurred in carrying out his tasks. But for the Statute of Frauds, there would be no need to consider transactions in terms of a dichotomy between guarantees and indemnities, and in other respects, it is a false dichotomy. The real question is, what has G undertaken to do in any particular case?

Whether an arrangement is a guarantee or an indemnity depends on the intention of the parties. But since they may use the words interchangeably, and may not have understood the need to distinguish, or may not have adverted to the matter, problems may arise. Clearly, the use of one word or the other is not conclusive, given the widespread ignorance of the distinction. If D is not in fact contractually bound to B (as G and B know) it may be construed as an indemnity.[10] If the arrangement is oral, there may perhaps be a tendency to treat it as an indemnity, so as to save it.[11] If G receives a payment for giving the promise, it may be construed as an independent obligation, that is, as an indemnity.[12] It has been said that arrangements are to be strictly construed, and that no liability should be imposed on G which is not clearly provided for.[13] Thus, any ambiguity would be resolved in G's favour, which would generally mean that the arrangement would be construed as a guarantee. Usually, however, the bank forms make the liability clear.

20.04 The bank may prefer an indemnity, though G (if it is explained to him) may be unwilling to agree to this. It has been said, indeed, in *Standard Chartered Bank Ltd.* v. *Walker* that if a clause makes G liable for a greater sum than D is liable for, the clause would be unenforceable by reason of the Unfair Contract Terms Act 1977.[14] The extent of this proposition is doubtful. The case concerned a receiver's duty to the guarantor to get in the best

---

[7] *Birkmyr* v. *Darnell* (1704) 1 Salk. 27; *Moschi* v. *Lep Air Services Ltd.* [1973] A.C. 331; *Yeoman Credit Ltd.* v. *Latter* [1961] 2 All E.R. 294; *Heald* v. *O'Connor* [1971] 2 All E.R. 1105; *Argo Carribean Group Ltd.* v. *Lewis* [1976] 2 Lloyds Rep. 286; *General Produce Co.* v. *United Bank Ltd.* [1979] 2 Lloyds Rep. 255.

[8] For a general discussion of the difference, see *Moschi* v. *Lep. Air Services Ltd.* [1973] A.C. 331.

[9] *i.e.* the parties, the promise and the subject-matter. If one document refers to another, and the terms are clear from both together, that is sufficient; *Elias* v. *George Sahely & Co.* (Barbados) Ltd. [1983] 1 A.C. 646.

[10] *Lakeman* v. *Mountstephen* (1874) L.R. 7 H.L. 17.

[11] See *Guild & Co.* v. *Conrad* [1894] 2 Q.B. 885.

[12] See *e.g.* *Goulston Discount Co. Ltd.* v. *Clark* [1967] 2 Q.B. 493.

[13] See *First National Finance Corpn. Ltd.* v. *Goodman* [1983] B.C.L.C. 203.

[14] See *Standard Chartered Bank Ltd.* v. *Walker* [1982] 3 All E.R. 938, 943, *per* Lord Denning M.R.

price on realisation of secured assets. That duty is clearly owed to the debtor, and Lord Denning is perhaps only saying that it would be odd if in these circumstances G is liable for more than D is liable for. In any case, the Unfair Contract Terms Act can apply only if the bank attempts to exclude a liability,[15] and cannot otherwise affect the nature of the obligation which G himself undertakes.

The distinction, as just mentioned, often arises in relation to companies and infants. Except in cases of illegality, where it would contravene public policy to allow G to agree to indemnity B for D's illegal debt,[16] G's liability is a matter for contract, and he may either agree to a guarantee, or to an indemnity, whereby he becomes principally liable for the debt, or to a form of liability intermediate between a guarantee and an indemnity. Given that G's liability depends upon what he agrees to do, the strict dichotomy between guarantee and indemnity is misleading, and has probably been encouraged only by the Statute of Frauds and the need for guarantees to be written. An intermediate case would be where G agrees to become liable only on D's default, but even if D is not liable.[17]

The two most obvious cases where D is not liable concern companies acting *ultra vires*, and minors[18] where G's guarantee would be worthless if the company or minor (D) is not liable. Thus, in *Coutts & Co.* v. *Browne-Lecky and Other*[19] a minor's overdraft was guaranteed by adults. Advances to minors being absolutely void[20] the bank was unable to enforce the guarantee. Oliver J. suggests that this applies "where all the parties know the facts," in which case it would not apply if, say, the minor misrepresented his age. But this limitation seems contrary to principle, and, it is submitted, is false. The decision in this case has been doubted.[21] It is necessary here to distinguish between the principle, and the decision on the facts. The principle, which the case correctly represents, is that the liability of G is a matter for contract, and that if he contracts on the basis that he is liable only if D is liable, there is no ground for imposing a different liability.[22] The factual question, as to which the case is of debateable authority, is as to whether G has contracted on this ground. In *Yeoman Credit Ltd.* v. *Latter and Another*[23] the Court of Appeal concluded that an adult's promise in respect of a minor's hire-purchase agreement[24] was an indemnity. Harman L.J. said that where all know that D is a minor "the court should incline to construe the document as an indemnity, for that must have been the intention of [G and B]. Otherwise the whole transaction is a sham." It is respectfully submitted

20.05

---

[15] The situation which s.4 of the Act aims to prevent.
[16] *c.f. Swan* v. *Bank of Scotland* (1836) 10 Bli. (N.S.) 627, and see Consumer Credit Act 1974, s.113(1–2).
[17] See *General Produce Co.* v. *United Bank Ltd.* [1979] 2 Lloyds Rep. 255.
[18] Persons (at least those domiciled in England) under 18 years of age.
[19] [1947] K.B. 104. See also, *Temperance Loan Fund Ltd.* v. *Rose* [1932] 2 K.B. 522; *Robinson's Motor Vehicles Ltd.* v. *Graham* [1956] N.Z.L.R. 545. The case of *Wauthier* v. *Wilson* (1911) 28 T.L.R. 582, was distinguished. There a parent signed a joint and several promissory note with his minor son, for the amount of an advance, and was held liable as a principle to the note. Oliver J., in *Browne-Lecky*, says (correctly, it is submitted) that this was a contract of indemnity.
[20] Infants Relief Act 1874.
[21] Paget, *op. cit.*, 32, 499.
[22] Cohn, 10 M.L.R. 40; Megrah, Gilbart Lectures, 1950 "Contractual Incapacity in the Banker's Customer."
[23] [1962] 2 All E.R. 294.
[24] Which was headed "Hire Purchase Indemnity and Undertaking."

that this observation deserves to be treated with the very greatest of caution. As Paget remarks[25] otherwise the defendant must be regarded as having been fraudulent from the start. An example of the technique is to be found in *Garrad* v. *James*[26] where D was a company, not liable on the transaction guaranteed by two of its directors, because the transaction was *ultra vires*. The directors had agreed to pay on D's default, and they argued that there could be no "default" if D was not legally obliged to pay. The court concluded that "default" included "failure" and "omission," and was not confined to "breach of a legally enforceable obligation." The intention of the parties had been that if D did not pay, G would pay.[27]

20.06   It is submitted, therefore, that where G knows the facts, even if he does not realize the legal consequences of infancy or of *ultra vires* transactions,[28] then unless the agreement makes it clear that G's liability is limited to that of D's liability, the agreement should be construed as an indemnity, which simply means to say that if D does not pay, for whatever reason, G will pay.[29]

In any case, bank guarantee forms will usually make the position clear. It is generally not stated simply that G is to be liable as an indemnifier, for the debt. Instead, the document begins with G guaranteeing D's liabilities, and contains a clause stating (for example) that the bank may recover from G "notwithstanding that D, being a limited company, corporate or unincorporate body or committee, may have exceeded its borrowing powers or that the borrowing from the bank may be *ultra vires*, or that D, being a person lacking in contractual capacity, shall not be liable in law to repay B, or that for any other reason the bank shall have no legal remedy against D for all or any part of the liabilities heretofore mentioned." There is no need to ask whether this a guarantee or an indemnity. The question is, what has G agreed to do, and here it is clear. If, as usual, G guarantees "the due payment" by D, then G is liable only if D defaults, in the sense of not paying at the proper times, or on demand, and it hardly matters what name one gives to the agreement.[30] Again, some clauses in bank guarantees, discussed below,[31] allow the bank to discharge D while leaving G liable.

20.07   If, however, there is a clause imposing a primary liability upon G (an indemnity), and B has a contract with D which B repudiates, G may also be discharged (but not by a non-repudiatory breach by B). This seems to depend, however, on some implied term in the indemnity, and some "linkage" between G's obligations and D's rights, so that it could not apply if the indemnity is entered before the contract between B and D and not in expectation of it. It may also be subject to any contrary term in the indem-

---

[25] *Op. cit.*, 499.

[26] [1925] 1 Ch. 616.

[27] This approach was accepted in *Heald* v. *O'Connor* above, n. 7. For other cases to the same effect see *Yorkshire Rly. Wagon Co.* v. *Maclure* (1881) 19 Ch. D. 478 aff.'d. (1882) 21 Ch. D. 309; *Munster and Leinster Bank* v. *Barry* [1931] I.R. 671.

[28] Or whatever the problem is.

[29] See Paget, *op. cit.*, 500, to the same effect.

[30] For another form of clause see *Barclays Bank Ltd.* v. *Trevanion* (1933) The Banker 98, where the clause said "As a separate and independent stipulation G agrees that all sums of money which may not be recoverable from the undersigned on the footing of a guarantee whether by reason of any legal limitation disability or incapacity on or of the principal or any other fact or circumstance and whether known to B or not shall nevertheless be recoverable from the undersigned as sole or principal debtor(s) thereof"

[31] Below, para. 20.28.

nity.[32] A contrary term, however, may be construed as an exemption clause, and may be subject to the Unfair Contract Terms Act 1977.[33]

B. General legal requirements of guarantees or indemnities

1. WRITING

We have observed that guarantees, but not indemnities, must be in writing.[34] G's signature is usually witnessed, sometimes by two bank officials, but this is strictly unnecessary.

20.08

2. CONSIDERATION

Liability arises on a contract, which requires consideration, or a deed. The consideration need not be stated in the document[35] though it is usual to do so. Past consideration—such as past advances—is insufficient. Whatever consideration is stated must be proved: thus, if it is for "further advances" these must be shown to have been made.[36] A nominal consideration may be provided by the bank, but usually that bank takes advantage of the rule that as long as consideration moves from B it need not move from B to G, and consideration is "manufactured" by the bank either stating that it will continue to afford banking facilities to D, or by demanding repayment from D and then promising to forbear to sue D for a time. Such forbearances may be inferred by the court, even if not stated.[37]

20.09

3. CAPACITY

Under English law, capacity of natural persons or corporations is determined by G's domicile, not by the place of contracting or a place of residence, or any choice of law in a contract. In the case of a minor, domicile is the domicile of his parents. Adults may acquire a domicile of choice. Corporations have the domicile of the place of their incorporation. Foreign countries may have different laws relating for example to the age of majority, to the contractual status of women, to the borrowing powers of companies, or to the power to give guarantees, all of these being questions of capacity, and thus determined by the (foreign) law of the domicile.

20.10

English domiciled infants, the mentally unsound and persons who are actually incapacitated by drunkenness cannot give guarantees.

In the absence of a special trade custom in particular cases, a partner has

---

[32] *National Westminster Bank PLC* v. *Riley* [1986] F.L.R. 213.

[33] Though this was not raised in the case, previous note.

[34] Extrinsic evidence may sometimes be introduced to explain a guarantee; *Perrylease Ltd.* v. *Imecar A.G.* (1986) 136 New L.J. 987.

[35] Mercantile Law Amendment Act 1856.

[36] See *Provincial Bank of Ireland* v. *Donnell* [1934] N.I. 33 (where the bank had no intention of making further advances); *Burton* v. *Gray* (1873) 8 Ch.App. 932 (£1000 to be lent to C within 7 days, but sums falling short of that lent to him); *Bank of Montreal* v. *Sperling Hotel Co. Ltd.* (1973) 36 D.L.R. (3d.) 130; *Royal Bank of Canada* v. *Salvatori* [1928] 3 WWR 501, P.C.; *National Bank of Nigeria* v. *Awolesi* [1964] 1 W.L.R. 1311 (if guarantee refers to existing account, opening a new one is not sufficient.) See also *U.D.T. Ltd.* v. *Beech* [1972] 1 Lloyds Rep. 546, 551 (block discounting facilities are not "banking facilities" where latter are promised).

[37] *Glegg* v. *Bromley* [1912] 3 K.B. 474, 491.

no usual (implied) authority to give a guarantee,[38] and the signature of all partners is required to bind the partnership.

After the abolition of the *ultra vires* rule a company will have full power to give guarantees, and any director may bind the company unless an outsider knows of a limitation on the director's powers. Until that time there must be an express power.[39] Additionally, the exercise of the power by directors may (at present) be made in circumstances where it is not for the benefit of the company, and this, if known to B, removes the ostensible authority of the directors.[40] It is forbidden, generally, for companies to give guarantees in connection with purchases of shares in the company.[41] At present, guarantees must be made in accordance with the Articles of the Company, if these say anything. Sometimes a deed may be required.[42] Unless a particular director is given power, the guarantee is authorised by the whole board of directors. This may be done by a resolution of the board, authorising the signing, in which case the directors are given a bank guarantee form referring to that resolution and to which in turn the resolution refers back. Alternatively, the board may be provided with a bank form of guarantee containing space for the resolution, which all the directors sign. In either case the Company Secretary certifies these as genuine resolutions of the company.

20.11   In the case of group guarantees, difficulties may arise if new members are to join the group, and if the guarantee is to be extended to them. In that case (a) the original agreement must contemplate and allow for the addition of new guarantors, or all the original members must agree to the addition of the new member, or the new member must sign a separate guarantee, and (b) there must be consideration for the new member, or it must be done by deed, and (c) the new member must follow the procedures which are correct for it. In *Ford & Carter Ltd.* v. *Midland Bank Ltd.*[43] five companies in a group gave mutual guarantees to the bank. Later another member of the group purported to enter the transaction, and gave a security as well, and the memorandum endorsed on the guarantee was signed by two officers of the company, one of whom was finance director of the parent company. None of the old signatories signed again. The guarantee and security failed[44] for two reasons: first, there was no resolution of the board of the new member, and, secondly, there was no agreement by the original five members that the parent company had authority to introduce a new party to the guarantee in this way. The consent of the original signatories had to be obtained. This principle is not, of course, limited to company law, but applies to any guarantee to which a new party is to be added.[45] The Ford and Carter case demonstrates the separate legal personality of members of a group of companies.

It may be that the Articles will provide for a certain quorum for any reso-

---

[38] *Brettel* v. *Williams* (1849) 4 Exch. 623.

[39] s.35, C.A. 1985 may apply.

[40] *Rolled Steel Products (Holdings) Ltd.* v. *British Steel Corpn.* [1985] 3 All E.R. 52. Contrast inter-group guarantees; *Charterbridge Corporation Ltd.* v. *Lloyds Bank Ltd.* [1970] Ch. 62. Ratification is possible, and s.35, C.A. 1985 may apply.

[41] C.A. 1985, ss. 151–154, above, para. 17.15 *et seq.*

[42] See *TCB Ltd.* v. *Gray* [1986] Ch. 621 where a requirement that a debenture be signed by a director was not fulfilled if signed by an attorney for a director.

[43] (1979) 129 N.L.J. 543.

[44] And the receiver under the security was held liable in damages for trespass.

[45] Below, paras. 20.14–20.15.

lution of the board of directors. If constructive notice of Articles is abolished, this will cease to be a problem, but at present, a particular problem may arise if directors "interested" in a transaction are prohibited from voting. If, for example, a director has already guaranteed a company's overdraft when the company gives a debenture for that overdraft, then the director is an interested person, and should not vote.[46] It would be otherwise if the director's guarantee is taken simultaneously with or after the company's debenture. At present, the bank is deemed to know the terms of the Articles, but the bank may be protected (i) by the Articles themselves (they may say that no outsider is to be affected), or (ii) the rule in *Turqunad's* case[47] may apply if the bank does not know that the director voted, or (iii) section 35 of the Companies Act 1985 may protect the bank.

4. UNDUE INFLUENCE, THE DUTY TO EXPLAIN TERMS, MISTAKE, AND MISREPRESENTATION, THE DUTY TO DISCLOSE D'S AFFAIRS, AND ESTOPPEL

These were discussed elsewhere as they do not affect only guarantees.[48]   **20.12**

5. APPLICABLE LAW

If B is dealing with persons outside England or Wales, or even with foreign   **20.13**
persons or corporations within the country, the contract should say if it is governed by English law, and it may be desirable in some cases to have a choice of jurisdiction clause whereby G submits to alternative jurisdictions in which action may be taken against him. Contracts signed in England, where G's duty is to perform here would, in any case, be governed by English law.

6. GUARANTEES BY MORE THAN ONE PERSON

Multi-party guarantees may be several (that is, quite separate and independ-   **20.14**
ent), or joint (that is, there is a single obligation, each being liable for the whole amount guaranteed), or joint and several. There is nothing wrong with several guarantees, except that a single document may be more convenient. At one time, if liability was joint only, then if the bank sued one party, that "exhausted" the action, and the others could not subsequently be sued. This is not now the case.[49] However, the death of a joint guarantor would result in the liability passing to the other joint guarantors, by survivorship, and not to the deceased's estate, and for that reason joint and several liability is still to be preferred.

(i) If a new guarantor is to be added, the consent of existing parties is required, failing which the new guarantor is not bound by the agreement.[50]

(ii) If G1 agrees to sign provided that G2 and G3 do so, (whether on joint, or joint and several guarantees) then if G2 or G3 do not sign, G1 is dis-

---

[46] *Victors Ltd.* v. *Lingard* [1927] 1 Ch. 323.
[47] Above, para. 17.06.
[48] Above, Chap. 19.
[49] Civil Liability (Contribution) Act 1978, s.3.
[50] Above, para. 20.11.

charged from the guarantee.[51] In these circumstances, an apparently several guarantee given by G3 would seem, if it is on the same terms as others, not to be "several" at all, but only a separate piece of paper embodying a joint and several, or maybe a joint liability together with G1 and G2. Liability would, perhaps, be several only if there are different obligations, although even such an agreement could be "linked" if it is understood by the several guarantors that the others would sign their several guarantees.

(iii) The same rule applies if G3's signature is forged.[52] Thus, in *National Provincial Bank of England Ltd.* v. *Brackenbury*[53] four persons were to be joint and several guarantors, and after three had signed the bank advanced the money, but the fourth guarantor then died before signing. Although this was a "hard case for the bank, and a curious result of the equitable doctrine," the guarantee was unenforceable. The doctrine seems, in fact, not to be equitable at all, but a simple application of elementary contractual principles, that where A's liability under a contract is subject to a condition precedent, the prescribed event must occur in order to make him liable.[54]

20.15 (iv) Similarly, if in the circumstances already described, G3 when he signs, alters the terms (so far as regards himself) in a material way, the others are discharged, for the condition precedent to their liability is not then fulfilled.[55]

(v) Similarly, if in the circumstances already described, the guarantee or separate "linked" guarantees are entered into by the parties, then if any of the terms are subsequently materially changed for G3, or if G3 is discharged from liability by the bank, then all are discharged, unless the guarantee provides otherwise, or all agree at the time.[56]

The result of these matters is that (a) the original agreement should provide for the addition of new members, or the consent of all should be obtained, or a separate guarantee should be taken from any new party, and (b) that where there are to be joint or joint and separate guarantors, no money should be advanced until all have signed in the same terms, and (c) likewise, no alteration of the terms or discharge or accommodation should be made to any guarantor unless all agree, whether originally or at the time.

With either joint and several or joint liability, if the bank were to sue G3 only, it is likely that he would join the others in the action, since they must indemnify him to the extent of their share.[57] This is described as the right of "contribution" which exists if there is no agreement to the contrary, where one guarantor of a common liability has paid more than his fair proportion of the debt, whether he is sued for it, or not.[58] It is because of this right of contribution that any change in G3's liability may discharge the others, because their right to contribution may be affected.

[51] *Evans* v. *Bremridge* (1855) 15 L.J. Ch. 102 aff'd (1856) 266 L.J. Ch. 334; *Hansard* v. *Letherbridge* (1892) 8 T.L.R. 346.
[52] *James Graham & Co. (Timber) Ltd.* v. *Southgate Sands and Others.* [1985] 2 All E.R. 344.
[53] [1906] 22 T.L.R. 797.
[54] See *James Graham & Co. (Timber) Ltd.* v. *Southgate Sands and Others.* [1985] 2 All E.R. 344, *per* O'Connor L.J.
[55] *Ellesmere Brewery Co.* v. *Cooper* [1896] 1 Q.B. 75.
[56] See *Ward* v. *National Bank of New Zealand* (1883) 8 App.Cas. 755; *Smith* v. *Wood* [1929] 1 Ch. 14. That the contract may provide to the contrary is shown by *Perry* v. *National Provincial Bank of England Ltd.* 1910 4 Ch. 464.
[57] And this may be more convenient than several actions against several guarantors.
[58] See, *e.g. Ellesmere Brewery Co.* v. *Cooper* [1896] 1 Q.B. 75; *Scholefield Goodman & Sons Ltd.* v. *Zyngier* [1985] 3 All E.R. 105, P.C. (above para. 14.04 *et seq.*) and s.1(1) Civil Liability (Contribution) Act 1978.

A several surety has the same right of contribution as a joint surety.[59] It **20.16** follows, therefore, that release of any surety may injure a several surety, who may be discharged.[60]

7. SINGLE AND CONTINUING GUARANTEES

Some "single" guarantees may be limited to a single transaction. Others **20.17** (most bank guarantees) are intended to cover a series of transactions (*e.g.* on a fluctuating overdraft balance) spread over a period of time. These are "continuing guarantees." A single guarantee would be discharged by the first advance up to the agreed limit: *i.e.* G would be liable for that sum, which might thereafter be reduced by the operation of *Clayton's case* upon an active current account.[61] A continuing guarantee, however, is not discharged in that way, as it covers all debts on the account. Whether a guarantee is single or continuing is a question of construction of the agreement to determine the intention of the parties.[62] The simplest way is to express the guarantee so that it covers the "ultimate balance" of the account, whatever that may be at any time. The words "continuing security" may additionally be used. A clause might say "and this guarantee shall be a continuing security applicable to the ultimate balance that shall become due from D to B from time to time and at any time."

8. LIMITED AND UNLIMITED GUARANTEES

In most guarantees, there will be an extensive clause referred to as the **20.18** "whole debt" clause, where G promises to become collaterally liable for any liabilities of D. Such a clause might say "I hereby guarantee all advances, liabilities, bills and promissory notes whether made, incurred or discounted before or after the date hereof, to or for D, either alone or jointly with other persons together with interest, commission and other banking charges including legal charges and commission."[63] There may be a reference elsewhere to liability for the "ultimate balance" of all D's accounts. A guarantee so phrased is "unlimited." It is, however, common for guarantees phrased in this way to be followed by another term to the effect "Provided that the amount for which G shall be liable shall not exceed £X and interest on such sum or on such less sum as may be due at the rate of Y from the date of D's default until payment." This is a "limited" guarantee, notwithstanding the whole debt clause. If the guarantee is to be made unlimited, this proviso need only be deleted and initialled by the parties.

As later explained,[64] a limited guarantee is phrased in this way so that on D's bankruptcy, even where G pays up to his agreed limit, B may pay the sum into a suspense account and may then prove against D in his bankruptcy for the whole debt, while because of the rule of "double-proof" G has no right to prove in the bankruptcy in competition to B.

---

[59] *Ward v. National Bank of New Zealand* (1883) 8 App.Cas. 755; *Whiting v. Burke* (1871) 6 Ch.App. 342.

[60] This is expressed in a hesitant way in the cases previous note, saying that the surety must show his right of contribution and the loss of it, or injury to it. It is difficult to see what this adds. Theory apart, it is difficult to see why a several surety should be discharged by what happens to the contract of a stranger, unless his contract is somehow linked by express or implied agreement with that other contract.

[61] Above, para. 13.24 *et seq.*

[62] *Cf. Westminster Bank Ltd.* v. *Sassoon* (1926) L.D.A.B. 19.

[63] See *Ellis* v. *Emmanueal* (1876) 1 Ex. D. 157.

[64] Below, para. 28.113 *et seq.*

C. Guarantor and debtor (G and D)

20.19   If G, having been requested by D[65] to give the guarantee in the first place, pays the whole (and not merely part) of D's debt,[66] then he is subrogated to the rights of B[67] in relation to that debt.[68] Thus, he is entitled to an indemnity from D,[69] and is also entitled to any securities[70] held by B unless (i) he agrees otherwise with B, or (ii) the securities also secure further advances by B (as is likely).

20.20   However, G's right to an indemnity from D exists only if his guarantee is called on by B or if it is determined by G or in some other fashion, so that G's liability is fixed.[71]

If G gives notice to determine his liability for the future, this fixes his liability, and he remains (contingently upon D's default) liable for debts already incurred by D. One way to reduce this contingent liability is for G to pay the amount of his liability to the bank. Since his liability is fixed, G has a right of indemnity at law against D, if G has paid. But where he has not paid, G also has an equitable right of exoneration, to require D to pay off the debt. The latter possibility is demonstrated by *Thomas* v. *Nottingham Incorp. Football Club, Ltd.*[72] where G guaranteed a football club's overdraft with Lloyds Bank. G gave notice to B to determine the guarantee, and then called on D to pay off the overdraft and thus to reduce G's liability. In the usual way, the bank had broken the account, and opened a new one. The debt in the broken account, therefore, simply remained as before. The guarantee stated (as most do) that G was liable only when D was in default, for example, when demand was made by B, and not complied with. Here, B had not demanded repayment, and D's argument was that as G's liability was merely contingent, G had no right to call on D to repay. But the court held that it was unreasonable that a man should always have the cloud of liability hanging over him, and in equity he had a right to have the overdraft paid off.[73] If, of course, D cannot repay, he may become bankrupt, in which case B will call upon G, so that the course of action adopted in *Thomas's* case may not always be advantageous to G. Terms in guarantees often restrict G's right to sue D until the ultimate balance is paid to the bank, but it would seem that such terms are not intended to prevent the sort of action brought in *Thomas's* case, since the result of his action was, of course, that the bank is repaid, to which it may have no objection. If, however, on its true construction a term does prevent such a person from demanding that his liability be thus discharged, the term may well be unreasonable, and contrary to public policy (analogous to clogs on the equity of redemption) or it may perhaps be unreasonable under the Unfair Contract Terms Act

---

[65] This is essential; *Owen* v. *Tate* [1976] Q.B. 402 (volunteer guarantor acted so as to help another guarantor); *The Zuhal K*, (November, 1986).

[66] Even if the guarantee continues and he pays the amount owing to date; *Davies* v. *Humphreys* (1840) 6 M. & W. 153.

[67] See Mercantile Law Amendment Act 1856, s.5, and above, Chap. 14, on subrogation.

[68] *Wilkinson* v. *London & County Banking Co.* (1884) 1 T.L.R. 63 (and not to any other debt).

[69] *Ascherson* v. *Tredegar Dry Dock & Wharf Co. Ltd.* [1909] 2 Ch. 401.

[70] Mercantile Law Amendment Act 1856, s.5. This is so even if securities are acquired by B after the guarantee is taken. See *Forbes* v. *Jackson* (1882) 19 Ch.D. 615; *Duncan, Fox & Co.* v. *North and South Wales Bank* (1880) 6 App.Cas. 1.

[71] *Morison* v. *Barking Chemicals Co. Ltd.* (1919) 122 L.T. 423.

[72] [1972] Ch. 596. See also *Watt* v. *Mortlock* [1964] Ch. 84; *Tate* v. *Crewdson* [1938] Ch. 869.

[73] The order declares G's right of exoneration, and orders D to pay, or to secure the debt.

1977[74] unless B has good reason to resist repayment. A good reason would presumably be that a term loan, not repayable earlier, has been made to D.

D. Guarantor and bank (G and B)

(i) Strictly, on a guarantee, G is liable if D is liable, and to the same extent, and only on D's default, but with an indemnity G has a separate liability, not depending on D's liability or default. Bank guarantees, however, make G liable if D does not make "due payment." On a term loan, for example, time must expire, or D must repudiate his obligations. On an overdraft, D must repudiate his obligations, or demand must be made for repayment, and D must fail to repay.[75]

20.21

(ii) Guarantees are strictly construed, and G is liable only for what he has agreed.[76] If G guarantees advances up to £1000 and B advances £1500, G is liable for £1000. But if G agrees to guarantee payment of a bill of exchange for £1000, and the bill is drawn for a greater amount than that, he has no liability at all, for it is a different thing in law. If G agrees to guarantee a given mortgage debt and "any further advances" then if the debt increases because the term is extended and the interest rate increased, these are not "further advances" for which G is liable.[77] Where G guaranteed a loan by B to enable D to buy two properties, and the guarantees were to exist so long as one property (Balfour Place) remained part of the security, and on default by D, B had the properties (including Balfour Place) sold, G was not liable for the deficiency, for Balfour Place had ceased to "form part of the security."[78]

If the guarantee refers to debts by D "due or owing," then there is a risk that if D does not owe the sum guaranteed, it cannot be recovered from G. Thus in *Re Moss, ex p. Hallet*[79] it was held that on D's bankruptcy his liability for interest ceased, and accordingly G's liability for interest ceased. This result is avoided if G guarantees to pay not what is due and owing from D but all moneys unpaid by D including interest thereon.[80]

(iii) However harsh the result may be, G is liable for what he agrees, in the absence of undue influence, misrepresentation, etc. In *First National Finance Corporation* v. *Goodman*[81] G and his co-directors guaranteed an advance by B1 to their company, renewable after a year. After a year, G ceased to be a director of the company, or to be connected with it, and B1 merged with B2 (the plaintiff here). The company subsequently borrowed more money, and when it was wound up B2 sought to make G liable on his

20.22

---

[74] s.3(2)(b), on the ground that the contract enables B to "render a contractual performance substantially different from that which was reasonably expected of him." But it is unclear if such a term relates to B's performance at all.

[75] Above, para. 20.06.

[76] See *Hyundai Shipbuilding and Heavy Industries Co. Ltd.* v. *Pournaras* [1978] 2 Lloyds Rep. 502; *First National Finance Corpn. Ltd.* v. *Goodman* [1983] B.C.L.C. 203.

[77] *Burnes* v. *Trade Credits Ltd.* [1981] 2 All E.R. 122.

[78] *Lloyds and Scottish Trust Ltd.* v. *Britten and Another* (1982) 44 P. & C.R. 249. In addition, B had foreclosed on another property. Foreclosure terminates the rights of the mortgagee to sue the mortgagor. If B could not sue D, then G also was discharged, for G is liable only if D is liable.

[79] [1905] 2 K.B. 307.

[80] *Re Moss* suggests also that D's debts are extinguished on bankruptcy; this is incorrect, even if any right of action against D is unavailable; see *Bank of Montreal* v. *McFatridge* (1959) 17 D.L.R. (2d.) 557.

[81] [1983] B.C.L.C. 203.

guarantee. The court held that as the guarantee covered G's liability to B1 or its successors and assigns or any company with which it might amalgamate, and as the other terms were clear, G was liable, even though the result was harsh. G should have given notice to determine the guarantee, when he left the company. In such cases, the Unfair Contract Terms Act will not assist G, since B is not attempting to exclude his liability or to render a performance substantially different from that expected of him, etc.

(iv) G is liable only if the promised consideration is given (to D, normally.)[82]

(v) If B brings a fruitless action against D, without giving notice to G so as to enable G to intervene, G remains liable on the guarantee, but is not liable for the cost of the action.

(vi) G becomes liable on a guarantee when D is in default, but the document may be worded so that (whether D is at fault or not) G is liable if D does not make "due" payment, which would seem to mean, at the time agreed, or on demand to D.

20.23   If the agreement does not (as it usually does) require a demand to G, then once D is liable for such "default," no notice to G or demand for payment is required to establish his liability, with the results (a) that B need not sue D first, and (b) G's liability for any debit item may be discharged not only by the effect of *Clayton's case*, but also (with a relatively dormant account) by the passage of time, causing the Limitation Act 1980 to apply.[83] Except on "default," the limitation period could not run against individual debit items if the guarantee is continuing.[84] As noted above, if called upon by B to pay, G has the right to require B to call on D to pay, and B cannot then sue G until doing so.

However, if (as is very common) the agreement requires G to pay "on demand" then demand must be made, with the consequences that (a) no cause of action against G accrues in the bank until D is in default and B makes demand of G, and (b) the statutory limitation period for sueing G[85] does not start to run against the bank until it actually does make demand.[86] It is usual to specify the means by which demand may be made: *e.g.* in writing, and so that demand is deemed to be made within a certain time of posting, whether received, or not.

Once demand is made of G, no further debits may be made to D's account, unless notice is given to G at the time of demand that there may be further outstanding items, such as cheques not yet cleared. (The call upon G fixes his liability at that time.)

---

[82] Above, para. 20.09.

[83] *Parr's Banking Company Ltd.* v. *Yates* [1898] 2 Q.B. 460, holding that time begins to run when a debit item is made, and is not paid. This must presuppose a default in D in not repaying. Paget criticized this decision: 1 L.D.A.B. 278, and see Paget, *op. cit.*, 521, referring to *Hartland* v. *Jukes* (1863) 1 H. & C. 667. However, although demand by B may be required of D himself to establish his default (or, see, *e.g.* demand of a mortgagor, in *Lloyds Bank Ltd.* v. *Margolis* [1954] 1 W.L.R. 644) the decision seems correct in principle.

[84] See *Wright* v. *New Zealand Farmer's Co-Operative Assn. of Canterbury Ltd.* [1939] A.C. 439, P.C.

[85] Six years, for liability on a simple debt, and 12 years for liability on deeds—see ss.5, 8 Limitation Act 1980.

[86] See *Bradford Old Bank* v. *Sutcliffe* [1918] 2 K.B. 833, where the death of one co-surety discharged the other for the future, but where B continued D's account, and did not sue the remaining surety until 15 years later. The action was not out of time.

While D may be expected to know the amount of his own liability, B can **20.24** never sue G nor call upon him to pay and hold him in default for not doing so, unless B tells G of the amount of G's liability.[87]

(vii) Before D's default some counter-claims or set-offs which D has against B are available to G[88] (whose liability is co-extensive with D's, under a guarantee).[89] After D's default, G cannot set-off against the debt any sums which fall due thereafter from B to D.

It might be thought that any deposit belonging to D and held by B before D's default could be relied upon by G, (who is liable only for B's debt, which must be calculated by looking at the overall state of indebtedness of D to B). Generally, this is the case, because bank guarantees secure the "ultimate balance" of D's account, and in such a case the bank must combine all accounts, even if at different branches, to determine the extent of G's liability.[90] It might be agreed between B and D that accounts will not be combined, and this should bind G, but such an agreement could not survive D's insolvency, because the mandatory "statutory set-off" provisions then apply and as against D the bank must set-off all accounts.[91]

Assuming that there is no "ultimate balance" clause, then if G guarantees one account, he may still rely upon D's deposit held by the bank in another account, provided that the deposit is given to secure transactions on the guaranteed account only. But if the deposit is given by D to secure liabilities on other accounts as well, it should not be available to G.[92]

(viii) If G pays B, he is subrogated to B's rights against D, and may claim securities belonging to D held by B, unless (as usual) the contrary is agreed. The contrary agreement may be made between G and B, or between B and D. An example of the latter would be if D's account is not closed, and the security was taken by B as a continuing security for all advances. But on D's insolvency, G would be entitled to a proportionate part of the security, after B is satisfied.

(ix) At any time, unless otherwise agreed, G is entitled to a statement of **20.25** his liability. Given the bank's duty of confidence, it must not reveal excessive detail concerning D's account, though there is in such a case implied consent to necessary disclosure. If G has guaranteed a certain sum, and D's debt is less than that sum, G may be told the exact sum. If D's debt exceeds that sum, G is told simply that his guarantee is being fully relied upon. It is prudent for banks to avoid disputes (and these may occur if D denies to G the extent of D's liability) as to the amount of liability, and a common course is for the guarantee to contain a clause to the effect that "In the event of any action or other proceeding brought against G upon this guarantee, a copy of D's account (or of the account for the preceding six months if the account shall have extended beyond that period) signed by the manager for the time being of the branch or office at which the account shall be kept, or by some other officer of the bank, shall be conclusive evidence against D of the amount for the time being due to B from D." The Court of Appeal has accepted the efficacy of such a term, on the ground of the high standing in

---

[87] *Bunbury Foods Pty. Ltd.* v. *National Bank of Australasia Ltd.* (1984) 58 A.J.L.R. 199 (H.C. of Australia).
[88] *Bechervaise* v. *Lewis* (1872) L.R. 7 C.P. 372.
[89] Though not under an indemnity.
[90] *Re Sherry, London and County Banking Co.* v. *Terry* (1884) 25 Ch.D. 692, 706.
[91] Below, Chap. 27.
[92] *York City and County Banking Co.* v. *Bainbridge* (1880) 43 L.T. 732.

the commercial world of bankers.[93] This being so, it would seem that such a term may not be questionable under section 2 or 3 of the Unfair Contract Terms Act 1977, as an unreasonable term, because the standing of bankers "is so high that their work is to be trusted."[94]

20.26   (x) Even after the guarantee is taken, the bank has no duty to tell G of any change in D's circumstances, (and has a duty not to tell G of D's affairs) though from a sense of moral obligation, the bank may, in an appropriate case, take some action, such as making demand on D, or arranging a tripartite meeting at which, with D's consent, the matter may be discussed with G.[95]

(xi) A bank-appointed receiver of D's property is under a duty of reasonable care towards G, to secure a good price, and sometimes the bank may be liable (either directly, or on an indemnity to the receiver) for his failure to do so.[96] The guarantee usually specifies that B is under no obligation to realise any securities held, and there would seem to be no obligation to do so anyway,[97] though G would be entitled to the securities if G pays B.[98] But it was held in *Bank of India* v. *Trans Continental Commodity Merchants*[99] that where G guaranteed performance of twelve foreign exchange contracts by D, it was no defence to G to argue that the bank was negligent in not ensuring that D actually signed the contracts. Bingham J. held that

> "The true principle is that while a surety can be discharged if the creditor acts in bad faith towards him, or is guilty of concealment amounting to misrepresentation, or causes or connives at the default of the debtor in respect of which the guarantee was given, or varies the term of the contract in such a way as to prejudice the surety, other conduct on the part of the creditor, even if irregular, and even if prejudicial to the interests of the surety in a general sense, does not discharge the surety."

While this statement[1] was undoubtedly correct before *Standard Chartered Bank* v. *Walker*[2] we must now at least add "or where the creditor sells (or has his agent sell) any security of D's for an undervalue." But with this qualification, it is respectfully submitted that the decision in the *Bank of India* case is not affected by the decision of the Court of Appeal in the *Walker* case, for there is no reason to suppose that if a bank does not assume a duty to supervise D, that any such duty is imposed by law. That is, the true principle of the *Bank of India* case is that the bank was not negligent, for negligence presupposes a duty. The *Walker* case decided that there is a duty owed

[93] *Bache & Co. (London) Ltd.* v. *Banque Vernes et Commerciale de Paris.* [1973] 2 Lloyds Rep. 437; *R. D. Harbottle (Mercantile) Ltd.* v. *National Westminster Bank Ltd.*[1978] Q.B. 146.
[94] *Ibid.* Prima facie, the Act applies, because there is clearly a duty to give a correct account, and a conclusive evidence clause excludes or restricts liability for breach of the duty. See s.13 of the Act.
[95] Above, paras. 19.21–19.22.
[96] Below, Chap. 23.
[97] See *Duncan, Fox & Co.* v. *North and South Wales Bank* (1880) 6 App.Cas. 1, 10, 14, 18, 20, and *Ewart* v. *Latta* (1865) 4 Macq. 983, 987. Paget, 515–516.
[98] It seems unlikely that refraining from selling could be affected by the Unfair Contract Terms Act 1977, and even s.3(2)(b) should not apply, since the bank is not "rendering" a contractual performance to G substantially different than that which he reasonably expects.
[99] [1982] 1 Lloyds Rep. 506.
[1] Generally approved by the C.A. in [1983] 2 Lloyds Rep. 298, 302—the court did not wish to "shut the door" on circumstances where G could be discharged.
[2] [1982] 1 W.L.R. 1410.

to guarantors by a receiver selling the debtor's assets. But it does not establish any general duty in a bank to supervise the conduct of the debtor, unless such a duty is expressly undertaken.

If B fails to register a security taken from D, and if D's security is contemplated by the parties when G enters his agreement, then the non-registration prejudices G, who is released to the extent of the loss caused to him thereby.[3] But there could be no duty in B to register any security not contemplated by G when he entered his guarantee. The *Walker* case dealt with the disposal of D's assets, which directly and necessarily concerns G, and affects his liability in a way which the parties must have contemplated. But the non-registration of an uncontemplated security is no concern of G's. If this is so, then a provision in the contract protecting B should be effective[4] and unaffected by the Unfair Contract Terms Act 1977.[5]

20.27

(xii) G may make a part payment to B before D becomes bankrupt. This may be done either as an indication of worth—that is, to show that he has the ability to perform his obligations—or it may be done to reduce G's ultimate liability, being made in circumstances where D's default seems likely. In the former case, the money is simply paid into a separate deposit account, to earn interest for G, and on D's bankruptcy it is called on[6] only after proving against D. In the latter case, unless G agrees otherwise, in the guarantee, or at the time of payment, the money should be paid into D's account.[7] The effect of part payments on B's and G's ability to prove in D's insolvency is further considered elsewhere.[7a]

(xiii) Any indulgence given by B to D or to a co-surety (G2), or any variation of the contracts of D or G2 prejudicial to G will discharge G from both existing and future liabilities under the guarantee.[8] It is otherwise if the change is "insubstantial or cannot be prejudicial to the surety."[9]

20.28

Even if it does not prejudice G[10] a binding agreement to give time to D will discharge G[11] but merely giving time may not do so, not being a variation of D's liability.[12] There would seem to be no prohibition on a mere fluctuation of the extent of D's liability, pursuant to the previous contract (*e.g.* if his overdraft fluctuates within an agreed limit), nor on any non-contractual variation or indulgence, such as a non-binding indication by the bank that it will not sue D.

Another form of "variation" is the release of D, which will discharge G.[13] The contract may specify otherwise, but whether this is effective depends on what G has undertaken to do. If he agrees to pay D's "debts,"

---

[3] *Wulff* v. *Jay* (1872) L.R. 7 Q.B. 756.

[4] See *Bauer* v. *Bank of Montreal* (1980) 110 D.L.R. (3d.) 424, where such a clause was held not to be an exemption clause, or unreasonable.

[5] Even by s.3(2)(b), because B is not "rendering a contractual performance."

[6] Generally, D's debt will be greater, so that proof against D is still required.

[7] *Mackinnon's Trustee* v. *Bank of Scotland* (1915) S.C. 411.

[7a] Below, para. 28.113 *et seq.*

[8] *Ward* v. *National Bank of New Zealand* (1883) 8 App.Cas. 755, 763; *Holme* v. *Brunskill* (1878) 3 Q.B.D. 495; *Webb* v. *Hewitt* (1857) 3 K. & J. 438; *Swire* v. *Redman* (1876) 1 Q.B.D. 536; *Pledge* v. *Buss* (1860) John. 663. For co-sureties, see above, para. 20.14.

[9] Neill J. in *Coal Distributors Ltd.* v. *National Westminster Bank Ltd.* (1981) unreported, referred to Encyclopedia E(2056).

[10] See *Ward* v. *National Bank of New Zealand* (1883) 8 App.Cas. 755, 763.

[11] *Polak* v. *Everett* (1876) 1 Q.B.D. 669; *Rouse* v. *Bradford Banking Co.* [1894] A.C. 586, 590, 594.

[12] *Overend Gurney & Co.* v. *Oriental Finance Corpn.* (1874) L.R. 7 H.L. 348.

[13] *Perry* v. *National Provincial Bank of England* [1910] 1 Ch. 464.

then his liability depends not on the protective provision alone, but also on whether the agreement between B and D is an "accord and satisfaction" whereby, in return for some consideration, D's debt is discharged. In that case, there is no debt upon which G is to be made liable, and an agreement preserving the bank's rights in fact preserves nothing.[14] On the other hand, the bank may not release D, but may simply agree not to sue D, thus waiving its rights against D, and in this case, B's rights against G may be preserved by an agreement.[15] If a bank enters what looks like a release of D's debt (which would release G also) but there is a term in the release preserving rights against G, this may be construed not as a release of D but as an agreement not to sue him.[16]

20.29   Where there is a novation, by which D is released and D1 introduced in his place, this discharges G. He is not liable for D1's debts, because he has never agreed to be liable, and he is not liable for D's debts because those debts are discharged.[17]

In relation to the cases just mentioned, it must be recalled that banks may ask G not to guarantee D's debts, but only to pay such sums as D has originally agreed to pay, if for whatever reason, D does not pay. A release of D here would not release G.

The situations just described must be distinguished from one where B merely permits D to enter a transaction under which G is not liable, because it is a transaction which he has not guaranteed. If G guarantees account No. 1, and B allows D to open another account, No. 2, this does not necessarily discharge G. That is, G may not be liable for debts on account No. 2, but he should not be discharged from liability on account No. 1, unless there is an express or implied agreement that the account will not be opened. What business is it, otherwise, of G's? It may be, for example, that it has been arranged for statements of the No. 1 account to be sent to G at regular intervals, so that he can observe the extent of D's liabilities, and the risk to G. In that case, it could be said that it was impliedly agreed that B would not open a second account for D. It is established that where the parties contemplate that D has and shall have only one account, then if D is allowed to open another account this is a variation affecting G's liability and G is discharged.[18] It might be said that this is a breach of an agreement with G, rather than a variation of a contract with D, and the same would apply even if the variation with D is non-contractual.

20.30   Similarly, although securities deposited by D or others may often be no concern of G's, it may be contemplated by the parties that securities will be deposited before further advances are made, and in such a case, G may be discharged if the securities are not provided.[19] Again, where it is contemplated that B will hold securities, and B releases these so as to prejudice G, G may be discharged[20] not because G is prejudiced, but because it is agreed

[14] See *Commercial Bank of Tasmania* v. *Jones* [1893] A.C. 313, 316, P.C.
[15] *Ibid.* See also *Price* v. *Barker* (1855) 5 E. & B. 760.
[16] *Green* v. *Wyn* (1869) 4 Ch.App. 204, 206; *Re Whitehouse* (1887) 37 Ch.D. 683, 694; *Duck* v. *Mayeu* [1892] 2 Q.B. 511, 514. Paget, 512.
[17] *Commercial Bank of Tasmania* v. *Jones* [1893] A.C. 313; *Bradford Old Bank Ltd.* v. *Sutcliffe* [1918] 2 K.B. 833.
[18] *National Bank of Nigeria Ltd.* v. *Awolesi* [1964] 1 W.L.R. 1311. The consideration was the continuation of "the existing account."
[19] See *Royal Bank of Canada* v. *Girgulis* (1980) 98 D.L.R. (3d.) 335.
[20] Perhaps only to the extent of the value of the security; *Rose* v. *Aftenberger* (1970) 9 D.L.R. (3d) 42; *Wulff* v. *Jay* (1872) L.R. 7 Q.B. 756.

332

between them, impliedly or expressly, that the securities will not be released.[21] Thus, in order to discharge G, it is submitted that there must be either a breach of an agreement directly with G[22] or a contractual variation of the terms of the contract with D which prejudices G. As we have seen, there is otherwise no duty in B to refrain from acting in a way which harms G's interests, except in realising D's assets (which deprives G of a possible fund from which, if all the proceeds do not go to B, G may claim his indemnity from D).

It is established that where G guarantees D's obligation (to pay by instalments), and D repudiates his obligation, B's acceptance of the repudiatory breach is not a variation of that contract such as to discharge G from his obligations. On the contrary, G's obligation immediately crystallizes.[23] In other words, G's liability extends not only to D's "primary" obligation to repay B, but also to D's "secondary" liability to pay damages to B for breach of the primary obligation.

To an extent, much of this is academic so far as banks are concerned, **20.31** since bank guarantees are phrased in terms which enable B to make the widest variations in D's liabilities. An example is a clause which (in conjunction with a promise to pay not D's debts, but whatever advances etc. are made to D, if D does not repay) allows B "full discretionary power, without any further consent from G, and without in any way affecting G's liability under this guarantee, to renew any advance, and to hold over, renew or give up in whole or in part and from time to time any (bills, securities, etc.) or to make any other arrangement with D in respect of (bills, securities, etc.) held by B, and to grant time or indulgence or consideration to D or to compound with D or release D from any liability, or to vary the term or the interest rate of any liability of D to B." At common law terms of this sort may be effective,[24] but the effect of the Unfair Contract Terms Act 1977 cannot be taken for granted. It seems difficult to argue that the bank has any "duty" not to release D or grant him indulgence, so that sections 2 and 3(2)(a) (which refer to breach of duty by the bank) would not apply. Possibly, however, section 3(2)(b) applies, and in acting in the way stated towards D the bank may be rendering to G a contractual performance substantially different from that which G reasonably expected. If the section does apply, the term must be reasonable. It is difficult to imagine that a court would hold unreasonable a provision enabling the bank to be lenient to D. If it were to do so, banks would be bound always to pursue remedies against debtors, however hopeless D's position.

If there is an indulgence clause, it must cover what happens. In *Burnes* v. *Trade Credits Ltd.*[25] B extended the term of D's mortgage, and increased the interest rate. This clearly would have discharged G, but it was argued that the contract allowed "any indulgence or consideration" to be given to D. But G was discharged, because his guarantee covered only the original mortgage and "any further advances," and the extension of the term, etc.,

---

[21] See *Wulff* v. *Jay* (1872) L.R. 7 Q.B. 756, 766; *Re Wolmershausen* (1890) 62 L.T. 541.

[22] As in the last group of cases mentioned.

[23] *Moschi* v. *Lep. Air Services Ltd.* [1973] A.C. 331; *Hyundai Heavy Industries Ltd.* v. *Papadopoulos* [1980] 2 All E.R. 29.

[24] See *Perry* v. *National Provincial Bank of England* [1910] 1 Ch. 464; *Union Bank of Manchester Ltd.* v. *Beech* (1865) 3 H. & C. 672, though see *Boultbee* v. *Stubbs* (1811) 18 Ves. 20 that B's reservation of rights against G will be ineffective if G has no remedy against D.

[25] [1981] 2 All E.R. 122.

was not a further advance. The "indulgence" clause did not require G "to shoulder an added liability." This was a variation of G's liability rather than an indulgence to D.

20.32   (xiv) While D's accounts are in operation, B has no duty to apply monies received for D to the particular account guaranteed, if only one is guaranteed.[26] Payments may even be placed in a new account, provided that there is no agreement with G not to open such an account.[27] In other words, the bank retains, as against D and G, the normal rights of appropriation, and need not appropriate between accounts, or within an account, (to the secured part of the account). None of this matters, if G guarantees the ultimate balance, because then any cash deposits are available at the time of D's default. But G may complain, if cash deposits are withdrawn by D earlier. It would seem that if a separate account exists, B may appropriate credits received to that account, if he wishes. But it has been suggested that (on an ultimate balance guarantee) it is wrong to open a new account especially for such deposits, if the effect is to deprive G of the benefit of them.[28]

D, of course, retains the right to appropriate payments between his accounts as he chooses, unless he agrees otherwise with the bank. In that case, presumably the bank need not consider G's interests and could place the funds in a new account. After all, if B refuses this request, D can take the money elsewhere, which will not assist G.

(xv) If G guarantees all of D's liabilities, this includes interest payable by D. For tax or other purposes it may matter whether what G pays is interest or principal. In *Re Hawkins*[29] it was held that if what D pays is interest and G pays it, it is still interest. It does not change its character just because G pays it. On the other hand, if tax relief is available for interest on a "loan," and G guarantees the loan, G's payments under the guarantee are not payments of interest on a "loan," for no loan is made to G.[30] Interest should be stipulated to run against G until "payment" of the sums guaranteed, and not on unpaid "debts" of D, for on D's bankruptcy, debts cease to be recoverable from him, and interest would be irrecoverable from G.[31]

(xvi) Whether guarantees are affected by the rules relating to transactions at an undervalue, or preferences, is discussed elsewhere.[32]

E. Determination of the guarantee

1. GENERALLY

20.33   Although many guarantors seem to misapprehend the position, the determination of the guarantee means only that G is excused from further liabilities incurred thereafter by D. G is not excused from liabilities which have already accrued. In *Westminster Bank Ltd.* v. *Sassoon*[33] the guarantee stated "This guarantee will expire on June 30, 1925." When, three months after that date, demand was made of G, she claimed that she was not liable, on

---

[26] *Williams* v. *Rawlinson* (1825) 3 Bing. 71; *Re Sherry* (1884) 15 Ch.D. 692; *Deeley* v. *Lloyds Bank Ltd.* [1912] A.C. 756.
[27] See the cases in previous note. Contrast *National Bank of Nigeria Ltd.* v. *Awolesi* [1964] 1 W.L.R. 1311, discussed above, n. 18.
[28] *Re Sherry* (1884) 15 Ch.D. 692, 706, *per* Cotton L.J.
[29] [1972] 3 All E.R. 386.
[30] *Hendy (Inspector of Taxes)* v. *Hadley* [1980] 2 All E.R. 554. See Finance Act 1978, s.49.
[31] *Re Moss* [1905] 2 K.B. 307; *Re Fitzgeorge* [1905] 1 K.B. 462.
[32] Below, para. 28.90 *et seq.*
[33] (1927) 5 L.D.A.B. 19.

the ground that her liability ceased on the day in question, not merely for the future, but entirely. The court, however, construed the words to mean that, in the usual way, the expiry of the guarantee did not discharge G from liabilities of D already accrued.

However, in the case of D's current account, the rule in *Clayton's case* will have the effect of gradually discharging G's liability, for the debts for which he became liable were "fixed" at the time the guarantee was determined. This may be prevented if the guarantee contains a term such as "G's liability for the amount due from D at the time when the guarantee is determined shall remain notwithstanding any subsequent payment into or out of the account by or on behalf of D."[34] Alternatively, the bank may stop D's current account, and open another one for him. In practice, it seems that banks do include terms such as those mentioned, but also stop the account. In *Re Sherry*[35] it was held that the bank had a right, on the determination of the guarantee, to break D's account, and that, even on D's death, the breaking of the account was effective to protect against the discharge of D's debt. Usually, bank forms expressly state this right. As already noted, however, accounts already opened must be combined on D's default, if the guarantee secures the ultimate balance, and it is mandatory to combine on D's insolvency.

2. DETERMINATION BY REVOCATION BY THE GUARANTOR

Even if guarantees are for a specified time, they are revocable by G giving reasonable notice,[36] unless they are (a) expressly stated to be irrevocable, or (b) impliedly irrevocable.[37] They may be impliedly irrevocable if given for a single lump sum consideration,[38] and in such a case, if alternative security cannot be arranged, D may, notwithstanding G's protests, be allowed to continue to draw on the account up to the maximum sum agreed, if any. Guarantees to secure a fluctuating overdraft would not be impliedly irrevocable. **20.34**

Bank guarantee forms generally allow G to withdraw by giving a fixed period of notice. Three months is a common period, and it is always stated that it must be in writing. In case of G's death, it is stated that his estate will continue to be liable until his personal representatives give three months notice. G's liability will be established at the end of the period of notice, (although it is still a contingent liability, depending of D's default) and at that time he is told the extent of it. The period of notice enables the bank to consider whether further securities should be arranged, or whether demand should be made of D, thus fixing G's liability immediately (and not when the notice expires). If further security is not available, G may agree not to withdraw if the consequences of a demand upon D is explained to him. Although again it may disturb G greatly, it is (probably) perfectly permissible for D to continue to increase the debt in the period of notice, though if D abuses this right, and particularly if G has made his fears of D's abuse known to the bank, it would seem to be an ethical practice for the bank,

---

[34] See *Westminster Bank Ltd.* v. *Cond* (1940) 46 Com. Cas. 60, where such a clause was held to be efficacious.

[35] (1884) 25 Ch. 692. See also *Deeley* v. *Lloyds Bank Ltd.* [1912] A.C. 756.

[36] *Offord* v. *Davies and Another* (1862) 12 C.B.(N.S.) 748.

[37] *Morrison* v. *Barking Chemicals Ltd.* (1919) 122 L.T. 423.

[38] *Lloyd's* v. *Harper* (1880) 16 Ch.D. 290 (irrevocable on both sides, so that the bank could not dishonour the agreement and refuse to provide D with the sum agreed).

perhaps with G's consent, to "fix"G's liability by making demand of D.[39] It is clear that if D's bill of exchange is accepted by B, it can be covered by the guarantee even if the bill matures in the period of revocation.

On occasion, the bank may allow G to determine the guarantee without notice, subject to payment by D of any outstanding cheques drawn by D and dated on or before the date of determination, and, as noted earlier, in such a case G is allowed, or may be requested, to discharge his existing liability by making a payment to the bank, to be held in a suspense account in case of D's default.

3. DETERMINATION BY REVOCATION BY ONE JOINT GUARANTOR

20.35   (a) Where there is a joint, or joint and several guarantee, the withdrawal of one joint guarantor ("co-surety") may[40] terminate the further liability of all the guarantors, unless otherwise agreed. It does not terminate liability for existing debts. In *Beckett* v. *Addyman*[41] it was held that the death of a joint and several co-surety did not release the others from future liability. But it may be different where G does not die, but withdraws.[42]

(b) However, it seems that any co-surety could give reasonable notice to withdraw, unless the contrary is agreed expressly, or as noted above, impliedly.[43] As this may have the effect of terminating the further liability of all of the guarantors, then on receipt of the notice, the bank should ask the others for fresh securities, or else make demand of D to fix the liability of all parties.

(c) The release of a co-surety may be a variation discharging the other parties.

(d) The contract may[44] provide for one co-surety to give notice to withdraw, without this affecting the liability of co-sureties. In this case, the liability of the one who withdraws is fixed on the expiry of the period of notice, and since the liability was joint, he is liable for the whole of the debt at the time. It is possible in such a case for all of the parties to agree to apportion the debt, but none are obliged to do so. If apportionment is agreed, consideration is required to release the departing guarantor from part of this liability, or it must be done by deed, but one way to provide consideration is to take new guarantees from the remaining guarantors in return for continuing the account, and to take a new several guarantee from the departing guarantor, on the same consideration, but limiting the amount for which he is liable. In such a case, D's account will be broken for the reasons explained above, unless the withdrawing guarantor pays off the amount of his liability (which may often be a condition of apportionment).

20.36   (e) The contract may provide for the bank to agree to release one co-surety (allow to withdraw), without discharging the others. That is, apart from any formal right in any guarantor to give notice, the bank "shall have full discretionary power, without any further consent from [any co-surety],

---

[39] It has been said that B must behave "equitably" towards G; *Holland* v. *Teed* (1848) 7 Hare 50, but in the light of *Bank of India* v. *Trans. Continental Commodity Merchants* [1982] 1 Lloyds Rep. 506, discussed earlier, the extent of this is doubtful.

[40] It is not clear if this is so, nor if there is a difference between joint, or joint and several, liability: see the case in the next note.

[41] (1882) 9 Q.B.D. 783.

[42] See Paget, 510, where it is suggested that this is "another matter."

[43] See *Kalil* v. *Standard Bank of South Africa* [1967] 4 S.A. 550 (A.D.).

[44] Bank guarantees invariably do this, as well as providing for (e) below.

and without in any way affecting the liability under this guarantee [of any co-surety] to release any security and to discharge or grant time or indulgence to or compound with any person liable jointly with or as surety."[45] If the bank exercises this power, there may be no point in breaking D's account and opening a new one, but the departing guarantor may be required to pay off a share of the indebtedness as a condition of the bank's agreement.

(f) If there is a provision for withdrawal on the giving of notice by "the undersigned," this has been held to mean that all of the co-sureties had to give notice in order to entitle any to resign.[46] An appropriate phrase to use instead is "all or any of the undersigned."

4. DETERMINATION BY THE BANK

The bank may demand repayment from D, and if D defaults, this fixes G's **20.37** liability, and will terminate the guarantee as a continuing obligation, unless otherwise specified. The account is broken, for the reasons given.

In the normal course of events, if the bank releases D, this will release G, not only from further obligations, but entirely, from all obligations.[47] But an appropriate clause in the agreement will give the bank the right to release or modify D's obligations without discharging G.[48] The same rules apply to the release by the bank of a co-surety.

5. DETERMINATION BY CHANGE IN THE CONSTITUTION OF D OR B, BY DEATH OR OTHERWISE

If the constitution of either D or B changes, the liability of G may be dis- **20.38** charged. Thus, a partnership (D) may lose or gain a member and the old partnership may then be dissolved, in which case G's guarantee would end for the future, since he guarantees the debts of the old partnership only, unless otherwise agreed.[49] Similarly, if D dies, the guarantee is determined for the future, for unless otherwise agreed, G does not promise to guarantee debts incurred by D's personal representatives. Similarly, if the constitution of B changes, as by amalgamation[50] with another bank, the guarantee is discharged, since G's promise was given to another person.[51] In all these cases contrary provision can be, and in bank guarantee forms usually is, made. For example, the term "the bank" may be defined so as to include "the bank's successors and assigns" and the benefit of the guarantee may be said to be enforceable "notwithstanding any change in the name of the bank, and shall enure for the benefit of any banking company with which the bank may become amalgamated and to which the bank shall assign it." It would

---

[45] In *Barclays Bank Ltd.* v. *Trevanion*, above, n. 30 the clause (there reproduced) was held not to be appropriate for this purpose when a bank released two out of three guarantors who agreed to pay a fixed sum each. The third guarantor was released entirely.

[46] *Egbert* v. *National Crown Bank* [1918] A.C. 903.

[47] *Samuel* v. *Howarth* (1817) 3 Mer. 272; *Perry* v. *National Provincial Bank of England Ltd.* [1910] 1 Ch. 464; above, para. 20.28.

[48] *Ibid.*

[49] s.18, Partnership Act 1890.

[50] Not just by absorption of the business—see Paget, 523.

[51] See *First National Finance Corpn.* v. *Goodman* [1983] B.C.L.C. 203, and Paget 524. The mere change of name by a corporation does not affect the guarantee: s.28(7) C.A. 1985.

seem such a clause is not necessary if the bank merely assigns the benefit of the guarantee, for it has the right at common law to do so.[52]

6. DETERMINATION BY CHANGE IN G'S CONSTITUTION, BY DEATH OR OTHERWISE

20.39 We have seen, for example, that where G is a co-surety his departure (by death or resignation) will discharge the others for the future, unless otherwise agreed. If G is a partnership, the dissolution of the partnership will end the guarantee for the future, but the personal liability of the partners in the original partnership, for existing debts, remains. The original partners may agree either that the partnership is not dissolved, or that their liability for the future continues in any case, but any new partner will not be bound by the guarantee, and so a new guarantee from that new partner will be necessary. If G is a natural person, it has been held that it is not his death alone, but notice of his death given to B which ends the guarantee, so that his estate will remain liable for new debts until the personal representatives give notice to B.[53] Even then, bank documents may provide otherwise, and often say that the liability of G's estate continues until the personal representatives actually give notice of their intention to determine the guarantee, and a normal period of notice (*e.g.* of three months) is required. Similarly, if G makes his liability irrevocable, this binds his representatives also. Thus, a guarantee of a single lump sum advance is impliedly irrevocable, and would be unaffected by G's death.[54] From this, it seems that the effect of death is merely that it acts as a form of notice, since it has no effect unless the bank is told, it has no effect at all if the guarantee is irrevocable, and it has no effect if there is any term to the contrary. It seems probable that constructive notice is insufficient for the purpose under discussion, and that the bank must have actual notice of G's death.[55]

20.40 On learning of G's death it is a frequent practice that the bank will inform the personal representatives of the guarantee and of their right to determine it by notice, etc. In the absence of special circumstances, it is unnecessary for the bank to make demand of D so as to fix the liability of G's estate. One circumstance in which it should do so is where D is the personal representative, even if not the only one, for in that case D faces a conflict of interest, about which B knows.[56] Similarly, if G's estate is left on trust to another, the bank, if it knows this, cannot claim against those assets in respect of future advances.[57] In these cases the normal procedures are followed.[58]

There is a special case, where there are multiple guarantors under a joint (but not joint and several) guarantee. In that case, on G's death, the operation of the doctrine of survivorship discharges the liability of G's estate, and the liability passes to the surviving co-sureties. But on a joint and several guarantee, the normal rules apply, for the estate is severally (separately) liable.

---

[52] *Ford Financial Trust Ltd.* v. *Obikoya* (1982) unrep. C.A.

[53] *Bradbury* v. *Morgan* (1862) 1 H. & C. 249; *Harriss* v. *Fawcett* (1873) 8 Ch. 866.

[54] *Lloyd's* v. *Harper* (1880) 16 Ch.D. 290.

[55] Contra *Coulthart* v. *Clementson* (1879) 5 Q.B.D. 42, but see *Re Silvester, Midland Railway Co.* v. *Silvester* [1895] 1 Ch. 573, and *Re Crace, Balfour* v. *Crace* [1902] 1 Ch. 733, 739.

[56] He may be tempted to increase the debt, knowing that the loss falls on G's estate.

[57] *Hariss* v. *Fawcett* (1873) 8 Ch.App. 866.

[58] *i.e.* demand made of D, other securities taken if possible, the account broken and a new one opened where appropriate, etc.

7. UNSOUNDNESS OF MIND OF G OR D

20.41 Once G or D loses contractual capacity, the guarantee will be determined for the future.[59] It is thought that as with death, notice to the bank would be required, and many bank forms so provide.[60]

8. BANKRUPTCY OF G

20.42 If G is insolvent, G's liability, even if contingent, (which it is if no demand is made of D) is a provable debt. But he will not be liable for future debts of D, since obligations of G arising after commencement are generally not provable.[61] There would be an exception for debts incurred by D pursuant to an obligation entered by D before commencement. Although demand need not be made of D in order to prove for G's debt, demand should be made so that G's liability is not contingent, in order to more clearly ascertain the amount for which G is liable. Other effects of insolvency upon G's guarantee, especially in relation to undervalues and preferences are discussed below.[62]

9. BANKRUPTCY OF D

20.43 D's bankruptcy does not affect G's liability,[63] but when the bank discovers D's bankruptcy it will stop D's account, since D can then incur no new debts to the bank, and G's liability is then fixed. The normal practice is to prove first against D, and in the result of an insufficiency, to sue or to prove against G, since this gives the bank two sources if G's funds prove insufficient. Other effects of insolvency upon guarantees are noted below.[64]

F. General features of bank guarantee forms

20.44 Many references have been made already to the terms in a bank's guarantee form. Forms vary greatly, of course, between one bank and another, and depending on whether G is an individual, an infant, an adult, or is to accept joint and several liability with another, and whether liability is to be limited or not, and so on.

The general structure may be something like this:

(a) The consideration clause.[65]

(b) The "whole debt" or "all moneys" clause, whereby G guarantees all types of D's liabilities, and the ultimate balance of his accounts, and any expenses of the bank in connection with D's debts or recovering under the guarantee.[66]

(c) The proviso to the "whole debt" clause, where the guarantee is to be limited, whereby G's liability, notwithstanding (b), is limited to a stated figure.[67]

(d) The continuing security clause, so that G is not discharged when D's overdraft first reaches the figure limited, and to exclude *Clayton's case*.[68]

---

[59] *Bradford Old Bank Ltd.* v. *Sutcliffe* [1918] 2 K.B. 833.
[60] *Ibid.*
[61] Below, Chap. 28.
[62] *Ibid*, esp. at para. 28.90 *et seq.*
[63] This was formerly stated in ss.16, 18 Bankruptcy Act 1914, and is now in s.281(7) I.A. 1986.
[64] See above, n. 62.
[65] Above, para. 20.09.
[66] Above, para. 20.18.
[67] Above, para. 20.18.
[68] Above, para. 20.17.

(e) The demand clause, whereby G is to pay on written demand to him, and providing for "machinery;; concerning the demand (*e.g.* deemed to be made 48 hours after posting).[69]

(f) The determination clause, whereby G is allowed to give notice to determine liability for the future, and where events such as his death may be dealt with.[70]

(g) The variation and release clause, whereby the bank is allowed to vary the contract or release D, co-sureties, or securities, (or not to do so) without discharging G, and to agree to compositions, arrangements, etc. made by D, and to prove against D and receive dividends, etc.[71]

(h) The clauses preventing G from competing with the bank, either in taking security from D or in proving against him on bankruptcy, or in suing him at any time.[72]

(i) The constitutional change clauses, providing that the guarantee is effective notwithstanding any change in the bank's constitution, or the dissolution of D if D is a partnership, of D's bankruptcy, liquidation or death.[73]

20.45 (j) The continuation clause, whereby B is entitled to continue D's account after determining the guarantee, or to open a new one, and that *Clayton's case* is not to operate so as to reduce the debt.[74]

(k) The conversion-to-indemnity clause, in case D is not liable as principal debtor, so that G will be liable nevertheless.[75]

(l) The additional security clause, so that this guarantee is additional to other guarantees, if any, given by G to B, and so that the bank has a lien on any securities of G which come into its hands.

(m) The part-payment clause, whereby payments received from G may be put in a suspense account, and not applied so as to discharge D's liability.[76]

(n) The conclusive evidence clause, to avoid disputes as to the extent of D's liability.[76a]

(o) The joint and several liability clause if the guarantee is or may be for multiple guarantors (and who may be released, etc., as in (g) above.)[77]

(p) The currency conversion clause, if the guaranteed indebtedness is or may be different currencies.

(q) The choice of law clause.[78]

(r) The retention clause, whereby the bank keeps the right to retain the guarantee or securities for a certain time after determination, (*e.g.* six months—two years) in case, say, D has repaid B, but D's payment is a preference, or is made after realisation of assets under a floating charge which is subsequently avoided by the liquidator. In addition, it is stated that G is not discharged if payments from D turn out to be invalid (though this is the case, anyway, probably.)

---

[69] Above, para. 20.33.
[70] Above, para. 20.33 *et seq.*
[71] Above, paras. 20.83–20.31.
[72] Below, para. 28.113 *et seq.*
[73] Above, para. 20.38.
[74] Above, para. 20.20, 20.33, 20.37.
[75] Above, para. 20.02 *et seq*, esp. para. 20.06.
[76] Above, para. 20.27.
[76a] Above, para. 20.24.
[77] Above, para. 20.14.
[78] Above, para. 20.13.

(s) The general waiver clause, whereby G waives all or any of his rights against B or D so far as may be necessary to give effect to any of the provisions of the guarantee. This is put in just for good measure.

LETTERS OF COMFORT

Guarantees or indemnities are legally binding contracts. A letter of comfort **20.46** is not susceptible of precise definition. The significant characteristic of many letters of comfort is that they are understood not to be legally binding, because they lack either consideration, or intention to create legal relations, or both. Such a letter may be in the form of a guarantee, but stated to be binding "in honour only, as a gentleman's agreement." Often, letters of comfort are given by parent companies in respect of subsidiaries, perhaps foreign subsidiaries, and amount to an indication of the parent company's intention to support its subsidiary in its business ventures, often up to a certain limit of debt. This may be given simply because the parent has a policy of not giving guarantees, or financial or legislative constraints may prevent it from doing so. Since it is not legally binding, by intention, the value of such a letter depends entirely on the standing of the parent company in the business and financial world.

There is, however, a danger in assuming that what is called a "letter of comfort" is not legally binding. In fact, so-called letters of comfort are phrased in many different ways, and some may be binding guarantees or other obligations,[79] others binding in some respects, and some entirely ineffective in law.

---

[79] In *Chemco Leasing S.P.A.* v. *Rediffusion Ltd.* (1987) a "put option" was created.

21. Company Securities

A. Introduction

21.01   At the time of writing, major reforms in the law relating to securities are proposed, and these reforms, if carried out, may bring some coherence and comprehensibility to the law relating to securities other than land. Unlike the proposed reform of the law relating to *ultra vires*,[1] the proposals as to securities are not at present in such form as to permit their incorporation in this work. In anticipation of major changes, however, the discussion of the present law has been curtailed.

   Securities given by companies differ (or have differed) from those given by individuals in at least four respects. Firstly, they have been affected by the doctrine of *ultra vires* (the abolition of which is expected).[2] Secondly, most securities given by companies are subject to registration under the Companies Act 1985, in addition to specific registration provisions relating to different types of property, such as land, ships, aircraft, etc., whereas securities given by individuals have a general registration requirement only in relation to chattel mortgages.[3] Thirdly, a company, but not an individual, can create a floating charge over its assets (including goodwill) so that it remains free to deal with the asset until specified events occur (such as liquidation), in which event the secured creditor may obtain priority over all creditors except preferential creditors and those with fixed charges. Fourthly, an individual's charge or mortgage may not provide that it shall never be redeemed, or contain any other unreasonable clog (such as non-redeemability for a very long time, or on onerous conditions). This is usually expressed by saying that there may not be a clog on the equity of redemption. However, by virtue of s.193, C.A. 1985, a company may create an irredeemable debenture,[4] or one redeemable only on the happening of a contingency, or after the expiration of a certain time. This is a significant advantage for a company, though a bank is unlikely to take a perpetual debenture as security from a company.[5]

B. The doctrine of *ultra vires*

21.02   In view of the proposed abolition of the doctrine of *ultra vires*, the doctrine will not be further discussed here. Any company will have full power to give securities, and any directors will have at least ostensible authority unless an outsider knows of and understands limitations upon the director's authority. Restrictions in the Articles as to the manner in which the security must be executed[6] will not affect an outsider unless he knows of them, and the security may be executed in any manner prescribed by law. For example, a legal mortgage of land must be made by deed, but an equitable

---

[1] Mentioned above, Chap. 17.

[2] Above, esp. para. 17.08 *et seq.*

[3] Under the Bills of Sale Acts 1878–91. A particular assignment of an individual's book debts is not registerable.

[4] "Debenture" includes mortgages and charges.

[5] Though it is possible that a bank loan (and security) will not be repayable for a specific period, and banks as corporations may issue their own perpetual bonds or debentures.

[6] *e.g.* that they be made by deed.

mortgage can be made by simple agreement or deposit of title deeds. A company may enter deeds simply by using the company seal, but the Articles may impose other requirements (*e.g.* who can use the seal, what other signatures are needed). But under the new rules, these prohibitions will not affect a contracting party unaware of them, and in any case, by virtue of s.74, L.P.A. 1925, notwithstanding any provision in a company's Articles referring to the execution of deeds, in favour of a purchaser a deed is deemed to have been properly executed by a company if it bears the company's seal, and is attested by the secretary (or clerk or other permanent officer or his deputy) and a member of the Board (or council or other governing body). The Board may appoint an agent to execute any transaction not requiring a deed (notwithstanding any contrary provisions for formalities).[7] The Articles or Memorandum may, however, authorise any additional "mode of execution or attestation" other than those just described,[8] but in any case, provisions in the articles will, in future, affect only those who know of them.[9]

In the light of the proposed changes, the previous recommended practice whereby an authority to give security was conferred by a resolution of the directors[10] (if not reserved to the General Meeting) would seem unnecessary, and unless the bank has actual knowledge of prohibitions on powers of individual directors, the security (if in the form approved by law) may bind the company. It would seem that any director would have ostensible authority to apply the company seal so as to bind the company to a deed.

C. Debentures

The word "debenture" is used a good deal in the Companies Act 1985[11] but the definition in s.744 is vague: " 'Debenture' includes debenture stock, bonds and any other securities of a company, whether constituting a charge on the assets of the company or not." Chitty J. said that "a debenture means a document with either creates a debt or acknowledges it, and any document which fulfils either of these conditions is a 'debenture'."[12] Doubts still exist whether certain instruments (such as depositary receipts or issues of sterling commercial paper) constitute debentures.[12a] Generally, however, people use the word "debenture" as if it were synonymous with "secured debenture." For present purposes, since we are concerned with securities, a debenture is a document which creates a debt or acknowledges a debt or promises to advance money, thus creating a debt (possibly on a contingency), and which provides for security to be given for the debt in ques-

21.03

---

[7] s.74(2), L.P.A. 1925.

[8] s.74(6), L.P.A. 1925.

[9] Article 101 of the Companies Act's Table A (S.I. 1985/805) provides that "The seal shall only be used by the authority of the directors or of a committee of directors authorised by the directors. The directors may determine who shall sign any instrument to which the seal is affixed and unless otherwise so determined it shall be signed by a director and by the secretary or by a second director. . . . "

[10] The bank takes a certified copy of this.

[11] *e.g.* ss.190–197.

[12] *Levy* v. *Abercorris Slate and Slab Co.* (1887) 37 Ch. D. 260, 264, speaking of the word in the Bills of Sale Act 1882.

[12a] Though subsequent to the Financial Services Act 1986, it matters less, if at all. (A "debenture" needed a prospectus, if issued to the public. The prospectus rules have now been clarified in relation to the instruments mentioned in the text).

tion.[13] The rights given to the debenture holder are a matter for contract and the company's Memorandum and Articles, and debentures come in many forms. They may, for example, be in registered or bearer form, single or series, perpetual or redeemable, and so on. The kind of debenture with which we are here concerned is a single redeemable debenture taken by the bank as security for a debt.

D. Standard form debentures

21.04 Banks generally have standard forms, and certainly, where the debenture secures an overdraft rather than a specific loan it is generally of the "All Monies" type. This provides for the following[14]:

1. The company agrees to pay on demand,[15] existing or future debts or liabilities, on any account, whether it is solely or jointly liable, whether as principal or surety, and including charges, interest and any costs to the bank.[16]

2. The company charges certain property with repayment of the debts just specified. Generally, there is a legal fixed charge over any freehold and leasehold property, and perhaps over fixed machinery, if any, and these assets will be specified in a schedule. A fixed equitable charge can be taken over any such property which may be obtained in future. Fixed charges, which may be legal or equitable, are taken over uncalled or unpaid capital, over shares in and securities of subsidiaries, over book debts, and over goodwill. In relation to future property of this sort, the charge must be equitable. Finally, a floating security is taken over the "undertaking" of the company and all its other assets (not already charged) either existing or which may afterwards be acquired. For reasons later stated[17] the taking of a floating charge is important, even if most of the company's property is subject to fixed charges.

21.05 3. There are generally prohibitive clauses:

(a) a negative pledge clause, prohibiting the creation of liens or securities ranking equally or ahead of this one.

(b) In relation to land, the bank is to hold all title deeds, etc., and in relation to equitably charged property the company is to execute legal charges when called on.

(c) The company is not to dispose of the undertaking or any part of it, unless the bank agrees.

(d) There are prohibitions on dealing with charged debts, except for getting them in and paying to the bank account, and the company is to execute an assignment in such form as the bank requires, if called on to do so.

4. There will be a "crystallisation" or "realisation" clause, specifying the events on which the bank debt is repayable and the security is enforceable. Relevant events may be (a) a demand made by the bank for repayment, (b) a

---

[13] This working definition would not cover, for example, an unsecured bond issue, though the issue seems in the light of s.744, C.A. 1985 clearly to be a debenture for the prospectus rules under that Act (now modified by the F.S.A. 1986).

[14] We follow the model in the Encyclopedia, I (921).

[15] For the time element involved, see below para. 23.04.

[16] This covenant to repay on demand (a) does not affect the existence or nature of debts, so that if the debenture is released, the separate debt is still actionable—*Barclays Bank Ltd.* v. *Beck* [1952] 2 Q.B. 47—(b) does not change the terms of loans previously granted for fixed terms, unless this is made clear—*Williams and Glyn's Bank Ltd.* v. *Barnes* (1980) unrep.

[17] In relation to "Administrators," below, para. 23.01.

breach of the prohibitive clauses or failure to repay interest or capital as agreed (*e.g.* for 14 days), (c) presentation of a petition for winding up, (d) appointment of a receiver (*i.e.* by someone else), (e) if distress is levied or any form of execution issued (including garnishee orders), (f) if the company ceases to carry on substantially the whole of its business.

5. There is provision for the bank to appoint a receiver and manager, who is to be the company's agent, not the bank's, and whose powers are extensively described and include realising the assets secured, (including, of course, the whole business), and managing the company and doing all things relevant thereto.

6. There is provision for the distribution of the proceeds of realisation.

7. There is an irrevocable power of attorney appointing the bank as agent to do what is necessary to enforce the debenture, and to appoint others as substitute agents for the bank.

8. In relation to land, there are covenants to repair, maintain and insure (this last applies to all property), and in default the bank may remedy the failure and its costs will be secured also. **21.06**

9. The company is not to lease or accept surrenders of leases unless the bank consents.

10. The company must pay all debts, etc., as they fall due, and inform the bank of any proceedings against the company. It must keep its records in good order. It must supply copies of accounts and notices of meetings to the bank.

11. The security is in addition to existing securities, not in substitution for them. It is a "continuing security for all debts liabilities and obligations from time to time of the company to the Bank" and is unaffected by payment of any monies to the bank (*i.e. Clayton's case* is not to operate to reduce the original debt and replace it with a new one which is not secured).

12. The bank is given powers on learning of charges, etc., to others to break the account and to open a new one, and is deemed to do so anyway (again, so that *Clayton's case* will not affect its claim, as against another mortgagee, etc.). It may combine accounts, if there is a credit balance elsewhere.

13. It is certified that the charges do not contravene the Memorandum or Articles. (The directors will be liable on a warranty of authority anyway, but this makes it clear.) Following the reform of *ultra vires* rules, this becomes less important.

14. There may be administrative provisions, about interpretation, the making of demands, service of documents, etc.

E. Registration of charges

Section 395, C.A. 1985 requires, in effect, the registration of most company **21.07** charges (including mortgages)[18] with the Registrar of Companies. The aim is to prevent the company fraudulently charging the same asset to more than one creditor. Strictly, the statutory obligation is not to register a charge, but to deliver to the registrar the details required within 21 days of the charge's creation, and if this is done, the charge is not void, even if never placed on the register.[19] On registration, any person may inspect the regis-

---

[18] s.396(4), C.A. 1985.
[19] See the words of s.395(1); *National Provincial & Union Bank of England* v. *Charnley* [1924] 1 K.B. 431; *Slavenburg's Bank N.V.* v. *Intercontinental Natural Resources Ltd.* [1980] 1 All E.R. 955.

ter, and take copies.[20] Delivery of particulars has the effect of giving notice of the existence of the charge, and this affects the common law rules of priority between charge holders. Non-delivery of particulars makes the charge void against the liquidator, administrator and other creditors.[21] This "registration requirement" applies not only to English companies, but also to foreign companies having an established place of business in England,[22] even though the foreign company has no other details (such as an address) registered.[23]

21.08 An unconditional agreement to create a charge in future creates a present equitable charge, and this is registerable,[24] although (a) the later charge need not be registered[25] and (b) if the later charge is registered and the earlier one is not, the later charge is valid.[26] But a conditional agreement, merely to execute a charge if called upon to do so, is not an existing equitable charge, and is not registerable.[27] Such an "inchoate" security right, however, may be affected by insolvency rules concerning preferences,[28] and the position may be affected by the proposals for reform already mentioned in the Introduction to this Chapter.

There is no objection in principle to a lender taking successive unregistered charges, each within the 21 day period for registration. This will give the lender priority against the liquidator. There is, of course, a risk that subsequent registered charges will obtain priority.

1. REGISTERABLE CHARGES

21.09 Section 396(1), C.A. 1985 states that the charges which must be registered (*i.e.* particulars delivered) are the following:

(a) a charge for the purpose of securing any issue of debentures.[29]

(b) a charge on uncalled share capital of the company.

(c) a charge created or evidenced by an instrument which, if executed by an individual, would require registration as a bill of sale. This covers chattel mortgages or charges if (i) written, and (ii) if not subject to certain exceptions. An individual need not register charges of particular book debts, hence (e) below.

(d) a charge on land (wherever situated) or any interest in it, but not including a charge for any rent or other periodical sum issuing out of the land.[30]

(e) a charge on book debts of the company. This refers to fixed charges.

(f) a floating charge on the company's undertaking or property. This would include floating charges over book debts.

(g) a charge on calls made but not paid.

---

[20] s.401.

[21] Below, para. 21.24 *et seq.*

[22] s.409.

[23] Such details are kept in what is now often called the "Slavenburg" register, after the case above, n. 19.

[24] See *Property Discount Corpn. Ltd.* v. *Lyon Group Ltd.* [1981] 1 All E.R. 379.

[25] *Re William Hall (Contractors) Ltd.* [1967] 2 All E.R. 1150.

[26] *Re Columbian Fireproofing Co. Ltd.* [1910] 2 Ch. 120.

[27] *Williams* v. *Burlington Investments Ltd.* (1977) 121 Sol. Jo. 424; *Re Gregory Love & Co.* [1916] 1 Ch. 203.

[28] Below, para. 28.90 *et seq.* See ss.238–240 I.A. 1986, and *Re Jackson & Bassford Ltd.* [1906] Ch. 467; *Re Eric Holmes (Property) Ltd.* [1965] Ch. 1052.

[29] "Issue," here, refers to a series of debentures, and means that a single bank debenture is not covered by this provision. See s.397 for the procedure.

[30] Land may have other registration requirements.

(h) a charge on a ship or aircraft, or any share in a ship.[31]

(i) a charge on goodwill, on a patent or a licence under a patent, on a trademark or on a copyright or a licence under a copyright.[32]

2. NON–REGISTERABLE MATTERS

For various reasons, the following are not registerable:

21.10

(a) Charges over stocks and shares owned by the company, unless the charge is floating. Charges are normally taken by taking physical possession of bearer certificates, or by registration of title to registerable shares, and this would warn others.

(b) Charges over life policies. Equitable charges (assignments) are made by taking physical possession of the policy, and with legal charges additionally, the life office concerned is notified, and notification gives priority.

(c) Charges over chattels subject to one of the exemptions for individuals: for example, charges over goods in foreign parts or at sea, or over identified imported goods, or goods represented by documents of title used in the ordinary course of business, or if the charge is additionally secured by possession of the goods, and so on.

(d) Completed pledges of goods, even if the goods are subsequently released to the pledgor by way of trust receipt. In this case and the previous exception, the trust receipt and release usually specifies that the proceeds of goods belong to the lender: this is not registerable, even though the proceeds are a book debt of the company, as this is deemed to be no more than a consequence of the non-registerable right (the pledge) which already exists. But if the owner of the goods had already sold them to another at the time he purports to create the original pledge, and if no exception to the *nemo dat* rule operates so that the original pledge is void,[33] then the subsequent reference to the proceeds of sale can only operate as a (non-exempt) charge, which will be void if not registered.[34]

(e) Deposits of bills of exchange by way of security do not amount to a registerable charge of the company's book debts.[35]

(f) Only "charges" which are "created" by the company are registerable. Rights such as liens and equitable or statutory set-off are not charges, and are not, in any case, "created" by the company, and are not registerable.[36] This includes a bank's lien over securities deposited with it in the way of banking.[37] But a lien arising by operation of law is destroyed by the granting of some contractual security right. If, therefore, an unpaid vendor (who has a lien) takes a legal mortgage over the asset in question the lien disappears, and is not resurrected if it turns out that the mortgage is void for non-registration.[38] Similarly, if title deeds are deposited with the intention of creating a security right, this creates an equitable mortgage (which may be

21.11

---

[31] These also must be separately registered.

[32] Patents and trademarks are also registerable elsewhere.

[33] *e.g.* if the lender knows of the sale—otherwise the exception to *nemo dat* in s.25, Sale of Goods Act 1979 will operate.

[34] *Ladenburg Co.* v. *Goodwin Ferreira & Co. Ltd.* [1912] 3 K.B. 275.

[35] s.396(2).

[36] *e.g.* an unpaid vendor's lien for the price of land sold—*London and Cheshire Insurance Co. Ltd.* v. *Laplagrene Property Co. Ltd.* [1971] Ch. 499—or a solicitor's lien over title deeds, etc., for his costs.

[37] Above, Chap. 13.

[38] *Burston Finance Ltd.* v. *Speirway Ltd.* [1974] 3 All E.R. 735.

registerable) and this cannot co-exist with the lien.[39] If not registered, where required, the bank will have no rights. If a charging order is made against the company's property, this is not registerable, not being "created" by the company.[40] A Romalpa (reservation of title) clause may be effective in relation to non-mixed goods, and not being a "charge" it is not registerable: but in relation to mixed goods (the products of the original goods and others) or proceeds of sale, it is likely that it operates as a registerable charge.[41]

(g) Property already subject to a charge when the company acquires it is subject to a quasi-exception: it is still registerable, but the consequence of non-registration is merely that the company and its officers may be fined, not that it is void.[42] Where, however, a company buys property without paying the full price, and the vendor takes a mortgage for the unpaid amount, the mortgage cannot exist before the property is acquired, so that the mortgage is subsequent to acquisition and the normal rule (void for non-registration) applies.[43]

(h) If a bank has a contractual set-off clause relating to a deposit held by it, it is unclear whether (i) conceptually this can be a charge,[44] (ii) whether if so, it is intended to be in particular cases, (iii) whether it is a registerable charge over a "book debt." Even if it is a charge, it seems not be a charge over a book debt.[45] It is more certain that "flawed asset" arrangements are not charges, and are not registerable. But if not charges, either of these may be affected by the *pari passu* rule in case of the depositor's insolvency.[46]

(i) Charges over choses in action not specifically mentioned in section 396,[47] are not registerable.

3. DEBTS AND OTHER MATTERS: WHETHER REGISTERABLE

a. Book Debts

21.12 These are an important registerable class. They are debts owing to the company which arise out of the normal carrying on of its business, so that they would appear in the books of the company, if well-kept.[48] On one view "The distinction to be drawn is probably between debts accruing to the company in the course of carrying on the business for which it was formed,

---

[39] *Re Molton Finance Ltd.* [1968] Ch. 325; *Wallis and Simmonds (Builders) Ltd.* [1974] 1 All E.R. 561 (title deeds deposited by company acting as surety).
[40] *Re Overseas Aviation Engineering (G.B.) Ltd.* [1963] Ch. 24.
[41] Below, Chap. 22.
[42] ss.400, 409.
[43] *Capital Finance Co. Ltd.* v. *Stokes* [1969] 1 Ch. 261.
[44] See *In Re Charge Card Services Ltd.* [1986] 3 All E.R. 289 where a "retentions clause" was held not to create a charge, this being conceptually impossible.
[45] In *Re Stevens, Stevens* v. *Keily* [1888] W.N. 110, a partnership's balance with its banker was held not to be a book debt, when that phrase was used in a will.
[46] Below, Chap. 28. The "flawed asset" clause merely says that a bank need not repay the deposit until the customer's debt is repaid, or somesuch arrangement, without a right expressed to set off the deposit.
[47] *i.e.* the uncalled share capital, calls made but not paid, floating charges, charges over book debts, goodwill, patents, licences, trademarks, and copyrights.
[48] *Shipley* v. *Marshall* (1863) 14 C.B. (N.S.) 566 (a "debt connected with and growing out of the plaintiff's trade"); *Dawson* v. *Isle* [1906] 1 Ch. 633 ("debts accruing in the ordinary course of trade and entered in the books"); *Independent Automatic Sales Ltd.* v. *Knowles and Foster* [1962] 3 All E.R. 27 ("a debt arising in due course of a business . . . [which] would or could in the ordinary course of such a business be entered in well kept books relating to that business").

and debts which are merely incidental to carrying on that business, or which, although *intra vires*, are totally unconnected with it."[49] If, for example, a company set up to make goods sells goods to C, C's debt is a book debt of the company. But if the company deposits money with a bank to secure an advance to the bank, the debt owed by the bank is probably not a book debt, being incidental to carrying on the business, and not arising from the carrying on of the business itself. Similarly, if the company disposes of surplus land, not needed for its manufacturing purposes: the debt owed by the purchaser is probably not a book debt.

There are two separate questions: first, what sort of debts or obligations may be charged, and secondly, which of the charges so identified need to be registered.

b. Existing Debts

These may be payable now or payable at some future time. Both of these **21.13** can be charged, and the charge is registerable. An example is the charging (*e.g.* by way of deposit) of hire-purchase agreements as security for a loan: this is a charge over the book debts due under the agreements, even though payable in future.[50]

c. Contingent Debts

A debt is contingent if under the terms of a contract it may or may not arise. **21.14** It has been decided that a charge taken over a contingent debt is not registerable, because it is not a book "debt" for the purpose of registration, even though a contingent obligation is a sufficient obligation to maintain a security interest.[51] Thus, a charge over an existing contractual right (to the benefit of an export credit insurance policy) has been held not to be registerable where no book debt then exists, even though a book debt may come into existence if the policy money becomes payable.[52] Such a contingent debt is not a book "debt."[53]

d. Potential Debts

It may be difficult to distinguish contingent debts from existing debts. If **21.15** payment is to be made for a house when built, the builder cannot sue for the money until at least substantial completion, and the debt may seem not yet to exist. But for the purpose of security interests, the debt is deemed not to be contingent or future because there are legal obligations on both sides which if fulfilled will inevitably result in the debt becoming owing. The fact that either party may break his contract is legally irrelevant, and there are no other contingencies. The debt is regarded as "growing" from an existing

[49] Pennington, 421.

[50] *Independent Automatic Sales Ltd.* v. *Knowles & Foster* [1962] 3 All E.R. 27. This must be distinguished from a sale (at a discount) of the agreements, which is a common form of financing: see *Re George Inglefield Ltd.* [1933] Ch. 1; *Lloyds and Scottish Finance Ltd.* v. *Prentice* (1977) 121 Sol.Jo. 847.

[51] See *Re Rudd* [1986] 2 C.L. 333, where a lender was entitled to refuse to vacate a mortgage created by an all monies debenture where the only obligation remaining was a contingent liability under a performance bond if the beneficiary of the bond or guarantee ever called for its enforcement. Goode C.L., 743 says there is merely an inchoate security interest. This may be so, but it is sufficient to prevent the discharge of the mortgage if that was intended by the parties—*Re Rudd*, above n. 51.

[52] *Paul and Frank Ltd.* v. *Discount Bank (Overseas) Ltd.* [1967] Ch. 348.

[53] Even if it was not contingent, it may have been incidental to the business, and not a "book" debt, though Pennington, 421, thinks it may be, as a substitute for payment of the goods supplied by the company.

contract, and as being inseparably connected with it, and as presently exist-ing. It is sometimes called "potential" property.[54] It would seem, therefore, that a debt is "contingent" and a charge upon it is not registerable if there is some contingency or condition or event, other than breach of a presently enforceable obligation, upon the occurrence or non-occurrence of which the existence of the debt depends. Until the event occurs, the existence of the debt remains hypothetical. Charges over truly contingent debts are not registerable: charges over merely potential debts are registerable because the property is deemed to have present existence.

e. Future Debts

21.16 A future debt is one which may arise under a contract not yet entered. Such debts are merely hypothetical: a company, for example, may expect each month to have certain debts owing to it, but until the contracts of sale, etc., are made, the debts cannot exist, and there is no guarantee that they ever will. It is established that even if the property is future, it is possible in equity (though not at law) to charge it.[55] For the purpose of establishing priorities between security interests, according to *Tailby* v. *O.R.*[56] an inchoate security interest exists from the date of agreement, and an equit-able charge attaches when the debt comes into existence, without the need for further action, and for priority purposes, relates back to the date of cre-ation of the security interest. This establishes that future debts can be charged, but not that the charges are registerable, and there is confusion sur-rounding this point.

Since book debts which may arise in the future under trading contracts not yet entered into are merely hypothetical, it might seem that they are contingent on all sorts of eventualities, and should be treated the same way as contingent debts. Yet it has been said that charges over future debts of this kind are registerable, on the ground that they are not contingent.[57] That they are not contingent is, it is respectfully submitted, a peculiar and inde-fensible view. In *Paul and Frank Ltd.* v. *Discount Bank (Overseas) Ltd.*[58] Pennycuick J. agrees that contingent debts are non-registerable. The examples he has in mind concern debts under contracts of insurance, guar-antee and the like. These are clear examples of contingent debts, but it is submitted that debts which may arise under contracts which may or may not ever be entered into are just as much contingent as debts arising under contracts of guarantee. Indeed, they are more contingent, since the con-tracts in question may not ever be entered into. Yet the result of the view criticised is that one is compelled to say that a debt which arises under a con-tract that may not ever be entered into is not contingent, and a debt which may arise under a contract which has been entered into is contingent. It is submitted that both are contingent, and that either both are registerable or

[54] See Goode, C.L., 742, referring to *G. & T. Earle Ltd.* v. *Hemsworth R.D.C.* (1928) 140 L.T. 69; *Norman* v. *Federal Commissioner of Taxation* (1963) 109 C.L.R. 9; *Hughes* v. *Pump House Hotel Co. Ltd.* [1902] 2 K.B. 190. The same applies to charges on growing goods—*e.g.* wool which may grow on a sheep. This is seen as a charge on existing property.
[55] See *Holroyd* v. *Marshall* (1862) 10 H.L.Cas. 191, 220 "At law property, non-existing, but to be acquired at a future time, is not assignable; in equity it is so": *Tailby* v. *O.R.* (1888) 13 App.Cas. 523; *Re Lind* [1915] 2 Ch. 345.
[56] Previous note.
[57] See *Independent Automatic Sales Ltd.* v. *Knowles & Foster* [1962] 3 All E.R. 27; *Paul and Frank Ltd.* v. *Discount Bank (Overseas) Ltd. and the Board of Trade* [1967] 1 Ch. 348.
[58] Previous note.

neither are registerable. The preferrable view, it is submitted, would be that both should be registerable,[59] and that despite *Paul and Frank Ltd.* v. *Discount Bank (Overseas) Ltd.*, the phrase "book debts" in section 396(1)(*e*), C.A. 1985 should be interpreted to include all future and contingent book debts.

Even with future debts there is an important exception, for if the charge allows the chargeor to deal with debts as they come into existence, and only attaches on some event such as liquidation, etc., then the charge is a "floating" charge, and is registerable, even though the property is future.[60]

f. Quistclose Trust

An arrangement which creates a Quistclose trust may not create a charge, but even if it does, there is a trust as well, and this is not registerable. Thus, if A, being indebted to a company, pays money to the company's account with a bank specifically so that the money should repay creditors of the company, then the money in the account is held by the company on trust for the creditors, and is not impeachable by the bank or others as an unregistered charge.[61]

21.17

g. Irrevocable Authority

If a bank desiring security for the repayment of advances takes an irrevocable authority from a company, entitling the bank to require the company's debtors to pay directly to the company's bankers, this "authority" will create a charge over the book debts concerned.[62] This may be avoided if the bank has the debts absolutely assigned to them by way of repayment of the advances: this would be non-registerable sale of the debt, not a charge. The bank would be owner, and the payments to it would discharge the debt.[63]

21.18

4. METHOD AND TIME FOR REGISTRATION

The statutory obligation is not to register but to deliver to the Registrar of Companies the "prescribed particulars of the charge together with the instrument (if any) by which it is created or "evidenced."[64] This must be done within 21 days of the creation of the charge. The regulations[65] provide for the use of a form (form 395)[66] and this must show the company name, the date and description of the charge instrument, (or the date on which property already subject to a charge was acquired), the amount owing on the security, names, addresses and descriptions of the chargees, and a short

21.19

---

[59] In *Property Discount Corpn. Ltd.* v. *Lyon Group Ltd.* [1981] 1 All E.R. 379 it was said that a charge over property part of which did not yet exist was registerable.

[60] Below, para. 21.43 *et seq.*

[61] *Carreras Rothman Ltd.* v. *Freeman Mathews Treasure Ltd.* [1985] Ch. 207.

[62] *Re Kent and Sussex Sawmills Ltd.* [1947] Ch. 177. It was admitted that the debts in question were book debts: the question was whether it was a charge.

[63] "Absolute" here means without proviso for redemption: a mortgage of a chose in action can be made by an assignment which is "absolute" in another sense, so that it can be a legal assignment, within the meaning of s.136, L.P.A. 1925, even though it is undoubtedly registerable because there is a proviso for redemption. There must be an outright sale, not just a mortgage, to escape registration.

[64] s.395(1). For property outside the U.K., a copy of the instrument may be used, and the 21 day period dates from the time the copy could, in due course of post if dispatched with due diligence, have been received in the U.K. For property to be registered in Scotland or N.I., a copy is used, plus a certificate concerning presentation for registration, s.398.

[65] S.I. 1985/854 Companies (Forms) Regulations 1985, reg. 4 and Sched. 3.

[66] Formerly form 47, under C.A. 1948.

description of the property charged.[67] The prescribed particulars should be shown on the form, and not by way of cross-referencing to other attached documents.[68] The Registrar may correct "obvious clerical or typing errors"[69] without returning the form, but except for this, delivery of incorrect documents is not a delivery at all, and the statutory requirement will not be fulfilled. In case correction is needed, documents should be delivered as early as possible, marked "Mortgage Section" of the registry. The duty to register is placed upon the company[70] but any "person interested" in the charge may do so, and recover the fees from the company.[71] It is a wise precaution for the bank to undertake registration, and it is thought that this is usually done. The registrar keeps a register of charges which contains the relevant particulars[72] and which can be inspected by any person without fee. He issues a certificate of registration of the charge.[73] The instrument of charge is returned to the company, which must keep a copy of the instrument creating the charge, at its registered office[74] and must keep there a register of charges showing the property, amount, and chargee (unless a bearer security).[75] The register can be inspected by creditors and shareholders without fee, and by others for a fee of 5p. This applies to foreign companies with a place of business here, in which case the register is to be kept at the principal place of business.[76]

21.20   A charge is created (and the 21 day period begins to run) when executed by the company, and not at the later date when money is first advanced.[77] If there is an agreement later to give a legal mortgage, the agreement creates an immediate registerable equitable charge, but even if time for registration of that charge expires, the legal charge, if later executed, is valid and can be registered within 21 days of its execution.[78]

If the particulars are not delivered in time (and this includes cases where defective particulars are delivered) or if there is an omission or misstatement of any particular, then a further charge may be taken (but it may be subject to other securities taken by others in the meantime) or the bank may apply to the court under section 404 for an extension of time, and the court has a discretion to extend the time or rectify the mis-statement, "on such terms and conditions as seem to the court just and expedient." This may be done if the mistake was "accidental or due to inadvertence or to some other sufficient cause, or is not of a nature to prejudice the position of creditors or shareholders, . . . or that on other grounds it is just and equitable to grant relief." Orders under section 404 will always be made subject to a condition that the position of any creditor who has acquired proprietary

---

[67] For debentures issued in series additional requirements are stated in s.397.

[68] *R.* v. *Registrar of Companies, ex p. Central Bank of India* [1986] 1 All E.R. 105, [1986] Q.B. 1114 where it was said to be "unwise" not to put particulars on form 47.

[69] *Ibid.*, approving the Registrar's statement of November 16, 1984.

[70] s.399.

[71] *Ibid.*

[72] s.401.

[73] A copy of this must be endorsed on any debenture subsequently issued by the company which is secured by that charge—s.402.

[74] s.406.

[75] s.407.

[76] s.409.

[77] *Esberger & Son Ltd.* v. *Capital and Counties Bank Ltd.* [1913] 2 Ch. 366.

[78] *Re Columbian Fireproofing Co. Ltd.* [1910] 2 Ch. 120, above, para. 21.08.

rights after the 21 day period expired is not to be affected.[79] Since such a condition does not give another creditor with a second debenture priority where the two debentures were created on the same day,[80] or within the 21 day period, it may be advantageous (despite the expense) to apply under section 404, rather than to take a new security. "Sufficient cause" can be shown by demonstrating, for example, confusion between different officers[81] but it seems anyway that the court takes a liberal approach, given the protective nature of the condition always imposed. Possibly only serious negligence giving rise to a suspicion of a deliberate delay would debar an extension. Similarly, when a mistake is discovered, an application should immediately be made for an extension, and the court will look askance at a chargee who deliberately delays.[82] Normally, however, an order will not be made after the company has gone into liquidation,[83] or where a winding up petition has been presented or is imminent,[84] unless the circumstances are wholly exceptional.[85] If an extension of time is allowed, then any term allowing time for repayment of the sum secured would be re-instated, having been automatically terminated (and money immediately repayable) when the charge originally became void.[86]

5. EFFECT OF REGISTRATION

a. Perfection

When the prescribed particulars have been delivered in time, whether regis-   **21.21**
tered or not, the charge cannot be impugned for invalidity on the ground of non-compliance with section 395. Compliance with section 395 is said to "perfect" the security. It may still be challenged on other grounds, even if registered—for example, that there was duress, or no consideration, or formalities missing, etc.

b. Certificate Conclusive

When the charge is registered, the registrar delivers a certificate of registra-   **21.22**
tion, and according to section 401(2) "The certificate—(a) shall be either signed by the registrar, or authenticated by his official seal, and (b) is conclusive evidence that the requirements of this Chapter as to registration have been satisfied." It is now established that once the certificate has been issued, compliance with section 395 cannot be challenged whether in an ordinary action or by special administrative actions or procedures.[87] If the

---

[79] See *Re Ehrmann Bros Ltd.* [1906] 2 Ch. 697; *Watson v. Duff, Morgan and Vermont (Holdings) Ltd.* [1974] 1 All E.R. 794.

[80] *Ibid.*

[81] *Re Kris Cruisers, Ltd.* [1949] Ch. 148.

[82] *Victoria Housing Estates, Ltd. v. Ashpurton Estates, Ltd.* [1982] 3 All E.R. 665, [1983] Ch. 110.

[83] *Re Eric Holmes (Property) Ltd.* [1965] Ch. 1052; *Re Mechanisations (Eaglescliffe) Ltd.* [1966] Ch. 20.

[84] *Victoria Housing Estates, Ltd. v. Ashpurton Estates, Ltd.* above, n. 82.

[85] See *Re R. M. Arnold & Co. Ltd.* [1984] B.C.L.C. 535, where there appeared to be no unsecured creditors to be prejudiced, and where priority between secured creditors needed to be established.

[86] *Goode, C.L.,* 776, n. 124. See s.395(2).

[87] *National Provincial & Union Bank of England v. Charnley* [1924] 1 K.B. 431 (subject matter improperly described); *Re Mechanisations (Eaglescliffe) Ltd.* [1966] Ch. 20 (amount mis-stated); *Re Eric Holmes (Property) Ltd.* [1965] Ch. 1052 (date mis-stated); *Re C. L. Nye Ltd.* [1971] Ch. 442 (date mis-stated); *R. v. Registrar of Companies, ex p. Central Bank of India,* above, n. 68 (registrar accepted late resubmission of originally defective form, and the challenge to the certificate by certiorari, was held to be impermissible).

form submitted to the Registrar does not contain the prescribed particulars, the Registrar has no discretion to accept a late re-submission, and if he does so he acts *ultra vires*, although the certificate still cannot be challenged. The older practice of allowing resubmission out of time has ceased since 1984, and the Registrar's decision to cease doing so was approved by the Court of Appeal in *R. v. Registrar of Companies, ex p. Central Bank of India*.[88] It is admitted in all these cases that there would be an exception for fraud, where, for example, an attempt is made to deceive the registrar by deliberate falsification of the date.[89]

c. Notice and Priorities[90]

21.23 The third effect of registration is that it gives notice of existence of the charge and notice may affect the rules of priority between charges, discussed below. Registration does not create priority except by virtue of notice, though non-registration may defeat an existing priority. It is an important and presently unresolved question as to what aspects of charges registration gives notice. One possibility (the narrowest) is that registration gives notice only of the existence of a charge, and not of its contents. An intermediate view is that, having deemed notice, a prospective purchaser or mortgagee should in his own interests expect at least to see the prescribed particulars, and that he will have "factually inferred" constructive notice of at least these. The widest view is that he would have notice of everything put upon the register, and this would include such things as negative pledge clauses, preventing the creation of charges with priority. This matter may be expected to be resolved by the proposed reforms, and we do not discuss it further, except to say that in our view, negative pledges in both fixed and floating charges are now so very common that persons in commercial life would be very surprised not to find them, especially in a bank debenture form. If the position has been reached when commercial people would expect to find a particular provision in most charges, the prospective chargees ought to be taken to have factually inferred constructive notice of such a provision if they do not at least make the reasonable inquiry of searching the Companies Register. It seems almost to amount to turning a blind eye to disregard the prevalence of such clauses.[91]

If that suggestion is correct for negative pledges, the question arises whether anyone has factually inferred notice of a fixed charge over future book debts (first established by *Siebe Gorman & Co. Ltd. v. Barclays Bank Ltd.*)[92] That case decided that a subsequent purchaser had no notice of the nature of the charge. Since then, however, it has become common for charges over book debts to be of the "fixed" kind, rather than floating charges, and the position may now be different.

---

[88] Previous note, and see the Registrar's statement of November 16, 1984.

[89] In the *Central Bank* (above, n. 68) case the court left open the possibility of challenge by judicial review in "special kinds of cases" without specifying what these were. It is thought that except for fraud the only cases may be ones involving general invalidity of the charge (*e.g.* for lack of formalities) in which case the charge could be challenged in any sort of action, not only by way of judicial review.

[90] In the expectation of changes, the discussion of these problems has been shortened drastically (though it now seems that the changes may be delayed).

[91] This argument is put by Farrar (1974) 38 Conv. 315, and appears in *Buckley on the Companies Acts* (14th edn. 1981), 625. It is not accepted by Goode, C.L., 774, by Pennington, 385, or by Gower, 475. The treatment in the Encyclopedia, E(1113) is somewhat ambiguous.

[92] [1979] 2 Lloyd's Rep. 142, below, para. 21.43.

6. EFFECT OF NON–REGISTRATION[93]

1. If a charge is not registered, it becomes void against the liquidator, the **21.24** administrator, or any creditor of the company.[94] This affects priorities, so that, for example, A's unregistered first legal charge would be defeated by B's second registered equitable charge.

It is uncertain what happens if both A and B fail to register. Strictly speaking, and taking a literal view of the statute, both are "creditors," and the charges of both should be void against the other, so that neither should have any priority.[95] Another view is that as between two or more unregistered charge holders the second unregistered charge holder takes priority.[96] A third view might be that their priorities between themselves should simply be determined by normal rules about notice, and the nature of the charge. This may be the fairest view, but to reach it it is necessary to read the section as if "any creditor" meant "any creditor (in liquidation) other than another unregistered creditor." Whether the courts are prepared to go so far remains undecided.

2. The unregistered charge remains effective against the company itself (*i.e.* if it is not in liquidation, and no other creditor claims priority).[97] It has been held, therefore, that if the debenture holder seizes and realises the asset in question, before liquidation begins, he may not be required by the liquidator to return the proceeds.[97a]

3. While the company is not in liquidation, (and possibly, while it is not **21.25** subject to an administrator) the holder of an unregistered charge will still rank ahead of unsecured creditors. That is to say, "creditor" in section 395 means secured creditor or execution creditor who has completed execution, but does not refer to an unsecured creditor unless the company is in liquidation (or possibly while the company is subject to the administrator).

4. The company's personal obligation or contract to repay the money remains enforceable.[98] It is, in other words, only the charge, and not the debt, which is affected.

5. The money secured by the charge becomes immediately payable, regardless of any term originally allowed.[99]

6. A purchaser (as opposed to a creditor) may perhaps be bound by an unregistered charge, since purchasers are not named in section 395.[1] Possibly, however, to the extent he has not received from the company that for which he contracted, the purchaser may be regarded as a creditor of the company, and the charge may be void against him. But unsecured creditors can only rely on section 395 if the company is in liquidation, so that unless this happens, the purchaser will be bound by the charge. This very odd position may be expected to change in the proposed reforms.

---

[93] *i.e.* non–delivery of prescribed particulars.
[94] s.395, C.A. 1985, as amended by I.A. 1986.
[95] Pennington, 430, reaches this conclusion.
[96] Goode, C.L. 777.
[97] See *Independent Automatic Sales Ltd.* v. *Knowles & Foster* [1962] 3 All E.R. 27 (company not a proper party to proceedings to have charge declared void).
[97a] *Mace Builders (Glasgow) Ltd* v. *Lunn* [1986] Ch. 459; [1986] 3 W.L.R. 921 (C.A.).
[98] s.395(2).
[99] s.395(2).
[1] Goode, C.L. 777.

F. Priorities of charges

21.26 Certain types of property (such as land) are subject to other registration requirements, and even if section 395, C.A. 1985 is complied with, and if otherwise a certain charge would have priority, that priority may be lost by reason of non-compliance with (*e.g.*) the Land Registration Act 1925. Here, we consider only general principles, and the effect of the Companies Act, and consider only tangible property.[2]

1. PRIORITIES OVER PHYSICAL PROPERTY

21.27 Charges may be of three kinds: fixed (specific) legal charges, fixed (specific) equitable charges, and (necessarily equitable) floating charges.

A fixed charge is one which, when made, immediately attaches or "fixes on" to the asset so as to change title or to act as an encumbrance. A better word would be "affixed." If the charge was by way of mortgage of goods, for example, property in the goods would pass immediately to the mortgagee. If the charge (as the statute[3] refers to either mortgages or charges) is not a mortgage but a true "charge," then the asset is immediately encumbered by it. Because the charge attaches immediately, *the right and ability of the owner to continue to deal with the asset is immediately affected*, so that a disposition or purported disposition would affect the purchaser. If no exceptions to the nemo dat rule apply, (and if the charge is not defeated by non-registration) then purchasers could not obtain good title to the property. Even if sold, the proceeds would belong to the chargeholder, and could not be used for the company's purposes.

A floating charge, on the other hand, is one which (while it creates a kind of immediate security right) creates no immediate change of title to or encumbrance upon the assets, *so that the company owner is free to continue to dispose of the assets* (maybe subject to conditions or restrictions) until certain events occur (such as the appointment of a receiver). Until those events occur, the charge does not attach to the asset (in the sense of encumbering it, or causing a change in title.) There is, nevertheless, an immediate security right, in the sense that (a) even before the charge becomes fixed, the debenture holder may apply to the court if his security is in jeopardy, for the appointment of a receiver[4] and (b) that a priority may be established between creditors, so that, for example, a first floating charge will ordinarily take priority over a later one. Here, therefore, by "attachment" we mean only that no encumbrance attaches immediately to the asset, and not that no proprietory rights (in the debenture holder) attach.

A different terminology might refer not to "fixed" and "floating" charges, but to "charges affecting subsequent dealings," and those not doing so, this being the real difference between them.

21.28 It follows that fixed charges, whether legal or equitable, rank ahead of floating charges, for the former have encumbered the asset, while the latter have not. As between fixed charges (attached encumbrances), priorities depend (a) on notice, (b) on the type of charge, (c) on registration, and (d) on other statutory rules. Registration (delivery of particulars) affects priorities by giving deemed notice of the existence of the charge and (probably) of

---

[2] For charges over debts see above, para. 21.12 *et seq.* and below, paras. 21.36, 21.43.
[3] Companies Act 1985, s.396(4).
[4] *Re Borax Co.* [1901] 1 Ch. 326.

its prescribed particulars, and (possibly) of certain of its contents,[5] and notice affects priorities. Non-registration affects priorities by rendering the charge void against the liquidator (and unsecured creditors in the liquidation) and the administrator, and thus defeats priorities otherwise established.[6] An example of "another statutory rule" is that applying to charges created as floating charges, which in insolvency not only rank behind previously attaching charges, but also behind preferential creditors.[7]

As to the type of charge, the established common law rule is that as between attached charges of the same kind (e.g. legal charge v. legal charge) the first in time prevails, and as between attached charges of different kinds (i.e. legal v. equitable), a legal charge will prevail over the equitable charge. This is the case even if the legal charge attaches after the equitable charge, provided that the legal charge is taken bona fide, for value and without notice of the prior equitable charge.

Registration, however, gives notice of prior charges, so that if all charges are registered, and registration in each case occurs before the next charge is created, then there cannot be a purchaser "without notice" and even a prior equitable fixed charge will prevail over a subsequent legal charge. But the bona fide purchaser rule could still operate if the charges are both created before the prior equitable one is registered, because notice is given only on delivery of particulars, and cannot work backwards. Since, however, a floating charge is designed for the very purpose of not preventing dealings with the assets to which it applies, then mere knowledge (actual, or by registration) of the existence of a floating charge does not prevent a subsequent sale, charge or other disposition of the asset, and a subsequent fixed chargeholder (whether equitable or legal) would take priority over a prior floating charge.

2. PRIORITIES IN RELATION TO FUTURE PROPERTY

An agreement to give security over future property is not recognised at law **21.29** as creating a security interest, but only as a contract between the parties. It was, however, recognised in equity.[8] Thus, although there is no property to which anything can have attached, a present security right is created. The significance of this is first, that if a subsequent creditor[9] takes a similar agreement from the same debtor, then if an asset comes into existence the first creditor would take priority. Secondly, the security interest automatically attaches to property later acquired, without new value being given, and even after the commencement of bankruptcy.[10] The security right is deemed to exist earlier than acquisition, so that no new value is needed, and so that the onset of bankruptcy does not defeat it.[11]

---

[5] Above, para. 21.23.
[6] This is the effect of s.395, C.A. 1985.
[7] s.175, I.A. 1986 (replacing s.614, C.A. 1985), and s.196, C.A. 1985. See further below, Chap. 28.
[8] See *Holroyd* v. *Marshall* (1862) 10 H.L.Cas. 191.
[9] Not being a purchase-money creditor.
[10] *Re Lind* [1915] 2 Ch. 345; *Re Reis* [1904] 2 K.B. 769. These cases are discussed by Goode, L.P.C.S. 7–8. See also, Matthews [1981] 2 L.M.C.L.Q. 40, and Goode (1980) 1 Co.Law 123, 125–126.
[11] But the transaction may in some circumstances be a void preference, under the I.A. 1986: below, para. 28.90 *et seq.*

3. PRIORITIES BETWEEN A CHARGEHOLDER AND A SUBSEQUENT PURCHASE–MONEY FINANCIER

21.30   As just described, ordinarily A's prior charge over future property would defeat B's later charge, and A would certainly obtain priority over a later chargeholder who is not supplying purchase money. Nevertheless, if the debtor borrows money from B to finance the purchase of the asset, and gives B security over the asset, it is right that B should have priority, and sometimes equity achieves this result, depending on how B takes his security. If the debtor acquires the asset, and later gives security to B, A's charge will take priority, for where there has been a moment of time in which the debtor has the unencumbered asset, A's charge will attach to it, and C's charge can only attach subsequently, thus giving A priority.[12] But if the agreement to give B security is made before the debtor agrees to buy the asset, B's security rights will attach to the asset when the debtor acquires his rights in it, and will have priority over A's charge.[13]

4. FIXED AND FLOATING CHARGES

21.31   A floating charge is a present security right over existing or future property under which, until certain events occur, no encumbrance attaches to the assets in question, so that the debtor may meanwhile continue to deal with them. The document creating the charge is generally worded so as to apply to all of a company's assets and its whole undertaking (*i.e.* its whole business, and goodwill), but specific assets are often additionally identified as the subject of a fixed charge. The floating charge could apply to a single asset, or to a single class of assets. It can apply to land, goods, or choses in action, and to all three simultaneously. In *Re Yorkshire Woolcombers Association*[13a] Romer L.J. said that floating charges had the following characteristics: "(1) If it is charge on a class of assets of a company present and future. (2) If that class is one which in the ordinary course of the business of the company would be changing from time to time; and (3) If you find that by the charge it is contemplated that, until some future step is taken by or on behalf of those interested in the charge, the company may carry·on its business in the ordinary way so far as concerns the particular class of assets I am dealing with."[14] It seems that only the last of these three characteristics is necessary, so that, for example, if the assets which are covered are only existing assets, or are not to be renewed on sale, it is still a floating charge.[15]

---

[12] *Church of England Building Society* v. *Piskor* [1954] 1 Ch. 553. See Goode, L.P.C.S. pp. 55–57, for criticism.

[13] See *Wilson* v. *Kelland* [1910] 2 Ch. 306; *Re Connolly Bros. Ltd. (No. 2)* [1912] 2 Ch. 25; *Security Trust Co.* v. *The Royal Bank of Canada* [1976] A.C. 503.

[13a] [1903] 2 Ch. 284, 295, (aff'd sub. nom: *Illingworth* v. *Houldsworth* [1904] A.C. 355).

[14] See also *Evans* v. *Rival Granite Quarries Ltd.* [1910] 2 K.B. 979, *per* Buckley L.J. at 999—it "is not a future security; it is a present security, which presently affects all the assets of the company . . . not a specific mortgage of the assets, plus a licence to the mortgagor to dispose of them . . . but a floating mortgage applying to every item . . . but not specifically affecting any item until some act or some act or event occurs or some act on the part of the mortgagee is done which causes it to crystallise into a fixed security." See also *Government Stock and Other Securities Investment Co.* v. *Manila Ry. Co.* [1897] A.C. 81, 86; *Illingworth* v. *Houldsworth* [1904] A.C. 355, 358; *Driver* v. *Broad* [1893] 1 Q.B. 744, 748; *Hubbuck* v. *Helms* (1887) 56 L.J.Ch. 536, 537.

[15] *Re Bond Worth Ltd.* [1979] 3 All E.R. 919 [1980] Ch. 228 (assets to be sold and proceeds payable to chargeholder).

The purpose of the floating charge is to enable the company to continue **21.32** to deal with the unencumbered asset, and to give good title to a purchaser, without requiring any formalities in "discharging" the charge, while permitting the charge to crystallize (attach as an encumbrance) when specified events occur, so that the debenture holder may resist the claims of liquidators or other creditors,[16] or may enforce the then fixed charge against the debtor company by the appointment of a receiver (under the terms of it, usually, but by the court's inherent power, if not). The form usually taken permits the chargeholder to appoint a receiver and manager to manage the whole undertaking, instead of selling specific assets. This is more likely to enable the sale of the business as a going concern, with a consequently better price. We have seen that only companies may create floating charges, so that this possibility is a substantial business advantage which companies (as opposed to individual traders, or partnerships) alone enjoy. A further advantage may be that a creditor with a floating charge covering substantially the whole of the company's assets may block the appointment of an administrator.[17] If, however, an administrator is appointed, he requires the court's authorisation to dispose of an asset subject to a fixed charge, but (since the floating chargeholder has consented to the administration) needs no such consent in the case of a floating charge. Finally,[18] whereas assets covered by an individual's charges must be "specifically described" according to the forms of the Bills of Sale Acts 1878–91, this is not required for company charges, so that "all our business and assets" is sufficient.[19]

Notwithstanding the undoubted benefits of floating charges, fixed charges are preferrable if the asset is valuable, easily identifiable and not subject to regular change or turnover. Fixed charges will (a) bind those with notice, which may be given by registration, and this prevents unauthorised dispositions of the assets, (b) generally have priority over floating charges,[20] (c) not be subject to the rights of preferential creditors[21] (d) not be void in liquidation under the "12 months[22] rule" discussed below.[23] In addition, all floating charges require registration, while some fixed charges may not.[24]

The ideal combination, therefore, is a fixed charge over all appropriate assets, and a floating charge over all assets for the time being, and the company's whole undertaking and business.

5. EFFECT OF NEGATIVE PLEDGE CLAUSES

A "negative pledge" is a contractual restriction in the charge aimed at pre- **21.33** venting the debtor from creating subsequent charges, or subsequent charges with priority over this charge. Since floating charges do not create an encumbrance, and leave a company apparent authority to deal with the

---

[16] For execution creditors, see below, para. 21.37.
[17] Below, Chap. 23.
[18] This applies to fixed or floating charges.
[19] Listing all assets otherwise might be impossible or at least extraordinarily time-consuming. It is this difficulty, together with the fact that an individual cannot effectively charge future goods, that makes an individual's floating charges impossible. Reputed ownership was also a factor, though that doctrine is abolished by I.A. 1986.
[20] Above, para. 21.28.
[21] Below, para. 21.35.
[22] Two years for persons connected with the company.
[23] Below, para. 21.38.
[24] Above, paras. 21.10–21.11 e.g. a charge over a debt which is not a book debt, or over stocks and shares.

asset, it seems that a negative pledge clause can only be a contractual restriction, not creating security right in the asset, and not binding a purchaser without notice of it. It may be, however, that negative pledge clauses are now so common that if details are filed with the registrar of companies so that an inspection would reveal them, a person who does not investigate would be held to have constructive notice, and would not be able to rely upon apparent authority.[25] Even so, if the clause does not create proprietary rights in the chargeholder, the company remains full owner of the asset, and has power to dispose of it, and at most the effect of a clause on a subsequent chargeholder would be to make him liable in taking the charge for the tort of "inducing breach of contract."[26]

6. EVENTS OF CRYSTALLIZATION

21.34   A floating charge may be made to attach as an encumbrance (or "crystallize") by the following events (all of which in some way reflect the termination of the company's right or ability to manage the assets in question):

(i) if winding up commences, whether in a compulsory[27] or voluntary[28] winding up,

(ii) if a receiver is appointed out of court[29] or the creditor takes possession of the assets subject to the charge,[30]

(iii) if the chargeor ceases to carry on business[31] or disposes of the whole of its undertaking or assets with a view to the cessation of trading.[32]

21.35   In these cases the charge crystallizes as a matter of law. It is now established that other contractual provisions may cause the charge to crystallize—say, by the giving of a notice, or even "automatically" as by failure to repay money on demand.[33] Since this may occur before the events discussed above, where crystallization occurs by reason of the general law, it may be called "pre-crystallization."[34] An advantage of pre-crystallization was previously that if the charge became fixed before the appointment of a receiver, or the commencement of winding up, then as a fixed charge it took priority over preferential creditors. But now, preferential creditors take priority over any charge which "as created" was a floating charge,[35] so that causing the charge to crystallize early cannot secure priority for the debenture holder over preferential creditors.

Pre-crystallization may still secure priority over (*e.g.*) a later fixed charge, but difficult questions of priority may then arise.[36] A particular problem arose in *Re Woodroffes (Musical Instruments) Ltd.*,[37] where the first charge (1) was a fixed and floating charge in favour of a bank. The second charge (2) was a fixed and floating charge in favour of W, though this was expressly

[25] Above, para. 21.23.
[26] The extent of which is doubtful.
[27] *Re Colonial Trusts Corpn. ex p. Bradshaw* (1879) 15 Ch. D. 465, 472.
[28] In *Re Roundwood Colliery Co.* [1897] 1 Ch. 373.
[29] *Evans* v. *Rival Granite Quarries* [1910] 2 K.B. 979.
[30] *Re Hamilton's Windsor Ironworks, ex p. Pitman & Edwards* (1879) 12 Ch. D. 707, 710.
[31] *Re Woodroffes (Musical Instruments) Ltd.* [1986] Ch. 366.
[32] *Hubbuck* v. *Helms* (1887) 56 L.J.Ch. 536.
[33] *Re Woodroffes (Musical Instruments) Ltd.* [1986] Ch. 366; *Re Brightlife Ltd.* [1987] 2 W.L.R. 197.
[34] See Goode, L.P.C.S., pp. 35–40.
[35] ss.175 and 251, I.A. 1986.
[36] Goode, L.P.C.S. 36–38, Gilmore (1961) 71 Yale L.J. 53, Gough, Company Charges (1978), Loo (1986) L.M. & C.L.Q. 519.
[37] *Re Woodroffes*, above n. 33.

declared to be subject to (1). There was a provision for (2) to become fixed by the giving of notice to the company, and this was given, causing (2) to crystallize before (1). Preferential creditors were also involved, and the court held that as between (1) and (2) and the preferential creditors, the priority was charge (1) (to the extent of W's interest under (2)), then the preferential creditors, then (1) to the balance of the bank's claim, then (2). "The reason for this rather odd result is that the bank, although a floating chargee, ranks prior to [W] who, as a fixed chargee, ranks prior to the preferential creditors."[37a] At first sight it appears that a mere contractual provision agreed between debenture holders (1) and (2) caused (2) to "leapfrog" over the preferential creditors. But the case is best understood[38] as a situation where the floating chargeholder is in fact subrogated to the position of the fixed chargeholder, so that the former collects from the liquidator in right of the latter the amount due to the latter. Thus, the floating charge does not truly leapfrog over the preferential creditors, but claims in the right of the fixed chargeholder and only to the same extent. In any case, W would not now rank ahead of the preferential creditors, so the order would be the preferential creditors, then (1), and (2). Problems may still arise where preferential creditors are not involved.

7. PRIORITIES IN RELATION TO FLOATING CHARGES OVER BOOK DEBTS

21.36

Normally, priorities over choses in action are determined by the rule in *Dearle* v. *Hall*,[39] which is to say, by the order in which notice is given to the debtor. But that rule cannot apply to floating charges over book debts, "for the floating charge, having impliedly authorised the subsequent fixed charge, cannot jump ahead by being the first to give notice to the debtor after the charge has crystallized."[40] (Nevertheless, the debtor would be entitled to a good discharge if he paid the first legal assignee to give notice.)

8. OTHER PRIORITY QUESTIONS OF FLOATING CHARGES

21.37

An execution creditor is bound by a charge if it crystallizes before he completes his execution, by seizure and sale of the assets.[41] A landlord, however, may levy distress for rent regardless of whether the charge has attached or not.

A subsequent floating charge will not have priority over an earlier floating charge relating to the same assets, even if the later charge attaches first and even if the earlier debenture expressly allows the company to create later charges.[42]

Rights of set-off between the company and a third party debtor may continue to accrue, and will affect a floating charge covering the debts in question, even if the third party knows of the charge.[43] Probably even an

---

[37a] *Ibid.*, at p. 375.
[38] Goode, L.P.C.S. 55.
[39] (1828) 3 Russ. 1.
[40] Goode, L.P.C.S., p. 43, citing *Ward* v. *Royal Exchange Shipping Co. Ltd.* (1887) 58 L.T. 174; *Re Ind Coope & Co. Ltd.* [1911] 2 Ch. 223.
[41] *Re Standard Manufacturing Co.* [1891] 1 Ch. 627; *Re Opera Ltd.* [1891] 3 Ch. 260.
[42] *Re Benjamin Cope & Sons Ltd.* [1914] 1 Ch. 800; *Re Automatic Bottle Makers Ltd.* [1926] Ch. 412; *Re Household Products Co. Ltd.* (1981) 124 D.L.R. (3d.) 325. It would be different if the earlier charge allowed later charges "with priority."
[43] See *Biggerstaff* v. *Rowatt's Wharf Ltd.* [1896] 2 Ch. 93; *Rother Iron Works Ltd.* v. *Canterbury Precision Engineers Ltd.* [1974] Q.B. 1.

(unknown) early crystallization would not affect the matter, since the company would still have apparent authority to deal with the debtor.

Rights of lien arising before crystallization may also be asserted against the floating charge, and if someone contracts for possession of assets for a purpose which may give rise to a lien, the relevant priority date is the date of the contract, not (if later) the date at which possession is actually taken.[44]

The effect of Romalpa (or retentions) clauses is considered elsewhere.[45]

9. THE "TWELVE MONTHS" RULE, AND FLOATING CHARGES

21.38   Section 245 of the Insolvency Act 1986,[46] provides that where a company creates a floating charge at a time when it is unable to pay its debts (or becomes unable to pay its debts as a result of the transaction creating the charge, because, for instance, it is deprived of valuable assets), then the charge, if made within 12 months of the commencement of the liquidation, may be invalid. In the case of a person connected with the company[47] the period is two years, and the charge may be invalid even if the company is able to pay its debts. Charges made after the presentation of a petition for an administration order are also affected in the same way. The charges are declared by section 245(2) to be invalid:

> "except to the extent of the aggregate of—(a) the value of so much of the consideration for the creation of the charge as consists of money paid, or goods or services supplied, to the company at the same time as, or after, the creation of the charge; (b) the value of so much of that consideration as consists of the discharge or reduction, at the same time as, or after, the creation of the charge, of any debt of the company; and (c) the amount of such interest (if any) as is payable on the amount falling within paragraph (a) or (b) above in pursuance of any agreement under which the money was so paid, the goods or services were so supplied or the debt was so discharged or reduced."

In some cases, section 245 must be considered together with provisions in section 239 concerning preferences. These are considered fully below,[47a] but the period is two years for connected persons or six months for others, and the section also applies where a company is unable to pay its debts. For example, supposing that a bank is not "connected" then in the six months before liquidation, both sections might apply, and if the bank does not contravene one section, it may contravene the other. Certainly, section 245 does not apply to fixed charges, while section 239 clearly could apply to fixed charges, and, it is thought, to floating charges also.

21.39   The apparent aim of section 245 is to prevent dominant creditors from obtaining an unfair advantage over others by insisting on a floating charge at a time when they know or suspect that the company is in financial difficulties. Only the charge is invalid: the debt is unaffected, and the creditor may claim as an unsecured creditor. A charge may be partially saved, for it

---

[44] *George Barker (Transport) Ltd.* v. *Eynon* [1974] 1 All E.R. 900.
[45] Below, Chap. 22.
[46] Replacing s.617, C.A. 1985, formerly s.322, C.A. 1948, both of which had a single 12-month limit.
[47] *i.e.* a director, shadow director, associate of one of these, or an associate of the company. A shadow director (s.251) is one in accordance with whose directions the company is accustomed to act, and it is not inconceivable that this may in some circumstances seek to a bank, if it is in the position of dominant creditor.
[47a] para. 28.90 *et seq.*

is invalid "except to the extent" specified in the three paragraphs. There is no objection to a charge if the company was solvent at the time,[48] or if the charge is for a genuine consideration. Previous provisions[49] saved only charges given for cash paid to the company. Now, paragraph (a) relates not only to money paid, but also to goods or services. Paragraph (b) is also new, and applies to any consideration which reduces the company's debts. Thus, if a bank paid a creditor of the company directly, instead of paying to the company, this would be protected. Similarly, if a guarantor paid money to a bank to discharge a debt owed by the company, and the guarantor is given a charge, this is now saved, though previously it was not, even if made pursuant to a previous agreement.[50] Paragraph (c) is also new, and enables the security to extend to amounts of interest payable on money, etc., advanced and so on.[51]

If, when money is advanced, an unconditional promise is given to give security at some time in the future, the security is treated as having been created when the original contract of loan was made, and time runs from then.[52] But if the agreement is conditional—e.g. to give security if called on to do so, or when called on to honour a guarantee—the charge is created when later executed and time runs from then.[53]

If the terms of a charge cover later loans, the bank may make loans thereafter which will have the benefit of the security, even though the bank is under no obligation to make the loans.[54]

If a creditor attempts to avoid the rule by entering into a paper transaction purporting to advance money to the company, secured by a charge, on the understanding that the "new" loan would immediately be used to pay off the old debt of the same amount, this was previously invalid, the consideration being past, and the courts looking past the sham transaction.[55] An example is *Re G. T. Whyte & Co. Ltd.*[56] The bank made an advance to the company, using the agency of a bank subsidiary to make payment and take security. Later, the subsidiary called in the advance, and the bank provided a replacement advance, of a fixed amount, not accounted for in an active current account, and securing this with a floating charge. Ten months later, the company was wound up, and the liquidator challenged the charge. The bank claimed to have advanced fresh money at the time of the charge, but the court held that having regard to the way the loans had been arranged between the bank and its subsidiary, the two loans could not be regarded as being made by separate entities. Thus, the bank was treated as having entered a paper transaction to substitute its own "old" debt with apparently "new" debt, and the charge was held to be void. It depends, however, on whether the transaction was in any sense genuine or not. In *Re Mathew Ellis*

21.40

---

[48] "Unable to pay its debts"—this has the meaning in s.123 (below, para. 28.11).
[49] Above, n. 46.
[50] See *Re Orleans Motor Co. Ltd.* [1911] 2 Ch. 41.
[51] Previously, interest was fixed at 5 per cent. or such other amount prescribed by statutory instrument.
[52] *Re Columbian Fireproofing Co. Ltd.* [1910] 2 Ch. 120; *Re F. and E. Stanton Ltd.* [1929] 1 Ch. 180.
[53] *Re Gregory Love & Co,* [1916] 1 Ch. 203.
[54] *Re Yeovil Glove Co. Ltd.* [1965] Ch. 148.
[55] See *e.g. Re Destone Fabrics Ltd.* [1941] 1 All E.R. 545, [1941] Ch. 319.
[56] (1982) F.T. December 14, 1982, [1983] B.C.L.C. 311.

Ltd.[57] a company owed about £2000 to X, and X advanced £3000 to the company in return for a security. £2000 was to be repaid to X so as to discharge the old debt, and the balance of the money went in cash to the company. This security was held to be enforceable by X. The company had some prospect of succeeding, and to do so it needed goods. X was the only firm which would provide it with goods on credit, and the court took the view that if X did so, it was right that he should be secured. The transaction, therefore, was "genuine," inasmuch as it was a real attempt to keep the company in business, and it was not only to protect a desperate creditor.

21.41 It may be, however, that the new provisions allow creditors to take valid charges to the extent of consideration which "consists of the discharge or reduction . . . of any debt." If section 245(2)(*b*) is taken at face value, this is now allowed, though this seems strange. It is thought that the provision is probably meant to refer only to cases, for example, where a bank pays off debts of the company owed to third parties. This argument is reinforced by the word "consideration," for past consideration is not good consideration, and if a creditor takes a charge for his own past debt there is no consideration. If, however, he pays off a third party's debt for the company, in return for a charge, he provides consideration. If this is incorrect, and banks can take valid floating charges for past consideration, it may very well be that charges taken within six months of liquidation amount to either a transaction at an undervalue, or a preference within section 239.

21.42 In any case, banks enjoy a singular advantage, which flows from the effect upon current accounts of the rule in *Clayton's case*, by virtue of which the normal operation of a current account will cause the gradual elimination of "old" debt in the account, even though the total amount of debt remains constant, or even reduces. The subsequent withdrawals are then seen as "new" debt, representing money advanced to the company after the creation of the charge, even though total indebtedness remains constant and the company is required to pay in before it may draw out.[58]

Goods and services supplied cannot be valued at an exorbitant price, but are valued at a reasonable market price.[59]

It has been held that if a creditor realises his security before liquidation, he cannot be forced to repay, because the underlying debt is not affected, and the payment to the creditor discharges the company's liability.[60] It seems that the reason for this is that the charge was only invalid "where a company is being wound up. . . . " Until that time, the charge was valid. There is now, however, no such limitation upon the operation of section 245 and if the charge is invalid, the debentureholder (or his receiver) is not the company's agent, and he should be liable in conversion for wrongly handling the property of the company (the company could refuse to recognise his authority, and prevent the sale). In addition, if there is no charge, it can hardly "crystallize," and even those subsequent chargees who know of a so-called crystallization would take priority, so that it would seem that the creditor wrongs those chargees, as well as the company.

---

[57] [1933] Ch. 458.
[58] *Re Yeovil Glove Co. Ltd.* [1965] Ch. 148, in relation to s.322, C.A. 1948. See also *Re Thomas Mortimer Ltd.* (1925) 4 L.D.B. 3.
[59] s.245(6).
[60] *Re Parkes Garage (Swadlincote) Ltd.* [1929] 1 Ch. 139; *Mace Builders (Glasgow) Ltd.* v. *Lunn* (C.A.), above, n. 97ª.

10. FIXED CHARGES OVER FUTURE BOOK DEBTS

The advantage of a fixed charge is that it takes priority over floating **21.43** charges, over later fixed charges, and particularly, that in winding-up, it takes priority over the preferential creditors. This is all the more important now that pre-crystallization gives charges created as floating charges no priority over preferential creditors. Until 1978, however, some doubt existed as to whether it was possible to word a charge so that it creates a fixed charge over future book debts when they come into existence. There seems to be no objection in principle to allowing the charge to become fixed at that time, by a contractual provision (as opposed to an event such as liquidation, crystallizing the charge). If pre-crystallization is possible, there is no reason to prohibit charges of this sort. This is now reasonably well established.

The essential point about an effective charge, is not that it refers to a "fixed" charge, for whether a charge is fixed or floating is a matter of substance, not of descriptive words. A floating charge allows the company liberty to deal with the asset, which is unencumbered. A fixed charge encumbers the asset, and the company has no free right to deal with it except with the creditor's consent. One looks to this matter of substance, not the descriptive words of the charge.

In *Siebe Gorman & Co. Ltd.* v. *Barclays Bank Ltd.*[61] the defendant bank **21.44** took a debenture which charged to it by way of first fixed charge all book debts and other debts then and from time to time due or owing to the company. The company agreed further to pay all monies received in respect of such debts into the company's account with the bank, and not to assign or charge the same to any other person unless the bank gave its written consent. Amongst the debts affected by the debenture were some bills of exchange held by the bank (which were held for the purpose of the debenture to be or represent "book" debts). These bills, held by the bank, were later assigned outright (by way of sale so that registration was not needed) by the company to the plaintiffs, so as to discharge part of a debt owed by the company to the plaintiffs. The defendant bank collected the bills, and claimed to be entitled to retain the proceeds against the plaintiffs. One of many issues was whether the charge was a floating charge, for if it was, the company had the power to dispose of the assets to the plaintiffs. Slade J. held that the charge was truly a fixed charge on the ground that the restrictions on assignment, and the requirement to pay to the bank alone removed the essential element of a floating charge (the debtor's freedom to dispose of the asset as he chose). However, the bank had misled the plaintiff as to the bank's rights, and he had no notice of the real nature of the charge. Registration merely gave notice of the existence of a charge, and not of its contents. There could be no constructive notice, because the plaintiffs would not have expected unusual terms such as these.[62] The plaintiff's assignment, therefore, took priority over the bank's fixed charge.[63] This decision is supported by other authority, and seems correct in principle.[64] In *Re*

[61] [1979] 2 Lloyd's Rep. 142.
[62] This may be different now: above, para. 21.23.
[63] The bank could assert a prior legal lien, which was effective against the later legal title of the plaintiff: but the account had been continued, and the passing of funds through it had caused the original debt to be almost completely discharged by virtue of *Clayton's case*.
[64] See also *Evans Coleman & Evans Ltd.* v. *R. A. Nelson Construction Ltd.* (1959) 16 D.L.R. (2d.) 123; *Re Keenan* (1986) (N.I., C.A.); *Re Brightlife* [1987] 2 W.L.R. 197.

Brightlife,[65] the *Siebe Gorman* case was distinguished, in a case where a non-bank creditor had left the company free to pay the receipts into its own bank account, where they would be at the company's free disposal. A non-bank creditor should arrange for payment of the debts to the creditor or his nominee or bank, or at least prohibit use of funds paid into the company's bank account. A bank creditor need only prohibit assignments, etc., and arrange for payment to the bank, and prohibit withdrawals without its consent.[66]

11. WAIVER OF SECURITY INTERESTS

21.45   A bank may ask a secured creditor to waive his security rights in the bank's favour as a condition of making further advances to the company, or the bank may be asked to waive its rights. Alternatively, the secured creditor may enter into a subordination agreement. Where a floating charge is involved, the bank may not be willing to give a waiver, but may be prepared to give a certificate that nothing has happened which as yet has caused the charge to crystallize. If a certificate of non-crystallization is given, then it should be expressed not as an absolute statement, but as a statement of the bank's non-awareness of any crystallizing event.

If a waiver is given, then it is revocable by reasonable notice unless it is under seal, for valuable consideration, or unless the party to whom it is given relies on it so that it would be inequitable for the party giving it to retract it (this is the doctrine of estoppel).[67] Thus, once the other party has advanced money on the strength of the waiver, retraction would be impossible in relation to any transactions covered by the waiver. If a secured lender were to waive his rights, and later to assign the debt and security to another, that other would be bound by the waiver, because the assignee's rights can be no greater than those of the assignor—he takes "subject to equities."[68]

A subordination agreement is like a waiver, except that the two parties merely agree to swap priorities.[69] We have observed a particular problem of priorities that may arise where a fixed chargee agrees to subordinate himself to a floating chargee, and where there are preferential creditors in a liquidation.[70]

G. Assignment of securities

21.46   A security being a property right it may be assigned to another, and the normal rules applying to assignments apply.[71] Bank forms usually make this clear by expressly providing that the debenture enures for the benefit of the Bank's successors and assigns. Where a customer changes banks, assignment by the former bank to another is rare, and the usual procedure is for the company's new bank to arrange for discharge of the old debenture and to take and register a new debenture.

---

[65] Previous note.
[66] As in *Re Keenan*, above, n. 64.
[67] See Treitel, *The Law of Contract*, (5th ed.), pp. 81 *et seq.*
[68] Goode, L.P.C.S., p. 53, noting that it may be different in the case of land.
[69] Goode, L.P.C.S., p. 54.
[70] Above, para. 21.35.
[71] *e.g.* under s.136 L.P.A. 1925, for choses in action.

H. Discharge of securities

A security interest is terminated if the customer ceases to be indebted in any **21.47** way to the bank, and the customer may demand that the security be vacated. If an overdraft was secured, the original debt (which is alone secured) might be discharged by the operation of *Clayton's case*,[72] but this is avoided with "all monies" debentures which cover all debts from time to time in the account. If it is agreed, the bank may retain the security for contingent liabilities. In *Re Rudd & Son Ltd.*,[73] a bank's forms said that it would surrender the mortgages if the companies repaid sums "which shall for the time being be owing to the bank" (these words suggest an accrued debt). However, it went on to refer to the liabilities in question as "including" a number of matters, which included contingent liabilities. On the liquidation of the companies, the bank refused to vacate the mortgages, on the ground of the contingent liabilities under a performance bond, and were held to be justified in so doing, notwithstanding the unfortunate wording of the debentures.

When the security interest is terminated, (on the customer ceasing to be **21.48** indebted) the bank may (if legal title had been transferred to it) still hold legal title to an asset, though it would hold this on trust for the customer, until retransfer. With a mortgage of registered shares, for example, the shares would require to be re-transferred to the mortgagor, and until then the legal rights would remain with the mortgagee.[74] With a mortgage of registered land, the entry on the land register would require to be corrected, and until then the mortgagee would retain his legal charge (or lease, if the mortgage is made that way). If the security is registered at the companies register, the entry may be removed if the company makes a statutory declaration in the prescribed form to the registrar, who will enter a memorandum of satisfaction on the register.[75] We have just seen that where this was agreed the bank may refuse to vacate its legal title to an asset or its legal lease or charge over land,[76] even for unaccrued liabilities, so that its security interest would exist even against a subsequent purchaser.

---

[72] Above, para. 13.24.

[73] In *Re Rudd & Son Ltd.*, *in Re Fosters & Rudd Ltd. The Times*, January 22, 1986, [1986] 2 C.L. 333.

[74] And the company is not rquired to take notice of any trust—s.360, C.A. 1985, and see s.211(4).

[75] s.403, C.A. 1985.

[76] Or with an equitable interest, it might refuse to agree to the removal of a caution on the register.

22. Reservation of Title Clauses

A. Introduction

22.01 It has become common in recent years for sellers of goods to sell them on terms that property in the goods will not pass to the buyer until the price is paid, and that if the goods are sold, the proceeds will belong to the original seller. The aim has been to avoid the more complicated procedure involved in taking, and registering a charge,[1] for the seller asserts not a security right, but ownership. He has not given property to the buyer (so that the latter does not "return" to the seller a registerable charge) but retains it in himself. Such clauses have not previously been used for individual traders, because (a) an individual's charges over specific book debts are not registerable,[2] and (b) in any case the doctrine of reputed ownership in bankruptcy[3] prevented a retentions clause from operating effectively. Now, however, the Insolvency Act 1986 has abolished the doctrine of reputed ownership, and it may well be the case that retentions clauses will become more common with individuals, for even though an individual's charge over receivables from a sale needs no registration, a charge over the original goods does require registration as a Bill of Sale, and for technical reasons this is often impracticable. A retentions clause would protect the seller in case of the bankruptcy of the individual while he still has the goods. Retentions clauses have had a chequered history: the courts have been loathe to deny ordinary principles of law, but have tended to regard such clauses with disfavour. In the first place, they act as an "invisible" type of security, since they are not registerable as charges, and this may be regarded as an unfair advantage against which others cannot protect themselves, and in the second place, difficult questions about part-payments by the buyer, and windfall profits from capital appreciation of the goods, or from mixing with other goods, have had to be dealt with.

The efficacy of retentions clauses was considered in *Aluminium Industrie Vaassen B.V.* v. *Romalpa Aluminium Ltd*[4] (generally called "the *Romalpa* case," and from which retentions clauses have acquired the title "Romalpa clauses"). The clause here provided that legal ownership remained in the seller until payment in full; that the product of the goods were held by the buyers as "fiduciary owners" (bailees) and should be stored separately from other stock on the supplier's behalf as "surety" for the remainder of the price; and that the products might be sold by the buyers as agent for the original sellers. On the buyer's insolvency, it was held that the plaintiff seller could assert ownership of goods (unmixed with other goods, as it happened) in the buyer's hands at that time, against the receiver. A fiduciary relationship existed because the buyer was bailee and agent, and this entitled

---

[1] Under s.395, C.A. 1985.
[2] Though a general assignment of book debts is registerable.
[3] s.38, Bankruptcy Act 1914, by which goods apparently belonging to the debtor are part of his divisible property.
[4] [1976] 1 W.L.R. 676.

368

the plaintiff to trace.[4a] The court was prepared to imply a term that the proceeds of sale belonged to the original seller.

Since the *Romalpa* case it has been held that if a clause refers to "equitable and beneficial" ownership remaining with the seller, this implies that legal title passes to the buyer, and the agreement therefore constitutes a registerable charge.[5]   **22.02**

It is necessary to consider the position relating to (a) the original goods, if they remain identifiable, (b) new or "mixed" goods, made from the goods in question, and other goods, which may have been the property of the buyer, or some other seller, and (c) the proceeds of sale of the original goods, or of the mixed goods.

B. Original goods

It appears from the *Romalpa* case itself that the easiest case relates to the original identifiable goods. If a seller provides goods to the buyer, and retains title, his legal title may remain so long as the goods supplied remain identifiable, so that he may trace at law into the goods or proceeds (while the latter are also identifiable). Indeed, it would seem that if he can show that he is still owner, he need not bother with tracing at all, and may simply assert against the liquidator or receiver that he is the owner of the goods, and the ordinary personal actions (*e.g.* for conversion) are available to him. In the *Romalpa* case, however, the receiver had sold the original goods, and had the proceeds of sale in a mixed fund, to which there were other claimants. Nevertheless, it is submitted that the plaintiff might simply have brought a personal action against the receiver, for wrongly converting the plaintiff's goods.[6]   **22.03**

After *Romalpa* itself, the leading case is now *Clough Mill Ltd.* v. *Martin*[7] where the plaintiffs supplied yarn, to be used in the manufacture of fabrics. The risk was to pass on delivery, but ownership was to remain with the seller. If payment was overdue, re-possession was permitted. Payment became due if any act or proceedings was taken in relation to the buyer's solvency. If the yarn was incorporated into any other property, this became the original seller's property also, and all his rights extended to such a product. The company's receiver claimed that this was a charge, void against him for non-registration. The plaintiffs sought damages, but lost at trial. On appeal the argument was only about the original goods (which remained identifiable) though there are *obiter* dicta concerning "new" goods, manufactured from a mixing of the original goods with others. As to the original goods, it was held that title was in, and remained in, the sellers, so that the buyers never had property over which they could confer a charge, and the plaintiffs were entitled to damages. This is a comprehensible proposition: if the "buyer" never had property, he cannot give a charge to the "seller" who retains full property in the goods.

Arguments were put to the court as to the intentions of the parties in relation to their respective rights concerning part-payments already made by the buyer, and as to capital appreciation of the goods. In relation to the orig-

---

[4a] *i.e.* to apply for a tracing order to follow his property into the proceeds of sale, and to claim the latter.
[5] *Re Bond Worth* [1979] 3 All E.R. 919, [1980] Ch. 228.
[6] Lack of space has prevented a full treatment of tracing: see, *e.g.* Hanbury and Maudsley, *Modern Equity* (12th ed., 1985), pp. 630–652).
[7] [1985] 1 W.L.R. 111.

inal goods, the court held that if on breach by the buyer the seller seized the goods, and sold them while the contract *subsisted* (*i.e.* if the buyer's repudiatory breach was not accepted by the seller), the intention of the parties under the still-governing terms of the contract was (a) that he could sell only enough to discharge the balance of the price still owing from the original buyer, and (b) that if he sold more, the proceeds belonged to the original buyer. But if the sale took place when the original contract had been *terminated* (*i.e.* discharged for breach) then the seller sold his own goods free of any implied contractual restraints, and could keep any profit. He must, however, repay the buyer for any part of the purchase price already paid. Further, though this agreement did not do so, an agreement might specify that the seller could keep legal title as trustee for the buyer, so that any balance received by the seller on resale belonged to the buyer, after discharging his liability for the price.

C. Mixed goods

22.04   But frequently, goods will be supplied so that they can be mixed with other goods, and the original product loses its identity. In this case, the contract may provide that legal ownership of the mixed goods passes directly to the original seller, or it may provide merely that he has a proprietary right of an equitable sort (so that in effect, he would seek to trace on bankruptcy of the buyer). An essential element of tracing in equity is some fiduciary element.

In *Borden (U.K.) Ltd.* v. *Scottish Timber Products Ltd.*[8] the original goods became mixed with other goods, and it was held that they ceased to be identifiable. There was no provision for separate storage of the mixed product, or provision for ownership in the mixed product remaining with the original seller.[9] The retentions clause failed.

In *Clough Mill Ltd.* v. *Martin* the product of the original goods and other goods was not in question, but the court considered the matter, *obiter*. The first question was whether an agreement that title in mixed or new goods should pass directly to the seller necessarily amounted to a charge. The title to the original goods could not remain in the seller once the identity of those goods were destroyed, and title to the mixed goods must vest in someone. In the normal course of events, title would vest in the buyer. The Court held, however, that an agreement that the title to the new goods should vest directly in the seller did not amount to a charge. If the buyer never owned the new goods, it could not be a charge. The seller owned the original goods, and now he owned the product. This was not a charge.

But a difficult problem arose. The new goods were the product of the seller's goods, and of goods belonging either to the buyer, or to other sellers. Conceivably, the seller's goods subject to the retentions clause were

---

[8] [1979] 3 All E.R. 961, [1980] 1 Lloyds Rep. 160.

[9] Retentions clauses failed in *Hendy Lennox (Industrial Engines) Ltd.* v. *Grahame Puttick Ltd.* [1984] 2 All E.R. 152, where there was no attempt to deal with mixed or manufactured goods, no express obligation to store new goods separately, and no mention of "fiduciary" obligations; in *Re Andrabell* [1984] 3 All E.R. 407, where the clause had these defects and also provided for property to pass after payment for each consignment (in *Romalpa*, it was only on full payment of all debts), where there was no provision for the supplier to have any benefit against a sub-purchaser, no provision for the buyer's sub-sale as agent for the supplier, no obligation to keep the proceeds of sale separate, and credit given to the buyer showed that in the meantime it could use the proceeds as it saw fit; and in *Four Point Garage Ltd.* v. *Carter* [1985] 3 All E.R. 12. See also *Re Peachdart Ltd.* [1983] 3 All E.R. 204; *Specialist Plant Services Ltd.* v. *Braithwaite* [1987] B.C.L.C. 1.

a very minor part of the new goods. In the court's view, without the clearest possible words, it could not have been intended that on termination of the contract the seller would gain the "windfall" of the full value of the new goods. This, it is submitted, is undoubtedly correct. What buyer would have agreed that a seller of, say, 100th part of the new goods should obtain title to the whole? The court concluded, therefore, that the clause must have been intended to create either a trust, or a charge. A trust (where the seller had legal title which he held in trust to the extent of windfall profits, for the buyer) seemed unlikely, because any seller with a Romalpa clause should suspect that other suppliers of goods might also have an identical Romalpa clause, and they could not both have the same rights as trustees. Therefore, a charge must have been intended, and this must be registered. The clause, therefore, was effective in relation to unmixed goods, but would not have been effective in relation to mixed goods, had any been in issue. For a seller, there are at least two theoretical ways around the decision: the first is expressly to say that all mixed goods and their windfall profits do indeed belong to the seller. No buyer properly advised would agree to this, but it may be that the small print of many supply contracts is rarely examined with care. The second is to say that a trust is intended. But it may prove to be impossible effectively to choose the trust option, as a way of dealing with mixed goods. If supplier A and supplier B both supply goods to a company, and it mixes the goods, and both A and B rely on a retentions clause under which both have legal title to the mixed goods, how could this ever be given effect? It may be that they would become joint legal owners, though legal ownership is said to depend on intention, and clearly neither the company nor either seller intended joint ownership.[10] If the only way one can envisage a trust in this circumstance is by ignoring the intention of the parties as expressed in their clause, then it is very dubious that the court will comply.

D. Proceeds of sale

Despite the difficulties with mixed goods and, therefore, their proceeds, it seems possible, as we have seen, to draft an effective retentions clause relating to unmixed goods, and to their proceeds. It has been said, however, that the clause must be drafted so as to deal with the separate "storage" of the proceeds of sale, and a restriction on their use.[11] **22.05**

E. "All liability" clauses

It has been argued that there is a distinction between "single contract" retentions clauses, whereby the seller reserves title until the goods delivered under the single contract in question have been paid for, and an "all liabilities" clause, whereby title is retained so long as any liability of buyer to seller under this or other contracts is not discharged.[12] The reasoning is that if it is truly a retention of title, as opposed to a charge, then if the seller recovers the goods, he must refund the purchase price to the buyer—but where different contracts are involved he would not wish to do this, so that it must have been intended to be a charge. If, for example, the seller sells **22.06**

---

[10] See Goode.

[11] See cases at n. 9 above. It is not clear why this should be so—tracing is possible into a mixed fund, and this sems to be a denial of this possibility.

[12] See Jones and Goodhart (1980) 43 M.L.R. 489; Goodhart (1986) 49 M.L.R. 96.

two lots of goods, both at £1000, and the buyer pays for the first contract, but not the second, the seller may seize both lots of goods and sell them. If he receives £1200, he may use this to satisfy his claim to £1000 of damages for breach of the second contract, but must refund the price of the first lot of goods, for there has been no breach of that contract, so he is left only with £200. He is better off if this is a charge, and this, therefore, should be said to be the intention of the parties. This persuasive argument, however, appears at first sight inconsistent with the reasoning in *Clough Mill Ltd.* v. *Martin* (though that was a "single contract" case), where it is said simply that there is no charge if all along the seller retains title in himself. In reply to this, it has been argued[13] that the seller retains legal title, but the buyer is intended to have beneficial title once he pays for the goods delivered under the contract in question, and the buyer grants a charge over his beneficial interest over those goods to secure liabilities under other contracts. It is thought, with respect, that there is considerable force in this argument, though it remains unresolved as yet by judicial decision. In principle, any argument which reduces the scope of Romalpa clauses is welcome.

F. Effect of Insolvency Act 1986

22.07 Under section 11 of the Insolvency Act 1986, if in a company insolvency an administration order is made, no steps may be taken to enforce any security over the company's property, or to repossess goods under a hire purchase agreement, unless the court gives leave.[14] However, this seems not to cover retentions clauses because the property is not that of the company, and in this section "hire-purchase" means the same as in the Consumer Credit Act 1974[15] which apparently excludes retentions clauses.[16] If, however, the seller does not repossess his goods for breach of the agreement, then under section 15, the administrator may with the court's agreement sell the goods, if the property was subject to a security or to a hire purchase agreement, and the original seller must be paid from the proceeds of sale.[17] (In this section, "hire-purchase agreement" also extends to conditional sale agreements, chattel leasing agreements and retention of title agreements.)[18] The section is mandatory in that the court must impose a condition that the monies payable under the retentions clause shall be discharged from proceeds of sale. Presumably, the section refers to a "valid" retentions clause: *i.e.* to one affecting the original goods, rather than one affecting mixed goods which is invalid under principles discussed above, or invalid as an unregistered charge. It cannot have been meant to cure defective retentions clauses.

SUMMARY

A retentions clause may (if properly drawn) be effective for the original unmixed goods and their unmixed proceeds, but there are considerable doubts concerning mixed goods or mixed proceeds, in respect of which the clauses may create charges, void for non-registration. "All liability" clauses are more likely to create charges than "single contract" types.

[13] (1986) 49 M.L.R. 96, 100–101.
[14] s.11(3)(c).
[15] See s.436.
[16] See s.189 of the 1974 Act.
[17] s.15(5).
[18] s.15(9).

23. Realisation of Securities: Receivership

A. Introduction

Considerations specific to realisation of land are discussed elsewhere, though much of what appears here is equally relevant to the realisation of a security in land. Except for the realisation of land, receivers are not generally appointed in the case of individuals, and the emphasis here is, accordingly, on the realisation of company securities.

23.01

The security may be realised whether or not liquidation or bankruptcy has occurred, by a receiver, or by an administrator, or in liquidation or bankruptcy by a liquidator. It is generally preferable that a bank's security be realised by a receiver, for the timing of the sale is then a matter entirely for the bank, whereas a liquidator may consider the interests of general creditors. But a liquidator must pay out the proceeds of sale in the same order as a receiver, and except for the bank's lack of control over timing, etc., the security rights of the bank are unaffected.

An administrator may also consider the interests of the company and of the general creditors. Once an administrator is appointed, no debenture holder can realise his security[1] except with the court's consent or that of the administrator,[2] and the administrator may compel any receiver to vacate office.[3] The appointment of an administrator can be blocked by the holder of a floating charge (provided that charge and any other fixed charges cover together substantially the whole of the company's assets), but not by the holder of a fixed charge.[4] A floating security may be realised as the administrator wishes (the debenture holder has consented to his appointment). The floating charge holder has the same priority over the proceeds of realisation as he had over the original property.[5] The administrator becomes responsible for paying preferential creditors.[6] The administrator's remuneration, expenses, and some other debts are paid in priority to a floating charge holder[7] which appears to be another very good reason for banks to refuse to agree to the appointment. Holders of fixed charges cannot block the appointment of an administrator, and the securities may be realised by the administrator (a) by agreement with the fixed debenture holder[8] or (b) by application to the court, where the court agrees that this will promote the purposes of the administration. In the latter case, the fixed charge holder is to receive at least the market price which could be obtained in an unforced sale (so that any deficiency because of a forced sale must be made up).[9] There is no similar "market-value" provision in respect of floating charges.

---

[1] s.11(3)(c) and (d).
[2] *Ibid.*
[3] s.11(1) and (2). Receivers under floating charges must vacate office, and those under fixed charges must do so if required to do so. Their remuneration, etc., is a charge on, and paid out of, the charged property: s.11(4).
[4] Below, this para.
[5] s.15(4).
[6] s.11(5).
[7] s.19(4).
[8] See s.11(3)(c), (d).
[9] s.11(5) and (6).

It is obvious that banks should take fixed charges which are as extensive as may be, while taking a floating charge over the rest and the whole "undertaking" (even if only as a residual security).

The procedure under section 9 of the Insolvency Act 1986 is this: if an application is made to appoint an administrator, the court shall give notice to anyone entitled to appoint an administrative receiver (*i.e.* to the floating charge debentureholder who has a charge over substantially the whole of the company's assets). Under the Insolvency Rules (rules 2.6 and 2.7) at least 5 days notice of the hearing must be given, and then the court shall dismiss the petition if it is satisfied that there is an administrative receiver, unless the debentureholder has consented to the administration order, or unless the charge is invalid for some reason (*e.g.* contravening the "12 months rule" under s.245). In other words, the bank must decide within 5 days whether to appoint an administrative receiver or not, for if it does not actually appoint, the court is free to grant the administration order, which will (a) prevent the bank from realising the asset, (since the administrator is under no obligation to do so), (b) permit the administrator to dispose of assets subject to a floating charge, and (c) permit the administrator to sell assets subject to a fixed charge if the court permits it. The bank will not lose its security rights but may only be entitled to the proceeds of realisation, which may occur at the administrator's discretion, if at all. Generally, banks will oppose the appointment of administrators where they can, and will take floating charges in future even where in the past a fixed charge would have sufficed, so that they have this option. The 5 days given to decide will also cause receivers to be appointed precipitately, and may bring about the very collapse that the appointment of an administrator was designed to avoid.

It should be observed that the administrator must, within 3 months normally, produce proposals for creditors (under section 23) and that a meeting of creditors is then summoned (section 24) to approve the proposals. If they do not do so, the administration order may be discharged. According to Insolvency Rule 2.28, the meeting decides by a majority in value of those present and voting, so that at this stage a bank which has ·had second thoughts, or which could not prevent the appointment of the administrator, may be able to terminate the proceedings, depending on the value of its debt, etc. It is also possible under section 27 for any creditor to oppose the administrator's actions on the ground that he is managing the company's affairs in a manner "unfairly prejudicial" to some or all of the creditors.

If an administration order is made, the effect (according to section 11) is that there is a "freezing" of actions against the company: no winding up petition can proceed, the administrative receiver must vacate office and any other receiver must do so if required, and without the administrator's consent or the court's approval, no steps can be taken to enforce any security or to repossess goods, no other proceedings and no execution or legal process may be commenced, or distress levied. It is this freezing of the position which is at the heart of the administration procedure, being designed to allow the company a respite, in which proposals for reorganisation, etc., can be put to the creditors. Otherwise, the "voluntary arrangements" which under Part 1 of the Act a company may put to its creditors, may not have the chance to succeed. But where a bank with a floating charge is involved, the general practice will be to refuse to consent to the appointment of an administrator, so that the collapse of the company subsequent to the receivership will generally be inevitable. This may be compared with the position of an individual bankrupt who, if he is insolvent, may apply to the court under section 253 for an interim order to "freeze" his position, pending the putting of proposals to his creditors, supervised by an insolvency practitioner. No secured creditor can prevent this, in the way possible with floating charges, and company debtors.

B. Remedies of debenture holder

Remedies become exercisable not only on breach but also whenever the bank's debenture permits (commonly, for non-repayment "on demand," whether or not that is a breach). In summary, the remedies are: (i) to sue for debt, or for damages if there is a breach of contract, by reason of non-payment of principal or interest; (ii) to apply to the court for an order for foreclosure (which makes the debenture holder the owner of the asset and is not allowed for land) or for sale of the asset. The court will normally prefer sale (unless perhaps the asset is obviously worth less than the debt) in order to prevent unearned enrichment of the mortgagee; (iii) to sell without reference to the court under an express or implied power. Powers of sale are implied for mortgages[10] but must be expressly given for other forms of security, such as a floating charge; (iv) to present a winding-up petition if the debt exceeds the "bankruptcy level"[11]; (v) above all, there is the remedy of receivership, and it will be recalled[12] that the appointment of a receiver causes the crystallization of floating charges.[13]

23.02

C. Receivers

The functions of a receiver are (a) to realise the company's assets comprised in the security, (b) to distribute the proceeds to the debenture holders in satisfaction of their claims, (c) to return any surplus and any unrealised assets to the company. Because it may be advantageous to be able to sell the company (or parts of it) as a going concern, the security should cover the company's whole undertaking[14] and the receiver will have under the debenture or the general law[15] the right to manage the company's business and to sell the whole. Frequently, the receiver will "hive off" part of the company: that is, he forms a new subsidiary company, transfers to that subsidiary such parts of the company's assets and business as will form a viable new undertaking, and sells the shares in the subsidiary to the highest bidder, who thus obtains a debt-free business.

23.03

1. APPOINTMENT[16]

Bank debenture forms will always expressly allow the bank to appoint a receiver on default, etc. The receiver appointed under a floating charge is called an "administrative receiver" (if that charge, together with any other charges, cover substantially the whole of the company's property),[17] and

23.04

---

[10] s.103, L.P.A. 1928.
[11] £750 or other amount prescribed by S.I.: s.267(4), I.A. 1986.
[12] Above, para. 21.34.
[13] *Re Panama New Zealand and Australian Royal Mail Co.* (1870) 5 Ch.App. 318.
[14] Though a charge on "the property" of a company has been held to include a charge on its business—*Re Leas Hotel Co.* [1902] 1 Ch. 332.
[15] The Insolvency Act 1986, esp. ss.42–44 and Sched. 1.
[16] See I.R. 1986, Part 3.
[17] See also s.29(2)(b).

the receiver under a fixed charge or under a partial floating charge is called simply a "receiver."[18] Where no distinction is to be made we shall refer to "any receiver" or "no receiver."

No receiver may be a body corporate[19] and no undischarged bankrupt may be any receiver or manager.[20] An administrative receiver must be an insolvency practitioner.[21]

The court has an inherent power to appoint a receiver.[22] On a winding up it can appoint the official receiver.[23] Appointment by this method is slow, expensive, and does not apply to administrative receivers (who must be managers of the company).

The debenture holder may make the appointment when entitled to do so by the terms of the debenture. Even term loans may contain a term entitling the bank to demand repayment if in its opinion a "materially adverse" change in the position of the borrower has occurred, and bank overdrafts or ordinary advances are invariably repayable on demand.[24] Where the debtor is required to pay on demand, a default[25] is easily engineered by the bank making a demand and then giving the debtor a very short time to get the money. It is established by *R.A. Cripps & Son Ltd.* v. *Wickenden*[26] that the debtor need not be given time to negotiate a deal which might produce the money, but need only be allowed time to get the money from a convenient (nearby) place, supposing that he has it there. Thus, in the case in question, the demand was made at 10.45 a.m. and the default (for a debtor located in Brighton) was held to have occurred by 12.30 a.m. It is, therefore, extremely significant that overdrafts and advances are made "on demand," since this enables a receiver to be appointed very swiftly.

23.05   In appointing a receiver, the bank must act in good faith, but has no duty to consider such matters as whether a company might be able to finance itself in the near future. No injunction will be given on these grounds to prevent a receiver acting.[27]

The appointment of any receiver must be in writing[28] but need not be under seal, even if the receiver is to transfer a legal estate in company land.[29] It takes effect not when it is prepared, signed and dated, but whenever it is received by and accepted by any receiver within the permitted time, even if

---

[18] See s.29.

[19] s.30, I.A.

[20] s.31, I.A.

[21] s.230(2), I.A. and Part XIII.

[22] Supreme Court Act 1981, s.37(1).

[23] s.32, I.A.

[24] This may be so even in the domestic mortgage market, where a "term" (of say, 25 years) is used merely to calculate the repayment schedule.

[25] The debenture need not provide that this is a breach of contract, but only that it is an event entitling the appointment of a receiver.

[26] [1973] 2 All E.R. 606. See also *Brighty* v. *Norton* (1862) 3 B&S 305, 312; *Toms* v. *Wilson* (1863) 4 B&S 442, 453; *Moore* v. *Shelley* (1883) 8 App. Cas. 285, 293; *Massey* v. *Sladen* (1868) LR Ex. 13; *Windsor Refrigerator Co. Ltd.* v. *Branch Nominees Ltd.* [1961] Ch. 375; *Bank of Baroda* v. *Panessar* [1987] 2 W.L.R. 208. Cf. *Kay* [1986] 4 J.I.B.L. arguing that the true principle is that a reasonable time is required, but that where the creditor is obviously without resources, a very short time is reasonable. See *Ronald Elwyn Lister Ltd.* v. *Dunlop Canada Ltd.* (1978) 85 D.L.R. (3d) 321: (1979) 105 D.L.R. (3d.) 684; (1982) 135 D.L.R. (3d.) 1, and *A.N.Z. Banking Group (NZ) Ltd.* v. *Gibson* [1981] 2 N.Z.L.R. 513.

[27] *Shamji and others* v. *Johnson Matthey Bankers Ltd.* [1986] 4 B.C.L.C. 278.

[28] s.109(1), L.P.A. 1925.

[29] *Windsor Refrigerator Co. Ltd.* v. *Branch Nominees Ltd.* [1961] Ch. 375.

tacitly.[30] The handing of an appointment letter by a bank's head office to a receiver's assistant who is to take them to a branch office of the bank will be insufficient, and appointment would take place when the branch manager handed the letter to the receiver.[31] Acceptance of an appointment must be made by the receiver or his agent by the end of the business day next following the receipt of the letter[32] and must be confirmed in 7 days.[33] Joint receivers may be appointed, and are subject to similar rules[34] and the appointment should say if they may act separately or only together.[35] Before appointment, the bank should check (a) that the charge is valid, (b) that the appointment is valid in other respects (for example, that the demand specifies the correct amount owing, and not too much), and (c) that there are sufficient assets to cover the receiver's fees and expenses. If the appointment is bad, he would have to be withdrawn and then re-appointed.[36] To lessen the risk of challenge by the company or its liquidator on the ground of invalid appointment[37] the directors may be asked by the bank formally to request the bank to appoint any receiver. The receiver will usually take an indemnity in case of invalidity but by statute, if any appointment is invalid (because a debenture is invalid or perhaps because of a faulty method of appointment) the person "by whom or on whose behalf the appointment was made" may be required to compensate any receiver against any liability.[38]

A person dealing with an administrative receiver in good faith and for **23.06** value shall not be concerned to inquire if he is acting within his powers[39] so that it seems that someone in possession of company property, apparently with the company's consent, and apparently acting as receiver, has a kind of ostensible authority to bind the company to any disposition. It is provided that the acts of an administrative receiver are valid, notwithstanding defects in his appointment, nomination, or qualifications.[40] It may be that the second of these provisions relates to technical defects in the appointment, rather than to appointments under invalid debentures, and that the former applies only to an administrative receiver appointed under a valid debenture (the purpose being to indicate the wide powers of such a receiver). It would seem that a person appointed under an entirely invalid debenture (or none at all) could not be intended to have power to bind the company.

After appointment, an administrative receiver must send a notice to the company and publish the fact of his appointment, and within 28 days send a notice to all the creditors of the company of whose addresses he is aware, even if he is also the liquidator.[41] Notice of the appointment of any receiver or manager must appear on every invoice, order for goods or business letter

[30] *R. A. Cripps & Son Ltd.* v. *Wickenden* [1973] 2 All E.R. 606, and s.33(1), I.A.
[31] *Ibid.*, though it may be otherwise if the receiver expressly appoints an agent to receive and accept.
[32] s.33(1), I.A.
[33] I.R. 3.1(1).
[34] s.33(2), I.A. and I.R. 3.1(2).
[35] s.231, I.A.
[36] *Cripps* v. *Wickenden,* above, n. 30.
[37] The receiver would be liable to repay money received, and may be a trespasser. If he is invited by the company, he is not a trespasser until the invitation is withdrawn, or the liquidator challenges him: *Ford and Carter Ltd.* v. *Midland Bank Ltd.* (1979) 129 New L.J. 543.
[38] s.34, I.A.
[39] s.42(3), I.A.
[40] s.232, I.A.
[41] s.46, I.A. and I.R. 3.2.

on which the company's name appears and issued by or for the company or the receiver or manager or liquidator.[42] On appointing any receiver or manager (or obtaining an order for appointment) the debenture holder must notify the registrar of companies within 7 days, and the registrar enters the fact in the register of charges[43] so as to warn others who may deal with the company. When a receiver or manager ceases to act, he must inform the registrar[44] and in the case of an administrative receiver 14 days is allowed for notification.[45]

The administrative receiver may be removed by the court, or he may resign, and shall vacate office if he ceases to be a qualified insolvency practitioner.[46] Although it has been common for debentures to provide for the removal of any receivers, the independence of the insolvency practitioner is now confirmed inasmuch as an administrative receiver may not now be removed other than by order of the court—for example, not by the debenture holder or by the appointment of a liquidator.[47]

2. RECEIVER AS AGENT OF COMPANY

23.07   The debenture may so provide (and normally does) that an administrative receiver shall be the company's agent[48] and it is now provided that this is "deemed" to be the case unless the company is in liquidation.[49] He can, therefore, bind the company, though it does not mean that he owes all the duties of an agent to a principal, such as the duty to take instructions.[50] Unlike an ordinary agent, any receiver is personally liable on any contract entered into by him in the carrying out of his functions (but the contract may provide otherwise), and on any contract of employment adopted by him in carrying out his functions. He cannot contract out of liability on adopted employment contracts, but is not to be "taken" to adopt them by virtue of anything done or omitted to be done within fourteen days of his appointment (as by not informing employees that they are no longer employed). What happens thereafter is debatable: if he adopts the contracts, there may be a large burden of accrued rights under their existing contracts. If the receiver is to become liable for these, his ability to continue trading beyond two weeks is very questionable. "Adoption" may suggest a positive act which unequivocally indicates his intention, and if so he may safeguard his position by not doing anything positive to adopt. Otherwise, he may be required positively to inform employees (or a group of them) that he does not adopt their contracts, even if he is prepared to permit them to continue working for the company on a short–term basis. It seems probable that the mischief at which the statute aims is that of a receiver who "leads on" the workforce to believe that their employment continues past the 14 day period.[51] In *Nicholl* v. *Cutts*[52] the receiver allowed the plaintiff managing director to continue in position, but the receiver was held not liable for the

---

[42] s.39, I.A.
[43] s.405, C.A. 1985.
[44] *Ibid.* No time is specified.
[45] s.45, I.A.
[46] s.45, I.A.
[47] s.45(1). But liquidation may affect his powers: see s.44(1)(a), and below para. 23.12.
[48] See also s.109(2), L.P.A. 1925 for receivers appointed under that Act.
[49] s.44(1)(a), I.A.
[50] *Re B. Johnson & Co. (Builders) Ltd.* [1955] 2 All E.R. 775, [1955] Ch. 634.
[51] ss.37 and 44, I.A.
[52] [1985] *The Times*, May 20, [1986] 5 C.L. 298.

plaintiff's salary, since the older provision[53] only made the receiver liable for "any contract entered into by him." Under the new provision, the receiver might possibly have "adopted" the contract previously entered between company and director.

An administrative receiver (properly appointed) has ostensible authority **23.08** to bind the company.[54] Although the company is liable on contracts, the receiver is also personally liable,[55] (but he may contract otherwise) so that the other party may choose whom to sue. If the receiver is sued, he may have a right to a contractual or statutory indemnity. An administrative or other receiver is entitled by statute to an indemnity from the company's assets.[56] However, (although there may be a contractual indemnity) there is no statutory indemnity in respect of contracts entered "without authority."[57] In the cases[58] where a receiver can be liable to the company or its liquidator or guarantors for "negligently" entering contracts, the statutory indemnity would not apply, for that applies to liability "on any contract," which is not the case where those persons sue the receiver (they sue in tort, for negligence). Even so, a contractual indemnity for that negligence could be given.

The law formerly was that to be agent was not automatically to be manager, and when an administrative receiver was appointed, he did not necessarily supersede the powers of the directors, though in practice, acting as agent, he might do so. If, however, (as is usual) the administrative receiver is by the debenture also made manager of the company, then his appointment does suspend the powers of the directors.[59] Under the Insolvency Act 1986 the powers of the administrative receiver (listed in schedule 1) are so extensive that it may now be true to say that to be agent with those powers is, automatically, to be manager, and that the powers of the directors are automatically suspended. His appointment by the debenture holder does not automatically dismiss the employees,[60] but if he is appointed by the court, it will do so,[61] though he can re-employ some or all.[62] His appointment does not affect the company's liability for existing contracts,[63] and he is not liable (even as manager) on contracts entered into by the company before his appointment. He is not liable if his realisation of assets prevents the company from carrying out its contracts (*e.g.* if goods for sale cannot be made, or by disposing of vehicles so that contracts to carry cannot be performed), though the company is liable in damages, and specific performance may be available against it.[64] While, however, he may freely realise assets subject to the charge, he should not otherwise break any contract in such a way as to damage the company's goodwill, unless with leave of

---

[53] s.492, C.A. 1985.
[54] s.42(3), I.A. He has, of course, wide actual authority: see below para. 23.15, for his powers.
[55] s.44(1)(b) I.A..
[56] ss.37(1)(b) and 44(1)(c) I.A.
[57] ss.37(3) and 44(3), I.A.
[58] Below, para. 23.10.
[59] *Reid* v. *Explosives Co. Ltd.* (1887) 19 Q.B.D. 264; *Re Foster Clark Ltd.'s Indenture Trusts* [1966] 1 All E.R. 43.
[60] *Re Foster Clark Ltd.'s Indenture Trusts*, previous note; *Re Mack Trucks (Britain) Ltd.* [1967] 1 All E.R. 977.
[61] *Reid* v. *Explosives Co. Ltd.* (1887) 19 Q.B.D. 264.
[62] And may then be personally liable: above, para. 23.07.
[63] *Parsons* v. *Sovereign Bank of Canada* [1913] A.C. 160.
[64] See *Airlines Airspares Ltd.* v. *Handley Page Ltd.* [1970] Ch. 193; *Freevale Ltd.* v. *Metrostore (Holdings) Ltd.* [1984] Ch. 199 (specific performance of sale of land).

the court, for he owes a duty to the company not to diminish its goodwill. The court's leave will not be given just because there is an advantage to the debenture holder.[65] Thus, the receiver might be liable to the company, though not to the third party involved.[66]

23.09   Any receiver's powers as agent to bind the company to new contracts (and, in that sense, his right to manage) ceases on liquidation.[67] He could not, for example, bring an action in the company's name. However, his powers to manage the company's assets for the purpose of realisation and to deal with the secured assets are unaffected.[68]

A receiver appointed under a floating charge in England can exercise his powers in Scotland, and vice versa.[69]

3. RECEIVER'S LIABILITY FOR NEGLIGENCE

23.10   We have observed that in disposing of the assets charged, the receiver is not liable even if this has the effect that the company must break its contract with another. It does not amount to negligence for him to do so, for he is entitled to give priority to the interests of those who appointed him. Again, if, for example, he sells in a forced sale, it may well be that prices will be lower than on a more leisurely disposition: but he is not liable for this, for he is entitled to realize his debt when he can.[70] On the other hand, the receiver must have a proper regard for the company's interests, and if, for example, he failed properly to advertise a sale, or to take expert advice, this may be negligence.[71] In *Standard Chartered Bank Ltd.* v. *Walker*[72] it was held that the receiver owed a duty to guarantors of the company's debts, to get the best price when disposing of the assets, and it was held that he should not sell at a particularly unfavourable time, even though the sale was by auction. The sale was in February, during severe weather, and none of the customers on the company's large mailing list had been informed. The bank debenture holder was liable[73] because it had interfered in the receivership, instructing the receiver to seek a quick sale, and thus making him the bank's agent. It is debatable whether the same result would follow merely because of a quick sale, without the lack of advertising,[74] and it may be that the true principle is that as against the company or guarantors a receiver may sell

---

[65] See *Re Newdigate Colliery Co. Ltd.* [1912] 1 Ch. 468. (Receiver wished to break contract to supply goods because market price had now risen—leave refused.)

[66] *Airlines Airspace Ltd.* v. *Handley Page Ltd.* [1970] Ch. 193.

[67] Administrative receivers are provided for in s.44(1)(a), I.A. but the same is true at common law, of any receiver: see cases, next note.

[68] *Gosling* v. *Gaskell* [1897] A.C. 575 (compulsory winding-up); *Thomas* v. *Todd* [1926] 2 K.B. 511 (voluntary winding-up); *Sowman* v. *David Samuel Trust Ltd.* [1978] 1 All E.R. 616.

[69] s.72, I.A.

[70] See *Re B. Johnson & Co. (Builders) Ltd.* [1955] Ch. 634.

[71] See *Cuckmere Brick Co. Ltd.* v. *Mutual Finance Ltd.* [1971] Ch. 949 (must take reasonable care to get best price available at time of sale: negligent not to advertise that property being sold had planning permission increasing its value); *American Express International Banking Corpn.* v. *Hurley* [1985] 3 All E.R. 564 (receiver failed to advertise in specialist magazines or take specialist advice, and received a lower price than possible. A bank debenture holder claimed against defendant director on his guarantee, but director able to rely on negligence because on special facts receiver was agent of bank.); see also *Tse Kwong Lam* v. *Wong Chit Sen* [1983] 3 All E.R. 54.

[72] [1982] 3 All E.R. 938.

[73] As in the *Hurley* case, above, n. 71.

[74] It would not, as far as the company is concerned.

when he wishes, if he allows sufficient time for the proper advertising of the sale.

4. RECEIVER AND OTHER SECURED CREDITORS

If another creditor has securities with priority, an administrative receiver **23.11** may ask the court to authorise a sale of the assets in question.[75] A sale may be ordered provided that the other secured creditor(s) receives at least the market price available in an unforced sale.[76] The registrar of companies must be notified within 14 days.

It would seem that an unauthorised disposal of secured assets (with priority) would nevertheless give good unencumbered title to a bona fide purchaser for value, since the administrative receiver has, by statute, ostensible authority to make the disposition.[77] But the administrative receiver would clearly be liable to the other secured creditor.

5. RECEIVER AND THE LIQUIDATOR

Liquidation so frequently follows the appointment of an administrative **23.12** receiver that people talk commonly as if "receivership" was synonymous with "liquidation." We have observed that on the appointment of the liquidator, the administrative receiver's powers of agency and management cease.[78]

If, (as on liquidation) a receiver's powers as agent for the company cease, it does not automatically follow that the receiver becomes agent for the debenture holder, and normally he will not (debentures generally say so, in any case). In exceptional cases, however, if he is treated by the debenture holder as the latter's agent, as by giving him instructions or by interfering in the process or realisation, then the receiver may be treated as the debenture holder's agent, whatever the debenture says.[79] As it is common for receivers to refer back to those who appointed them, and unrealistic to expect them not to do so, the implications of this are of some concern to banks, for it cannot be said when exactly expressions of opinion, concern, advice, or desire become "interference." If there is interference, then a direct contractual relationship is established between bank (debenture holder) and mortgagor (company) in relation to the conduct of the receivership, and the bank is liable if the receiver is guilty of negligence.[80] The bank, however, is entitled to an indemnity from the receiver for any liability so caused, under an implied term in the contract.[81] But this implied right of indemnity will not exist if, on the contrary, there is an express indemnity given by the bank to the receiver, as there often is. In such a case the loss will probably fall upon the bank, for even if its contractual duty to indemnify the receiver does not apply to negligence, the maxim *expressio unius est exclusio alterius*[82] may apply to exclude an implied term that the receiver should indemnify the bank. Obviously, bank debenture forms

---

[75] s.43, I.A.

[76] In order of priorities, if there are more than one.

[77] s.42(3), I.A.

[78] Above, para. 23.09.

[79] *American Express International Banking Corpn.* v. *Hurley* [1985] 3 All E.R. 564 following *Standard Chartered Bank Ltd.* v. *Walker* [1982] 3 All E.R. 938.

[80] As in the cases, previous note.

[81] *Ibid.*

[82] To express one thing is to exclude (the implication of) another.

should provide for an express indemnity from the receiver for his negligence where this can be agreed. At any rate, the mortgagor's choice is to sue the bank directly (if it is liable on the agency principle just described) or he may sue the receiver (who may sometimes be able to rely against the bank on a contractual indemnity covering negligence).

23.13 Any receiver may be appointed after liquidation commences,[83] but to save costs the court may in a compulsory winding-up often appoint the liquidator as receiver, and the debenture holder's receiver may not then take possession of the company's assets unless authorised by the court. The court always has power to remove any receiver, but where he is appointed and in possession before the liquidator, it will not ordinarily do so unless this is to the debenture holder's advantage.[84]

If the receiver (as manager) brings an action in the company's name, he may continue this after winding-up[85] though probably he cannot commence new actions thereafter.

In windings up by the court, the liquidator may take into his custody "all the property and things in action to which the company is or appears to be entitled."[86] Notwithstanding this, any receiver appointed before the liquidator may still (without the court's permission) take or retain and dispose of the property comprised in the debenture, and may use the company's name for the purpose of agreeing a sale, and the debenture holder is still entitled to use a power of attorney to effect a conveyance, etc.[87] If, however, any receiver is appointed after the liquidator, then the court's permission is needed if the receiver is to dispose of the assets.[88]

In a voluntary winding up, the agency rights of any receiver cease, but his rights to take and dispose of assets are unaffected by the appointment of a liquidator, whoever is appointed first, unless the liquidator applies to the court for directions[89] and the court gives a contrary direction. The court also has powers to appoint a special manager.[90] It seems doubtful that these powers would be exercised so as to prevent any receiver from carrying out his functions.

6. GENERAL DUTIES OF RECEIVER

23.14 A variety of duties are imposed on an administrative receiver, concerning notification of his appointment, the taking of statements about the affairs of the company, the making of a report on his receivership, and the calling of a creditor's meeting.[91] We do not further consider these, here, except to say that the duties include the making of a report for creditors (for which the bank pays, if the assets are insufficient), and that he must give a creditors' committee (if established) such information as it may reasonably require.

---

[83] *Re Northern Garage Ltd.* [1946] Ch. 188.
[84] *Re Joshua Stubbs Ltd.* [1891] 1 Ch. 475: *Re Henry Pound, Son and Hutchins Ltd.* (1889) 42 Ch.D. 402.
[85] *Gough's Garages Ltd.* v. *Pugsley* [1930] 1 K.B. 615.
[86] s.144, I.A.
[87] *Gosling* v. *Gaskell* [1897] A.C. 575; *Sowman* v. *David Samuel Trust Ltd.* [1978] 1 All E.R. 616.
[88] *Re Henry Pound, Son & Hutchins Ltd.* (1889) 42 Ch.D.42.
[89] Under s.168(3), I.A.
[90] s.177, I.A.
[91] See I.A. Part III, and I.R. 3.3

7. OTHER POWERS OF RECEIVER

So far as third parties are concerned, administrative receivers have osten- **23.15**
sible authority to dispose of property.[92] The actual powers of the administrative receiver have formerly been listed in debentures, but the statutory
powers are now very extensive, and are listed in schedule 1 to the Insolvency Act 1986. These seem to cover most eventualities, but could be
extended or restricted by the debenture.[93]

8. ORDER OF DISPOSITION OF PROCEEDS

Like the liquidator, the receiver must distribute the proceeds according to **23.16**
an order laid down by law. This order is discussed further when we consider insolvency, but by way of summary the order is:

1. The true owners of assets (*e.g.* where the company has goods on hire
purchase). If he is not negligent, and disposes of such property, believing
reasonably that he is entitled to seize or dispose of it, then the administrative
receiver is not liable to any person for loss or damage, and has a lien on the
property or proceeds of sale for his expenses (but otherwise the proceeds
would belong to the true owner).[93a] This does not apply to other receivers.
It may particularly affect retentions of title clauses.

2. Costs and expenses. When the receiver vacates office (as on finishing
the task) his remuneration and expenses and any indemnity are charged on
and paid out of the company's property which he holds in priority to the
debenture holder's rights.[94] The costs of the receivership and the receiver's
remuneration have priority over other debts.[95] When there is a liquidation,
the receiver's remuneration may be challenged by a liquidator[96] and fixed
by the court.[97] Where a liquidator is also appointed, then priority between
him and the receiver may depend on whether the receiver is appointed
before the winding-up, or not.[98]

3. The holder of a fixed charge, for principal and interest. Priorities
between fixed chargeholders were considered elsewhere.[99]

4. Preferential creditors. Whether or not the company is being wound up, **23.17**
the receiver must pay preferential debts[1] out of assets in his hands in priority
to claims under debentures secured by a charge which "as created" was a
floating charge.[2] We have observed that this prevents "pre–crystallisation
clauses" from giving any priority.[3] Additionally, under the previous law[4] a
charge was treated as no longer floating after the receiver is appointed, so

---

[92] s.42(3), I.A.
[93] s.42(1), I.A.
[93a] s.234, I.A. This applies also to liquidators and administrators.
[94] s.37(4), I.A.
[95] s.109(6), L.P.A. 1925, and generally on priorities see *Batten* v. *Wedgwood Coal and Iron Co.* (1884) 28 Ch.D.317; *Re Glyncorrwg Colliery Co. Ltd.* [1926] Ch. 951.
[96] s.36, I.A.
[97] See *Re Potters Oils Ltd.* [1986] 1 W.L.R. 201, where the remuneration and costs were challenged under s.494, C.A. 1985 on the ground that the receiver's appointment needlessly
duplicated the work of the liquidator. The court declined to accept this argument, and said
that it would not exercise its discretion unless the receiver's claim was manifestly excessive.
[98] See *Re Barleycorn Enterprises Ltd.* [1970] Ch. 465.
[99] Above, Chap. 21.
[1] These are mainly taxes, and certain employees wage rights: see below, para. 28.104.
[2] s.40, where the company is not in liquidation, s.175 where it is. See also s.250 (definition of
"floating charge").
[3] Above, para. 21.35.
[4] As stated in *Re Griffin Hotel Co. Ltd.* [1941] Ch. 129.

that preferential claims arising thereafter did not have priority: this is now changed. Between themselves, preferential creditors rank equally among themselves after the expenses of the winding up and shall be paid in full, unless the assets are insufficient to meet them, in which case they shall abate in equal proportions.[5]

5. The holder of a floating charge for principal and interest.[6]

6. Unsecured creditors. Unless the charge is invalid for some reason[7] secured creditors rank ahead of unsecured creditors.[8]

7. If there is any surplus, it will go to the members of the company.

---

[5] s.175(2)(a), I.A.
[6] For subrogation of a fixed charge holder, apparently placing the floating chargeholder first, see above, para. 21.35.
[7] e.g. for non-registration, or under the "12 months rule" discussed above, Chap. 21.
[8] Other grounds for invalidity are discussed below, para. 28.90 et seq.

24. Land as Security[1]

A. Introduction

The law relating to interests in land is a large and complicated subject, **24.01** encompassing not only what is generally called "land law" but also equity and trusts, the law of torts, and contracts. It is our intention primarily to deal with land as a security, though we begin with a brief introduction to the doctrine of estates, and the methods of creation and transfer of interests in land. Land is referred to as realty or real property, and is distinguished from personalty or personal property. It is an excellent form of security, even where most of the security value resides in buildings on the land, for buildings can be insured, and the whole tends to increase in value. It may be the subject of a fixed or floating charge, though the latter, obviously, is found only where the customer is in a business which involves acquiring and disposing of interests in land fairly frequently.

B. The nature of interests in land

1. THE DOCTRINE OF ESTATES AND INTERESTS[2]

People commonly talk of "owning" land, but our system of land law relates **24.02** back to a system of "tenure" where different persons "held" rights in the same land, all deriving title ultimately from the Crown. Thus, the Crown (while retaining residual rights) might grant rights to a nobleman (or tenant in chief) who (while retaining residual rights) granted rights to a tenant, and so on. Each of those below the Crown held the tenure of an "estate" or bundle of rights in the land, though none of them "owned" the land in the same way that they might own a horse or cattle. In modern times there are essentially two forms of estate, these being leasehold and freehold. The term "freehold" is an indication that the tenant or freeholder owes no obligations to a superior tenant in respect of his holding. The term "leasehold" signifies that the tenant obtains his estate from a superior tenant, to whom he owes obligations (such as rent, or the obligation to repair, and above all, perhaps, the obligation to give the property back when the lease expires). This superior tenant may be either another leaseholder or a freeholder. It is nowadays common practice to talk only of leaseholders (or sub-leaseholders) as tenants, and we shall adopt this practice, referring often to the superior tenant as the "landlord." When people talk of the ownership of "flats" or "maisonettes" it generally (but by no means always) signifies leasehold title. In law, the title is to the land itself, and any buildings on the land are seen as part of the land, so that while, for example, the ordinary purchaser of land may be more concerned with the building, the lawyer continues to speak of the land, and of rights in the land.

As with other property, different persons may still have different (or the same) rights in the same land. Thus, one person may be freeholder and

---

[1] On land as security, reference may be made to the Encyclopedia, Section E, and also to Megarry and Wade, *Law of Real Property*, (5th ed.), or to Megarry, *Manual of the Law of Real Property*, (6th ed.), or to Cheshire and Burn, *Modern Law of Real Property*, (13th ed.).

[2] We vastly simplify this account, and it may, be, therefore, technically inaccurate in some respects, though not greatly misleading.

another leaseholder, and they have different rights. Or, two persons may own jointly in one of the forms of joint ownership, and may have the same, or similar rights. Or, one person may be legal owner, and another may be equitable owner, having different rights.

2. FREEHOLD AND LEASEHOLD ESTATES AND INTERESTS

24.03   Freehold estates (once called socage tenure) are of various kinds, though by far the most common is called the "fee simple absolute in possession." "Fee" means that the land is inheritable by the heirs of the present free-holder, (though, of course, he may sell or leave it to someone else, thus "alienating" the land); "simple" means that it may be inherited by his general heirs (as opposed to an "entailed" estate, where say, only the male heirs may be entitled to inherit or where another kind of descent is speci-fied); "absolute" means that it is not conditional, nor determinable in any way (as opposed, say, to a life interest); and "in possession" means either in actual physical possession or having the right to receive rents or profits[3] so that a freeholder who has leased his property to a tenant is still "in pos-session." Other types of freeholds include those which are entailed, those which (being granted by another freeholder) are for the life of an individual (a "life interest" or "freehold for life"), and those which are to last until some event occurs, such as remarriage (a "conditional" or "determinable" fee simple). If say, land is gifted by A, a fee simple owner[4] to B for life, A would be said to own the "reversion," and on B's death the land would revert to A or his heirs.[5] If the land was left by will to B for life and then to C, C is described as the remainderman, as he has a remnant (or remainder) of an estate expectant on the life estate created at the same time as that estate.

24.04   A leasehold estate (called a chattel real) exists where a freeholder has from his own estate made a grant of a lesser estate (*i.e.* other than a freehold) to another person.[6] He who grants the lease is the lessor and he who receives it is the lessee. The freeholder will have the reversion, though his greater free-hold interest continues to exist throughout. The leasehold interest may (if the period of the estate is definite or capable of definition) be referred to as a "term of years," though it may last for less than a year.[7] The estate may be "a term of years absolute," which means that it is to last for a certain fixed period, unless it ends earlier by forfeiture for breach, or by redemption of a mortgage lease,[8] or by operation of law. Other forms of leasehold estate (not terms of years, because the period is not definite) are periodic leases (automatically repeating, say from year to year, or week to week, unless either party gives notice to the contrary); tenancies at will, where no specific term is agreed, but the tenancy may be determined by the landlord's notice; a tenancy for life (of the tenant); a tenancy for the life of another (*pur autre vie*); a tenancy at suffrance (where a lawful tenant ceases to be a lawful ten-ant, but stays in possession wrongly). Leases may not be made perpetually renewable, for this operates as a grant of a 2,000 year lease.[9] They may,

---

[3] s.205, L.P.A. 1925.
[4] We will refer to him as owner, henceforth.
[5] Thus, if a bank's customer claims to have a reversion, he should be sent not to a pscyhiatrist, but to a valuer, for valuation of the interest.
[6] If it is not a lesser estate then he is conveying or assigning his estate, not granting a lease.
[7] s.205, L.P.A. 1925.
[8] The lease contains a "proviso for cesser on redemption."
[9] L.P.A. 1922, s.145, Sched. 15.

however, be made renewable at intervals (*e.g.* for three or seven or 15 years) provided that the period does not exceed 60 years from the end of the lease in question.[10] Business leases are made renewable by statute,[11] on terms similar to the original lease, (including the term) but at a new market rent, and this must be remembered where the bank's customer appears to have a limited (and, therefore, not very valuable) term.[12] A lease to begin from a past date is a lease in possession, and one to begin at some future date is called a "reversionary" lease. A lease must be distinguished from a mere licence (or permission to remain on land without being a trespasser), such as a hotel guest would have.

A leaseholder may grant to another person a leasehold interest of a lesser **24.05** term: this is a sub-lease or an underlease or derivative lease. Any number of such sub-leases may be created (assuming there are no prohibitions on so doing). The person who grants the underlease is referred to as the under-lessor, and his lessee as the underlessee.

Generally, a leaseholder pays rent to his lessor—*i.e.* a periodical payment. Sometimes, however, leases may be granted for a single payment. There must always be at least one obligation owed by lessee to lessor (apart from the obligation to pay rent) for the lessee must surrender possession on the expiry of the lease. Generally, there are a number of obligations, either express or implied. These obligations are of concern to banks and other lenders, since the lessor may have a right to determine the lease if the obligations are broken. Forfeiture of the lease in this way will deprive the bank of its security, and this is considered below.

Apart from freehold and leasehold estates, other rights or "interests" in land are recognized by law or equity, and may be valuable enough for security purposes, or may be of importance because they affect a security interest detrimentally. For example, there are easements (or rights of an owner of land over the lands of another, such as rights of way or of light or to a flow of water); profits à prendre (or rights of taking the produce from another's land, such as rights of common, or of pasture); rentcharges[13] (*i.e.* annual or periodic sums charged on or issuing out of land, other than rent under a lease, or sums payable by way of interest); and a mortgage by way of charge (some mortgages, for example, may be by way of lease).

3. LEGAL AND EQUITABLE RIGHTS

At one time England had two systems of courts, known as courts of law **24.06** and of equity. A court of law might recognize the rights of A to a certain piece of land, while a court of equity might recognize the superior rights of B to the same land. In this "conflict," the courts of equity were generally successful, inasmuch as the remedies of a court of equity were aimed at the person. This is to say, if the court of equity decided that B's rights were superior, A would be prevented by injunction from enforcing the rights given to him by a court of law, and would be ordered, where necessary, to carry out promises made to B (by an order for specific performance) even though the court of law would, perhaps, not recognize the effect of such a promise. A's penalty for disobedience to the court of equity might involve

---

[10] *Ibid.*

[11] There are exceptions.

[12] Landlord and Tenant Act 1954, Part II.

[13] No new rent charges may be created and existing ones will be extinguished in the 60 years from 1978-Rent Charges Act 1977.

imprisonment for contempt of court, and in that case the fact that a court of law upheld his claim would achieve little. In this sense, the rules of equity were superior. Thus, it is often said that the law acts against or has concern for the "thing" (legal rights are held *in rem*), while equity acts against or has concern for the person (equity acts *in personam*). When the dual system of courts was abolished (from the middle of the 19th century onwards) the same court continued to apply the dual system of rules. Thus, it is still possible for one person to be recognized as the "legal owner," while another is regarded as the "equitable" (or "beneficial") owner.

The legal owner (or trustee) holds the legal title in trust for the beneficiary (equitable owner, or *cestui qui trust*), and the profits of the use of the land belong to the latter. One may think of the legal owner having the "paper" title, while the beneficiary has the "real" or beneficial title. This division of titles has lent itself to a system of land management, for it is convenient often to separate managerial functions (in the legal owner) from beneficial functions (in the equitable owner), just as one does, though in a different way, if one invests in a company, which is managed by others. Obligations are imposed upon the trustee to manage the trust property for the benefit of the equitable owner.

24.07   Equitable titles could be created by will, if A leaves to B to hold for A's children, C and D. B could dispose of his legal title (appoint another trustee) and C and D could dispose of their equitable titles (*e.g.* by mortgaging them). Equitable titles can be created by a person in his life, simply by declaring himself irrevocably to be a trustee for the benefit of another (for land, the declaration is unenforceable unless evidenced in writing). Another common way in which an equitable title is created, not necessarily by design, is where the law insists on the observance of certain formalities (such as a deed) to dispose of an interest in land, and some other form of disposal is adopted. In that case the person attempting to dispose of his interest will not divest himself of his legal interest, but will dispose of an equitable interest, thus "splitting" ownership, as described already. Naturally, there may not be a separate equitable owner: *i.e.* as is commonly the case, the legal owner is also the beneficial owner. Such a legal and beneficial owner may dispose of both his legal and beneficial interest, or only his equitable interest. If there is a separate equitable owner, then the legal owner may dispose of his legal interest, and an equitable owner may dispose of his equitable interest. As to a mortgage of land, this may be taken from the legal and beneficial owner, either as an equitable mortgage or a legal mortgage (depending on the formalities observed); and it may be taken from an equitable owner as an equitable mortgage. Subject to what we shall shortly say, there is little point in taking a mortgage from a person who is known to be merely legal owner, for the mortgagee would only obtain the "paper" title of the legal owner.

There is, however, one respect in which the paper title of the legal owner assumes a considerable importance. A legal owner may, in breach of trust, purport to dispose of both the legal title, and the beneficial title. An accomplice would obtain no rights, but the purchaser may be a bona fide purchaser, who paid a fair price for the property (gave value), and who at the time of purchase had no notice of the title of the beneficiaries. As between the two innocent parties—the bona fide purchaser and the beneficiary—the courts of equity favoured the bona fide purchaser (for value, and without notice) leaving the beneficiaries to their remedies against the trustee for his breach of trust. He has, of course, to account to them, and he may be criminally liable as well. In this way, however, although he has only paper (legal) title, the trustee may be able to defeat the interest of the beneficiaries, and may be able to give the bona fide purchaser both legal and beneficial title. Nowadays, the beneficiaries may be protected by a system of registration of title, which gives notice to prospective purchasers, and also by other means.

It should not be assumed, from the foregoing, that the trustee always **24.08** commits a wrong by selling.[14] An adult beneficiary may consent to the trustee's disposition. In any case, the trustee may be permitted to sell by the terms of the trust deed (for management or investment purposes, or where there is more than one beneficiary, it may be necessary to sell so as to be able to distribute the proceeds of sale to the beneficiaries).

Statutory provisions may also allow sale. For example, a common trust is on marriage, to trustees for the benefit of husband and wife, and after the death of the survivor, the land is to be sold, and the proceeds held on trust (*e.g.* for their children, if any). This creates a "trust for sale" which[15] in theory is not a trust of the land at all, but a trust of the proceeds of sale. The effect of a trust for sale is that any purchaser (including a mortgagee) may safely take legal title from two trustees or a trust corporation, even knowing of the beneficiaries' rights, and the trustees can give a good receipt to the purchaser for the proceeds of sale.[16] This is described as the "overreaching" of the beneficiaries' rights. Overreaching is possible with registered land even if a person with rights in the land is in occupation, but is not possible if a person with rights in the land has his rights protected by entry on the land register. Trusts for sale are also created if land is devised or conveyed to two or more persons as equitable tenants in common or joint tenants, and also in other cases.[17] Where there is a trust for sale, and the trustees will not sell, it is possible for an equitable owner (or one of them) to apply to the court for an order for sale under section 30 of the Law of Property Act 1925, and the "court may make such order as it thinks fit." The mortgagee of such an interest has a similar right.

After the property legislation of 1925, there are now only two estates in land which may be legal estates (they may, of course, be held equitably by another than the legal owner). In the case of freeholds, this is the fee simple absolute in possession, and in the case of leaseholds, this is the term of years absolute. There are a variety of other interests to which there may be legal title: such as an easement or profit held in perpetuity or for a term of years absolute, a rent charge in possession held in the same way, a reversion in a term of years, and a legal mortgage by way of charge. Of course, these legal interests, such as a legal mortgage, can only be granted over a legal estate. Any of these potentially legal estates or interests may, however, be equitable, if, for example, A holds the legal interest on trust for B under a will, or if A purports to dispose of his interest but not in a manner sufficient to do so at law. All other estates and interests, such as freeholds or interests for life, or determinable freeholds and interests, or future interests (reversions or remainders or executory interests), are equitable. Tenancies in common are necessarily equitable, but joint tenancies may be either legal or equitable.

[14] See below, para. 24.33 *et seq.*
[15] Subject to overriding interests, below, para. 24.23.
[16] See Cheshire and Burn, *Modern Law of Real Property*, (10th ed.), pp. 78–79, and see particularly ss.23–32, L.P.A. 1925.
[17] *Op. cit.*, above, n. 16, 198–199.

4. CO-OWNERSHIP

24.09 Whereas the distinction between legal and equitable owners is mainly a distinction between those managing property and those entitled to the benefit of it, the law recognises co-ownership between legal owners, and also between equitable owners.

There are essentially two forms of co-ownership, and these are joint tenancy and tenancy in common. The only form of legal co-ownership is by way of joint tenancy (though there may be an equitable joint tenancy). There may not be more than four legal joint tenants. Equitable co-ownership may be by joint tenancy or by tenancy in common.

A joint tenancy exists if two or more persons each own the whole interest, and do not have distinct and separate shares in it. Each owns the whole, and yet neither is entitled to exclusive possession of any part of it. The most significant characteristic is that there is a right of survivorship: that is to say, when one of the tenants dies, the others automatically succeed to the rights of the deceased.[18] If there is a disposition of land on joint tenancy to A, B, C, D, E, and F, the first four named are the legal owners of the land, and E and F are equitable joint tenants, A, B, C, and D holding on trust for A, B, C, D, E and F. The trust is a trust for sale. Because of the right of survivorship, if C dies, legal title vests in A, B, and D, and in this way, legal title is concentrated in fewer, and not more, hands. It is not possible[19] for one tenant to sell or mortgage his legal rights, for the legal joint tenancy cannot be severed. But a joint tenant may sell or mortgage his equitable rights, and if he so disposes of his equitable joint tenancy then this severs the equitable joint tenancy, so that between the new tenant (or mortgagee) and those remaining, there is now an equitable tenancy in common (though still an equitable joint tenancy between those who remain, if more than one). The bankruptcy of a joint tenant also severs the equitable joint tenancy, and passes his title to the trustee in bankruptcy. On conversion to a tenancy in common, the interest still operates as a trust for sale.

A tenancy in common exists where two or more persons own land (or other property) in undivided shares. That is, each does not own the whole, but has a share in the land, though that share is not identifiable in the sense that the land is divided up. The shares may be equal or unequal. There is no survivorship, so that if one tenant dies, his share does not go to the others, but goes to his personal representatives (who dispose of it according to his will, or the rules of intestacy, etc.). There cannot be a legal tenancy in common, so that if the legal estate is subject to co-ownership, the co-owners (trustees) must hold as legal joint tenants, on a trust for sale for the equitable owners. If land is conveyed in undivided shares to A, B, C, D, E, and F then this operates as a legal joint tenancy between A, B, C, and D, and as an equitable tenancy in common as between A, B, C, D, E and F. The first four hold the legal title as trustees for all six of them on a trust for sale. If A and F die, legal title vests in B, C and D as joint tenants, and equitable title vests in B, C, D, E, and A and F's personal representatives.

The result of this is:

(a) that a legal mortgage may not be taken except from all the legal joint tenants, and

(b) that two or more legal joint tenants may (as trustees for sale, and sub-

[18] They have the *Jus accrescendi*.
[19] Since 1925—*op. cit.* above, n. 16, 219.

ject to complications with registered land) give a good mortgage over the equitable interest of a tenant under the trust for sale, and

(c) that with an equitable joint tenancy an equitable mortgage may be taken from a single tenant over his rights (severance occurs).

(d) with an equitable tenancy in common any single tenant may mortgage his equitable tenancy in common, and

(e) in either of the last two cases, a bank mortgagee may apply to the court for an order for sale if occasion arises, but the court need not order a sale (and with registered land and an overriding interest, cannot order a sale). A further complication is that where, A (a husband) is legal owner and B (his wife) is equitable owner or co-owner, B may authorise the mortgage by A. If B knows of it and assents, even by conduct (as by living in a property acquired partly with B's money and partly by mortgage funds) then A mortgages as B's agent, and B is bound.[20] But while this is so with unregistered land, it may not be so with registered land if B is in occupation and no "enquiry" is made of her.

C. Creation and transfer of estates and interests in land

We are not concerned here to discuss the disposition of interests in land by way of will, or by the rules of intestacy, nor with declarations of trust.[21] Our concern is with commercial transactions *inter vivos*, that is, with sales and mortgages.

24.10

1. REGISTERED AND UNREGISTERED LAND

In England and Wales, we are in the process of moving to a system whereby title to land is registered, so that each parcel of land has a file in the land registry and a file number by which it is referenced, and the name of the owner of the legal estate (the proprietor) is registered, together with any other interests which may effect the land, such as mortgages or equitable interests. Land not yet within the system is referred to as unregistered land. Some areas of the country are known as areas of compulsory registration, so that on a registerable disposition of the property, it will come within the system, and must be registered in two months, while other areas as yet are still areas of voluntary registration, and on a disposition of land here it may, or may not, be registered. Even in compulsory areas it is only compulsory to register leases with terms of more than 40 years to run. In voluntary areas, if land is once registered, any subsequent disposition is also subject to compulsory registration. Some leaseholds are not registerable in any area: for example, leases with less than 21 years to run, those with absolute prohibitions against assignments[21a] and those created for the purpose of mortgage where the mortgagor has a right to redeem. (When we say that these estates are not registerable, we mean that they are not registered as titles. They may, however, and generally should be protected by some other form of entry on the register.)[22] The land register (*i.e.* entries affecting any piece of land) has three parts to it: first, the property register, describing the property and its location, secondly, the proprietorship register, describing the

24.11

---

[20] *Bristol and West Building Society* v. *Henning* [1985] 2 All E.R. 606.
[21] By which anyone may declare himself to be trustee of his rights for the benefit of another. This is binding, without a contract, even for dispositions of land, if in writing.
[21a] Discussed below, para. 24.76.
[22] This is discussed below, para. 24.15 *et seq.*

owner and his rights, and thirdly, the Charges register describing certain rights (such as mortgages) affecting the land.

The land register and the land registry (for *registered* land) should not be confused with the land charges register and registry which deals with certain rights (including mortgages) over *unregistered* land.

2. THE SALE OF LAND

24.12   In relation to unregistered land, the stages of disposition by way of sale (at lease of a dwelling house) are often as follows: first, the purchaser makes an offer to buy "subject to contract" at a certain price. If this is accepted, no contract is created, and it is only a gentleman's agreement, from which either party is free to resile, for any reason or none. (It need not be done this way, and if the words "subject to contract" are omitted, there will be an immediate concluded sale). The purchaser has no mortgageable interest at this stage. Usually a small sum will be deposited with the estate agent concerned to hold as a stakeholder. This is merely an earnest of good faith, and is returnable to the purchaser if he does not proceed, for whatever reason, unless otherwise agreed. Next, the solicitors for the purchaser investigate the title of the vendor to the land. They "deduce" title from the title deeds, which are documents relating to past dealings in the land. Unless the parties agree to a longer period, the obligation on the vendor is only to deduce a good title at least 15 years back.[23] This gives no guarantee of good title in the vendor, but it does protect the purchaser from equitable titles not registered elsewhere or disclosed in the documents, and he will take free of these. If the equitable title is registered, but through no fault of his own the purchaser cannot discover it, there is a compensation system. It is possible that there may be a legal mortgage of the land, involving a deposit of the title deeds with the mortgagee. This will not be registered, but the absence of the deeds will alert the purchaser.

When good title has been deduced, and when the purchaser has arranged finance, the parties exchange contracts. Probably also, a list of questions will have been sent by the purchaser's solicitor to the vendor (called "inquiries before contract") seeking some information about the land. Searches will have been made of local authorities, concerning various matters. Contracts must be in writing, or evidenced in writing (even if after the contract) or are unenforceable. The parties may already have physically exchanged these, and the contract is entered by a "telephone exchange" or acknowledgement by the solicitors concerned that the contract is now in effect. At this stage the parties are bound, and it is common for the purchaser to pay 10 per cent. of the price, which is not refundable if he breaks the contract, but is otherwise recoverable. Insurance schemes are beginning to replace these deposits, and there will accordingly be a reduction in the need for finance of deposits. After exchange the purchaser is in equity the owner of the property, and his interest is mortgageable, though if he defaults, the vendor may rescind the contract and equitable title will revest in him, defeating any mortgage. The risk of destruction of any buildings (or even of the land, by slippage, etc.) is now on the purchaser, and he must insure, although the vendor is liable for any damage negligently caused by him in the meantime. Finally, the purchaser's solicitor prepares a deed of

---

[23] Of course, if no binding contract is yet entered the purchaser can refuse to ahead, unless a longer period of good title is shown.

conveyance, and this is given to the vendor to sign. On the day for completion, this is handed to the purchaser or his solicitor in return for the rest of the purchase price, usually paid by bank draft. At that moment, the purchaser becomes the legal owner. Where the finance is provided by, say, a bank, the bank's representative hands across the money in exchange for an instrument of mortgage of the land, so that the conveyance takes place only momentarily before the mortgage.

In the case of registered land, the procedure is the same, except that after completion, the purchaser's title is registered, where necessary, and instead of deduction of title from deeds, one looks at the land register.

3. LEASEHOLD ESTATES

Whereas freeholds are "conveyed," leaseholds are either "granted" (or **24.13** "created") by a freeholder or leaseholder, or are "assigned," if they already exist, by one leaseholder to another. A leaseholder may grant a lease (an underlease) by granting a term which is less than his own. This is a separate estate, carved out of his greater estate. If he disposes of his whole term, he is assigning it.

As to creation, a legal lease exceeding three years must be created by deed, but if the legal lease is for less than three years, it may be created orally, in writing or by deed. Of course, only the legal owner can create a legal lease, so that a lease granted by an equitable owner by deed is an equitable interest. Equitable leasehold interests exceeding three years can be created either orally (if followed by part performance, such as the lessee going into possession and paying rent) or in writing, and need not be by deed. The grant of a sub-lease is a matter between the under-lessor and the under-lessee only, and the latter takes neither the benefits nor the burdens of the lease between under-lessor and superior lessor.

As to assignment, all legal assignments of legal leases must be by deed, and equitable assignments may be in writing. The legal assignment of the lease transfers to the assignee both the benefit of the lease and its burdens: *i.e.* the landlord may sue the assignee for non-compliance with the terms of the lease. The equitable assignment of a lease transfers the benefits, but not the burdens, so that the landlord seeks his remedy against his immediate lessee, who sues his immediate under-lessee and so on (each will have covenanted with his superior lessor to observe the terms).

D. Complications of mortgages of registered land

The proprietorship register may show that the mortgagor has various titles **24.14** (and he will accordingly be given a certificate—the land certificate—showing that title). The first available title is "Title Absolute" which is a guarantee of title, subject to what follows. Sometimes the owner will have been able to give the registry some evidence, but not conclusive evidence of his title, but shows that he is in possession. In that case he may have a certificate of possessory title. This gives no guarantee that there are no other rights affecting the land, but (a) freeholders may convert this to a certificate of absolute title after 15 years, and (b) a leaseholder may obtain a certificate of good leasehold title after 10 years. The third kind of title is "qualified" and this is extremely rare. Such land would be bad security. The fourth title (for leasehold only) is that of "good leasehold." This would be given to a leaseholder who shows a good lease, but where the freeholder's title is not absolute. In other words, if the freehold is good, the leasehold is good. An absolute title may be given after 10 years in possession by the leaseholder (or his successors).

It follows that the best security comes from absolute title in the mortgagor. However, it is insufficient that the mortgagor is registered proprietor with absolute title if there is (i) an entry in the Charges register, (ii) a minor interest noted on the register, or (iii) someone with an overriding interest.

1. ENTRIES IN THE CHARGES REGISTER

24.15 Anything here binds the purchaser or mortgagee, as later discussed.[24] Legal mortgages and charges would appear here, as would leases of the land, and certain incumbrances (*e.g.* rights of way).

2. MINOR INTERESTS

24.16 Minor interests are any interests that are not registered within two months (as legal titles, or as legal charges) or protected on the register within that time, and which are not overriding interests.[25] Minor interests must be equitable in nature, so that a mortgage in legal form is a legal mortgage to begin with, but unless it is registered as such in the Charges register within two months, it will cease to have effect as a legal mortgage, and operates as an equitable mortgage, with the legal rights revesting in the mortgagor. A purchaser (including a mortgagee) takes free of any minor interests unless they are protected by an entry on the register. It follows that a mortgagee must inspect the land register before taking the mortgage, to see if there are prior mortgages or other rights, and must protect his own mortgage by entry on the register.

Entries protecting such interests may appear in the Proprietorship register or the Charges register. They are Notices, Inhibitions, Cautions, or Restrictions. We do not deal here with the technicalities of these entries on the register. Inhibitions are court orders or directions by the registrar forbidding (absolutely or conditionally) dealings with the land, either absolutely, or until a certain time, or event. It is routinely used in bankruptcy cases, where a vesting order is made, to prevent the registered proprietor from disposing of his land. Restrictions are of similar effect, but are made usually by application of the registered proprietor. Notices, Cautions and other entries are described in the next paragraphs.

a. Protection of Mortgages: Notices, Cautions, and Registration

24.17 The present discussion considers the protection of a mortgage, but will serve also to indicate those entries which banks should investigate before taking a mortgage, and the effect of the entries.

Equitable mortgages may be protected by Notices and Cautions. Mortgages may be protected in those ways or alternatively by registration of the mortgage. That is, protection is given in the following ways:

(i) by a Notice in the Charges register. This can be entered only if the mortgagee has the Land Certificate or it is on deposit at the land registry, as where there is a prior registered charge.[26] As the name implies, a Notice

---

[24] Below, para. 24.17.
[25] s.3(xv), L.R.A. 1925.
[26] This rule requiring the Land Certificate has been described as "irrational": Megarry and Wade, *The Law of Real Property*, (5th ed.), p. 212.

gives notice, and anyone taking an interest in the land takes it subject to rights protected by the Notice (supposing the rights—say a company charge—to be valid).[27]

(ii) by a Caution lodged by any person interested in the registered land or in any charge. This does not require production or deposit of the Land Certificate. Cautions against the land appear in the Proprietorship register, and if against the charge, appear in the Charges register. The effect is that if anyone attempts to deal with the land in such a way that the register is to be affected (or the proprietor attempts to remove or "warn off" the Caution) then the registrar must inform the person who lodges the Caution, who then has 14 days in which to act (*e.g.* by seeking an injunction). During that time no change will be made to the register. Matrimonial Homes Act charges are protected by Notices, not Cautions.

Cautions give no priority against a purchaser, and a later purchaser will not obtain priority by entering a Caution.[28] The only protection they give is a right to object to dealings within 14 days. If a mortgagee is informed by the registrar of a sale, the purchaser would have produced the Land Certificate, and the mortgagee could now place a Notice on the register. If informed of a second mortgage, and if he or the second mortgagee produces the Land Certificate, he can either request a Notice (preserving his priority) or register his own first mortgage. This would have priority because the first in time prevails until the purchaser or second mortgagee obtains a legal interest on registration. Fairly, but somewhat illogically, if the registry fails to give notice to the cautioner, then a purchaser (who is aware of the Caution) takes subject to the interest protected by the Caution.[29] But this would not be the case if being properly notified, the cautioner takes no steps to object. Thus, while a Caution is not as satisfactory as a Notice, it gives reasonable protection.

(iii) by entering in the Charges register a notice of deposit of a Land Certificate (obviously, the mortgagee must have the Land Certificate). This operates not as a Notice, but as a Caution.[30] If, thereafter, the mortgagee is notified of a proposed dealing, he need only seek to register his mortgage (if under seal), or otherwise to protect it by Notice (if he agrees to deposit the Land Certificate with the Registry so as to enable registration of the subsequent purchaser's title) and he will obtain priority.[31]

(iv) by registering a charge in the Charges register. This is the normal procedure, but it is possible only for a legal mortgage[32] and only if the mortgagee can produce the Land Certificate or that certificate is already lodged with the registrar. In return for the Land Certificate, the registrar returns a Charge Certificate to the applicant. If the mortgage is a second mortgage, the Charge Certificate shows details of the earlier charge. A mortgage which is not registered as a legal mortgage within two months of its creation is treated as an equitable mortgage[33] and must be protected as a Minor Interest in the other ways already mentioned.

---

[27] s.52, L.R.A. 1925.
[28] *Barclays Bank Ltd.* v. *Taylor* [1974] Ch. 137.
[29] *Parkash* v. *Irani Finance Ltd.* [1970] Ch. 101.
[30] L.R.R. 1925, r. 239.
[31] See *Re White Rose Cottage* [1965] Ch. 940.
[32] Not, *e.g.* for a company floating charge, which must be equitable, and is protected by Notice or Caution.
[33] s.106, L.R.A. 1925.

b. Effect of Registration of a Legal Interest

24.18 Registration (of a title, or of a mortgage) will achieve the following effects:

(i) secure the legal title of the transferee or grantee, who will not be bound by prior minor interests (not being overriding) even those of which he knows, unless they appear on the register;

(ii) determine priorities: as between two registered mortgages priority is generally determined by the order of entry in the Charges register, and not by order of creation.[34] The normal order of priority may be affected by agreement between the various incumbrancers, and the proprietor, usually by a "deed of priority" which varies the charge. The alteration is entered on the register, provided that all the Charge Certificates are presented to the registrar.[35] In addition, some statutory charges (which may be registered as local land charges) have priority even over pre-existing mortgages.[36]

c. Effect of Non-registration (and Non-protection on the Register)

24.19 If an interest (a title, such as the legal fee simple, or a charge such as a legal mortgage) which can be registered is not registered, the interest may cease to be a legal interest, if the area is a compulsory registration area, and a registerable transaction relating to a sale of the freehold or a lease for more than 40 years or a legal charge is not registered within two months. It is void as to the legal estate.[37] The unregistered transaction has effect as a minor interest, needing protection by Notice or Caution. In voluntary areas there is no time limit even if registration is compulsory because the title has already been registered.[38]

d. Minor Interests and Later Legal Interests

24.20 A minor interest which is not overriding may be defeated by a subsequent purchaser or mortgagee if:

(i) the trustees have power to dispose of the property subject to the equitable interest (e.g. by consent, or by the terms of the trust deed, or by overreaching, or by court order). The subsequent legal purchaser will take priority whether he knows of the prior equitable title or not; or

(ii) if the interest is not protected by an entry on the register (and is not overriding) then it will not bind a transferee or grantee of a legal estate for valuable consideration, whether or not he has notice of it.[39] Only an entry on the register serves to give notice to any legal transferee or grantee.[40]

e. Minor Interests and Later Minor Interests

24.21 If minor interests are not overriding, they take priority between themselves in order of time of creation.[41] If, therefore, a (potentially) legal mortgage is not entered on the register, it takes priority as a minor interest over a later equitable mortgage, even if the latter is protected by a Caution.[42] A similar

---

[34] s.29, L.R.A. 1925.

[35] L.R.A. 1925, ss.31, 64.

[36] See below, para. 24.31.

[37] L.R.A. 1925, s.123(1). The grantor would hold the legal estate on trust for the guarantee.

[38] Megarry and Wade, op. cit. 200, L.R.A. 1925, ss.19, 22.

[39] L.R.A. 1925, s.20(1).

[40] There is an exception for fraud: see Lyus v. Prowsa Developments Ltd. [1982] 1 W.L.R. 1044.

[41] If the "equities are equal."

[42] Barclays Bank Ltd. v. Taylor [1974] Ch. 137. In some cases, however, a form of estoppel may operate on the ground that it is usual to register a potentially legal charge, and that failure to do so misleads the later mortgagees—see Megarry and Wade, op. cit. 225, n. 7, and Megarry, Manual of the Law of Real Property, (6th ed.), pp. 70, 104, 129, n. 12.

principle may apply even to an equitable mortgage (*e.g.* created by deposit of the Land Certificate). Retention of the certificate itself protects against any transaction for which its production is required, so that no purchaser could obtain legal title. But because it is standard practice to protect interests by some entry on the register, a subsequent equitable mortgagee may claim to have been misled, so that an estoppel operates.[43] The misleading of a subsequent party may be prevented by the use of a Caution. Frequently, when banks take equitable mortgages, the bank requests the customer to execute a legal mortgage form, though to save expense, this is not registered. If protected by a Caution, then on being informed of any proposed dealing with the land, the bank has a period of time in which to seek the registration of its legal charge, and this will give it priority.

f. Effect of Search Period

The absence of the Land Certificate is an indication of a prior equitable **24.22** mortgage which will take priority. (The later mortgage cannot become a registered mortgage, which would have priority, without the Land Certificate.) Possibly the earlier mortgagee is still within the two months within which he can register, and has forms entitling him to do so. If an application for an official search is made on a certain day the rules confer a "priority period" of 30 working days afterwards[44] providing that during that period an application for registration of the mortgage is submitted. If any entry by another person is made in the register in that priority period, it will be postponed to the later mortgagee, who made the earlier official search. This is no hardship to the party whose interest is postponed, for the fact that a search is being made is entered on the register, and can itself be discovered by search.[45]

3. OVERRIDING INTERESTS

Overriding interests bind any purchaser (including a mortgagee) of regis- **24.23** tered land, even though he does not know of them, and even though there is no entry in the register.[46] The most important classes of overriding interests are (a) easements and profits, except equitable easements, (b) certain liabilities to repair (*e.g.* highways, embankments, sea walls), (c) rights of persons in occupation, (d) local land charges unless protected by entry on the register, (e) leases[47] for not more than 21 years at a rent without a fine[48] including agreements for a lease which create an immediate tenancy. It is expressly declared that a spouse's statutory right of occupation under the Matrimonial Homes Act 1983 is not an overriding interest. This must be protected by entry on the register.[49]

The most difficult and important class of these is the third here mentioned, which appears in section 70(1)(g) of the Land Registration Act 1925. This is "The rights of every person in actual occupation of the land or in receipt of the rents and profits thereof, save where enquiry is made of such person and the rights are not disclosed." Thus, the owner of any minor

[43] Hayton, *Registered Land*, (3rd ed.), Chap. 8.
[44] Expiring at 11 a.m. on the 30th working day after the application.
[45] Land Registration (Official Searches) Rules 1981.
[46] L.R.A. 1925, s.70(1).
[47] Not an agreement for a lease—*City Permanent Building Society*. v. *Miller* [1982] Ch. 840, though the tenant may fall within (c) being in occupation.
[48] A premium payable for grant or renewal of the lease.
[49] s.2(8), M.H.A. 1983.

interest who is in actual occupation is protected, even though his interest is not protected by any entry on the register. A bank, dealing with the legal owner, must inquire of the equitable owner. This naturally causes significant problems in the taking of the mortgage, for it may be difficult in dealing with a (fraudulent) legal owner to discover who has what equitable rights in the property. The legal owner should be asked, but may not tell the truth. If the bank can discover whether anyone lives in the property, other than the legal owner, then that person should be asked whether he has any interest in the land. If the answer is in the affirmative, the bank should either ask him to join in the mortgage, or at least to waive his rights in writing.

It is perhaps necessary to stress that the overriding interest must exist at the time of the bank's mortgage. Provided that it protects its mortgage, the bank is unconcerned with other rights arising subsequently.

Rights in the Land

24.24 In addition to the occupation of land, there must be "rights" in the land. These rights must be of a proprietary nature in the land, but equity does not require a formal disposition and may hold that there has been an implied (or resulting) trust in a beneficiary's favour, of the nature of a proprietary interest. Even some oral arrangement may suffice to confer rights, if the trust is not express, but is implied by law. For example, if land is conveyed to A, but the purchase money or part of it is provided by B, then A may be said to hold in trust (or to hold a share in trust) for B. This is said to depend on the intentions of the party, and is rebutted by evidence of contrary intention, such as that B intended to make a gift to A.[50] Again, if B spent money on buildings or improvements on A's land, a trust in B's favour could be found, if not rebutted by evidence of intention.[51]

Problems frequently arise in respect of spouses and persons cohabiting, whether of the same or different sex. A trust may be implied if A and B acquire a home in the name of one of them with the joint intention of sharing the ownership between them. This agreement can be inferred at the time of acquisition or subsequently, though it will not be inferred to have been made subsequently merely from contributions of money (*e.g.* to the mortgage). Thus, in *Winkworth* v. *Edward Baron Development Co. Ltd.*[51a] a wife contributed money to a company controlled by her and her husband, and the company was legal owner of their house. The payment reduced the company's overdraft, but was not necessarily referable to an intention to confer a beneficial interest upon her. However, later contributions may be evidence of an earlier intention. Equity will not assist a volunteer (one who does not pay) and the courts will look for evidence of a financial contribution (or money's worth) to the purchase or subsequent maintenance of the home.[52] No equitable interest arises just because a husband defrauds a wife:

---

[50] If A was B's wife or child, this was presumed to be the case: B was presumed to intend A's "advancement." Megarry and Wade, *op. cit.*, 471, *et seq.*

[51] See *Hussey* v. *Palmer* [1972] 1 W.L.R. 1286. (B was mother-in-law of A, and spent money for extension to house for B's accommodation: trust in B's favour found.

[51a] [1986] 1 W.L.R. 1512 (C.A.); [1987] 1 All E.R. 114 (H.L.).

[52] See *Gissing* v. *Gissing* [1971] A.C. 886; *Heseltine* v. *Heseltine* [1971] 1 W.L.R. 342; *Pettitt* v. *Pettitt* [1970] A.C. 777.

equity operates on conscience, but is not influenced by sentimentality.[53] If, therefore, there is (i) an intention such as described, and (ii) a financial contribution, a co-occupant may have "rights" within section 70(1)(g) which will give him an "overriding interest." Since banks cannot possibly judge these things, the only solution is that they become "snoopers and busibodies"[54] and make inquiries of all occupants of whose existence they know. Surveyors and the like may be asked to look for evidence of occupation.

The position has been made significantly more difficult by the decision of **24.25** the House of Lords in *Williams and Glyn's Bank Ltd.* v. *Boland.*[55] Where persons share equitable ownership the legal owner holds on trust for sale, and it was thought that the rights of the equitable tenants did not amount to an interest in land, but only to the proceeds of sale, and that they could not amount to an "overriding interest." In that case, a disposition by the legal owner would be effective even if the purchaser knew of the existence of the equitable rights, because the legal owner acted within his powers as trustee for sale.[56] But in the *Boland* case the House of Lords decided that the rights of a tenant in common did amount to an "interest subsisting in reference to" land, and that because of shared occupation the right was an overriding interest. The case concerned a matrimonial home. The wife's statutory right of occupation is not an overriding interest. The wife had, however, contributed financially to the purchase, and the court held that the parties had intended equitably to share ownership, though the husband was registered proprietor. Thus, the wife had an equitable interest, and although this was on trust for sale, it was held to be an interest in land, and an overriding interest. The bank should have made inquiry of the wife, and if her interest was disclosed, she should have been asked to join in the mortgage or to waive her rights.

In such a case, the bank's remedies are (a) to sue the proprietor on his personal obligation to pay, though he may be insolvent, (b) to obtain a charging order on his beneficial interest in the property and then to apply for sale or (c) to apply to the court as a person interested under the trust for sale for a sale under section 30, Law of Property Act 1925. This is possible because the mortgage is at least an effective mortgage over the equitable interest of the proprietor (it would sever any joint equitable tenancy).[57] Since, however, a sale would affect the equitable tenant in common, the court may not order a sale. Indeed, since lenders are now aware of the problem, the court may look askance at any lender who has not taken the precaution of inquiring of persons in occupation, and of spouses, and of seeking their consent where necessary.

The decision in the *Boland* case was met with some dismay, not merely by **24.26** bankers but by the Law Commission[58] but an attempt in 1985 to change the law was abandoned by the Government in the face of suggestions by opponents that the decision should not be restricted, but extended. In *City of London Building Society* v. *Flegg* it was held in the Court of Appeal[58a] that the

---

[53] *Winkworth* v. *Edward Baron Development Co. Ltd.*, above, n. 51a.
[54] *Caunce* v. *Caunce* [1969] 1 W.L.R. 286, 294.
[55] [1981] A.C. 487.
[56] See *Cedar Holdings Ltd.* v. *Green* [1981] Ch. 129.
[57] Above, para 24.08, below, paras. 24.30, 24.33.
[58] Law Com. No. 115 (1982).
[58a] [1986] 2 W.L.R. 6/6, [1986] Ch. 605.

principle of *Boland* even extended to cases where there was not one, but two trustees for sale, despite the "overreaching" provisions applicable to two trustees. But in the House of Lords[58b] it was held that where there are two trustees for sale, the "overreaching" provisions apply, and the two trustees can defeat even an overriding interest. A bank may, therefore, request a single trustree to appoint a co-trustee, and if both sign the mortgage, the bank is protected from any third party rights not entered on the register, even if it knows of the existence of beneficiaries.

In some cases, A may forge B's signature to a mortgage deed. This apparent consent is no protection for the mortgagor.[59] The only way the mortgagee can fully protect himself against this risk is to have all those in occupation of the property physically attend for the signing of the agreement, and in many cases this may be a wise precaution. On the other hand, it seems that an overriding interest may exist even though an equitable owner (who has not joined in the mortgage or waived his rights in writing) knows of and has actually or ostensibly authorised the sale, for the interest ceases to be overriding not if consent is given, but where "enquiry" is not made and the interest not disclosed.[60]

It is possible that inquiry ought to be made even of young children, who may have an interest in the property. What sort of inquiry is one to make of a baby? It may be, however, that inquiry can be made of their legal guardians.

Nor is it clear what "actual occupation" means. In the *Boland* case the House of Lords said that occupation meant simply physical presence, coupled with a right to exclude others not possessing similar rights. But it would seem that it ought to mean occupation of some degree of permanency, and that that temporary absence, say on holiday, would not prevent the person concerned from asserting actual occupation. Conversely, an equitable owner who happens to stay in the property on the day of the mortgage, but who otherwise lives elsewhere, is surely not in actual occupation.

E. Unregistered land: land charges

24.27   In the case of unregistered land, interests known as "land charges" may be registered in the Land Charges register.[61] Unlike the land registration scheme, they are registered against the name of the proprietor, not the land.

There are six classes of land charges, known as classes A–F. Classes A and B are statutory charges. Class C covers puisne mortgages, limited owners charges, general equitable charges, and estate contracts. Class D covers restrictive covenants, death duty charges and equitable easements. Class F covers a spouse's charge under the Matrimonial Homes Act 1983. These classes do not cover all interests. Most legal rights are not registerable, including legal mortgages protected by deposit of the title deeds. An equitable mortgage protected by deposit of the title deeds, and any trust for sale, are not registerable.

[58b] *The Times*, May 18, 1987.
[59] *Winkworth* v. *Edward Baron Development Co. Ltd.*, above, n. 51a.
[60] Contrast unregistered land: *Bristol & West Building Society* v. *Henning*, above, n. 20.
[61] Under the Land Charges Act 1972.

1. NON-REGISTRATION

If registerable interests are not registered the interest is generally void **24.28**
against a subsequent purchaser for value (including a subsequent mortgagee, whether legal or equitable)[62] whether or not the subsequent interest
is itself registered anywhere.[63] However, estate contracts, restrictive covenants, equitable easements and inland revenue charges, are made void only
against subsequent legal purchasers, while bankruptcy petitions and receiving or vesting orders[64] are void only as against a subsequent legal purchaser
without notice of a petition.

2. REGISTRATION

Registration gives notice to others, and notice will prevent a subsequent **24.29**
purchaser from obtaining title free of the incumbrance. A prior (registered)
equitable mortgagee would, therefore, take priority over a subsequent
(registered or not) legal mortgagee. The purchaser is not bound even if he
has actual notice of an unregistered interest,[65] and even if he acts in collusion
with the vendor.[66] Unlike registered land, it does not matter that the interest holder was actually in possession or occupation of the land.[67]

Registration gives notice as between the interest holder and a subsequent
purchaser or mortgagee, but does not prevent the latter from suing his vendor or mortgagor[68] if the vendor has misrepresented the existence or extent
of any interest.[69]

A system of "priority notices" enables a rapid sequence of transactions.
If, for example, a purchaser agrees on purchase to a restrictive covenant,
and is to raise the money by mortgage from a bank, the sale and covenant
and the mortgage will in practice follow only moments apart. To enable the
vendor to protect his (registerable) covenant against the bank (a subsequent
purchaser, against whom an unregistered prior interest would be void) the
vendor may give a "priority notice" to the registry at least 15 days before
creation of the covenant, and it will take priority over the bank if registered
within 30 days after the priority notice was entered.

Searches of the register may be made in person, or by official search.
Only the latter is conclusive in favour of a purchaser (in respect of those persons he specifies, and if he correctly specifies the land). Protection is given
also against incumbrances registered in the interval between search and
completion.[70] If it is negligent, the registry may be sued.[71] There is a
scheme of compensation if a purchaser fails to discover a registered land
charge of a person not involved in his particular transaction.[72] Since charges

---

[62] L.C.A. 1972, ss.4–7.
[63] Contrast registered land, above, para 24.21.
[64] Registerable as pending actions or as writs and orders.
[65] *Coventry Permanent Economic B.S.* v. *Jones* [11951] 1 L11 E.R. 901, 904; *Hollington Bros. Ltd.*
v. *Rhodes* [1951] 2 T.L.R. 691, 696.
[66] *Midland Bank Trust Co. Ltd.* v. *Green* [1981] A.C. 513.
[67] See *Hollington Bros. Ltd.* v. *Rhodes*, above, n. 65.
[68] Or from rescinding the contract.
[69] L.P.A. 1969, s.24.
[70] If the latter is not more than 15 days late than the certificate date, and there is no priority
notice.
[71] *Ministry of Housing* v. *Sharp* [1970] 2 Q.B. 223. But see s.10(6), L.C.A. 1972 where the applicant does not check that the particulars supplied are those requested.
[72] L.P.A. 1969, s.25.

are registered against names, and may appear against the name of a previous owner, a failure to discover is quite possible.

3. UNREGISTERED LAND, AND TRUSTS FOR SALE

24.30   Trusts for sale are not land charges, and cannot be registered.[73] Two trustees for sale (or a trust corporation) have the power to dispose of land subject to trust for sale to a bona fide purchaser of a legal estate (including a mortgagee)[74] thus "overreaching" the equitable titles (even if in occupation). A legal mortgage may, therefore, safely be taken from two trustees of unregistered land, if the bank does not know of bad faith.

If, however, there is one trustee for sale—say, the husband—and the wife or cohabitee, unknown to the bank, has an equitable interest, the trustee (the sole legal owner) cannot give a good receipt for capital money, so that the overreaching provisions do not apply. On the other hand, however, the doctrine of the bona fide purchaser[75] applies, so that if the purchaser (including mortgagee) has no notice of the equitable title, he will, at common law, take priority over the equitable title.

The important question is as to what counts as notice. It cannot come from registration, since the interests are not registerable. Actual notice of the equitable rights is, of course, binding, and a prospective mortgagee should then seek the equitable owner's consent. Constructive notice is more difficult. The position seems to be that (i) as regards a person not in occupation, the mortgagee is affected only by actual notice of rights, and (ii) if the mortgagor is not himself in occupation, inquiry should be made of the person in occupation,[76] and (iii) that if the mortgagor is in occupation but the circumstances are suspicious, inquiry should be made of those who might have rights (even if the fact of their occupation not known) and (iv) inquiry may possibly be required, even if the mortgagor is in occupation and there are no suspicious circumstances, if the existence of someone who may have rights (such as a wife) is known, even if that person is not in occupation. *Caunce* v. *Caunce*[77] decided, however, that a mortgagee has no constructive notice of a wife's interest merely because both husband and wife occupy the premises, even if they both banked with the same branch, and from a close comparison of their accounts it could be deduced that the wife had contributed to the property. The wife's presence was "consistent with the title offered." This suggests that inquiry need not be made if the mortgagor himself is in possession, but subsequent cases suggest that even then an inquiry ought to be made of other occupiers.[78] In *Kingsnorth Trust Ltd.* v. *Tizard*[79] a building society was dishonestly told by the mortgagor that he was single, but when the agent for the society visited the property evidence of occupation by children was available and the mortgagor said he was separated from his wife. The court held that the building society, through the agent, knew of the wife's existence and that it should have made inquiry of her rights. The agent should not have made a pre-arranged visiting time,

---

[73] Above, paras. 24.08, 24.26 for trusts for sale.
[74] s.27(1), L.P.A. 1925.
[75] Above, para. 24.07.
[76] *Hunt* v. *Luck* [1902] 1 Ch. 428. This seems to presuppose that A's presence is apparent on reasonable inspection, see L.P.A. 1925, s.199(1)(ii)(a).
[77] *Caunce* v. *Caunce* above, n. 54.
[78] See *Hodgson* v. *Marks* [1971] Ch. 892, and *Williams & Glyn's Bank* v. *Boland* [1981] A.C. 487.
[79] [1986] 1 All E.R. 54.

which would enable a fraudulent mortgagor to arrange for the absence of his wife. The precise effect of this decision is as yet unknown. The fact that the mortgagor lied about his status was surely a very suspicious occurrence, indicating that he might be seeking to conceal the rights of his wife. It may be that there is no duty to inquire of a person in occupation if the mortgagor is also in occupation and there are no suspicious circumstances, but the safe course is to make inquiry of any occupant whose existence is known. In this respect, the position resembles that applicable to registered land.[80]

Where, however, a mortgage is taken which is defeated by the equitable title, the legal owner (the trustee) nevertheless has power to mortgage his own equitable title, thus severing the equitable joint tenancy (if there is one, rather than a tenancy in common). While the bank (in the position of equitable co-owner) may then apply for a sale of the property under section 30 of the Law of Property Act 1925, such an order is in the court's discretion, and will not be ordered if the court feels that this would cause hardship to the other equitable co-owner.[81] Non-occupation by the equitable co-owner may perhaps make an order for sale more likely.

F. Other registers

Whether the land is registered or not, there are a variety of other registers which, in an appropriate case, must be examined. The main ones are as follows.   **24.31**

(i) Companies Register. Company charges may be registerable under section 395 Companies Act 1985, as well as being registered under the Land Charges register or with the Land Registry.[82] Floating charges over land need not be registered as a land charge[83] and like other charges which are not registerable as land charges (e.g. mortgages with deposit of the title deeds) may nevertheless be invalid for non-registration with the Registrar of Companies. With registered land, all enforceable charges fall into the class of registered charges, protected minor interests, or are overriding interests. Any of these, even overriding interests, would be affected by non-registration under the Companies Act.

(ii) Local Land Charges. These are kept by London boroughs or by district councils, and relate to governmental land charges which may be imposed by public authorities upon land under statutory powers relating to health, housing, highways and town and country planning, etc. Sometimes they may prevail even over prior mortgages.[84] Charges are registered against land. Failure to register does not make the charge unenforceable, but a purchaser suffering loss is entitled to compensation, provided that either a personal or official search has been properly made.[85]

(iii) Commons and town and village greens. Rights over common land and town and village greens are registerable under the Commons Registration Act 1965 with county and county borough councils. Some land is out-

---

[80] Above, para. 24.23 et seq.
[81] See above, para. 24.08, and *Thames Guaranty Ltd.* v. *Campbell* [1985] Q.B. 210, and *First National Securities Ltd.* v. *Hegerty* [1984] 3 All E.R. 641.
[82] Above, Chap. 21.
[83] L.C.A. 1972, s.3(7): *Property Discount Corp. Ltd.* v. *Lyon Group Ltd.* [1981] 1 All E.R. 379.
[84] See *Westminster City Council* v. *Haymarket Publishing Ltd.* [1981] 1 W.L.R. 677 (rating surcharge on unoccupied premises).
[85] Local Land Charges Act 1975, s.10.

side the Act[86] but otherwise rights in land not registered by July 1970 are now extinguished. Registration is conclusive evidence as to the land being common land and as to the rights of common over it. A mortgage taken over such land would, therefore, be subject to the rights of common.

(iv) Agricultural charges. Charges given by farmers over farming stock and agricultural assets may be registered under the Agricultural Charges Act 1928.

G. Matrimonial Homes Act 1983

24.32 The Matrimonial Homes Act 1983 gives a statutory right of occupation of the matrimonial home to a spouse who is not entitled by reason of a contract or interest in the land to occupy it. The protected spouse cannot be evicted or excluded by the other except by leave of the court. During the continuance of the marriage, this right of occupation has the effect of an equitable charge on the land. Even if the spouse leaves the house, the right to occupy is not extinguished.[87] The charge does not itself affect a third party purchaser or mortgagee unless the charge is registered as a land charge (for unregistered land) or protected by a Notice[88] (for registered land). It is *not* an overriding interest, *even if* the protected spouse is in occupation. If there is such a charge, and it is protected, then the mortgagee should ask for its withdrawal, or take a written postponement of priority from the protected spouse. Given the development in the *Boland* case,[89] then notwithstanding the trust for sale, the wife may have a quite separate equitable interest in registered land, sufficient to give her an overriding interest, and even if there is no protected matrimonial homes charge, "enquiry" ought to be made of the wife for that purpose.

H. Who may mortgage land?

24.33 (a) *Minors.* Persons under 18 may not hold legal estates in land,[90] and a minor would not be bound by a mortgage.[91]

(b) *Mentally disordered persons.* Dispositions by such persons are voidable if the other party knew of the facts from which the disorder could be inferred.[92] If the Court of Protection appoints a receiver, dispositions would in any case be void.[93] If a power of Attorney is made under the Irrevocable Powers of Attorney Act 1985 the power may be exercised after the disorder comes to exist, subject to the safeguards of the Act.

(c) *Bankrupts.* The bankrupt's property vests in his trustee, and any disposition by the bankrupt (except perhaps of after acquired property) after the petition is void, although some valid debts may be incurred between the order and the vesting order, and such debts could be enforced through a prior security.

---

[86] *e.g.* in Epping Forest, and the New Forest.
[87] *Watts* v. *Waller* [1973] Q.B. 153.
[88] Not a Caution, since February 14 1983.
[89] Above, para. 24.25.
[90] ss.1(6) and 19, L.P.A. 1925, s.27 Settled Land Act 1925.
[91] Infants Relief Act 1874. The lender might be subrogated to the vendor's rights as unpaid vendor entitled to a lien: see *Nottingham Permanent Building Society* v. *Thurstan* [1903] A.C. 6.
[92] *Imperial Loan Co. Ltd.* v. *Stone* [1892] 1 Q.B. 599.
[93] *Re Marshall* [1920] 1 Ch. 284.

(d) *Trustees.* Trustees may mortgage land (i) if the trust deed so specifies, (ii) if permitted by order of the court,[94] (iii) if there is power under the general law. The powers of two trustees for sale have been mentioned, and are an example of a power under the general law.[95] With registered land the powers are effective even if there is an overriding interest.[96] With unregistered land the bank must have no notice (actual or constructive) of the equitable rights.[97] Another case is where the trustees are directed by the trust deed to pay or apply capital for a purpose, when they may mortgage trust property in order to raise capital for the purpose.[98] Mortgages cannot be given in order to purchase the land in question. A mortgagee acting in good faith who does not know of an unauthorised purpose is safe to deal with the trustee provided the money is paid to at least two trustees or to a trust corporation.[99]

(e) *Personal representatives.* Executors and administrators may mortgage property comprised in the deceased's estate.[1] An executor's title derives from the will, and he may act immediately on the death of the testator. However, if the will proves invalid then dispositions would also be invalid so that a bank should wait until probate is granted. An administrator's title derives from the court's grant of letters of administration, and like a grant of probate is conclusive of the representative's authority.[2] Personal representatives disposing of land subject to trust for sale are subject to the "two-trustee" rule relating to receipts.[3]

24.34

(f) *Co-owners.* If the legal title is in more than one, then a transfer of the legal title requires the signature of all legal owners. The equitable title will be held on trust for sale[4] and we have observed the consequences of that.[5] There should be no dealings with a sole survivor of a tenancy in common, since that person cannot (even as personal representative) give a good receipt (two trustees are needed), but if the mortgagor is the sole survivor of an unsevered joint tenancy then he is the sole beneficial (and legal) owner and may mortgage and give receipts.

(g) *Corporations.* The difficulties here concern the authority of agents, the powers of the company to borrow and give security, and registration of securities.

(h) *Agents.* An agent authorised to do so may dispose of any interest for his principal, but if the disposition is to be by deed, the agent must be appointed by deed. Thus, a power of attorney must be by deed if the agent is to be able to give a legal mortgage of an interest in registered land, but an agent otherwise appointed may dispose of an equitable interest. Hence a bank which takes an equitable mortgage may also take a power of attorney under seal, for this purpose, enabling a sale without recourse to the courts.[6]

---

[94] *e.g.* under s.57 Trustee Act 1925 a trustee may apply to the court for authorisation.
[95] Above, paras. 24.08, 24.26, 24.30.
[96] *City of London B.S.* v. *Flegg*, above, n. 58[b].
[97] Above, para. 24.30.
[98] s.16, Trustee Act 1925.
[99] ss.95, 110 Settled Land Act 1925, s.27 L.P.A. 1925, ss.14, 17 Trustee Act 1925.
[1] Adminstration of Estates Act 1925, esp. s.39.
[2] s.204, L.P.A. 1925.
[3] Above, at n. 99.
[4] ss.34–37, L.P.A. 1925. For joint ownership see above, para. 24.09.
[5] Above, paras. 24.08, 24.26, 24.30 and esp. para. 24.09.
[6] Below, para. 24.44.

I. The taking of the mortgage

1. LEGAL MORTGAGES

a. Method of Creation

24.35   Mortgages may be legal or equitable. There may be a legal mortgage of a legal estate[7] or of legal interests.[8] Legal mortgages[9] may be created in two ways.

The first method is by way of conveyance of a legal estate. Freeholders may grant a lease of land for a term of years[10] absolute, subject to a provision for cesser on redemption. Leaseholders may grant a sub-lease for a lesser term[11] than remains to the mortgagor. If the land is registered, these legal rights are registered not as estates (in the proprietorship register) but as a charge, and if not registered within two months, they become equitable minor interests.[12] Because leases are involved, the mortgagee has the power immediately to go into possession, but obviously this is rarely done, and never by banks, except in case of default, when the bank may exercise the right which exists all along.

The second method is to make a charge by deed expressed to be by way of legal mortgage. There is no conveyance of a legal estate, but in terms of the mortgagee's protection, powers and remedies in case of default, the charge method has the same effect as if (for freehold) a 3000 year lease had been granted or (for leasehold) a term less by one day than the mortgagor's term had been granted.[13] This method is (a) simpler,[14] and (b) it can be used for either freehold or leasehold and for a mortgage of parcels of land comprising both interests.[15] Additionally, if a leasehold mortgagor's lease contains a prohibition on sub-leases, a charge may still be possible.[16]

Neither of these methods involve (as with goods) a transfer of the whole title subject to a proviso for redemption. Since 1925 an attempt to create a mortgage in that fashion results in a lease for 3000 years[17] or a term ten days less than that expressed to be assigned,[18] respectively.[19]

Legal mortgages may be protected by deposit of the title deeds, and the first mortgagee has a right to demand the deeds.[20] With unregistered land, mortgages so protected are not registerable, but otherwise (as puisne mortgages) they are registerable land charges. With registered land, the Land Certificate must be surrendered on registration, and a Charge Certificate is returned to the mortgagee.

Although in practice a conveyance to a purchaser and the taking from him of a mortgage occur practically simultaneously, on the day for completion, in theory the money is advanced and the security can only then be

---

[7] The legal fee simple absolute in possession or the legal term of years absolute.
[8] Though some, like easements and restrictive covenants, are unsuitable, having little value.
[9] Governed by s.85, L.P.A. 1925.
[10] Commonly 3,000 years.
[11] Commonly less by one day only.
[12] Above, para. 24.14 *et seq.*
[13] s.87, L.P.A. 1925.
[14] It does not require the long forms usually used with leases.
[15] Called a "compound" mortgage.
[16] See below, para. 24.78.
[17] Or, for a second mortgagee, a term one day longer than that of the prior mortgage.
[18] Or, for a second mortgagee, a term one day longer than that of the prior mortgage.
[19] s.85, L.P.A. 1925.
[20] L.P.A. 1925, s.85(1), s.86(1).

taken. If money is to be advanced at an earlier time, the bank may rely upon an equitable mortgage.[21]

No provision in a charge over registered land may prevent the proprietor from disposing of his interest by registered disposition[22] (*e.g.* by subsequent charge).[23] But the prior mortgagee can protect himself by an entry on the register, and a Caution will give him the right to object on the ground of a contractual prohibition, which will, therefore, appear in bank mortgage forms.[24] A prohibition in a charge of unregistered freehold land cannot prevent subsequent dispositions, (though it may be a breach of contract) but problems may arise with leaseholds.[25]

b. Terms of the Mortgage Deed

(i) Personal liability to repay principal and interest. Bankers' mortgage forms may (a) secure a fluctuating overdraft, (as with business mortgages) or (b) secure a loan for a fixed amount (*e.g.* in the increasing home-mortgage business done by banks). Financing by secured term loans is becoming more common, especially with larger businesses,[26] but except for term loans the customer is usually obliged to repay on demand, even if it is understood (though not promised) that domestic customers will not be required to repay unless there is a default in repayments of principal and interest. The customer's obligation is to repay on demand all amounts of principal, interest, bank charges and other sums (such as insurance premiums) from time to time payable. There is sometimes a covenant to this effect,[27] with the security then taken over the sums so covenanted to be paid,[28] although sometimes the covenant is omitted (since the obligation exists anyway)[29] and the security is simply over all monies presently and from time to time owing. In the case of home-mortgages, the customer will also agree to repay amounts of principal and interest from his account maintained for the purpose at certain intervals, usually of one month, but this agreement need not be and usually is not part of the actual mortgage. (It can be quite informal, because the bank always retains the right to demand repayment). By contrast, building society mortgages are usually for fixed terms, not on demand, and the customer covenants to repay principal and

24.36

---

[21] Created, *e.g.* by an agreement to give a legal mortgage; future property may be mortgaged, but in any case the purchaser has an equitable interest when he formally exchanges contracts.

[22] L.R.A. 1925, s.25(3).

[23] He can be prevented from granting leases: ss.99–100, L.P.A. 1925.

[24] Below, para. 24.36 *et seq*, esp. at 24.40, 24.44.

[25] Below, para. 24.78.

[26] Even these may contain "material change of circumstances" clauses which make them resemble demand loans.

[27] *e.g.* "The mortgagor hereby covenants . . . that he will on demand in writing repay all monies, interest, bank charges, and other sums which from time to time and for the time being . . . be due or owing or incurred to the Bank by the mortgagor whether actually or contingently and whether solely or jointly with any other person and whether as principal or surety including interest discount commission or other lawful charges and expenses . . . "

[28] *e.g.* "The mortgagor as beneficial owner hereby charges by way of legal mortgage ALL THAT the property referred to in the schedule hereto . . . as a continuing security for the payment or discharge on demand of all monies and liabilities hereby covenanted to be paid or discharged by the mortgagor."

[29] With registered land, it is implied by s.28, L.R.A. unless there is a negativing clause, and it is implied in law with unregistered land: *Sutton* v. *Sutton* (1883) 22 Ch.D. 511, 515. No obligation to repay is implied with unregistered land if the mortgage is given by one who is merely a surety for another's debt to the bank, but bank forms may impose such an obligation.

interest by fixed instalments, in default of which the building society may exercise its security.

The bank's right to interest is nearly always expressed to be at a floating rate.[30]

24.37 **(ii) Type of charge.** The simplest method (for a legal mortgage) is to say that the mortgagor as beneficial owner "hereby charges by way of legal mortgage" the property described in a schedule.

24.38 **(iii) Beneficial owner.** The mortgagor may covenant as trustee or personal representative,[31] but if he covenants expressly as beneficial owner this impliedly covenants that he has the power to convey the property, that the mortgagee will be entitled to possession on default, that he will execute further documents, if required by the mortgagee, to perfect the latter's title, and that in the case of leaseholds, that the lease is valid, and that all obligations under it have been and will be performed.[32] Obviously if there is a breach of some of these covenants, the security is gravely impaired, and although there is a personal remedy for damages, this is hardly the point of taking security.

(iv) "All estate" clause. A mortgage will pass to the mortgagee such rights of the mortgagor as he has power to convey[33] and no problem should arise where the mortgagor is sole legal and beneficial owner. If he is sole legal owner but there are doubts as to the rights of others, then the mortgagee should seek the participation of those others.[34] If he is a joint legal owner he may not create an effective legal charge but may charge his own equitable interest, if any (severing any equitable joint tenancy). If the mortgagee cannot obtain the agreement of co-owners, but is agreeable to taking security over whatever interest the mortgagee has, even so, the mortgage will probably still purport to charge the whole beneficial interest, though a cautious lender may wish expressly to specify that a charge is taken over the whole interest of the mortgagee, whatever that may be.[35]

24.39 **(v) Other common clauses.**[36] (a) As to the making of demand by letter to the last known place of business or abode, and the time at which the demand is deemed to be made.

(b) Excluding the mortgagor's power to grant, or accept surrenders[37] of, leases or tenancies unless the Bank consents.[38]

---

[30] Expressed by some term such as "and including interest . . . which shall be computed and compounded according to the usual mode of the Bank both after and before any demand is made or judgment is obtained hereunder . . . "

[31] Whereby he impliedly covenants that he has not done anything to prevent the mortgage operating according to its terms.

[32] s.76, L.P.A. 1925.

[33] s.63, L.P.A. 1925. See the example above, n. 28.

[34] Above, paras. 24.09, 24.23, 24.30.

[35] *e.g.* in addition to the charge in the form already discussed, the form may say "And by way of further security the mortgagor assigns to the bank All That the beneficial interest of the mortgagor in the property and the proceeds of sale thereof" subject to cesser on redemption. (This is expressed as a conveyance, because this is possible where the interest is equitable. It could be expressed as a charge.)

[36] Many different mortgage forms are in use: what follows merely illustrates the most common terms.

[37] *e.g.* so as to grant another lease.

[38] Mortgagors in possession have such powers, by ss.99–100, L.P.A. 1925, but except for agricultural land the sections may be excluded by the terms of the mortgage—s.99(13), L.P.A. 1925.

(c) Excluding section 93 of the Law of Property Act 1925, thus enabling the bank to "consolidate" mortgages (to insist that if one is redeemed, all must be).[39] In fact, an "all monies" mortgage generally means that the bank does not have separate mortgages.

(d) Excluding section 103 of the Law of Property Act 1925 (which prohibits sales for a three months period after default) and providing for an immediate power of sale after demand.

(e) Providing for the appointment of a receiver and manager of the property after demand or on the mortgagor's request, and for the payment and powers of the receiver, and excluding the bank's liability for moneys not actually received by it. The receiver's costs are declared to be a debt which is also charged on the property.

(f) Extending the bank's statutory powers of sale, etc., so that it can grant leases of the whole or any part of the property and on terms which it thinks fit.[40]

(g) Irrevocably appointing the bank and the receiver as the joint and several attorneys of the mortgagor with power to execute deeds, etc. This eliminates the need for any assistance from the court in disposing of the property (if help is needed).[41]

(h) Covenanting for insurance of the property, and to keep it in good repair, in default of which the bank may do so and the moneys so expended are to constitute a secured debt. The bank is given power to apply insurance moneys either to repairing the property or to discharging the debt.

(i) The bank may pay bills of exchange, etc., on which the mortgagor is liable, without affecting his liability under this security.

24.40

(j) The security is declared to be a continuing security notwithstanding any settlement of accounts, etc. It is not to prejudice or affect any security which may have been previously given (*e.g.* by deposit of title deeds) or relating to other property, and is not replaced by subsequent security given.

(k) On learning of any subsequent disposal or incumbrance of the property the bank may close the account and open new accounts, and no money paid into the new account shall discharge any part of the amount due under the closed account.[42] An express power to combine accounts may be given, for the avoidance of doubt, and if so it will specify that no notice to the debtor is required beforehand.[43]

(l) In order to facilitate sale the bank may remove and sell chattels, and pay the net proceeds to the mortgagor.[44]

(m) If the title is not registered, no person (including the mortgagor) is to be registered as proprietor without the bank's consent, and if anyone is

---

[39] s.93, L.P.A. 1925 excludes consolidation unless the contrary is expressed.

[40] Any mortgagee has some powers of leasing by s.99, L.P.A. 1925, but only for agricultural leases less than 50 years, or building leases less than 999 years, and subject to certain conditions. The powers can be increased in the mortgage deed—s.99(14), L.P.A. 1925.

[41] Below, para. 24.67 *et seq.*

[42] This is to prevent *Clayton's case* from operating to discharge the debt. Sometimes an account is "deemed" to be opened.

[43] The right exists anyway: above, Chap. 13.

[44] Some agreements for individual mortgagors will say that the bank is to have no right of set off or retention of these proceeds against the debt, to prevent the term being construed as a chattel mortgage, void for non-registration as a bill of sale. But probably the absence of the qualification does not create a chattel mortgage, in which case combination with the proceeds would be possible. An individual mortgagor might well object to this.

registered, the Land Certificates must (if not deposited with the Land Registry) be given to the bank (so that it can register the charge).

(n)It is certified that a company charge does not contravene the Articles or Memorandum of the company. This acts as an express[45] warranty of authority by the directors, so that they are personally liable in damages if it is false, and if the company is not bound by the charge.[46]

(o) Mortgagor is defined so as to include his successors in title, and bank is similarly defined. There may be other interpretive provisions.

2. EQUITABLE MORTGAGES

24.41 These are not uncommon, even for legal estates, being taken perhaps for short-term loans, or those arranged in haste (pending a legal mortgage), or for customers not wanting the record of a registered charge (even one which is discharged) appearing against the property, or sometimes simply wishing to avoid the expense of a legal mortgage. In addition, a mortgage of an equitable estate or interest must be equitable. They are simpler to take than legal mortgages, and (with registered land) more easily discharged. Theoretical disadvantages such as the lack of a statutory power of sale (which exists for legal mortgages)[47] may be overcome by special terms.

a. Methods of Creation

24.42 There are four ways to create an equitable mortgage. In every case, while the property may be future,[48] equity will not assist the mortgagee unless he has actually advanced money, for the consideration must be executed.[49] In each case, banks may ask the customer to sign a Memorandum of Deposit, both for evidential purposes[50] and because it contains an undertaking by the customer to execute a legal mortgage if called on to do so, and (probably) an irrevocable power of attorney or other useful terms. In addition, if the memorandum (or any of the types of equitable mortgage described here) is under seal, this makes the transaction a mortgage by deed, which entitles the mortgagee to all the powers given by the section 101 of the Law of Property Act, which includes the power of sale. The power of attorney also enables him to sell a legal estate, if the mortgagor had one.

1. The first method is by deposit of title deeds or (for registered land) the Land Certificate.[51] There need be no written agreement or memorandum,[52] but a Memorandum of Deposit is commonly taken.

It should be emphasized that the mere delivery of deeds does not create a security interest, unless so intended (as shown by the Memorandum). Likewise, the bank has no "banker's lien" over documents deposited with it otherwise than in the business of banker.[53] A company charge by deposit of deeds must be registered,[54] even if the debt secured is owed by a third

---

[45] One would be implied, anyway.
[46] This will become unnecessary if the Prentice report becomes law: above, Chap. 12.
[47] s.101(1), L.P.A. 1925.
[48] *Re Clarke, Coombe* v. *Carter* (1887) 36 Ch.D. 348.
[49] See *Rogers* v. *Challis* (1859) 27 Beav. 175; *Holroyd* v. *Marshall* (1862) 10 H.L.Cas. 191; *Tailby* v. *O.R.* (1888) 13 App.Cas. 523.
[50] To show that the documents are not held as security, rather than, *e.g.* safe-keeping.
[51] See L.R.A. 1925, s.66.
[52] It is a form of part performance within s.40(2), L.P.A. 1925—see *Re Wallis and Simmonds (Builders) Ltd.* [1974] 1 All E.R. 561.
[53] Above, Chap. 13.
[54] Under s.395, C.A. 1985.

party,[55] and if not, no lien by operation of law can arise instead,[56] but the charge is affected only in liquidation or on an administration.[57]

In respect of unregistered land this form of mortgage is not a land charge and cannot be registered, but possession of the deeds normally gives security. If, however, the prior equitable mortgagee by deposit of title deeds (not registerable as a land charge) deliberately or by negligence in relation to the title deeds enables the mortgagor to raise a further loan on the basis that there is no prior mortgage, then the second mortgage, even if equitable, takes priority by virtue of the "doctrine of postponement of priority by estoppel."[58] This might occur if the deeds were deliberately left with the mortgagor to enable him to raise money, or where by some sort of gross negligence, the mortgagor was enabled to recover possession of the deeds. A bank, therefore, ought not (with such mortgages) allow the mortgagor to have the deeds, though they might be entrusted to his solicitor from whom an appropriate undertaking is obtained.

Furthermore, even if there is no negligence by the mortgagee, and even though the absence of title deeds often acts as constructive notice to subsequent purchasers of unregistered land, it has been held that where there is a prior *equitable* mortgage, then if a subsequent bona fide purchaser of the *legal* interest (including a mortgage) is given a reasonable explanation for the absence of the deeds, he takes priority over the prior equitable mortgagee (not over prior legal mortgagees).[59] A reasonable explanation prevents the subsequent legal purchaser from having constructive notice of the prior equitable rights, and the bona fide purchasers rule applies. Since the mortgage cannot be registered as a land charge, any equitable mortgage of unregistered land by deposit of title deeds can never be entirely safe from a fraudulent mortgagor. (With registered land, they may be protected by a Caution or a Notice).

24.43

2. Secondly, an equitable mortgage may be made by way of "equitable charge." This needs only a signed written memorandum identifying the property concerned, and indicating that the mortgagor intends his property to be security for money advanced, and it can be very simple.

3. Thirdly, where a mortgagor agrees to execute a legal mortgage or charge in favour of another for moneys actually advanced, equity regards the other as having an immediate equitable mortgage.[60]

4. Fourthly, if the estate or interest is equitable, the whole may be conveyed, subject to a proviso for cesser on redemption, for this is prohibited only with legal estates. This must be in writing, but need not be by deed, and needs no special form of words if the meaning is plain.[61]

---

[55] *Re Wallis & Simmonds (Builders) Ltd.* [1974] 1 All E.R. 561.

[56] *Re Molton Finance Ltd.* [1968] Ch. 325.

[57] Above, Chap. 21.

[58] See *Clarke* v. *Palmer* (1882) 21 Ch.D. 124; *Brocklesby* v. *Temperance Permanent Building Society* [1895] A.C. 173. But see *Northern Counties Fire Ins.* v. *Whipp* (1884) 26 Ch.D. 482.

[59] *Agra Bank Ltd.* v. *Barry* (1874) L.R. 7 H.L. 135 (mortgage made in England of property in Ireland, and deeds said to be in Ireland: a reasonable excuse); *Hewitt* v. *Loosemore* (1851) 9 Hare 449 (farmer mortgagee, not legally advised, told by solicitor mortgagor that he was busy and would show deeds later: a reasonable excuse). See also *Hudston* v. *Viney* [1921] 1 Ch. 98. There is no difference if the second mortgage is not registered as a land charge, for this affects subsequent, not prior purchasers: L.C.A. 1972, s.4.

[60] *ex p. Wright* (1812) 19 Ves. 255, *Parker* v. *Housefield* (1834) 2 My. & K. 419; *Swiss Bank Corpn.* v. *Lloyds Bank Ltd.* [1979] Ch. 584, [1980] 3 W.L.R. 457 (C.A.).

[61] s.53, L.P.A. 1925.

The first method (deposit of deeds) does not create a registerable land charge (for unregistered land) but all the others do. The first three methods operate by way of charge, not conveyance, but the fourth is a conveyance, and is an alternative to the first two methods of equitable mortgage. The third, obviously, can be used only by legal owners or those who may become legal owners. With registered land all methods create a minor interest, requiring protection on the register by Caution or Notice.

b. Bank Forms for Equitable Mortgages

24.44   These tend to be much simpler than for legal mortgages, though, for the reason already given, they are under seal.

(a) There is a covenant to repay[62] then the charge clause. This is usually a charge, though it could be a conveyance (method four, above). The charge may extend to property not yet owned by the mortgagor, for this may be the subject of an equitable mortgage. Future property is most commonly mortgaged with company customers.[63]

(b) There is a covenant to execute a legal mortgage if called on to do so. Consideration is expressed for this, in the usual form of provision of banking facilities, etc., because equity will not help a volunteer even where there is a deed.

(c) The bank is given an irrevocable power of attorney to execute the legal mortgage or to execute a conveyance of the legal estate. As an alternative, the borrower could declare that he holds the legal title as trustee for the execution of a legal mortgage and the bank is to have the statutory power to remove him and appoint new trustees in his place.

(d) (For registered land) no-one else is to be registered as proprietor[64] and the costs of putting a Caution on the register are to be deemed to be properly incurred (and a secured debt, therefore).

(e) The bank is to have the same right to possession as it would have if the charge hereby created had been a legal mortgage created by way of a demise for 3000 years.

c. Terms of Equitable Mortgage with Memorandum of Deposit

24.45   Where the mortgage is created by deposit of title deeds, a Memorandum of Deposit (under seal) may, for reasons given already, be signed by the mortgagor. The terms of this may be almost the same as those just mentioned, except that the first clause states that the documents have been deposited to the intent that the property is equitably charged and the borrower as beneficial owner hereby charges, etc. If the deposit is simultaneous with or later than the Memorandum, it is the latter which creates the charge, and the deposit is not a second or additional charge.[65]

J. Restrictions upon the mortgagor's right of redemption

24.46   A maxim of equity is "once a mortgage, always a mortgage."[66] That is, where a security interest is intended, the courts insist on the mortgagor's right to to redeem the property by paying off the principal, interest, and any costs, whether the mortgage is legal or equitable, and whether made by way

---

[62] Unless omitted: above, para. 24.36.
[63] Above, Chap. 21.
[64] Above, para. 24.35, for the effect of this.
[65] *Re White Rose Cottage* [1965] Ch. 940.
[66] *Samuel* v. *Jarrah Timber and Wood Paving Corpn. Ltd.* [1904] A.C. 323, 329.

of conveyance or charge. This right may be exercised even though there is a date for redemption stated in the mortgage which has passed. The right to redeem, or "equity" is itself seen as a proprietary interest, capable of being disposed of like any other interest. The equity remains until it is extinguished, which may occur in only four ways. These are (a) if the mortgagor gives it up ("releases") to the mortgagee, (b) if the mortgagee goes into possession and stays in possession for 12 years, (c) if the mortgagee sells or agrees to sell the land on the mortgagor's default, and (d) if the mortgagee obtains from the court an order absolute of foreclosure ("forecloses").

Because of this equity, agreements to make the security irredeemable are against public policy, and unenforceable. It is not generally possible to "clog the equity of redemption." This, however, needs qualification. First, the equity can be extinguished in the four ways mentioned. Secondly, section 193 of the Companies Act 1985 provides that a company's debenture may contain conditions making the debenture irredeemable or redeemable only on the happening of a remote contingency or on the expiration of a long period "any rule of equity to the contrary notwithstanding." Thirdly, some reasonable restrictions may be permitted.

The types of restrictions commonly found are (i) postponements of redemption (prohibitions on repayment); (ii) clauses restraining the activities which may be carried on by the mortgagee (restraint of trade clauses); (iii) provisions requiring additional sums to be paid (premiums, or penalties, or index-linking clauses); and (iv) clauses giving to the mortgagee some "collateral advantage" (a type, perhaps, of restraint of trade clause, giving a benefit to the mortgagee, rather than simply restraining the mortgagor).

Postponement of the right to redeem may be permissible if not unreasonable, undue or oppressive, or where the mortgagor is a company. If a commercial borrower with an existing mortgage, not being under any pressure, transfers his mortgages to an "arms length" mortgagee to secure a better rate of interest, and, to ensure that the repayments could be spread over a period, and would not be called in at any time, asks for the term to be fixed at (say) 40 years, a prohibition on repayment is reasonable.[67]

"Collateral advantages" arise, for example, where the mortgagor (being a **24.47** garage or publican) "ties" himself to a petrol company or brewery for a period, in return for the mortgage.[68] These clauses may be struck down under the quite separate doctrine relating to unreasonable "restraints of trade" (which can apply even if there is no security). It is difficult to argue that a clog which is unfair or unconscionable is a reasonable restraint, and it seems probable that the doctrines converge to a large degree, so that a reasonable restraint is not an unreasonable clog, and vice versa. But the doctrine of restraint of trade may require, for example, that the clause be reasonable not merely between the parties, but also as to the public interest, and (sometimes) that a clause be no wider than is needed to protect some

---

[67] *Knightsbridge Estates Trust Ltd.* v. *Byrne* [1939] Ch. 441 (affirmed [1940] A.C. 613, on the ground that the mortgagor was a company); *Santley* v. *Wilde* [1889] 2 Ch. 474, (10 year lease, irredeemable until payment of proportion of the net profits from the lease, which could not be calculated until the end of the lease, held reasonable). *c.f. Fairclough* v. *Swan Brewery Co. Ltd.* [1912] A.C. 565, (JC) (restriction on redemption until six weeks before the expiry of a 17 year lease unreasonable).

[68] See *Esso Petroleum Co. Ltd.* v. *Harper's Garage (Stourport) Ltd.* [1968] A.C. 269.

proprietory interest. There may also be a difference between those mort-gages in which the property is acquired with the loan in question, and those where it is already acquired, and then mortgaged.[69] Collateral advantages may or may not depend upon a postponement of repayment: if so, then both the postponement and the collateral advantage must be reasonable. An advantage is more likely to be seen as fair if it ceases with the mortgage.[70] Even so, a modern court is likely to distinguish between ordinary commer-cial transactions, and those involving oppression, and a tie made on fair commercial terms which continues, after redemption, may be upheld.[71]

24.48   It may be reasonable to index-link repayments to a foreign currency. This was decided in *Multiservice Bookbinding Ltd.* v. *Marden*, even though the original sum more than doubled as a result, and despite objections that unfa-vourable movements of currency might act as a disincentive to redemption and were an unfair collateral advantage.[72]

A premium on prepayment requires the borrower to pay his mortgagee a sum of money for the privilege of early repayment. Whether true premiums are enforceable (where there is a security) depends on all the facts: the rela-tive strengths of the parties[73] the availability of independent legal advice, the size of the premium, and so on.

24.49   If there is no security, a premium cannot be a "clog" on the equity of redemption, and is enforceable unless it amounts to a "penalty." A clause cannot be a penalty, unless it is payable on default (breach of contract). If payable on default, it is a penalty unless it is a genuine pre-estimate of the likely losses.[74] An example of a "genuine pre-estimate" may be found in the compensation clauses found in some term loans where the lending bank funds itself in the interbank market for a fixed period, and where the loan provides for repayments to occur at periods matching the bank's funding periods. Losses may occur if early repayment causes a mismatch of interest rates, and a term providing for the prepayer to compensate the bank for such losses would not be objectionable. A clear penalty would be a pro-vision for an increase in the rate of interest, not related to possible losses.

---

[69] See generally, Treitel, *The Law of Contract*, (5th ed.) p. 337 *et seq.*

[70] As in *Biggs* v. *Hoddinott* [1898] 2 Ch. 307 (reasonable postponment of mortgage for five years, tie to brewery ceased on redemption—held to be reasonable). Contrast *Noakes & Co. Ltd.* v. *Rice* [1902] A.C. 24 (26 year lease, mortgage of uncertain duration, tie to last for term of lease—held to be unreasonable); *Bradley* v. *Carritt* [1903] A.C. 253 (shares mortgaged, mortgagor promised to use best efforts to see that mortgagee was "always hereafter" broker for the company—held unreasonable).

[71] *Kreglinger* v. *New Patagonia Meat and Cold Storage Co. Ltd.* [1914] A.C. 25 (five year tie involved mortgagor selling products only to the mortgagee, at ruling market price, held to be enforceable when five year loan repaid early).

[72] [1979] Ch. 84:—borrower was small expanding company, with benefit of independent legal advice, loan irredeemable for 10 years (allowable, being a company). Interest was at floating rate two per cent. above bank rate, (over the period it was about 16 per cent.) with capitali-zation of arrears of interest after 21 days—so that interest was payable on interest. Both capi-tal and interest were index-linked to the Swiss franc. Court held that the bargain was hard, but not unfair and unconscionable. It did not fall into that category unless one of the parties imposed the objectionable terms "in a morally reprehensible manner, that is to say, in a way which affects his conscience." See also *Nationwide Building Society* v. *Registry of Friendly Societies* [1983] 3 All E.R. 296.

[73] See *Cityland and Property (Holdings) Ltd.* v. *Dabrah* [1968] Ch. 166 (mortgagor "obviously of limited means" buying from landlord, at premium of 57 per cent. of loan—held unreason-able).

[74] See *Re Anglo-Danubian Steam Navign. and Colliery Co.* (1875) L.R. 20 Eq. 339; *Re Phillips ex p. Bath* (1884) 27 Ch.D. 590; *Booth* v. *Salvation Army Building Assn. Ltd.* (1897) 14 T.L.R. 3; *Cato* v. *Cato* (1972) 116 Sol Jo. 138.

Even here there are ways around the rule: for example, if instead of increasing the rate on default, a high rate is originally set and then reduced for prompt payment. this is not a penalty, and is enforceable.

The result seems to be that:

(a) with unsecured loans, a prohibition on prepayment or a premium for prepayment (not being a default) is unobjectionable;

(b) with secured loans, a prohibition on prepayment or a premium (other than on default) is acceptable if the borrower is a company, and otherwise is acceptable if not unfair and oppressive;

(c) collateral advantages, separate from the prepayment (if there is one) are not necessarily void, even if they may last after prepayment, and will be enforceable if not unfair and oppressive; provided that if they amount to restraints of trade they fulfil all the requirements of the restraints of trade doctrine;

(d) index linking, even to foreign currencies, is not in itself unfair and oppressive;

(e) sums of money payable on breach and not as a genuine pre-estimate of losses, are penalties, and unforceable.

K. Transfers of mortgages

A mortgage is assignable, though assignment by banks of domestic mortgages has not been common. One possibility is that instead of redeeming a mortgage by repayment, the mortgagor (or another incumbrancer) may require the mortgagee to assign the debt and mortgage to a third party, and a bank faced with such a request must comply.[75] Similarly if B (a guarantor, say) who does not have the equity of redemption, pays A's debt so as to discharge the mortgage, without any reconveyance or surrender or release, the mortgage may be assigned to B.[76] If, therefore, a bank's customer wishes to obtain mortgage finance elsewhere, the new lender may pay the bank directly, and take a transfer. This has the advantage of preserving the priority of the original mortgage, rather than taking a new mortgage, though the new lender is subject to the terms of the old mortgage[77] unless they are subsequently varied. With any assignment, there may, however, be difficulty with an "all monies" mortgage securing an overdraft. The security covers all debts of mortgagor to the assignor, but (unless varied) not all debts between mortgagor and assignee, so that the assignee could enforce it only in respect of the debt as it was assignor and debtor at the time of assignment.[78] If the mortgagor does agree, this probably constitutes a new mortgage entered at that time, and the discharge of the old.[79]

With unregistered land, legal mortgages may be transferred by deed, which transfers the debt, the security right, and all associated remedies.[80] There is a simple statutory form of transfer.[81] The transfer may be made by separate instrument, or it may be endorsed on the original mortgage instrument. A legal assignment may use some other form, if under seal.[82] An

24.50

---

[75] s.95, L.P.A. 1925. Naturally, the bank is simultaneously repaid.
[76] Though not in all cases. See s.95(2), L.P.A. 1925.
[77] A reason why banks may refuse, preferring new mortgages on their own forms.
[78] References in the mortgage to the bank's heirs and assigns can make no difference.
[79] *i.e.* it may operate as a novation.
[80] s.114(1), L.P.A. 1925.
[81] In the third schedule to the L.P.A. 1925.
[82] s.52(1), L.P.A. 1925.

equitable assignment may be made otherwise than by deed, but must be made in writing, and for valuable consideration,[83] but in that case the assignee could not give a good discharge for the debt. A mortgage made by deposit of title deeds, can be transferred merely by delivery of the deeds to the transferee,[83a] though some Memorandum is desirable for evidential purposes. The debt for which the security is given can be transferred separately, according to the ordinary rules of assignments, and this may by implication transfer the security.[84] If not, the security cannot be enforced by the original creditor if he is no longer legal owner of the debt.

24.51   With registered land, a transfer of a registered charge must be by deed in a form prescribed.[85] The transferee's title is not subject to any defects in the charge, of which he had no notice. The assignment is complete only on registration of the transfer, and if this is not done the transferor remains proprietor, though the assignee has a good equitable right. Unregistered (and, therefore, equitable) mortgages could be transfered as already discussed for unregistered land, and then be protected by Cautions, etc.

Transfer of only part of a debt is necessarily an equitable assignment, and although the legal title and right to the security can be owned jointly,[86] the right to realise the property cannot be separately exercised, so that the parties must act together in realising the whole security.

For perfection purposes[87] notice must be given to the mortgagor, but his consent to a transfer is strictly unnecessary, though desirable inasmuch as the deed recites the amount of the debt, and this will bind him against the transferee. Otherwise, he may contest the debt.[88] Similarly, he is prevented from relying on any matter (such as misrepresentation) which might have made the mortgage voidable, and he is estopped from asserting that it is void. Further, where part of the debt is to be assigned the mortgagor's consent makes it possible to split the mortgage between assignor and assignee (i.e. both being legal owners of part). If the debt secured is the same, this may not change priorities in relation to subsequent incumbrancers, or a liquidator, and so on, as it may be seen as an alteration of an existing mortgage rather than a new mortgage.[89] Because bank mortgages are repayable on demand, the bank is (legally, though not necessarily, morally) in a strong position when in any of these cases it asks for consent.

L. Sub-mortgages

24.52   A sub-mortgage occurs where a mortgagee mortgages the rights which he has under the mortgage.[90] Sometimes, the bank's customer will himself be mortgagee (e.g. a mortgage company), and as an alternative to assigning the debt outright, or to calling in the debt, he may sub-mortgage it in order to raise money. The bank has the double security of the personal liability of

---

[83] s.53(1), L.P.A. 1925.

[83a] *Brocklesby* v. *Temperance Permanent Building Society* [1895] A.C. 173.

[84] Transfer of the security certainly transfers the debt.

[85] L.R.A. 1925, s.33(1), L.R.R. 1925, r. 153, and form 54.

[86] And they can be jointly registered, for example. They could have legal title jointly, or the assignor could declare himself to be a trustee of the mortgage for them jointly.

[87] *i.e.* to create a complete legal assignment, with legal title in the assignee.

[88] See *De Lisle* v. *Union Bank of Scotland* [1914] 1 Ch. 22; *Turner* v. *Smith* [1901] 1 Ch. 213.

[89] Encyclopedia, E(361), n. 1. The editors submit this "confidently," though there is some doubt.

[90] *i.e.* it is a "mortgage of a mortgage." The first mortgage is referred to as the "head mortgage."

both original mortgagor and original mortgagee on their covenants to repay, and it has the land as well. Sub-mortgages, however, are not very commonly encountered by banks. They may be legal (if made by deed, and if registered, in the case of registered land) or equitable, and are made by way of assignment of the mortgage, with a proviso for redemption.[91] If, say, a mortgage company gives a floating charge to its bankers, the crystallization of the charge operates as an equitable assignment of the mortgages held by the company, and therefore, as a sub-mortgage.[92] The rights under the assignment are perfected by giving notice to the original mortgagor. The sub-chargee will have the rights and powers of the original mortgagee.[93]

M. Discharge of mortgages

1. BY REDEMPTION

The mortgagor retains an equity of redemption, until that is finally ext-inguished.[94] The right of redemption is exercisable by the mortgagor or by any person who has an interest in the mortgaged property.[95] Bank mortgages are repayable on demand, and unless otherwise agreed, the mortgagor may repay when he wishes. Some loans for fixed periods may have a premium for early repayment (structured as a reduced rate for timely payment, to avoid the "penalty" rule).[96] Bank forms usually exclude the right of consolidation, though it may be unnecessary for all monies mortgages.

With registered land, Form 53 may be used for the discharge, though the Registrar may act on any sufficient proof of satisfaction, such as an endorsed receipt for the principal money plus interest.[97] Discharges by a company must be executed under seal. With banks a signature by someone of comparable or greater standing than a branch manager will be accepted by the Registrar. He then cancels the entry on the title.[98] The Registrar returns the Land Certificate. For unregistered charges, Cautions or Notices are withdrawn on the same proof.[99] The mortgagee returns the Land Certificate to the mortgagor or if it holds for safe custody, notes the change in purpose of the deposit.

With unregistered land, a receipt which is on or annexed to the instrument (often on the reverse) is usually indorsed. The receipt need not be under seal, but often is when standard forms are used. If this names a third

24.53

24.54

---

[91] For the form of the sub-mortgage see the Encyclopedia, E(383–385).

[92] See *Sowman* v. *David Samuel Trust Ltd.* [1978] 1 All E.R. 616; *Barrows* v. *Chief Land Register* [1977] CLY 315.

[93] Provided that, for example, with registered land he seeks registration.

[94] Above, para. 24.46.

[95] *e.g.* subsequent mortgagee, tenant, (subrogated) surety for the mortgagor, spouse with right of occupation.

[96] Above, para. 24.48. These are mostly used by building societies.

[97] Or a conveyance of the land with discharge endorsed on it—form 55 may be used for this.

[98] A line is drawn through it, and a stamp put next to this. The entry remains visible until the Charges register is next tidied up, as on a change of title number.

[99] With Notices, there is a withdrawal form on the reverse side of the Notice which the mortgagee has. With Cautions, form 71 is used, signed by the cautioner.

party as payer it operates as a transfer to him[1] and discharges the mortgagor against the original mortgagee.[2] The party redeeming may, however, demand in lieu of the receipt a reassignment, surrender, release or transfer, and this is necessary anyway if not at all of the money is then repaid.[3] Commonly, redemption occurs on sale of the property, at which time the actual instrument of conveyance may carry the receipt and be endorsed by the mortgagee, so that the property is conveyed free of the mortgage. Equitable mortgages can be discharged by payment accompanied by (a) receipt (for evidential purposes), or (b) deed, if the mortgage was under seal, or (c) return of deeds, if created by deposit of deeds. In the first two cases, a registered land charge may be vacated.[4] All documents of title are returned to the mortgagor, and the bank has no duty to search out subsequent incumbrancers and hand the documents to them. If, however, the bank knows of them (other than by registration of a land charge) it must return the deeds to them, and not the mortgagor.[5]

With company mortgages, whether discharge occurs by redemption or by release the company may[6] apply for removal of the entry from the Companies registrar.[7]

2. BY RELEASE

24.55 A release without redemption of the debt may occur, for example, if (a) only part of the property is to be released, the rest now being of sufficient value to cover the debt, either because the debt is reduced, or the property has increased in value; or (b) if substitute security is to be given; or (c) if the mortgagor wishes to sell and the property is of insufficient value even to repay incumbrances which have priority over the bank's mortgage.[8] Registered land is released by using Form 53. For unregistered land a deed of release will suffice.

3. BY LAPSE OF TIME

24.56 The mortgagee's right to sue for principal and to enforce the mortgage may become barred if he does take action within 12 years of the date to receive it accrues.[9] In the case of loans repayable on demand, however, there is no "right to receive" until a demand is made, so that time bars will not affect a bank.[10]

---

[1] Above, para. 24.50.
[2] If it is for all the money secured—s.115(1), L.P.A. 1925.
[3] s.115(4), L.P.A. 1925.
[4] Form K11 is used.
[5] s.96, L.P.A. 1925, as amended.
[6] Under s.403, C.A. 1985.
[7] A memorandum of satisfaction is filed, supported by a declaration by the secretary, and a director.
[8] In which case, because prior incumbrances can always exercise their power of sale, the bank may as well agree.
[9] ss.8 and 20, Limitation Act 1980.
[10] Above para. 3.05: rights to interest for arrears could be barred after six years.

N. The mortgagee's rights and powers[11]

1. WHILE THE MORTGAGE IS IN FORCE

a. The Right to Possession[12]

A legal mortgagee is entitled to possession of the property (without any **24.57** default) immediately the security is executed,[13] even if the mortgage is by way of legal charge rather than lease,[14] unless the instrument expressly[15] or impliedly[15a] provides to the contrary.[16] An equitable mortgagee probably has the same right if he has a covenant for a legal mortgage, and a power of attorney.[17] Naturally, banks would rarely exercise this right unless there is a default, or a business mortgagor is in difficulty, and demand is made for repayment. Possession would be taken, for example, in order to receive rents, or to secure the property while waiting for more favourable market conditions for sale, or in order to sell a business mortgaged under a floating charge, but even so the appointment of a receiver is a better remedy. The reason is (apart from administrative inconvenience) that once in possession, the mortgagee is (a) liable for negligence causing damage to the property, and (b) liable to account strictly to the mortgagor for the greater of what he has received or what he might have received by diligent management. This is often described as liability for "wilful default," but liability for negligence would be a more appropriate description.[18] In addition, the mortgagee may be liable to third parties: for example, under the Occupier's Liability Act 1957, or for nuisance. Further, on sale, there might be a complaint against the bank that it has failed to achieve the best price. These problems are avoided by appointing a receiver, who is the agent of the mortgagor, not the bank.

Possession is achieved by taking the management of the estate out of the mortgagor's hands, even if the mortgagor is still in physical occupation.[19] It is, however, a criminal offence for anyone to threaten violence against a person who is present on any premises, in order to gain entry,[20] or (whether the resident mortgagor is temporarily absent or not) physically to enter residential premises without a court order.[21] If, therefore, the mortgagor (or anyone else) is in the premises, or if it is dwelling house, a court order must be sought.[22] It is not a criminal offence honestly to break into non–residential premises if the mortgagor[23] is temporarily absent. Where an action for possession is brought, any co–occupier must be joined.

---

[11] [1986] 3 C.L. 174. See also, above, Chap. 23, concerning realisation of securities.
[12] What is said here is relevant also to cases of default.
[13] *Four-Maids Ltd.* v. *Dudley Marshall (Properties) Ltd.* [1957] Ch. 317.
[14] ss.95(4), 87(1), L.P.A. 1925.
[15] As is common.
[15a] As perhaps with domestic mortgages.
[16] Unless the mortgagee gives notice of intent to take possession the mortgagor has many of the normal rights of a full owner, such as the right to rents, or to sue for trespass, and so on; s.98, s.141, L.P.A. 1925.
[17] Encyclopedia, E(501); *Barclays Bank Ltd.* v. *Bird* [1954] Ch. 274.
[18] See *Mayer* v. *Murray* (1878) 8 Ch.D. 424.
[19] *Noyes* v. *Pollock* (1886) 32 Ch.D. 53.
[20] Criminal Law Act 1977, s.6.
[21] Protection from Eviction Act 1977.
[22] Carefully forcing a door may not be "violence": Encyclopedia E(511), but see Smith and Hogan, *Criminal Law*, (5th ed.), p. 754, n. 5.
[23] And employees, etc.

b. The Right to Additional Property

24.58 A mortgage of land includes fixtures,[24] and anything later affixed becomes subject to the mortgage.[25] Similarly, if the mortgagor of leasehold property manages, because of his status of tenant, to acquire a new lease or the freehold reversion, the new interest becomes subject to the original mortgage.[26]

c. The Right to Documents of Title

24.59 Except with registered land where the mortgage is registered and the mortgagee has a Charge Certificate, a first legal mortgagee is entitled to all the title deeds,[27] though the mortgagor is entitled to inspect them and make copies, etc., at his own expense.[28] An equitable mortgagee, where the mortgage is made otherwise than by deposit of the deeds, is not entitled to them unless it is so stipulated.

d. Granting and Surrendering Leases

24.60 Either party, if in possession, and if not prohibited by the mortgage[29] has a statutory power to grant leases not exceeding 50 years.[30] Either party, if entitled to exercise this power of leasing may for that purpose, (unless prohibited)[31] accept the surrender from a tenant of all or part of a leasehold interest which is part of the mortgaged property.[32] With agricultural land, exclusion of the mortgagor's powers to lease is impermissible[33] so that the possibility of a tenancy affects the valuation of the land. A business tenant has in many cases a statutory right of renewal of his lease, and if the landlord is mortgagor his duty to renew cannot be excluded.[34]

A grant by the mortgagor of a lease in breach of a prohibition does not bind a non–consenting mortgagee[35] unless the agreement to lease was made before or simultaneously with the mortgagor's acquisition of title to the land. In the latter event, the lease is regarded as affecting the title as soon as it is acquired, while the mortgage takes effect only after the acquisition and the lease[36] (which takes priority).[37]

A lease granted by the mortgagee, otherwise than under the statutory power, is subject to the mortgagor's right to redeem, except in the unlikely case that the lessee.[38] is a bona fide purchaser, who may defeat the equity of redemption. A lease granted by the mortgagor, otherwise than under the

---

[24] For a discussion of fixtures, see Megarry and Wade, *The Law of Real Property*, (5th ed.), 730 *et seq.*

[25] *Reynolds* v. *Ashby & Son* [1904] A.C. 466.

[26] *Leigh* v. *Burnett* (1885) 29 Ch.D. 231; *Chelsea Estates Investment Trust Co. Ltd.* v. *Marche* [1955] Ch. 328.

[27] ss.86, 87, L.P.A. 1925.

[28] s.96, L.P.A. 1925.

[29] As is normal, because tenants may reduce the value of the property: above, para. 24.39.

[30] Or building leases not exceeding 999 years. See generally, s.99, L.P.A. 1925.

[31] As normal: above, para. 24.39.

[32] s.100, L.P.A. 1925.

[33] Agricultural Holdings Act 1948, s.2.

[34] Landlord and Tenant Act 1954, s.36.

[35] *Dudley and District Benefit Building Society* v. *Emerson* [1949] Ch. 707.

[36] This is a "lease by estoppel." The acquisition of legal title by the mortgagor "feeds the estoppel."

[37] See *Rajapakse* v. *Fernando* [1920] A.C. 892; *Church of England Building Society* v. *Piskor* [1954] Ch. 553; the same rule applies to registered land: *Woolwich Equitable Building Society* v. *Marshall* [1952] Ch. 1.

[38] Who will generally know that he is dealing with the mortgagee or otherwise have notice of the mortgagor's rights.

statutory power, will be subject to the mortgage unless the lessee is a bona fide purchaser, etc., and the mortgage is not properly protected.

e. The Right to Protect the Property

Bank mortgages should contain terms concerning maintenance of the property, insurance, and so on. Even without express terms, there are common law and statutory powers to restrain deliberate damage,[39] to do necessary repairs,[40] and to insure against fire.[41] Only necessary repairs may be charged to the mortgagor, so that express provision is desirable. If the mortgagee goes into possession to effect the repairs, he must account strictly for what he does, and a better course is to appoint a receiver[42] for the purpose. The statutory right to insure against fire exists only if the mortgage is by deed, and is only to the extent of two-thirds of reinstatement value, and does not cover other risks, so that express provision should be made.

24.61

f. The Right to Tack, and its Effect on Subsequent Mortgages

Tacking is the right of a secured lender to add further monies to the security so that the further monies are also secured. Bank mortgages usually provide that the mortgage secures any advances.[43] The main problem concerns the priority of mortgages subsequent to the "original mortgage" in relation to the amounts tacked on.

24.62

With unregistered land, further advances made under a legal or equitable mortgage rank in priority to subsequent legal or equitable mortgages if (i) the original mortgage obliges (not merely permits) the mortgagor to advance further money,[44] or (ii) if the original mortgagee does not know of later mortgages when he advances the money, or (iii) if by agreement the subsequent mortgagees subordinate their securities to the original mortgagee.[45] The first of these would not apply where a bank gives an overdraft limit secured by mortgage, since there is no "obligation" to maintain the limit, which remains repayable on demand.[46] But some large term loans are made in terms of a commitment by a bank, and the borrower is entitled to draw-down certain amounts at certain periods if he chooses. A security over subsequent draw-downs would have priority over subsequent incumbrances. As to the second case, registration of the subsequent mortgage as a land charge, after the original mortgage, and after the last search by the mortgagee, does not give notice to a mortgagee whose mortgage secures a current account or further advances (but searching is advisable, in case the "subsequent" mortgage was in fact before the original mortgage, though registered after). Actual notice binds the original mortgagee, and subsequent incumbrancers ought to give written notice when their mortgages

---

[39] *Ellis* v. *Glover & Hobson Ltd.* [1908] 1 K.B. 388.
[40] *Sandon* v. *Hooper* (1844) 14 L.J. Ch. 120.
[41] s.101, L.P.A. 1925.
[42] As mortgagor's agent.
[43] *e.g.* "all moneys and liabilitites which shall for the time being . . . be due owing or incurred . . ."
[44] s.94, L.P.A. 1925. (Even if the original mortgagee knows of subsequent mortgages.)
[45] Either by a formal contract, or merely by waiver, since estoppel would then operate.
[46] *Hopkinson* v. *Rolt* (1861) 9 H.L.C. 514.

are made. Notice will not prevent tacking under the first (obligatory) case.[47]

With registered land, there are special statutory rules for registered charges: first, any obligation to advance further monies is entered on the register, so that subsequent incumbrancers know of it and take subject to further advances.[48] Secondly, where there is no obligation, but the charge covers further advances, the land registry is obliged to notify the proprietor of the charge of proposed entries affecting his priority, (so that he may decide whether to advance further sums or not).[49] Thirdly, a subordination agreement may be entered by deed, and put on the register,[50] though a simple contract, or an estoppel, or an estoppel, would bind consenting subsequent incumbrancers.

24.63 If the original mortgage is protected by Notice or Caution, but not registered, further advances have no priority over subsequent registered mortgages (which, once registered, take priority over the earlier mortgage protected only by a Caution, not only over further advances). Further advances probably have no priority if the original mortgagee has notice of the subsequent mortgagee (whether registered or not), even if through entries on the register.[51]

Since notice generally prevents taking of further advances, if a bank mortgagee receives notice of a subsequent mortgage, and the debt secured is an overdraft on a current account, normal procedure involves breaking the account, and opening a new one, which is either kept in credit or secured by alternative security.[52] This procedure avoids the effect which the rule in *Clayton's case* would otherwise have in reducing the size of the secured debt.[53] *Clayton's case* causes transactions through the current account continually to replace the original debt with new debt, so that although the total amount outstanding remains the same or even increases, the bank makes "further" advances, which have no priority once the bank has notice of a subsequent incumbrancer. The rule in *Clayton's case*, however, is merely a rule as to the presumed intention of the parties, and can be rebutted.[54] An express term can rebut the presumption[55] and the "deemed" opening of a new account should be sufficient. Sufficient terms would include: "the rule in *Clayton's case* shall not only apply to the secured debt," or "money paid in or carried to the mortgagor's credit on any current account shall first be appropriated towards and have the effect of discharging the most recent debit items on the said current account(s)." Nevertheless, cautious banks break the account, though it seems unnecessary.

---

[47] *West* v. *Williams* [1899] 1 Ch. 132, was reversed by s.94(1), L.P.A. 1925.

[48] L.R.A. 1925, s.30.

[49] *Ibid.* After the date when that notice ought to be received, subsequent incumbrancers have priority. If the notice is not sent or received, the original mortgagee is entitled to compensation, provided he gave the correct address (hence, if the branch dealing with the account changes, the land registry should be told). See L.R.A. 1925, s.83.

[50] s.31, L.R.A. 1925.

[51] L.R.A. 1925, ss.29, 30, 48, 49, 55, and L.R.R. 1925, r. 218.

[52] Above, para. 24.40, esp. at n. 42, for terms, which may "deem" a new account to be opened at the moment the bank receives notice.

[53] Above, Chap. 13: the bank has no obligation to advance further sums, and the rule relating to obligatory tacking, which could overcome *Clayton's case*, is inapplicable.

[54] *Deeley* v. *Lloyds Bank* [1912] A.C. 756.

[55] *Westminster Bank and Cond* (1940) 46 Com.Cas. 60.

2. WHILE THE MORTGAGE IS NO LONGER IN FORCE

A mortgagee may be entitled to some rights (such as possession) even with- **24.64**
out default. Bank mortgages normally enable the bank to make demand at
any time, and thus "manufacture" a default. Demand may be effective notwithstanding the death of the mortgagor.[56] On default the mortgagee's
remedies are (a) to sue on the personal covenants, for any breach, and for
capital and interest, (b) to apply for foreclosure, (c) to sell the property. If
repairs are necessary, or to safeguard the property, or to manage, or to sell
it, he may go into possession, or may appoint a receiver.

a. Effect of Consumer Credit Act 1974

The Consumer Credit Act 1974 applies to mortgages given to individuals if **24.65**
the credit does not exceed £15000[57] and if none of the exemptions apply.
Banks are not exempt, though building societies are. Given the financial
limit, it would primarily affect second mortgages.[58] If the Act applies, the
mortgage may be enforced (*e.g.* possession, or sale) only on a court order,
unless the mortgagee consents.[59] The court has power to re-open the credit
agreement if it is extortionate[60] though this may be unlikely to affect any
English bank. The debtor has power to redeem prematurely at any time,
and any term to the contrary is void,[61]

b. Possession

This is discussed above.[62]   **24.66**

c. Sale

The power of sale is the most important right. There are statutory rights, **24.67**
though standard forms contain an express power or modifications to the
statutory power.

(i) The statutory power. A statutory power of sale is given for mortgages **24.68**
made by deed.[63] Sale can be of the whole, or parts of the property, can take
place by auction or private contract, and may be subject to such conditions
"as the mortgagee thinks fit."[64] The power of sale may be exercised by
"any person for the time being entitled to receive and give a discharge for
the mortgage money."[65] The conveyance on sale may be made in the name
of either mortgagor or mortgagee,[66] though the latter is most common.[67]
    The mortgagee may exercise his power of sale even though the mort-
gagor has himself agreed on a sale which would produce enough to pay off

---

[56] *Barclays Bank Ltd.* v. *Kiley* [1961] 2 All E.R. 849.
[57] S.I. 1983, No. 1878.
[58] If the Act applies, the agreement must be in a specified form, and the mortgagee must have
    been given a seven day period in advance in order to change his mind.
[59] s. 126, 173(3).
[60] ss. 137–140.
[61] s. 173(1), and above for postponement terms.
[62] Above, para. 24.57.
[63] s. 101(1)(i), L.P.A. 1925.
[64] See also s. 101(2), L.P.A. 1925, enabling restrictive covenants to be imposed on the pur-
    chaser: mines and minerals to be sold separately; and reservations of rights of way and so on,
    to be made.
[65] s. 106(1), L.P.A. 1925.
[66] ss. 88, 89, L.P.A. 1925.
[67] A sale of registered land has effect as a sale by the registered proprietor, and the charge and
    all entries of lower priority are cancelled: s. 34, 1.R.A. 1925.

the whole mortgage debt.[68] Tender of the whole sum, however, would prevent the mortgagee's sale, so long as the equity of redemption has not yet been extinguished[69] by sale, or even by the entering of an unconditional contract to sell. Thereafter, the mortgagor cannot redeem even by tender of all of the purchase money, but his equity revives if the contract for sale does not proceed.[70]

The statutory power exists "when the mortgage money has become due," which will be on default of repayment on demand. The statutory power may be varied, extended or wholly excluded by the mortgage.[71] Express clauses[72] may extend the power as between bank and purchaser, so that the power is exercisable at any time (even if, between bank and mortgagor demand should be made). In fact, purchasers have statutory protection from verifying that the power has become exercisable,[73] but this protection will not exist if they become aware of any impropriety,[74] and an express clause may reduce assertions of improper exercise of the power.

Restrictions in section 103 of the Law of Property Act are usually excluded by banks. These require demand for payment followed by the default continuing for three months, or interest remaining in arrears for two months, or breach of some other covenant (other than payment of principal and interest). The mortgage may contain other rights, relating, for example, to sale of chattels in the property (with an individual's mortgage), or to separation and separate sale of fixtures (with a company mortgage). In leasehold mortgages there may be terms allowing the mortgagee to sell by granting leases at a premium,[75] or allowing the mortgagee to charge the mortgagor for landlord's obligations to leaseholders. It is desirable to retain and exercise the statutory power, for this has the effect of discharging not only the mortgagee's own mortgage, but also any subsequent incumbrances, thus giving the purchaser clear title.[76] Otherwise, the consent of the subsequent incumbrancers would be required.

On sale, the purchaser obtains good title to the whole estate, subject only to mortgages prior to those of the mortgagee who sells. The sale extinguishes the security of the selling mortgagee, and any mortgages with lower priority.[77]

24.69 **(ii) Equitable mortgages.** The statutory power covers equitable mortgages if made by deed, and the legal estate can be sold (if the mortgagor is legal owner). Equitable mortgages not by deed give no power to transfer the legal estate, though the mortgagee may transfer good equitable title. In

[68] *Duke* v. *Robson* [1973] 1 All E.R. 481.
[69] Above, para. 24.46.
[70] *Lord Waring* v. *London and Manchester Assurance Co. Ltd.* [1935] Ch. 310; *Property and Bloodstock Ltd.* v. *Emerton* [1968] Ch. 94 (where dicta suggest that a conditional sale does not extinguish the equity).
[71] s.101(3–4), L.P.A. 1925.
[72] *e.g.* "Section 103 of the Law of Property Act 1925 shall not apply to this security but the statutory power of sale shall as between the Bank and a purchaser from the Bank arise on and be exercisable at any time after the execution of this security provided that the Bank shall not exercise the said power of sale until payment of the moneys hereby secured has been demanded but this proviso shall not affect a purchaser or put him on inquiry whether such demand has been made."
[73] s.104, L.P.A. 1925.
[74] *Lord Waring* v. *London and Manchester Assurance Co. Ltd.* [1935] Ch. 310.
[75] *i.e.* not for a regualar rent.
[76] s.104(1), L.P.A. 1925.
[77] ss.88, 89, 104, L.P.A. 1925.

practice, therefore, an equitable mortgagee of a legal estate must apply to the court for an order of sale.[78] An irrevocable power of attorney may be separately taken, but again, the legal title cannot be transferred under such a power unless it is by deed.[79] A declaration of trust by the mortgagor that he held legal title for the mortgagee, coupled with a power in the bank to remove the trustee and appoint another, would be affective,[80] and is sometimes done even where the memorandum of deposit is made by deed. With registered land, however, even if the bank has thus ensured the power to sell the legal estate, it probably may not do so while the mortgage remains equitable, and it must first become legal mortgagee (which the mortgage usually allows) and register the charge.[81] If the mortgage (unusually) contains no provision entitling the mortgagee to the execution of a legal mortgage he must, therefore, apply to the court. (The devices of the power of attorney or the trust would, it seems, enable him to have a legal mortgage executed.)

(iii) Duty of care in relation to price. This is discussed elsewhere.[81a] **24.70**

(iv) Proceeds of sale. The mortgagee is trustee of the proceeds and to **24.71** avoid breach of trust must pay in this order: (i) to prior incumbrancers[82] (ii) the costs of sale, (iii) the moneys payable under the mortgage agreement, (iv) any subsequent mortgagee,[83] (v) the mortgagor himself. Other incumbrancers may be discovered from a "proceeds search" of entries on the land register, or (with unregistered land), the Land Charges register. In case of dispute between incumbrancers, the money should be paid into court.[84] A subsequent incumbrancer whose mortgage is not registered but whose existence is known should be paid, unless someone claims priority over him, for his mortgage is defective only against later purchasers, etc. But if a search is made, and through no fault of its own the bank had no notice of a subsequent mortgagee, and paid any surplus to the mortgagor or another incumbrancer, the bank is not liable.[85]

If instead of receiving cash on the sale the mortgagee leaves all or part of the price outstanding, by way of mortgage to the purchaser, he must immediately give credit to the mortgagor for the whole of the agreed purchase price.[86] If on this basis he has notionally "received" a surplus, that would have to be distributed as stated above.

d. Action for Foreclosure

Foreclosure is rarely sought, and can only be obtained in an action brought **24.72** by a legal mortgagee or an equitable mortgagee who is entitled to a legal mortgage.[87] All other incumbrancers must be parties, and must be satisfied.

---

[78] The court has power under ss.90 and 91, L.P.A. 1925. The court can vest title in the purchaser, or appoint a person to convey the land, or vest a term in the mortgagee so that he can sell as if legal mortgagee.

[79] Powers of Attorney Act 1971; s.52, L.P.A. 1925.

[80] The bank appoints a nominee who is willing to convey the legal title.

[81] ss.59(2), 106(2), L.R.A. 1925; Encyclopedia, E(586) n. 8. But this step is unnecessary for unregistered land. *Re White Rose Cottage* [1965] Ch. 940.

[81a] Above, Chap. 23.

[82] s.105, L.P.A. 1925: these may be discharged, or the money paid into court.

[83] Who pays himself, then subsequent mortgagees, then the mortgagors.

[84] s.63, Trustee Act 1925.

[85] s.30(1), Trustee Act 1925 says the trustee is only liable for "his own wilful default."

[86] See *Kennedy v. De Trafford* [1897] A.C. 180.

[87] *Re Owen* [1894] 3 Ch. 220.

If an order is awarded, it extinguishes the title of the mortgagor so that for all purposes the mortgagee is entitled to the mortgagor's rights in the property. The court may,[88] and generally will, order a sale instead, to establish the price of the property, and to prevent unjust enrichment of the mortgagee.

e. Appointment of Receiver

24.73 Receivers may be appointed (a) under a statutory power, (b) by the court, (c) under an express power. If the mortgage is by deed, there is a statutory right to appoint a receiver so as to collect income from the property, but the appointment cannot be made until the statutory power of sale has become exercisable.[89] The statutory power and this restriction, may be varied, extended or excluded.[90] It is common, therefore, for mortgages to provide for appointment of a receiver and manager "At any time after the bank shall have demanded payment of any moneys hereby secured or if requested by the Mortgagor . . . " The receiver is given powers in the name of the mortgagor to take possession of the property, and to sell or lease or mortgage it, and so on. The mortgagee has the statutory powers to grant leases, and may delegate them to the receiver.[91] The receiver's sale may (like a mortgagee's sale) discharge the appointing mortgagee's charge, and all subsequent incumbrances, though it is usual for the receiver to seek the consent of all subsequent incumbrancers, and their releases, and in default, for the mortgagee to exercise his statutory powers. The mortgage under which the receiver is appointed is released by him after the conveyance, for otherwise he will have released the document entitling him to act, and he will have no power of sale. A transferee of a charge over registered land cannot exercise the statutory power to appoint a receiver until he is registered as proprietor of the charge.[92] If before such registration he exercises a contractual right to appoint, the receiver will be his agent, and not that of the mortgagor.

If (unusually) there is an equitable mortgagee with no express power, the court has inherent power to appoint a receiver.

The role of the receiver is most important with companies or individual business mortgages, but even with an individual domestic mortgage, the administrative burden of realisation is removed from the bank, and the receiver's costs are recouped from the assets in question. The great advantage of the receiver is that he is not the bank's agent, unless the bank interferes with him and gives him directions[93] and his negligence, therefore, may not ordinarily be laid at the foot of the bank.[94]

24.74 The receiver owes the same duties, and to the same parties, that a mortgagor does. He must apply the proceeds of sale in the following order[95]: (a) in discharge of rents, taxes, rates and outgoings affecting the property, (b) in keeping down all annual sums and interest on principal sums which have priority to his mortgage, (c) in paying his commission,[96] and pre-

[88] s.91, L.P.A. 1925.
[89] s.109, L.P.A. 1925.
[90] s.101.
[91] ss.99 and 100, L.P.A. 1925.
[92] L.R.A. 1925, ss.33, 34.
[93] Above, Chap. 23.
[94] Although the bank may agree to indemnify him.
[95] s.109(8), L.P.A. 1925.
[96] Five per cent. of gross receipts, unless a lower rate is agreed on his appointment or the court allows a higher rate.

miums on insurances properly payable, and the cost of any necessary or proper repairs directed by the mortgagee in writing, (d) in paying the interest accruing due under his mortgage, (e) in discharging the principal money if so directed in writing by the mortgagee, and (f) the residue goes to those entitled to the mortgaged property. If he acts under a floating charge, he must pay preferential creditors in priority to all other debts, though most bank advances will contain fixed charges over land, even if there is also a floating charge.[97]

O. Second mortgages

Any number of mortgages may simultaneously be granted over the same land to the same or different mortgagees. As described already,[98] notice of the second mortgagee may affect the first mortgagee, but the first mortgagee may sometimes have the obligation to tack, and his further advances will then give him priority over subsequent mortgagees.[99] If there is no obligation, notice to the prior mortgagee[1] will prevent this from occurring, and notice may come either through the register with registered land, or from actual notice with unregistered land. A sale by the first mortgagee under his statutory powers extinguishes the title of the subsequent mortgagees, who are only entitled to the surplus, if any. Despite the disadvantages, second mortgages are common, since rising property values tend to leave surplus value in the land.[2]

24.75

P. Leasehold mortgages: special problems

1. THE NATURE OF THE LEASEHOLD INTEREST: FORFEITURE

Leasehold tenants will owe obligations to their landlord (*e.g.* to pay rent). This may, for example, include the duty to repair. Such a duty not only affects the valuation of the property, but if the tenant is in default, the landlord will have certain remedies, one of which is the right of forfeiture, by which the landlord may become entitled to re-enter the premises and re-take them, ending the lease prematurely. Naturally, if the leasehold interest is the security and the leasehold is terminated, the security vanishes.

24.76

Forfeiture is possible if (a) the tenant denies the landlord's title, (b) there is a covenant expressed to give a right to forfeiture on breach, or (c) the tenant's particular obligation is worded as a condition of the lease, or (d) there is a general forfeiture clause applying to any breach of any covenant. The landlord may expressly or impliedly waive the breach. He must strictly prove his entitlement to forfeit, even at law. In equity, the tenant may be granted relief against forfeiture on the grounds of his non-payment of rent. In addition, there is statutory relief against forfeiture on other grounds.

If the bank discovers non-payment of rent, it should pay arrears itself, and seek to realise the security. Otherwise, the landlord may make formal demand for rent from the tenant[3] and bring an action for possession. The

---

[97] Above, Chaps. 21, 23.
[98] Above paras. 24.62–24.63.
[99] *Ibid.*
[1] Often with a request for acknowledgement, for details of the amount outstanding, and for information as to any obligation to tack. There is no obligation on the mortgagee to reply to this.
[2] For the relation between first and second mortgages, see above, para. 24.62.
[3] In some cases this is excused—*e.g.* if the lease says so.

tenant may pay all arrears of rent before costs, and stay proceedings.[4] Alternatively, he may claim relief in equity, which considered the right of forfeiture to be a kind of security with a kind of equity of redemption in the tenant. If it is just and equitable, and if the tenant pays the rent and the landlord's expenses, equity will give relief and reinstate the lease. This can be done normally within six months of the order for possession,[5] but relief is discretionary and may not be given in all cases (*e.g.* if the landlord has agreed to lease to others). Any underlease will also end on termination of the lease, as will any right of security given by mortgage. The underlessee and mortgagee, however, may also apply for relief.

24.77   For breaches other than non-payment of rent, generally the landlord must serve a statutory notice,[6] specifying the breach and requiring its remedy and any compensation desired, and otherwise the forfeiture is void. The tenant must be given a reasonable time (usually three months) to comply with the notice, and if he does not, the landlord may enforce the forfeiture by action.[7] At any time after the notice is served *but before the landlord actually enters*, even if judgment for possession is ordered, the tenant can apply for relief, at the court's discretion. If granted, it is as if the lease was never forfeited. A sub-tenant or mortgagee may also apply for relief, and the court may make a vesting order, vesting the whole or part of the premises in such an applicant, on any conditions the court thinks fit.[8] It is most important to note that the relief cannot be given after the landlord has entered, even if the application by the mortgagee (or tenant) is within the six months after judgment. The relief is only available "where a lessor is proceeding by action or otherwise to enforce a right of re-entry of forfeiture." In *Di Palma* v. *Victoria Square Property*[9] the Court of Appeal decided that the statutory provisions in section 146 of the Law of Property Act 1925 ousted any inherent equitable jurisdiction to grant relief.[10] Again, in *Smith* v. *Metropolitan City Properties Ltd.*[11] Walton J. held that relief could be given only while the landlord was still proceeding, and not once he had enforced by re-entering (as he did here, for lack of repairs). The bank could, of course, apply for relief, but only if it knows of the tenant's breach and the landlord's proceedings. In most leases there is no provision for landlords to notify the tenant's mortgagee that he is exercising a right to re-enter, and it is hardly in the landlord's interest to do so, as he will acquire a valuable property right which may be resold. The tenant may be required to inform the bank, but if he tells his mortgagee he simply compounds his troubles, since the security will ordinarily be realised. A bank taking a leasehold as security may wish to consider, therefore, if there is a provision in the lease requiring the mortgagee to be informed by the landlord. If not, the landlord may be asked to

[4] This statutory right is (strangely) only available if at least six months rent is in arrear.
[5] It is more complicated than this, and sometimes a longer period is allowed. See Megarry and Wade, *The Law of Real Property*, (5th ed.) p. 677. The main statute governing much of this is the Common Law Procedure Act 1852.
[6] Under the L.P.A. 1925, s.146.
[7] He could simply enter, but is subject to the provisions about violence, etc., discussed above, para. 24.57.
[8] The mortgagee has to take a new lease, and becomes directly responsible to the landlord. This is not the equivalent of foreclosure, because the mortgagor still has his equity of redemption against the new lease.
[9] [1985] 2 All E.R. 676, [1986] Ch. 150.
[10] Overruling *Abbey National Building Society* v. *Maybeech* (1894) 171 E.G. 995.
[11] September 2, 1985.

agree to a deed of variation. But if he will not give it, there is a serious danger in taking leasehold interests as security. Clearly, legislation is called for.

2. PROHIBITIONS ON ASSIGNMENT[12]

Some leases contain prohibitions on assignments and on other transactions. **24.78** If there is no prohibition, the tenant is free to mortgage, assign, etc. If there is a prohibition it is a contractual matter between landlord and tenant, and the tenant still has power to assign. The trouble is, that for breach of the covenant, the landlord may be given the power to forfeit the lease, with the consequences which we have seen. Relief is unlikely to be available, because such a breach can hardly be "remedied" if the mortgagee insists on his security or the assignee on his interest.

A prohibition may be absolute or conditional. A conditional prohibition refers generally to the landlord's consent as the condition of assignment, etc. An absolute prohibition prevents assignment, etc., in any case. A landlord with an absolute prohibition cannot be compelled to consent, though he may agree to do so and thus waive his rights. If the prohibition is conditional, statute requires that the landlord shall not unreasonably withhold his consent.[13] Some prohibitions are not worded as such but require the tenant to offer to surrender his tenancy to the landlord before assigning or underletting, etc. These seem to be perfectly effective: they do not require consent, and are not subject to any reasonableness test, but have the same effect as if consent were required, since the landlord may refuse the surrender.[14]

Secondly, whether a prohibition in a lease affects the mortgage is a matter of construction. Often, the prohibition is against "assignment, underletting or parting with possession" of all or any part of the premises. In such a case, a mortgage made by sub-lease is a breach[15] but one made by deposit of the title deeds (which operates as a charge) is not a breach.[16] Even if there is no prohibition on "parting with possession" a sub-lease is an "underletting"[17] and a mortgage in this form is a breach. It is generally thought, however, that unless there is a prohibition against a "charge"[18] a mortgage made at law or in equity by way of charge is unaffected by the prohibition, whether it be absolute or conditional.[19] However, if there is a prohibition against parting with possession, the mortgagee perhaps cannot go into possession,[20] though he could still exercise the statutory right of sale or could sell by court order, without breach.[21]

Clearly, therefore, not all leases are suitable for mortgage purposes.

---

[12] See generally, Megarry and Wade, *op. cit.*, 712, *et seq.*
[13] Under the Landlord and Tenant Act 1927, s.19.
[14] *Bocardo S.A. v. S. & M. Hotels Ltd.* [1980] 1 W.L.R. 17; *Adler v. Upper Grosvenor Street Investment Ltd.* [1957] 1 W.L.R. 227.
[15] *Serjeant v. Nash, Field & Co.* [1903] 2 K.B. 304.
[16] *Doe d. Pitt v. Hogg* (1824) 4 Dow. & Ry. 336.
[17] See *Matthews v. Smallwood* [1910] 1 Ch. 777.
[18] *i.e.* actually using the word, or making the intent clear.
[19] See *Doe d. Pitt v. Hogg* (1824) 4 Dow. & Ry. 336; *Gentle v. Faulkner* [1900] 2 Q.B. 267; *Grand Junction Co. Ltd. v. Bates* [1954] 2 Q.B. 160.
[20] Megarry & Wade, *op. cit.*, 925 n. 89, *contra* Encyclopedia, E(583) arguing with force that it is an ordinary incident of a mortgage.
[21] *Slipper v. Tottenham & Hampstead Junction Ry.* (1867) L.R. 4 Eq. 112; *Doe d. Mitchinson v. Carter (No. 1)* (1798) 8 T.R. 57.

3. EXERCISE OF POWER OF SALE BY LEASING

24.79 If a bank lends say, to a developer so as to build flats, on the security of a mortgage over the whole, and the leases have not yet been granted, it is uncertain whether the statutory power of sale entitles the mortgagee to grant leases.[22] Mortgages of such properties should, therefore, contain an express power to grant leases at a premium.[23]

4. SALE OF "FLYING FREEHOLDS"

24.80 It is considered undesirable in England and Wales that a freehold property should be divided horizontally with freehold titles. That is, where there is a building, which is broken up into flats or other divisions, it is not thought desirable that each flat should be given a freehold title (as "flying freeholds"). The reason is the very good one that there will be common parts of the building (such as roof, stairs, walls, foundations, drains, etc.) in which all tenants have an interest, and over which all or some may have an obligation. But is difficult to arrange things between freeholders in a convenient legal way so that in case of breach of covenant by one, the others may enforce. It is much more satisfactory if there is a separate freeholder (maybe one of the flats) with the right and preferably the duty to enforce the obligations, and thus to maintain the common structure. One solution is to vest the freehold in a company, in which all the tenants of a building have shares, with provision for meetings to be held and votes to be taken, and the company to enforce the covenants according to the wishes of the meeting. This may work, but is cumbersome. Suggestions have now been made for legislation to introduce "strata titles"[24] or "condominiums"[25] under schemes which solve these problems.[26]

5. LEASEHOLD REFORM ACT 1967

24.81 This Act enables the leaseholder of a "house" originally let for a term greater than 21 years to buy the freehold or to ask for a 50 year extension of the lease, in certain cases.[27] A tenant sharing a house with other leaseholders cannot rely on the Act, and a business tenant may not be able to say that his shop is a "house."[28] A purchase of freehold by a leasehold mortgagor would increase the value of his security, and the mortgagee would not object.

---

[22] It ought to, but the Land Registry disagrees.

[23] The leases, when granted, should contain terms which relieve the mortgagee from any liability once he sells the freehold.

[24] As known in New Zealand, for example.

[25] As they are known in Australia.

[26] Not necessarily a problem, but mentioned for the sake of completeness.

[27] Depending on the rateable value: tenancies before February 18, 1966, £750 or £1500 in Greater London, tenancies after then £500 or £1000 in Greater London.

[28] Though a tenant of a whole house for mixed purposes—*e.g.* the ground floor used as a shop, and the top floor as a flat—can do so: *Tandon* v. *Trustees of Spurgeon Homes* [1982] A.C. 755.

25. Stocks and Shares and Other Securities

In the present context, "securities" may refer to documents representing choses in action, such as stocks and shares, and bonds or debentures. Other forms of tradeable securities include certificates of deposit, bank bills, and American depositary receipts. All of these things are capable of providing security, in the legal sense, by way of mortgage or charge or pledge. One may thus speak of taking security over securities.

Here, we examine particularly company securities of the bearer or registered kind, and their use as security (or "collateral" security). Naturally, the valuation of shares in a private company is difficult, and the security value debateable, but shares in public companies, though variable in value, are easily valued.

A. Bearer securities and negotiable instruments

Negotiable instruments are documents of title to a chose in action, capable **25.01** of transfer by delivery, or by delivery and indorsement, so as to make the transferee the legal owner of a perfect title to the chose in action, regardless of any defects in his transferor's title, provided that the transferee takes a document which is complete and regular on its face, for value, in good faith, and without notice of any defect in his transferor's title. If, however, the instrument (or "security") is capable of being transferred by delivery alone, it is a bearer security. Bearer securities are designed in such a way that they do not require registration to perfect C's title against B, and generally contain an order to or promise by B to pay "Bearer," or at least are not payable to a named payee, or to order. The obvious risk to the owner of bearer certificates is that a thief could transfer good title to an innocent purchaser.

If bearer securities are delivered to a bank by way of security for a fresh advance, they are taken for value. If taken as security for a past advance, the consideration must be expressed as being for continuing the account. If, however, a bill of exchange is deposited as security, the bank takes for value if the customer is presently indebted, for past consideration is good consideration for liability on a bill.[1]

The bank has no duty to inquire as to the ownership of securities deposited as security,[2] though it would, perhaps, not take in good faith if facts were actually present to put it on enquiry.

On delivery of the security to the bank, it becomes legal owner, if a mortgage is intended, or pledgee if a different security interest is intended. Either of these carries with it the right of sale, and so there is no need to specify which is intended. If the security is not sold outright to the bank to discharge liabilities, a Memorandum of Deposit may refer to the receipt of the

---

[1] s.27, Bills of Exchange Act 1882.

[2] See *London Joint Stock Bank Ltd.* v. *Simmons* [1892] A.C. 201, where the customer was a stockbroker who pledged bonds belonging to his clients, and *Lloyds Bank Ltd.* v. *Swiss Bankverein Ltd.* (1913) 108 L.T. 143, where the court held that a negotiable instrument is not to be impressed with vendor's lien, implied trust, or constructive notice. Contrast *Colonial Bank* v. *Cady and Williams* (1890) 15 App.Cas. 267, where the instruments were not negotiable (below, n. 7).

security "by way of security." As already noted, even if not deposited by way of security, but for some other function of a banker's business, the banker has a lien for the customer's debts, and an implied right of sale.

The realisation of the security is also achieved by delivery.[3]

It may be added that delivery may be constructive. Bonds or debentures, for example, may be held by a depository or clearing house. If third parties acknowledge the title of another, and agree to hold for that other, that is sufficient delivery to transfer legal title. Internationally traded securities, for example, may be held by clearing houses.

It follows that security over bearer certificates is easy to take, that realisation is simple, and that because the security is negotiable, the bank faces no risks as to the customer's title.

B. Registered stocks and shares

25.02 The register referred to here is, of course, that kept by the company, in which the names of the legal owners are recorded. Legal title is transferred not by delivery of a document alone, but by a proper transfer followed by registration.

1. LEGAL AND EQUITABLE TITLE

25.03 A certificate under the company seal is prima facie evidence of legal title to the shares.[4] It is not evidence of equitable title[5] and the share certificate is not a negotiable instrument.[6] If, therefore, the bank has actual or constructive notice of the existence of an equitable owner, the bank will take subject to his rights.[7] Otherwise, if the bank acquires legal title as a bona fide purchaser without notice, it will, in the normal way, defeat the equitable title. In order to acquire legal title, the proper method of transfer must be used (described below) and the bank must be registered[8] as legal owner with the company. Until it is registered, it has an equitable title only, and the company is not bound to give any recognition to the rights of an equitable owner.[9] However, registration is insufficient to confer legal title, unless the proper method of transfer is used.[10] This includes the requirement for the signature of the registered owner or of his authorised agent. A forgery on a transfer will, therefore, confer no legal title even though the bank has the share certificate (which is only prima facie evidence of title) and obtains registration. In this event, the true legal owner may bring an action for rectification of the register, if the company disputes his title.

25.04 If a share certificate is issued, the company is estopped from denying the truth of any statement in it against a person who acts on the faith of it, and

---

[3] The provisions of the Consumer Credit Act 1974 do not apply to pledges of documents of title (s.114) or to bearer bonds: s.38(2), Banking Act 1979.

[4] s.186, C.A. 1985.

[5] *Shropshire Union Railways and Canal Co.* v. *R.* (1875) L.R. 7 H.L. 496.

[6] *Swan* v. *North British Australasian Co. Ltd.* (1862) 7 H. & N. 603.

[7] See *Colonial Bank* v. *Cady and Williams* above, n. 2, where executors signed blank transfers and gave them to stockbrokers for sale. The brokers pledged them to a bank for their own purposes. The court held that the bank was put on inquiry as to the brokers' authority. This was distinguished in *Fry* v. *Smellie*, [1912] 3 K.B. 282. See also, *Société Général de Paris* v. *Walker* (1885) 11 App.Cas. 20; *Moore* v. *North Western Bank* [1891] 2 Ch. 599.

[8] Company articles always require this.

[9] s.360, C.A. 1985.

[10] *Powell* v. *London and Provincial Bank* [1893] 2 Ch. 555, 566.

suffers loss.[11] If, therefore, a thief steals a certificate, forges a transfer, and obtains registration, and the bank relies on the new certificate then issued showing that the thief is owner, the bank has a remedy against the company. But if the thief, having stolen the old certificate, produces it and a forged transfer to the bank, and the bank obtains registration, the bank has no remedy against the company, for it has relied not on the company's statement, but on the forgery. Furthermore, in that case, if the bank obtains registration and later sells the shares to another, the buyer has a remedy against the bank for selling him what the bank did not own, or against the company on whose new certificate naming the bank he relied. But if he sues the company, the company has a remedy against the bank, for the company relied on the transfer form sent in by the bank, which is taken, therefore, impliedly to promise to indemnify the company.[12] The issue of the new certificate to the bank does not assist it, for that is obtained by its own mis-representation, and it cannot rely on it against the company.[13] In all these cases, the original "true" owner may have the register rectified, and will suffer no loss.[14] Any dividends received by the bank belong to the true owner. It follows from all of this that there are risks in dealing with a person whose signature is unknown, even if he has the share certificates. The clear-est possible identification, therefore, is required. It may be added that there is no substantial risk from a forgery of the share certificate itself (as opposed to forgery of a signature) since when the bank sends that in for registration, the company (unless it is negligent) will identify the forgery.

It is not uncommon for the bank to remain content with equitable title. **25.05** This may be obtained (i) merely by a memorandum evidencing the security right, (ii) (preferably) by taking possession of the certificates, or (iii) if a (reliable) third party who holds them agrees to hold them for the bank. In this case (and, indeed, even if the bank proposes to take legal title) a Memorandum of Deposit may be used, to establish the purpose for which the bank has the certificates. This memorandum may cover all securities deposited, or only those mentioned in a schedule. In either case, it is stated to be a continuing security for all moneys from time to time owing and on any account. This prevents *Clayton's case* from discharging the debt, and the security. Where the securities belong to a third party surety, there will be terms similar to those in guarantees[15] entitling the bank to vary arrange-ments with the debtor-customer, and so on. Other terms give the bank a power of sale, the right to demand the execution of further documents if required to perfect the bank's title, the right to substitute equivalent securi-ties on redemption,[16] and perhaps a clause entitling the bank to "re-pledge" the securities as security for re-financing operations.[17] Where a memoran-dum is signed by two parties it should be joint and several, so as to cover not only joint holdings and liabilities, but also separately owned holdings and separate liabilities.

---

[11] *Balkis Consolidated Co.* v. *Tomkinson* [1892] A.C. 396.

[12] *Sheffield Corporation* v. *Barclay* [1905] A.C. 392; *Bank of England* v. *Cutler* [1908] 2 K.B. 208; *Oliver* v. *Bank of England* [1902] 1 Ch. 610.

[13] See especially the first case mentioned in the previous note.

[14] If the company discovers the forgery before registration, the bank cannot compel the com-pany to register the bank's title: *Simm* v. *Anglo-American Telegraph Co.* (1879) 5 Q.B.D. 188.

[15] Above, Chap. 20.

[16] The originals may be transferred to a nominee company for administrative purposes, and if it handles large volumes, it may be administratively difficult to keep the originals separate.

[17] Another reason for providing for substitute securities.

Unless the bank protects itself, on default, realisation would have to be effected by application to the court for sale or foreclosure.[18] To avoid that one or more of the following may be done: (i) it is normal practice for the owner to sign a transfer form, leaving other details blank,[19] so that in case of default, the bank may sell and simply insert the name of the purchaser, or its own name, (ii) an irrevocable power of attorney may be taken as an alternative, enabling the bank to sell as agent, (iii) where the memorandum of deposit is made by deed, there will be a power of sale under the Law of Property Act 1925, section 101.

25.06   If on taking equitable title with a signed transfer, a deed of transfer is used, (*e.g.* being required by the articles, and the shares being partly paid so that a stock transfer form cannot be used) the details (including the date) must not be left blank, because this is not a valid deed, and the bank will have only equitable title.[20]

The equitable title may be defeated by a bona fide purchaser for value and without notice of the bank's rights,[21] but the possession of the certificates is some protection against such an occurrence. It is not complete protection, because there is a procedure for a registered owner to obtain a replacement certificate on certifying the loss or destruction of the originals. It is difficult for the bank to protect itself against this slight risk, because the company is entitled to disregard any equitable interests.[22] It may be prepared to note on its records that the bank has the certificates, so as to avoid making duplicates available to anyone else, but need not do so. However, a "stop notice"[23] may be served on the company, requiring the company to give the bank (or other equitable owner) eight days warning of intention to transfer the shares, and enabling time for notice to be given to the purchaser, or for an injunction to be obtained. This, however, requires the expense and delay of an application to the court, and as the purpose of taking a mere equitable title is to save time and expense, this defeats the purpose of the exercise. Another risk which may be avoided is the risk that the company may claim a lien against the shares for debts owed by the registered owner to the company. This risk, which does not exist for fully paid shares of a public company,[24] is avoided by sending a "notice of lien" to the company, after which no new rights of lien may be acquired effective against the bank.[25]

These risks aside, the equitable title will assure priority to the bank in the event of the registered shareholder's insolvency. In that event, if the bank has an executed transfer form (or power of attorney, or deed giving a statutory power of sale) it may sell or become legal owner. Otherwise, the trustee or liquidator may execute the transfer, or the court may order a sale of the shares and payment of the bank's share of the proceeds to it. As between

---

[18] See *Harrold* v. *Plenty* [1901] 2 Ch. 314.

[19] The efficacy of blank transfers was approved in *Ireland* v. *Hart* [1902] 1 Ch. 522, 527.

[20] See *Powell* v. *London and Provincial Bank* [1893] 2 Ch. 555; once dated it must be stamped within 30 days: Stamp Act 1891.

[21] See *Coleman* v. *London County and Westminster Bank Ltd.* [1916] 2 Ch. 353; *Fry* v. *Smellie* [1912] 3 K.B. 282; Contrast *Colonial Bank* v. *Cady and Williams*, above n. 2.

[22] s.360, C.A. 1985.

[23] Under R.S.C., Ord. 50, rr. 11–15.

[24] s.150, C.A. 1985 prohibits liens or charges in favour of a public company unless for partly paid shares or where the company's business includes moneylending, and for shares quoted on the Stock Exchange, the rules of the Exchange prohibit it.

[25] *Bradford Banking Co. Ltd.* v. *Henry Briggs, Son & Co. Ltd.* (1886) 12 App.Cas. 29; and see *Mackereth* v. *Wigan Coal and Iron Co. Ltd.* [1916] 2 Ch. 293.

equitable titles, the first in time will prevail,[26] but if the later equitable owner holds a blank transfer form, his registration will make him legal owner, and he will take priority, if bona fide,etc.

The advantages of taking legal title are (i) that registration protects against later legal titles, (ii) that registration defeats an earlier unknown equitable title, (iii) that the bank has full control over the securities, being able to sell without recourse to the courts, and being entitled to all rights such as bonus shares, rights issues, dividends, votes, etc. The disadvantages or risks of legal title, apart from those arising from the slight risk of a forged share transfer, include the fact that the registered shareholder may be under certain obligations, such as liability for calls on unpaid shares.[27] In addition, there is more administrative work, and some customers may object to being deprived of legal title. An example is the director who is obliged to own qualification shares in order to remain a director.

25.07

On the other hand, the taking of equitable title is administratively simple, cheap and private, does not expose the bank to any liability on the share obligations, and does not affect the customer's legal title (the director's qualification shares). The disadvantages include (i) the risk that the customer will fail to pay calls, and will be deprived of title, thus defeating the bank's title, (ii) defeat by prior equitable title, (iii) fraud by the registered shareholder leading to a bona fide purchaser obtaining good legal title through duplicate certificates, thus defeating the bank, (iv) the issue of bonus or rights issues, etc., to the registered shareholder, and not to the bank. In particular, on a rights issue, the registered owner should either sell the shares allotted to him or buy them, for the increase in numbers of allotted shares will depress the price of all shares somewhat. While the memorandum taken by the bank entitles it to new issues, a risk remains until the certificates come into its possession. The theoretical difficulty of the need for application to court for sale is avoided, as stated earlier, by taking an executed transfer form, irrevocable power of attorney or Memorandum under deed.

2. METHOD OF TRANSFER

Where legal title is to be obtained by registration, a document (transfer form) must be used, notwithstanding anything in the company's articles.[28] The articles of the company may prescribe a certain form of transfer, say, by deed (if not, the transfer may be by deed, or otherwise in writing ("under hand")) but notwithstanding anything in the articles,[29] a "stock transfer form" may often be used.[30] This simplified form is the most widely used method of transfer, although it cannot be used except for fully paid up registered securities.[31] The stock transfer form may be used not only for company securities (shares, stock, or debentures), but also for securities of any body incorporated in Great Britain (except a building society or an Industrial and Provident society), and for Government securities (other than National Savings stock or bonds or certificates), local authority securities,

25.08

---

[26] *Coleman* v. *London County and Westminster Bank Ltd.* [1916] 2 Ch. 353.

[27] Or a similar liability on winding up.

[28] s.183, C.A. 1985.

[29] See s.182, C.A. 1985.

[30] Under the Stock Transfer Act 1963.

[31] Stock Transfer Act 1963, s.1(4). Where shares are traded on the Stock Exchange, a different form is provided. See S.I. 1979, No. 277, and Stock Transfer act 1982.

or unit trust units or shares. The form is signed by the transferor, and a company transferor must affix its common seal.[32] If the registered shareholder is dead, his personal representative may sign[33] and because a transfer form must be used, the company may not register even those to whom the deceased's estate has passed on his death.[34] Once the transfer is lodged with it, the company has two months to prepare and deliver the certificates, or to give notice of refusal to register.[35]

If a transferor wishes to transfer (by way of sale or security) only part of the holding represented by a single certificate, he lodges his certificate and a transfer form with the company, which keeps the certificate and marks the transfer form "Certificate Lodged" or in some similar fashion. The company thus represents only that it has seen documents which on their face show a prima facie title. It is not a representation that the transferor has title. If the company has seen documents as represented, and if it is not negligent, it is not liable. But if it is negligent, it is liable as if it was fraudulent.[36] Where the Stock Exchange certifies transfers, as an alternative, the Exchange is under no liability. The transfer form may then be given by the transferor to the bank which sends that to the company, which in due course delivers new certificates to the bank and transferor for the appropriate shareholdings.

Transfer is usually to a nominee company (a subsidiary) of the bank, which permits easier devolution of duties, especially on re-transfer, so far as concerns use of the bank's seal.

To avoid stamp duty payable on non-governmental securities, either on transfer or re-transfer, a nominal consideration (say 50p) is stated, and a certificate, signed by a bank representative, is attached stating that the transfer is by way of security or that the transfer is exempt from the relevant provision.[37]

3. SCRIP, AND RIGHTS ISSUES, AND BONUS ISSUES

25.09 "Scrip" is a word used by some to indicate that the certificate is of a provisional nature and by others to refer to bonus issues. For example, a provisional certificate may be issued where shares are not fully paid. These are usually negotiable by delivery. On a rights issue, where the company issues new shares to existing shareholders, usually at favourable terms,[38] letters of allotment may be used instead. These may be personal to the allottee, but more usually are renounceable (within a certain period) in favour of someone else. The allottee completes the form of renunciation contained in the letter, and delivers it to the transferee, who completes the form and lodges it with the company. But if the allottee is committed to the purchase, the usual transfer forms as already described are used, with the letter of allottment merely filling the role of the as yet unissued share certificate. Since the value of all shares will decrease with the increased number of shares on a rights issue, it is important that the allottee either renounce his rights in favour of another to whom the rights are sold, or that he buys the

[32] Or a facsimile seal, with the word "securities" on it, under s.40, C.A. 1985.
[33] s.183(3), C.A. 1985.
[34] See *Re Greene* [1949] Ch. 333.
[35] ss.185, 183, C.A. 1985.
[36] s.184, C.A. 1985.
[37] s.74, Finance (1909–10) Act 1910. This is allowed if a bank is party to the transaction.
[38] No shareholder can be compelled to take more shares: s.16, C.A. 1985.

new issue. If he simply renounces, his existing shareholding will decrease in value, with no corresponding gain elsewhere.[39] Rights issues in public companies will be saleable. The risk to the bank of partly paid shares have been mentioned, and they are either of forfeiture by non-payment of instalments, where the bank has only equitable title, or of liability for payment, where the bank has legal title.

Bonus shares are fully paid issues allotted to existing members. These will be issued to the bank, if legal owner, and to the registered shareholder, if the bank has an equitable security. Again, the price will fall, and again the bank is at risk until it obtains the new certificates.

It is uncertain whether the charge over shares includes bonus shares or rights issues,[40] but the memorandum of deposit will expressly extend the charge to cover these things.

[39] There is usually a warning on the rights issue documents.
[40] See Paget, 453.

26. Life Assurance

26.01 Life assurance policies are of interest to bankers for two separate reasons. First, if a customer is indebted to the bank, say, by way of a 25 year mortgage loan, the life policy preserves the bank's position if the customer dies. It may be a simple temporary insurance, for this purpose. Secondly, if the policy has a surrender value, the assured person's contractual right to that value is good security, being easy to value, transfer and realise, and the value increases with premiums paid. In both cases, the benefit of the policy is assigned to the bank by way of security. Valuation (by asking the insurer) and realisation (by surrender) of the policy is simple. Accident policies, of course, have no surrender value, and are not useful for security. Retirement annuity policies[1] are not surrenderable or assignable, and are not useful for security. Policies in which age is not admitted may be affected by misrepresentation of age, and a birth certificate should be sought from the customer, and an admission sought from the insurer, before the insurance is taken.

The main legal problems are as to the insurable interest, the doctrine of *uberrimae fidei*, and the effect of crime, and suicide. We shall refer briefly to these before considering the taking of the security.

A. The insurable interest

26.02 For reasons of public policy[2] no life assurance may be made so as to benefit a person who has no pecuniary interest in the life (being the life of another) which is insured.[3] Moreover, where there is an interest, the amount recoverable under the policy may not exceed the amount of that interest. The rule is satisfied so long as the insurable interest exists when the policy is made, even if it ceases thereafter.[4] If the rule is broken, the policy is completely void and confers no rights, and no premiums are recoverable.[5] It may perhaps be unlikely that an insurance company of repute would seek to insist upon this rule to avoid payment to an innocent third party assignee, such as a bank.

The following persons, however, have pecuniary (insurable) interests in the lives of those named second: (i) spouse, in spouse:[6] the amount of interest here is unlimited; (ii) creditor, in debtor, to amount of the debt[7]; (iii) surety or guarantor, in principal debtor, to amount of guarantee; (iv) employer in employee[8]; (v) trustee, in life of his beneficiary[9]; (vi) dependent

---

[1] Under the Finance Act 1971.
[2] Both to prevent gambling, and murder.
[3] Life Assurance Act 1774.
[4] *Dalby* v. *India and London Life Ass. Co.* (1854) 15 C.B. 365.
[5] See *Harse* v. *Pearl Life Ass. Co.* [1904] 1 K.B. 558. Premiums are recoverable if the assured is misled by the insurer: *Hughes* v. *Liverpool Victoria Legal Friendly Soc.* [1916] 2 K.B. 482.
[6] *Griffiths* v. *Fleming* [1909] 1 K.B. 805 (husband, in wife); *Reed* v. *Royal Exchange Assurance Co.* (1795) Peake Add.Cas. 70 (wife, in husband).
[7] *Anderson* v. *Edie* (1795) 2 Park's Mar.Ins. (8th. ed.), 914.
[8] *Hebdon* v. *West* (1863) 3 B. & S. 579.
[9] *Tidswell* v. *Ankerstein* (1792) Peake, 151.

child, in parent[10]; (vii) litigant, in life of his judge.[11] There is no insurable interest between siblings or other relatives, or from parent, in the life of a child, unless there is some pecuniary interest in a particular case.[12] A banker has an insurable interest in the life of one indebted to him, and could take out a policy over that life, but this is not usual.

The rule applies to the original contract of insurance itself, not to subsequent assignments, so that if it is desired to avoid this rule, where B has no pecuniary interest, this is done in one of two ways. First, A may insure his own life, for his own benefit[13] and subsequently assigns the benefit of the policy moneys to B.[14] B may then, in turn, assign his rights, as security. Alternatively, A insures his own life and makes a declaration of trust, appointing a trustee to hold for B's benefit. B may assign his rights as beneficiary under the trust.

B. The duty to disclose

Certain classes of contracts, of which insurance contracts are one, are said to be contracts *uberrimae fidei*, which means to say "of the utmost good faith." The significance of this is that persons entering such contracts have a duty to disclose any material facts which affect the insurance. A material fact is one which "would influence the judgment of a prudent insurer in fixing the premium, or determining whether he will take the risk" and is a question of fact in each case.[15] If a material fact is not disclosed, the insurer may avoid the contract, and refuse to pay. Examples of material facts are: failing to disclose convictions for dishonesty (material for house insurance),[16] failing to disclose that a number of other insurers had declined the risk of life assurance,[17] and failing to disclose doubts about the assured's mental health, (which might have made him suicide prone).[18]

26.03

The position is not uncomplicated

(i) Proposal forms often contain a list of specific questions. An untrue answer is a misrepresentation, entitling the insurer to avoid the policy, although the fact must still be "material." However, it is often stated that the truth of statements made is a condition of the insurer's liability. Thus, the duty to disclose can be extended even to non-material facts.[19] Conversely, the form may restrict the duty to disclose, so that the policy is avoided only for wilful failure to disclose, or positive misrepresentation.

(ii) Contracts of insurance are excluded from the effect of the Unfair Contract Terms Act 1977, and no terms need be reasonable, so that the *uberrimae fidei* rule, and "accuracy" clauses are unaffected.

(iii) The list of questions specifically asked does not, by implication,

---

[10] *Howard* v. *Refuge Friendly Soc.* (1886) 54 L.T. 644 (not a child being supported).

[11] This is not uncommon, where the trial may be long.

[12] See *Halford* v. *Kymer* (parent, in child) (1830) 10 B. & C. 724; *Evanson* v. *Crooks* (1911) 106 L.T. 264 (sisters).

[13] *i.e.* that of his estate.

[14] For the validity of this, see *Ashley* v. *Ashley* (1829) 3 Sim. 149.

[15] See s.18(2) and (7) of Marine Insurance Act 1906, said to be generally applicable in *Locker and Woolfe* v. *Western Australian Insurance Co. Ltd.* [1936] 1 K.B. 408, and see *Banque Keyser Ullman SA* v. *Skandia (U.K.) Ins. Co* [1987] 1 Lloyds Rep. 69; *Kelsall* v. *All State Ins. Co.* (1987) *The Times*, March 20.

[16] *Woolcott* v. *Sun Alliance and London Ins. Ltd.* [1978] 1 W.L.R. 493.

[17] *London Assurance* v. *Mansel* (1879) 11 Ch.D. 363.

[18] *Lindenau* v. *Desborough* (1828) 8 B. & C. 586.

[19] See *Dawsons Ltd.* v. *Bonnin* [1922] 2 A.C. 413.

exclude the duty to disclose, unless it is expressly excluded by the insurer. In *Woolcott* v. *Sun Alliance and London Ins. Ltd.*[20] a house purchaser obtained a building society mortgage, and the society gave him a form for insurance purposes. He answered all questions asked, without disclosing a conviction for armed robbery several years before. When his house was later damaged by fire, the insurers were held to be justified in refusing to pay. The conviction related to dishonesty, and this was a material fact.

26.04   (iv) Any material changes between the date of the proposal and the policy date must be disclosed.[21]

(v) Facts which the insurer should already know, or which reduce the risk, or which both parties have equal means of knowing, or general topics of speculation, or facts the disclosure of which are waived, or facts which the assured does not know (such as a hidden illness), need not be disclosed.

The difficulty with the rule, therefore, is that matters which the assured thinks irrelevant may be relevant to the hypothetical "prudent insurer"; the presence of questions on the form may make the assured think that is all he need answer; if the proposal forms make accuracy a condition, even insignificant errors may vitiate the policy; and if there is an omission, the insurer can avoid the policy even though (as it happened), the omission was irrelevant to the cause of the claim.[22] All of this may affect the bank's security, for (from sound reasons of economy) insurance companies usually reserve thorough checks until the time at which a claim is made. If the assured fails to disclose to the insurer, he is unlikely to disclose to the bank. Some insurers have stated that they will not rely on the disclosure rule. Others will not rely on it against innocent assignees. Many have agreed to make very clear on the proposal form the duty to disclose material facts. There is an insurance ombudsman, who has power to make awards up to a certain monetary limit, but his attitude in any given case cannot very well be predicted, and should hardly be relied upon. There is a temptation to say that the rule should be abolished, but given the enormous number of factors which may vary from individual to individual, there is some force, perhaps, in the insurers' claims that no proposal form could be developed which could satisfactorily deal with all material matters, without becoming ridiculously complicated. Perhaps, however, a rule to protect innocent assignees might be justified, or, perhaps, a rule to allow the assured's estate to recover if it can be proved that there is no causal connection between the non-disclosed fact and the death.

C. Murder and unlawful killing

26.05   No-one may benefit from his own unlawful act, so that a murderer may not make a claim on the life of his victim.[23] In cases of unlawful killing other than murder[24] the Forfeiture Act 1982 gives the court a discretion to allow

---

[20] [1978] 1 W.L.R. 493.
[21] *Canning* v. *Farquhar* (1886) 16 Q.B.D. 727, where after making his proposal, the assured was seriously injured.
[22] *e.g.* a potential suicide fails to disclose mental ill-health, but dies in an aeroplane crash.
[23] *Amicable Society* v. *Bolland* (1830) 4 Bli. N.S. 194; *Cleaver* v. *Mutual Reserve Fund Life Assn.* [1892] 1 Q.B. 147.
[24] *i.e.* for manslaughter, or murder reduced to manslaughter by reason of provocation or diminished responsibility.

recovery where it thinks just, and this may apply to some insurance policies.[25]

D. Suicide

Suicide is not a crime, though it remains an offence to aid and abet a suicide.[26] Most policies will state what will occur in case of suicide.[27] If not, the rule is still that laid down by *Beresford* v. *Royal Insurance Co. Ltd.*[28] that a sane suicide cannot take the benefit of an assurance, because it is against public policy. The coroner's finding that the assured took his life while the balance of his mind was temporarily disturbed will allow recovery[29] (unless the policy states otherwise).[30] The Forfeiture Act 1982 does not apply to suicides, because it applies only to killings of "another." It is not clear whether the public policy rule would override any contrary provision in the agreement,[31] but presumably no insurer would refuse to pay where the policy allowed for payment to a sane suicide, particularly to an assignee.

26.06

E. Conflicts of laws

The policy will be governed by the objectively determined proper law, or by a chosen proper law. It is thought that all U.K. policies will state that law which is to apply. If a policy is governed by foreign law, it may be subject to complications concerning third party rights, which may affect the bank, as assignee. An assignment is a further contract, which will be governed by its own proper law as to most matters, although so far as compliance with the formalities for making the assignment it will probably be sufficient to comply either with the proper law or with the law of the place of contracting.[32]

26.07

The place of performance (payment) of a policy[33] is the place fixed by the policy, but if none is fixed, it is the life office where the contract was made.[34] Even if the contract were governed by English law, an illegality affecting the policy at its place of performance would invalidate the policy according to English law.[35]

F. Cooling-off

Persons taking life policies have a ten-day period in which to change their mind.[36] This is unlikely to affect a bank because the policy will not be issued to the assured in the cooling-off period, and a mere determinable contract would not be acceptable as security.

26.08

---

[25] A possible case might exist where a wife, under provocation, kills her husband and then herself. The children might be allowed to recover as next of kin under a policy in favour of the wife.

[26] Suicide Act 1961.

[27] *e.g.* protecting assignees, or perhaps all parties, where suicide does not occur within the first few years of the policy.

[28] [1938] A.C. 586.

[29] See *Moore* v. *Woolsey* (1854) 4 E. & B. 243.

[30] See *Ellinger & Co.* v. *Mutual Life Insurance Co. of N.Y.* [1905] 1 K.B. 31.

[31] See the discussion in *Beresford* v. *Royal Insurance Co. Ltd.* [1938] A.C. 586.

[32] The *lex loci contractus*: see, generally, Vol. 2 of this work, in Chap. 1.

[33] *Lex loci solutionis.*

[34] *New York Life Insurance Co.* v. *Public Trustee* [1924] 2 Ch. 101.

[35] *Ralli Bros.* v. *Compania Naviera Sota y Aznar* [1920] 2 K.B. 287.

[36] ss.75–76, Insurance Companies Act 1982. This may be extended to 14 days by rules to be made by the Securities and Investments Board, under the Financial Services Act 1986.

G. The beneficiary

26.09 It will be appreciated that assignment is taken from the person entitled to the benefit which forms the security value: that is, the person to whom a surrender value, or monies payable under a policy, are payable. This "beneficiary" may or may not be the life assured. The beneficiary must be 18 years of age, or the assignment will be ineffective. Generally, unless there is a trust of the policy, the life assured would be entitled to surrender the policy and claim the surrender value. In that case, both life assured (for the surrender value) and the beneficiary (for the policy monies) should join in the assignment. If the policy monies alone are in question, only the beneficiary need be party to an assignment. But if a policy is taken out by A, payable to B, it is possible that A is a trustee for B. If so, both the surrender value and the capital monies payable under the policy belong to B, who must always join in the assignment.

Not all cases where a beneficiary is involved, creates a trust. If a man or woman effects an insurance on his or her life, which is expressed to be for the benefit of the other, or for their children, or both, a trust is created, and an interest immediately vests in the wife, etc., who must be party to the assignment.[37]

In other cases, a trust is created only if there are express words not merely making the monies payable to B, but "pointing to the conclusion that the insurance money was to be a fund to which the [person named] was to be entitled."[38] The use of words such as "held in trust" are quite clear. One consideration is that with a true trust the trustee is under an obligation not to let the policy lapse, for that is a breach of his duty to the beneficiary.[39] If there is any doubt as to the entitlement of the "beneficiary"named, he should be asked to join in the mortgage, though in the case of a trust "for my wife and children," say, the children may not have contractual capacity, depending on their age, and there may well be other children.

It may be that a policy either names the beneficiary[40] or else identifies the beneficiary by reference to a description such as "my wife," or "my wife and children." Where the beneficiary is named, as "my wife Jane," then if there is a trust, her interest is vested in her and she would not cease to be entitled to whatever rights she may have by divorce or where the wife predeceases her husband.[41]

26.10 Where, however, the beneficiary is not named, but is identified by a description, the beneficiary must correspond with the description at the time the policy monies become payable. Thus, if the description is "my wife," and the wife at the time the policy was taken out has died, or is divorced, no monies would be payable to the wife.[42] Where, for example, a policy was made for "my wife and children," and the first wife divorced and the husband remarried the benefits were shared by the second wife and by the children of both marriages. This affects the security value of the policy. If there

---

[37] Married Women's Property Act 1882.

[38] *Re Webb, Barclays Bank Ltd.* v. *Webb* [1941] Ch. 225; see also *Perrin* v. *Dickson* [1930] 1 K.B. 107; *Re Sinclair's Life Policy* [1938] Ch. 799.

[39] *Re Sinclair's Life Policy* [1938] Ch. 799.

[40] This word, here, means only "the person to whom the insurance monies are payable."

[41] *Cousins* v. *Sun Life Assurance Society.* [1933] 1 Ch. 126, approving *Prescott* v. *Prescott* [1906] 1 I.R. 155.

[42] See *Re Browne's Policy, Browne* v. *Browne* [1903] 1 Ch. 188.

is a trust in favour of "my children" it is possible that there may be more children subsequently, who would not be bound by an assignment.

But even where there is a trust for a named wife, if the parties agree jointly and severally to pay the premiums, then in case of the wife's death the husband is entitled to a lien on the policy monies to the extent of the premiums paid by him since the wife's death.[43]

H. Non-payment of premiums

The risk of non-payment of premiums may be reduced if they are paid **26.11** through the bank account by standing order, and if the customer has insufficient funds to do so the bank can (i) pay overdue premiums and realise the (endowment) security, or (ii) continue to pay premiums, if near maturity, or (iii) (if the policy allows it) convert the policy into a fully paid one. All this will be allowed by the charge forms, though in any case the mortgagee has a right to safeguard his security.

When taking the security, the bank will obtain the current premium receipt. The customer will covenant to pay premiums, and the security covers these as well (in case the bank pays them), but if the policy holder becomes bankrupt, the bank cannot prove for future unpaid premiums.[44]

The effect of non-payment depends on the policy in question. With some policies, the assurance is "renewable" (*i.e.* it may continue only so long as premiums are paid), and with others the policy may be "continuing," but subject to forfeiture if the premium is not paid. In either case, a period of grace is usually allowed. With the renewable type, payment within the period of grace is usually allowed even after the assured's death, subject to deduction of the premium. With the continuing type, unless the policy states otherwise, the payment may be made within the period of grace even if the assured has died.[45] Some policies provide for conversion to fully paid policies (of a smaller amount) in case of default in payment of the premiums.

I. Method of assignment

Unless the contract provides to the contrary,[46] the assignment is taken from **26.12** the beneficiary, not from the life assured, where they are different. Problems of undue influence must be considered.[47] Minors will not be bound by the assignment, so that a policy to "wife and children" would be good security only to the wife's share. Company insurances of the life of directors do not require registration under section 395 of the Companies Act 1985, on assignment by way of charge.

Where English law governs, the assignment may be either legal or equitable. No legal assignment is possible if this is prohibited by the policy.[48] An agreement to assign in those circumstances would be effective between assignor and assignee, but might be ignored by the insurer.

---

[43] *Re Smith's Estate, Bilham* v. *Smith* [1937] Ch. 636; *Grabiner* v. *Brew* (1964) 108 Sol.Jo. 1030.
[44] *Deering* v. *Bank of Ireland* (1886) 12 App.Cas. 20.
[45] *Stuart* v. *Freeman* [1903] 1 K.B. 47.
[46] This is occasionally the case.
[47] Above, Chap. 19.
[48] This is uncommon.

1. LEGAL ASSIGNMENTS

26.13   These are made in accordance with the Policies of Assurance Act 1867.[49] The Act requires that the assignment be signed and witnessed. It need not be made by deed, though these are often used. The assignment may be effected on the policy itself, or by separate instrument.[50] The insurer must be informed of the date and effect of the assignment,[51] the place for notification being stated on the policy. Where a written receipt is required, a small fee is payable.[52] A convenient practice is for the bank to give duplicate notices to the insurer, which returns one copy as receipt.

A bank's assignment may be taken as security for a fixed sum, but generally is for all monies covenanted to be paid, with the customer convenanting to repay all advances etc., on any account, and including interest, and as a continuing security.[53]

The effect of a legal assignment of a life assurance policy is like that of most assignments, as follows:

(i) After receiving notice, the insurer is bound to pay the assignee only, and is discharged by earlier payment to another.[54]

(ii) The insurer is entitled to defences or set-offs or counterclaims existing between himself and the assured before notice.[55]

(iii) The priorities between successive assignees are regulated by the order in which notice is received by the insurer. (This is the "rule in *Dearle* v. *Hall*")[56] This priority rule, however, applies only if the second assignee (who gives notice first) has no notice himself at the time of contracting[57] of the prior assignment. Such notice may be actual or constructive,[58] and since constructive notice may be found as a fact where the bank has taken insufficient care to discover the facts, non-production to the assignee by the assignor of the policy may amount to constructive notice.[59] Thus, where the policy is not produced, no further advances should be made in reliance upon the security unless the bank has full details of prior assignees[60] or some reasonable explanation for the absence of the policy is given.[61] Assuming that the bank has no notice of prior assignees, and that it gives notice to the insurers, its legal charge defeats prior equitable assignees (if they have not given notice to the insurers) and subsequent legal or equitable assignees. As a matter of procedure, the insurers should be asked before making further advances whether there is any outstanding incumbrance.

If a bank lends on the security of a policy, and learns of a subsequent charge, the bank will not have priority for further advances over the sub-

---

[49] s.136, L.P.A. 1925 is stated not to affect the provisions of the 1867 Act: s.136(2), L.P.A. 1925.

[50] s.5 of the 1867 Act.

[51] *Ibid.*, s.3.

[52] *Ibid.*, ss.4, 6.

[53] As with guarantees (above, Chap. 20), land (above, Chap. 24), stocks and shares (above, Chap. 25).

[54] s.3 of the 1867 Act.

[55] *Ibid.*, s.2.

[56] (1828) 3 Russ. 1.

[57] Possibly, the time of giving notice to the insurer.

[58] *Newman* v. *Newman* (1885) 28 Ch.D. 674; *Re Weniger's Policy* [1910] 2 Ch. 291.

[59] *Spencer* v. *Clarke* (1878) 9 Ch.D. 137.

[60] Either from the insurer or the customer.

[61] *e.g.* that it has been destroyed by fire, and a fire is proved to have occurred.

sequent chargeholder,[62] and if the account is current, it should be broken to prevent the operation of the rule in *Clayton's case*.

As legal assignee the bank has the power to surrender or sell the policy, and to give a good discharge to the insurer for payment of the monies. The assignee may, of course, sue in his own name.[63]

2. EQUITABLE ASSIGNMENTS

These may be made simply by an oral agreement, or by written memoran-**26.14**
dum,[64] or by deposit of the policy with intent that it be security.[65] The last of these is, of course, the safest, though there is still a risk that the assured may declare the policy lost and obtain a replacement from the insurer. Obviously, given the simplicity of taking a legal assignment, that ought to be (and nearly always is) preferred except in special cases. A Memorandum of deposit could be (but rarely is, it seems) taken in the usual way to explain the purpose of deposit. If so, this should be under seal and contains a promise by the assured to make a legal assignment if called on to so. This may give the bank a power of sale on default.[66] In addition, the bank may take an irrevocable power of attorney, entitling it to sell in the name of the assignor. If no Memorandum is taken, or the document is not under seal, and there is no separate power of attorney, realisation could be effected only by application to the court.

As with legal assignments, the priority between competing equitable assignees is determined by actual or constructive notice of prior assignments, or where there is no notice, by order of notice to the insurer.[67] They are defeated by earlier legal assignments. The bank will have priority over the assignor's liquidator or trustee.[68]

---

[62] Above, para. 24.62 (relating to land: the same common-law principles apply here).
[63] s.1 of the 1867 Act.
[64] *Myers* v. *United Guarantee and Life Ass. Co.* (1855) 7 De G. M. & G. 112.
[65] See *Spencer* v. *Clarke* (1878) 9 Ch.D. 137.
[66] Under s.101, L.P.A. 1925.
[67] Although the insurer has no obligation to formally note on his records any equitable interest, he may do so, but in any case notice is necessary, even if he disregards it.
[68] *Re Wallis, ex p. Jenks* [1902] 1 K.B. 719.

Section Five

Insolvency

27. Statutory Set-off

"Statutory-set off" refers to the right available under section 323 of the Insolvency Act 1986, which has replaced that under section 31 of the Bankruptcy Act 1914. It will be necessary to refer to cases concerning the previous statutory provision, and this chapter examines the differences between the new provision and the old.

27.01

Section 323 of the Insolvency Act 1986 provides as follows: (words in square brackets represent modifications for companies).[1]

"(1) This section applies where before the commencement of the bankruptcy [liquidation] there have been mutual credits, mutual debts or other mutual dealings between the bankrupt [company] and any creditor of the bankrupt [company] proving or claiming to prove for a bankruptcy debt [in the liquidation].

(2) An account shall be taken of what is due from each party to the other in respect of the mutual dealings and the sums due from one party shall be set off against the sums due from the other.

(3) Sums due from the bankrupt to another party shall not be included in the account taken under subsection (2) if that other party had notice at any time they became due that a bankruptcy petition relating to the bankrupt was pending [that a meeting of creditors had been summoned under section 98 or (as the case may be) a petition for the winding up of the company was pending].

(4) Only the balance (if any) of the account taken under subsection (2) shall be provable as a bankruptcy debt or, as the case may be, be paid to the trustee as part of the bankrupt's estate." [Only the balance (if any) of the account is provable in the liquidation. Alternatively (as the case may be) the amount shall be paid to the liquidator as part of the assets.]

Section 31 of the Bankruptcy Act 1914 provided as follows:

"Where there have been mutual credits, mutual debts or other mutual dealings, between a debtor against whom a receiving order shall be made under this Act and any other person proving or claiming to prove a debt under the receiving order, an account shall be taken of what is due from the one party to the other in respect of such mutual dealings, and the sum due from the one party shall be set off against any sum due from the other party, and the balance of the account, and no more shall be claimed or paid on either side respectively; but a person shall not be entitled under this Section to claim the benefit of any set-off against the property of a debtor in any case where he had, at the time of giving credit to the debtor, notice of an act of bankruptcy committed by the debtor and available against him."

In considering statutory set-off, our attention will be focused primarily on the position of a bank which holds a credit balance for a customer, and to the rights of the bank to set-off the customer's debts against that credit

---

[1] Under I.R. 4.90 (section 31 applied to company liquidations by virtue of section 612 of the C.A. 1985).

balance. (The remedy is not, of course, confined to banks or to such occasions as these.)

A. Statutory set-off, under both sections 31 and 323

The following points may be made about statutory set-off, and they seem to apply whether one considers the old section 31, or the new section 323.

1. SECTION IS MANDATORY

27.02 The provision is mandatory, and cannot be excluded by contrary agreement. Thus, in the *Halesowen* case[2] the bank had agreed with its customer to freeze an overdrawn account and not to reduce the debit balance in the absence of "materially changed circumstances." On the customer's winding-up, the bank wished to combine accounts, notwithstanding its agreement. The House of Lords decided that (a) even at common law the agreement was terminated, and the right of combination could be exercised,[3] and (b) that in any case section 31 applied, and its provisions were mandatory, and could not be excluded by prior agreement.

2. APPLIES TO CLAIMS OF DIFFERENT TYPES

27.03 The two claims to be set-off need not be of the same type. This right is thus differentiated from the common-law right of combination, which does not apply to unliquidated claims, contingent or future liabilities, or non-contractual claims. In the normal run of events, the bank will merely combine different accounts, in respect of contractually created debts. There may be occasions, however, when the debt is not created by contract, or is not liquidated, etc. Statutory set-off enables an unliquidated claim to be set off against a liquidated debt, or a future debt, and (probably) now a contingent liability may be set off against a present debt,[3a] while a contractual claim may be set off against a non-contractual claim.[4] The distinction arises because, unlike combination, set-off is not a matter of accounting, but involves two different claims which, as a matter of procedure, may be set-off instead of one party being compelled to pay the whole of the other's claim and then being compelled to bring his own action.[5] The Crown can set off against a claim from a government department a claim due to a different department, and a person owing money to a government department can set off money owing to him by a different department. But set-off cannot be claimed against a claim for taxes, duties or penalties.[6]

---

[2] *National Westminster Bank Ltd.* v. *Halesowen Presswork and Assemblies Ltd.* [1972] 1 All E.R. 641 (H.L.), above, para. 13.31.

[3] In fact, the case is somewhat ambiguous, leaving it unclear if that particular agreement (referring to "material changes" was not intended to survive bankruptcy), or whether all agreements would automatically terminate, though on balance it seems that the latter was intended.

[3a] Below, para. 27.08.

[4] See *Hitchens, Harrison, Woolston & Co.* v. *Jackson & Sons* [1943] A.C. 266.

[5] "It arose to prevent the injustice of such a man having to pay in full what he owed in respect of such dealings while only receiving a dividend on what the bankrupt owed him in respect of them." *per* Lord Cross in the *Halesowen* case, above n. 2, at p. 655. Another example of a non-contractual claim might be a director's liability under a warranty of authority, which might be set off against his personal credit balance.

[6] See R.S.C. Ord. 77, r. 6, *Re D. H. Curtis (Builders) Ltd.* [1978] 2 All E.R. 183 (Crown's debt for goods supplied to government department set off against fiscal liabilities of company); *Cullen* v. *Nottingham H.A.* (unrep.).

3. MUST BE MONEY PAYMENTS

The two claims must, however, resolve themselves into money payments, **27.04** so that a claim for the return of goods could not rank as a set-off[7] (though the claimant might claim damages instead, and this could be set-off).

4. ENGLISH OR WELSH BANKRUPTCIES ONLY

The section applies only to English bankruptcies or liquidations (whatever **27.05** the nationality of the individual or company).

5. CLAIMS IN SAME RIGHT

The claims must arise in the same right—the statute expresses this by saying **27.06** that the debts or claims must be "mutual." As with combination, therefore, no set off is available between a personal debt and a joint account or vice versa, or a trust account and a personal debt, etc.[8]

Mutuality was in issue in the *Halesowen* case[9] and it was decided that a debt which appeared in one account was nevertheless mutual despite an agreement to keep that account separate and not to combine it. Buckley L.J. said[10]:

> "It is well settled that the expression 'mutual credit' here extends to cases where the party receiving the credit is not a debtor *in praesenti* to him who gave the credit . . . provided that the credit is one which must eventually ripen into a debt presently due. A comparatively recent case of this kind is *Rolls Razor Ltd.* v. *Co.*[11] . . . where . . . the retention fund held by the plaintiff company on account of the defendant salesman was not payable at once but by three instalments. See also *Re Daintrey, ex parte Mant,*[12] where the amount to be paid by Messrs. Mant was not even ascertainable at the date of the receiving order."

A problem with claims in different rights may arise from the rules relating to constructive trusts. In particular, it was held in *Neste Oy* v. *Lloyds Bank* P.L.C.[13] that where a bank knew (only) that its customer had ceased trading, and that a receiver had been appointed, but received a payment which was credited to the customer's bank account, the payment received could not be combined because the bank ought to have inquired as to the circumstances of the receivership. This would have revealed that the funds

---

[7] *Rolls Razor Ltd.* v. *Cox* [1967] 1 Q.B. 552.

[8] On trust funds see *Re European Bank, Agra Bank Claim* (1872) 8 Ch.App. 41; *Union Bank of Australia Ltd.* v. *Murray-Aynsley* [1898] A.C. 693; on Quistclose trusts, see *Barclays Bank Ltd.* v. *Quistclose Investments Ltd.* [1970] A.C. 567; *Stumore* v. *Campbell & Co.* [1892] 1 Q.B. 314; on constructive trusts see *Barnes* v. *Addey* (1874) 9 Ch.App. 244; *Neste Oy* v. *Lloyds Bank p.l.c.* [1983] 2 Lloyds Rep. 658; on money paid by mistake of fact see *Kerrison* v. *Glyn, Mills, Currie & Co.* (1911) 81 L.J.K.B. 465; *Scottish Metropolitan Assurance Co.* v. *P. Samuel & Co.* [1923] 1 K.B. 348; on joint debts see *Watts* v. *Christie* (1849) 11 Beav. 546; *Re Willis, Percival & Co. ex p. Morier* (1879) 12 Ch. D. 491. See also the *Halesowen* case, above, n. 2, in the House of Lords at 651–2, *per* Lord Simon, who says "I prefer to say that money is paid for a special (or specific) purpose so as to exclude mutuality of dealing within section 31 if the money is paid in such circumstances that it would be a misappropriation to use it for any other purpose than that for which it is paid."

[9] Above, n. 2.

[10] In the Court of Appeal, [1970] 3 All E.R. 473, 490.

[11] [1967] 1 All E.R. 403.

[12] [1900] 1 Q.B. 546.

[13] [1983] 2 Lloyds Rep. 658.

were the subject of a trust in favour of the receiver. If this case is correct in holding that a constructive trust may arise from what amounts to negligence on the bank's part, then the same principle would apply to statutory set-off (but the case perhaps goes too far).[14]

6. PREFERENTIAL DEBTS

27.07   In relation to preferential debts (say, on a Wages account) the position is no different, in that these must be set-off against credit balances held. It is possible, however, that the bank may have both a preferential and a non-preferential debt. In such a case the bank's preferred position would be to set-off first against the non-preferential debt, leaving the largest possible preferential debt for proof in bankruptcy. In *Re E. J. Morel (1934) Ltd.*[15] Buckley J. suggested *obiter*,[16] that the credit balance must first be set-off against the preferential debt. This dictum was disapproved of in *Re Unit 2 Windows Ltd.*,[17] where Walton J. held that the correct solution was to apply the credit balance rateably between the preferential and a non-preferential debts, so that if, for example, the preferential debt was twice the size of the non-preferential debt, then two-thirds of the credit balance would be allocated to the former. It is submitted that this is the "only logical and sensible solution," (as the learned judge said).

It is necessary to distinguish *Re William Hall (Contractors) Ltd.*,[18] in which a secured creditor realised his security and then purported to appropriate the money to a non-preferential debt in an account containing both a preferential and a non-preferential debt.[19] It is established that a debt remains preferential although it is not kept in a segregated account.[20] In other words, even though it is in a single account, with non-preferential debts, it has to be regarded as a separate debt, subject to different rules regarding preference. It is also established that a banker has a right of appropriation of moneys received to any debt the banker chooses,[21] unless agreed otherwise with his customer.[22] Both these rules, therefore, regard individual debit items in a single account as separate debts for the purpose in question. *Re William Hall (Contractors) Ltd.* follows these rules, inasmuch as it shows that where the bank does not rely on the right of combination, or the right of statutory set-off, but on the separate right of appropriation to an account, it is unaffected by considerations applicable to the other rights. It is submitted, therefore, that the rule in *Re William Hall (Contractors) Ltd.* is unaffected by the decision of Walton J. in *Re Unit 2 Windows Ltd.*, although the former decision does not enable the bank, once it has appropriated money to any account, subsequently to combine accounts so as to destroy only a non-preferential debt. The appropriation must be made when the money is received, because it is at the moment of appropriation that debts are, according to the principle, discharged. It is further submitted that the appropriation principle has nothing to do with the fact that the bank is

---

[14] Above, Ch. 10.

[15] [1962] Ch. 21.

[16] He held that there was no preferential debt, because the bank had made no "advance" for wages.

[17] [1985] 3 All E.R. 647.

[18] [1967] 2 All E.R. 1150.

[19] So far as appears, it seems to have been a single account.

[20] See, *e.g. Re Primrose Builders Ltd.* [1950] Ch. 561.

[21] *Devaynes* v. *Noble, Clayton's Case* (1816) 1 Mer. 572.

[22] *Westminster Bank Ltd.* v. *Cond* (1940) 46 Com.Cas. 60.

secured, or not.[23] Unless otherwise agreed expressly, or by implication, the right of appropriation is a general right, not confined to cases of realisation of securities.

B. Section 323 and Insolvency Rule 4.90

1. CONTINGENT, UNLIQUIDATED, AND FUTURE LIABILITIES

Contingent debts may probably be set off under the new provisions, which refer to debts or bankruptcy debts, defined as follows[24]: "For the purposes of references in this Group of Parts to a debt or liability it shall be immaterial whether the debt or liability is present or future, whether it is certain or contingent or whether its amount is fixed or liquidated, or is capable of being ascertained by fixed rules or as a matter of opinion . . . "

27.08

An example of a contingent liability is that of a customer who discounts a bill to the bank (which the customer endorses) and who then becomes bankrupt. Another example is the bank's contingent liability under a performance bond. The bank may at some future date, have to proceed against the customer, but until maturity his liability is merely contingent: there is no present debt. Under the older law, it was debatable whether contingent debts or liabilities could be set off. One recent case held that this was possible[25] but the better view may be that it was not possible unless the insolvency was treated by the creditor as a repudiation of a contract, entitling the creditor to a present action for unliquidated damages.[26] This could be done in most cases, and if so, it solves the problem.

Although there is little doubt that Parliament intended section 323 to cover contingent debts, there is a serious drafting error in the section. Under section 31 of the old Act, sums could be set-off (a) only if "due", and (b) only if "at the time of giving credit" the party had no notice of a pending bankruptcy petition. Under section 323 sums can be set off (a) only if "due", and (b) only if "at any time they became due" the party had no notice of a pending bankruptcy petition (or the company equivalent). If "due" means "payable" then even contingent debts arising before notice of the petition would be affected by subsequent notice of the petition. This cannot have been intended, and it is submitted that for the purposes of this section "due" must mean "at the time the contract is entered under which a debt may become due, regardless of when it becomes due." It is to be hoped that the fact that this directly contradicts the words used in section 323 will not dissuade the courts. In *Re Charge Card Services Ltd.*,[26a] the court held that under section 31, contingent debts could be set-off. That case is under appeal at the time of writing, but if upheld on this point, then if "due" under section 31 includes contingent liabilities, this would also be the case for the new section 323, and "due" must mean "when the contract was made under which they might arise."

The preceding suggestion, however, raises another problem. Suppose bank A is owed a sum of money by the debtor, and bank B holds a deposit from the debtor. If bank A assigns the debt to bank B, bank B can combine

---

[23] Though *Re William Hall (Contractors) Ltd.* relied on older cases concerning the rights of secured creditors.

[24] s.382(3), 385, I.R. 12.3, 13.12.

[25] *Re Charge Card Services Ltd.* [1986] 3 All E.R. 289.

[26] See Shea, [1986] 3 J.I.B.L. 192.

[26a] Above, n. 25.

accounts, or set–off in insolvency. Outside of insolvency, this would appear unobjectionable, but it can hardly be thought that the courts will welcome the attempt in an insolvency case, if the banks know of a pending petition. But if "due" means "when the contract was made under which the debts arise" (and not "at the time of the assignment") then on the face of it the assignment is permissible, since the debts became "due" before the assignment, and at the time they became due, neither bank had notice of a pending petition. This may be avoided if, as seems likely, the courts read the word "due" as meaning "due to him" (*i.e.* the party seeking the set–off). In the example given, the debt becomes due to bank B only after the assignment, at which time B's knowledge of the petition will debar him. This argument would, of course, apply not only to contingent liabilities, but also to existing debts owed to bank A. The banks could not trade either existing, or contingent debts in the manner mentioned, so as to give themselves rights of set–off, after knowledge of a petition.

27.09   When, it may be asked, should "contingent" claims and unliquidated claims be set–off? Under section 323 the relevant time for establishing a set–off is the date of the bankruptcy order. Under section 31, the relevant date was the earlier date of the receiving order, which then preceeded the bankruptcy order. If the amount to be set–off cannot be known after the receiving order (under the old system) or until after the bankruptcy order (under the new system) then it would seem to be necessary to include in the right of set–off a right in the bank to retain the credit balance until the amount of its claim has been satisfied. If a bank can set–off for unliquidated or contingent claims, there must with a section 323 set–off be a similar right of retention,[27] provided perhaps that the amount it seeks to retain is a reasonable estimate. Under the new insolvency scheme, where contingent debts can be set–off the problem of quantum is dealt with by section 322(3) of the 1986 Act, which provides that if a contingent debt does not bear a certain value, the trustee is to estimate the amount, and this is the amount provable, unless the creditor appeals against this.[28]

2. FUTURE LIABILITIES

27.10   An example of a future liability is the case where a customer with an outstanding loan, payable at sometime in the future, becomes bankrupt.[29] An immediate proof may be made for the debt or if the bank has some credit balance on another account, this may be set off. The debt is owing at present, though repayable only in future.[30] The Insolvency Act 1986 expressly provides in section 382(3) that it is immaterial if a debt is "present or future" and such a debt is a "bankruptcy debt" which can be set–off within section 323.

3. DEBTS AND DEPOSITS

27.11   There are some obscurities in the Insolvency Act 1986, and the following discussion must, therefore, be somewhat tentative.

Section 323 does not enable mutual debts to be set off if they occur

---

[27] Goode, L.P.C.S. 112 argues that such a right is implied in a contractual set–off agreement.
[28] *E.g.* under s.303.
[29] For an example of a "future" debt see *Rolls Razor Ltd.* v. *Cox* [1967] 1 Q.B. 552 (debt repayable in instalments).
[30] *Debitum in praesenti, sed solvendum in futuro.*

(i) after knowledge of a pending petition for bankruptcy or winding up, or of a meeting for creditors to consider winding up, or (ii) after the commencement of bankruptcy or liquidation, or (iii) if the debt is not a "bankruptcy debt" or "debt." It is necessary, therefore, to look closely at the meaning in the Act of "commencement of bankruptcy or liquidation" and "bankruptcy debt" (or, at least, "debt").

Under the new system, there are in the case of an individual bankrupt three relevant periods, which are in chronological order: the date of the petition, the date of the bankruptcy order, and the date of the order vesting the property in the trustee. Apart from section 323 itself, the key sections for present purposes are sections 283–285 (for individuals) and section 127 (for companies). Section 283 declares that the bankrupt's estate, which is vested in the trustee, includes all property vested in the bankrupt at the commencement of the bankruptcy. Bankruptcy commences on the date of the bankruptcy order.

In the case of a company the commencement of liquidation in a compulsory winding up is when the petition is presented, (or at the time of passing of a resolution by the company for a winding up, if there is one).[31] With a voluntary winding up, the commencement of liquidation is at the time the company passes a resolution to wind up.[32]

It will be appreciated that the bank may be dealing with two types of situations: (a) where a payment is received by the bank, (which wishes to set it off against an unchallenged debt) and this payment to the bank is challenged as belonging to the trustee or liquidator, and (b) where the bank has an unchallenged deposit to set off but where the debt against which it is to be set-off is challenged as one which should not have been incurred. The question of what payments the bank may keep, and what debts may be incurred, is dealt with elsewhere.[33]

In the case of an individual, by way of summary, the position *may* be as follows:

(i) For transactions after the petition and before commencement, (a) payments into an overdrawn account may be kept, (b) payments into a credit account belong to the trustee, (c) debts incurred by payments from overdrawn accounts without notice of the petition are provable, and can be set off, (d) debts incurred with notice of a petition are void and may not be set-off.

(ii) After commencement the position seems to be (a) that payments into an account are recoverable by the trustee, and cannot be set off, (b) that payments from an account (whether in credit or not) cannot be debited to the account, and are not provable, and cannot be set off, (c) however, as later discussed[34] some payments out may create debts which are deemed, by section 284, to occur before commencement (and then on the same terms as for payments between the petition and commencement).

27.12

(iii) Payments and debits, etc., after vesting are completely unprotected, and unprovable, and cannot be set off, though the trustee may permit the conduct of an account, and it may be that some property is "after-acquired" and may be retained by the bank unless claimed by the trustee. But this is irrelevant to statutory set-off.

[31] s.129.
[32] s.86.
[33] Below, para. 28.78 *et seq.*
[34] Below, para. 28.78 *et seq.*

In the case of a company the position is more straightforward, because commencement occurs at the time of the petition or resolution to wind up.

(i) In compulsory windings up, any dispositions of the company's property after commencement are void, and this includes payments into an overdrawn account.[35] No payments may be received, nor any new debts incurred, unless ratified by the court.[36]

(ii) In voluntary windings up, the directors are deprived of ostensible authority to deal with the property of the company by the Gazetting of the resolution, and this would prevent them incurring new debts or making valid payments to the bank, which could either be proved, or set off.[37]

(iii) In either a compulsory or voluntary winding up, the knowledge of a petition or a pending creditors meeting under section 98 would prevent further debiting of the account, so the debits cannot be proved or set off.

---

[35] *Re Gray's Inn Construction Co. Ltd.* [1980] 1 All E.R. 814.
[36] Below, para. 28.78.
[37] Below, para. 28.78.

28. Insolvency

INTRODUCTION

In this chapter, we consider together, as far as may be, the processes of cor- **28.01**
porate insolvency and liquidation, and individual insolvency and bankruptcy, with some reference to the bankruptcies of partnerships. Section A
concerns the "insolvency regimes." Section B concerns corporate insolvency. Section C deals with certain effects of corporate insolvency upon
directors. Section D concerns individual bankruptcy. Section E considers
together matters affecting property transactions relating to corporate or
individual insolvency. Section F concerns provable debts and priorities of
payment (for both companies and individuals). Section G considers some
matters affecting the bank's conduct of accounts with insolvent persons.
Only the barest outline of procedures in insolvency is provided (in Sections
B and D).

Insolvency means, generally, inability to pay debts. A frequent, but not
necessary consequence of insolvency is, in the case of corporations, the process of liquidation or "winding-up" of the company, and in the case of an
individual, the process of bankruptcy. Liquidation involves the cessation of
the company's existence, and the disposal of all its assets. Bankruptcy
involves the disposal of some of the assets of the individual, but leads to his
eventual rehabilitation.

The main provisions affecting both types of insolvency are to be found in
the Insolvency Act 1986 and rules made thereunder (primarily The Insolvency Rules 1986). The Insolvency Act 1985 introduced new concepts, but
few of its provisions came into force. The Insolvency Act 1986 which came
into force on December 29, 1986 codified the law relating to insolvency and
repealed the 1985 Act. *All references in the text or notes are to the 1986 act, unless
otherwise stated.*

INSOLVENCY PRACTITIONERS

The Insolvency Act 1986 lays down[1] requirements for qualifications to be **28.02**
held by those, other than the official receiver, who practise as insolvency
practitioners: *i.e.* as liquidators, administrators, administrative receivers,
supervisors of voluntary schemes, or trustees of individual bankrupts.
These provisions are designed to ensure a certain level of competence, but
also of independence, amongst those concerned.

A. Insolvency régimes

With an insolvent corporation there are four "régimes" or courses of action **28.03**
available: these are receivership, administration, voluntary arrangements,
and winding up. In addition to these régimes banks have often taken part in
"bank rescues" of companies in difficulty.

With individuals receivership of mortgaged property may occur but is
not considered an insolvency régime, and no administrator may be
appointed, though there may be a supervisor of a voluntary scheme: gener-

---

[1] In Part XIII.

ally, then, the insolvency régimes for individuals are voluntary arrangements and bankruptcy.

1. BANK RESCUES

Bank rescues of corporations might take place (for example) where in the bank's opinion a company had temporary cash flow problems, but its position was not hopeless (assets exceeded liabilities). Generally the company or its group was required to give the bank full debentures affecting all their assets, in return for addition or continued finance from the bank. We have observed that although the bank may take fixed charges for this purpose, the creation of additional floating charges for "old" debt is prohibited, but that if new advances are made (even by the operation of *Clayton's case*) there is no objection.[2] Sometimes rescues may involve the bank insisting upon a change of management: this may cause problems with the new concept of "wrongful trading."[3]

2. RECEIVERSHIP

28.04 This may be receivership *simpliciter*, as where a bank acting under a fixed charge seizes and sells particular assets, or it may be "administrative receivership" where under a floating charge the receiver takes over the whole company and its management and business, with a view to selling it or perhaps hiving parts of the business off. Receivers are considered elsewhere.[4]

3. ADMINISTRATION

28.05 This is a new process introduced by the Insolvency Acts 1985–86, designed to facilitate the rehabilitation of companies in difficulty, or to improve the prospects of beneficial realisation of its assets or business. The effect of an administration order is to freeze the rights of secured and unsecured creditors. So long as the order is current, it prevents winding up, or the appointment of an administrative receiver. But we have observed that the holder of a debenture creating a floating charge over substantially the whole of the company's assets may block the appointment of a receiver, and we have considered the effect of the administrator upon the realisation of securities.[5]

4. VOLUNTARY ARRANGEMENTS BY COMPANIES

28.06 These may occur under the Companies Act 1985, s.425.[6] These fall into the classes of arrangements, assignments and compositions. An arrangement could include a reorganisation of the company's share capital whereby creditors convert some debt into equity (though "scheme of arrangement" is a term used for any voluntary scheme). A composition is an agreement of creditors not to take action against the company, in return for an agreement by the debtor company—for example, payment of part (a dividend) of their debt, or payment over a period, and so on. An assignment involves transfer of the company's property to the creditors (or to a nominee for them all). The creditors benefit from avoiding the delays and expense of liquidation.

[2] Above, Chap. 21, esp. at para. 21.38 *et seq.*
[3] Below, section D, para. 28.40.
[4] Above, Chap. 23.
[5] Above, para. 23.01.
[6] Or under s.539(1)(e) if by the liquidator, and ss.582,593 for voluntary windings up.

Section 425 requires an application to the court by the company or a creditor, and if $\frac{3}{4}$ in value (and a majority in number present and voting) of the voting creditors of a particular class (*e.g.* secured, unsecured) agree, at a class meeting, the court may sanction the agreement and it then binds all creditors of that class (the largest advantage of such schemes).[7] These schemes were little used, being slow (a court order, and class meetings, were required) complicated and fairly expensive (because of the need for applications to the court). The company would often "die" while awaiting the scheme, when creditors petitioned for winding up or secured creditors enforced their security. It may be that new penalties imposed on dilatory directors may encourage voluntary arrangements at an earlier time, especially where the major creditor is a bank. Such schemes are confidential and allow directors to retain control and to avoid public disgrace.

Additionally to section 425, a liquidator may make a compromise and the court or committee of inspection may agree to this under section 539(1)(e).[8]

The Insolvency Act 1986 introduces[9] a new scheme of voluntary arrangement. Unlike section 425, this requires supervision by an insolvency practitioner, as "nominee." A proposal is made to the company and its creditors, by directors, the liquidator, or the Administrator, and may be made if the company is being wound up, or is subject to an administration order, or at any time. The proposal appoints a nominee to implement the scheme. Class meetings are not required, only meetings of all the creditors together, so that these schemes may be speedier than those under section 425. Again, however, the delays involved may themselves lead to the death of the company. It must be observed that no meeting of creditors under a voluntary scheme can approve a proposal which affects the rights of a secured creditor to enforce his security, nor shall the proposal affect the priority of a preferential debt, or cause any a preferential creditor to be paid an amount proportionately less than other preferential creditors, unless in each case the creditor affected agrees. It may be, then, that such schemes will be most advantageous in conjunction with the appointment of an administrator, for his appointment freezes all proceedings against the company, preventing fixed or floating chargeholders (if the latter agree to the administration order) from realising their securities, and preventing any creditor from petitioning for winding up.

5. VOLUNTARY ARRANGEMENTS BY INDIVIDUALS

28.07 These may be made as a deed of arrangement under the Deeds of Arrangement Act 1914[10] or a voluntary arrangement under the Insolvency Act 1986, Part VIII (ss.252–263).

a. Deeds of Arrangement

28.08 These include any instrument, whether made under seal or not, made for the benefit of creditors generally, or made by an insolvent debtor for the benefit of three or more creditors. The individual might assign his property, or agree to a composition, and where the creditors obtain control over his property or business, the class of instruments includes a "letter of licence"

[7] See next note, for another provision.
[8] s.601, C.A. 1948 (s.306, C.A. 1948), now replaced, provided for arrangments to be made binding for a company in liquidation.
[9] In ss.1–7.
[10] As amended by I.A. 1986, Sched. 14.

459

and "deed of inspectorship" whereby the creditors agree not to sue for a time and allow the debtor to continue his business, or to wind it up.[11] These "deeds" are void, unless (i) registered with the Department of Trade within seven days of execution and properly stamped,[12] and (ii) assented to by a majority in number and value within 21 days of registration, and (iii) within 28 days of registration a statutory declaration is filed confirming that the assents have been obtained, and (iv) within a further seven days the trustee gives security (unless the creditors dispense with this).[13] The problem with deeds of this sort is that they do not prevent dissenting creditors from presenting a bankruptcy petition.

b. Voluntary Arrangements under the Insolvency Act 1986

28.09 These may be made where a debtor (or his trustee or the official receiver, where he is an undischarged bankrupt) proposes a composition or scheme to his creditors, under which an insolvency practitioner (the nominee) is to supervise the implementation of the agreement. No application may be made while a debtor's bankruptcy petition is pending, if the court has appointed a person to inquire into the bankrupt's affairs. The substantial advantage of the procedure (as opposed to company proposals) is that while an application is pending, the court may grant an interim order, under which it has wide powers at its discretion to allow a "moratorium," staying actions, or execution, etc., against the debtor's property or person.[14] Additionally, no bankruptcy petition against the debtor may be presented or proceeded with. These interim orders do not endure for longer than 14 days (unless extended on the nominee's application), but the freezing of the debtor's position may be most valuable in enabling him to reorganise his affairs. To prevent abuse, the debtor must genuinely intend to make a proposal, and he must be an undischarged bankrupt or be in a position where (from the level of his debts) he is able to petition for his own bankruptcy, having made no previous application in the past 12 months. The nominee must be a qualified insolvency practitioner who is willing to act.

Before the interim order ceases to have effect, the nominee shall submit a report to say whether the creditors should be called to a meeting to consider the proposals (in which case the interim order is extended). The debtor must provide the nominee with details of his debts, liabilities and assets. The order may be discharged if on the nominee's application the court is satisfied that the debtor has not complied with his obligations under this provision, or that it is inappropriate to call a meeting of creditors.

If the meeting approves the proposal, the arrangements bind those who in accordance with the rules had notice of and were entitled to vote at the meeting, whether they came, or voted, or not, as if they were parties to the arrangement. Bankruptcy petitions stayed by interim orders which cease subsequent to a meeting approving proposals shall be deemed to have been dismissed. As with companies, the meeting may not affect the rights of secured or preferential creditors, without their consent. The Deeds of Arrangement Act 1914 does not apply to the approved arrangement. If the debtor is an undischarged bankrupt, the court may annul the bankruptcy

---

[11] s.1, 1914 Act.

[12] *Ibid.*, s.2.

[13] In default of this last, the court may declare the deed void, or appoint a new trustee—s.11, 1914 Act.

[14] ss.252–254.

order and/or give such directions with respect to the conduct of the bankruptcy as it thinks fit.

B. Winding-up of companies

"Winding-up" or "liquidation" are equivalent terms for the process by
which a company's existence is terminated (the company is "dissolved")
and its remaining assets distributed. Usually, this occurs on insolvency, but
not necessarily: for example, the company may simply have achieved the
purposes for which it was established. **28.10**

Winding-up may occur in only two ways. First, there is a form of compulsory winding-up, by the court, and secondly, there is the more common
form of voluntary winding-up, which may be by way of member's winding-up (broadly, where the company is solvent), or creditor's winding-up.
Compulsory winding-up starts ordinarily with a petition by a creditor, and
voluntary winding-up starts with a resolution by the company.

1. WINDING-UP BY THE COURT (COMPULSORY WINDING UP)

a. Grounds for Petition

A petition may be presented to the court for compulsory winding-up in the
following two cases: **28.11**

(a) under section 440 of the Companies Act 1985 the Secretary of State
may petition where he thinks it expedient in the public interest as a result of
a report from inspectors, under section 437, or from information or documents gained under sections 447–448;

(b) under section 18 of the Banking Act 1979[14a]: The Bank of England
may petition in relation to recognised banks or licensed institutions in certain cases.

In addition, petitions may be presented in circumstances laid down in section 122 of the Insolvency Act 1986. The main[15] provisions are:

(a) if the company so resolves, by special resolution;

(b) if the company does not commence its business within a year from its
incorporation or suspends its business for a whole year;

(c) if the number of members is reduced below two, (which is the minimum for any company);

(d) if the court is of the opinion that it is just and equitable that the company should be wound up. This ground is rarely used, and is available
generally for small private companies where, for example, the management
has become deadlocked, or a director is "frozen out" or excluded, in circumstances where, if it were a partnership, the partnership might be dissolved.[16]

(e) if the company is unable to pay its debts. This is the most commonly
used ground. According to s.123 it is deemed to occur in these cases: **28.12**

(i) "Insolvency Notice": if a creditor (by assignment or otherwise) to
whom the company is indebted in a sum exceeding £750,[17] then due has
served on the company at its registered office a written demand in the
prescribed form requiring the company to pay, and the company has

---

[14a] Similar provisions in the Banking Act 1987 will replace this.

[15] There are special rare grounds affecting public companies.

[16] See *Re Yenidje Tobacco Co. Ltd.* [1916] 2 Ch. 426; *Re Lundie Bros. Ltd.* [1965] 2 All E.R. 692;
Ebrahimi v. *Westbourne Galleries Ltd.* [1973] A.C. 360. See also s.125(2), I.A. 1986.

[17] The sum may be varied by Regulation.

within three weeks neither paid, nor secured or compounded for the sum to the creditor's reasonable satisfaction. An order will not be made if in good faith the company disputes the debt. It applies only to undisputed debts (*e.g.* those not in fact disputed, or judgment debts).[18] The calculation of periods of time is done by ignoring fractions of a day, and by excluding the day on which the demand is served.[19]

(ii) "Unsatisfied execution": if execution or other process by a judgment creditor is returned unsatisfied in whole or in part.

(iii) "Proved insolvency": if it is proved to the satisfaction of the court that the company is unable to pay its debts as they fall due. The court may consider any evidence it deems to be sufficient, and it has been held[20] that the fact that the company's assets exceed its liabilities does not show that it is solvent if in fact it cannot pay its debts as they fall due. It is a question of fact: the assets may be very illiquid, justifying winding-up, or they may be realisable in a few days, and be sufficient to discharge all immediate liabilities, in which case the order may be refused.[21] The court clearly has some discretion.[22] Naturally, where a bank has a standard form charge, it may make demand, and appoint a receiver in a very short time indeed,[23] and the seizure of assets may enable the bank or another creditor more easily to show inability to pay debts thereafter.

(iv) "Asset test": if it is proved to the satisfaction of the court that the value of the company's assets is less than the amount of its liabilities, taking into account its contingent and prospective liabilities. This "asset test" was new in 1985, and is very wide. From time to time it may affect many companies whose balance sheets show a deficit,[24] but it should be recalled that the court need not order a winding-up, and may dismiss the petition,[25] or make an administration order. It may be that the balance sheets display inappropriate values for assets, being set deliberately artificially high, or having been affected by depreciation or, for that matter, showing inappropriately low values due to increasing property values, and presumably it is the true market value, not the book value, which counts. While contingent liabilities must be considered, it is unclear if equal contingent assets should be taken into account.

b. Who May Petition?

28.13 In the special cases mentioned the Secretary of State, or the Bank of England may petition. In the other cases, section 124 allows the petition to be presented by the company, or by majority of the directors,[26] or any creditor(s), including contingent or prospective creditors, or by any contributory(ies).[27] When a company is being wound up voluntarily, the official receiver may additionally petition, but the court shall not make a winding-

[18] See *Re London and Paris Banking Corpn.* (1874) L.R. 19 Eq. 444.
[19] *Re Lympne Investments Ltd.* [1972] 2 All E.R. 385.
[20] *Re Patrick and Lyon Ltd.* [1933] Ch. 786.
[21] See *Re Capital Annuities Ltd.* [1978] 3 All E.R. 704.
[22] See also, s.125.
[23] Above, Chap. 23.
[24] It has been said that on this criterion, half the companies in England are unable to pay their debts.
[25] s.125.
[26] The plural form suggests majority action.
[27] s.124(2)–(3) limits the rights of contributories.

up order unless the voluntary winding up cannot be continued with due regard to the interests of the creditors or contributories.[28]

Contributories are those defined in section 79[29] as every person liable to contribute to the assets of a company in the event of its being wound up.[30] Section 74 states that every past and present member is liable to contribute to the assets of the company if it is wound up, so as to pay its debts and liabilities, though past members are not to be called on until after existing members, nor for debts after their membership ceased, nor incurred more than a year before winding up commenced. Contribution is limited to the extent of any sums unpaid on shares held. This provision is at the heart of the "limited liability" of companies. Today, most shares are fully paid, so that there are few contributories.

c. After the Petition

The following steps may occur: **28.14**

(i) Before a winding-up order, the court may appoint a provisional liquidator.[31] This "freezes" the position, by taking powers away from the directors to dispose of property, etc. It is often done at the time of filing the petition, by an application to a judge in chambers.

(ii) The company, or any creditor or contributory may apply to have a stay of any action or proceeding against the company.[32]

(iii) The court may dismiss the petition, adjourn the hearing conditionally or unconditionally, or may make an interim order, or any other order it thinks fit,[33] but it should not refuse to make a winding up order just because the company has no assets, or because they are heavily mortgaged.[34] In reaching its decision the court will have regard to the wishes of the majority of creditors and contributories. It may order a meeting of creditors and contributories to be summoned to determine the wishes of the majority.[35] Where a petition is brought by members of the company (contributories) the court will not order a winding up against the wishes of the majority.[36] If a petition is brought by creditors, the majority view (in value) will usually, but not necessarily be followed. It may be that a single large creditor is using the petition as a means of enforcing a disputed debt[37] or that he will obtain no benefit from the order[38] and it may then be refused.

d. After Commencement

Section 129 states that in compulsory windings up the commencement date **28.15** is the time of the presentation of the petition (or the time of passing of a resolution by the company for voluntary winding up, if there is one). After the commencement the following occur:

(i) dispositions of the company's property are affected[39];

(ii) any attachment, sequestration, distress or execution put in force

---

[28] s.124(5).
[29] See ss.79–83.
[30] Or their personal representatives: *Re Bayswater Trading Co. Ltd.* [1970] 1 All E.R. 608.
[31] s.135.
[32] s.126.
[33] s.125.
[34] *Ibid.*
[35] s.645, C.A. 1985, now replaced by s.195, I.A. 1986.
[36] *Re London Suburban Bank* (1871) 6 Ch.App. 641.
[37] *Holt Southey Ltd.* v. *Catnic Components Ltd.* [1978] 2 All E.R. 276.
[38] *Re Krasnapolsky Restaurant and Winter Garden Co.* [1892] 3 Ch. 174.
[39] Below, section E, para. 28.78 *et seq.*

against the estate or effects of the company is void[40] and proceedings against the company may be affected[40a];

(iii) the company ceases to carry on business, except so far as is necessary to carry on the winding up. The powers of directors cease.[41] The employees are automatically dismissed,[42] although the liquidator may re-employ some of them temporarily.

e. The Official Receiver

28.16 Where the court has made a winding-up order or appointed a provisional liquidator, the official receiver must investigate the affairs of the company, and the causes of its failure, and must report to the court, and his report shall, in any proceedings, be prima facie evidence of the facts therein.[43] He may (and sometimes must) apply to the court for the public examination of certain persons, or can require statements from them.

f. The Liquidator

28.17 The official receiver is *ex officio* liquidator, but another liquidator may be appointed by a meeting of creditors.[44] The functions of a liquidator being wound up by the court "shall be to secure that the assets of the company are got in, realised and distributed to the company's creditors and, if there is a surplus, to the person entitled to it."[45] Some of his wide powers are subject to the sanction of either the court, or of the committee of creditors. The court may control the exercise of any power, on application by a creditor or contributory. In order to establish the wishes of creditors or contributories, he may call general meetings, and he must do so if meetings direct him to do so or if one tenth in value of the creditors or contributories direct him to do so.[46] He may apply to the court for directions in relation to any particular matter, and this power may be useful not only where there is doubt as to his powers or duties, but where he faces obstruction. He may (subject to the Act) use his own discretion in managing and distributing the company's business and assets.[47] Any person aggrieved by his acts or decisions may apply to the court, which may confirm, reverse or modify the act or decision complained of.[48] The court also has certain powers, described below, and some of these are delegable to the liquidator as an officer of the court, and subject to the court's control.

g. Committees

28.18 Meetings of creditors and contributories may decide to establish a committee to exercise various functions (not if the official receiver is liquidator). Many of the liquidator's powers[49] are subject to the sanction of the court or of the committee.

---

[40] Below, section E, para. 28.68.
[40a] Below, para. 28.69.
[41] *Fowler* v. *Broad's Patent Night Light Co.* [1893] 1 Ch. 724; *Measures Bros Ltd.* v. *Measures* [1910] 2 Ch. 248.
[42] *Re General Rolling Stock Co., Chapman's case* (1866) L.R. 1 Eq. 346.
[43] s.132.
[44] Or contributories: s.136.
[45] s.135. His powers are largely specified in ss.165–167.
[46] s.168(2).
[47] s.168(4).
[48] s.168(5).
[49] Those listed in Parts I and II of Sched. 4.

h. Powers of Court

Those not already mentioned include the following: (a) to stay the winding up on the application of the liquidator, official receiver, creditor or contributory,[50] (b) to settle a list of contributories (unless calls on contributories are unnecessary) and cause the company's assets to be collected and applied in discharge of its liabilities,[51] (c) to order contributories to pay money due to the company,[52] (d) to make calls on contributories,[53] (e) to exclude creditors who do not prove their debts within a time stated by the court,[54] (f) to adjust the rights of contributories among themselves and distribute any surplus among those entitled,[55] (g) to allow creditors and contributories to inspect the company's books and records,[56] (h) where assets are insufficient to satisfy the liabilities, to make an order for payment of expenses of winding up in such order of priority as the court thinks just,[57] (i) to arrest absconding contributories and have their books, papers and movable property seized.[58] The powers thus given are in addition to any other powers which the court may have.[59] All of the court's powers in relation to certain matters may be delegated to the liquidator as an officer of the court, and subject to the court's control.[60] These delegable matters are as to the holding of meetings, the settling of lists of contributories and the collection and application of assets, the payment, delivery, etc., of money, property, books, etc., to the liquidator, the making of calls, and the fixing of a time within which debts and claims must be proved.

28.19

i. Final General Meeting of Creditors

If it seems to the liquidator that the winding-up of the company is for practical purposes complete, he shall summon a final general meeting of creditors to receive his report, and to determine if he should have his release under section 174.

28.20

j. Dissolution

When the registrar of companies is informed that the winding-up of a company is complete, he shall register the notice, and three months later, the company shall be dissolved, unless the Secretary of State defers the date.[61]

28.21

2. VOLUNTARY WINDING UP

Voluntary winding up is more common than winding up by the court, being not only quicker than winding up by the court, but less expensive.

28.22

---

[50] s.147.
[51] s.148.
[52] s.149: note ss.151, 152.
[53] s.150.
[54] s.153.
[55] s.154.
[56] s.155.
[57] s.156.
[58] s.158.
[59] s.159.
[60] s.160.
[61] s.205.

a. Grounds for Voluntary Winding Up

28.23   It may occur in the following cases[62]:

(i) Where the Articles impose some condition (either as to time, or otherwise) upon which the existence of the company depends, and the time having expired or the event having occurred, a general meeting passes an ordinary resolution for winding up. This is rare.

(ii) Where the company resolves by special resolution (requiring 21 days notice) that it be wound up voluntarily.

(iii) Where the company resolves by extraordinary resolution (requiring 14 days notice) that it cannot by reason of its liabilities continue its business, and that it is advisable to wind up. This enables some saving of time if the position is hopeless and the creditors are pressing.

b. Effect of Resolution for Winding Up

28.24   (i) On penalty of fine, notice of the resolution must be published in the London Gazette.[63]

(ii) Winding up commences at the time of the passing of the resolution.[64]

(iii) After commencement, the company "shall" cease to carry on its business, except so far as may be required for its beneficial winding up, although its corporate status and powers continue until dissolution.[65]

(iv) Any transfer of shares not approved by the liquidator, and any alteration in the status of the members, is void.[66]

(v) The directors' powers to dispose of property, etc., is affected, as later described.[67]

c. Types of Voluntary Winding Up

28.25   There may be a members' voluntary winding up, or a creditors' voluntary winding up.[68]

28.26   **(i) A members' voluntary winding up** is distinguished by a "statutory declaration of solvency." It may occur when within five weeks of the resolution and before it (even if on the same day) at a meeting of directors a majority of them make a statutory declaration that they have made full inquiry into the company's affairs and have formed the opinion that it will be able to pay its debts and interest thereon within a period (not greater than 12 months) specified in the declaration. A recent statement of the company's assets and liabilities must be included in the declaration, and (on penalty of fine) the declaration is to be delivered to the registrar of companies within 15 days of the resolution. If after such a declaration the company's debts are not paid in full, within the period specified, it is to be presumed unless the contrary is shown, that the directors did not have reasonable grounds for their declaration. If directors do not have reasonable grounds, the penalty is a fine, or imprisonment.[69]

The resolution for winding up follows this declaration, and the company in general meeting "shall" appoint one or more liquidators to wind up the

---

[62] s.84.
[63] s.85.
[64] s.86.
[65] s.87.
[66] s.88.
[67] Below, section E, para. 28.78.
[68] s.90.
[69] s.89.

company's affairs and distribute its assets. If the liquidator believes that the company will be unable to pay its debts and interest thereon in full within the period specified, he calls a meeting of creditors, and from the day on which the creditors' meeting is held, the winding up continues thereafter as a creditors' winding up, with the meeting having the normal powers of a creditors' meeting (*e.g.* to appoint a committee).

(ii) A creditors' voluntary winding up also depends on a resolution being passed by the company. Then within 14 days a meeting of creditors must be notified, advertised and called to consider the resolution (the directors must attend and preside at the meeting). The company meeting, and the creditors' meeting may appoint a liquidator (in case of conflict, the creditors' liquidator prevails). The creditors and the company may appoint a committee, which may sanction the continuance of the directors' powers, or some of them.[70] The liquidator requires the sanction of the committee (or of the court) to exercise certain of his powers, but is free to deal with property except that if he disposes of company property to a person connected with the company, he must give notice to the committee.[71] Apart from this, the main function of the committee is simply to act as a more coherent and manageable body than the whole body of creditors, better able to monitor the progress of the winding up.

28.27

d. Dissolution

Once the company's affairs are fully wound up, the liquidator makes up a full account showing what has occurred, and calls separate meetings of company and creditors to consider and explain his account, and sends to the registrar of companies a copy of the account and a return as to the meetings. The registrar registers the account and the returns received, and the company is then dissolved in three months, unless the court defers the date.[72]

28.28

e. The Liquidator

Except where the committee's sanction is needed the liquidator (in a members' or creditors' winding up) may without sanction exercise any of the other powers given by the Companies Act to a liquidator in a compulsory winding up.[73] As in that case, he is to use his own discretion in the management of the estate and in its distribution among the creditors, and he may apply to the court for directions in relation to any matter concerning the winding up.[74] In *Leon* v. *York-O-Matic*[75] it was held that the court might not interfere with the liquidator's day to day administration, nor question the exercise in good faith of his discretion, nor might he be held accountable for an error of judgment, if, say, he sold at an undervalue.[76] Notwithstanding this, he owes to the company some, at least, of the duties of a trustee, though under the previous insolvency scheme he was not liable for negli-

28.29

---

[70] s.103.
[71] s.167(2).
[72] ss.106, 201.
[73] Above, para. 28.17.
[74] ss.168, 112.
[75] [1966] 3 All E.R. 277.
[76] Contrast receivers, above, Chap. 23.

gence, but only (a) for behaviour amounting to fraud,[77] or (b) for the mis-application of the assets of the company, for example, paying debts in the wrong order, or admitting and paying an invalid claim,[78] or (c) making a secret profit from his position. His safeguard, whenever he is in doubt, is to apply to the court for directions,[79] or the determination of any question, or for the exercise of any power which the court might exercise in a winding up.[80] Any contributory may also apply to the court for the determination of questions, or exercise of power[81] but we have just observed that the court may be reluctant to interfere. Although section 212 allows the court to make certain orders where there is misfeasance, it seems that this does not impose additional duties on liquidators.

It is the liquidator's duty to swell the assets of the company, not merely by disposing of property, but by collecting in all debts, bringing actions to establish and enforce liabilities, recovering sums which may be owed by the directors or the officers of the company (if, for example, they have behaved improperly), and by challenging transactions as being *ultra vires* the company, beyond the powers of the directors, made by an unauthorised agent, or amounting to a transaction at an undervalue, or a fraudulent preference. Naturally, he scrutinises securities to ensure that they are valid, not being void for non-registration, or being floating charges given for past consideration, etc.

He is to pay the company's debts, and adjust the rights of contributories amongst themselves.[82] As with a court winding up, he may not prevent a secured creditor from realising the assets in question, and he may not dispose of assets owned by another[83] or subject to a trust.[84]

One of the liquidator's powers (with sanction of court, committee or company) is to accept shares in another company as consideration for the sale of the company property,[85] and the shares may be distributed among the members of the company in liquidation. Or he may sell in return for a profit-sharing scheme, or other benefit. But without special arrangements, this is unlikely to be approved by the committee in a creditors' winding up, because the benefits go to the members of the company in liquidation. What the liquidator may do instead, in either form of liquidation, is to "hive off" the assets. He has the power to dispose of the company's assets and business. For this purpose he may form a new company, and transfer to it the old company's assets and business. This new company may pay for its acquisition of property and goodwill, etc., by an issue of shares to the liquidator (who holds them as an asset of the old company) and then the liquidator may be able to sell the "hived off" new company and its business as a going concern, unencumbered by debt (for it is not responsible for the debts of the old company). By this means, a better price may be obtained than by piecemeal realisation of parts of the company's assets.

---

[77] *Knowles* v. *Scott* [1891] 1 Ch. 717; *Re Hills Waterfall Estate and Gold Mining Co.* [1896] 1 Ch. 947.
[78] *Re Windsor Steam Coal Co., (1901) Ltd.* [1929] 1 Ch. 151; *Pulsford* v. *Devenish* [1903] 2 Ch. 625.
[79] s.168.
[80] s.112.
[81] s.112.
[82] s.165.
[83] *e.g.* subject to hire-purchase, or a retentions clause.
[84] *Re Kayford* [1975] 1 All E.R. 604.
[85] ss.110,111.

f. Appointment of Special Manager

Whether in a corporate or individual insolvency, the liquidator, or trustee, **28.30** etc., may apply to the court for the appointment of a special manager of the business or property of a debtor (including an undischarged bankrupt), where it appears to them that this is required from the nature of the estate, property or business, or the interests of the creditors require it. The special manager shall have such powers as are given to him by the court. He shall give such security as may be prescribed, and keep accounts and produce them to the Secretary or such others as are prescribed.[86]

C. Personal liability of directors and others

1. CIVIL LIABILITY

The point of forming a limited company is that the company, and not its **28.31** members or managers should primarily be liable if the company becomes insolvent. To this principle, however, there are numerous exceptions, when directors (or others) may be personally liable to compensate persons dealing with the company, who suffer loss. When an insolvent company is wound up, the exceptions may assume considerable importance.

a. Guarantees[87]

Especially in small private companies it is common for banks to take guar- **28.32** antees from directors, often secured over the personal property of the directors (who, in small companies, are often the major, or only, shareholders). In that case, the bank may ignore the guarantee and other third party securities, and seek its remedies under its company securities, or by proving for debts, against the company, and if it is then unsatisfied, it may proceed against the directors. This would be the normal procedure, but alternatively, the bank may immediately proceed against the guarantor, if it wishes. In relation to public companies, guarantees from directors are rarer, but some directors may be other companies in the group and in that case (and even if others in the group are not directors) the taking of guarantees is more common. To this extent, when dealing with liability to banks, the "limited liability" achieved by the corporate structure is often an illusion, although valuable in relation to trade creditors, who are generally unsecured and unprotected by guarantees. A principle similar to that of guarantees is that any agent, contracting for a principal, may agree to be personally liable on the contract, and is then liable as co-principal.[88]

b. Warranty of authority

If a company's borrowings are *ultra vires*, or if the board of directors have no **28.33** authority to act, or if a particular director borrows without authority those who thus act on behalf of the company are liable for having expressly or impliedly warranted their authority.[89] The very fact that the director negotiates on behalf of the company impliedly represents his authority to do so. For example, he is liable if he negotiates a loan to his company and this

---

[86] ss.117, 370.
[87] Above, Chap. 20.
[88] See, *e.g. The Swan* [1968] 1 Lloyd's Rep. 5, and above, para. 15.26, and also para. 15.36 for personal liability undertaken by the form of signature.
[89] See above, para. 15.28.

causes the company to exceed a borrowing limit in the memorandum.[90] The directors are liable even if under the rule in *Royal British Bank* v. *Turquand*[91] the bank could treat the transaction as valid[92] and it is thought that the same would apply even if the bank could rely upon section 35 of the Companies Act 1985 to save the improper transaction, for section 35 does not validate the transaction, but merely disallows the company, as against the other party, from relying on lack of power or authority as a defence.

c. Promoters

28.34 A person who contracts with a company before it is formed is liable on the contract unless it is expressly agreed that he should not be liable.[93] It is not an express agreement to the contrary to sign "per pro" the company.[94] There may subsequently be a novation with the company, discharging the person concerned.

d. Memorandum

28.35 A company's memorandum may provide (or be amended to provide) that the liability of its directors, or of the managing director, shall be unlimited.[95]

e. Tort

Directors will be liable if they obtain a loan by negligent or fraudulent misrepresentation, for this is an independent tort, for which the misrepresentor is personally liable. The same applies if they undertake any other personal duty, which they perform negligently.[96]

f. Bills of Exchange

28.36 Anyone who, while acting for the company, signs a bill of exchange in his own name, will be liable,[97] unless by words such as "For" or "per pro," or "for and on behalf of," or by signing "as agent for the company," he indicates that he is not signing so as to bind himself. If S signs "S Ltd., S, Managing Director" the company, and not S is liable.[98] A mere description of his occupation may be insufficient for the purpose. Thus, if X signs, "X, agent for Y," or "X, managing director of Y," this may show only that he has that occupation in life, not that on this occasion he signs for Y. If he signs a cheque in his own name but the company's name is printed on the cheque and there is an account number (which is that of the company) this may indicate that liability is attached in relation to the holder of that account, so that if it is the company account, the company alone is liable.[99]

---

[90] *Weeks* v. *Propert* (1873) L.R. 8 C.P. 427; *Chapleo* v. *Brunswick Permanent Building Soc.* (1881) 6 Q.B.D. 696; *West London Commercial Bank* v. *Kitson* (1883) 12 Q.B.D. 157.
[91] (1855) 5 E. & B. 248, 6 E. & B. 327.
[92] *Cherry and McDougall* v. *Colonial Bank of Australasia Ltd.* (1869) L.R. 3 P.C. 24.
[93] s.36(4), C.A. 1985.
[94] *Phonogram Ltd.* v. *Lane* [1982] Q.B. 938.
[95] ss. 306, 307, C.A. 1985.
[96] *Edgington* v. *Fitzmaurice* (1885) 29 Ch.D. 459 (fraud); *Fairline Shipping Corpn.* v. *Adamson* [1975] Q.B. 180 (negligently failed to exercise personal skill and care where duty undertaken to do so).
[97] Under s.26, Bills of Exchange Act 1882. *cf.* s.37, C.A. 1985 on the circumstances in which the company is bound. Signatures are discussed above, para. 15.36 *et seq.*
[98] *Chapman* v. *Smethurst* [1909] 1 K.B. 927; contrast *Elliott* v. *Bax-Ironside* [1925] 2 K.B. 301 (where a similar signature was also put on the back of an acceptance); *Rolfe Lubell & Co.* v. *Keith* [1979] 1 All E.R. 860.
[99] *Bondina Ltd.* v. *Rollaway Shower Blinds Ltd.* [1986] 1 All E.R. 564.

g. Company's name

If an officer of a company signs or authorises to be signed any bill of **28.37** exchange or promissory note, endorsement, cheque or order for money or goods in which the company's registered name does not appear, he is liable to a fine and is personally liable to the holder of the document[1] unless it is duly paid by the company.[2] The company's "name" means its registered, not trading name[2a] and must be exactly as registered.[3] However, the plaintiff may be estopped, if the omission by the defendant is the plaintiff's fault.[4] If a bank prints the cheque form wrongly, the bank may be liable in negligence to the signatory who is liable to the payee.[5] The holder need not be misled by the omission of the name.[6] In all cases, the company will be liable where it is a sufficiently identified principal[7] so that the cases in which the bank will seek to apply the principle will normally be those where the company is in liquidation and unable to pay.

h. Registrar's Certificate

If a public company carries on business without the registrar of companies' **28.38** certificate, and allots shares, the directors are jointly and severally liable with the company to anyone who suffers loss.[8]

i. Two Members

If the number of members falls below two, and the company carries on **28.39** business for more than six months, the remaining member-director is jointly and severally liable with the company for its debts thereafter.[9]

j. Fraudulent and Wrongful Trading

The directors (or others) may be civilly and criminally liable for fraudulent **28.40** trading. First, section 213 of the Insolvency Act 1986[10] provides that where in a winding up it appears that any business of the company has been carried on with intent to defraud creditors of the company (or of any other person) or for any fraudulent purpose, the court may, on the liquidator's application, declare that any persons who were "knowingly parties" to the carrying on of the business in the manner mentioned are liable to make such contributions to the company's assets as the court thinks proper. Where the knowing party is a creditor of the company, his liability to contribute to the

---

[1] Even if an order form is lost: *Civil Service Co-operative Society* v. *Chapman* (1914) 30 T.L.R. 679 (the person concerned need not be "holder" in the sense used with bills, etc.).

[2] s.349(4), C.A. 1985.

[2a] *Maxford Spa* v. *Mariani & Goodvill Ltd.* [1979] 2 Lloyds Rep. 385.

[3] See *British Airways Board* v. *Parish* [1979] 2 Lloyds Rep. 361 ("Ltd." omitted, signatory liable); *Hendon* v. *Adelman* (1973) 117 Sol.Jo. 631 ("&" missing, signatory liable).

[4] *Durham Fancy Goods Ltd.* v. *Michael Jackson (Fancy Goods) Ltd.* [1968] 2 All E.R. 987 (plaintiff drew the bill wrongly, using "M" instead of "Michael," acceptor for company not liable).

[5] *Hendon* v. *Adelman* (1973) 117 Sol.Jo. 631.

[6] *Scottish & Newcastle Breweries Ltd.* v. *Blair* (1967) S.L.T. 72.

[7] *Goldsmith (Sicklesmere) Ltd.* v. *Baxter* [1970] Ch. 85.

[8] s.117(8), C.A. 1985.

[9] s.24, C.A. 1985.

[10] Formerly s.630, C.A. 1985, s.332, C.A. 1948.

assets may be charged against his own rights against or security interests in the company, and his rights may be ranked by the court behind all other debts and interest on them. However, the contributions received are general assets, and a particular creditor who is defrauded has no preferential rights.[11] A most important decision is *Re William C. Leitch Brothers, Ltd.*[12] in which it was held that it is fraudulent to continue to trade when the directors know that there is no reasonable prospect of paying debts. Later decisions have perhaps qualified this, insisting on "actual dishonesty involving, according to current notions of fair trading among commercial men, real moral blame."[13] In *R. v. Grantham*[14] it was held that it need not be proved that there is no prospect of the company's creditors ever receiving payment: all that is necessary is that if a person obtains credit, or further credit, for the company, he must know that there is no reasonable ground to think that funds will be available to pay the debt at or about the time it falls due. Knowing that the creditor will not be paid at the time he should be, therefore, may amount to intent to defraud. But a stupid, but optimistic director, is not liable.[15] Gower says[16] "in practice this section represents a potent weapon in the hands of creditors which exercises a restraining influence on over-sanguine directors. The mere threat of proceedings under it has been known to result in the directors agreeing to make themselves personally liable for part of the company's debts." It is immaterial that only one creditor is defrauded, and by a single transaction.[17] It has been said that there must be a positive step to carry on the business, and mere inertia is insufficient[18] but the case in question concerned a company secretary, not concerned in "carrying on the business," and it would seem to be otherwise with the directors of the company where they deliberately refrain from acting. In *Re Sarflax Ltd.*[19] a company ceased to trade and transferred its assets to its parent company, to which it was indebted. Although effectively it closed down its business, this was held to be "carrying on" the business. However, the court also decided that merely giving preference to one creditor over the others is not "an intention to defraud" (even though it may be a "fraudulent" preference for other statutory provisions).

28.41   Although the section is helpful in restraining directors, there were numerous scandals in which it seemed to the public that persons deliberately allowed their companies to run into debt, although fraud was difficult to prove. There is now a separate new provision relating to "wrongful trading" in section 214 of the 1986 Act. The provision is similar to section 213, applying where the liquidator applies to the court, and enabling the court to make charging orders, or to rank a creditor's claim last, and so on, but it applies if:

---

[11] *Re William C. Leitch Brothers Ltd. (No. 2)* [1933] Ch. 261.
[12] [1932] 2 Ch. 71.
[13] *Re Patrick & Lyon Ltd.* [1933] Ch. 786, 790–791; *Re Maidstone Buildings Provisions Ltd.* [1971] 1 W.L.R. 1085.
[14] [1984] Q.B. 675.
[15] *White v. Osmond (Parkstone) Ltd.* [1960] unrep. Because of this, it was sometimes said that there was a "sunshine" defence (if the director thought the sun would shine again on the company).
[16] *Principles of Modern Company Law*, (4th ed.), 115.
[17] *Re Gerald Cooper Chemicals, Ltd.* [1978] Ch. 262.
[18] *Re Maidstone Buildings Provisions, Ltd.* [1971] 1 W.L.R. 1085.
[19] [1979] 2 W.L.R. 202.

(a) the company has gone into insolvent liquidation, (not when it is unable to pay its debts, but when its assets are insufficient to pay its debts, liabilities, and the expenses of liquidation)[20] and

(b) where the defendant at some time before commencement "knew or ought to have concluded that there was no reasonable prospect that the company would avoid going into insolvent liquidation," and

(c) where at the relevant time (when he should have so concluded) the person was a director of the company.

The first and last of these requirements are somewhat narrower than the fraudulent trading provisions of the Companies Act, but the second requirement extends liability to cases of negligence. However, to protect the director who, having realised that the company has no reasonable prospect of avoiding insolvent liquidation, does what he can to avoid loss to creditors (perhaps in the face of opposition by other directors), it is provided that no order shall be made against a director if, where he knew of the prospect of insolvent liquidation he took every step with a view to minimising the potential loss to the creditors that "he ought to have taken." The section refers to "every" step, not every reasonable step, but the severity of this may be modified by the phrase "ought to have taken." In deciding this, it is to be assumed that he knew that there was no reasonable possibility of avoiding insolvent liquidation. In deciding what he ought to know or conclude and what steps he ought to take, the court is to have regard to what a reasonably diligent person would think or do if he had both the level of skill, knowledge and experience that may be reasonably expected of a person carrying out the functions of the director in question (or which are entrusted to him to carry out), and to the general skill, knowledge and experience which the director in question has. That is to say, he is expected to have a minimum level of skill, (which will vary from company to company, of course and also within a given company, depending on the position each director holds) and he cannot defend himself by pleading abnormal stupidity. But if in fact he has a greater degree of skill than the minimum, he must exercise it, and cannot plead that he did what acceptable, but less skilled, directors would have done.[21]

It is not impossible that these provisions will inhibit the behaviour of **28.42** banks, in attempting to rescue or stave off the insolvency of a company in difficulties. The liability for wrongful trading (not fraudulent trading) may attach to "shadow directors"[22]: these are persons in accordance with whose directions or instructions the company is accustomed to act.[23] It is not clear what "accustomed" means. A person may possibly be "accustomed" on the first occasion he accepts instructions, if prepared generally to do so (although this is not a widely held view). When companies are in difficulty, and come cap in hand to the bank, it is not unknown for directors to accept the instructions of the bank. Great care must, therefore, be exercised, for a bank would be a clear target for a liquidator. A bank might be expected to have a considerable degree of skill, and if it is a shadow director, it must

---

[20] s.214(6).
[21] s.214(4).
[22] s.214(7).
[23] s.251. Professional advisers are excluded, but this probably does not apply to a bank creditor.

attempt to minimise loss to all the creditors, not just to itself. There are very real dangers, here. The section covers managers, so that there is a definite risk to the administrative receiver who carries on trading, pending sale of the company. He also has a clear duty to take every step to minimise loss to the company's creditors. It is unclear if this includes the manner in which he disposes of the company's property (*e.g.* by forced sale). Possibly one must distinguish between his roles as seller of property and as manager of the company.

Banks are (it is understood) advising branch managers to be most careful in phrasing their discussions with directors in terms of "advice" rather than instructions. It may be that this will be sufficient, if the bank merely informs the company of the terms upon which the bank is prepared to continue its support, or to refrain from calling in loans, enforcing security etc., without actually giving instructions to the company. But until the attitude of the courts is known, there remains a risk (which must be greater if the bank has a nominee upon the board) that even "advice" so phrased will be considered to be a disguised instruction, which the company is accustomed to accept. It may well be the case that the matter is to be looked at from the directors' point of view: if, despite the phrasing used, the director thinks (and admits in court) that he believed he was being told what to do, and if the court thinks that was a reasonable understanding, then the bank may be liable. The director has every incentive to make such a claim, for he may defend himself from a wrongful trading accusation by arguing that he thought he was taking the most appropriate steps to minimise loss to creditors by following the bank's instructions, and thus securing the continuation of a line of credit. It is to be hoped that the courts do not accept these arguments, for this would lead to the earlier collapse of many companies, and to the collapse of some which might have been saved, given the inevitable tendency of banks in that situation simply to enforce their securities, and to appoint receivers. A rescue could, of course, be mounted by the appointment of an administrator, which may be the intention of the legislation: but for reasons already given, banks are expected to oppose the appointment of administrators.

Parent companies are likely to be particularly affected, given the universal presence of nominated directors on the board of the subsidiary company. (Under the Companies Act 1985, s.741, parents are not shadow directors merely because the subsidiary is accustomed to act according to its directions, but this definition is modified for the purposes of the Insolvency Act 1986, by section 251 of that Act). The giving of group guarantees may also help to establish a "connection." There is no immunity for non-executive directors. Nor can a director who is concerned about his company, necessarily escape liability by resigning, for he must still show he has taken every step which he could take (trying to persuade the other directors, etc.) Directors should ensure that accounts are properly kept; that the Board and individual directors have a clear picture of the company's financial and trading situation; that a sensible corporate plan to reduce expenditure and increase income and guarantee cash flow is established; that appropriate professional advice is taken; that major creditors are informed as early as possible. At some stage, it may be a fault to fail to apply for an administration order. Minority directors should insist upon the minuting of their recommendations and having repeatedly insisted upon changes, resign and record their reasons in writing.

474

k. Disqualified Persons, and Prohibited Names

A person "involved in the management of the company" (*i.e.* if he is a **28.43** director, or concerned, directly or indirectly, or takes part in, the management) shall be personally responsible jointly and severally with the company,[24] for the debts and liabilities of the company, if:

(a) he is a person disqualified under statutory provisions[25] from acting as a director (he is liable for debts incurred while he is involved), or

(b) he acts or is willing to act on instructions given without leave of the court by such a disqualified person (he is liable for debts incurred while he acts or is willing to act on the instructions of the disqualified person). Once a person has accepted instructions from a person he knew to be disqualified, he is presumed thereafter to be willing to do so, unless he proves the contrary.

Similar provisions in section 217 impose liability on anyone who is involved in management, or accepts instructions from another person, while the company is trading under a prohibited name.

l. Misfeasance, etc.

Liability may be imposed under section 212 of the Insolvency Act 1986. **28.44** Liability includes liability for misfeasance and breach of fiduciary duty. The director's duties include acting in the best interests of the company, exercising their powers for the proper purposes, exercising care and skill in the management of the company's property and business, and duties of loyalty and good faith (*e.g.* avoiding secret profits, conflicts of interest, and so on). The court may order restoration of money or property, or the contribution of a compensating sum to the company's assets. This section has considerable potential importance.

The section applies also to the liquidator, administrator, or administrative receiver, or to any person who has been concerned in the management, promotion or formation of the company, or who has been trustee of an individual bankrupt's estate. If these persons have misapplied or retained, or become accountable for any money or other property of the debtor, or been guilty of any misfeasance or breach of any fiduciary duty in relation to the debtor then the court may, on the application of the official receiver, liquidator or of any creditor or contributory, or of an individual bankrupt[26] examine the conduct of the person in question, and order him to repay money or restore or account for property or to contribute such sum to the company's assets by way of compensation, as the court thinks just. In the case of a company it is stated that misfeasance and breach of fiduciary duty include references to these matters in connection with the carrying out of the functions of liquidator or administrator. The power of a contributory to apply (*i.e.* in a company insolvency) requires leave of the court, but is exercisable even if the applicant will not benefit from any order. A bankrupt similarly needs leave to apply. The power to apply in relation to a liquidator, administrator or trustee needs the leave of the court, where these persons have had their release.

---

[24] And with any other persons liable like himself under this provision, which comes from s.15, C.D.D.A., 1986.

[25] Which includes undischarged bankrupts, disqualified under s.11, C.D.D.A. 1986, below, para. 28.46.

[26] Or the Secretary of State in an individual bankruptcy.

2. CRIMINAL LIABILITY

28.45 Penalties are imposed on administrators, liquidators, receivers, officers of the company and others for failure to comply with the various duties imposed. In addition to those, there are various other offences, and liabilities.[27] Generally, where a body corporate commits an offence and the offence has been committed with the consent or connivance of, or is attributable to neglect by, any director, manager, secretary or other similar officer, (or the members, where they manage the company) he or they shall also be guilty of the offence.[28]

3. DISQUALIFICATION OF DIRECTORS

28.46 We have seen that where disqualified persons act, they may be personally liable. They also commit a criminal offence.[29]

Disqualification orders may be made under the Companies Directors Disqualification Act 1986, disqualifying persons from being directors, liquidators, administrators, or receivers or managers, or from taking part directly or indirectly in the promotion formation or management of a company, for up to 15 years.[30] An order may be made (a) on conviction for an indictable offence in connection with a company[31] or (b) for persistent defaults in complying with obligations under the Companies Act[32] or (c) where in the course of a winding up it appears that a person has been guilty of an offence of fraudulent trading[33] or of any other fraud in relation to the company or his duties as officer, liquidator, etc.,[34] or for wrongful trading[35] or (d) where in a five year period before a summary conviction for a Companies Act offence a person has had made against him or been convicted of at least three default orders and offences[36] or where a director has been a director of an insolvent company and he is unfit to be concerned in the management of a company[37] and in certain other cases.[38] A register of disqualification orders is kept.[39] An undischarged bankrupt may not act as director, or be concerned in the formation, promotion, or management of a company.[40]

4. RESTRICTION ON USE OF COMPANY NAMES

28.47 Provision is made so that persons involved with insolvent companies should not be able to start up new companies, under a similar name to the insolvent company, relying on the fact that the previous trading or company name is well known, but that the public are unaware of the fact that the original company had gone into liquidation. If, therefore, a company

---

[27] See, *e.g.* ss.206–211, 218–219, 164, I.A. 1986.
[28] s.14 C.D.D.A. 1986, in relation to offences concerning disqualification orders.
[29] s.13, C.D.D.A. 1986.
[30] Five years, for "persistent default" under s.3, C.D.D.A. 1986.
[31] s.2, C.D.D.A. 1986.
[32] s.3, C.D.D.A. 1986.
[33] Under s.458, C.A. 1985, or (by s.10, C.D.D.A. 1986.) s.213, I.A. 1986.
[34] s.4, C.D.D.A. 1986.
[35] Under s.214, I.A. 1986: s.10, C.D.D.A. 1986.
[36] s.5, C.D.D.A., 1986.
[37] s.6, C.D.D.A. 1986.
[38] See ss.8, 11, C.D.D.A. 1986.
[39] s.18, C.D.D.A. 1986.
[40] s.11, C.D.D.A. 1986.

(the liquidated company, below) has gone into insolvent liquidation, and a person was a director or shadow director in the 12 months before liquidation commenced, then unless the court gives leave, such a person may not for a period of five years after the company went into liquidation, be a director or be concerned in the promotion, formation, management, or be concerned in the carrying on of a business conducted by, any other company if that other company or business uses a name by which the liquidated company was known at any time in the 12 months mentioned, or is a name so similar to any such name as to suggest an association with the liquidated company.[41]

D. Individual bankruptcy

The purposes of bankruptcy are not to punish the debtor, but on the contrary, to protect him from his creditors, and to protect all creditors from unfair advantage being gained by any other creditor (this is the *pari passu* principle).[42]   **28.48**

1. THE PETITION

The process begins with a petition to the court made by (i) the debtor or (ii)   **28.49** by a creditor or creditors jointly, or (iii) by the supervisor of, or by a person bound by, an approved voluntary arrangement under the Insolvency Act 1986[43] or (iv) in criminal bankruptcy cases by the Official Petitioner and similar persons.[44]

No petition by the debtor or a creditor is allowed unless the debtor (a) is domiciled in England and Wales, or (b) is personally present there on the day on which the petition is presented, or (c) at any time in the three years before the petition has been ordinarily resident, or has had a place of residence in, or has carried on business[45] in England and Wales.[46]

In order to prevent threats of bankruptcy being used to exact payment, and also to prevent the buying off of particular creditors, no petition is to be withdrawn without leave of the court.[47]

2. CREDITOR'S PETITION

Each creditor who petitions must be owed, and must petition in respect of,   **28.50** "debts owed by the debtor." The debts in question must at the time of the petition:

(a) be equal to (or equal in aggregate, where creditors join together) the "bankruptcy level" (which is a statutory minimum figure set initially at £750)[48] and

(b) be for a liquidated sum payable to the creditor(s) either immediately or at some certain future time (this excludes contingent and unliquidated debts, which are otherwise "debts" under the Act), and

(c) be unsecured, as further discussed shortly, and

[41] s.216. See para. 28.43, above, for civil liability.
[42] Below, para. 28.63
[43] Above, para. 28.09.
[44] s.264.
[45] Including a business carried on by a firm or partnership of which he is a member, or a business carried on by an agent or manager for the debtor or the partnership.
[46] s.265.
[47] s.266(2).
[48] s.267(4).

(d) be debts which the debtor is either unable to pay or to have no reasonable prospect of being able to pay. Inability to pay is proved by (and only by):

(i) the statutory demand: the petitioning creditor(s) (and not other creditors) serves a demand on the debtor (requiring him to pay or to secure or compound for the debt), if the demand is neither complied with nor set aside in accordance with the rules within three weeks, or

(ii) execution in favour of the petitioning judgment creditor(s) being returned unsatisfied in whole or in part.

Lack of "reasonable prospect of being able to pay" is proved, only where the debt is not immediately payable, by (and only by) a statutory demand (serving a notice requiring the debtor to establish that there is a reasonable prospect of him being able to pay when the debt falls due, and the notice not being complied with, as above).[49]

No petition can be brought if the debtor has applied to set aside a statutory demand, and the application has not yet been determined by the court. The three week limitation on the statutory demand for existing debts may be accelerated (expedited) and a petition brought earlier, if the petition states that there is a serious possibility that the debtor's property or its value will be significantly diminished during the period[50] (although no bankruptcy order can be made until the three weeks elapse).[51]

Secured creditors may not petition, with exceptions. Security means mortgage, charge, lien or other security, though not a lien on books, papers or other records unless they are documents of title to property and held as such.[52] The exceptions are:

(i) only security over the debtor's property counts[53] so that third party securities are irrelevant for this purpose.

28.51
(ii) a secured creditor may petition if his petition contains a statement of his willingness to surrender the security for the benefit of all the bankrupt's creditors,[54] (on the making of a bankruptcy order on that petition he is deemed to have surrendered his security).[55]

(iii) a secured creditor may petition if his petition is expressed not to be made in respect of the secured part of the debt, and contains a statement by the creditor of the estimated value at the date of the petition of the security for the secured part of the debt.[56] (The secured and unsecured parts of the debt are treated as separated debts.)[57] In other words, the creditor may estimate that his security will not cover all of the debts owed to him, and may petition, and prove for, the balance. In order to prevent creditors from setting their estimates of the value of goods too low, so as to be able to petition and prove for greater amounts, it is provided elsewhere that the security may not be realised if the official receiver[58] or trustee[59] serves a notice on the secured creditor, and that where such a notice has been served, the trustee or

[49] Unwillingness to pay a future debt is not a ground for bankruptcy.
[50] s.270.
[51] s.271(2).
[52] s.383(2) and (4).
[53] s.383(2).
[54] s.269(1).
[55] s.383(3).
[56] s.269(1)(b).
[57] s.269(2).
[58] s.285(5).
[59] s.311(5).

official receiver may inspect the goods (this applies only to goods, not land) and may exercise the bankrupt's right of redemption in respect of the goods (at the value stated in the petition, because a value given in the petition cannot be revalued except with the leave of the court).[60]

(iv) a secured creditor might realise the security and he could then petition on the ground of any deficit after deducting the net amount realised (he must not be secured "at the time the petition is presented").[61]

3. THE BANKRUPTCY ORDER

No bankruptcy order is to be made on the petition unless the court is satisfied that the debts on which the petition is based (or one of them) is either: **28.52**

(i) a debt payable at the time of the court's consideration which has been neither paid nor secured or compounded, or

(ii) a debt which the debtor has no reasonable prospect of being able to pay when it falls due.

The petition may be dismissed if the court is satisfied that (i) the debtor is able to pay all his debts, including contingent and prospective liabilities, or (ii) he has made an offer to secure or compound for a debt on which the petition is based and that acceptance of the offer would have required the dismissal of the petition, and that the offer has been unreasonably refused.[62]

4. DEBTOR'S PETITION

Bankruptcy may be seen by a debtor as a kind of refuge from his creditors, and the debtor himself may petition. The only ground for this is that the debtor is unable to pay his debts.[63] **28.53**

Special procedures are available for small estates, and these may result in a court sponsored voluntary arrangement, or a certificate for the summary administration of the estate.[64]

5. AFTER THE PETITION, AND BEFORE THE BANKRUPTCY ORDER

In the period between the petition and the bankruptcy order the following may occur: **28.54**

(a) An interim receiver of the debtor's property may be appointed if necessary for the protection of the debtor's property (the official receiver is appointed).

(b) Certain dispositions and dealings with the debtor's property may be affected (if a bankruptcy order is subsequently made).[65]

(c) Proceedings against the debtor may be stayed,[66] and execution against him may be affected.[66a]

[60] I.R. 1986, r. 6.115(2).
[61] s.267(2).
[62] s.271.
[63] s.272. There is no definition of this.
[64] ss.273–276.
[65] Below, para. 28.78 *et seq.*
[66] Below, para. 28.69.
[66a] Below, para. 28.68.

6. EFFECT OF THE BANKRUPTCY ORDER

a. Receivership Before Trustee Appointed

28.55 A bankruptcy order terminates any interim receivership.[67] If the bankrupt's estate does not immediately vest in the trustee in bankruptcy, the official receiver is receiver and manager of the estate and has a duty to act as such. His function is to protect the bankrupt's estate and any property which may be claimed for the estate by the trustee, and he may sell or dispose of any perishable goods or those of which the value may diminish if not disposed of. He may summon a general meeting of creditors, and the court may direct this. He is protected if, not being negligent, he wrongly seizes property not belonging to the debtor.[68] The bankrupt must provide the official receiver with specified information, and attend when reasonably required, and the official receiver investigates the conduct and affairs of the bankrupt (before and after the order) and may report to the court if he thinks fit. He may at any time before discharge apply to the court for the public examination in court of the bankrupt, and shall do so (unless otherwise ordered by the court) if required to do so by any creditor with the concurrence (including that creditor) of not less than one-half in value of all creditors.

b. Appointment of Trustee

28.56 This takes effect only if the person appointed accepts his appointment and then at the time specified in his certificate of appointment.[69]

Except in special cases, the trustee is appointed by creditors at a meeting. The official receiver may call this, or a creditor supported by $\frac{1}{4}$ in value may requisition a meeting. If none is called, the official receiver is trustee.[70]

7. CONTROL OF TRUSTEE, AND OF THE BANKRUPTCY PROCEDURE

28.57 A meeting of creditors may establish a committee to exercise various functions (like those of the committee in a winding up).[71]

If the bankrupt, or a creditor or any other person is dissatisfied with decisions of the trustee he may apply to the court, which may give the trustee such directions as it thinks fit. The trustee may also apply to the court for directions.[72]

Every bankruptcy shall be under the general control of the court, which shall have full power to decide all questions of priority and questions of law and fact, and which may give binding directions to the bankrupt.[73] The court may order the Post Office to redirect (for up to three months) any mail addressed to the bankrupt.[74] It may extend any time limits as it thinks fit.[75]

---

[67] s.286. See previous paragraph.
[68] s.287.
[69] s.292.
[70] ss.292–294.
[71] Above, para. 28.18.
[72] s.303.
[73] s.363.
[74] s.371.
[75] s.376.

Duties and Powers of Trustee in Bankruptcy

The official name of the trustee in bankruptcy is "the trustee of the estate of **28.58** (name), a bankrupt,"[76] and his function shall be to get in, realise and distribute the estate in accordance with the Act, and in carrying out that function he is entitled (subject to the Act) to use his own discretion.[77] He must co-operate with the official receiver. His general powers are listed in section 314 and schedule 5, and as with a liquidator in a voluntary winding up, he may exercise some of them without sanction, and others with the consent of the committee or the court. The permissions given by court or committee in all these cases are to be specific, not general. No person dealing with the trustee in good faith and for value shall be concerned to see that permission has been given. If he acts without permission, his acts may be ratified by the court, or by the committee if he acted in an emergency and promptly sought ratification.

If the trustee (not being the official receiver) disposes of property to an associate of the bankrupt or employs a solicitor, he must give notice to the committee, if one is established.[78]

The trustee may also summon at any time a general meeting of the creditors, and shall do so if requested by a creditor with the concurrence of not less than one-tenth in value of the creditors (including the creditor who makes the request).[79] He may exercise his powers outside England and Wales.[80] There are complicated provisions enabling him to disclaim onerous property.[81]

8. FINAL MEETING OF CREDITORS

Once it appears to the trustee that the administration of the estate is "for **28.59** practical purposes complete" then (if he is not the official receiver) he is to summon a final general meeting of creditors to receive the trustee's report of his administration and to decide if he should have his release.[82]

9. DURATION OF BANKRUPTCY AND EFFECT OF DISCHARGE

Bankruptcy commences when the bankruptcy order is made and continues **28.60** until discharge. Discharge occurs[83] (i) in cases based on criminal bankruptcy orders, by order of the court, (ii) where the debtor had been an undischarged bankrupt at any time in the previous 15 years before this commencement, by order of the court, (iii) where a certificate of summary administration is issued and not revoked before discharge, in two years from commencement, (iv) in any other case, in three years from commencement. In the last two cases, the official receiver may apply to the court on the ground that the bankrupt is not complying with his obligations, and the court may suspend the running of time for a period, or until conditions are fulfilled. In the first two cases, an application for an order of discharge may be made by the bankrupt at any time after five years from commencement,

---

[76] s.305(4).
[77] s.305(2).
[78] s.314(7).
[79] s.314(7).
[80] s.314(8).
[81] ss.315–319.
[82] ss.331–332.
[83] ss.278–280.

and the court may refuse, or discharge him absolutely, or on conditions as to subsequent income or property, or on other conditions.

The effect of discharge[84] is that the bankrupt is released from all those bankruptcy debts to which he is subject at commencement or may become subject to after commencement by reason of any prior obligation.[85]

Discharge does not affect the following: (i) the unfulfilled functions of the trustee (in relation to the estate, etc.), (ii) the right of any creditor to prove in the bankruptcy for any bankruptcy debt from which the bankrupt is released, (iii) the right of any secured creditor to enforce his security for a released debt, (iv) any bankruptcy debt or forbearance obtained by fraud (to which the bank was party), (v) any liability for a fine imposed for an offence, or for any liability under a recognisance[86] or under a confiscation order for drug trafficking,[87] (vi) (unless and to the extent which the court directs) any liability for a bankruptcy debt arising under family or domestic proceedings, or consisting of a liability to pay damages in respect of personal injuries[88] to any person, (vii) from any other not provable debts as are prescribed.

The bankrupt's release does not release any other person (such as partner, or co-trustee or surety for the bankrupt) from their liabilities.[89]

The court has powers to annul a bankruptcy order in certain cases (even after an apparent "discharge.")[90]

10. BANKRUPTCY OFFENCES

28.61 Where a person is bankrupt, he may before discharge[91] (and sometimes even before commencement) commit a variety of offences.[92] The offences may be committed even outside England and Wales. No prosecution may be brought except by the Secretary of State or by or with the consent of the Director of Public Prosecutions. Some of the offences require an intent to defraud or to conceal the state of his affairs. They cover such matters as failure to disclose property or its disposal or to hand over property to the trustee, or concealment, removal or failure to account for loss of any debt or property; failure to deliver up books and records, etc; misinforming the trustee, or not telling him of false debts proved; fraudulently disposing of his property or having done so within five years of the commencement, or concealing property within two months before an unsatisfied judgment for payment is obtained against him; absconding with property; disposing of property obtained on credit and not paid for; obtaining any form of credit exceeding a certain amount while being undischarged and not revealing the fact; engaging in business in a different name (without disclosing it); carrying on business without proper accounts; or if gambling contributed to his insolvency, or to loss of property. For these offences he may be fined or imprisoned.

---

[84] s.128.
[85] s.382.
[86] Essentially, an obligation under a "binding over" by a court—*e.g.* to keep the peace.
[87] I.R., 6.223.
[88] Defined broadly in s.281(8).
[89] s.281(7).
[90] ss.282, and 260–261.
[91] s.350.
[92] ss.350–362.

11. DISQUALIFICATION FROM PUBLIC OFFICE

An undischarged bankrupt is disqualified from sitting or voting in the **28.62** House of Lords, or House of Commons (and from being elected to that), or in any committee of either House. Elected members of the Commons must vacate their seats at the end of a period of six months disqualification.[93]

E. General effect of bankruptcy or liquidation on debtor's property and on dealings with him

1. THE PARI PASSU PRINCIPLE

It is a principle of insolvency law that, except for secured and preferential **28.63** creditors, all creditors should be treated equally. This is the case for companies[94] or individuals[95] and the effect of this principle is that a creditor may obtain an advantage over other creditors if he is either (i) a preferential creditor, or (ii) if he takes a valid security right (perfected by registration if necessary, and not offending rules such as the "12 months" rule for floating charges), but that any mere contractual provision giving the creditor an advantage in winding up over other creditors is contrary to policy, and void.[96] Some contractual rights of set-off or over deposits would, if merely contractual, seem to offend the principle.[97] The *pari passu* principle does not affect non-contractual rights such as the right of combination, or of lien.

Sometimes creditor A agrees to subordinate himself to creditor B (with whom, say, he otherwise ranks equally). It is unclear if this is permissible. There seems to be nothing objectionable in it, for the *pari passu* principle aims to prevent a person gaining an advantage over creditors generally, not from subjecting himself to a disadvantage. If A subordinates himself to B, he must subordinate himself to other creditors ranking equally with B. Whether subordination faces other (purely contractual) difficulties is discussed elsewhere.[98]

2. SECURED CREDITORS, AND VALIDITY OF CHARGES

In relation to securities it is necessary to consider (a) the validity of charges, **28.64** (b) the priority of charges, (c) matters relating to the proof or provability of debts, where a creditor is secured. Here, we consider validity by way of summons, only.

a. Companies

1. Company charges will be void against the liquidator, administrator, **28.65** and creditors if not registered in accordance with section 395 of the Companies Act 1985.[99]

2. All company charges, whether fixed or floating, may be affected in

---

[93] s.427.

[94] s.107: previously s.597, C.A. 1985.

[95] s.328(3).

[96] See *British Eagle International Airlines Ltd.* v. *Compagnie Nationale Air France* [1975] 1 W.L.R. 758.

[97] Above, para. 21.11. In *Re Charge Card Services Ltd.* [1986] 3 All E.R. 289, contractual retentions clauses were held to be merely contractual, not creating charges. The *pari passu* point was not argued.

[98] Above, para. 14.12 *et seq.*

[99] Above, Chap. 21 (para. 21.07).

some way by the appointment of an administrator, but the holder of a floating charge may block the appointment.[1]

3. Floating charges may be invalidated in whole or in part by the "twelve months" rule.[2]

4. Floating charges will not now be able, by early crystallisation, to gain priority over the claims of preferential creditors.[3]

5. All charges may be given in circumstances amounting to a "preference" or an "undervalue" in which case they may be void or subject to a variety of orders.[4]

6. All charges may be void if associated with an extortionate credit transaction.[5]

7. All charges may be void if not sanctioned by the court and made after the commencement of liquidation.[6]

8. All charges may be void if they amount to "transactions defrauding creditors."[7]

b. Individuals

28.66 If an individual is engaged in business and makes a general assignment of his existing or future book debts, or any class of them, and is subsequently adjudged bankrupt, the assignment is void against the trustee as regards book debts which were not paid before the presentation of the bankruptcy petition unless the assignment was registered under the Bills of Sale Act 1878.[8] Assignment includes assignment by way of security or charge. But this provision does not apply to debts which are (i) due at the date of the assignment from specified creditors, or (ii) debts becoming due under specified contracts, or (iii) included either in a transfer of a business made in good faith and for value, or in an assignment of assets for the benefit of creditors generally (*i.e.* to a trustee for all creditors).

3. INDIVIDUAL AND COMPANY LIENS

28.67 Liens on books, papers, etc., shall be unenforceable to the extent that their enforcement would deny possession to the official receiver or trustee, but this does not affect liens over documents which give a title to property and which are held as such.[9]

4. EFFECT UPON EXECUTION OR ATTACHMENT

28.68 Execution is the process of seizing the debtor's property and selling it (done by the sheriff). Attachment is a similar process, in relation to debts owed to the debtor. Sequestration is a kind of court receivership, ordered until someone complies with a court instruction.

If a company is being wound up by the court, any attachment, sequestration, distress or execution against the company's estate or effects is void if put in force after commencement.[10]

[1] Above, Chap. 23 (para. 23.01).
[2] s.245, above, para. 21.38.
[3] Above, para. 21.35.
[4] ss.238–240, and 339–341, below, para. 28.90.
[5] s.244.
[6] s.127.
[7] s.423.
[8] s.344.
[9] ss.246, 349.
[10] s.128.

If a company is being wound up voluntarily, and a judgment creditor has issued execution against company property or has attached any debt due to it, and the company is wound up, he may keep the benefit of his execution or attachment against the liquidator only if the process was complete before winding up commenced. An execution of goods is complete on their sale or by the making of a charging order; an attachment of a debt is completed by receipt of the debt; and execution against land is completed by seizure or the appointment of a receiver or the making of a charging order. However, (a) if a creditor has notice of a meeting to consider a resolution for voluntary winding up, he must have completed before that date, (b) a person buying company goods in good faith under a sheriff's sale obtains good title, and (c) the court may set aside the liquidator's right in favour of the creditor.[11] Provision is made for recovery of goods from the sheriff, where they have been seized in execution.[12]

Similar provisions apply to individual bankruptcies.[13] An additional provision here[13a] relates to a landlord's rights over rent, and the remedy of distraint (the process is referred to as "distress" and is the right to enter the property in certain defined circumstances, to take goods, and sell them to pay for the rent). The basic rule is that before discharge a landlord may distrain for six months rent accrued due before commencement. If he distrains for more, or for rent due after the distress, this must be held for the trustee. But even in relation to the six months rent, if the debtor is adjudged bankrupt within three months, the proceeds, etc., become subject to a charge in favour of the preferential creditors (if they are not satisfied from the rest of the estate), although where the landlord surrenders such property or money to the trustee, he ranks as a preferential creditor himself in relation to the rest of the bankrupt's property (not in relation to the property the landlord surrendered). If the landlord arranges for execution for rent to be carried out by the sheriff or other officer, the preceding rule would not apply, for they are not liable to account for sums paid to them before they were served with notice of the bankruptcy order. These rules apply to others than landlords, if levying distress. None of these provisions affect a landlord's right to prove for a bankruptcy debt in respect of the rent, and they do not affect other rights of distraint other than for rent, nor are such rights affected by the vesting of the property in the trustee.

5. RESTRICTIONS ON PROCEEDINGS

In a compulsory winding up, after a winding up order is made or a provisional liquidator is appointed, no action or proceedings may be commenced or proceeded with against a company or its property except by leave of the court.[14]

28.69

In a voluntary winding up, there is no automatic bar in England and Wales, but the liquidator may apply to the court for a stay of action,[15] and the court may stay actions if it will be "just and beneficial" to do so.[16]

---

[11] s.183.
[12] s.184.
[13] s.346.
[13a] s.347.
[14] s.130.
[15] s.112.
[16] This means, to the creditors, not, say, to the directors: *Re J. Burrows (Leeds) Ltd*. [1982] 2 All E.R. 882.

In an individual bankruptcy, if a bankruptcy petition is pending, or if an individual has been adjudged bankrupt, the court considering the petition may stay any action, execution or other legal process against the debtor's person or property, and a court where other proceedings are pending may either stay the proceedings or allow them to continue on such terms as it thinks fit.[17]

After the bankruptcy order, no person who has a provable debt shall have any remedy against the property or person of the bankrupt for the debt, nor before discharge commence any action, etc., unless the court gives leave.[18] This does not affect the right of a secured creditor to enforce his security, but we have observed the right of the official receiver or trustee to inspect goods and to exercise the bankrupt's right of redemption.[19]

6. WHAT ASSETS OF THE DEBTOR ARE DISTRIBUTABLE?

a. Companies

28.70 Since the company is to be wound up, it has no need to retain property, and all is available for the creditors of the company.

In a compulsory winding up, where a provisional liquidator has been appointed, or winding up order is made, the liquidator or provisional liquidator is to take all company property into his custody,[20] and the court may direct that all or part of the property vests in the liquidator.[21] Even if not vested in the liquidator, dispositions of the company's property *made after the commencement* are void unless sanctioned by the court.[22]

In a voluntary winding up, the company ceases business but its corporate powers continue until it is dissolved[23] and the liquidator is appointed to exercise the company's powers over its property (the powers of the directors ceasing except as the liquidator permits).[24] There is, therefore, no need to vest the company's property in the liquidator, since he acts for the company, to bind it in distributing its property.[25]

b. Individual Bankrupts

28.71 The provisions relating to individual bankrupts are considerably more complicated, since provision must be made for the retention by them and their families of the necessities of life, and since their existence (unlike that of companies) is not to be terminated by the insolvency process. The Insolvency Act 1986 accordingly provides for the distributable property of the bankrupt to vest in the trustee, but for the bankrupt to retain some of his assets. It also makes provision to distinguish between property which he has at the commencement of bankruptcy, and property which he acquires while an undischarged bankrupt, and after discharge from bankruptcy. Commencement occurs when the bankruptcy order is made.[26]

---

[17] s.285.
[18] s.285.
[19] Above, para. 28.51.
[20] s.144.
[21] s.145.
[22] s.127, discussed below, para. 28.78.
[23] s.87.
[24] s.103.
[25] ss.165, 167 and Sched. 4, Part II, para. 5 and Part III, paras. 6, 7, 9, 13 particularly.
[26] s.278.

(i) Property originally owned. When the trustee is appointed or the **28.72** official receiver becomes trustee, the bankrupt's estate immediately vests in the trustee, without any conveyance, assignment or transfer.[27] The bankrupt's estate comprises all property belonging to or vested in the bankrupt at the commencement of the bankruptcy and any other property treated by the Act as being comprised in the estate.[28] It may include powers (such as options) exercisable by the bankrupt over property.[29] It can be seen, then, that the trustee's title "relates back" to commencement of the bankruptcy (time of the order) even if appointed afterwards. In fact, his rights are extended further than that, even back to the petition.[30] It is to be noted that owing to a drafting error, the Act has two different provisions relating to the period between commencement and vesting. One is contained in sections 283–284, which say that all property held by the bankrupt in this period automatically vests in the trustee. The other is contained in section 307 (after acquired property) which says that property acquired after commencement has to be claimed by the trustee. Section 307 should have referred to vesting, not commencement.

The estate does not include (a) tools, books, vehicles and other items of equipment as are necessary to the bankrupt for use personally by him in his employment, business or vocation; or (b) such clothing, bedding, furniture, household equipment and provisions as are necessary for satisfying the basic domestic needs of the bankrupt and his family.[31] But even such property may be claimed by the trustee if it appears to him that the realisable value of the whole or part of it exceeds the cost of a reasonably adequate replacement for it. If he serves a notice claiming it,[32] the property vests in him, and except against a bona fide purchaser for value, his title relates back to the commencement of bankruptcy (the order). He must then apply funds in the estate to purchase a reasonable replacement, and this duty has priority over his obligation to distribute the estate to creditors.[33]

The estate does not include property held on trust by the bankrupt for any other person.[34] The vesting of the property in the trustee is also subject to the rights of any person other than the bankrupt thereto, (such as a secured creditor, or hirer of goods, or tenant of property) but rights given up in accordance with the rules, or surrendered by a secured creditor who so states in his petition[35] shall be disregarded.

The restrictions on proceedings, enforcement and execution, which we have observed, continue, of course, after the bankruptcy order. They protect the bankrupt, but also reflect the fact that his estate will be vested in the trustee, for the benefit of all creditors.

(ii) After-acquired property.[36] Property acquired by, or which devolves **28.73** on the bankrupt, after commencement but before discharge, does not automatically vest in the trustee, but may be claimed by him by serving a notice

---

[27] s.306.
[28] s.283.
[29] s.283(4).
[30] Below, para. 28.78.
[31] s.283(2).
[32] Normally within 42 days of first learning about the property.
[33] ss.308–309.
[34] s.283(3).
[35] Under s.269: above, paras. 28.50–51.
[36] s.307, which is partly contradicted by ss.283–284.

normally within 42 days after he learned about the property. Property to which the notice relates vests in him, and his title relates back to the time the bankrupt acquired the property. If, however, (whether before or after such a notice) a bona fide purchaser for value acquires property without notice of the bankruptcy, or a banker enters into a transaction in good faith and without such notice, the trustee has no remedy against such persons or others deriving title through them. In the preceding paragraph, we have noted the conflict in the Act, between sections 283 and 307, and we suggest that section 307 should be interpreted as applying to the period after the vesting order.

The trustee cannot claim property if it is of the type which would not originally have vested in him, and cannot normally claim property acquired after discharge.[37]

28.74 **(iii) Income payments.**[38] The trustee may apply to the court for an "income payments order" claiming for the estate income (including every payment in the nature of income, and payments from the carrying on of any business or from any office or employment) earned by the bankrupt, in such amounts and for such a time as is specified in the order. No order shall be made so as to reduce the bankrupt's income below what appears to the court to be necessary for meeting the reasonable domestic needs of the bankrupt and his family. The order may direct the bankrupt, or the person paying the bankrupt, to pay the trustee. Any attachment of earnings order that is in force may be varied or discharged. Payments received will become part of the estate. Orders are not to be made after discharge and should not have effect after discharge unless the order (made earlier) specifically provides that it will not continue for more than three years (from the date of the order) or unless continuation is a condition imposed where discharge is ordered by the court[39] (rather than occurring by expiry of time).

28.75 **(iv) The bankrupt's house.** The bankrupt's dwelling house is liable to be sold by the trustee. This is so even if a spouse has an existing charge under the Matrimonial Homes Act 1983 (no new rights of occupation can arise after the petition)[40] and even if the house is owned jointly or as tenants in common (in law or in equity) by another. In either case the trustee may apply for an order for sale under section 30 of the Law of Property Act 1925. If both co-owners are trustees for sale (having legal ownership) or the wife has a Matrimonial Homes Act charge, the application is to the bankruptcy court, and that court shall make such order as it thinks just and reasonable having regard to the interests of the creditors, the conduct of the spouse, etc., so far as contributing to the bankruptcy, to the needs and financial resources of the spouse, etc., and to the needs of the children, and to any other circumstances "other than the needs of the bankrupt."[41]

The bankrupt's position is stronger if he has children under 18 who have their home in the house at the time of the petition, provided that the bankrupt is entitled to occupy the house by virtue of an equitable interest (even if he has legal ownership). Then, the bankrupt (if in occupation) has a right not to be evicted by the trustee except with leave of the court. If not actually

---

[37] But see ss.307(2) and 280.
[38] s.310.
[39] Under s.280.
[40] s.336(1).
[41] s.336.

in occupation he has a right with leave of the court to enter and occupy. These rights are a charge on the trustee's interest just as if the bankrupt had a spouse's charge under the Matrimonial Homes Act. Applications for leave to enter, or for sale under the Matrimonial Homes Act, are considered by the bankruptcy court, which is to make such order as it thinks just and reasonable having regard to the interests of the creditors, the bankrupt's financial resources, the childrens' needs, and all the circumstances "other than the needs of the bankrupt." But if the bankrupt applies for leave to enter later than one year after the vesting of the estate in the trustee, the court is to assume, unless in exceptional cases, that the creditors' interests outweigh all other considerations.[42]

Where the house is occupied by the bankrupt or his spouse or former spouse and the trustee is, for any reason, unable for the time being to realise that property, the trustee may end his supervision and administration of the property by applying to the court for an order charging the property. The house then vests in the bankrupt (subject to the charge) and the estate (the creditors) have the benefit of the charge.[43] The bankrupt could sell the house, but the charge would bind the purchasers, who should pay the trustee.

Where premises are comprised in a bankrupt's estate and occupied by him on condition of payment towards liability under a mortgage or other outgoings, the bankrupt shall not by virtue of the payments acquire any interest in the property. (Otherwise, he might acquire equitable rights, which would be after-acquired property.)[44]

7. COMPANIES AND INDIVIDUALS: DISCLAIMER OF ONEROUS PROPERTY

Whether in a winding up or in an individual bankruptcy, the liquidator or trustee has power to disclaim onerous property (which means generally, unprofitable contracts, or unsaleable property). Notice must be given before he does so.[45] The complicated provisions relating to this are not further considered here. **28.76**

8. COMPANIES AND INDIVIDUALS: SEIZURE OF PROPERTY

There are wide powers for the office holders (liquidators, trustees, etc.) to seek a court order to take possession of property, books, papers, or records to which the debtor (company, or individual bankrupt) is or appears to be entitled, which are in the possession or control of the debtor or someone else.[46] (In the case of an individual there are powers to break and enter premises and to issue a search warrant.) A variety of criminal offences are imposed upon debtors, in relation to concealment, etc., of property.[47] If the office holder seizes or disposes of the wrong property, he is given special **28.77**

---

[42] s.337.
[43] s.313.
[44] s.338.
[45] ss.178–182, 315–321.
[46] ss.234, 365.
[47] Above, paras. 28.45, 28.61.

protection provided that he had reasonable ground to believe that he was entitled to seize or dispose of it, and he has a lien on the property or its proceeds for his expenses of sale or seizure.[48] (He is liable for losses which he negligently causes to the property.) In the case of a company, persons who are or have been officers, or who within the past year took part in the formation of the company, or were employees, or employees of another company which was an officer of the company, must provide the office holder with such information as he may reasonably require, and attend on him, etc.[49]

The court has a power to arrest and detain an individual bankrupt at any time, and to seize and detain his goods or property if there are reasonable grounds to think he has or may abscond or may remove his goods, or conceal or destroy any goods, books, papers, etc., or if he has removed goods exceeding a certain value, or if he has failed to attend an examination ordered by the court, without reasonable excuse.[50]

The trustee shall take possession of all books, papers, and records concerning the estate and belonging to the bankrupt or in his possession or control. For the purpose of taking control of the estate, the trustee is to be treated as a receiver appointed by the High Court, so that he is an officer of the court to which he may apply for assistance, and interference with him is contempt of court. If the property is stocks and shares, he may transfer these as the bankrupt could have done. Choses in action are deemed to be assigned to the trustee, but he need not give notice of the assignment.[51]

In an individual bankruptcy, the bankrupt, official receiver, ex-trustee or supervisor of a composition or scheme under a voluntary arrangement must deliver up possession of books, records, papers to the trustee.[52] Any banker or agent or other person holding property to the account of, or for the bankrupt, must pay or deliver such property which is part of the estate, and "which he is not by law entitled to retain as against the bankrupt or trustee."[53] A banker could, of course, exercise a right of lien, or set-off, or a valid security right under a pledge, and his receiver in possession could retain possession. It is contempt of court for anyone not to comply with these obligations, without reasonable excuse. But if goods are held by way of pledge, pawn or other security the trustee may serve a notice to inspect them (unless the official receiver has already served the notice), and may in any case exercise the bankrupt's right of redemption in respect of the goods.[54]

The bankrupt has duties to give the trustee such information, and to attend on him at such times and do such acts as are reasonably required.[55] This applies even after his discharge. He must inform the trustee of property acquired by or devolving on him, or any increase in his income. It is contempt of court to fail to comply.

---

[48] s.234(3–4), 304(3–4). In Chap. 23, we noted that this also protects an administrative receiver.
[49] s.235.
[50] s.364.
[51] s.311.
[52] s.312(1–2).
[53] s.312(3).
[54] s.311(5).
[55] s.333.

9. EFFECT OF INSOLVENCY ON DISPOSITIONS OF THE PROPERTY OF THE DEBTOR

a. Companies

In the case of a voluntary winding up, the directors lose all powers to dispose of the company's property once the liquidator is appointed, and the question so far as dispositions by them are concerned, becomes a problem of agency and of ostensible authority. They lose ostensible authority on the Gazetting of the fact of liquidation. The liquidator has power to sell or mortgage company property, etc.[56] and he could continue a bank account for the purpose of winding up.

28.78

In the case of compulsory winding up, the important time is the commencement of winding up, which will normally be at the time of the petition.[57] After commencement all dispositions of company property are void unless the Court consents (at the time, or subsequently).[58] No valid purchase, or security, etc., could be taken, unless in pursuance of a pre-existing unconditional agreement.[59]

In relation to bank accounts, transactions on the account after commencement should not be permitted without the court's order. Any payment into an overdrawn account would otherwise be repayable, and any debit to the account would otherwise be unsecured, and not even provable. This applies even if the bank is unaware of commencement, but if it acted in good faith, before the Gazetting of the petition, and without negligence, the court would probably sanction such transactions retrospectively. Cheques, etc., presented for payment are returned marked "Winding up petition presented." (It is, of course, a serious libel if this is incorrect). In deciding whether to exercise its discretion the court will consider the interests of all pre-liquidation unsecured creditors, for it may be unfair to them if the bank is allowed to receive payments, or to incur new, provable, debts, or if other creditors are paid first. If, therefore, the company is to be permitted to trade (and the liquidator may wish to continue trading so as to permit better realisation) the court may grant approval subject to freezing of the old account, with all new transactions taking place on a new account (in respect of which combination or statutory set-off will not be possible). A "validation order" will be on condition that continued trading is at a profit, and for the benefit of creditors generally.[60]

In *Re Gray's Inn Construction Co. Ltd.*[61] between the time of the petition and the order an account was continued, with £25,000 odd being paid in and £24,000 odd being paid out. The liquidator at first claimed either the payments in, or out, as being "dispositions" of the company's property, but subsequently claimed only the losses to the company incurred because of the continued trading (£5,000). At first instance, Templeman J. held that payments in were not "dispositions," and he validated the payments out. The Court of Appeal, however, held that both payments in (to an overdrawn account) and out were "dispositions," and payments should not be

28.79

---

[56] Above, para. 28.29, and refer to para. 28.17.
[57] Above, para. 28.15.
[58] s.127, replacing s.522, C.A. 1985, which replaced s.227, C.A. 1948.
[59] Above, see *Re Columbian Fireproofing Co. Ltd.* [1910] 2 Ch. 120: *Re F. and E. Stanton Ltd.* [1929] 1 Ch. 180; contrast *Re Gregory Love & Co.* [1916] 1 Ch. 203.
[60] See *Re Gray's Inn Construction Co. Ltd.* [1980] 1 All E.R. 814, considering s.227, C.A. 1948.
[61] Previous note.

validated if this might result in any creditor being paid in full while others received only a dividend. This might apply either to the bank itself, where a payment in, to an overdrawn account, discharged a pre-liquidation debt, or to other creditors, who benefit from a payment out. Thus, a bank should preferably seek the court's consent before continuing the account, although the court will be more likely to validate transactions if it increases, or at least does not reduce the value of the company's assets. If the bank decides to continue the account without an order, it should freeze the old account, and insist on subsequent dealings being dealt with on a separate account, taking a personal assurance from the directors that payments out will not be used to discharge pre-liquidation debts, and will relate to new business. Applying these principles, the court in the *Gray's Inn* case validated credits received up until the day after the petition was advertised, but not a credit received four days later. No credits after the bank should have known of the (Gazetted) advertisement were allowed to reduce the overdraft. Sums paid out for pre-liquidation debts were recoverable from the bank, but only if recovery could not be obtained from the recipients, from whom recovery should first be sought.[62] The decision in this case marks a change of judicial attitudes, for courts had previously been thought to regard more benevolently the continued trading of the company, and the continuation of its account.[63]

Once a winding up order is made, the account will be stopped entirely, and the liquidator will be paid the credit balance. The bank may be secured, and may look to its security,[64] though if the liquidator has already taken possession, the bank needs the consent of the court (in a winding up by the court) to take possession of secured assets.[65] In relation to other debts, the bank may be a preferential creditor.[66] It must prove for these debts, and for other unsecured debts.[67]

If the petition is dismissed then if the bank has not called in the debt, the account may be continued as normal.

b. Individual Bankrupts

28.80   Property vests in the trustee from commencement[68] (date of bankruptcy order)[69] and the bankrupt thereafter has no power to dispose of it, since it belongs to the trustee. Dispositions by the bankrupt then become a question of authority (from the trustee) or lack of it. The trustee, however, may not be appointed until after the bankruptcy order, perhaps after a meeting of creditors (the official receiver may be appointed pending his appointment).[70] Provision is made, therefore, affecting earlier dispositions. But the

---

[62] The court's view of the meaning of "disposition" may be contrasted with that taken in *Re Mal Bower's Macquarie Electrical Centre Pty. Ltd.* [1974] 1 N.S.W.L.R. 254, cited by Paget, 62.

[63] See *Re Wiltshire Iron Co., ex p. Pearson* (1868) 3 Ch.App. 443; *Re Park Ward & Co. Ltd.* [1926] Ch. 828; *Re T.W. Construction Ltd.* [1954] 1 All E.R. 744 (loan after commencement, to pay wages, validated: bank knew company expected money under export contracts.); *Re Clifton Place Garage Ltd.* [1970] Ch. 477.

[64] See *Sowman* v. *David Samuel Trust Ltd.* [1978] 1 All E.R. 616.

[65] See *Re Pound, Son and Hutchins* (1889) 42 Ch.D. 402. It is otherwise if the receiver is already in possession.

[66] Below, paras. 28.104 and 28.110.

[67] Below, para. 28.101.

[68] s.283.

[69] s.278.

[70] s.287.

provisions thus made may have an effect even before commencement, going back to the time of presentation of the petition. It must be remarked that the section which governs this—section 284—is very badly drafted and extremely obscure. What follows is merely a tentative view of what is possibly the present position.

(i) Dispositions and payments between the petition and commencement. Section 284 makes provision for the period between the petition, and the time when the estate vests in the trustee. The section applies only if a person is adjudged bankrupt, and although strictly the trustee's title is not "related back" to the petition, the effect is similar.[71] In the period in question, any "disposition" of property "made by" the bankrupt is void unless made with the consent of the court or subsequently ratified by the court. The same rule applies to "payments" by the bankrupt (whether or cash or otherwise) and where a payment is void the person paid shall hold the sum for the bankrupt as part of his estate.[72]

28.81

(a) Payments into an overdrawn account. "Disposition" is not defined, but in a case concerning a company, decided under the previous insolvency scheme, it was held that "disposition" included payments by the bankrupt into his overdrawn bank account, (this being a disposition in favour of the bank) as well as payments from an account in credit to third parties.[73] Thus, a payment to an overdrawn bank account after the petition seems to be void both as a disposition and as a "payment," unless ratified by the court. However, there is to be no remedy against any person in respect of any property or payment which he received before the bankruptcy order, in good faith, for value and without notice that the petition had been presented.[74] If the account is overdrawn, therefore, or if the debtor owes debts on other accounts to the bank, it would seem that the bank takes payments in for value and is protected in receiving them if it has no notice or suspicion as to the petition.

28.82

(b) Payment from account in credit. If after the petition the debtor pays money from an account in credit to a third person, this prima facie is a "payment" made by the bankrupt, and void. What is unclear is whether the bank can debit the account because of this "void" payment or disposition by the debtor of his money. There is no remedy against the payee, if ignorant of the petition[75] so that the trustee's only source of repayment is the bank. It would appear that (as with company debtors after commencement) even payments made in ignorance of the petition require ratification by the courts, even though a debt incurred in those circumstances would be provable, being before commencement. That is, unless ratified, the bank must repay the trustee and prove for the debt.

28.83

(c) Payments from overdrawn accounts. If, on the other hand, the account is overdrawn at the time of a debit this is not a disposition of the bankrupt's property, but of the bank's property, and the question is not whether the trustee can recover it from the bank, but whether the debit is validly made so that the bank can prove for the debt. Debts occurring before the com-

28.84

---

[71] The section, therefore, resembles s.127, discussed above.
[72] s.284(2).
[73] *Re Gray's Inn Construction Co.* above, n. 60.
[74] s.284(4): nor in respect of any interest in property deriving from an interest in respect of which there is no remedy.
[75] s.284(4).

mencement of the bankruptcy are provable, and it would seem that the bank may, therefore, prove for the debt.[76]

28.85   *(d) Payments made with notice of the petition.* If, however, the bank has notice of the petition, then debits to the account made between the petition and commencement *may* be unenforceable, whether the account was then in credit or overdrawn. This is *perhaps* the effect of section 323, which applies where before commencement there have been mutual credits, mutual debts or other mutual dealings between bankrupt and any creditor proving for a bankruptcy debt. An account is to be taken as to what is due from each to the other, and the sums shall be set off. But sums due from the bankrupt shall not be included in the account if the other party had notice that a bankruptcy petition was pending. Only the balance (if any) of the account thus taken is provable as a bankruptcy debt. This appears to exclude debts incurred with notice of a petition (the court could not ratify such transactions). The section may not (and on the face of it, does not) apply if at the time of the payment there are no mutual debts, where, say, the bank owes nothing to the bankrupt. But that could produce a strange result, for if the bank owed a tiny sum to the debtor there would be mutual debts, and notice of the petition would operate against all transactions, whereas in the absence of that sum the bank's notice of a petition would not affect it if, for example, it debited an already overdrawn account. The section would seem to apply if at any time before commencement "there have been mutual credits . . . ," etc. Possibly, therefore, the section does render void all debits on a current account made with notice of a pending petition, (or it may be that it apples only if the bank owes the debtor money, so that in that sense, there are (mutual) credits).

28.86   **(ii) Payments into an account, after commencement, before vesting.** These are recoverable by the trustee either as his own property (if owned by the bankrupt before commencement) or (if he gives notice) as after-acquired property.

28.87   **(iii) Payments from an account (whether in credit or not) after commencement, before vesting.** Section 284(5) provides that where a void payment occurs after the commencement (time of the bankruptcy order) and the making of the void payment incurs a debt to a banker or other person, the debt is deemed to have occurred before the commencement unless the banker or other person had notice of the bankruptcy before the debt was incurred, or it is not reasonably practicable for the payment to be recovered from the payee. The effect of this is to treat some debts which, in fact, occur after commencement as if they occurred before commencement. They become provable debts, therefore.

It is unclear whether this applies to credit accounts, or to overdrawn accounts. In relation to a credit account, while the banker debits the account following a payment, no debt is "incurred" to the banker, for the account is in credit. The question is whether "debit" and "debt" are synonymous, and on the face of it they are not. If this is the case, then a payment from a credit account is a payment or disposition of the bankrupt's property, requiring the court's ratification before the debit can be made. In any case, if debit and debt are for this purpose to be treated alike, the debit is deemed to be made before the bankruptcy order, in which case, as already said, ratification is

---

[76] s.382, defining "bankruptcy debt," and s.322 (proof).

also necessary. It seems, then, that the subsection refers only to debits which leave the account overdrawn, so that a debt is incurred to the banker. All payments from a credit account need ratification.

In relation to an overdrawn account, the debit represents a debt incurred after commencement, and is not provable.[77] It might be thought that a payment from an overdrawn account is a payment of the bank's money, not a payment of the bankrupt's money (and not, therefore, "a payment which is void under this section"). If so regarded, the section would not save payments from an overdrawn account. But this cannot be intended, for we have just excluded debits on a credit account, and that being so, the subsection must apply to debits on an overdrawn account. It is difficult to see, otherwise, how a payment could ever result in the bankrupt incurring a debt to the banker or other person mentioned in the subsection. The subsection must, therefore, refer to payments from an overdrawn account, which incur debts, which are then made provable. But this is not so if the bank knew of the bankruptcy (which must, it seems, refer to the bankruptcy order, for there is no bankruptcy merely because a petition is presented), nor if the money cannot be recovered by the trustee from the payee. In other words, it is treated as a payment of the bankrupt's money only if the trustee can get it back from a third party, and if he can the bank is allowed to prove for it, if ignorant of the fact of the bankruptcy. If the trustee cannot recover from the third party, the money is treated as a payment of the bank's money, and being after commencement, it is not provable.

(iv) Payments and debits after the vesting order. Debits after the vesting order are not provable, and any dealing with the property is a dealing with the trustee's property, or with after-acquired property. **28.88**

10. EFFECT OF SECOND BANKRUPTCY

A bankruptcy order may be made against an undischarged bankrupt. In that case certain dispositions or distributions by the existing trustee (under the earlier bankruptcy) after notice of the later petition shall be void unless the court consents or ratifies it. This applies to after-acquired property which has become vested in him by his notice to acquire it, to money received by him under an income payments order, and to property or money representing these, or their proceeds. Such property is to be comprised in that estate dealt with by the trustee under the subsequent bankruptcy, subject to a charge for the existing trustee's expenses. However, otherwise than as just stated, property comprised in the estate for the purposes of the first bankruptcy, is not comprised in the estate for the purposes of the second bankruptcy. Creditors under the earlier bankruptcy are not to prove for the same debts in the later bankruptcy, though the existing trustee may prove for the unsatisfied balance of the earlier debts and interest and expenses (he will rank after all other debts and interest).[78] **28.89**

11. TRANSACTIONS AT AN UNDERVALUE AND PREFERENCES[79]

These matters are dealt with in a very similar way for both companies (sections 238–240) and individuals (sections 339–341). The court (on the application of liquidator, administrator, or trustee) may make an order affecting **28.90**

[77] s.382.
[78] ss.334, 335.
[79] Formerly misleadingly called "fraudulent preferences."

the prohibited matters, so as to restore the position to what it would have been if they had not occurred.

a. A Transaction at an Undervalue

28.91 This occurs where in relation to another person the debtor (company, or individual) makes a gift, or enters a transaction providing for the debtor to receive no consideration or a consideration the value of which in money or money's worth is significantly less than the value of the consideration provided by the debtor. The consideration of marriage for an individual debtor is also an undervalue.[80]

In the case of a company debtor, no order is to be made if the company entered the transaction in good faith and for the purpose of carrying on its business, if at the time it did so there were reasonable grounds for believing that the transaction would benefit the company.[81] This provision might, for example, protect a guarantee (and security) given to a bank by one company in a group on behalf of another company in the group (which, otherwise, are prima facie undervalues).[82] Another example may be promotional offers made at a nominal consideration, or free.

b. A Preference

28.92 This requires an effect, a motive and a recipient. The recipient is a creditor of the debtor, or a surety or guarantor for his debts or liabilities. The effect occurs where the debtor does or allows anything to be done which has the effect of putting the recipient into a position which, in the event of the debtor's insolvent liquidation or bankruptcy will be better than the position he would have been in if that thing had not been done. It should not be difficult to prove that this effect has occurred. The motive to be shown is that the debtor "was influenced in deciding to give it by a desire to produce" the effect of a preference.[83] Thus, mere knowledge of the effect is insufficient, but the desire to produce the effect need not be the main, or only influence. A debtor who paid a creditor in order to obtain further deliveries of goods would, presumably, know of the effect, but not be influenced by a desire to produce it. A debtor who responded to a threat of legal action, or an insolvency petition, might possibly be influenced by a desire to produce the effect of a preference. Despite the use of the word "preference" the sections do not require the motive to prefer one creditor over another: it requires only that the creditor "preferred" has his position improved, over what it would otherwise have been. The sections apply even if the debtor believes himself to be solvent.

If the person who receives the preference was connected with or an associate of the company debtor, or is an associate of the individual debtor, a motive to prefer is presumed,[84] unless the contrary is proved.[85] A person connected with a company is a director or shadow director, or an associate of these, or an associate of the company.[86] "Associate" is widely defined, and includes spouses, relatives, partners (and their spouses or relatives),

---

[80] s.339(3)(b).
[81] s.238(5).
[82] Below, para. 28.96 *et seq.*
[83] ss.239(5), 340(4).
[84] But unlike undervalues, it is not presumed that the company went into insolvent liquidation.
[85] ss.239(6), 340(5).
[86] s.249.

trustees who may benefit under a trust, employees (including directors), and controllers of companies. Two companies are associates if the same person controls both, or he controls one and his associates the other, and also in other cases.[87] There might be a risk to a bank if it is considered to be a shadow director[88] in which case even the advance of further funds in a rescue would be deemed to be a preference, unless the contrary is proved.

Possibly to prevent debtors aquiescing in legal actions by certain creditors, it is possible that something may be a preference even if done by order of a court.[89]

Like predecessor provisions, these sections do not require that the person preferred (*e.g.* a guarantor) should be the person paid (*e.g.* the bank) under the preference. If a debtor pays a bank this may reduce the liability of a guarantor for the debtor: the bank is paid, but the guarantor is preferred.[90] The court could order the bank to repay.[91] This difficulty is met by giving some protection to innocent persons in such cases.[92]

c. Relevant Times and Circumstances

Undervalues and preferences are affected only if made within certain periods, and in certain circumstances.   **28.93**

For a company, the "relevant time" is commencement of the winding up or the date of a petition for an administration order. Transactions are affected then if they occur within the following periods before the relevant time: (a) two years for transactions at an undervalue, (b) six months for ordinary preferences (not being undervalues), (c) two years for preferences given to connected persons.

But in these cases, even transactions within the periods mentioned are unaffected unless the company was unable to pay its debts[93] at the time, or becomes unable to pay its debts because of the transaction or preference.[94] But if a transaction at an undervalue is entered into with a connected person, inability to pay debts, etc., is presumed unless the contrary is proved (not so with preferences).

An additional "relevant period" occurs between the date of a petition for an administration order, and the making of an order on the petition. This is not protected by the requirement of inability to pay debts.

In the case of *an individual bankrupt*, the periods are times before the date of the petition for bankruptcy, and are: (a) five years for transactions at an undervalue, (b) six months for ordinary preferences, (not being undervalues) (c) two years for preferences given to an associate (not being undervalues).[95]

Even so, preferences are not prohibited unless the individual is insolvent at the time or becomes insolvent because of the preference. Transactions at an undervalue are subject to the same rule, except that those made less than two years before the petition are affected even if the individual is then sol-

[87] s.435.
[88] Above, para. 28.42.
[89] ss.239(7), 340(6).
[90] Below, para. 28.97.
[91] This is expressed in ss.241(2), 342(2).
[92] Below, para. 28.94.
[93] Above, para. 28.11.
[94] s.240(2).
[95] Above, para. 28.91.

vent.[96] "Insolvent" means[97] unable to pay his debts as they fall due, or where the value of his assets is less than his liabilities, (including his contingent and prospective liabilities). In the case of transactions at an undervalue (not preferences) given to an associate of the bankrupt, insolvency is presumed unless the contrary is proved.[98]

An additional period when transactions and preferences is prohibited is in criminal bankruptcy cases, if entered or given after a date specified in the criminal bankruptcy order (no proof of insolvency is required).[99]

d. Effect

28.94 Once it is established that a transaction or preference is wrongful under these provisions, the court may[1] make a variety of orders, particular examples of which are listed.[2] Thus, the court may require, for example, retransfer of the property (or its proceeds, etc.) or its vesting in the trustee or company, or the release or discharge of any security given by the debtor, or requiring payments to be made to the debtor. It may provide for guarantors or sureties whose obligations were released or discharged (if, say, the debtor paid a debt to his bank, thus releasing a guarantor of the account from his liability) to be under such new or revived obligations as the court thinks appropriate. Since the person preferred—here the guarantor—need not be the person paid, revival of obligations may be fair to third parties (such as the bank), who were unaware of the preference. Further, where the court imposes an obligation, it may order the person concerned to provide security for the discharge of his obligation, and for the obligation to be charged on any property, and the security thus taken may be made to have the same priority as the security or charge released or discharged because it was made under a prohibited transaction or preference. Further, the court may make orders as to the extent to which a person affected by orders taking property or imposing obligations is to be allowed to prove in the liquidation or bankruptcy in respect of debts or liabilities thus arising, or for debts and liabilities which had been released or discharged when the prohibited transaction or preference was entered or given to be revived.

As noted already[3] the order made may affect persons other than those who entered the prohibited transaction or to whom the preference was given, but is not to prejudice any interest in property acquired from someone other than the debtor, in good faith, for value, and without notice of the relevant circumstances,[4] or any interest derived through such an interest. Nor shall an order require a person who received a benefit in good faith for value and without notice of the relevant circumstances[5] to pay a sum to the office holder or trustee, unless the recipient was a "party to the transaction," or the payment is to be "in respect of a preference given to that person" (the recipient) at a time when he was a creditor of the debtor.[6]

---

[96] s.341(2).

[97] s.341(3).

[98] s.341(2).

[99] s.341(4–5).

[1] ss.241, 342.

[2] *Ibid.*

[3] Above, para. 28.92.

[4] *i.e.* of the preference or undervalue, or of the liquidation or administration order, or bankruptcy order—s.241(3), 342(4).

[5] Previous note.

[6] ss.241(2), 342(2).

This last provision probably protects a bank creditor who innocently receives money from the debtor, (receipt into an overdrawn account being "for value") where the debtor intends to prefer a guarantor or surety. The aim of the sections seems to be to affect gifts, or parties to the undervalue or those to whom the preference is "given." In accordance with the references to notice, "party" presumably means "knowingly party" being aware not only of the effect of the preference (which the bank would know of) but knowing of the debtor's motive. The bank is not the creditor to whom such a preference is "given" (the guarantor is preferred). If, however, the bank is not innocent, and must repay, the court could order the guarantor's obligations to revive.

Although an innocent bank need not repay, the court may revive the guarantor's obligation: but this alone may do little good, for if the bank is paid, it has no debt on which the guarantor is liable, and the guarantor is not liable to anyone else. It may be, however, that the court may impose an obligation on the guarantor, "redirecting" his liability. The sections say clearly that the court "may . . . impose any obligation on, any person . . . " (whether or not preferred, etc.)[7]

e. Guarantees and Preferences and Undervalues

A guarantee may be affected by these rules either because the Guarantor (G) becomes insolvent, or because the debtor (D) becomes insolvent. **28.95**

(i) G's insolvency. Where G becomes insolvent, then the guarantee may be a preference, if given at the prohibited times, provided that: **28.96**

(a) at the relevant time G is unable to pay its debts, or becomes unable to pay its debts in consequence of the giving of the guarantee. It would seem that this means, as a direct consequence of the transaction, and not simply because, at some later date, the guarantee is called on. It would seem to be unlikely that a guarantee would be taken from G if G is unable to pay its debts, (or, for an individual, is insolvent) but perhaps this is a possibility in inter-group guarantees.

(b) the bank (B) must be a creditor (or surety or guarantor) of G. For this reason, it seems that many guarantees are unlikely to be a preference, because the nature of the transaction is such that B is a creditor of D's.

(c) Additionally, the guarantee must put B, in relation to G, in a "better position" in G's insolvency, whereas (unless secured) it puts B in a better position against D.

As to undervalues, supposing the guarantee is given within the periods affected, they are affected if G "receives" no consideration or a consideration "significantly less" than the value of the consideration provided by G. Guarantees must be supported by consideration, but the consideration (affording D time to pay, or facilities, etc.) moves to D, not to G. Does G "receive" consideration? If not, it is a transaction at an undervalue. The alternative statement of undervalue does not require "receipt" of the consideration by G, so long as G's consideration is matched by a consideration of equivalent value. This may be the case with guarantees (the consideration being given by B to D). In any case, if G is a company the court is not to make an order if the court is satisfied that G entered the transaction "in good faith and for the purpose of carrying on its business" and that at the time there were reasonable grounds for believing that the transaction would ben-

---

[7] ss.241(2), 342(2), and see ss.241(1)(*d*) and 342(1)(*d*).

efit" G. There is no such restriction for individuals. It has been said that the making of an inter-group guarantee may be for G's benefit[8] and possibly, therefore, it will be saved. It must be shown that the transaction is for G's "business" which may be the case in inter-group guarantees. But if G is an individual, the court must find either that G receives consideration, or that there is matching consideration given to D, or else guarantees given within six months of G's bankruptcy are affected.

28.97 **(ii) D's insolvency.** As to D's insolvency, the question is not as to transactions at an undervalue, but as to preferences. It was, and still is the law, that the preference need not be given to the bank (B). Thus, if D, contemplating his insolvency, and in order to favour G, pays money to B, then although there is no intention to prefer the bank,[9] there is an intention to prefer G, and that is enough to require the court to set the payment aside.[10] As noted, this is express in the sections in question. If G is connected with, or an associate of D (as a member of a group may be) D's intention to prefer G is presumed. Unfortunately, it is the bank, which receives the payments, and not G, the person preferred, who must refund the payments.[11] The "saving" provisions relating to good faith and lack of notice (for non-parties), are mentioned above and are of vital importance.

If there is a preference, then it appears that nothing happens until the court makes an order, so that until that time B has been validly paid and G is discharged from liability. Hence, G's liability may be revived by the court.[12] In fact, bank forms will probably expressly specify that G remains liable, and in order to avoid problems of proof, etc., and the need for a written memorandum,[13] will provide that the bank may retain the guarantee form for a period of six months (which should be extended to two years if G is connected with D). If the bank holds G's securities only, and not his personal promise to repay the debt, then the bank may have given up the security. It may reserve to itself a right not to do so for six months, etc., but if the security is given up, the court may renew the security.

In short, then, where D is insolvent, there may be a fraudulent preference of B if D pays to his account desiring to prefer B or G, but (i) G remains liable, or his liability can be renewed by the court, and (ii) the bank is protected from repayment if it received in good faith, for value, and without knowledge of the circumstances, and is not the party preferred or otherwise a party to the transaction.

It may be possible to avoid some problems of undervalues and preferences by lending jointly to the members of a group, thus providing "consideration." Given a joint debt, the bank needs no guarantee.

It should not be forgotten that if the bank as recipient of funds is unaware in any case that directors are in breach of their fiduciary duties (lending for matters not to the benefit of the company) then the bank may be liable for

---

[8] *Charterbridge Corpn. Ltd.* v. *Lloyds Bank Ltd.* [1970] Ch. 62, though see *Rolled Steel Products Ltd.* v. *B.S.C.* [1986] Ch. 246.

[9] There may be such an intention: see *R. F. P.& C. H. Matthews Ltd.* [1982] Ch. 257.

[10] See *R. M. Kushler Ltd.* [1943] Ch. 248.

[11] *Re T. N. Barling & Co. Ltd.* (1937) unrep., *Re Lyons, ex p. Barclays Bank Ltd.* v. *Trustee* (1934) 152 L.T. 201; *Re Conley* [1938] 2 All E.R. 127.

[12] Above, para. 28.94.

[13] See the Scottish cases: *MacKinnon's Trustee* v. *Bank of Scotland* (1915) S.C. 411; *Simpson* v. *Jack* (1948) S.L.T. (Notes) 45.

constructive trust.[14] This, however, will become less problemmatical given either the reforms suggested by Dr. Prentice[15] or, at present, express powers in the Memorandum and Articles to give guarantees in a wide range of circumstances.

f. Charges

The question arises whether charges can be affected by these rules. (As to third party charges, everything said above about guarantees is relevant, except that on D's insolvency a question of undervalues may well arise.) Floating charges, it will be recalled, are subject to a rule under which they may be void to the extent that they are not given for fresh consideration. Fixed charges given for past debts are not subject to that rule, but might be preferences or undervalues. If the company receives no "consideration" (past consideration is not good consideration) then this is an undervalue, but the transaction is saved if there were reasonable grounds to think that it might benefit the company. Possibly the continuation of banking facilities might be regarded as the "benefit" or as the consideration provided to the company. It can hardly be the case that there is a special 12 months rule for floating charges, but a stricter, 2 year rule, for fixed charges, and it is thought that the courts are unlikely to hold charges of either kind to be undervalues if the consideration is the continuation of banking facilities.

In relation to preferences, the position is more difficult. The bank's position is improved by the giving of the charge; it is a creditor, and the only question seems to be as to the motive of the debtor. Was he influenced in giving the preference by a desire to produce the effect of putting the bank in a position which would be better if insolvency occurred? It might be said that his "desire" was to have continuation of banking facilities, just as the desire of the debtor who pays one creditor in order to induce him to deliver more goods is to obtain the goods. In each case the debtor knows he will produce the effect of the preference, but that is not his desire. In other words, where there is some genuine expectation of some benefit being obtained from the creditor who is preferred, the debtor's desire may be said to obtain that benefit, rather than to produce the effect of the preference, even if he knows about the latter (as he does). If this is the case, then even a charge given for past consideration should be saved if genuinely given in the hope of continued banking facilities. The case which may be caught is that of the creditor who offers nothing new, and the continuation of no facilities, but threatens, say, legal action in order to obtain his charge. It may be that here the courts would hold that the desire is to produce the effect of the preference, in order to avoid the legal action (this seems to be a fair result, though the logic of the distinctions is debateable).

12. TRANSACTIONS DEFRAUDING CREDITORS (FRAUDULENT UNDERVALUES)

Sections 423–425 affect both companies and individual bankrupts.[16] These "fraudulent undervalue" provisions apply where the debtor (company, or individual) enters a transaction at an undervalue (as already defined). If a fraudulent undervalue is proved, then the court may make an order to restore the position, and to protect the interests of those who are, or who

28.98

---

[14] Above, Chap. 10.
[15] Above, Chap. 17.
[16] s.172, L.P.A. 1925 is repealed.

are capable of being, prejudiced (a "person prejudiced" below). The differences between these provisions and those as to undervalues already examined ("ordinary undervalues") are as follows:

(i) Ordinary undervalues make no reference to the purpose of the transaction. A fraudulent undervalue requires proof of one of two purposes: *i.e.* that the transaction was entered into "for the purpose of putting assets beyond the reach of a person who is making, or may at some time make, a claim" against the debtor, "or of otherwise prejudicing the interests of such a person" in relation to such a claim. It is not the effect of the transaction alone which counts, but the purpose for which it is done. It must (a) be at an undervalue, and (b) be for one of the forbidden purposes. There is no need to prove fraud (*i.e.* dishonesty) but only one of the two purposes mentioned. In the case of a company, it is thought that the purpose must be the purpose of those who make the decision to enter the transaction.

(ii) With ordinary undervalues, the classes of applicants for an order are limited to the administrator, liquidator, or trustee. But with fraudulent undervalues, application may be made even outside insolvency. In appropriate circumstances (*e.g.* the trustee applies on an individual bankruptcy) application may be made by the official receiver, trustee, liquidator, administrator, supervisor of a voluntary arrangement, or by any person prejudiced.

(iii) With ordinary transactions at an undervalue only transactions within certain periods are affected, but there is no temporal limitation with fraudulent undervalues.

(iv) The orders which the court may make are like those in relation to ordinary transactions at an undervalue, or preferences, except that (a) there is no particular mention of provision being made for a person on whom obligations are imposed being permitted to prove as a bankruptcy debtor[17] and (b) the provisions protecting persons receiving benefits in good faith, for value and without notice are wider than for undervalues and preferences, the only restriction here relating[18] to those who are parties to the transaction (*i.e.* preferred creditors are not mentioned).

Clearly, these provisions are important, being unlimited in time, and available even outside bankruptcy. The circumstances when it might be used outside of bankruptcy would perhaps be unusual, but perhaps the provision would enable a speedy application to the court (like the jurisdiction under a Mareva injunction) to prevent assets being removed from the jurisdiction. Generally, the provision will (like its predecessors) be used where, say, a husband (or father) gives assets to his wife (or children) so that in the event of his bankruptcy the assets will remain in the family. Similarly, if a company in a group of companies disposed of assets to another in the group, or to a nominee, for the same purpose, the transaction could be upset if not for bona fide commercial reasons.

13. FRAUDULENT RECEIPT OF PROPERTY FROM INDIVIDUAL BANKRUPT

28.99 If in the 12 months before the petition, or between the petition and the commencement of the bankruptcy, a person acquires or receives property (including receiving it by pawn or pledge) from the bankrupt knowing or

---

[17] Compare ss.241(1)(*g*), 342(1)(*g*).
[18] s.425(2)(*b*).

believing (not merely suspecting) that the bankrupt owed money in respect of the property and that the bankrupt did not intend, or was unlikely to be able, to pay the money he owed, the recipient is guilty of an offence. No offence is committed if the transaction was in the ordinary course of a business carried on by the bankrupt at the time, and in deciding this, particular regard may be had to the price paid for the property.[19] There is a defence of "no intent to defraud or to conceal the state of affairs."[20] Although it is not stated, if it is a criminal offence so to receive the property, the transaction is presumably void as a matter of contract, and could not pass property to the recipient, and would be recoverable by the trustee.

14. EXTORTIONATE CREDIT TRANSACTIONS[21]

These matters affect both companies and individual bankrupts. Where a **28.100** debtor (company, or individual) has been a party to a transaction involving the provision to him of credit, the administrator, liquidator, or trustee may apply to the court for an order on the ground that the transaction is or was extortionate. The transaction must have been entered within three years before the making of the administration order, the commencement of liquidation, or the commencement of an individual's bankruptcy. The provider of credit must prove that the transaction is not extortionate. It will be extortionate if, having regard to the risk accepted by the provider of the credit, either the terms of it are such as to require grossly exorbitant payments to be made (even if on contingencies), or it otherwise "grossly contravened ordinary principles of fair dealing."

If a transaction is extortionate, the court may set aside the whole or part of the obligation, or vary the terms (or the terms of any security), or require a party to pay sums of money to the office holder or trustee, or to surrender security, or to direct that accounts be taken between any persons. Money or property thus received will be part of the debtor's distributable assets.[22] Powers given by this provision are exercisable concurrently with any powers given if the same transaction should also be a transaction at an undervalue.

In the case of an individual debtor, the right of the bankrupt or his trustee to re-open an extortionate credit transaction under the Consumer Credit Act 1974, s.139(1)(a) is excluded (the matter being covered by the foregoing provisions).[23]

F. Provable debts and priorities

1. GENERAL

In a voluntary winding up the liquidator is to pay the company's debts[24] **28.101** and except for secured creditors and preferential debts[25] he pays the debts *pari passu* with any surplus going to the members of the company according to their rights under the Articles or otherwise.[26] The same applies to com-

---

[19] s.359.
[20] s.352.
[21] ss.244, 343.
[22] s.343(5).
[23] s.343(6).
[24] s.165(5).
[25] ss.107, 175.
[26] s.107.

pulsory windings up.[27] In an individual bankruptcy, the trustee shall distribute dividends amongst the creditors "in respect of the bankruptcy debts which they have respectively proved."[28]

Whether in a corporate or individual insolvency, creditors must claim against the liquidator or trustee for their debts, and even in the case of a secured creditor,[29] the liquidator is entitled to be shown proof of the debt and security. The claim made by the creditor is described as his "proof," and the process of claiming as "proving" and this takes place under the Rules.[30]

In the case of a company, the Act refers to "debts,"[31] while in the case of an individual it refers to "bankruptcy debts" but the definitions are essentially the same.[32] Subject to that, provable debts[33] are in the case of an individual,

(i) debts or liabilities to which the debtor is subject before commencement (the date of the bankruptcy order), or

(ii) those to which he may become subject thereafter (even after discharge) by reason of an obligation incurred before commencement;

(iii) amounts specified in a criminal bankruptcy order;

(iv) where a debt bears interest, the interest is provable except for interest payable after commencement.

In the case of tortious liability, the "debt" arises for these purposes when the cause of action accrues, so that, for example, damage caused to another's property before commencement is a bankruptcy debt.[34]

It seems that (i), (ii) and (iv) apply also to company windings up.[35]

It is immaterial whether the debt or liability is present or future, whether it is certain or contingent or whether its amount is fixed or liquidated, or is capable of being ascertained by fixed rules or as a matter of opinion.[36] Subject to that, "liability" means an obligation to pay money or money's worth.[37] Where, because of a contingency or any other reason, a debt does not bear a certain value, the liquidator,[38] or trustee[39] is to estimate its value, and the amount provable is the amount of the estimate. If a ("pre-adjudication") contract was made with a person subsequently adjudged bankrupt, the court may make an order discharging obligations under the contract, on such terms as to payment of damages as seem to be equitable. If the damages are payable by the bankrupt, they shall be provable as a bankruptcy debt.[40]

Debts in foreign currency are converted into sterling at the official rate of

---

[27] ss.143, 167, 168, 175 and I.R. 4.179–184. I.R. 4.181 states the *pari passu* principle in compulsory windings up.

[28] s.165.

[29] I.R. 4.75(1)(g), 6.98(1)(g).

[30] s.322, 411, 412, Scheds. 8 (paras. 12,13), 9 (paras. 17,18).

[31] s.385.

[32] s.382, I.R. 12.3, 13.12.

[33] See s.382(1), I.R. 12.3, 13.12.

[34] s.382(2).

[35] Because of the definition of "debt" in ss.385 and 382(3). See also s.189 (interest) and R.4.94 (future debts).

[36] s.382(3), 13, 12

[37] s.382(4), I.R. 13.12(4).

[38] R.4.86.

[39] s.322(3); or court: s.303.

[40] s.345.

exchange prevailing on the date the debtor went into liquidation.[41] Rent and periodical payments may be proved so far as due and unpaid up to the date winding up commenced or the bankruptcy order was made.[42] Debts due after the date of liquidation may be proved, but any dividend distributed before the date of payment is discounted at $\frac{5}{12}$ per cent. per month.[43]

2. STATUTORY SET-OFF

We have observed[44] that where there are mutual debts, the rules of statutory set-off operate[45] and the debts must be set-off and are provable (to the extent of any balance).

28.102

3. UNENFORCEABLE DEBTS

It has already been observed[46] that (a) transactions after the date winding up commences may not give rise to enforceable debts, (b) that transactions taking place after a bankruptcy petition may (possibly) be affected if there is notice of the petition, but (c) that some debts after commencement of an individual bankruptcy may be treated as having occurred before commencement (and are provable, as above).

28.103

4. PRIORITY OF DISTRIBUTION

a. Companies

(1) Creditors with fixed charges. These are paid from the proceeds of the secured assets (if the assets in question are sold by the receiver, instead, his expenses would be paid first). Priority between different secured creditors was discussed earlier.[47] If the secured assets are insufficient to satisfy the secured debts of the creditors concerned, they fall into the class of unsecured creditors to the extent of the shortfall.

28.104

(2) Expenses. In the case of a voluntary winding up, the expenses of winding up (including the liquidator's remuneration) are payable in priority to all other "claims."[48] In a compulsory winding up, the court has a discretion to order payment of expenses in such priority as it thinks fit.[49]

(3) Next are paid the debts of preferential creditors.[50] Amongst themselves, preferential debts rank equally after the expenses of winding up and are paid in full, but if the assets are insufficient to meet them, they abate in equal proportions.[51]
Preferential debts are defined in section 386 of the Act, as debts listed in schedule 6. They are debts arising in certain periods before the insolvency, but not later than the following "relevant dates" (only some of which are given): (a) voluntary arrangements, the date of approval of the arrange-

---

[41] I.R. 4.89, 6.111.
[42] I.R. 4.92, 6.112.
[43] I.R. 4.94, 6.114, 11.13.
[44] Above, Chap. 27.
[45] Under s.323 and R.4.90.
[46] Above, para. 28.78 *et seq.*
[47] Above, Chap. 21.
[48] s.115.
[49] s.156: for detailed rules of priority of expenses see I.R. 4.218–220.
[50] ss.107, 175.
[51] s.175.

ment, (b) compulsory winding up, the date of the appointment of a provisional liquidator, or, if none, the date of the winding-up order, (c) receiverships, the date of the appointment of the receiver, (d) bankrupts, the date of the bankruptcy order (unless there is an interim receiver appointed, in which case it is that date).

Preferential debts (arising before the relevant dates just mentioned) are as follows:

(i) Certain deductions from wages which the (now insolvent) employer ought to have made under the P.A.Y.E. scheme, or for sub-contrators in the building industry, in the 12 months before the relevant dates,

(ii) value added tax payable in the six months before the relevant dates, and certain other excise duties,

(iii) certain social security contributions due from the debtor in the 12 months before the relevant date,

(iv) certain contributions to occupational pension schemes which the debtor should have made,

(v) (most important for banks) amounts payable for wages or salary (including various payments such as holiday pay, sick pay, etc.), and "any sum owed in respect of money advanced for the purpose as has been applied for the payment of a debt which, if it had not been paid" would have been preferential under this provision. The wages debts have priority only if incurred in the four months before the relevant date, and only if they do not exceed a sum made by order (presently £800). The reference to money advanced for the purpose of paying preferential debts means that a bank which advances money to an insolvent employer for the payment of wages becomes a preferential creditor. This is further considered below.[52]

28.105   (4) The next in priority[53] are the holders of floating charges to the extent of the assets covered by their charges (bank floating charges will normally cover all the assets.) Priority between different floating charge holders was discussed earlier.[54] Charges rank behind preferential creditors even if they crystallise (become fixed) before liquidation, for what counts is whether "as created" the charge was floating.[55] Hence, wherever possible, banks will take fixed charges, even though they also take a floating charge over the whole enterprise.[56]

(5) Next come the unsecured creditors who rank *pari passu*, which means not equally, but in proportion to their claims. We have observed that mere contractual devices not amounting in law to a proprietory security interest, will not be enforced so as to give priority to creditors.[57]

(6) Next comes interest on debts.[58] (Secured creditors would already have taken interest on their debts.) "Interest" includes so much of any debt as represents interest on the remainder—*i.e.* interest is payable on interest owing. The capital of the unsecured or preferential debts is paid first, and then any surplus is to be applied in paying interest on the debts for the periods during which they have been outstanding since the company went

[52] Below, para. 28.110 *et seq.*
[53] s.175(2)(b).
[54] Above, Chap. 21.
[55] s.251.
[56] Above Chaps. 21, 23.
[57] Above Chap. 21, esp. para. 21.11.
[58] Payable under s.189.

into liquidation. All interest ranks equally, regardless of whether the unsecured debts rank equally. The rate of interest is the greater of a statutory rate[59] and the rate applicable to the debt apart from the winding up. Thus, with a bank overdraft on which the bank set a standard rate, the standard rate would be payable if higher than the statutory rate.

(7) Finally, come the members of the company, if any assets remain. If there are assets left at this stage, the company was not insolvent on the "asset" test.[60] The division at this stage depends on the Articles or perhaps on subordination agreements. For example, preference shareholders might have preference as to capital, taking ahead of the "equity" shareholders.

The order of priority is the same whether the assets are sold by a receiver or by the liquidator.[61] A bank normally prefers sale by a receiver, so that it has more control over the timing of sales and the disposition of assets.

b. Individuals

Subject to the provisions of any other enactment[62] the priorities are as follows: **28.106**

(1) The bankrupt's estate is subject to the rights of secured creditors which have not been surrendered.[63] To the extent of the security, they belong to the secured creditor. They claim from the property itself, and are not subject to the trustee's expenses, etc. Secured creditors are further discussed, below. No question of floating charges arises with individual debtors.

(2) Secondly, if a trustee sold otherwise exempted property of the bankrupt and replaced them with cheaper items,[64] the cost of buying replacement goods has priority over any distribution.

(3) The trustee must retain such sums as may be necessary for the expenses of the bankruptcy, and the expenses of a final meeting, before making a distribution.[65]

(4) Next, the trustee must pay preferential debts which rank equally between themselves after the expenses of bankruptcy and are paid in full or abate in equal proportions between themselves.[66] Preferential debts have the same meaning as for companies, and advances by a bank for wages also become preferential.[67]

(5) Next come the debts of ordinary unsecured creditors, which rank equally between themselves and are paid in full or abate in equal proportions between themselves.[68]

(6) Any surplus then goes to pay interest for the period since bankruptcy

---

[59] Under s.17, Judgments Act 1838 on the day liquidation commenced.
[60] In s.518(1A), C.A. 1985.
[61] For receivers, see above, Chap. 23.
[62] s.328(6).
[63] s.283(5).
[64] s.308, above, para. 28.72.
[65] s.324(1), 331(4).
[66] s.328(2).
[67] Below, para. 28.110 *et seq.*
[68] s.328(3).

commenced[69] on the preferential or ordinary debts[70] and the preferential debts have no priority here.[71]

(7) Next come debts for credit provided by a person who was the bankrupt's spouse at the commencement of the bankruptcy, with interest.[72]

(8) Finally, any surplus goes to the bankrupt.[73]

5. MANNER OF DISTRIBUTION OF ESTATE

28.107 Whenever the trustee or liquidator has sufficient funds in hand he shall declare and distribute dividends among creditors for the debts which they have proved, according to the priorities just mentioned. He is to give notice of the dividend and of how it is proposed to distribute it, with details of the debtor's assets or estate. He shall make provision for persons who by reason of distance of their place of residence have had insufficient time to tender and establish their proofs, or for debts which are the subject of claims not yet determined, and for disputed proofs and claims. Creditors who have not proved before the dividend shall not disturb the dividend, but may be compensated in priority to others in future dividends. No action lies against the liquidator or trustee for dividends, but if he refuses to pay, the court may order him to do so and be personally responsible for interest and the costs of proceedings. Property which cannot be readily or advantageously sold may be divided amongst the creditors, with the committee's permission. In criminal bankruptcy cases no distribution shall be made while an appeal is pending.[74]

When the liquidator or trustee has realised all of the estate, or so much of it as can, in his opinion, be realised "without needlessly protracting" the liquidation or trusteeship, he shall give a notice (containing prescribed information concerning the assets or estate, etc., and with a final date for claims to be established) of intention to declare a final dividend, or that no dividend or further dividend, will be declared. The final date thus set may be postponed by the court. After the final date the liquidator or trustee is to defray any outstanding expenses of the insolvency out of the assets or estate, and where he intends to declare a final dividend, he is to do so and to distribute it without regard to any debts not already proved. Any surplus goes to members of the company or the bankrupt.[75]

6. SECURED CREDITORS

28.108 The rights of secured creditors[76] are, as we have seen, unaffected by the insolvency, except in the case where an Administrator of a company is appointed,[77] or where the security is not perfected by registration, etc. The priorities are stated above.[78] We have seen that a secured creditor may not

[69] Interest payable beforehand is provable.
[70] At the higher of the agreed rate or that under s.17 of the Judgments Act 1838 at commencement.
[71] s.328(4–5).
[72] s.329.
[73] s.330(5).
[74] ss.324–327, I.R. 4.179–186.
[75] s.330, I.R. 4.186.
[76] Defined widely in s.383(2) to include mortgages, charges, liens and other security.
[77] Above, para. 23.01.
[78] para. 28.104, and Chap 21.

be permitted to petition for bankruptcy,[79] unless he is willing to give up the security, or values it and claims for the unsecured part of the debt. The position otherwise, as to proof, is as follows:

(i) the secured creditor need not prove at all if he is content to rely upon his security.

(ii) if he wishes to prove, he must (a) value his security (as below) and prove for the balance (running the risk that the liquidator or trustee will, as stated below, redeem at that value, which he may not be able to amend), or (b) give up the security and prove for the whole debt, or (c) realise the security and claim for the balance of his debt.[80] If he realises the security, (even if required to do so by the liquidator, as stated below), the net amount realised is substituted for the value in his proof.[81]

(iii) any proof must contain particulars of a security,[82] and the value which the creditor puts upon it, and the liquidator or trustee is entitled to proof of the debt.

(iv) the secured creditor can re-value his security only with the agreement of the liquidator or trustee or by leave of the court (only the latter if he petitioned for winding up or bankruptcy or has voted with the creditors).[83]

(v) if he omits to disclose his security in his proof he must surrender it for all the creditors unless the court excuses him for inadvertency or honest mistake.[84]

(vi) if the liquidator or trustee wishes, he may redeem the security at the value put upon it in the creditor's proof (subject to re-valuation, as above). The creditor may call on the liquidator or trustee to say if he will redeem, and they have six months to decide.[85] If they are dissatisfied with the creditor's valuation, (not, with individual bankrupts, where the court approved the revaluation) they may require the property to be offered for sale (in which case they, or the creditor may bid at an auction).[86] We have seen that with goods, the liquidator or trustee may inspect the goods, and after his written notice to this effect, the goods may not be realised until he has a reasonable chance to inspect them and to decide if he will redeem them.[87]

28.109

(vii) in all of this, third party securities may be ignored and are irrelevant to the proof, because they are not assets of the debtor. Only those securities which, if given up, would augment the assets or estate of the debtor need be taken into account.[88] But if the debtor and a third party jointly own an asset, which is jointly charged to the bank, then the security must be taken into account.[89] Liens count as securities, and must be taken into account.[90]

Generally speaking, the bank's choice is between realisation of the asset and valuation. It would be rare to surrender the security, and waiver of proof would occur only if the value if the security is obviously sufficient to cover the debt. Valuation might be adopted with securities like land, when

---

[79] s.267, 269.
[80] I.R. 4.88, 6.109.
[81] I.R. 4.99, 6.119.
[82] I.R. 4.75 and 6.98.
[83] I.R. 4.95, 6.115.
[84] I.R. 4.96, 6.116.
[85] I.R. 4.97, 6.117.
[86] I.R. 4.97, 6.118.
[87] Above, para. 28.50–28.51.
[88] *Re Turner, ex.p. West Riding Union Banking Co.* (1881) 19 Ch.D.105.
[89] *Re Rushton*, (a bankrupt) *ex p. National Westminster Bank Ltd.* v. *O.R.* [1972] Ch. 197.
[90] s.383(2).

realisation may be slow, while realisation might occur with easily realisable securities (such as shares, or life policies).

7. STATUTORY SUBROGATION: WAGES ACCOUNTS AND PREFERENTIAL DEBTS

28.110 We have seen that one preferential debt is for employees' wages in the four months before the bankruptcy, not exceeding at present £800 per employee.[91] Additionally, anyone advancing money for payment of wages, providing that the money is actually used for the purpose, is given preferential status (is subrogated to the preferential position of the employees).

There must be a legal relation of employer—employee between the customer and his workforce, so that, for example, the relation between employer and sub-contractors is insufficient.[92] If the bank has preferential status, it ranks equally with other preferential creditors (the main one ordinarily being the Inland Revenue or Customs and Excise) and in case of insufficiency of assets, the claims of all preferential creditors abate rateably, in proportion to their claims.

Because of this provision for statutory subrogation, which formerly related only to companies, banks have developed the practice of operating special wages accounts. It is clear that this is not a legal necessity[93] but is adopted (a) for administrative purposes, (b) so as to prevent the operation of the rule in *Clayton's case* from eliminating the preferential debt from the ordinary (and more active) current account, and (c) so as to avoid argument about the purpose for which the money was advanced. In *Re Rampgill Mill Ltd.*[94] the bank failed to keep a separate wages account. The court accepted the bank's preferential status for £5,000 applied to wages, but the bank lost preference to the extent of £3,000 because of the rule in *Clayton's case*.

The general practice as to wages accounts is for drawings for remuneration to be made on this account only, and when a debit loses priority after four months, it is cleared by transferring it to the current account, so that the wages account gives an up to date picture of the bank's preferential status.

It must be stressed that the statute refers not only to the purposes of the advance, but to its application for that purpose. The bank must show that the money was actually used for payment of wages,[95] but it seems that if it shows this it will be presumed that the banker advanced money for the purpose, even if it is not advanced from an account set up for the purpose. This was held in *Re Rampgill Mill Ltd.*,[96] where Plowman J. adopted this "benevolent construction" which avoided the need for the bank to show that it made a particular advance for this purpose only—a difficult thing to prove, given a general purpose account. Accordingly, the bank need not have the intent to achieve preferential creditor status.

28.111 It is essential that there be what in law amounts to an "advance." In *E. J. Morel (1934) Ltd.*[97] a company operated a wages account, on terms that the

---

[91] See the case below, n. 94.
[92] *Re C. W. and A. L. Hughes Ltd.* [1966] 2 All E.R. 702.
[93] See *Re Primrose (Builders) Ltd.* [1950] Ch. 561.
[94] [1967] Ch. 1138.
[95] Hence, companies are often asked to certify this, showing employees' names, amounts paid, etc.
[96] Above, n. 94
[97] [1962] Ch. 21.

credit in the current account was always to exceed the debit in the wages account, that wages would be paid by debit from the wages account, and that old debts (over four months old) in the wages account would be "moved" to the current account by a credit to the wages account being made from the current account which was then debited. This arrangement was entered because there was a third account, heavily in debit, which had by agreement been frozen. Buckley J. held that the way this account was operated meant that the accounts were completely interdependent. The bank would not meet a cheque on either account without considering the combined position of the two accounts taken together. Accordingly, the accounts should be regarded as a single account. It followed, therefore, that regarding them thus, there was no overall "advance" made by the bank which could be preferential, since the combination of the two accounts always left the company in credit overall. In other words, wages were paid for not by the bank, but by the company, and the book-keeping arrangements merely disguised this. It is submitted, with respect, that this conclusion was unavoidable, given the way this account was operated. A different conclusion might be reached if, as is often the case, the current account is not so "tied" to the debit on the wages account. Indeed, sometimes the wages account is not opened until the company is overdrawn on the current account, and the bank simply attempts to stabilise or gradually reduce the overdraft there, while opening a wages account for preferential treatment of wages payments. There is no problem in this case: clearly the bank advances its own money. (Strictly, it is not an "advance," if made by way of overdraft, but although the word "advance" is used in the statute, this distinction has never been taken, and appears not to be significant.) The problem in *Morel's* case arose because instead of maintaining, stabilising, and gradually reducing the overdraft on the current account, the bank froze that account and opened a new current account which was closely tied to the wages account.[98]

In *National Provincial Bank Ltd.* v. *Freedman and Rubens*[99] a company's overdraft had increased to an extent which aroused the bank's concern, and the bank followed the practice of refusing to meet cheques drawn for wages unless the same amount was at the same time paid into the account. On the company's liquidation, the bank claimed a preference, for wages. The liquidator claimed that there had been no "advances," for the bank had merely exchanged cash for the cheques paid in each week. Happily, the court rejected the argument. The payments in, on normal principles, discharged the oldest existing liabilities first, and could not be related, as the liquidator argued, to the most recent debits. *Clayton's case* here operated to the bank's advantage.[1]

Provided that the current account remains overdrawn, even an agreement which closely ties together the current and wages accounts will not be held to be subject to the principle in *Morel's* case. Thus, in *Re James R. Rutherford* **28.112**

[98] See Ryder, "Combination of Bank Accounts in Winding Up of Customers," (1961) J.B.L. 278.

[99] (1934) 4 L.D.A.B. 444.

[1] *Clayton's case* is expressly the ground for the decision in *Re Primrose (Builders) Ltd.* [1950] Ch. 561, on very similar facts to the case just discussed. These cases show that the rule in *Clayton's case*, which can be displaced by agreement, needs a fairly express kind of agreement to displace it.

& *Sons Ltd.*[2] transfers were made weekly to the wages account from the overdrawn current account, on condition that they should repay the earliest advances made for wages on that account.[3] On the company's liquidation, it was held that not only the debit on the wages account, but also the debits to the current account made when the transfers to the wages account occurred, had preferential status. Pennycuick J. said, without specifying, that the facts here were different from those in *Morel's* case "in an essential particular." It is submitted that this is correct, and that the essential particular is that in *Morel's* case the balance on the two accounts in question was never a debit balance, while in *Rutherford's* case it was. In the former case the bank advanced nothing, while in the latter it did.

We have observed elsewhere[3a] that if a customer is in debt to the bank, the bank may appropriate payments received to whichever account the bank chooses (if not specifically appropriated by the customer to meet a particular liability), and that it may subsequently combine accounts, although the effect of the latter is that the credit will go rateably to preferential and non-preferential elements of the debt. If however, the bank exercises the former option, and appropriates when the credit is first received, it appears from *Re William Hall (Contractors) Ltd.*[4] that it may appropriate entirely to the non-preferential debt, if it chooses.

Can the bank assign its preferential right gained by way of subrogation? This is undecided. Section 614, and schedule 19, para. 13, C.A. 1985 gave the right to "the person by whom the money was advanced." But the new provision contains no such qualification.

8. DOUBLE PROOF, AND ASSOCIATED PROBLEMS

28.113 This rule of equity stops two creditors claiming for the same debt, and it may be troublesome from time to time, especially in relation to guarantees.[5] We may say the following:

(i) Naturally, no creditor may claim more than 100 pence in the pound. If, for example, a guarantor pays 50p of the debt, the bank cannot prove against the debtor for more than 50p, even though this is a third party security.

(ii) Guarantors (G) may pay sums to the bank before the commencement of winding up or a vesting order, so as to reduce their liability. If credited to the debtor's (D's) account these reduce the liability of D and the proof must take account of them.[6] The bank will generally prefer to prove first against D and then to claim under the guarantee against G. To enable this, a clause in the guarantee enables the bank to place such payments in a separate "suspense" account, so that the payments are not appropriated to the debts so as to discharge them. The bank may then prove for the whole debt, and have recourse to the guarantor's payments if not fully satisfied.[7] If not prevented,

---

[2] [1964] 1 W.L.R. 1211.

[3] As would happen anyway, by *Clayton's case*, unless the account was used for other purposes. See *Re Yeovil Glove Co. Ltd.* [1963] Ch. 148.

[3a] Above, Chap. 13.

[4] [1967] 2 All E.R. 1150.

[5] Below, this para.

[6] *Re Daintry* [1900] 1 Q.B. 546; *Mackinnon's Trustee* v. *Bank of Scotland* (1915) S.C. 411.

[7] *Commercial Bank of Australia* v. *O.A. of the Estate of Wilson* [1893] A.C. 181; *Ulster Bank* v. *Lambe* [1966] N.I. 161 (where B first demanded the difference from D, and then sued D for the whole sum.

as shortly described, the guarantor could prove for his contingent liability even where a suspense account is used.

(iii) There are three reasons why a guarantor may not be able to prove for his debt or contingent liability: these are (a) the whole debt clause, (b) merely partly paying a separate debt, and (c) contractual agreement to the contrary.

(a) The first reason concerns the rule against double proof, and the "whole debt" clause found in guarantees. Most guarantees are not phrased so that the guarantor (G) guarantees a specific sum, but are phrased so that he guarantees the whole debt of the debtor (D). If a limitation on G's liability is desired, there is a proviso that his liability shall not exceed a certain sum. If this is done, then on D's bankruptcy, even if G pays the bank (B) his limited sum, the bank (which pays into a suspense account so as not to discharge D), is entitled to prove in D's bankruptcy for the whole debt, and G cannot prove against D's estate for a dividend on the amount paid by him to B.[8] The reason for this result is that where G agrees to be responsible for the whole debt, with a limitation, the guaranteed indebtedness of D is regarded as undivided, and G cannot prove for it while B proves for it, for two persons cannot prove for the same debt.[9] Thus, G must give way to B.

(b) Suppose, however, that G agrees to be liable simply for a stated amount. This is treated as a guarantee of a separate debt of D (*i.e.* the debt is regarded as divided), and unless (as usual) he agrees otherwise, he may prove for the debt. But this is possible only if he pays the whole of his separate debt, for otherwise he and B would again be competing against D for the same debt. Thus, a mere partial payment of his separate debt does not enable G to prove.[10]

28.114

(c) Thirdly, G normally contracts not to compete in D's bankruptcy. Bank forms of guarantee normally provide that on D's bankruptcy B may, without discharging G's liability, enter into any "compromises, compositions or arrangements" with D "or to prove and to rank as creditors . . . and to receive dividends" so that G's liability extends to the ultimate balance after deduction of these payments (though not payments made by co-sureties), and so that G's rights to compete against the bank (by proving against D) are excluded. Thus, the foregoing is agreed "to the entire exclusion and surrender of all my rights as surety in competition with B." The aim of this is that the share of the assets available to the bank should be enlarged (it could claim against G, but he may become insolvent). Such a term prevents G from proving against D for an independent debt owed by D to G (nothing to do with the guarantee). Goode argues[11] that this invariable practice might be improved upon, and that the bank should in fact provide that G shall be obliged (if B so desires) to prove against D, and shall hold the proceeds on trust for B, in such amounts as needed to discharge G's liability (a power of attorney could be taken in case G refuses). The effect of that would be that as the sum of the claims of B and G is greater than the claim of B alone, the dividend of B and G together will also be greater, as against other creditors, and it will all accrue to the bank unless, perhaps, G is also

---

[8] *Re Houlder* [1929] 1 Ch. 205; *Rees, ex p. National Provincial Bank of England* (1881) 17 Ch.D. 98; *Re Sass, ex p. National Provincial Bank of England* [1896] 2 Q.B. 12. Similarly, G cannot set off against a debt owed to D, G's right to indemnity from D: *Re Fenton* [1931] 1 Ch. 85.

[9] *Re Fenton* [1931] 1 Ch. 85; Goode, L.P.C.S. 64, 70.

[10] *Goodwin v. Gray* (1874) 22 W.R. 312; *Re Sass* [1896] 2 Q.B. 12.

[11] L.P.C.S. 71.

bankrupt (but even then, he holds in trust for the bank, which would take priority, unless the arrangement is entered in circumstances where it is a preference). Nevertheless, this interesting suggestion might not work satisfactorily, if there is a whole debt clause, (for the rule against double-proof prevents G from proving together with the bank), and if there is a partial guarantee, G must have paid the whole of his debt to the bank, or the same rule prevents him from proving. Assuming a limited guarantee and a full payment by G, Goode's suggested arrangement might work, but if G is insolvent, it might be attacked as a preference, etc. There seems to be no reason, other than that, why one cannot declare a trust of or charge over a dividend in bankruptcy. The arrangement is probably not a registrable charge on G's book debt (the dividend right).

(iv) Payments by a guarantor made subsequent to commencement of winding up or a vesting order, may be ignored in the proof.[12] Since the bank need not reduce its proof, it follows that the guarantor cannot prove for his payment, for they would be claiming for the same debt. By way of exception to this principle, where G is an indorser of a bill of exchange on which D is liable, G's position is analogous to a surety, but in this case with the difference that any part payment by him received before B put his proof in must be taken into account in B's proof.[13]

G. The bank and the bankrupt customer

28.115 There is little the bank can do if it is unaware of the commencement of winding up or the presentation of a petition for bankruptcy. If it becomes aware, then it ought to take the following steps, although this depends on the effect, in relation to an individual bankrupt, of section 323. It may be that section 323 makes void any debt incurred after the petition with knowledge of it. Or it may be that this applies only where there have been "mutual credits . . . debts . . . or . . . dealings" and that this is not applicable to a single bank account.[14] If the former is the case (and even where it is not) then after the petition, or commencement of winding up the bank ought to take the following steps:

(i) Exercise any rights of set-off, and look to its securities, whether from the debtor or third parties, and consider whether to prove, realise, value, etc. Unless there are rights of set-off, the bank must surrender all property to the trustee or liquidator.

(ii) Cease to operate any account for the debtor, for transactions not ratified by the court may be affected as described earlier.[15] The account may, however, be debited for obligations already incurred by the bank on behalf of the customer. Cheques are returned marked appropriately.

(iii) Joint accounts should similarly be stopped, even if one party is solvent, to prevent the operation of *Clayton's case,* and the disposition of any of the assets now belonging to the liquidator or trustee. Cheques should be returned, marked carefully, so as not to damage the credit of any solvent party. The contents of the account are divided between the solvent party and the liquidator or trustee, with the bank interpleading in case of dispute. The normal possibilities of proof, etc., against the insolvent party, apply

---

[12] *Re Rees* (1881) 17 Ch.D. 98; *Re Sass* [1896] 2 Q.B. 12; *Re Fenton* [1931] 1 Ch. 85.
[13] *Re Blackburne,* (1892) 9 Mor. 294; *Re Houlder* [1929] 1 Ch. 205.
[14] Discussed above, para. 28.78 *et seq.*
[15] *Ibid.*

(survivorship does not operate so as to make the remaining partner alone liable) but the bank may, additionally, proceed against the other joint party.

(iv) Undischarged bankrupts may operate accounts with the consent of the trustee. Their wages may be paid into the account, for example. Those wages would be after-acquired property, and the trustee may claim them by notice under section 307. (An income payments order is likely.)[16] The bankrupt is required to tell the trustee of any after-acquired property,[17] but may fail to do so. A banker receiving after-acquired property of a bankrupt is protected, if the bank acts in good faith and without notice of the bankruptcy.[18] In any case, unless claimed, it is not part of the bankrupt's estate. The protection would not apply to wages innocently received by a bank if those wages are subject to an income payments order, since these form part of the bankrupt's estate.[19] Although there seems no direct requirement to do so, presumably the prudent step on learning that a customer is an undischarged bankrupt is to inform the trustee.[20]

(v) If the payee of a cheque is bankrupt, the chose in action represented by the cheque belongs (or, if after-acquired, may belong) to the trustee. For the sake of its customer, the drawer, a bank should not pay this cheque, since the trustee may say to the customer that he should pay again, for only the trustee can give a good discharge for the debt. Additionally, the bank could be liable (in conversion) to the trustee for handling his cheque (if ignorant of the bankruptcy, it is protected by section 60 of the Bills of Exchange Act 1882). The unpaid cheque should be marked "Payee bankrupt."

(vi) If a bankrupt customer has accepted bills payable at the bank, the bank will return the bills unpaid when presented. **28.116**

(vii) If the bank has discounted bills for a customer (drawer or indorser) and the customer is bankrupt while the bill is still current (not yet payable) then the bankrupt's liability is contingent (since, at maturity, the acceptor may pay). It may be that section 323 allows set-off of the contingent liability (depending on the meaning of "due" in that section) but the bank may in any case treat him as having repudiated his liabilities, and treat him as liable for liquidated damages, in which case it may prove immediately.[21] Other parties may, of course, be liable on the bill. The rule against double proof will prevent the bank from claiming more than 100 pence in the pound, from the various parties.

(viii) If the bank has discounted a bill for the customer and the acceptor of the bill becomes bankrupt, the bank has no immediate remedies against the customer. It may sue him at maturity, and it may prove immediately against the acceptor for the full amount of the bill (since at maturity he cannot pay).

(ix) If a bill of exchange is expressed on its face to be drawn against specific goods (which may happen if the bill is payment for a contract for the goods) then this does not of itself create a security against those goods (usually shipped by the drawer and bought by the acceptor). If, however, the drawer and acceptor both become insolvent, then the holder is entitled to the goods named, as security (and he can prove for any deficiency,

[16] Above, para. 28.74.
[17] s.333.
[18] s.307(4)(b).
[19] ss.307(5), 310(5).
[20] cf. s.47, Bankruptcy Act 1914.
[21] Above, Chap. 27.

etc.).[22] This assumes that another creditor has no security rights over the goods which take priority (as will often be the case). The most likely situation is one where the bill under bank A's commercial credit is negotiated to B and where the drawer C and the bank A both become insolvent, in which case B has a charge on the documents held by A.[23] The reason is that it is unjust that A keep the securities for payment while not discharging its own liabilities on the bill.[24]

[22] *Ex p. Waring* (1815) 19 Ves. 345.
[23] See *ex p. Dever (No. 2)* (1885) 14 Q.B.D. 611.
[24] *Banner* v. *Johnston* (1871) L.R. 5 H.L. 157.

Index

INDEX